Lecture Notes in Computer Science 8831

Commenced Publication in 1973
Founding and Former Series Editors:
Gerhard Goos, Juris Hartmanis, and Jan van Leeuwen

Xavier Franch   Aditya K. Ghose
Grace A. Lewis   Sami Bhiri (Eds.)

Service-Oriented Computing

12th International Conference, ICSOC 2014
Paris, France, November 3-6, 2014
Proceedings

 Springer

Volume Editors

Xavier Franch
Universitat Politècnica de Catalunya
UPC - Campus Nord, Omega 122, c/Jordi Girona 1-3
08034 Barcelona, Spain
E-mail: franch@essi.upc.edu

Aditya K. Ghose
University of Wollongong
School of Computer Science and Software Engineering
Wollongong, NSW 2522, Australia
E-mail: aditya@uow.edu.au

Grace A. Lewis
Carnegie Mellon Software Engineering Institute
4500 Fifth Ave., Pittsburgh, PA 15213, USA
E-mail: glewis@sei.cmu.edu

Sami Bhiri
Télécom SudParis
9 rue Charles Fourier, 91011 Evry Cedex, France
E-mail: sami.bhiri@gmail.com

ISSN 0302-9743   e-ISSN 1611-3349
ISBN 978-3-662-45390-2   e-ISBN 978-3-662-45391-9
DOI 10.1007/978-3-662-45391-9
Springer Heidelberg New York Dordrecht London

Library of Congress Control Number: 2014952601

LNCS Sublibrary: SL 2 – Programming and Software Engineering

Typesetting: Camera-ready by author, data conversion by Scientific Publishing Services, Chennai, India

Printed on acid-free paper

Springer is part of Springer Science+Business Media (www.springer.com)

Preface

Welcome to the proceedings of the 12th International Conference on Service-Oriented Computing (ICSOC 2014), held in Paris, France, November 3–6, 2014. ICSOC 2014 was co-organized by Télécom SudParis (Institut Mines-Télécom) and the Paris Dauphine University. These proceedings contain high-quality research papers that represent the latest results, ideas, and position and vision statements in the field of service-oriented computing. Since the first occurrence of the conference more than 10 years ago, ICSOC has grown to become the premier international forum for academics, industry researchers, and practitioners to share, report, and discuss their groundbreaking work. ICSOC 2014 continued along this tradition. In addition to traditional topics such as service-oriented architecture, service design, service description, and service composition, service change management is a key topic that reflects the need for services to adapt to dynamic environments. Cloud service management also naturally appears as a topic of intersection between service-oriented computing and cloud computing. This year's call for papers attracted 180 research and industry submissions from 31 countries and six continents. The submissions were rigorously evaluated by three reviewers, followed by a discussion moderated by a senior Program Committee (PC) member who made a final recommendation in the form of a meta-review. The PC was composed of 112 world-class experts in service-oriented computing from 22 different countries. The ICSOC 2014 program featured 25 full papers (acceptance rate of 13.9%) and 26 short papers. The conference program was highlighted by two invited keynotes (by Joseph Sifakis from RiSD Laboratory EPFL and François Bancilhon from Data Publica), lively panel discussions, multiple demonstrations, the PhD Symposium, and seven workshops on different aspects of service-oriented and cloud computing. We would like to express our gratitude to all individuals, institutions, and sponsors that supported ICSOC 2014. The high-quality program you are about to experience would have not been possible without the expertise and dedication of our PC and in particular of our senior PC members. We are grateful for the guidance of the general chair (Samir Tata), the effort of more than 60 external reviewers, the proceedings chair (Sami Bhiri), the local organizers (led by Walid Gaaloul and Daniela Grigori) and volunteers, and last but not least to the distinguished members of the ICSOC Steering Committee. All of them helped to make ICSOC 2014 a success. Finally, a special word of thanks goes to all researchers, practitioners, and students who contributed their presentations, questions, and active participation in the conference. We hope you enjoy these proceedings!

November 2014

Xavier Franch
Aditya K. Ghose
Grace A. Lewis

Organization

General Chair

Samir Tata   Télécom SudParis, France

Advisory Board

Paco Curbera   IBM Research, USA
Paolo Traverso   ITC-IRST, Italy

Program Chairs

Xavier Franch   Universitat Politècnica de Catalunya, Spain
Aditya K. Ghose   University of Wollongong, Australia
Grace A. Lewis   Carnegie Mellon Software Engineering
                       Institute, USA

Steering Committee Liaison

Boualem Benatallah   University of New South Wales, Australia

Workshop Chairs

Daniela Grigori   University of Paris Dauphine, France
Barbara Pernici   Politecnico di Milano, Italy
Farouk Toumani   Blaise Pascal University, France

Demonstration Chairs

Brian Blake   University of Miami, USA
Olivier Perrin   University of Lorraine, France
Iman Saleh Moustafa   University of Miami, USA

Panel Chairs

Marlon Dumas   University of Tartu, Estonia
Henderik A. Proper   Henri Tudor Center, Luxembourg
Hong-Linh Truong   Vienna University of Technology, Austria

PhD Symposium Chairs

Djamal Benslimane   Claude Bernard University of Lyon 1, France
Jan Mendling   WU Vienna, Austria
Nejib Ben Hadj-Alouane   ENIT, Tunisia

Publicity Chairs

Kais Klai   University of Paris 13, France
Hanan Lutfiyya   University of Western Ontario, Canada
ZhangBing Zhou   China University of Geosciences, China

Local Organization Chairs

Walid Gaaloul   Télécom SudParis, France
Daniela Grigori   University of Paris Dauphine, France

Publication Chair

Sami Bhiri   Télécom SudParis, France

Web Chairs

Chan Nguyen Ngoc   LORIA, France
Mohamed Sellami   Ecole des Mines de Nantes, France

Senior Program Committee

Samik Basu   Iowa State University, USA
Boualem Benatallah   University of New South Wales, Australia
Athman Bouguettaya   RMIT University, Australia
Fabio Casati   University of Trento, Italy
Flavio De Paoli   University of Milano-Bicocca, Italy
Schahram Dustdar   Technical University of Vienna, Austria
Mohand-Said Hacid   University of Lyon, France
Lin Liu   Tsinghua University, China
Heiko Ludwig   IBM Research - Almaden, USA
E. Michael Maximilien   IBM Cloud Labs, USA
Cesare Pautasso   University of Lugano, Switzerland
Barbara Pernici   Politecnico di Milano, Italy
Gustavo Rossi   National University of La Plata, Argentina

Michael Q. Sheng	Adelaide University, Australia
Stefan Tai	Technical University of Berlin, Germany
Zahir Tari	RMIT University, Australia
Mathias Weske	HPI/University of Potsdam, Germany
Jian Yang	Macquarie University, Australia
Liang Zhang	Fudan University, China

Program Committee

Rafael Accorsi	University of Freiburg, Germany
Rama Akkiraju	IBM, USA
Alvaro Arenas	Instituto de Empresa Business School, Spain
Ebrahim Bagheri	Athabasca University, Canada
Luciano Baresi	Politecnico di Milano, Italy
Alistair Barros	Queensland University of Technology, Australia
Khalid Belhajjame	Paris Dauphine University, LAMSADE, France
Salima Benbernou	Paris Descartes University, France
Sami Bhiri	Télécom SudParis, France
Domenico Bianculli	University of Luxembourg, Luxembourg
Walter Binder	University of Lugano, Switzerland
Omar Boucelma	University of Aix-Marseille, France
Ivona Brandic	Vienna University of Technology, Austria
Christoph Bussler	Tropo Inc., USA
Manuel Carro	IMDEA Software Institute and Technical University of Madrid, Spain
Wing-Kwong Chan	City University of Hong Kong, Hong Kong
Shiping Chen	CSIRO ICT, Australia
Lawrence Chung	University of Texas at Dallas, USA
Florian Daniel	University of Trento, Italy
Shuiguang Deng	Zhejiang University, China
Khalil Drira	LAAS-CNRS, France
Abdelkarim Erradi	Qatar University, Qatar
Rik Eshuis	Eindhoven University of Technology, The Netherlands
Marcelo Fantinato	University of Sao Paulo, Brazil
Marie-Christine Fauvet	University of Joseph Fourier, France
Joao E. Ferreira	University of Sao Paulo, Brazil
Walid Gaaloul	Télécom SudParis, France
G.R. Gangadharan	IDRBT, India
Dragan Gasevic	Athabasca University, Canada
Paolo Giorgini	University of Trento, Italy
Claude Godart	University of Lorraine, France
Mohamed Graiet	ISIMM, Tunisia
Sven Graupner	Hewlett-Packard, USA
Daniela Grigori	Paris Dauphine University, France

Jun Han	Swinburne University of Technology, Australia
Peng Han	Chongqing Academy of Science and Technology, China
Bernhard Holtkamp	Fraunhofer ISST, Germany
Fuyuki Ishikawa	National Institute of Informatics, Japan
Hai Jin	Huazhong University of Science and Technology, China
Dimka Karastoyanova	University of Stuttgart, Germany
Hamamache Kheddouci	University of Lyon, France
Kais Klai	University of Paris 13, France
Ryan Ko	University of Waikato, New Zealand
Gerald Kotonya	Lancaster University, UK
Patricia Lago	VU University Amsterdam, The Netherlands
Frank Leymann	University of Stuttgart, Germany
Ying Li	Zhejiang University, China
Xumin Liu	Rochester Institute of Technology, USA
Alessio Lomuscio	Imperial College London, UK
Zaki Malik	Wayne State University, USA
Massimo Mecella	Sapienza University of Rome, Italy
Lars Moench	University of Hagen, Germany
Marco Montali	Free University of Bozen-Bolzano, Italy
Michael Mrissa	University of Lyon, France
Nanjangud C. Narendra	Cognizant Technology Solutions, India
Surya Nepal	Commonwealth Scientific and Industrial Research Organisation, Australia
Srinivas Padmanabhuni	Infosys Labs, India
Helen Paik	University of New South Wales, Australia
Fabio Patrizi	Sapienza University of Rome, Italy
Olivier Perrin	Lorraine University, France
Radha Krishna Pisipati	Infosys Technologies Limited, India
Marco Pistore	Fondazione Bruno Kessler, Italy
Pascal Poizat	Paris Ouest University and LIP6, France
Artem Polyvyanyy	Queensland University of Technology, Australia
Karthikeyan Ponnalagu	IBM Research, India
Mu Qiao	IBM Almaden Research Center, USA
Manfred Reichert	Ulm University, Germany
Wolfgang Reisig	Humboldt University of Berlin, Germany
Hamid Reza Motahari-Nezhad	Hewlett-Packard, USA
Colette Roland	Paris 1 University, France
Antonio Ruiz-Cortés	University of Seville, Spain
Diptikalyan Saha	IBM Research, India
Jun Shen	University of Wollongong, Australia
Larisa Shwartz	IBM T.J. Watson Research Center, USA
Ignacio Silva-Lepe	IBM, USA
Sergey Smirnov	SAP, Germany

George Spanoudakis	City University London, UK
Jianwen Su	University of California at Santa Barbara, USA
Giordano Tamburrelli	University of Lugano, Switzerland
Roman Vaculin	IBM T.J. Watson Research Center, USA
Guiling Wang	North China University of Technology, China
Jianwu Wang	University of California - San Diego, USA
Yan Wang	Macquarie University, Australia
Zhongjie Wang	Harbin Institute of Technology, China
Ingo Weber	National ICT Australia, Australia
Lai Xu	Bournemouth University, UK
Yuhong Yan	Concordia University, Canada
Zheng Yan	Xidian University, China/Aalto University, Finland
Jian Yu	Auckland University of Technology, New Zealand
Qi Yu	Rochester Institute of Technology, USA
Weiliang Zhao	University of Wollongong, Australia
Andrea Zisman	City University London, UK

External Reviewers

Imene Abdennadher	LAAS-CNRS, Toulouse, France
Husain Aljafer	Wayne State University, USA
Nariman Ammar	Wayne State University, USA
Mohsen Asadi	Simon Fraser University, Canada
Nour Assy	Télécom SudParis, France
Yacine Aydi	University of Sfax, Tunisia
Fatma Basak Aydemir	University of Trento, Italy
George Baryannis	University of Crete, Greece
Mahdi Bennara	University of Lyon, France
Lubomir Bulej	University of Lugano, Switzerland
Mariam Chaabane	University of Sfax, Tunisia
Wassim Derguech	NUI, Galway, Ireland
Raffael Dzikowski	Humboldt University of Berlin, Germany
Soodeh Farokhi	Vienna University of Technology, Austria
Pablo Fernández	University of Seville, Spain
José María García	University of Innsbruck, Austria
Feng Gao	NUI, Galway, Ireland
Amal Gassara	University of Sfax, Tunisia
Leopoldo Gomez	University of Guadalajara, Mexico
Genady Grabarnik	St. John's University, USA
Gregor Grambow	Ulm University, Germany
Khayyam Hashmi	Wayne State University, USA
Dragan Ivanovic	IMDEA Software Institute, Spain
Nesrine Khabou	University of Sfax, Tunisia
Fayez Khazalah	Wayne State University, USA

Keynote (Abstracts)

Rigorous System Design

Joseph Sifakis

RiSD Laboratory EPFL
joseph.sifakis@epfl.ch

Abstract. We advocate rigorous system design as a coherent and accountable model-based process leading from requirements to implementations. We present the state of the art in system design, discuss its current limitations, and identify possible avenues for overcoming them. A rigorous system design flow is defined as a formal accountable and iterative process composed of steps, and based on four principles: (1) separation of concerns; (2) component-based construction; (3) semantic coherency; and (4) correctness-by-construction. We show that the combined application of these principles allows the definition of rigorous design flows clearly identifying where human intervention and ingenuity are needed to resolve design choices, as well as activities that can be supported by tools to automate tedious and error-prone tasks. An implementable system model is progressively derived by source-to-source automated transformations in a single host component-based language rooted in well-defined semantics. Using a single modeling language throughout the design flow enforces semantic coherency. Correct-by-construction techniques allow well-known limitations of a posteriori verification to be overcome and ensure accountability. It is possible to explain, at each design step, which among the requirements are satisfied and which may not be satisfied. The presented view has been amply implemented in the BIP (Behavior, Interaction, Priority) component framework and substantiated by numerous experimental results showing both its relevance and feasibility. We show in particular, how distributed implementations can be generated from BIP models with multiparty interactions by application of correct-by-construction transformations.

Applying Data Science to Firmographics

François Bancilhon

Data Publica
francois.bancilhon@data-publica.com

Abstract. Data science is now fashionable and the search for data scientists is a new challenge for headhunters. Even though both terms are fuzzy and subject to hype and buzzword mania, data science includes data collection, data cleansing, data management, data analytics, and data vizualisation, and a data scientist is a person who can master some or all of these techniques (or sciences). At Data Publica, we are applying data science to firmographics (firmographics is to organizations what demographics is to people), and we are using firmographics to answer the needs of B2B sales and marketing departments. This talk will present the techniques we use and some of the amazing results they produce.

Table of Contents

Service Design, Description and Evolution

Cloud and Business Service Management

Research Papers - Short

Ensuring Composition Properties

Quality of Services

Semantic Web Services

Service Management

Cloud Service Management

Business Service Management

Trust

Service Design and Description

Industrial Papers

Configuration Rule Mining for Variability Analysis in Configurable Process Models

Nour Assy and Walid Gaaloul

Computer Science Department, Telecom SudParis
UMR 5157 CNRS Samovar, France
{firstname.lastname}@telecom-sudparis.eu

Abstract. With the intention of design by reuse, *configurable process models* provide a way to model variability in reference models that need to be configured according to specific needs. Recently, the increasing adoption of configurable process models has resulted in a large number of configured process variants. Current research activities are successfully investigating the design and configuration of configurable process models. However, a little attention is attributed to analyze the way they are configured. Such analysis can yield useful information in order to help organizations improving the quality of their configurable process models. In this paper, we introduce *configuration rule mining*, a frequency-based approach for supporting the variability analysis in configurable process models. Basically, we propose to enhance configurable process models with configuration rules that describe the interrelationships between the frequently selected configurations. These rules are extracted from a large collection of process variants using *association rule mining* techniques. To show the feasibility and effectiveness of our approach, we conduct experiments on a dataset from SAP reference model.

1 Introduction

With the rapidly changing demands in today's business requirements, there is no doubt that new paradigms for managing enterprises' business processes turn into a pressing need. In such a highly dynamic environment, seeking reuse [1] and adaptability [2] become a strong requirement for a successful business process design. To this end, *configurable process models* [3] provide a way for modeling variability in reference models. A configurable process model is a generic model that integrates multiple process variants of a same business process in a given domain through variation points. These variation points are referred to as *configurable elements* and allow for multiple design options in the process model. A configurable process model needs to be configured according to a specific requirement by selecting one design option for each configurable element. In this way, an individual process variant is derived without an extra design effort.

Recently, several approaches addressed the problem of building configurable process models. Some of them propose to merge existing process variants [4–7], others try to mine one configurable process model from execution logs [8–10].

X. Franch et al. (Eds.): ICSOC 2014, LNCS 8831, pp. 1–15, 2014.

These research results highlight the need for means of support to derive individual variants as integrated models tend to be complex with a large number of configurable elements [11]. To fill this gap, some works propose to use questionnaires [12] or ontologies [13] in order to get business requirements and guide the configuration process. Others propose to use non functional requirements to assess configuration decisions on the process performance [14]. Although these works have made a considerable effort on process variability design and configuration, a less attention has been paid to understand the way a configurable process model is configured. That means *which configurations are frequently selected by the users* and *how configuration decisions may have an impact on others in the process model.* The configurations' frequencies and interrelationships have been identified in the requirements for a configurable modeling technique in [3].

In this work, we propose to enhance configurable process models with *configuration rules.* These rules reveal the frequency and association between the configuration decisions taken for different variation points in a configurable process model. Concretely, we propose to discover from a large collection of process variants the frequently selected configurations in a configurable process model. Then, taking advantage of machine learning techniques [15], in particular *association rule mining*, we extract configuration rules between the discovered configurations. These rules can be then used to support business analysts to develop a better understanding and reasoning on the variability in their configurable process models. For instance, business analysts can manage the complexity of existing configurable process models by removing or altering the configurations that were never or rarely selected. Moreover, the automated discovery of the interrelationships between configuration decisions can assist the configuration process by predicting next suitable configurations given the selected ones.

The remainder of the paper is organized as follows: in section 2, we present a running example used throughout the paper to illustrate our approach. Section 3 provides some concepts and definitions needed for our approach. In section 4, we detail our approach to derive configuration rules using association rule mining techniques. The validation and experimental results are reported in section 5. In section 6, we discuss related work and we conclude in section 7.

2   Running Example

Our running example is from SAP reference model for a procurement process management modeled with the Configurable Event-Driven Process Chain notation (C-EPC) [3] (see Fig. 1). The EPC notation consists of three elements: event, function and connector. An event can be seen as a pre- and/or post-condition that triggers a function. A function is the active element that describes an activity. Three types of connectors, OR, exclusive OR (XOR) and AND are used to model the splits and joins. In our example, we index connectors with numbers in order to distinguish between them. The C-EPC notation adds the configurability option for functions and connectors. A configurable function can be included or excluded from the model. A configurable connector can change its type

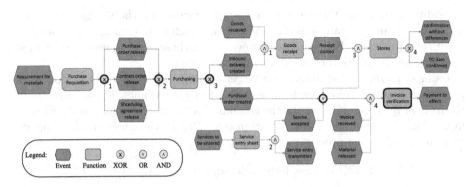

Fig. 1. An example of a configurable process model from SAP reference model

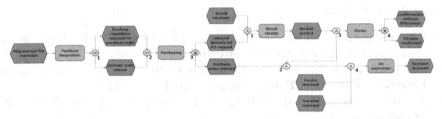

Fig. 2. A variant derived from the configurable process model in Fig. 1

(e.g. from OR to AND) or restrict it incoming or outgoing branches. Graphically, a configurable element is modeled with a thick line.

Returning to our example, the procurement process starts by detecting the need for new materials. A purchase request is sent to the corresponding provider. The purchase requisition type (for purchase order, for contract release order or for scheduling agreement schedule) is evaluated before the purchase starts. At this stage, either the goods delivery is followed until receiving goods or a purchase order is created. At the same time, a service entry sheet is created and transmitted. Last, the invoice is sent to the customer for verification and payment. We identified five configurable elements in the process: the connectors "$\times_1$", "$\times_2$", "$\times_3$", "$\vee$", and the function "invoice verification". This reference model is configured and used in a large number of companies that aim at reusing best practices for modeling their procurement processes.

Assume that a large number of configured process variants has been collected in a business repository from which we show one process variant in Fig. 2. This process is derived from the configurable process model in Fig. 1 through the following configurations:

1. Remove the outgoing branch starting with the event "Scheduling agreement release" from the configurable "$\times_1$";
2. Change the type of the configurable "$\vee$" to "$\wedge$", and remove the incoming branch ending with the event "service accepted";
3. Exclude the function "invoice verification" from the model.

In addition, some modifications have been performed on the configured model according to the company specific requirements such as renaming and/or adding events and functions. For example, the event "purchase order release" is renamed to "purchase requisition released for purchase order".

Using our proposed approach, we target to induce a set of configuration rules for each configurable element from available process variants. These rules are in the from of *if...then* and describe the combinations of the frequently selected configurations. For example, a configuration rule CR_1 for the configurable elements "$\times_1$" and "$\vee$" in the process model in Fig. 1 is:

$$CR_1 : < \times, \{\text{purchase order release, contract order release}\} >$$
$$\xrightarrow{S=0.7/C=0.65} < \wedge, \{\text{Purchase order created}, \wedge_3\} > \tag{1}$$

This rule means that:

- The configurable "$\times_1$" is frequently configured to a "$\times$" with the outgoing branches starting with "purchase order release" and "contract order release";
- The configurable "$\vee$" is frequently configured to an "$\wedge$" with the incoming branches ending with "Purchase order created" and "$\wedge_3$";
- $S = 0.7$ means that in 70% of the process variants, these two configurations are selected;
- $C = 0.65$ means that in 65% of the process variants, whenever the first configuration (that of "$\times_1$") is selected, then the second configuration (that of "$\vee$") is also selected.

In the following sections, we give a formal definition for our configuration rules. Afterwards, we detail our approach for extracting the configuration rules that explain all possible combinations of the frequently selected configurations in the configurable process model.

3   Preliminaries

In this section, we present the definition of the *business process graph* and *configurable process model* enhanced with our *configuration rules* definition.

3.1   Business Process Graph

A business process model is a directed graph with labeled nodes. There exist many notations to represent a business process model such as Event-driven Process Chain (EPC), Business Process Modeling Notation (BPMN), Unified Modeling Language (UML), etc. In this work, we abstract from any specific notation and we represent a process model as a directed graph called *business process graph*. This notation is inspired from [4] in which the elements are derived from the common constructs of existing graphical process modeling notations.

Definition 1. *(Business process graph) A business process graph*
$P = (N, E, T, L)$ *is a labeled directed graph where:*

- *N is the set of nodes;*
- *$E \subseteq N \times N$ is the set of edges connecting two nodes;*
- *$T : N \rightarrow t$ is a function that assigns for each node $n \in N$ a type t where t depends on the elements' types for each standard notation. In case of the EPC notation, $t \in \{event, function, connector\}$; Throughout the paper, we refer to functions and events by activities.*
- *$L : N \rightarrow label$ is a function that assigns for each node $n \in N$ a label such that if $T(n) = event \vee function$, then $L(n)$ is its name, and if $T(n) = connector$ then $L(n) \in \{\vee, \wedge, \times\}$ where $\vee = OR$, $\wedge = AND$ and $\times = XOR$.*

Let $P = (N, E, T, L)$ be a business process graph. We define the preset and postset of a connector $c \in N$ as the set of elements in its incoming and outgoing branches respectively.

Definition 2. *(preset $\bullet c$, postset $c\bullet$) The preset of a connector $c \in N$ denoted as $\bullet c$ is efined as $\bullet c = \{n \in N : (n, c) \in E\}$. The postset of c denoted as $c\bullet$ is defined as $c\bullet = \{n \in N : (c, n) \in E\}$.*

A connector "c" is a **split** if $|c \bullet| > 1$; it is a **join** if $|\bullet c| > 1$. For example, in Fig. 2, $\times_1 \bullet = \{$purchase requisition released for purchase, contract order release$\}$; $\bullet \wedge_4 = \{\wedge_2,$ invoice received, material released$\}$. "$\times_1$" is a split connector and "$\wedge_4$" is a join connector.

3.2   Configurable Process Model

A configurable process model, is a business process graph with configurable elements. A configurable element is an element whose configuration decision is made at design-time [3]. Configurable elements can be *functions* and/or *connectors*. A configurable function can be included (i.e. *ON*) or excluded (i.e. *OFF*) from the process model. A configurable connector has a generic behavior which is restricted by configuration. A connector can be configured by changing its type while preserving its behavior and/or restricting its incoming (respectively outgoing) branches in case of a join (respectively split). Table 1 presents the set of constraints identified in [3] for the configuration of connectors' types. A configurable connector is denoted by *[label]*^{c}. Each row in the table corresponds to a configurable connector which can be configured to one or more of the connectors presented in columns. The last column (i.e. *Seq*) corresponds to a simple "sequence". For example, the configurable "$\vee$" can be configured to any connector's type while a configurable "$\wedge$" can be only configured to an "$\wedge$". These configuration constraints are formalized through the partial order $\preceq$ that specifies which concrete connector may be used for a given configurable connector.

Definition 3. *(partial order $\preceq$) Let c^c be a configurable connector and c be a normal connector or a sequence (i.e. "Seq"). $c \preceq c^c$ iff $(L(c^c) = $ "$\vee$") $\vee (L(c^c) = $ "$\times$" $\wedge L(c) = $ "Seq") $\vee (L(c^c) = L(c))$.*

Table 1. Configuration constraints of configurable connectors

	$\vee$	$\wedge$	$\times$	Seq
$\vee^c$	✓	✓	✓	✓
$\wedge^c$		✓		
$\times^c$			✓	✓

Formally, the configuration of a configurable element, i.e. a function or a connector, is defined as:

Definition 4. *(Configuration Conf) The configuration of a node n^c such that $T(n^c) = 'function' \vee 'connector'$ is defined as:*

- *if $T(n^c) = 'function'$ then $Conf(n^c) \in \{ON, OFF\}$;*
- *if $T(n^c) = 'connector'$ then $Conf(n^c) = < n, \bullet n >$ (respectively $Conf(n^c) = < n, n \bullet >$) in case n^c is a join (respectively split) connector where:*
  1. *$n \preceq n^c$;*
  2. *$\bullet n \subseteq \bullet n^c$ (respectively $n \bullet \subseteq n^c \bullet$) in case n^c is a join (respectively split) connector*

For example, the process variant in Fig. 2 is derived from the configurable process model in Fig. 1 by configuring the "$\vee^c$" to: $Conf(\vee^c) = < \wedge_2, \{$purchase order created, $\wedge_3\} >$; the configurable function "invoice verification" to: $Conf($invoice verification$) = OFF$; etc.

Configuration rule. A configuration rule describes an association among the frequently selected configurations for different configurable elements in a configurable process model. It is defined as:

$$Conf_{h_1}, ..., Conf_{h_p} \xrightarrow{S,C} Conf_{b_1}, ..., Conf_{b_q} \qquad (2)$$

where $Conf_{h_i} : 1 \leq i \leq p$ is called the *rule head* and $Conf_{b_j} : 1 \leq j \leq q$ is called the *rule body*. The rule head and body represent the configurations of different configurable elements in a configurable process model. These configurations are retrieved from a business process repository. A configuration rule is parameterized by two well known metrics in association rule mining: the *Support S* and the *Confidence C*. The support is the fraction of process variants in the business process repository that contain the configurations of the rule head and body. It evaluates the usefulness of a rule. The confidence is the fraction of process variants that contain the rule body configurations among those that contain the rule head configurations. It represents the certainty of the rule. Let $\mathbb{P} = \{P_m : 1 \leq m \leq n\}$ be a business process repository. Formally:

$$S = \frac{|\{P_{hb} : 1 \leq hb \leq n \wedge Conf_{h_i}, Conf_{b_j} \in P_{hb}\}|}{n}$$
$$C = \frac{|\{P_{hb} : 1 \leq hb \leq n \wedge Conf_{h_i}, Conf_{b_j} \in P_{hb}\}|}{|\{P_h : 1 \leq h \leq n \wedge Conf_{h_i} \in P_h\}|} \qquad (3)$$

where $|\{P_{hb} : 1 \leq hb \leq n \wedge Conf_{h_i}, Conf_{b_j} \in P_k\}|$ is the number of process variants in $\mathbb{P}$ that contain the configurations in the rule head and body; $|\{P_h : 1 \leq h \leq n \wedge Conf_{h_i} \in P_h\}|$ is the number of process variants that contain the configurations in the rule head. The semantic of a configuration rule is: *if the configurations in the rule head are selected, then it is highly probably that the configurations in the rule body are also selected.* An example of a configuration rule is given in (1).

Definition 5. *(Configurable process model)* A configurable process model is denoted as $P^c = (N, E, T, L, B, Conf^c, CR^c)$ where:

- N, E, T, L are as specified in Definition 1;
- $B : N \rightarrow \{true, false\}$ is a boolean function returning true for configurable nodes;
- $Conf^c$ is the set of valid configurations according to Definition 4;
- CR^c is the set of configuration rules.

4 Configuration Rule Mining

In this section, we present our approach for mining configuration rules. Let $P^c = (N, E, T, L, B, Conf^c, CR^c)$ be a configurable process model and $\mathbb{P} = \{P_i = (N_i, E_i, T_i, L_i) : i \geq 1\}$ an existing business process repository. First, we extract from $\mathbb{P}$ the set of similar configurations for the configurable elements in P^c (see section 4.1). Then, using association rule mining techniques, we mine configuration rules from the retrieved similar configurations (see section 4.2).

4.1 Retrieving Similar Configurations

In this step, we extract from each process variant $P_i \in \mathbb{P}$ the configurations corresponding to the configurable elements in P^c. Nevertheless, retrieving exact configurations is not realistic as existing process variants may have similar but not exact parts with the configurable model. Thus, we aim at extracting *similar configurations* for the configurable elements. In order to match graph elements, we compute two similarities: the similarity Sim_A between activities and the similarity Sim_C between connectors.

Activities' similarity. Let $a \in N$ be an activity (function or event) in P^c and $a' \in N_i$ be an activity in the process variant P_i. To compute the similarity Sim_A between a and a', we use a combination of syntactic and semantic similarity metrics since they are popular for measuring the similarity between activities' labels in business process models [16]. We use a syntactic similarity based on Levenshtein distance [17] which computes the number of edit operations (i.e. insert, delete or substitute a character) needed to transform one string into another. For the semantic similarity, we use WordNet database [18] which a is lexical database for English words. The WordNet similarity package includes a set of algorithms for returning the synonyms between two words. We use in particular the *WUP* algorithm [19] which measures the relatedness of two words by considering their depths in WordNet database. After normalizing activities' labels (i.e. put all characters in lowercase, remove stop words, etc.) the total similarity is the average of their syntactic and semantic similarities.

$$Sim_A(L(a), L_i(a')) = \frac{LD(L(a), L_i(a')) + WUP(L(a), L_i(a'))}{2} \qquad (4)$$

where $0 \leq Sim_A \leq 1$, LD and WUP are functions returning the Levenshtein distance and the WordNet based similarity respectively between $L(a)$ and $L_i(a')$. We say that **a' is the best activity matching for a** iff: $Sim_A(L(a), L_i(a') \geq minSim_A \wedge \nexists a_x \in N_i : Sim_A(L(a), L_i(a_x)) > Sim_A(L(a), L_i(a'))$, where $minSim_A$ is a user specified threshold. For example, in Fig. 1 and 2, the similarity between the events "Purchase order release" and "Purchase requisition released for purchase order" is 0.735. For a $minSim_A = 0.5$, "Purchase order requisition for purchase order" is the best activity matching for "Purchase order release" as it has the highest similarity with "Purchase order release".

Connectors' similarity. Let $c \in N$ be a connector in P^c and $c' \in N_i$ be a connector in P_i. The similarity between connectors cannot be done in the same way as activities since connectors' labels do not have linguistic semantics. Hence, in order to compute the similarity Sim_C between c and c', we rely on (1) the partial order $\preceq$ (see Definition 3) which orders the connectors' labels based on their behavior and (2) the postset (respectively preset) similarities in case of split (respectively join) connectors. The similarity Sim_C between split connectors is computed as:

$$Sim_C(c, c') = \begin{cases} \frac{\#BM(c\bullet, c'\bullet)}{|c\bullet|} & \text{if } c' \preceq c \\ 0 & \text{otherwise} \end{cases} \qquad (5)$$

where $\#BM(c\bullet, c'\bullet)$ returns the number of best elements' matching in $c'\bullet$ that correspond to those in $c\bullet$. The join connectors' similarity is computed in the same way but with the consideration of their preset instead of postset. We say that **c' is the best connector matching for c** iff: $Sim_C(c, c') \geq minSim_C \wedge \nexists c_x \in N_i : Sim_C(c, c_x) > Sim_C(c, c')$ where $minSim_C$ is a user specified threshold. For example, in Fig. 1 and 2, the similarity between "$\times_1$" in the first process model and "$\times_1$" in the second one is $Sim_C(\times_1, \times_1) = \frac{2}{3} = 0.67$. For a $minSim_C = 0.5$, "$\times_1$" in the second process model is the best connector matching for "$\times_1$" in the first one.

Similar functions'/connectors' configurations. Having defined the similarity metrics for activities and connectors, we show how we retrieve for configurable elements in P^c the similar configurations from each process variant $P_i \in \mathbb{P}$.

A configurable function $f^c \in N$ can be configured to ON or OFF. A configuration $Conf(f^c) = ON$ is retrieved from a process variant P_i, if there exists a function $f' \in N_i$ such that f' is the best activity matching for f^c. Otherwise, the configuration $Conf(f^c) = OFF$ holds. For example, in our running example, for a $minSim_F = 0.5$, the configurable function "Invoice verification" in the configurable process model in Fig. 1 does not have any best activity matching in the process variant in Fig. 2. Thus from this process variant, we retrieve the configuration OFF.

A configurable split (respectively join) connector $c^c \in N$ can be configured w.r.t. its type and postset (respectively preset) (see Definition 4). A configuration $Conf(c^c) = <c, c \bullet>$ [1] is retrieved from a process variant P_i:

- if there exists a connector $c' \in N_i$ such that:
    1. c' is the best connector configuration for c^c,
    2. $L(c') = L(c)$ and
    3. $c \bullet$ is the set of elements in $c^c \bullet$ that have best element' matching in $c' \bullet$.
- else if $|c \bullet| = 1$ and there exists an element $e' \in N_i$ such that e' is the best element matching for $e \in c \bullet$. In this case, c^c is configured to a "sequence", i.e. $c = Seq$.

For example, for a $minSim_C = 0.5$, the configuration $Conf(\times_1) = <\times, \{$Purchase order release, contract order release$\}$ for the configurable connector "$\times_1$" in the process model in Fig. 1 is retrieved from the process model in Fig. 2 since (1) "$\times_1$" in the second model is the best connector matching for "$\times_1$" in the first model, (2) $L(\times_1) = L(\times_1)$ and (3) "Purchase order release" has "Purchase requisition released for purchase order" as the best activity matching; and "contract order release" has "contract order release" in the second model as the best activity matching.

4.2   Deriving Configuration Rules

In the previous section (section 4.1), we retrieved for each configurable element in P^c the set of similar configurations found in each process variant in $\mathbb{P}$. In this section, we use these configurations to mine our configuration rules using association rule mining techniques.

Association rule mining [20] is one of the most important techniques of data mining. It aims to find rules for predicting the occurrence of an item based on the occurrences of other items in a transactional database or other repositories. It has been first applied to the marketing domain for predicting the items that are frequently purchased together. Thereafter, it has manifested its power and usefulness in other areas such as web mining [21] and recommender systems [22]. The Apriori algorithm [23] is one of the earliest and relevant proposed algorithms for association rule mining.

In our work, we also use the Apriori algorithm for deriving our configuration rules. In order to be able to apply the Apriori algorithm, we store our retrieved configurations in a **configuration matrix**. The configuration matrix is a $n \times m$ matrix where n is the number of process variants in $\mathbb{P}$ (i.e. $n = |\mathbb{P}|$) and m is the number of configurable elements in P^c. A row in the configuration matrix

---

[1] We show the case for a split connector.

corresponds to one process variant in $\mathbb{P}$. A column corresponds to one configurable element in P^c. The entry for the row i and the column j contains the configuration retrieved from $P_i \in \mathbb{P}$ for the jth configurable element. An example of the configuration matrix for the configurable process model in Fig. 1 is presented in Table 2. For example, the second row corresponds to the configurations retrieved from the process variant in Fig. 2. For clarification purpose, we refer to the configurations by their identifiers denoted as $C[nb]$. Table 3 contains the retrieved configurations' identifiers for each configurable element.

Table 2. An excerpt of a configuration matrix

P_{id}	invoice verification	$\times_1$	$\times_2$	$\times_3$	$\vee$
P_1	$C2$	$C3$	$C3$	$C20$	$C27$
P_2	$C1$	$C4$	$C4$	$C21$	-
P_3	$C1$	$C4$	$C4$	-	$C28$
...	...	...	...	...	...

Table 3. An excerpt of the retrieved configurations associated to unique identifiers

N^c	$Conf$	$Conf_{id}$
invoice verification	OFF	$C1$
	ON	$C2$
$\times_1$	$< \times, \{\text{purchase order release, contract order release}\} >$	$C3$
	$< \times, \{\text{purchase order release, scheduling agreemenr release}\} >$	$C4$
	...	...
$\times_2$	$< \times, \{\text{purchase order release, contract order release}\} >$	$C8$
	$< \times, \{\text{purchase order release, scheduling agreemenr release}\} >$	$C9$
	...	...
$\times_3$	$< \times, \{\text{Inbound delivery created, Purchase order created}\} >$	$C20$
	$< Seq, \{\text{purchase order release}\} >$	$C21$
	...	...
$\vee$	$< \wedge, \{\text{Purchase order created}, \wedge_3\} >$	$C27$
	$< \times, \{\text{purchase order created, Service accepted}\} >$	$C28$
	$< \times, \{\text{Service accepted}, \wedge_3\} >$	$C29$
	...	...

The configuration matrix along with a user specified support and confidence thresholds are used as inputs by the Apriori algorithm. As output, the Apriori algorithm returns the set of configuration rules having a support and confidence above the user's thresholds. An example of a configuration rule returned by Apriori for a support $S = 0.5$ and a confidence $C = 0.5$ is given in (1).

5 Experimental Results

In order to evaluate the usefulness and effectiveness of our proposed approach, we conduct experiments on a dataset from SAP reference model which contains 604 process models in EPC notation [24]. These models are not configurable. To create configurable process models for our experiments, we merge the similar processes in SAP models into configurable EPC (C-EPC) models using the merging approach proposed in [4]. To do so, we cluster similar process models with the Agglomerative Hierarchical Clustering (AHC) algorithm using the similarity approach presented in [4]. We obtain 40 clusters of similar process models having a similarity higher than 0.5. Then, each cluster is merged into one configurable process model. The characteristics of each obtained cluster and the corresponding configurable models are reported in Table 4.

Table 4. The size statistics of the clusters and the configurable process models

	size			# configurable nodes		
	min	max	avg.	min	max	avg.
cluster	20.55	25.625	23	0	0	0
configurable model	2	162	34.175	0	36	5.575

In the first experiment, we calculate the amount of reduction in the number of allowed configurations for a configurable process model using our proposed approach. Since the exponential growth in the number of allowed configurations is a source of complexity in a configurable process model, reducing and linking configuration decisions to the frequently selected ones have a significant impact on the variability understanding in configurable process models. Therefore, for each configurable process model, we mine the configuration rules. Then, we compute the amount of reduction which is one minus the ratio between the number of valid configurations using our configuration rules and the total number of valid configurations. The amount of reduction is defined as:

$$R = 1 - \frac{\#C_R}{\#C} \tag{6}$$

where $\#C_R$ is the number of configurations using our configuration rules and $\#C$ is the total number of valid configurations. The results reported in Table 5 show that in average we save up to 70% of allowed configurations which are either infrequent configurations or never selected in existing process models. Note that this amount of reduction may vary depending on the selected *minSupport* and *minConfidence* thresholds which are set to 0.5 in our experiments.

In the second experiment, we evaluate the mined configuration rules in order to extract useful characteristics for the configuration decision. Since configuration rules can be represented as a graph where each node represents a rule

Table 5. The amount of reduction

	Size	$\#C_R$	$\#C$	R
min	2	2	6	0.6
max	162	10.5×10^4	70×10^4	0.85
Avg.	34.175	1.5×10^3	5×10^3	0.7

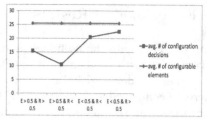

Fig. 3. The # of configuration decisions with varied emission and reception values

head or body and edges represent the implication relation between rules' head and body [25], we analyze this graph structure in order to derive interesting hypothesis for the configuration decision. We borrow the *emission* and *reception* metrics from the social network analysis domain [26] which measure the ratio of the outgoing and incoming relations respectively of a node in the graph. The reason for choosing these two metrics in particular is justified by the fact that a configuration node with a high emission have an impact on a large number of configurations in the process model. Therefore starting by its configuration may save the number of configuration decisions that should be taken by the user. Whereas a configuration node with a high reception depends on a large number of configurations. Therefore it may be useful to delay the selection of such configuration. The emission E_C and reception R_C ratios of a configuration node are computed as:

$$E_C = \frac{\#out_C}{max_i(\#out_{C_i})} \qquad R_C = \frac{\#in_C}{max_i(\#in_{C_i})} \qquad (7)$$

where $\#out_C$ (respectively $\#in_C$) is the number of outgoing (respectively incoming) relations of the node C and $\#max_i(out_{C_i})$ (respectively $\#max_i(in_{C_i})$) is the maximal number of outgoing (respectively incoming) relations among the configuration nodes C_i in the graph. Using these two metrics, we select the models having more than 10 configurable nodes. Then for each configuration node, we compute its emission, reception and the number of configuration decisions that must be taken when starting with such configuration. Then, we organized these nodes in four groups based on their high (> 0.5) or low (< 0.5) reception and emission. The obtained results are illustrated in Fig. 3. The straight line represents the average number of configurable elements and the curve line represents the average number of configuration decisions that must be taken when starting with a specific group of configuration nodes. These results show that selecting the configurations with a high reception and a low emission reduce the number of configuration decisions to 10 while there exist in average $25, 5$ configuration decisions (i.e. configurable elements) in the model.

6   Related Work

The limitation and rigid representation of existing business process models have led to the definition of flexible process models [27]. In this paper, we rely on the work presented in [3] where configurable process models are introduced. In their work, the authors define the requirements for a configurable process modeling technique and propose the configurable EPC notation. They highlight the need for configuration guidelines that guide the configuration process. These guidelines should clearly depict the interrelationships between configuration decisions and can include the frequency information. In our work, we demonstrate how using association rule mining techniques, we induce frequency-based configuration rules from existing process variants. These rules describe the association between the frequently selected configurations.

In order to match existing process models for merging, La Rosa et al. [4] use the notion of graph edit distance [28]. They compute the score matching using syntactical, semantic and contextual similarities identified in [16]. In our work, we propose to use existing process variants in order to analyze the variability in a configurable process model. This analysis can be used to improve the design and configuration of the configurable process model. We also use similar metrics for process model matching. However, instead of matching entire process models, we only search a matching for configurable elements.

To manage the variability in configurable process models, the researchers have been inspired from variability management in the field of Software Product Line Engineering [29]. La Rosa et al. [12] propose a questionnaire-driven approach for configuring reference models. They describe a framework to capture the system variability based on a set of questions defined by domain experts and answered by designers. Their questionnaire model includes order dependencies and domain constraints represented as logic expressions over facts. The main limitation of this approach is that it requires the knowledge of a domain expert to define the questionnaire model. In addition, each change in the configurable process model requires the update of the questionnaire model by the domain expert. This task manually performed may affect the configuration framework performance. While in our work, we propose an automated approach to extract the knowledge resulted from existing configurations using the well know concept of *association rules*. Our configuration rules can serve as a support for domain experts in order to define and update their configuration models.

Huang et al. [13] propose an ontology-based framework for deriving business rules using Semantic Web Rule Language (SWRL). They use two types of ontologies: a business rule ontology which is specified by a domain expert, and a process variation points ontology based on the C-EPC language. Using these ontologies, they derive SWRL rules that guide the configuration process. Different from them, we map the configuration process to a machine learning problem and use association rule mining instead of SWRL based rules in order to derive configuration rules. Our approach does not require any extra expert's effort and can be extended in order to classify the learned configuration rules w.r.t. specific business requirements.

7 Conclusion

In this paper, we present a frequency-based approach for the variability analysis in configurable process models. We propose to enhance the configurable process models with *configuration rules*. These rules describe the combination of the frequently selected configurations. Starting from a configurable process model and an existing business process repository, we take advantage of association rule mining techniques in order to mine the frequently selected configurations as *configuration rules*. Experimental results show that using our configuration rules, the complexity of existing configurable process models is reduced. In addition, metrics such as *emission* and *reception* applied to our configuration rules help in identifying the configurations that save users' decisions.

Actually, we are integrating our approach in an existing business process modeling tool, namely Oryx editor. In our fututre work, we target to define most sophisticated rules for retrieving similar connector' configurations. Instead of relying only on the connectors's direct preset and postset, we aim at looking for k-backward and k-forward similar elements. This in turn, would improve our preprocessing step and therefore our mined configuration rules. Moreover, we look for enhancing our configuration rules, besides the frequency, with other useful information such as the configuration performance, ranking, etc.

References

1. Fettke, P., Loos, P.: Classification of reference models: a methodology and its application. Information Systems and eBusiness Management (2003)
2. Schonenberg, H., et al.: Towards a taxonomy of process flexibility. In: CAiSE Forum, pp. 81–84 (2008)
3. Rosemann, M., van der Aalst, W.M.P.: A configurable reference modelling language. Inf. Syst. (2007)
4. Rosa, L., et al.: Business process model merging: An approach to business process consolidation. ACM Trans. Softw. Eng. Methodol. (2013)
5. Derguech, W., Bhiri, S.: Merging business process variants. In: Abramowicz, W. (ed.) BIS 2011. LNBIP, vol. 87, pp. 86–97. Springer, Heidelberg (2011)
6. Gottschalk, F., Aalst, W.M., Jansen-Vullers, M.H.: Merging event-driven process chains. In: OTM 2008 (2008)
7. Assy, N., Chan, N.N., Gaaloul, W.: Assisting business process design with configurable process fragments. In: IEEE SCC 2013 (2013)
8. Buijs, J.C.A.M., van Dongen, B.F., van der Aalst, W.M.P.: Mining configurable process models from collections of event logs. In: Daniel, F., Wang, J., Weber, B. (eds.) BPM 2013. LNCS, vol. 8094, pp. 33–48. Springer, Heidelberg (2013)
9. Gottschalk, F., Aalst, W.M.P.v.d., Jansen-Vullers, M.H.: Mining Reference Process Models and their Configurations. In: EI2N08, OTM 2008 Workshops (2008)
10. Assy, N., Gaaloul, W., Defude, B.: Mining configurable process fragments for business process design. In: Tremblay, M.C., VanderMeer, D., Rothenberger, M., Gupta, A., Yoon, V. (eds.) DESRIST 2014. LNCS, vol. 8463, pp. 209–224. Springer, Heidelberg (2014)
11. Dijkman, R.M., Rosa, M.L., Reijers, H.A.: Managing large collections of business process models - current techniques and challenges. Computers in Industry (2012)

12. Rosa, M.L., et al.: Questionnaire-based variability modeling for system configuration. Software and System Modeling 8(2), 251–274 (2009)
13. Huang, Y., Feng, Z., He, K., Huang, Y.: Ontology-based configuration for service-based business process model. In: IEEE SCC, pp. 296–303 (2013)
14. Santos, E., Pimentel, J., Castro, J., Sánchez, J., Pastor, O.: Configuring the variability of business process models using non-functional requirements. In: Bider, I., Halpin, T., Krogstie, J., Nurcan, S., Proper, E., Schmidt, R., Ukor, R. (eds.) BP-MDS 2010 and EMMSAD 2010. LNBIP, vol. 50, pp. 274–286. Springer, Heidelberg (2010)
15. Witten, I.H., Frank, E.: Data Mining: Practical Machine Learning Tools and Techniques, Second Edition (Morgan Kaufmann Series in Data Management Systems). Morgan Kaufmann Publishers Inc (2005)
16. Dijkman, R.M., et al.: Similarity of business process models: Metrics and evaluation. Inf. Syst. 36(2), 498–516 (2011)
17. Levenshtein, V.I.: Binary Codes Capable of Correcting Deletions, Insertions and Reversals. Soviet Physics Doklady (1996)
18. Pedersen, T., Patwardhan, S., Michelizzi, J.: Wordnet: Similarity - measuring the relatedness of concepts. In: AAAI, pp. 1024–1025 (2004)
19. Wu, Z., Palmer, M.: Verbs semantics and lexical selection. In: ACL 1994 (1994)
20. Agrawal, R., Imielinski, T., Swami, A.N.: Mining association rules between sets of items in large databases. In: ACM SIGMOD 1993, pp. 207–216 (1993)
21. Fu, X., Budzik, J., Hammond, K.J.: Mining Navigation History for Recommendation. In: IUI 2000, pp. 106–112 (2000)
22. Lin, W., Alvarez, S.A., Ruiz, C.: Collaborative recommendation via adaptive association rule mining. In: Data Mining and Knowledge Discovery (2000)
23. Agrawal, R., Srikant, R.: Fast algorithms for mining association rules in large databases. In: VLDB, pp. 487–499 (1994)
24. Keller, G., Teufel, T.: Sap R/3 Process Oriented Implementation, 1st edn. Addison-Wesley Longman Publishing Co., Inc., Boston (1998)
25. Ertek, G., Demiriz, A.: A framework for visualizing association mining results. In: Levi, A., Savaş, E., Yenigün, H., Balcısoy, S., Saygın, Y. (eds.) ISCIS 2006. LNCS, vol. 4263, pp. 593–602. Springer, Heidelberg (2006)
26. Scott, J.P.: Social Network Analysis: A Handbook. SAGE Publications (2000)
27. Bhat, J., Deshmukh, N.: Methods for Modeling Flexibility in Business Processes. In: BPMDS 2005 (2005)
28. Hart, P.E., Nilsson, N.J., Raphael, B.: A formal basis for the heuristic determination of minimum cost paths. IEEE Trans. Systems Science and Cybernetics 4(2), 100–107 (1968)
29. Clements, P.C.: Managing variability for software product lines: Working with variability mechanisms. In: SPLC, pp. 207–208 (2006)

ProcessBase: A Hybrid Process Management Platform

Moshe Chai Barukh and Boualem Benatallah

School of Computer Science & Engineering
The University of New South Wales, Sydney – Australia
{mosheb,boualem}@cse.unsw.edu.au

Abstract. Traditional structured process-support systems increasingly prove too rigid amidst today's fast-paced and knowledge-intensive environments. Commonly described as "unstructured" or "semi-structured" processes, they cannot be pre-planned and likely to be dependent upon the interpretation of human-workers during process execution. On the other hand, there has been a plethora of Social and Web 2.0 services to support workers with enhanced collaboration, however these tools are often used ad-hoc with little or no customisable process support. In order to address these challenges, we thus present: *"ProcessBase"*, an innovative Hybrid-Processes platform that holistically combines *structured, semi-structured* and *unstructured* activities. Our task-model proposed encapsulates a spectrum of process specificity, including: structured to ad-hoc Web-service tasks, automated rule-tasks, human-tasks as well as lifecycle state-tasks. In addition, our hybrid process-model enables the "evolution/agility" from unstructured to increasingly structured process design; as well as the notion of "cases" representing repeatable process patterns and variations. We further propose an incremental process-knowledge acquisition technique for curation, which is thereby utilised to facilitate efficient "re-use" in the form of a context-driven recommendation system.

Keywords: Business Process Management, Hybrid Process, Case Management, Service Oriented Architecture, Web-Services, Web 2.0.

1 Introduction

Many processes are difficult to model due to the ad-hoc characteristics of these processes [1], which often cannot be determined before the process begins. While certain characteristics could be predicted, the actual activities and ordering may differ. More so, information may only become available during the process, thus making human-beings and knowledge-workers in control of these processes [2–5].

An emerging discipline to deal with such processes (commonly referred to as "unstructured" or "semi-structured" processes) is Case-Management. The importance is well recognised since knowledge-workers who make up 25-40% of a typical workplace play a vital role on the long-term success of an enterprise [3]. However, while research in this area correctly highlights the importance of combining knowledge with process [3], and calls for increased flexibility [4],

X. Franch et al. (Eds.): ICSOC 2014, LNCS 8831, pp. 16–31, 2014.
© Springer-Verlag Berlin Heidelberg 2014

most existing implementations are yet to embrace these requirements [2]. As a result, case-management has often only intensely been managed manually, in circumstances where traditional BPM suites would otherwise prove too rigid.

On the other end of the spectrum, major advances in Web-technology, including Web 2.0, crowd- and cloud- computing, has also influenced a new wave of process-support. Cultivated by the services-oriented paradigm, *Software-as-a-Service (SaaS)* tools are extensively being used to complete everyday tasks, [6, 7]. Albeit there remains significant shortcomings: (i) Firstly, the re-use of such ready-made Web-apps often implies conforming to the embedded work-process allowing little room for customisation; (ii) Alternatively, even if a collection of such tools are used for different portions of the process, this inevitably leads to "shadow processes" [8], often only informally managed by e-mail or the like; (iii) Yet if none of the above suffices, a support system would have to be "developed" from scratch, and even when leveraging existing apps, it still requires considerable technical/programming skills; (iv) Finally, without the required skills or lack of resources, it may likely resort to "homebrewed" solutions (e.g. spreadsheets and/or office applications), resulting in untidy and hard-to-maintain products.

Not surprisingly, process-support technology has thus typically been portrayed in two extremes [2, 9]: Either highly *structured* and almost procedurally executed processes supported by BPMS, WfMS, ERP, etc.; whilst many *unstructured* and ad-hoc processes strive for support from various SaaS tools. The reality however, is that most processes rarely fit into only one of these two extremes; rather they usually comprise (sub-)fragments of various types of organisational activities that include a mix (or spectrum) of structured activities to other activities that may be very ad-hoc, [9, 10]. Moreover, there exist a variety of process paradigms/models/representations that are best suited to a specific domain. For example, BPEL for structured flows, state-models for monitoring, rules for ad-hoc functionality, etc. While systems may support a partial-hybrid approach with one or two types, they generally compete rather than leverage inter-domain support. The main challenge is thus facilitating *end-to-end* process-support.

To address this, we propose *ProcessBase — A Hybrid-Process Management Platform*, consisting of an extensible platform that encourages a new breed of hybrid-process-driven applications. We define domain-specific types and functions to represent process abstractions from *structured* to *unstructured* activities; which is thereby exposed via a programmatic API in order to provide enhanced in-App process-support. Moreover, *ProcessBase* acts as a knowledge-base, for the efficient "curation" and "re-use" of process-knowledge, supported via a context-based recommendation system driven by an incremental acquisition technique. More specifically, we make the following main contributions:

- In Section 3, we begin by analysing the technological landscape, as well as tracking the evolution from structured to unstructured process support, with respect to existing work. We use this to demystify the various concepts, identify key characteristics and provide directives for our proposed work.
- In Section 5, we then propose a *domain-specific model for hybrid-processes.* Most importantly, we support: (i) The ability to capture possibly repeatable "patterns"; whilst also (ii) Allowing the "evolution/agility" from an early

unstructured to increasingly structure design. We address this by separating a hybrid-process *definition* from the actual executional *tasks* by introducing a *logical* layer that enables *modularity, virtual-ordering* and *hierarchy* of activities. Moreover, to support (iii) Case-based "variations" we integrate the notion of *cases* and *variations*. The logical layer thus enables the organisation of process-knowledge without governing the execution. We model the executional components as a variety of 5 task-types, aiming to cover the range of process-specificity, including: Structured (i.e. BPEL) tasks, ECA Rule-tasks, Human-tasks, Web-services tasks as well as lifecycle State-tasks.

- In Section 6, we propose a novel *context-based recommendation system* for more efficient "re-use" of process-knowledge, via an incremental knowledge-acquisition technique. The first work to propose this, as far as we know.
- In Section 7, we delineate our proposed programmatic *Hybrid Process-as-a-Service (HPaaS)* API. In Section 8, we evaluate our work by implementing the reference scenario over a comparative experimental study. Finally, we conclude with a summary and directions for future work at Section 9.

2   Motivating Example

Consider the *"Software Development Change-Management"* process, as illustrated in the BPMN model shown in Figure 1.

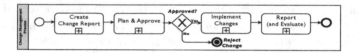

Fig. 1. Software Development Change Management Process

While the overall pattern may be followed, the specifics may vary between case-to-case. For example, a "formal" software-project often view changes as a non-typical event requiring a strict approval-process. However, even in a "formal" setting, structured activities may exhibit variations, but only based on preconceived conditions; an example is illustrated in Figure 2.

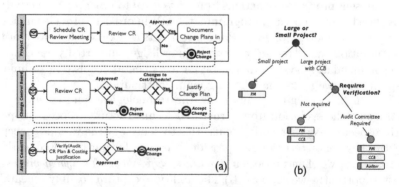

Fig. 2. (a) Formal Software Project Approval Process; (b) Process Variation Tree

In contrast however, "agile" (e.g. eXtreme programming) software-projects embrace change and thus are prone to a simplified approval process that could likely be reduced to a simple human-task, as illustrated in Figure 3. Moreover, in both cases, certain activities could nonetheless be inherently ad-hoc. For example, activities such as: *create change report*, and *implement changes* could directly depend upon the specific project's development environment. Such as, a change report could be generated using *GoogleDrive*, while another project could depend on a documents uploaded to *DropBox*. Likewise, some projects could employ *Git* while others may use *SVN*.

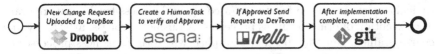

Fig. 3. Agile Software Development Change Management Process

3   Background and Related Work in Hybrid-Processes

Transitioning process-support from structured to unstructured domains, requires harnessing the capabilities that BPM had to offer for its application to unstructured processes; such that these ad-hoc style processes can be comparably visible, measurable and managed [8]. Essentially this means bridging the gap between *structured* and *unstructured* processes. We therefore dedicate this section in understanding the technological evolution and landscape, in order to recognise the potential gaps, from which we derive the main directives of our proposed work.

BPM vs Rule-based Systems. BPM and rule-based systems are two of the most conventional archetypical approaches, for structured versus less-structured support, respectively. BPMSs introduced the process-centric methodology, and offered a high-level model-driven approach that strongly appealed to non-technical domain-experts. However it suffered from a vital lack of agility. Rule-systems on the other hand, while inherently capable of dealing with the executional dynamics of orchestrations, their applicability in non-trivial contexts have meant limited success, due to the number of rules required to describe a process. The synergy therefore, between BPM and Rule-based systems has thus often been explored as a potential way for achieving the best of both worlds.

For instance, in 2008 the OMG joined forces with the BPM community and released the *Semantics of Business Vocabulary and Business Rules (SBVR)* standard. The goal was to express business knowledge in a controlled natural language, albeit it did not directly address the formal integration with process modelling diagrams. *Vanthienen et al.* thus proposed to implement SBVR into the business process management lifecycle using an SOA approach [11], consisting of a three-layer architecture. Similarly, *Agrawal et al.* proposed *Semantics of Business Process Vocabulary and Process Rules (SBPVR)* [12]. *Milanovi et al.* also offered to integrate BPMN with R2ML, developing a new modelling language *rBPMN (Rule-based Process Modelling Language)* [13], which extended existing BPMN elements with rule-based properties. Nonetheless these works are yet to be well adopted in mainstream, likely because they overarch the extensive range of business rule-types (i.e. integrity, derivation, reaction and deontic rules), thus clouding simplicity with over-rich vocabulary and semantics, [4, 8].

Event Driven Business Process Management (EDBPM). In an similar approach, EDBPM focuses primarily on "event-driven" *reaction-rules*. The motivation has been to merge BPM with Complex Event-Processing (CEP) platforms via events produced by the BPM-workflow engine or any associated (and even distributed) IT services. In addition, events coming from different sources and formats can trigger a business process or influence its execution thereof; which could in turn result in another event. Moreover, the correlation of these events in a particular context can be treated as a complex, business-level event, relevant for the execution of other business processes. A business process, arbitrarily fine or coarse grained, can thus be choreographed with other business processes or services, even cross-enterprise. Examples of such systems include: *jBPM* [14], and *RunMyProcess* [15]. However, these systems are usually implemented where the respective components sourced from BPM or CEP operate almost independently, (e.g. event-modeller vs. process-modeller; event-store vs. process-store; rules-engine vs. process-engine; process-instances vs. rules-instances, etc.). In fact, the only thing connecting these two systems together is the event-stream at the low-level, albeit this does not really directly benefit the process-modeller. These systems also tend to be dominated somewhat by the structured process side (e.g. a rudimentary process is always required, and even basic changes require restarting the process). They also do not encompass the full range of process-specificity support, however nonetheless they do provide the crucial step-ahead towards at least a partial hybrid-process methodology.

Case Management. As mentioned, the "case-management" paradigm has also been recognised as a promising approach to support semi-structured processes. Unlike traditional business-process systems that require the sequence and routing of activities to be specified at design-time (as otherwise they will not be supported) - case-management is required to empower the ability to add new activities at any point during the lifecycle and when the need arises, [4]. At the same time it also requires the ability to capture possibly repeatable process patterns, and variations thereof [3, 16]. However, although there has been several efforts to push this, (e.g. OMG is currently working on an appropriate standardisation), at present there are no concrete all-encompassing frameworks capable of adequately supporting these requirements. *Emergent Case Management* provides a slightly more modernised twist, suggesting a bottom-up approach. *Bohringer* [2], proposes such a platform which petitions the use of social-software (e.g. tagging, micro-blogging and activity-streams) in a process-based manner. It claims to empower people to be at the centre of such information systems, where the goal is to enable users to assign activities and artifacts independent of their representation to a certain case, which can be dynamically defined and executed by users. However, this work is currently only at its concept stage and is yet to be implemented and tested. Likewise case-management in general is rather yet only considered "a general approach" rather than being a "mature tool category".

Characteristics & Requirements for Hybrid-Processes. In light of the above analysis, we identify the following dimensions that may be used to *characterise* process-systems. Bridging the technological gap and avoiding fragmented support thus *requires* collectively supporting the various facets over a holistic model. Accordingly, this has precisely been the motivation of our proposed work.

Process Paradigms. Refers to the type of control-structure the process-system can handle, [17–20]. There are three main facets identified within this dimension: (A) *structured*; (B) *semi-structured*; and (C) *unstructured.*

Process Representation-Models/Languages. Represents the language, model or interface offered to the process-designer. Again, there are three identified facets: (A) *Activity-centric* models the flow of control between activities based on a specified sequence; (B) *Rules-centric* define statements that express a business policy, thus defining or constraining the operations of a "process", in a declarative manner; and (C) *Artifact-centric* have tasks (actions or events) defined in the context of process-related artifacts, as first-class citizens, [21–24].

4   *ProcessBase* Architecture Overview

Figure 4 illustrates the system design and interaction of the main components of the *ProcessBase* system, which are elucidated as follows:

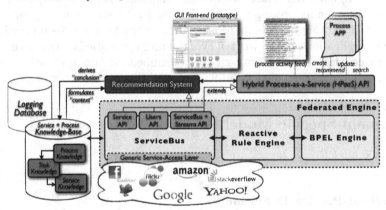

Fig. 4. ProcessBase System Architecture

The **Web-Services Layer** represents APIs available over the Internet, whose integration in processes offers vital potential: Services act as rich and real-time sources of data, as well as, providing functionality (software and tools), infrastructure building-blocks, collaboration mechanisms, visualisations, etc.

The **ServiceBus** components (leveraged from our previous work [6, 7]) acts as the middleware between outside Web-services and the platform back-end. Most importantly, it helps solve the inherent heterogeneity challenges: Services may differ in representation and access protocols, (e.g. SOAP vs. REST); as well as in message-interchange formats, (e.g. JSON, XML, CSV, or Media files, etc.). Moreover, APIs are constantly subject to change, (e.g. due to system updates, when data-structures are improved, errors fixed or new components introduced). The *ServiceBus* overcomes this by utilising our previously proposed *Unified Services Representation Model (USRM)*, which abstracts low-level logic and masks heterogeneity thereby exposing a common access and data-interchange interface. It relies on service-integration logic organised in the Services Knowledge-Base.

The **RuleEngine** enables reactive capabilities, via Event-Condition-Action (ECA) rules. When event patterns are matched, and their conditions are satisfied, the specified actions are then fired. Likewise, the **BPELEngine** component is delegated for executing and managing BPEL processes, which may represent a complete or more often a segment of a larger unstructured process. In both cases, these two engine components are federated with the *ServiceBus* for detecting and logging instance as well as activity-level events of running processes.

There are two **Storage** components: The *Knowledge-Base (KB)* extends the Services programming base with knowledge about hybrid-processes. Moreover, this combined Services+Process KB also maintains incremental *knowledge-capture rules* (different from event-rules mentioned earlier). Such a rule serves to map a process "context" (rule-condition) to an existing process "definition" (rule-conclusion). In this manner, when a new process starts formulation, and a similar "context" can be detected, the **Recommendation System** may suggest the closest matching process "definition" that could be re-used, either directly, or to create a template from. The other storage component is the *Logging-Database*, which curates ongoing process-instance data and artifacts, such as events and interactions data from services and tasks, for later analysis and/or processing.

Finally, applications can be written over the programmatic **Hybrid Process-as-a-Service (HPaaS) API**, which may be embedded into applications. (For instance, we have implemented a prototypical GUI front-end, for better support.)

5   Domain-Specific Model for Hybrid-Processes

In Figure 5, we presents the overall hybrid-process model:

5.1   Hybrid-Process Definition

At the highest level, a `HybridProcess` contains a set of logical `Activities` which in turn contains a set of functional `Tasks`. This provides a *light-weight* definition model for hybrid-processes. During execution, instance data may be recorded as `ProcessInstanceMessages`, which encapsulates a `Fact`, representing a data artifact from either an *event* or *action*, with various structure depending on its origin. A process may also require a `CorrelationCondition` (or set thereof called a `CorrelationSet`) to be specified, this is required in order to correctly partition messages and thus distinctly manage different running process-instance. We support the following types of correlation-conditions:

- *Key/Reference* based, refers to two messages being correlated if they share a field that are equal in value, (e.g. $M_x.f_i = M_y.f_j$);

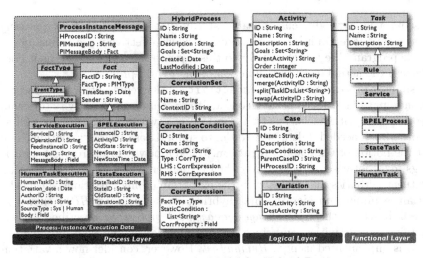

Fig. 5. Domain-Specific Model for Hybrid-Processes

- *Direct Reference* based, refers to when a message M_x can be directly correlated with a message M_y, by introducing a special uniquely identifiable field from M_x into M_y, (e.g. $M_x.f_i = M_y.\hat{f}$, where $\hat{f} := f_i$);
- *Semantic* based, refers to a special *reference-based* condition, where a relationship between messages M_x and M_y can be inferred using semantic-knowledge that are computed over the relative fields, (e.g. $email \equiv e-mail$).

5.2 Process Cases and Variations

In the absence of a process-schema based approach, unstructured processes are usually defined and managed as *instance*-only. However, even while such unstructured or ad-hoc processes may not be precisely repeatable, they may often have recurring elements and "patterns" that could be "re-used". Moreover, a pattern could also exhibit various case-based "variations". This is often expressed as *templates*, accessible via a template-library, or derived from existing instances. In our platform we adopt the latter approach. However, in either case a template

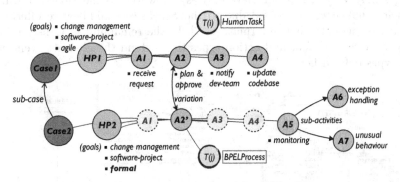

Fig. 6. Example of Hybrid Process Model (showing key nodes and relationships)

represents a light-weight, customisable at run-time abstraction for organising process components; unlike process-schemas, which effectively pre-define an executable program. We therefore refer to this layer as the *logical* layer, as it does not govern the actual execution/function of the hybrid-process.

To support process "patterns": An `Activity` entity represents a *logical* work-item, that may: be `ordered` between one another; contain a sub-activity (or chain thereof); `merge` with another activity; `split` into two sub-activities; as well as `swap` ordering if needed. Likewise, in order to support case-based "variations": we adopt the notion of `Case` and `Variation`. When a new hybrid-process begins it belongs to a root-case; sub-cases may then be defined which inherit the parent's constituent activities and tasks, with the exception of any variations specified.

As an example, consider the first hybrid-process (denoted *HP1*) shown in Figure 6, based on the *agile change-management process* we described earlier. It contains four activities, and since for an agile project, the *plan and approve* activity is implemented using a *HumanTask*. However, consider now a variation to this process for a *formal software project* instead. A new hybrid-process *HP2* can be defined as a sub-case, such that all activities are inherited (thus avoiding replication). However the designer specifies a variation: a new Activity *A2'* to replace the original *A2*, having the approval task implemented as a *BPELProcess* task instead. Similarly, additional activities (such as *A5-7*) can also be added.

5.3   Functional Tasks

We have identified a set of 5 domain-specific functional tasks that together encapsulate the required range of process-specificity:

Automated Rule Task. An automated `RuleTask`, shown in Figure 7, represents an ECA-style rule with a set of `EventTypes` and `ActionTypes`. A specialised `TemporalEvent` is also defined to enable triggering rules at specific times, or as part of temporal event conditions. `Conditions` are expressed as the triple $< path\_expr, comparator, value >$. Where a *path_expr* defines the query to reach the attribute value of the event message instance. While some event-types may have predefined message-models (e.g. a BPEL instance event), other types of messages may vary (e.g. from Web-services). However, as mentioned, the heterogeneity challenges are solved due to the *ServiceBus* middleware offering a uniform message-interchange format, [6, 7]. In the remaining sections for each task-type we define event and action types that extend the abstract event and action types defined here.

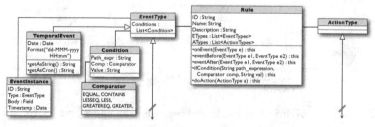

Fig. 7. Automated Rule Task Data-Model

Web-Service Task. To enable integration of Web-services, as illustrated in Figure 8, we define a `ServiceTask`. This is basically precisely akin to the model of `Service` defined in our previous work, [6, 7], we thus omit elaborating on the details. We support both WSDL and RESTful services, albeit the model could be abstracted into a unified set of entities, namely: `Service`, `OperationType`, `FeedType` (reference to a generic feed-endpoint), and `FeedInstance` (a specialised instance feed-type, with specific parameters defined, e.g. `&id=123`).

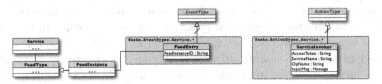

Fig. 8. Web-Service Task Data-Model

Structured-Process Task. Although well-structured process-support technology may not be feasible for a complete overall process, these frameworks are nonetheless useful in the case of routine and repeatable "fragments" of the overall process. We implement this type of task as a `BPELProcess`, as illustrated in Figure 9.

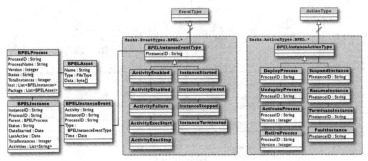

Fig. 9. Structured Process BPEL Task Data-Model

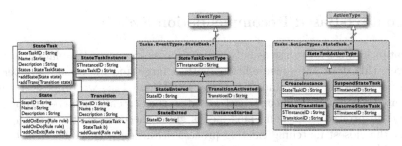

Fig. 10. Lifecycle State-Task Data-Model

Lifecycle-State Task. Data and resources are central to any process. However, since many process systems tend to be activity-centric, data-artifacts manipulated by these processes are seen as second-class citizens. In contrast, the "artifact"-centric approach stipulates an artifact modelled to have both an *information* and *lifecycle* model, [22]. We implement this archetype, as a Lifecycle StateTask as illustrated in Figure 10, consisting of States and Transitions. Modelled after a finite-state-machine (FSM), there are three kinds of state-actions (in our model represented as a Rule - where a pure action could just be with no event or condition): (i) *onEntry* is activated when the state is entered; (ii) *onDo* after finishing the entry-action and anytime while in that state; (iii) *onExit* when the state is deactivated. Likewise, in FSM terms, a transition is modelled as an *event*, *guard* and *action*. A guard is effectively a condition, which thus means we again re-use the notion of Rule which can thereby also be attributed to the Transition entity.

Human Task. Although there are several options for integrating human-worker frameworks into our platform, we have chosen to leverage *Asana*, due to its popularity, integration with other tools, and ease-of-use [25]. The model for a HumanTask has been illustrated in Figure 11. The entity Story represents any change or human/system activity performed during the execution of some human-task; which we represent in our system as events.

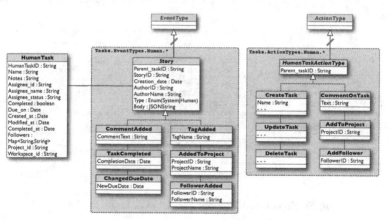

Fig. 11. Human-Task Data-Model

6   Context-Based Recommendation System

Current techniques for re-use usually utilise process schema or template libraries. However, this does not prove efficient with a large and increasing number of process definitions, cases, and variations. In *ProcessBase*, we propose a novel automated recommendation approach based on the currently detected "context" of a hybrid-process definition. This means given the context, the system may suggest the closest matching existing process definition, that could then be re-used and/or customised as required.

A context is matched based on existing process-knowledge. The hybrid-process model we presented thus far inherently curates this type of knowledge. However to make the system efficient in responding with a recommendation, we extend our model with knowledge-acquisition rules (denoted kRules to differentiate from ECA-rules) to incrementally capture process-knowledge. This means whenever an existing process is created anew, modified, or sub-case created, a new/updated context triggers a new knowledge-rule to be incrementally added.

To model kRules, we adopt the knowledge acquisition method *Ripple-Down-Rules (RDR)* [26], due to its simplicity, and its successful application in many other domains. However, it has never been applied to process-knowledge acquisition for the purpose of context-based re-use. We make use out of the *Single-Conclusion RDR (SCRDR)* approach, where the general form of this rule has two main components: if *[condition]* (i.e. when does the rule apply), do *[conclusion]* (i.e. what to recommend as a result). The knowledge-rules are organised in a tree-like hierarchy (in the order they are created). A new rule may be added as a child to another rule via a *true* branch (denoted $\triangle+$, if the current rule condition validates true but extra conditions are added), or via a *false* branch (denoted $\triangle\pm$, if the condition does not (fully) match, so a variation of the rule is created). During evaluation, starting at the top node, the inference engine tests whether the next rule node is true or false. If a rule node is true, the engine proceeds with the child nodes and again tests if they are false or true. The last rule node that evaluates to true is the conclusion given.

Applying this to our model, the kRule *condition* is thus represented as a hybrid-process "context", while the *conclusion* is a pointer to the matching hybrid-process, e.g. "HProcess_id". There could in fact be many different dimensions to formulate a process-context, for example: (i) the set of *goals* of the overall process; (ii) the set of *goals* of each constituent activity; (iii) the order of activities; (iv) the hierarchy of activities; (v) the type of Tasks assigned to each activity, etc. We've found the conjunction of the first two sufficient enough to formulate a viable context, (however, this could be customised as required).

To give an example (shown in Figure 12): Consider a designer starts with a blank process and simply specifies the process goals "software-project", "change-management". Assuming so far only an *agile* process has been defined, the system finds *Rule1* and thus recommends *HP1*. The designer may then create a sub-case

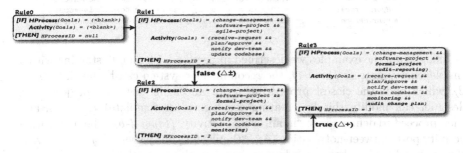

Fig. 12. Incremental Knowledge-Rules kRules

(for a "formal-project"), resulting in a new process *HP2*. However, since a new context has been defined, a new (*Rule2*) is added, as a variation to the parent. In another scenario, consider now the designer requires a more sophisticated formal change-process with *auditing*. Again, the designer may specify the relevant goals. This time we assume the process previously exists from someone else. Starting at the top, *Rule1* is checked however, since it evaluates to *false*, it proceeds down the "false" branch and encounters *Rule2*. Since it evaluates to *true*, it proceeds down the "true" branch ending at *Rule3*. The system thus recommends *HP3*, from which a *copy/template* can be created in order to be re-used.

7 Hybrid-Process-as-a-Service *(HPaaS)* API

We have exposed *ProcessBase* over a set of APIs. The benefit of this means hybrid-processes may be embedded in-Apps, and thus integrated at the programmatic level. We provide both a Java-client library (for backend integration); as well as, a RESTful API (suitable for front-end integration). In this section we show snippets of code highlighting the main features of the platform.

We have organised into two main APIs, as follows: Firstly, the `TasksAPI.*` offer CRUD operations over individual tasks (in cases where it could be used stand-alone and outside any process definition - this could be useful in very ad-hoc domains); Secondly, the `ProcessBase.*` API offer CRUD operations on hybrid-process definitions, in addition to other required operations.

TasksAPI.*	▪ `String id = create(Task t)` : registers the task on the knowledge-base	**C**
	▪ `Task task = get(String t_id)` : gets the task from the knowledge-base	**R**
	▪ `bool result = update(Task t)` : updates the task on the knowledge-base	**U**
	▪ `bool = result = delete(String t_id)` : deletes the task from the knowledge-base	**D**
	▪ `Fact fact = execute(ActionType at)` : executes the specified *Action*, returns data as a Fact.	
	▪ `String sub_id = subscribe(EventType et)` : creates a subscription to this *Event*	
	▪ `void addEventListener(sub_id, (@EventCallback)Object, String "handler_id")` : registers an event callback handler - such that events are asynchronously "pushed" to the callback	
ProcessBase.*	▪ `String id = create(HybridProcess hp)` : registers the hybrid-process on the knowledge-base	**C**
	▪ `HybridProcess hp = get(String hp_id)` : gets the hybrid-process from the knowledge-base	**R**
	▪ `bool result = update(HybridProcess hp)` : updates the hybrid-process on the knowledge-base	**U**
	▪ `bool result = delete(String hp_id)` : deletes the hybrid-process from the knowledge-base	**D**
	▪ `bool result = suspend(String hp_id)` : suspend processing of the specified hybrid-process	
	▪ `bool result = resume(String hp_id)` : resume processing of the specified hybrid-process	
	▪ `HybridProcess hp = createSubCase(String hp_id)` : create a sub-case of the h-process	
	▪ `HybridProcess hp = createTemplate(String hp_id)` : create a template of the h-process	
	▪ `HybridProcess hp = createCopy(String hp_id)` : create a copy of the specified h-process	
	▪ `HybridProcess hp = recommend(HybridProcess hp)` : invoke the recommendation system	

Using again the examples we described in Sections 5.2 and 6, starting with a simple/empty process *(Line 1)*, the recommender system can be invoked *(Line 2)*, which finds the closest process being for an "agile" software project. The designer can modify this by creating a sub-case (or template) *(Line 3)*, and then proceed to define a new "monitoring" activity, *(Lines 4-6)*. The monitoring activity posts a tweet-notification (e.g. "thanks for your patience!"), in the event the approval process has taken longer than 1-week to complete.

```
1.  HybridProcess hp = new HybridProcess.HybridProcessBuilder("formal_chng_mngmt")
                         .addGoal("software-project")
                         .addGoal("change-management"));
2.  HybridProcess hp_ = ProcessBase.recommend(hp);
3.  hp = ProcessBase.createSubCase(hp_);

4.  BPELProcess f_approval = new BPELProcess.BPELProcessBuilder("formal_approval")
                             .asset("approval.bpel");

5.  Rule delayed_approval = new Rule.RuleBuilder("delayed_approval")
                            .eventAfter(new TemporalEvent("0,0,*,*,0"),
                                        new ..BPEL.InstanceCompleted())
                  .onCondition(…)
                  .doAction(new ServiceInvoker("Twitter","postTweet",…));

6.  Activity monitoring = new Activity.ActivityBuilder("monitoring")
                          .setGoals("…")
                          .addTask(Twitter)          //"Twitter" ServiceTask
                          .addTask(approval)         //BPELProcess Task
                          .addTask(delayed_approval) //Automated Rule Task
7.  hp.addActivity(monitoring);
    ...
8.  ProcessBase.create(hp);
```

8   Evaluation and Analysis

A total of 5 potential platforms were considered: *Enhydra Shark, JawFlow, JBoss jBPM, JOpera, WFMOpen*; out of which the top-2 were chosen based on shortest installation and initial testing time; and quality of user-docs. We conducted 3 experimental studies, each comprising 4 comparative executional alternatives: (a) *ProcessBase*; (b) *jBPM*; (c) *JOpera*; and (d) Pure Java code-based solution.

Usability Study. Usability involves the criterion of *learnability* and *efficiency*. The former assessed by the time to install and run the initial tests: *ProcessBase* resulted in 26*m* and 39*m* respectively; compared to averages of 159*m* and 193*m*. The latter measured as the time to successfully implement the reference scenario: *ProcessBase* again proved superior in 72*m*, in contrast with an average of 203*m*.

Productivity Study. Given the task was fixed, productivity was measured based on the total number of lines-of-code (LOC) in order to produce the solution. The results in Figure 13(a-d), presents a distributed measure of LOC.

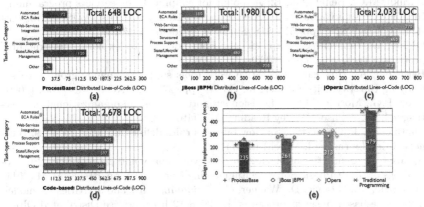

Fig. 13. Experimental Results of *Productivity* and *Performance* Studies

Performance Study. Finally, we measured the round-trip time (i.e. from when the change-request was issued, until updates were committed into *Git*). We repeated this study 5 times, taking the median; results as presented in Figure 13(e).

9 Conclusions

The work in this paper as far as we know, proposes the *first* all-encompassing complete hybrid-processes platform. Moreover, we propose an architecture where existing process-support technology (either domain-specific or partial-hybrid) can be leveraged, rather than compete with each other. In addition, our work is the first to propose a novel recommendation system using process context-detection - based on an incremental knowledge acquisition technique. Experimental results shows superior performance across all evaluated dimensions: *usability*, *productivity* and *performance*. Above all, we are optimistic this work provides the foundation for future growth into a new breed of enhanced process-support.

References

1. Marjanovic, O.: Towards is supported coordination in emergent business processes. Business Process Management Journal 11(5), 476–487 (2005)
2. Böhringer, M.: Emergent case management for ad-hoc processes: A solution based on microblogging and activity streams. In: Muehlen, M.z., Su, J. (eds.) BPM 2010 Workshops. LNBIP, vol. 66, pp. 384–395. Springer, Heidelberg (2011)
3. BPTrends: Case management - combining knowledge with process (July 2009)
4. de Man, H.: Case management: A review of modelling approaches (January 2009)
5. Holz, H., Rostanin, O., Dengel, A., Suzuki, T., Maeda, K., Kanasaki, K.: Task-based process know-how reuse and proactive information delivery in tasknavigator. In: Conference on Information and Knowledge Management, pp. 522–531 (2006)
6. Barukh, M.C., Benatallah, B.: ServiceBase: A programming knowledge-base for service oriented development. In: Meng, W., Feng, L., Bressan, S., Winiwarter, W., Song, W. (eds.) DASFAA 2013, Part II. LNCS, vol. 7826, pp. 123–138. Springer, Heidelberg (2013)
7. Barukh, M.C., Benatallah, B.: A toolkit for simplified web-services programming. In: Lin, X., Manolopoulos, Y., Srivastava, D., Huang, G. (eds.) WISE 2013, Part II. LNCS, vol. 8181, pp. 515–518. Springer, Heidelberg (2013)
8. Olding, E., Rozwell, C.: Expand your bpm horizons by exploring unstructured processes. Technical Report (2009)
9. Bernstein, A.: How can cooperative work tools support dynamic group process? bridging the specificity frontier. In: CSCW, pp. 279–288. ACM, New York (2000)
10. Keen, P.G., Morton, M.S.S.: Decision support systems: an organizational perspective, vol. 35. Addison-Wesley Reading, MA (1978)
11. Vanthienen, J., Goedertier, S.: How business rules define business processes. Business Rules Journal 8(3, March) (2007)
12. Agrawal, A.: Semantics of business process vocabulary and process rules. In: Proceedings of the 4th India Software Engineering Conference, pp. 61–68. ACM (2011)
13. Milanovic, M., Gasevic, D., Wagner, G.: Combining rules and activities for modeling service-based business processes. In: 2008 12th Enterprise Distributed Object Computing Conference Workshops, pp. 11–22. IEEE (2008)

14. JBoss: jbpm, http://www.jboss.org/jbpm/
15. RunMyProcess, https://www.runmyprocess.com/
16. Swenson, K.D., et al.: Mastering the unpredictable. How Adaptive Case Management Will Revolutionize the Way That Knowledge Workers Get Things Done
17. Berry, P.M.: Intelligent workflow - state of the art in workflow
18. Manolescu, D.A.: Workflow enactment with continuation and future objects. SIGPLAN Not 37(11), 40–51 (2002)
19. Wang, J., Kumar, A.: A framework for document-driven workflow systems. In: van der Aalst, W.M.P., Benatallah, B., Casati, F., Curbera, F. (eds.) BPM 2005. LNCS, vol. 3649, pp. 285–301. Springer, Heidelberg (2005)
20. Manolescu, D.: Micro-workflow: A workflow architecture supporting compositional object-oriented software development. Technical report, USA (2000)
21. Bhattacharya, K., Caswell, N.S., Kumaran, S., Nigam, A., Wu, F.Y.: Artifact-centered operational modeling. IBM Systems Journal 46(4), 703–721 (2007)
22. Cohn, D., Hull, R.: Business artifacts: A data-centric approach to modeling business operations and processes. IEEE Data Eng. Bull. 32(3), 3–9 (2009)
23. Bhattacharya, K., Gerede, C.E., Hull, R., Liu, R., Su, J.: Towards formal analysis of artifact-centric business process models. In: Alonso, G., Dadam, P., Rosemann, M. (eds.) BPM 2007. LNCS, vol. 4714, pp. 288–304. Springer, Heidelberg (2007)
24. Bhattacharya, K., et al.: A model-driven approach to industrializing discovery processes in pharmaceutical research. IBM Syst. J. 44(1), 145–162 (2005)
25. Asana: Asana project managements
26. Richards, D.: Two decades of ripple down rules research. Knowledge Eng. Review 24(2), 159–184 (2009)

A Multi-objective Approach to Business Process Repair

Chiara Di Francescomarino, Roberto Tiella, Chiara Ghidini, and Paolo Tonella

FBK-irst, Via Sommarive 18 Povo, 38050,Trento, Italy
{dfmchiara,tiella,ghidini,tonella}@fbk.eu

Abstract. Business process model repair aims at updating an existing model so as to accept deviant (e.g., new) behaviours, while remaining as close as possible to the initial model. In this paper, we present a multi-objective approach to process model repair, which maximizes the behaviours accepted by the repaired model while minimizing the cost associated with the repair operations. Given the repair operations for full process repair, we formulate the associated multi-objective problem in terms of a set of pseudo-Boolean constraints. In order to evaluate our approach, we have applied it to a case study from the Public Administration domain. Results indicate that it provides business analysts with a selection of good and tunable alternative solutions.

1 Introduction

Business process model repair can be used to automatically make an existing process model consistent with a set of new behaviours, so that the resulting repaired model is able to describe them, while being as close as possible to the initial model [4]. Differently from process discovery, in which a completely new process is discovered from the new observed behaviours, process model repair starts from an initial process model and it incrementally evolves the available model through a sequence of repair operations [4]. *Repair operations* range from simple insertion and deletion of activities in the model, to sophisticated sets of operations. In all cases, however, repair operations have a cost: they add complexity to the repaired models. Business analysts in charge of repairing existing models with respect to new behaviours are hence forced to choose whether to accept the increased complexity of a model consistent with all deviant behaviours, or to sacrifice consistency for a simpler model. In fact, some deviant behaviours may correspond to exceptional or error scenarios, that can be safely abstracted away in the process model.

In this work, we propose a multi-objective optimization approach to support business analysts repairing existing process models. It uses repair operations from state-of-the-art process repair algorithms to define a multi-objective optimization problem, whose two objectives are: (1) minimizing the cost of repair (in terms of complexity added to the repaired model); and, (2) maximizing the amount of new behaviours represented consistently in the model. We formulate such multi-objective optimization problem in terms of a set of pseudo-Boolean constraints and we solve it by means of a Satisfiability Modulo Theory (SMT) solver. The result provides business analysts with a set of Pareto-optimal alternative solutions. Analysts can choose among them based on the complexity-consistency trade-off that better fits their needs. The approach has been evaluated on a real life case study.

X. Franch et al. (Eds.): ICSOC 2014, LNCS 8831, pp. 32–46, 2014.

The contribution of the paper is twofold: (i) a multi-objective approach for business process model repair (Section 3); (ii) the results of our evaluation of the approach on a real-life case study (Section 4).

2 Background

Inputs to the automated process repair techniques are new process behaviours, which in modern information systems are captured through new execution traces recorded in log files, so the problem of automated repair can be stated as the problem of *repairing a process model with respect to a log file* [4]. In other words, given an *initial process model* M (either manually designed or automatically discovered) and a set of execution traces T (describing the new behaviours of the system), *automated process repair* aims at transforming M into a new model M' that is as close as possible to M and that accepts all traces in T, where an execution trace $t \in T$ is a sequence of events (i.e., system activities) $t = \langle e_1, ..., e_n \rangle$.

Among the different ways in which automated repair can be realized, two main categories of approaches can be identified in the literature: (i) the approaches performing *repair operations* on the initial model M by directly looking at its *differences* with the new traces [4]; (ii) the approaches that mine from T one (M_T) or more $(M_T = \bigcup(M_{t_i}))$ new process models describing the new behaviours, use delta-analysis [1] techniques for identifying differences between the new mined models and the initial one, M, and apply repair operations to M [7,6].

In both cases, the *differences* of the initial process model with respect to the deviant behaviours (described as execution traces or as mined process models) have to be identified (see e.g., [4] and [7]). Once such differences have been identified, a set of *repair operations* can be applied to the initial model M. The basic operations consist of *insertion* and *deletion* of activities in the model. For example, given the extract of Petri Net in Figure 1 and the execution traces $t_1 = \langle A, B, D, C \rangle$ and $t_2 = \langle A, C \rangle$, two basic repair operations, an insertion o_1 and a deletion o_2 (see Figure 2) can be applied to the Petri Net in order to make t_1 and t_2 accepted by the Petri Net. Since these operations might remove old behaviours of the net, some approaches (e.g., [4]) tend to be conservative and to introduce the addition or removal of behaviours only as an optional alternative to the old behaviours. Figure 3 shows how this can be realized in a Petri Net: the black transitions represent silent transitions, i.e., transitions that are not observed when the net is replayed. Note that while preserving old behaviours, repair operations can introduce extra-behaviours such as the one described by the execution $\langle A, D, C \rangle$.

In this work we use a repair technique belonging to the first group of approaches (repairs based on trace differences) and, in detail, the ProM[1] *Repair Model* plugin. This plugin implements the approach proposed by Fahland et al. [4] and takes as input a Petri Net describing the initial model M and a log. A cost is assigned to insertion and deletion operations. Correspondingly, an optimization problem is defined and the lowest-cost alignment between the process model and the set of input traces is computed. The outcome is a Petri Net M' which is able to accept all traces in T.

---

[1] http://www.promtools.org/prom6/

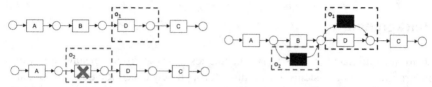

Fig. 1. An extract of M described as a Petri Net

Fig. 2. Base repair operations

Fig. 3. Base operations preserving old behaviours

On top of this base alignment algorithm and of the insertion and deletion operations described above, a set of variations are proposed in the approach by Fahland [4]:

Subprocess repair operations. In order to improve the precision of the repaired model M', i.e., to avoid having too many extra-behaviours (besides those in T), a *subprocess repair operation* is introduced. The idea is that whenever a sequence of inserted activities occurs at the same place in the model, instead of adding these activities incrementally, they are structured as a subprocess, which is mined starting from the set of subtraces that maximize the sequence of skipped activities in M. For example, considering the two traces $t_3 = \langle A, B, D, E, C \rangle$ and $t_4 = \langle A, B, E, D, C \rangle$, the subprocess $s1$ in Figure 4 is added to the net in Figure 1 to take care of the sequences of activities $\langle D, E \rangle$ and $\langle E, D \rangle$ that are inserted at the same place, i.e., after B. Moreover, according to whether the inserted actions represented by means of the subprocess are executed at most once, exactly once or more than once in T, a skipping transition is added to the net, the subprocess is added in sequence or it is nested in a loop block. In our example the subprocess is executed at most once and therefore a skipping transition that directly connects B and C is added to the net in Figure 4.

Loop repair operations. In order to improve the simplicity of the repaired model, a special repair operation is dedicated to the identification of loops in the traces. The identification of a loop, whose body represents a behaviour already described in the model, allows the addition of a simple *loop back* transition instead of a new subprocess duplicating the behaviour already contained in the initial model. For example, given the net in Figure 1 and a trace $t_5 = \langle A, B, C, B, C \rangle$ the silent transition (loop back transition) in Figure 5 is added to the net, instead of a new subprocess accepting the second sequence $\langle B, C \rangle$.

Remove unused part operations. In order to improve the precision and the simplicity of the repaired model M', the parts of M' that are no more used are removed, by aligning T with M' and detecting the parts of the model that do not contribute to the acceptance of a minimum number of traces.

In this paper we applied our technique on top of the results provided by the state-of-the-art ProM *Repair Model* plugin with the default configuration, which has been set by the authors to values providing the best results, according to their experiments [4].

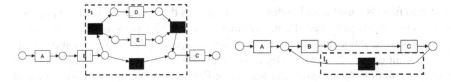

Fig. 4. An example of subprocess repair operation

Fig. 5. An example of loop repair operation

3 Process Repair as a Multi-objective Optimization Problem

To repair a model, a set of changes A (*repair operations*) are discovered and applied by the repair algorithm. Indeed, every subset $\bar{A} \subseteq A$ is able to partially fix the model M, so that a subset $\bar{T} \subseteq T$ of traces is accepted by the partially repaired model. Assuming that every operation $a \in A$ has a cost $c(a)$, we can formulate the problem of trading the number of traces accepted by the repaired model for the cost of repairing the model as a *multi-objective optimization problem* (MOP).

3.1 Multi-objective Optimization

In single-objective optimization, given a set X of alternatives and a function $f : X \to \mathbb{Z}$, which returns a cost (benefit) value associated with each alternative in X, the single-objective optimization problem consists of finding an element $x^* \in X$ which minimizes (maximizes) f. Multiple objectives can be expressed through a finite set of functions $\{f_i : X \to \mathbb{Z} | i = 1...n\}$ defined on the set X. Solving the optimization problem intuitively requires to find elements in X that give the best possible values for all the objective functions f_i at the same time. It is often the case that functions f_i assume their minimum/maximum in different points of X so that there is not a single point in X which simultaneously optimizes all f_i. For this reason the concept of *Pareto optimum* is introduced:

Definition 1 (MOP). *Multi-objective Optimization Problem (MOP) is defined by an n-tuple of functions* $(f_1, f_2, ..., f_n)$ *with* $f_i : X \to \mathbb{Z}$ *and a corresponding n-tuple of ordering operators on* $\mathbb{Z}$ $(o_1, o_2, ..., o_n)$ *where* $o_i \in \{\leq, \geq\}$, $o'_i \in \{<, >\}$.

Definition 2 (Pareto optimum). *A point* $x^* \in X$ *is a* Pareto optimum *for the MOP defined by* $\langle (f_i), (o_i) \rangle$ *if the following two conditions hold:*

- $\forall i \in \{1, ..., n\}$, $f_i(x^*) \, o_i \, f_i(x)$ *for all* $x \in X$,
- $\exists j \in \{1, ..., n\}$ *such that* $f_j(x^*) \, o'_j \, f_j(x)$, *for all* $x \in X$.

Definition 3 (Pareto front). *The image* $F^* = \{(f_1(x^*), f_2(x^*), ...f_n(x^*) | x^* \in X^*\}$ *of the set* X^* *of points* x^* *which are Pareto optima for the MOP defined by* $\langle (f_i), (o_i) \rangle$ *is called* Pareto front *for the MOP.*

Thus, a Pareto optimum provides a point that is equal or better than any other point for all the functions f_i and it is better than any other point for at least one function f_j.

The Pareto front is a useful tool to describe the options that a decision maker has at disposal and to identify preferred alternative among the available ones. In particular, when problems with two objective functions are concerned, a graphical representation of alternative solutions can be obtained by drawing the Pareto front points on the Cartesian plane. The solutions (points) that are not on the Pareto front are by definition worse at least in one objective than the solutions on the front and so they can be ignored in the decision process.

3.2   Process Repair as a MOP

Process model repair can be seen as a MOP if the power set of the repair operations $\mathcal{P}(A)$ is taken as the space of alternative solutions X, i.e. $X = \{\bar{A}|\bar{A} \subseteq A\}$ and for every element in X, namely $\bar{A} \subseteq A$, the following are considered objective functions:

- **Number of accepted traces:** $N(\bar{A}) = |\bar{T}|$, the size of the set $\bar{T}$ of traces accepted by the model repaired by the operations in $\bar{A}$
- **Total Cost:** $C(\bar{A}) = \sum_{a \in \bar{A}} c(a)$, the sum of the costs for all repair operations in subset $\bar{A}$

where function $N(\bar{A})$ is to be maximized, while function $C(\bar{A})$ is to be minimized.

Having expressed process model repairs as a MOP, we can find a solution by following the approach in [12], which transforms the MOP into a satisfiability problem. The method consists of assuming a maximum value $\bar{C}$ for the total cost function C and a minimum value $\bar{N}$ for the number of accepted traces function N, and writing a set of linear integer equations that describe the process repair problem under the constraints imposed by $\bar{C}$ and $\bar{N}$. Then, an SMT solver is used to find a solution or to establish that the problem is infeasible under constraints $\bar{C}, \bar{N}$. By varying $\bar{C}$ and $\bar{N}$ appropriately (e.g., incrementing $\bar{C}$ or decrementing $\bar{N}$ when no solution is found), the entire Pareto front can be precisely explored.

The first step for us is to translate the problem into a set of pseudo-boolean constraints (PBCs). A PBC is a formula involving booleans and linear integer arithmetics, having the form: $\sum_{i=1}^{n} a_i x_i \odot B$, where: $\odot \in \{<, \leq, =\neq, >, \geq\}$, $a_i, B \in \mathbb{Z}$, and all x_i range over the set $\{0, 1\}$. Figure 6 shows a simple

Operation	Cost	Accepted Traces
a_1	3	t_1, t_2
a_2	2	t_1, t_3
a_3	4	t_2, t_3, t_4

Fig. 6. An example of repair operations

example of process model repair, including the repair operations, their costs and the traces accepted by the model repaired by each operation.

The second step is to define, for a set $\bar{A} \subseteq A$ of repair operations, the vector $(\alpha_1, \alpha_2, ..., \alpha_{N_A})$ as the boolean-valued variables with the property $a_i \in B$ iff $\alpha_i = 1$. In other words, $(\alpha_1, \alpha_2, ..., \alpha_{N_A})$ gives the characteristic function of $\bar{A}$. Similarly, for a set $\bar{T} \subseteq T$ of traces, $\bar{T}$ can be characterized by the vector $(\tau_1, \tau_2, ..., \tau_{N_T})$ of the boolean-valued variables with the property $t_i \in \bar{T}$ iff $\tau_i = 1$. To make the notation easier to read, we overload the semantics of variables α_i and τ_i, making the assumption that when used in an integer context the boolean value *true* is interpreted as the integer value 1, *false* as 0.

The constraints on the objective functions "total cost" C and "number of accepted traces" N can be expressed as PBCs involving the variables α_j and τ_i, respectively:

$$\sum_{i=1,...,N_A} c_i \alpha_i \leq \bar{C} \qquad (1) \qquad\qquad \sum_{i=1,...,N_T} \tau_i \geq \bar{N} \qquad (2)$$

Let us define the matrix $\{m_{ij}\}$ with $i = 1, ..., N_T$ and $j = 1, ..., N_A$ such that $m_{ij} = 1$ if and only if trace t_i requires the repair operation a_j to be accepted by the repaired model. The following system of logical formulas model the relationship between repair operations and accepted traces:

$$\tau_i \leftrightarrow \bigwedge_{j=1,...,N_A \wedge m_{ij}=1} \alpha_j, \qquad \text{with } i = 1, ..., N_T \qquad (3)$$

Figure 7 shows the logical formulas for the example in Figure 6: the formula in the first row states that trace t_1 is accepted (τ_1 is true) if and only if repair operations a_1 and a_2 are applied ($\alpha_1 \wedge \alpha_2$ are true). Similar conditions for t_2, t_3 and t_4 are shown in the remaining rows of the table.

$$
\begin{array}{l}
\tau_1 \leftrightarrow \alpha_1 \wedge \alpha_2 \\
\tau_2 \leftrightarrow \alpha_1 \wedge \alpha_3 \\
\tau_3 \leftrightarrow \alpha_2 \wedge \alpha_3 \\
\tau_4 \leftrightarrow \alpha_3
\end{array}
$$

Fig. 7. Logical formulas for Figure 6

It can be proven that the set of formulas in Equation (3) is equivalent to the set of PBCs expressed by Equations (4a) and (4b), for all $i = 1, ..., N_T$. Figure 8 shows the set of PBCs obtained for the example in Figure 7.

$$\tau_i \geq 1 + \sum_{j=1,...,N_A} m_{ij}(\alpha_j - 1) \qquad (4a)$$

$$N_A \tau_i \leq N_A + \sum_{j=1,...,N_A} m_{ij}(\alpha_j - 1) \qquad (4b)$$

With this transformation, all constraints that must be satisfied to solve our MOP problem are expressed in pseudo-boolean form. Specifically, the set of PBCs (1), (2), (4a), and (4b) defines the model repair problem $MRP = \langle\{c_j\}, \{m_{ij}\}, \bar{N}, \bar{C}\rangle$ of finding a subset of repair operations that are required to accept at least $\bar{N}$ traces with a repair cost not greater than $\bar{C}$, given the action costs $\{c_j\}$ and the relation between actions and traces specified by matrix $\{m_{i,j}\}$.

$$
\begin{array}{l}
\tau_1 \geq 1 + (\alpha_1 - 1) + (\alpha_2 - 1) \\
\tau_2 \geq 1 + (\alpha_1 - 1) + (\alpha_3 - 1) \\
\tau_3 \geq 1 + (\alpha_2 - 1) + (\alpha_3 - 1) \\
\tau_4 \geq 1 + (\alpha_3 - 1) \\
3\tau_1 \leq 3 + (\alpha_1 - 1) + (\alpha_2 - 1) \\
3\tau_2 \leq 3 + (\alpha_1 - 1) + (\alpha_3 - 1) \\
3\tau_3 \leq 3 + (\alpha_2 - 1) + (\alpha_3 - 1) \\
3\tau_4 \leq 3 + (\alpha_3 - 1)
\end{array}
$$

Fig. 8. PBCs expressing the relation between applied actions and accepted traces for Figure 6

The problem MRP can be tackled by a Satisfiability Modulo Theory solver (YICES[2] was used in this work). If the problem

---

[2] YICES: http://yices.csl.sri.com/

turns out to be satisfiable, the accepted traces are identified by the true elements of $\{\tau_i\}$ and the required repair operations by the true elements of $\{\alpha_j\}$.

Computing the Pareto front. The Pareto front for the model repair problem MRP can be computed using Algorithm 1. First (step 1), we compute the point (C_T, N_T) of the front with maximum cost. Second (step 2), starting from $C = C_T$ and $N = N_T$, the maximum allowed cost C is reduced by one and the maximum number N of traces that can be accepted with that cost is searched, iteratively solving the problem $P(c, m, C, N)$ while decreasing N until a satisfiable problem is found. When found, the point (C, N) is added to the set F and every point (C', N') that is dominated by (C, N) is removed from F; the cost is reduced by one and the loop is repeated. Upon exit, the algorithm returns the set of points in the Pareto front.

Algorithm 1. Computing the Pareto front for the Model Repair MOP

Input:
> $c = c_1, ..., c_{N_A}$ vector containing the cost of repair operations,
> $m = (m_{ij})_{i=1,...,N_T, j=1,...,N_A}$, matrix specifying what traces are repaired by what operations

Output:
> F, a set of points (C, N) (cost, number of accepted traces),
> i.e. the Pareto front for the Model Repair MOP

// step 1: Compute the cost C_T to have a model that accepts the whole set of traces
$C_T = \sum_{i=1,...,N_A}(c_i)$
add (C_T, N_T) to F
// step 2: Follow the Pareto front
$C = C_T - 1$
$N = N_T$
while $C > 0$ **do**
  while $N > 0$ **do**
    if MRP problem $\langle c, m, C, N \rangle$ is satisfiable **then**
      add (C, N) to F
      remove any (C', N') dominated by (C, N) from F
      break
    end if
    $N = N - 1$
  end while
  if $N = 0$ **then**
    break
  end if
  $C = C - 1$
end while
return F

---

4 Experimental Results

In order to evaluate the proposed multi-objective approach, we formulate the following research questions:

RQ1 Does the Pareto front offer a wide and tunable set of solutions?
RQ2 Does the Pareto front offer solutions that can be regarded as repaired models of good quality?

RQ1 deals with the number and the variety of different solutions provided by *Multi-objective Repair*. In particular, the shape of the Pareto front and the number of the solutions in the Pareto front determine whether a wide range of alternatives that balance the two dimensions of interest is offered to business analysts. The Pareto front, in fact, might consist of points spread uniformly in the interesting region or it may be concentrated in limited, possibly uninteresting regions of the plane (e.g., near the totally repaired processes accepting almost all traces in T). In our specific setting the number of solutions available in the Pareto is dependent on the number of operations needed to repair the whole set of traces in T. In order to answer this research question, we look at the number of optimal solutions, as compared to the whole set of repair operations, and at the shape of the Pareto front.

RQ2 investigates the quality of the repaired models in the Pareto front. Specifically, two important quality dimensions for repaired models [3] are taken into account: (i) *Precision*, i.e., how many new behaviours are introduced in the repaired model with respect to the real process being modelled; and, (ii) *Generality*, i.e., how many yet unobserved behaviours of the real process are accepted by the repaired model.

In the following, we report the case study, the metrics, the experimental procedure, and the results obtained to positively answer **RQ1** and **RQ2**.

4.1 Process under Analysis

The process used in the case study is a procedure carried out in the Italian Public Administration (PA). It deals with the awarding of public tenders by contracting administrations. Before the winners can be awarded with the final notification, the contracting administration has to verify whether the winners have all the necessary requirements. In detail, the procedure is activated when the tender reports and a temporary ranking are available. According to whether anomalous offers can be accepted or not, a further step of evaluation is required or the letters for winners, non-winners as well as the result letter can be directly prepared and entered into the system. At this point, the requirements of the temporary winners have to be verified. If such verification is successful, an award notice is prepared and officially communicated; otherwise, further clarifications are requested to the temporary winners and the verification is iterated. The award notice can be published through the Web, through the Council notice board or, if the reward is greater than a given threshold, it has to go to print.

A Petri net M describing such public tender awarding procedure has been defined by a team of business experts as part of a local project. M takes into account the "ideal" procedure described in official documents and is composed of 35 transitions, none of which silent, and 32 places. No concurrent behaviours and no routing transitions occur in M, while there are three alternative choices and a loop, involving 5 routing places[3]. Since discrepancies were found between M and the actually observed execution traces T, a repaired model M' was produced from M using the ProM Repair Model plugin.

4.2 Metrics

In order to answer the above research questions, we use precision and generality metrics to compare M' to a gold standard model GSM. Differently from the initial model M which did take into account the generic "ideal" procedure described in official documents, the gold standard GSM has been manually defined by a team of business analysts working on the real process of a specific institution. It contains all and only behaviours that are legal in the specific setting. Model GSM contains 49 transitions and 38 places; it contains some parallel behaviours (2 routing transitions), several alternative paths and few loops (21 routing places). Transitions are decorated with transition probabilities estimated from real process executions.

Precision. Precision (P) of a repaired model M' measures the absence of extra-behaviour in M' with respect to the behaviour it should contain. It is computed as the percentage of execution traces generated by the repaired model and accepted by the gold standard model GSM:

$$P(M') = \frac{|acc(GSM, T_{M'})|}{|T_{M'}|} \tag{5}$$

where $acc(M, T)$ is the subset of T accepted by M and T_M is a set of traces stochastically generated by model M. It should be noticed that in the general case, where no GSM is available, measuring the precision of a model might be quite difficult and might involve substantial manual effort. We expect that good models are characterized by high precision.

Generality. Generality (G) measures the capability of the repaired model M' to describe unobserved behaviours of the real process. We compute it as the percentage of traces generated by GSM that are accepted by M':

$$G(M') = \frac{|acc(M', T_{GSM})|}{|T_{GSM}|} \tag{6}$$

where $acc(M, T)$ is the subset of T accepted by M and T_M is a set of traces generated by model M. We expect that good models are characterized by a high generality.

4.3 Experimental Procedure

The procedure followed in our experiments consists of the following steps:

---

[3] Detailed descriptions of the case study are available at the link http://selab.fbk.eu/mor/

1. **Trace generation.** Two sets of traces T and GT are generated from the gold standard model GSM (in our experiments, $|T| = 100; |GT| = 10$). Each trace is generated by a random execution of the Petri net: at each step, the transition to fire is chosen according to the probabilities associated with the enabled transitions. The execution ends when no enabled transitions exist;

2. **Model Repair.** The set of traces T is used to repair the initial model M, producing the set A of operations required to fix it. For each operation $a \in A$, its cost $c(a)$, estimated as the number of transitions added by the repair operation a, and the set of traces $T(a)$ accepted by the repaired model due to the specific repair operation a are stored;

3. **MRP Solver.** The Solver applies Algorithm 1 to obtain the *Pareto front*. Each point P_i in the Pareto front is associated with a repaired model M_i;

4. **Compliance Computation for Generality.** The set of traces GT is used to evaluate the generality of each repaired model M_i;

5. **Trace Generation from Repaired Models.** Each model M_i is used to randomly generate a set T_{M_i} ($|T_{M_i}| = 100$), using a uniform distribution of probabilities associated with the transitions;

6. **Compliance Computation for Precision.** Traces T_{M_i} are checked against GSM to measure the precision of model M_i.

Stochastic trace generation from GSM and from the repaired models M_i was repeated 10 times, to allow for the computation of average and standard deviation of the experimental metrics for precision and generality.

4.4 Results

Figure 9 shows the Pareto Front obtained by applying *Multi-objective Repair* to the presented case study. Each Pareto front point is associated with a model M_i, obtained by applying a different set of repair operations. The x-axis represents the cost of the repair operations applied to obtain model M_i, while the y-axis represents the number of traces in T that are accepted by the repaired model M_i.

The shape of the Pareto front offers an approximately linear set of solutions that are quite well distributed along the two axes. There are 6 points in the central area of the plot, distributed two by two along the Pareto front. For each pair, the point with the lowest cost is clearly associated with a better solution since the more costly solution accepts just one additional trace. For example, M_7 (indicated with an arrow in Figure 9) and M_8 represent a pair of close points. A business analyst, in charge to choose between the two repaired models, would probably prefer M_7, since this solution presents a lower cost, sacrificing only one trace.

Considering that 16 different repair operations have been identified by the ProM repair plugin – hence, 2^{16} different sets of operations can be potentially built – the 12 solutions provided by *Multi-objective Repair* represent, for a business analyst in charge of repairing the initial model, a good selection of different trade-off solutions, all ensured to be Pareto-optimal. Manual inspection of the whole space of solutions would be unaffordable. Based on these considerations, we can answer **RQ1** positively.

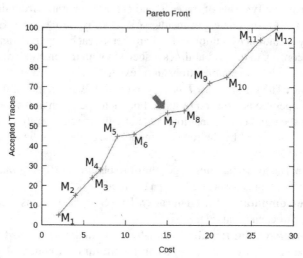

Fig. 9. Pareto Front obtained by applying *Multi-objective Repair* to the awarding of public tenders

Table 1 reports, for each repaired model M_i in the Pareto front, the number of traces in T accepted by M_i, the cost of the repair operations applied, and the values for precision and generality. Figure 10 plots the same data as a function of the repair cost. The low values for precision at increasing repair costs are due to the ProM repair algorithm, which tends to preserve old behaviours by introducing alternative silent transitions. These increase the number of extra-behaviours. As a consequence, the trend of the precision metrics is decreasing when the number of repair operations applied to the model grows.

The opposite trend can be noticed for the generality metrics (blue line in Figure 10). Starting from very low values for the poorly repaired models, the capability to reproduce new, unobserved behaviours increases together with the application of repair operations. It is worth noticing that in our case study the generality value for the repaired model accepting all traces in T, i.e., M_{12}, is exactly 1. In fact, the trace set T used to repair the initial model M provides exhaustive coverage of all possible process behaviours. Of course, this might not be true in the general case.

Table 1. Precision and generality for the models in the Pareto front

	# of accepted traces	Repair operation cost	Precision		Generality	
			Avg.	Std. dev.	Avg.	Std. dev.
M_1	5	2	1	0	0.04	0.07
M_2	15	4	1	0	0.13	0.17
M_3	24	6	1	0	0.22	0.08
M_4	28	7	0.51	0.04	0.26	0.1
M_5	45	9	0.53	0.07	0.41	0.08
M_6	46	11	0.29	0.03	0.41	0.1
M_7	57	15	0.51	0.04	0.51	0.11
M_8	58	17	0.3	0.03	0.51	0.11
M_9	72	20	0.4	0.03	0.66	0.1
M_{10}	75	22	0.25	0.02	0.66	0.1
M_{11}	94	26	0.26	0.03	0.98	0.04
M_{12}	100	28	0.13	0.01	1	0

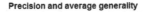

Precision and average generality

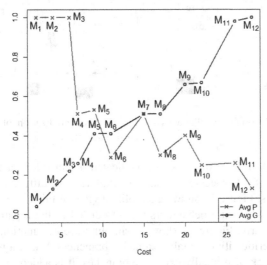

Fig. 10. Precision and average generality plots

The plot in Figure 10 shows that some of the intermediate solutions in the Pareto front (e.g., M_5, M_7 and M_9) offer quite interesting trade offs between precision and generality. For example, the repaired model M_7 is characterized by a precision and a generality of 0.51. At the same time, the additional complexity of this model in comparison with the initial model M can be approximately measured by the repair cost (15), which is half of the total repair cost (28) for the fully repaired model M_{12}. If we can accept only half of the overall model complexity increase, we get approximately half precision and generality.

We can conclude that the Pareto front built by *Multi-objective Repair* provides business analysts with a set of tunable and good quality repaired models. The possibility to consider intermediate solutions (i.e., solutions in the central area of the Pareto plot) and to choose "how much" to repair the model (hence, how much to increase the model complexity), provides business analysts with a lot of flexibility in the trade-off between model quality and complexity. Based on these considerations, we can answer **RQ2** positively.

4.5   Discussion

We have manually inspected the repaired models in the Pareto front. We found that some cheap operations (e.g., the introduction of silent transitions, realizing loop back/skipping activities, or of small subprocesses) enable the acceptance of almost half of the traces in T (see, e.g., M_7), at a cost that is around half of the total repair cost (28). Solutions located in the upper-right part of the Pareto, instead, are characterized by costly repair operations dealing with the acceptance of parallel behaviours.

The parallelization of activities and the management of mutually exclusive branches represent typical examples of challenging behaviours for repair techniques (in our case, for the approach implemented by the ProM plugin). The low precision values of some repaired models can be ascribed to these two types of criticalities. Concerning the first

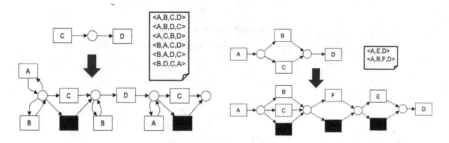

Fig. 11. Sequentialization of parallel activities

Fig. 12. Sequentialization of mutually exclusive activities

one (parallelization), indeed, the lack of a dedicated detector for parallel behaviours causes the insertion of subprocesses in charge of exploring the different interleavings of the parallel activities. Figure 11 shows a simplified view of this critical setting, which makes it also clear why extra-behaviours are introduced in the repaired model (e.g., $\langle C, B, D, C \rangle$). Similarly, Figure 12 shows a simplified representation of a particular case of the second criticality (mutually exclusive branches). When a new activity has to be added to a block of mutually exclusive branches, it is added in sequence at the join place as an optional activity, disregarding whether it is a new branch or part of an existing one. Figure 12 gives an idea of the extra-behaviour introduced in the repaired model (e.g., $\langle A, B, F, E \rangle$).

This analysis gives qualitative indications about the consequence of selecting a solution in the central area of the Pareto front (e.g., M_5 or M_7). A business analyst can repair the model at lower costs, while sacrificing execution traces involving more complex (and costly to repair) behaviours, such as parallel behaviours (M_7) or both mutually exclusive and parallel behaviours (M_5). The analysis provides also indications for the improvement of existing model repair algorithms, e.g., the need to introduce special rules dealing with parallelism and mutual exclusion.

4.6   Threats to Validity

Two main threats to validity can be identified in the presented case study, both related to the external validity, i.e., to the generalizability of the obtained results. The first threat concerns the investigation of a single case study. Results related to a single case study cannot be easily generalized. Nevertheless, the case study under analysis deals with a real procedure actually executed by Italian PA. The second threat is related to the specific repair tool and configuration used for identifying the set of repair operations. Different plugins and configurations would make the results more general. Nevertheless, the ProM plugin for process repair used in this work is among the most known in the literature.

5   Related Work

Reconciling execution information and process models, as done in process model discovery and repair, involves multiple, often contrasting, dimensions. Some works [5] apply post-processing analysis to simplify the discovered process models, while preserving the ability of the models to replay all the execution traces used for their generation. Others [9,3] use evolutionary algorithms to deal with these dimensions. De Medeiros et al. [9] apply a genetic algorithm to mine process models balancing the capability to reproduce behaviours traced in execution logs and extra-behaviours. Their algorithm optimizes a single-objective function, which combines under and over-generalization. A similar approach is taken by Buijs et al. [3], who use a genetic algorithm to discover a process model that not only balances under and over generalization, but also takes into account the model simplicity and generality, as well as the distance from an initial reference model. These works differ from ours because: (i) a new model is discovered rather than having an initial one repaired; and (ii) a single-objective function is used to combine all the dimensions to be optimized.

Multi-objective approaches have been applied to various fields of software engineering. For example, Harman et al. [13] present the first application of multi-objective optimization to the problem of test case selection. In their work, they study Pareto efficient genetic algorithms, such as NSGA-II, to maximize code coverage and minimize test cost during regression testing. Tonella et al. [11] introduce a multi-objective optimization algorithm to recover specification models that balance the amount of over- and under-approximation of application behaviours observed in traces. They show that multi-objective optimization performs outstandingly better than previous state-of-the-art approaches. Arito et al. [2] propose the formulation of the multi-objective problem of Test Suite Minimization (TSM) in terms of a set of pseudo-Boolean constraints. While our method adopts a similar formalization, the two considered problems differ in terms of involved constraints: in MRP a trace is accepted if and only if *all* associated repair operations are performed on the model, while in TSM each line of code can be executed by more than one test case, hence including *at least one* of them is enough to increase coverage.

Multi-objective optimization approaches have also been applied to the business process field, but never to optimize business process model repair. Marchetto et al. [8] apply a multi-objective technique to reduce intricate process models recovered from execution logs. In their work, two dimensions are investigated: complexity (measured in terms of analysts' understandability) and under-generalization. In Tomasi et al. [10], a third dimension is added to the two above: the business domain content of recovered processes. In both cases, the considered dimensions and the goal of the multi-objective optimization differ from the ones of this work.

6   Conclusions and Future Work

This paper presents a multi-objective approach to process model repair. It builds on top of state-of-the-art repair approaches and exploits the repair operations they provide to balance cost (in terms of complexity added to the recovered model) and advantages (in terms of traces accepted by the repaired model) of applying such operations to the initial model. Preliminary results, obtained by applying our approach to a real-life case study, indicate that: (i) the proposed *Multi-objective Repair* technique provides business analysts with a good selection of different solutions, all ensured to be Pareto-optimal; (ii) the returned solutions are tunable and good quality repaired models.

Future works will be devoted to performing further experiments involving larger case studies, as well as investigating the use of different configurations and tools for process model repair.

Acknowledgments. This work is partly funded by the European Union Seventh Framework Programme FP7-2013-NMP-ICT-FOF (RTD) under grant agreement 609190 - "Subject- Orientation for People-Centred Production".

References

1. van der Aalst, W.M.P.: Business alignment: Using process mining as a tool for delta analysis and conformance testing. Requir. Eng. 10(3), 198–211 (2005)
2. Arito, F., Chicano, F., Alba, E.: On the application of SAT solvers to the test suite minimization problem. In: Proc. of the 4th Int. Symposium on Search Based Software Engineering (SSBSE), pp. 45–59 (2012)
3. Buijs, J.C.A.M., La Rosa, M., Reijers, H.A., van Dongen, B.F., van der Aalst, W.M.P.: Improving business process models using observed behavior. In: Cudre-Mauroux, P., Ceravolo, P., Gašević, D. (eds.) SIMPDA 2012. LNBIP, vol. 162, pp. 44–59. Springer, Heidelberg (2013)
4. Fahland, D., van der Aalst, W.M.P.: Repairing process models to reflect reality. In: Barros, A., Gal, A., Kindler, E. (eds.) BPM 2012. LNCS, vol. 7481, pp. 229–245. Springer, Heidelberg (2012)
5. Fahland, D., van der Aalst, W.M.P.: Simplifying mined process models: An approach based on unfoldings. In: Rinderle-Ma, S., Toumani, F., Wolf, K. (eds.) BPM 2011. LNCS, vol. 6896, pp. 362–378. Springer, Heidelberg (2011)
6. Gambini, M., La Rosa, M., Migliorini, S., Ter Hofstede, A.H.M.: Automated error correction of business process models. In: Rinderle-Ma, S., Toumani, F., Wolf, K. (eds.) BPM 2011. LNCS, vol. 6896, pp. 148–165. Springer, Heidelberg (2011)
7. Li, C., Reichert, M., Wombacher, A.: Discovering reference models by mining process variants using a heuristic approach. In: Dayal, U., Eder, J., Koehler, J., Reijers, H.A. (eds.) BPM 2009. LNCS, vol. 5701, pp. 344–362. Springer, Heidelberg (2009)
8. Marchetto, A., Di Francescomarino, C., Tonella, P.: Optimizing the trade-off between complexity and conformance in process reduction. In: Cohen, M.B., Ó Cinnéide, M. (eds.) SSBSE 2011. LNCS, vol. 6956, pp. 158–172. Springer, Heidelberg (2011)
9. Medeiros, A.K.A.D., Weijters, A.J.M.M.: Genetic process mining: an experimental evaluation. Data Min. Knowl. Discov. 14 (2007)
10. Tomasi, A., Marchetto, A., Di Francescomarino, C.: Domain-driven reduction optimization of recovered business processes. In: Fraser, G., Teixeira de Souza, J. (eds.) SSBSE 2012. LNCS, vol. 7515, pp. 228–243. Springer, Heidelberg (2012)
11. Tonella, P., Marchetto, A., Nguyen, C.D., Jia, Y., Lakhotia, K., Harman, M.: Finding the optimal balance between over and under approximation of models inferred from execution logs. In: 2012 IEEE Fifth Int. Conf. on. Software Testing, Verification and Validation (ICST), pp. 21–30. IEEE (2012)
12. Van Veldhuizen, D.A., Lamont, G.B.: Multiobjective evolutionary algorithm test suites. In: Proc. of the 1999 ACM Symp. on Applied Computing, pp. 351–357. ACM (1999)
13. Yoo, S., Harman, M.: Pareto efficient multi-objective test case selection. In: Proc. of the 2007 Int. Symposium on Software Testing and Analysis, pp. 140–150. ACM (2007)

Memetic Algorithms for Mining Change Logs in Process Choreographies*

Walid Fdhila, Stefanie Rinderle-Ma, and Conrad Indiono

University of Vienna, Faculty of Computer Science, Vienna, Austria
{Walid.Fdhila,Stefanie.Rinderle-Ma,Conrad.Indiono}@univie.ac.at

Abstract. The propagation and management of changes in process choreographies has been recently addressed as crucial challenge by several approaches. A change rarely confines itself to a single change, but triggers other changes in different partner processes. Specifically, it has been stated that with an increasing number of partner processes, the risk for transitive propagations and costly negotiations increases as well. In this context, utilizing past change events to learn and analyze the propagation behavior over process choreographies will help avoiding significant costs related to unsuccessful propagations and negotiation failures, of further change requests. This paper aims at the posteriori analysis of change requests in process choreographies by the provision of mining algorithms based on change logs. In particular, a novel implementation of the memetic mining algorithm for change logs, with the appropriate heuristics is presented. The results of the memetic mining algorithm are compared with the results of the actual propagation of the analyzed change events.

Keywords: Change Mining, Process Choreographies, Memetic Mining, Process Mining.

1 Introduction

As a result of easier and faster iterations during the design process and at runtime, the management of business process changes, their propagation and their impacts are likely to become increasingly important [1]. Companies with a higher amount of critical changes list change propagation as the second most frequent objective. In particular, in around 50% of the critical changes, the change necessity stems from change propagation. Thus critical changes are tightly connected to change propagation in terms of cause and effects [2].

In practice, companies still struggle to assess the scope of a given change. This is mainly because a change initiated in one process partner can create knock-on changes to others that are not directly connected. Failures of change propagations can become extremely expensive as they are mostly accompanied by costly negotiations. Therefore, through accurate assessments of change impact, changes

---

* The work presented in this paper has been funded by the Austrian Science Fund (FWF):I743.

X. Franch et al. (Eds.): ICSOC 2014, LNCS 8831, pp. 47–62, 2014.

not providing any net benefit can be avoided. Resource requirements and lead times can be accounted for when planning the redesign process [3]. With early consideration of derived costs and by preventing change propagation, bears the potential to avoid and reduce both average and critical changes [2].

Hence it is crucial to analyze propagation behavior, particularly, transitive propagation over several partners. Note that change propagation might even be cyclic, i.e., the propagation affects either the change initiator again or one of the already affected partners. This is mainly due to transitivity; e.g., when a change propagation to a partner not only results in direct changes he has to apply, but also leading to redesigns in different parts of his process. In turn, this may have consequences on the change initiator or a different partner.

This paper is based on change event logs and uses mining techniques to understand and manage change propagation, and assess how changes propagate between process partners that are not directly connected (cf. Figure 1). A novel contribution is the implementation of a memetic mining algorithm coupled with the appropriate heuristics, that enables the mining of prediction models on change event logs, i.e., no information about the propagation between partners is provided.

In the following, Section 2 illustrates a motivating example, while Section 3 presents change log formats and gives the global overview of the problem. Section 4 follows up with a set of heuristics for change mining. Based on these heuristics, we introduce a memetic change mining algorithm in Section 5, which we discuss and evaluate in Section 6. In Section 7 we discuss related work and conclude in Section 8.

2   Motivating Example and Preliminaries

A process choreography is defined as a set of business partners collaborating together to achieve a common goal. Based on [4], we adopt a simplified definition of a process choreography $C := (\Pi, \mathcal{R})$ with $\Pi = \{\pi_i\}^{i \in \mathcal{P}}$ denoting the set of all processes distributed over a set of partners $\mathcal{P}$ and $\mathcal{R}$ as a binary function that returns the set of interactions between pairs of partner; e.g., in terms of message exchanges. Typical change operations comprise, for example, adding or removing a set of activities from a process model or modifying the interaction dependencies between a set of partners. A change operation is described by a tuple (δ, π) where $\delta \in \{Insert, Delete, Replace\}$ is the change operation to be performed on the partner process model π that transforms the original model π in a new model π' [4].

Consider the choreography process scenario as sketched in Figure 1 consisting of four partners Acquirer, Airline, Traveler, and TravelAgency. In this paper, we abstract from the notions private and public processes and assume that logs with change information on all partners exist (e.g. anonymized and collected). The Acquirer initiates a change of its process (δ, Acq) that requires a propagation to the direct partner Airline. In order to keep the interaction between Acquirer and Airline correct and consistent, the Airline has to react on the change by inserting a new fragment F3 into its process. This insertion, in turn, necessitates a

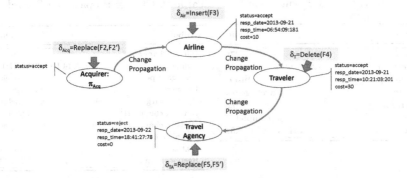

Fig. 1. Running Example: process choreography with Change Propagation

propagation to the `Traveler` that reacts by deleting process fragment F4. Finally, the change propagates to the `TravelAgency` that would have to replace fragment F5 by new fragment F5'. However, as the `TravelAgency` rejects the change, the entire change propagation fails. According to [4], such change propagation is defined as a function $\gamma : \{$Insert, Delete, Replace$\} \times \Pi \mapsto 2^{\{Insert, Delete, Replace\} \times \Pi}$ with $\gamma((\delta_i, \pi_i)) = \{(\delta_j, \pi_j)\}$. γ takes as an input an initial change on a given process model and generates the ripple effects on the different partners affected by the change.

The approach presented in this paper is based on change event logs collected from different partners. Figure 2 outlines the overall approach and distinguishes this work from previous ones. In [4], the overall picture of change propagation in process choreographies has been set out. Also the basic algorithms for change propagation are provided in [4]. We started analyzing change impacts in process choreography scenarios using a priori techniques in [5]. The latter work is based on the choreography structure only and does not consider information on previous change propagations that occurred between the partners.

3   Problem Formulation

In this section, we introduce two different change log types and give a global view on our approach.

3.1   Change Logs in Process Choreographies

Change logs are a common way to record information on change operations applied during process design and runtime for several reasons such as recovery and compact process instance representation [6]. For process orchestrations, change logs have been also used as basis for change mining in business processes in order to support users in defining future change operations [7].

Change logs can be also used for process choreographies. Here, every change log contains all individual change requests performed by every partner, where no propagation information are described in the log. At a certain time, all the public parts of the change logs owned by the partners participating in the collaboration

Table 1. Change Event Record

Attribute	Value
Initial Change ID	15d6b27b
Request time	2014-08-03T00:41:15
Change type	Insert
Partner	TravelAgency
Magnitude	0.6
Status	completed
Response time	2014-08-05T12:32

Table 2. Change Propagation Record

Attribute	Value
Initial Change ID	15d6b27b
Request time	2014-08-03T00:41:15
Change type	Insert
Partner	TravelAgency
Partner target	Airline
Derived change ID	c25b8c67a
Derived change type	Insert
Magnitude	0.6
Status	completed
Response time	2014-08-05T12:32

are anonymized [8], normalized, collected and put in one file to be mined. In the following, we refer to this type of log as CEL (Change Event Log).

In practice, it is also possible to have a change propagation log CPL (i.e. containing the change requests, their impacts and the propagation information as well). However, since the processes are distributed, it is not always possible for a partner to track the complete propagation results of his change requests (due to transitivity and privacy). To be more generic, we adopt change logs that contain solely change events CEL (without information about propagations) to be mined. However, in order to validate our mining approach, and assess the quality of the mined model from the CEL, we also maintain a log of the actual propagations CPL. The results of the predicted model from the CEL are compared and replayed on the CPL propagation events.

Anonymization of the logs represents an important *privacy* step [8], which is a trivial operation in a non-distributed setting. In a distributed environment a consistent anonymization scheme needs to be employed, where for example π_2 is consistently labeled as X.

Table 1 describes a sample of a change record. Each record includes information about the partner that implemented the change (anonymized), the change ID and type, the timestamps and the magnitude of the change. The latter is calculated using the number of affected nodes (in the process model), the costs (generated randomly), and the response time. Other costs can be added as needed. Table 2 describes a propagation record, with more propagation information.

3.2   Overview

As aforementioned, the main problem is to generate and analyze a propagation model by mining the change event log CEL, which contains all change events that occurred on the process partners involved in the choreography. Figure 2 gives a global overview of the main components for managing changes in collaborative processes. The first set of components (C^{3}Pro framework) provides support for specifying, propagating, negotiating, and implementing changes in choreographies. In particular, the change propagation component calculates the ripple effects of an initial change on the affected partners and checks the soundness of the collaboration if changes are accepted and implemented. The details

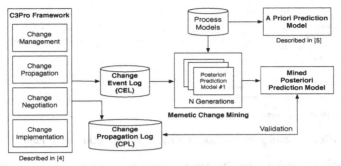

Fig. 2. Overview of the Approach

of the propagations are stored in the CPL, and all individual change events are stored in the CEL. Based on the change simulation data, posteriori and a priori techniques are provided to evaluate and understand the propagation behavior in the choreography through prediction models. The a priori technique [5] uses the choreography structure to assess and predict the impact of a change request. The posteriori technique, described in this paper, generates prediction models by mining the previously stored change data. Derived models are validated through a replay of the CPL.

In the CEL, the relationships between the change events are not explicitly represented. The changes are collected from different partners without any information if a change on a business partner is a consequence of a change on another business partner or if they are independent (because of the transitivity). In order to correlate between the change events and understand the propagation behavior, we adopted different heuristics related to change in process choreographies.

4   Heuristics

In this section we present 4 groups of heuristics that can be exploited for mining change events in process choreographies.

Time Related Heuristic (TRH): In connection with process mining [9,10,11], if two activities a and b whose most occurrences in the log are such as the completion time of a always precedes the start time for the execution of b, then we conclude that a precedes b in the process model. If there exist cases where the execution start time of b occurs before the completion of a, then we can say that a and b could be in parallel. In change mining, a partner π_2 that always performs changes directly after a partner π_1 has changed its process, may lead to the conclusion that the changes on π_2 are the consequences of the changes of π_1. However, this does not always hold true. Indeed, the change events are collected and merged from different sources, and several independent change requests can be implemented by different partners at the same time.

In addition, in process execution logs, each trace represents a sequence of events that refer to an execution case (i.e. an instance of the process execution).

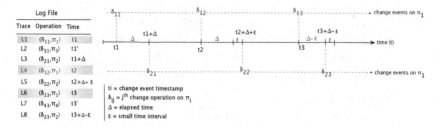

Fig. 3. Change Event Log (CEL): Representation over Time

The precedence relationships between events of a same trace are explicit. In change logs CEL, each trace represents solely one change event. Even if the timestamps give an explicit precedence relationship between different traces, it is not possible to directly conclude that they are correlated. For example, we assume that the actual propagation of two initial change requests on different partners (δ_1, π_1) and (δ_2, π_2) are such that:

- the actual propagation of (δ_1, π_1) results in (δ_3, π_3).
- the actual propagation of (δ_2, π_2) results in (δ_4, π_4).

Since, in this paper, we consider that we do not have the information about the propagations, and that each of these change events is logged separately by the partner which implemented it, then, according to the timestamps, the merging and ordering of these change events in the CEL may lead to the following sequence: $[(\delta_1, \pi_1), (\delta_2, \pi_2), (\delta_3, \pi_3), (\delta_4, \pi_4)]$. According to this ordering, (δ_2, π_2) may be considered as a consequence of (δ_1, π_1) and (δ_4, π_4) as a consequence of (δ_1, π_1). In order to avoid such erroneous interpretations of the log, we need to enhance the heuristic with new elements.

Figure 3 illustrates an example of a sample CEL and its representation over time. The Figure shows a log file containing traces of 8 change events occurred on process partners π_1, π_2, π_3 and π_4 at different times. We assume that the log is chronologically ordered. According to the timestamps, there is a strict precedence relationship between the change occurrences on π_1 and the change occurrences on π_2. However, we can not directly deduce that the latter are the effects of the changes on π_1. Therefore, it is necessary to find another correlation between the timestamps that is more relevant regarding the identification of the propagation patterns. In this sense, we can remark that each time a change operation δ_1 occurs on π_1 at time t, there is a change operation δ_2 that occurs on π_2 at $t + \Delta$ with a variance of $\pm\epsilon$. This deduction holds true when the number of change occurrences on π_2 in the interval $[t + \Delta - \epsilon, t + \Delta + \epsilon]$ becomes high, and when Δ corresponds to the average latency between partners π_1 and π_2. The identification of Δ and ϵ are calculated empirically and should consider the noise in the event logs (e.g. rare and infrequent behavior).

Window Related Heuristic (WRH): Figure 4 presents another example of change events extracted from a CEL. For instance, we consider a Replace on partner **Acquirer** (A) followed by an Insert on **Airline** (B), which in turn, followed by a Delete on the **TravelAgency** (C). We also consider Γ_i as the

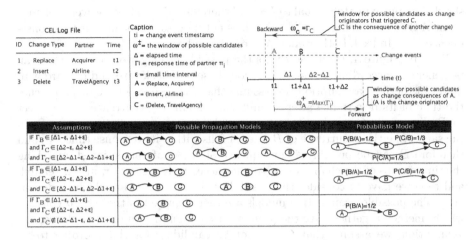

Fig. 4. Correlating change events using forward and backward windows

response time of partner i (the **average** time required by partner i to implement a change). When mining this log, the first challenge is to know if a change event is the originator or a consequence of another change. For this purpose, we define two types of windows; i.e., backward and forward. Given a change event, the forward window represents all the following change events that can be considered as effects of its propagation. In contrast, a backward window includes all previous change events that can be considered as the originators of the change event in question. For instance, in Figure 4, the forward window of A (i.e., ω_A^+), is defined by the maximum of the response times of all change events (i.e., $Max_{i \in \mathcal{P}}(\Gamma_i)$). Indeed, Γ_i is the time required by a partner to react and implement a change. So, with respect to A, if a following change event B was implemented at a time t_B such as $t_B - t_A > \Gamma_B$, then B cannot be considered as consequence of A. In turn, if $t_B - t_A < \Gamma_B$, then B might be a consequence of A (but not necessarily).

For a given change A, since we know that only change events that respect this constraint can be considered, then the possible candidate events as consequences of A should be within this window $\omega_A^+ = Max_{i \in \mathcal{P}}(\Gamma_i)$. According to this approach, in Figure 4, the possible change events that can be considered as effects of A are B and C.

This forward window allows to avoid parsing all change events that come after A to the end of the log CEL. However, a change event within this window does not necessarily imply that it is a consequence of A. for example, C is within the ω_A^+ window, but Γ_C **can be** such as $\Gamma_C < t_C - t_A < \omega_A^+$ or $t_C - t_A < \Gamma_C < \omega_A^+$. For instance, if we assume that in time scale, $t_A = 3$, $\omega_A^+ = 10$, $t_C = 9$ and $\Gamma_c = 4$, then $\Gamma_C = 4 < t_C - t_A = 6 < \omega_A^+ = 10$. In this case, C is within the window of A, but did not occur within its response time $t_A + \Gamma_C \pm \epsilon$ (ϵ is a variance value).

On the other hand, for a given change event C, the backward window ω_C^- includes all possible change events that can be considered as the originators that triggered C. In this sense, if C is a consequence of another change A, then $t_C - t_A$

should be approximately equal to Γ_C, and therefore $\omega_C^- = \Gamma_C$. However, a change event A that occurred at $t_C - \Gamma_C \pm \epsilon$ does not necessarily mean that C is consequence of A. Indeed, both events can be independent.

Back to Figure 4, the table shows the possible propagation models that can be generated according to the assumptions based on backward and forward windows. In the first assumption, we assume that the response time of B matches the time of its occurrence after A, and the time of its occurrence with respect to B. Therefore, C can be seen as a possible consequence of either A or B. In the same time the occurrence of B after A falls within its response time Γ_B, and therefore B can be possibly a consequence of A. As aforementioned, matching the timestamps of the change events do not necessarily mean they are correlated, and then we have to consider the possibility that the events might be independent. The possible propagation models are then depicted in the second column, which, merged together, give the probabilistic model in column 3. In the second assumption, we assume that C can not be candidate for A (according to its response time), and therefore the number of possible propagation models is reduced to only 4. In the last assumption, C can not be considered as consequence of both A and B, and then the number of models is reduced to 2.

To conclude, the forward and backward windows can be very useful in reducing the search space and highlighting the more probable propagation paths between the change events. In addition, the example of Figure 4 considers only a small window of events, where each event type occurred only once. In a bigger log, a same change event (e.g. a Replace on a partner) can occur several times, which may improve the precision of the probabilistic models.

Change Related Heuristics (CRH): The calculation of the prediction model could benefit from the relationships between change operation types. Indeed, from our experience [4], and considering solely the structural and public impacts, an initial change request of type Insert always generates insertions on the affected partners, and the same holds for Delete which generates only deletions. However, the Replace could generate all (three) types of changes. From this we deduce, that we can not have propagation of the type $(Insert, \pi_1) \rightarrow (Delete \vee Replace, \pi_2)$ or $(Delete, \pi_1) \rightarrow (Insert \vee Replace, \pi_2)$. Using these as punishments, the mining techniques could reduce the search space and therefore avoid incorrect behavior.

Choreography Model Heuristics (CMH): Another improvement consists in using the choreography model. The latter sketches all the interactions between the partners and gives a global overview on the collaboration structure. In this sense, we can use the dependencies between the partner interactions as a heuristic to identify transitive propagations (e.g. centrality). More details about heuristics that stem from the choreography structure can be found in [5]. These heuristics can be used to improve the mining results. For example, an identified **direct** propagation link between two partners through mining could be invalidated if the partners have no direct interactions together in the choreography model, and the change type is Delete. Because, unlike the Replace and Insert, the Delete does not result in new dependencies between the partners.

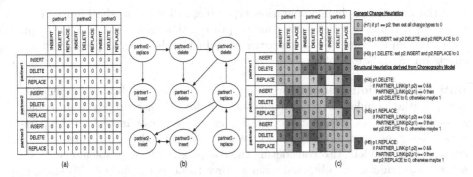

Fig. 5. (a) Genetic Encoding of a candidate solution (b) Candidate solution in graph form (c) Visualization of heuristics affecting a candidate solution

The implementation and the evaluation of the proposed heuristics within the memetic mining is described in the following sections.

5   Memetic Change Propagation Mining

In this section we outline the memetic algorithm for mining change event logs used to build change propagation models. This core algorithm is enriched with an implementation of the heuristics sketched out in the previous Section 4. Employing a change propagation model, predicting the behaviour of change requests in the choreography becomes possible. Memetic algorithms follow the basic flow of genetic algorithms (GAs) [12], which are stochastic optimization methods based on the principle of evolution via natural selection. They employ a population of individuals that undergo selection in the presence of variation-inducing operators, such as mutation and crossover. For evaluating individuals, a fitness function is used, which affects reproductive success. The procedure starts with an initial population and iteratively generates new offspring via selection, mutation and crossover operators. Memetic Algorithms are in their core GAs adding an inner local optimization loop with the goal of maintaining a pool of locally optimized candidate solutions in each generation [13].

Genetic Encoding: The genetic encoding is the most critical decision about how best to represent a candidate solution for change propagation, as it affects other parts of the genetic algorithm design. In this paper, we represent an individual as a matrix $\mathcal{D}$ that states the change relationships between the partners (the genotype). Each cell d_{ij} in the matrix has a boolean value equal to 1 only if a change on π_i is propagated to π_j, and zero otherwise. The matrix is non symmetric and the corresponding graph for change propagation is directed. This means that the probabilities of propagating changes from π_i to π_j and from π_j to π_i are not equal. This is due to the fact that the log file may contain more change propagations from π_i to π_j than from π_j to π_i. Figure 5(a) shows the representation of a candidate solution. Internally, the table rows are collapsed resulting in a *bitstring* of length $(m \times n)^2$ where n is the number of partners and

m is the number of change operation types (e.g., $(3 \times 3)^2$ in the Figure 5(a)). Figure 5(b) represents the corresponding propagation model graph. Figure 5(c) shows the importance of the heuristics in reducing the search space and their effects on candidate solutions.

Initial Population Generation: Two approaches are applicable for generating an initial population: (i) starting with random change propagation models by defining random paths for propagating change requests in each of the partners. This generated model may not respect the dependencies defined by the choreography model. Also considering the complexity of the problem caused by several constraints, the obtained results prove to be not sufficient. (ii) starting with an initial good solution using a part of the propagation dependencies existing in the log file. This solution could represent an incomplete behavior since some propagation paths of the log are not incorporated into the model. For the implementation we have chosen approach (ii) as it allows us to start with an approximate solution using that as the basis for search space exploration.

Heuristics: Here we briefly outline the implemented heuristics extracted from Section 4.

- **H1 (CMH)** - A change to a partner's process (π_1) never results in a propagation to him- or herself (e.g. $\pi_1 = \pi_2$). We can avoid solutions with this property in the search space by applying this heuristic.
- **H2 (CMH)** - Through our extensive simulations we can rule out the case where the originating change is of the type Insert and where the propagated change type is anything other than Insert (e.g. Delete and Replace).
- **H3 (CMH)** - Similarly to H2 we can rule out the cases where the originating change type is Delete, and the propagated change type is anything other than Delete (e.g. Insert and Replace).
- **H4 (CRH)** - Rule out propagated changes of type Delete $\iff$ the originating change is of type Delete, and there is no interaction between the two partners (i.e. $\mathcal{R}(\pi_1, \pi_2) \cap \mathcal{R}(\pi_2, \pi_1) = \{\emptyset\}$, $\mathcal{R}$ is defined in Section 2).
- **H5 (CRH)** - Rule out propagated changes of type Delete $\iff$ the originating change is of type Replace, and there is no interaction between the two partners (i.e. $\mathcal{R}(\pi_1, \pi_2) \cap \mathcal{R}(\pi_2, \pi_1) = \{\emptyset\}$).
- **H6 (CRH)** - Rule out propagated changes of type Replace $\iff$ the originating change is of type Replace, and there is no interaction between the two partners (i.e. $\mathcal{R}(\pi_1, \pi_2) \cap \mathcal{R}(\pi_2, \pi_1) = \{\emptyset\}$).
- **H7** - The mutation as well as the crossover operation change a solution candidate in random ways. We can limit candidates of lower quality by taking into consideration only those events where both the partner and the change operation type occur (in pairs) in the change event log.
- **H8 (TRH/WRH)** - Both the timestamp and the window related heuristics are implemented as H8. The goal of both is to probabilistically find the correct (i) affected events given an originating event and (ii) originator given an affected event. This is accomplished via the forward (i.e. ω_i^+) as well as the backward window (i.e. ω_i^-) concept to limit the filtering process

for the most probable candidate events. Both windows are determined by $Max_{i \in \mathcal{P}}(\Gamma_i)$, i.e. the maximum average response times over all partner response times. For change event candidate selection inside the window, the individual timestamps are used to determine Δ. For the actual selection, the variance value ϵ can be determined empirically. We have opted to base this value on the candidate partner's average response time.

Fitness Function: The fitness function measures the quality of a solution in terms of change propagation according to the change event log CEL. The fitness score is a major component in (i) parent selection, determining each individual's eligibility for generating offspring and (ii) survival selection, determining which individuals survive into the next generation to pass on their genes. The following scoring logic is implemented as the fitness function as follows.

$$fitness = w_1 \times completeness + w_2 \times precision \qquad (1)$$

Where w_1 and w_2 are weights, the completeness privileges individuals that are more complete according to the CEL and the precision penalizes propagation models that have extra behavior according to the CEL. We define ξ_{ij} as the probability that a change event type (i.e., Replace, Insert or Delete) on partner j is a consequence of a change event type on i. This probability is calculated based on the backward and forward windows, weighted by the number of occurrences of the same sequence of changes in the CEL. As illustrated in Figure 4, the individuals are probabilistic models that represent all or a subset of the change events of the CEL. A node in the propagation model σ is represented by a tuple (δ, π) containing a change type and a partner. The propagation probability between nodes i and j in σ is equal to ξ_{ij}. Then the completeness is given by the following weighted equation:

$$completeness = w_{11} \times \frac{\sum_{i \in \sigma} (\delta_i, \pi_i)}{\sum_{i \in CEL} (\delta_i, \pi_i)} + w_{12} \times \sum_{i,j=1..n} \xi_{ij} \times \phi_{ij} \quad with \; \phi_{ij} = \begin{cases} 1 & if (i,j) \in \sigma \\ 0 & otherwise \end{cases}$$
$$(2)$$

The first term concerns the percentage of traces of the CEL that are represented by the predicted model, while the second term calculates the percentage of the identified correlations between change events in the CEL that are considered by the propagation model. The attributes w_{11} and w_{12} are the weights given to each term of the equation.

$$precision = \sum_{i,j=1..n} (k \times \xi_{ij} - 1) \times \phi_{ij} \quad with \; \phi_{ij} = \begin{cases} 1 & if (i,j) \in \sigma \\ -1 & otherwise \end{cases} \qquad (3)$$

The precision penalizes individuals with extra behavior (noise), by accumulating appropriate negative scores for propagation paths with very low propagation probabilities. The variable k is used to define when an event is considered to be noise; e.g., k=5, means propagation edges with probabilities less then $1/5=0.2$ are considered as noise. Therefore, models containing several propagation paths with probabilities lower than 0.2 are classified as bad models. In this equation, we used a simple linear function to penalize noise $k \times \xi_{ij} - 1$, but can be changed to a more complex function (e.g. logarithmic). k is determined empirically.

6 Discussion and Evaluation

In this section we briefly describe the data set as well as the experimental setup in order to evaluate the memetic change mining algorithm coupled with the propsed heuristics for building change propagation models from change event logs (σ_{CEL}).

6.1 Data Set

The data used in this paper are obtained through our C^3Pro change propagation prototype[1]. During the simulation process, we generated change requests of type Replace, Insert and Delete. In total, 17068 change requests were created with an average of 682.7 requests per partner resulting in 49754 change propagation records in the CPL with an average of 2.9 derived propagations per initiated change request. In total 66822 change event records were generated and logged in the CEL. The logged data are in CSV format.

6.2 Benchmark Results

For the benchmark, the goal was on one hand to observe the effects of the applied heuristics on reducing the search space and on the other hand to validate the resulting mined model. Towards the former, each inclusion of a new heuristic should increase the maximal achievable score, as it takes less time to find an improved candidate solution. The benchmark was conducted in the following manner: (1) We start with creating distinct CEL slices with differing partner sizes of the range $[3, 16]$. $\Lambda = \{\lambda_i\}^{i \in [3,16]}$ (2) Then we define the heuristic sets to benchmark. The heuristic set *None* means we do not apply any heuristics, which practically reduces the memetic algorithm into a genetic algorithm. A heuristic set *H1-H3* means we apply heuristics *H1*, *H2* and *H3* within the local

Table 3. Benchmark Results: Memetic Mining of Change Logs. P=Partner Size. G=Generation. Score values are in range $[-\infty, 1]$ (inclusive), where 1 represents the best possible validation score.

| | P=3 | | | P=9 | | | P=15 | | |
	G=1	G=10	G=20	G=1	G=10	G=20	G=1	G=10	G=20
Heuristics									
None	-48.74	-48.26	-27.80	-268.75	-226.71	-186.64	-553.90	-502.61	-476.96
H1	-38.08	-30.03	-22.96	-241.34	-197.63	-168.61	-520.53	-482.92	-449.32
H1-H2	-25.94	-20.24	-17.17	-138.19	-106.18	-88.86	-337.45	-289.14	-250.25
H1-H3	**0.73**	**0.78**	**0.80**	0.50	0.55	0.56	0.54	0.55	0.55
H1-H4	0.72	0.76	0.75	0.53	0.58	0.55	0.57	0.55	0.61
H1-H5	0.72	0.77	0.75	0.56	0.50	0.64	0.60	0.62	0.56
H1-H6	0.72	0.77	**0.80**	0.50	0.63	0.63	0.62	0.65	0.67
H1-H7	0.72	**0.78**	0.77	**0.65**	0.67	0.56	**0.71**	**0.73**	0.72
H1-H8	0.71	0.77	0.75	**0.65**	**0.68**	**0.70**	**0.71**	**0.73**	**0.75**

[1] http://www.wst.univie.ac.at/communities/c3pro/index.php?t=downloads

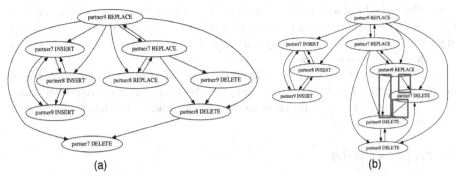

Fig. 6. Mined change propagation models (a) via CPL and (b) via CEL

optimization loop of the memetic algorithm. We have several such heuristic sets as can be observed by the rows in Table 3. (3) Each heuristic set is loaded into the memetic algorithm and executed on the change logs in Λ for up to 20 generations in turn. (4) For validating the mined model, we derive a propagation model from the CPL (i.e. σ_{CPL}), and compare it to the mined model (i.e. σ_{CEL}) by applying the following scoring function:

$$fitness_{validation} = completeness \times precision - penalites \qquad (4)$$

$$precision = \frac{Nb\_extra\_propagation\_paths}{Nb\_total\_propagation\_paths} \qquad (5)$$

$$completeness = \frac{Nb\_valid\_traces}{Nb\_total\_traces} \qquad (6)$$

This validation function returns score values in the range $[-\infty, 1]$, where 1 represents the best possible validation score, meaning the two models are identical. We repeat this process ten times, storing the average score into the respective cells in Table 3. Underlined values are the best scores identified for each column.

We can generally observe the following: regardless of the employed heuristics, with each increasing partner size we obtain a lower quality candidate, except in the case where H8 is introduced. This behaviour signals the positive effects of time related heuristics (TRH) as well as window related heuristics (WRH). Similarly, with each increasing generation, the best candidate solution score increases. This holds true, except in cases where the survival selection routine (tournament selection) misses the current best candidate solution, resulting in a lower fitness score. Finally, we can indeed conclude that the proposed heuristics reduce the search space, as the quality of the best candidate solutions increase as more heuristics are added to the memetic change mining algorithm.

In terms of validation, Figure 6(b) shows the mined change propagation model using the described memetic change mining algorithm (on the CEL) with parameters: $partners = 3$, heuristics H1-H6 applied, and $generation = 20$. In contrast, Figure 6(a) represents the change propagation extracted from the CPL. According to Table 3, the average validation score of these two models are 0.72.

The differences between these two models are visually illustrated in the annotations in Figure 6(b). As can be seen in that figure, the memetic change mining algorithm could find a good approximation for the prediction model, showing only three extraneous edges (i.e. $(Replace, \pi_8) \to (Delete, \pi_9)$, $(Replace, \pi_8) \to (Delete, \pi_7)$ and $(Delete, \pi_7) \to (Delete, \pi_9)$). Our proposed memetic change mining algorithm fared well in this instance. As more partners are added, more candidates are included as potential consequences, leading to bigger models with more extraneous edges.

7 Related Work

Only few approaches have been proposed to compute the changes and their propagation in collaborative process settings [4,14,15,16]. Most of these approaches use either the public parts of the partner processes or the choreography/collaboration model; i.e., the global view on all interactions, to calculate the derived changes. They mainly calculate the public parts to be changed, but cannot anticipate the impacts on the private parts, which in turn, could engage knock-on effects on other partners. Besides, in some collaboration scenarios, a partner may have access to only a subset of the partner processes, and consequently could not estimate the transitive effects of the change propagation.

Change impact analysis has been an active research area in the context of large complex systems and software engineering [17,18,19,20]. As pointed out in [5], we studied these approaches, but found major differences to the problem discussed in this paper. One difference is based on the different structure of the underlying systems. Moreover, the use of the structured change propagation logs combined with memetic as well as genetic mining has not been employed before in these fields.

There exist approaches on impact analysis of change propagation within choreographies, i.e., [19,21]. However, they do not consider previous change propagation experience to enhance the prediction models.

Also they do not take into consideration the different metrics related to the specific structure of business process choreographies. Our previous work [5] on analyzing change impacts in collaborative process scenarios is based on the choreography structure only, i.e., it does not take into consideration any information on previously applied changes.

8 Conclusion

Being able to predict the change propagation behavior in collaborative process scenarios can contribute to time as well as cost reductions, which can determine the overall success of the cooperative process execution. Towards this end we have shown a memetic change mining approach for building a posteriori prediction models based on change event logs (CEL). This approach helps in cases where change propagation logs (CPL) (i.e. those logs which include complete propagation information) are lacking. In addition to the CEL as input, we have proposed a set of heuristics embedded in the memetic change algorithm to guide the candidate selection process towards higher quality ones. The conducted benchmarks and validation of the mined models (see Table 3) show the positive effects of the defined heuristics for reducing the search space, thus reducing the exploration time for finding accurate prediction models. Future work aims at mining change propagation logs (CPL), and analyzing dynamic impacts of process choreography changes.

References

1. Wynn, D.C., Caldwell, N.H.M., Clarkson, J.: Can change prediction help prioritize redesign work in future engineering systems? In: DESIGN, pp. 600–607 (2010)
2. Maier, A., Langer, S.: Engineering change management report 2011. Technical University of Denmark, DTU (2011)
3. Ahmad, N., Wynn, D., Clarkson, P.J.: Change impact on a product and its redesign process: a tool for knowledge capture and reuse. Research in Engineering Design 24(3), 219–244 (2013)
4. Fdhila, W., Rinderle-Ma, S., Reichert, M.: Change propagation in collaborative processes scenarios. In: IEEE CollaborateCom, pp. 452–461 (2012)
5. Fdhila, W., Rinderle-Ma, S.: Predicting change propagation impacts in collaborative business processes. In: SAC 2014 (2014)
6. Rinderle, S., Jurisch, M., Reichert, M.: On deriving net change information from change logs – The Deltalayer-Algorithm. In: BTW, pp. 364–381 (2007)
7. Günther, C., Rinderle-Ma, S., Reichert, M., van Der Aalst, W., Recker, J.: Using process mining to learn from process changes in evolutionary systems. International Journal of Business Process Integration and Management 3(1), 61–78 (2008)
8. Dustdar, S., Hoffmann, T., van der Aalst, W.M.P.: Mining of ad-hoc business processes with teamlog. Data Knowl. Eng. 55(2), 129–158 (2005)
9. van der Aalst, W.M.P.: Process Mining: Discovery, Conformance and Enhancement of Business Processes, 1st edn. Springer (2011)
10. Buijs, J.C.A.M., van Dongen, B.F., van der Aalst, W.M.P.: Mining configurable process models from collections of event logs. In: Daniel, F., Wang, J., Weber, B. (eds.) BPM 2013. LNCS, vol. 8094, pp. 33–48. Springer, Heidelberg (2013)
11. Gaaloul, W., Gaaloul, K., Bhiri, S., Haller, A., Hauswirth, M.: Log-based transactional workflow mining. Distributed and Parallel Databases 25(3), 193–240 (2009)
12. Goldberg, D.: Genetic Algorithms in Search, Optimization and Machine Learning. Addison-Wesley Longman Publishing Co. (1989)
13. Eiben, A.E., Smith, J.E.: Introduction to Evolutionary Computing. Natural Computing. Springer, Berlin (2007)
14. Rinderle, S., Wombacher, A., Reichert, M.: Evolution of process choreographies in DYCHOR. In: Meersman, R., Tari, Z. (eds.) OTM 2006. LNCS, vol. 4275, pp. 273–290. Springer, Heidelberg (2006)
15. Fdhila, W., Rinderle-Ma, S., Baouab, A., Perrin, O., Godart, C.: On evolving partitioned web service orchestrations. In: SOCA, pp. 1–6 (2012)
16. Wang, M., Cui, L.: An impact analysis model for distributed web service process. In: Computer Supported Cooperative Work in Design (CSCWD), pp. 351–355 (2010)
17. Bohner, S.A., Arnold, R.S.: Software change impact analysis. IEEE Computer Society (1996)

18. Giffin, M., de Weck, O., Bounova, G., Keller, R., Eckert, C., Clarkson, P.J.: Change propagation analysis in complex technical systems. Journal of Mechanical Design 131(8) (2009)
19. Oliva, G.A., de Maio Nogueira, G., Leite, L.F., Gerosa, M.A.: Choreography Dynamic Adaptation Prototype. Technical report, Universidade de São Paulo (2012)
20. Eckert, C.M., Keller, R., Earl, C., Clarkson, P.J.: Supporting change processes in design: Complexity, prediction and reliability. Reliability Engineering and System Safety 91(12), 1521–1534 (2006)
21. Wang, S., Capretz, M.: Dependency and entropy based impact analysis for service-oriented system evolution. In: Web Intelligence, pp. 412–417 (2011)

Flexible Batch Configuration in Business Processes Based on Events

Luise Pufahl, Nico Herzberg, Andreas Meyer, and Mathias Weske

Hasso Plattner Institute at the University of Potsdam
{firstname.lastname}@hpi.uni-potsdam.de

Abstract. Organizations use business process management techniques to manage their core business processes more efficiently. A recent technique is the synchronization of multiple process instances by processing a set of activities as a batch – referred to as batch regions, e.g., the shipment of goods of several order processes at once. During process execution, events occur providing information about state changes of (a) the business process environment and (b) the business process itself. Thus, these events may influence batch processing. In this paper, we investigate how these events influence batch processing to enable flexible and improved batch region execution. Therefore, we introduce the concept of batch adjustments that are defined by rules following the Event-Condition-Action principle. Based on batch adjustment rules, relevant events are correlated at run-time to batch executions that fulfill the defined condition and are adjusted accordingly. We evaluate the concept by a real-world use case.

Keywords: BPM, Batch Processing, Event Processing, Flexible Configuration.

1 Introduction

Companies strive to manage their core business in a process-oriented fashion to be efficient and stay competitive in the market. For this attempt, business processes are documented as process models [25]. These process models can also be used for process automation by a Business Process Management System (BPMS) [18]. Usually, the instances of a process, i.e., the concrete executions, run independently in existing BPMSs, e.g., [3,4,13]. However, efficient process execution may require bundled processing of activities of different process instances. Hereby, efficiency refers to costs savings under the trade-off of increasing average waiting times. For instance, in an hospital, a nurse transports multiple blood samples of patients to the laboratory at once instead of each separately to save transportation costs. To cope with this challenge, batch activities were introduced in business processes, e.g., in [1,14,20,21]. In these works, further application domains as, for instance, logistics and event organization, are discussed.

The recent concept of batch regions [20] enables the synchronization of process instances with similar characteristics for a set of activities. Thereby, several configuration parameters allow the process designer to individually setup the batch execution, e.g., rule-based activation of a batch. However, specifying the rules at design-time does not guarantee optimal process execution, since expected and unexpected events occurring

X. Franch et al. (Eds.): ICSOC 2014, LNCS 8831, pp. 63–78, 2014.

during process execution do influence the execution [10]. Reacting on these events and changing the specified configuration parameters is required for process improvement.

In this paper, we apply event processing techniques to flexibly adapt these configuration parameters at run-time to react in real-time on changes of the business process execution environment and improve the batch execution. The contributions of this paper are (i) to provide an overview about changes on batch configuration parameters triggered by events and (ii) to describe a framework that implements the flexible adaptation of configuration parameters triggered through event occurrence.

The paper is structured as follows. Section 2 introduces the concepts of batch regions and event processing before Section 3 presents a motivating example originating from a real-world scenario in the healthcare domain. It leads to an analysis on how events may influence batch execution and corresponding requirements in Section 4. Section 5 presents the concept of flexible adaptation of batch regions based on event processing techniques. In Section 6, the framework is applied to the healthcare scenario from Section 3 as evaluation. Section 7 is devoted to related work and Section 8 concludes the paper.

2   Foundation

Batch Region. A batch region comprises a connected set of activities. For batch processing configuration, a batch region contains four configuration parameters: (1) a grouping characteristic to cluster process instances to be processed in one batch based on attribute values of utilized data, (2) an activation rule to determine when a batch may be processed while balancing the trade-off between waiting time and cost savings, (3) the maximum batch size indicating the maximum number of entities to be processed, and (4) the execution order of the processed entities [20].

Each single execution of the batch region is represented by a batch cluster collecting – based on the grouping characteristic – a number of process instances for synchronization. Thereby, a batch cluster passes multiple states during its lifetime [21]. It is initialized (state *init*) upon request of a process instance. The batch cluster transitions to state *ready* (enablement), if the activation rule is fulfilled and is then provided to a resource that decides to start execution at some point in time. The execution is indicated by state *running*. If more than one resource is available, several batch cluster can be executed in parallel. After initialization and before execution start, process instances may still be added until the maximum batch size is reached (state *maxloaded*). Termination of all process instances being part of the batch cluster successfully *terminates* it.

Collecting multiple objects, e.g., blood samples, may also be done by utilizing loop or multi-instance structures as specified in the workflow patterns [2]. This requires to merge multiple process instances into one handling the synchronization. However, batch regions do not merge instances to retain the single instances autonomy outside the batch regions. This enables dynamic process instance assignment to batch clusters, e.g., for run-time cluster adjustments as discussed in this paper or for error handling.

Events. Information about changes or exceptions in the business process environment are provided by events. Often those events are not stored at one place, but in several information systems and BPMSs [7]. We refer to events being unstructured and available in an IT system as *raw events*. Event processing techniques help to utilize these raw events and use them during process execution for process monitoring, adjustment, and control [5, 9, 10]. Structuring raw events according to a certain description referred to as *structured event type*, transforms raw events in a first step into *normalized events*. Normalized events are the basis for further processing by, for instance, combination, aggregation, and enrichment by context data [11]. We distinguish two event types being relevant for flexible batch processing: (a) *business events* and (b) *process events*. Business events base on normalized events enriched by business context information that are relevant for all running process instances. In contrast, a process event is correlated to a specific process instance and thus provides instance-specific information.

3 Motivating Example

The following healthcare process, the blood testing process in Fig. 1, is used to illustrate the need for flexible batch execution.

Instantiation of the process takes place, if there is a blood test required for a patient at the ward. First, the blood test order is prepared before a blood sample is taken from the respective patient. Afterwards, a nurse transports both to the laboratory, where the blood sample is first prepared for testing. Then, the actual test is conducted by a blood analysis machine. The laboratory possesses one machine for each type of blood test. As the blood analysis machines have an interface to the central hospital information system, the results are published so that they are accessible by the physicians in the respecting ward. There, they can evaluate the blood test result and can use it for diagnostic.

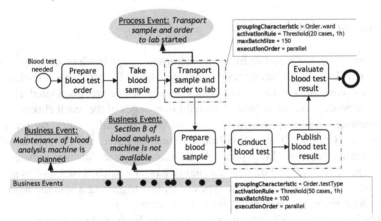

Fig. 1. Blood testing process

Within the given process, two batch regions are specified. As several blood test orders incur at a ward, the nurse would not bring each individually to the laboratory. In fact, a nurse delivers several blood samples together to save transportation cost which is captured by the first one comprising activity *Transport sample and order to lab*. The second batch region comprises activities *Conduct blood test* and *Publish test results* and enables to collect multiple blood samples before a test run on a blood analysis machine is started to save machine costs. So far, the configuration parameters are defined at design-time and can not be adapted at run-time. However, changes and exceptions within the business process or in its execution environment might require adaptation. Following, we discuss three example events being of relevance for batch regions in the blood testing process:

Planned maintenance of a machine: This business event indicates that a maintenance of a machine is planned. During the maintenance, the machine is not available to conduct tests of the specific type. Blood samples in not yet running batch clusters might expire, because the waiting time of the collected process instances increases by the maintenance time. Thus, in such situations, the blood analysis should be started shortly before the maintenance takes place to avoid expired blood samples.

Partly unavailability of a machine: Assume, a blood analysis machine contains four sections to process blood samples from which one fails. Then, the capacity of the machine is reduced by one quarter. Hence, the maximum number of process instances allowed to be contained by a batch cluster should be reduced accordingly.

Transportation of a set of blood samples of the same type is started: Assume, the timeout is almost reached for a batch cluster while a transportation of blood samples to the laboratory requiring the same test is started. The respective batch cluster may delay its activation until the instances arrive to improve cost savings.

These examples show that there exist various situations requiring a flexible adjustment of predefined batch processing behavior in order to (1) reduce costs, (2) avoid increased waiting time, and (3) ensure correct batch execution, e.g., a reduced capacity of the task performer. Next, we perform an analysis to set the requirements before we present our concept in Section 5.

4   Events and Batch Regions

As discussed above, it is valuable for organizations to design batch processing in a flexible manner. Thus, created batch clusters may be adjusted according to the changes of the process environment as described by business events or process related aspects as described by process events. Adjustments refer to changes of the batch cluster configuration parameters. Table 1 provides an overview how the configuration parameters (1) groupingCharacteristic, (2) activationRule, (3) maxBatchSize, and (4) executionOrder can be adjusted at run-time. More precisely, the table discusses how a parameter can be changed (*type of change*), the influence a change has on a batch cluster and its assigned process instances (*influence*), and the types of events triggering a specific adjustment (*events indicating*) and gives corresponding event *examples*.

In Table 1, all types of adjustments are considered. Each configuration parameter always contains a value that can be also *undefined* for the first three parameters. Usually, the configuration of a batch cluster is adapted as reaction on an event. In the case of changing the grouping characteristic, existing batch clusters have to be canceled and the corresponding process instances need to be reassigned to new ones, because the data view of the existing clusters do not fulfill the new grouping characteristic. For example, grouping characteristic *Order.ward* results in batch clusters with data views *General Surgery* and *Endoscopic Surgery*. If the grouping characteristic is adjusted to *Order.section*, the data views above are not valid anymore. Thus, both batch clusters need to be canceled and their instances reassigned to a cluster with data view *Surgery*.

Table 1. Classification on how batch clusters can be changed and by which events

Configuration parameter	Type of changes	Influence	Events indicating	Examples
groupingCharacteristic	- aggregate - refine - restructure	- cancel existing batch cluster and assign process instances to new clusters	- need for aggregation or division of batch clusters or batch cluster restructuring	- if staff gets ill, a nurse has to organize the transport of two wards
activationRule	- adapt rule parameter - use a new rule	- adapt configuration of batch cluster	- change in availability of task performer/material - the arrival/delay of instances - change of process instance properties	- maintenance of machine - start of the transport of several samples - blood sample expires
maxBatchSize	- increase - decrease	- adapt configuration of batch cluster and, if necessary, remove process instances	- a change in the capacity of task performer, used resource etc.	- section of a machine is not available
executionOrder	- select other type of execution	- adapt configuration of batch cluster	- change of resource or resource type	- usage of a replacement machine acting differently

Reducing the maximum batch size may result in batch clusters exceeding the newly set limit. Then, newest assigned process instances are removed from the corresponding clusters and get assigned to other or new batch clusters accordingly. The concept introduced in the next section covers all changes of Table 1 including these special cases.

As described in Section 2, during a batch cluster's lifetime, it may pass the states *init - ready - maxloaded - running - terminated*. When a task performer starts execution of a batch cluster, it transitions to state *running*. From this moment, no adjustments shall be done on the respective batch cluster anymore. Therefore, we assume that batch clusters can only be adjusted in states *init, ready,* or *maxloaded*.

Having presented multiple types of changes according to the configuration parameters and their implications, we derive three requirements to implement above observations. First, at design-time, event types relevant for batch cluster adjustment need to be identified (R1). Then, at run-time, occurring events must be correlated to respective batch clusters (R2) and they need to be adjusted accordingly (R3).

5 Flexible Configuration Based on Events

In the following, we describe the basic idea of our approach by referring to the example introduced in Section 3. Afterwards, the newly introduced *batch adjustments* and their *batch adjustment rules* are described, before we explain a method for process instance reassignment and introduce an architecture for realizing the presented approach.

5.1   Basic Idea

We assume that events are observed by an event processing platform. If a relevant event is observed, the corresponding batch cluster gets adjusted accordingly, cf. Fig. 2.

Our concept builds on structured events that are a derivation of an event object [16] consisting of an identifier, a timestamp, and some structured event content, e.g., a set of key-value-pairs or a tree-structure expressed in extensible markup language (XML). A structured event type describes a class of structured events that have the same format. Besides attributes specific for an structured event, a structured event type consists of some content description describing the

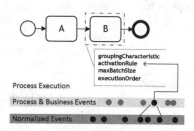

Fig. 2. Events influence the properties of batch clusters during run-time

structure of the event content of a structured event, e.g., by defining the attributes (keys) or by an XML schema definition (XSD).

We propose an approach that enables run-time flexibility of batch clusters by *batch adjustments* following a *batch adjustment rule*. A *batch adjustment* is triggered by a certain event and may result in the adaptation of some parameters of one batch cluster. The events to react on, the conditions that need to be met, and the adjustments that may need to be applied are defined in the *batch adjustment rule*. The structure of a batch adjustment rule follows the (E)vent-(C)ondition-(A)ction principle originating from the database domain [6]. Events to react on are described by their event type, e.g., an event indicating the maintenance of a machine. The condition information enables the correlation of the event to the corresponding batch cluster, e.g., only the batch clusters containing process instances with blood samples for this machine. The described action specifies the particular adjustment of a batch cluster, e.g., the immediate execution.

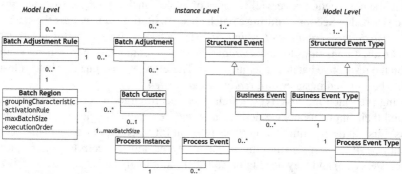

Fig. 3. Class diagram integrating batch region [20] and event processing [11] concepts. The model level shows the design-time concepts and the instance level shows their run-time implementation.

The connection of events and the batch region concept is illustrated in the class diagram of Fig. 3. One batch region can have an arbitrary set of batch adjustment rules which are provided by the process designer. A batch adjustment rule refers to at least one structured event type which can be a business or process event type. The structured event types describe based on which events a batch adjustment is triggered. If a structured event occurs which is relevant for a set of batch clusters, then for each batch cluster one batch adjustment is created. Thus, a batch adjustment rule can have a arbitrary set of batch adjustments being related to one or several structured events, but each adjustment is assigned to only one batch cluster. During the lifetime of a batch cluster, it can be adapted by an arbitrary set of batch adjustments.

5.2 Batch Adjustment Rule and Batch Adjustment

For connecting batch clusters and events during process execution, we introduce the concepts of *batch adjustments* and *batch adjustment rules*. A batch adjustment rule, following the ECA-principle, describes how and under which conditions a batch cluster needs to be adjusted during run-time.

The events that need to be considered for an adjustment of a batch cluster are described by their event type. For example, a business event type describes the business events that indicate a planned maintenance of the blood analysis machine, cf. Listing 1.1. The event should be provided one machine analysis run before the maintenance starts so that not started batch clusters can be activated and finished before the maintenance start. This information is composed of fine-grained information of normalized events indicating the maintenance need and the schedule of the service technician.

The business event $machineMaintancePlanned_b$ contains information about the name of the corresponding machine. Further, it holds an ID and a timestamp as these are mandatory fields of structured events. The ID of the resulting business event is uniquely generated (getGUID()) and the timestamp is set to the actual time of creation (getTime(now)). The remaining data is collected from two normalized events $machineStatus_n$ and $technicianSchedule_n$ that need to be correlated. This is done by defining constraints in the WHERE-clause of the SELECT statement. In the example, it is checked whether the events target the same machine followed by a check for the maintenance need of the machine and the action of a planned maintenance by the service technician. As mentioned, the event shall be created exactly one machine run before the maintenance

```
1   machineMaintancePlanned b . extraction  =
2   { machineMaintancePlanned b . id  =  getGuid ();
3       machineMaintancePlanned b . timeStamp  =  getTime (now);
4   SELECT
5           machineStatus n . name ,
6   FROM
7           machineStatus n ,
8           technicianSchedule n
9   INTO
10          machineMaintancePlanned b . MachineName
11  WHERE
12          machineStatus n . name  =
13      technicianSchedule n . machineID  AND
14      machineStatus n . status  =  "MaintenanceNeeded" AND
15      technicianSchedule n . state  =  "planned" AND
16      technicianSchedule n . time  −  getTime (now) <= machine (name) . getRuntime ()}
```

Listing 1.1. Definition of the business event type *machineMaintancePlanned_b* that captures the information about a maintenance in near future. This event results from events of the machine itself (event type $machineStatus_n$) and the technician schedule (event type $technicianSchedule_n$).

takes place. Thus, a time constraint is set to create the corresponding business event, if time until the maintenance is equal or lower to the time needed for a run of the machine (machine(name).getRuntime() returns the duration of a run of machine *name*).

This defined event type can be used as trigger for a batch adjustment rule that adapts the activation rule of batch clusters in case of a maintenance for avoiding expired blood samples. The proposed batch adjustment rule is shown in Listing 1.2, illustrating its basic structure. In the condition part of the batch adjustment rule, we ensure that batch adjustments are only created for batch clusters the event is relevant for. In our example, the events of type *machineMaintancePlanned$_b$* are relevant for all batch clusters that are intended to run in time where the maintenance is planned to be conducted. Those should be started before the maintenance takes place to avoid unnecessary waiting times for the blood samples. The relevant clusters are those that have the same blood testing type as the blood analysis machine to be maintained and that are not yet enabled for execution, i.e., in state *init*. The instances of the *blood testing* batch region are grouped based on their blood test type (cf. Fig. 1) with the grouping characteristics = *Order.bloodTestType*. Thus, the batch cluster's data view provides information which blood test type its assigned process instances requires, e.g., *BC1(BloodTestA)*. The data view of the batch cluster can be used for the condition, cf. Listing 1.2 line 2 and 3.

```
1   EVENT {machineMaintancePlanned_b}
2   CONDITION batchCluster.dataView == machineMaintancePlanned_b.name
3   batchCluster.state == "INIT"
4   ACTION batchcluster.activationRule=Threshold (50,0h)
```

Listing 1.2. Definition of a batch adjustment rule to start batch clusters before a maintenance takes place.

Based on this example, we can observe that a specific batch cluster or a set of specific batch clusters for which an event is relevant can be identified based on batch cluster specific characteristics, i.e., (1) data view, (2) current state of the cluster, (3) number of instances contained in a cluster, and (4) type of instances. If no condition is described, a batch adjustment is created for all batch clusters which are in the *init*, *ready*, or *maxloaded* state. Clusters being already accepted by the task performer are not adapted anymore.

The last part of the batch adjustment rule is the definition of actions that need to be performed when an event happened and the conditions are fulfilled. These actions can use information of the underlying events to specify the adjustments of the particular batch cluster. Referring to our example, the action would be to enable the batch execution before maintenance, cf. Listing 1.2 line 4. With this action, the activation rule of the cluster is adjusted so that either 50 blood sample are triggered or the batch cluster waits 0 hours, meaning that the cluster is immediately enabled to be finished before the maintenance starts.

Batch adjustment rules are utilized to create batch adjustments for batch cluster. A batch adjustment holds the ID of the corresponding batch cluster and the action that need to be taken to change certain parameters of the batch cluster. Applying the batch adjustment rule of our example, a batch adjustment as shown in Listing 1.3 will be generated for batch cluster 1234.

```
1   batchCluster.id = 1234
2   batchCluster.activationRule = "Threshold(50,0h)"
```

Listing 1.3. Exemplary batch adjustment created for batch cluster 1234.

The batch adjustment mentioned above will replace the activation rule *Threshold (50,1h)* of batch cluster 1234 by *Threshold (50, 0h)*. With regards to the generation of batch adjustments, if an event is received, it is immediately checked whether this event is relevant for any available batch cluster. For each relevant cluster, a batch adjustment is created. In case that the event is valid for a certain time period, the event is stored. For each further initialized cluster, it is checked whether this event applies. Upon invalidation of the event, it is removed from the event storage. After presenting the structure of batch adjustment rules and the generation of batch adjustments, the next section discusses the special case where a batch cluster is not only adapted, but a reassignment of process instances is necessary.

5.3   Reassignment of Process Instances

A batch adjustment usually results in the adaptation of the configuration of one batch cluster. Sometimes, it also triggers (a) the reduction of instances contained by the batch cluster in case of a decreased *maxBatchSize* or (b) the cancellation of a batch cluster in case of a changing *groupingCharacteristic*. The extended lifecycle of batch clusters with the *canceled* state is shown in Fig. 4; a cancellation is only possible from states *init, ready*, and *maxloaded*. In both cases, process instances have to be reassigned to other or new batch clusters.

Fig. 4. Lifecycle of batch cluster extended by *canceled* state

In general, process instances that arrive at a batch region, i.e., the enablement of the entry activity into the region, are temporarily deactivated and assigned to a queue of the so-called *batch cluster manager* in the order of their arrival time (first-in-first-out). The batch cluster manager organizes the assignment of process instances to batch clusters and, if necessary, initializes new batch clusters.

If a process instance, in case of an adjustment, is reassigned, it should be handled prioritized, because it already experiences a longer waiting time than newly arriving instances at the batch region. Thus, the to-be reassigned process instance is placed in the front of the queue based on its arrival time at the batch region. Then, it is assigned to an existing or new batch cluster. In the example of Fig. 5, the number of instances of the batch cluster BC1 have to be reduced because an event indicated that a section of machine A is not

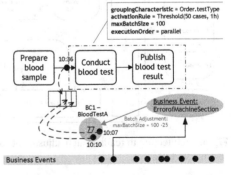

Fig. 5. Reassignment of process instances in case of a reduced *maxBatchSize*

working currently. Then, the newest assigned instances are removed from the size-reduced cluster. The process instance with the arrival time 10:07 is placed at the beginning of the queue, then the instance with 10:10 is added followed by the newly arrived instance at 10:36.

Often batch regions have an activation rule with a time constraint which describes the maximum waiting time for a process instance in a batch cluster. In the example process of Fig. 5, the threshold rule states that either 50 instances have to be available or the waiting time of 1h is exceeded to activate the batch cluster. For assuring the maximum waiting time also for reassigned process instances, we propose the usage of the batch adjustment concept here. If an instance is added to a batch cluster which was arrived at the batch region earlier than the batch cluster was created (or one of its instances), an event is created. This event triggers a batch adjustment which reduces the time constraint of the batch cluster by the difference between the batch cluster's creation time and the reassigned instance arrival time at the batch region.

5.4   Architecture

Next, we present an architecture showing details about a technical implementation to flexibly adapt batch cluster configurations. Fig. 6 presents the main components and their interactions as FMC block diagram [12]. The architecture is structured into three parts: event producer, *event processing platform*, and process control. The *process engine*, which controls process execution and batch handling, is an event producer and consumes event provided by the event processing platform at the same time. Besides the process engine, several event producers (*event sources*) can be connected via an appropriate *event adapter* to the event processing platform. These can be information systems as well as databases. The event processing platform normalizes the received raw events and creates business and process events based on defined rules. Event consumers are connected by an *event consumer interface*.

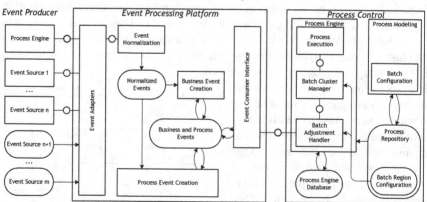

Fig. 6. Architecture to realize batch adjustments during process execution based on an event processing platform

Process control comprises the process engine and some modeling environment to create the process model to be executed within the process engine. After creation, a process model is stored in the process repository. While modeling a process, batch regions can be designed. Thereby, the process designer can define batch adjustment rules used at run-time to adapt the batch regions. Those are saved together with the process model in the process model repository. During process execution, the process engine retrieves the process model and the adjustment rules from the repository. For each designed batch region, the *batch cluster manager* assigns the process instances to batch clusters. The *batch adjustment handler* registers for events that are specified in the batch adjustment rules of a batch region at the event consumer interface. If the handler receives a registered event from the event processing platform, then the event is evaluated and the according action is triggered for the appropriate batch clusters. The batch adjustment handler has an internal list of all batch clusters which are in state *init*, *ready*, or, *maxloaded* as these are the only ones that might be affected by events.

6 Evaluation

The approach is evaluated by showing its applicability to a real world use case: the blood testing scenario introduced in Section 3 with a simulation. As described, the laboratory uses a batch region to synchronize several blood samples for the blood analysis to save machine costs. The blood analysis machine needs to be maintained regularly respectively on request. Based on an event informing about the maintenance some time before it actually starts, the configuration of a running batch cluster can be adjusted. With the adjustment, the cluster is started in-time to decrease the number of expired blood samples due to unavailability of the machine. A blood sample expires after a certain time frame, often 90 to 120 minutes, because the blood structure changes. Then, the blood sample is not useful for medical analysis. Each expired blood sample causes costs of taking a new one.

Simulation Setup. For the evaluation, a simulation is used to compare the number of expired blood samples in case of normal batch execution, i.e., without run-time adaptations, to flexible batch execution as presented in this paper. Therefore, the laboratory part of the blood testing process was implemented as simulation[1]
    with DESMO-J [8], a Java-based framework for discrete event simulation. The simulation starts with the arrival of process instances, i.e., blood samples, at the laboratory. Each process instance is terminated after finishing the blood test. At average, using an exponential distribution, every 12 minutes, a nurse brings 20 ± 5 blood samples (normally distributed) to the laboratory. For this simulation, we assumed that only one blood analysis machine exists. One run of the machine for analyzing blood samples takes 25 minutes. At maximum, the machine can handle 100 blood samples in one analysis.

For the simulation, the laboratory selected *ThresholdRule(50 instances, 1h)* as activation rule requiring 50 instances or a waiting time of one hour to enable a batch cluster (cf. Fig. 1). If a batch cluster fulfills this rule, it queues for being processed by the machine. The machine is already in use for a longer time period. Thus, twice a week, every 3.5 days with a deviation of 1 day, a maintenance is required. For the flexible batch handling, some time before the technician arrives, an event regarding the maintenance is

---

[1] The simulation source code and the reports of the different simulation runs are available at
http://bpt.hpi.uni-potsdam.de/Public/FlexibleBatchConfig

provided. When the technician arrives, he is prioritized, but a current analysis on the machine is not interrupted.

Results. We conducted several simulation runs for two scenarios to compare the impact of flexible batch adjustments. The scenarios differ in the expiration time for blood samples: 120 minutes and 90 minutes. Fig. 7 and 8 summarize the results of the simulation runs over a period of two years, one diagram for each scenario. In both diagrams, we compare the results for maintenance times of 45 minutes and 60 minutes (intercept 2 and 3) with the result where no maintenance takes place (intercept 1). The black bars provide the numbers of expired blood samples, if (1) no adjustments are made at run-time. The different gray bars (2)-(4) show the results for event triggered batch adjustments, if the event is sent 1, 1.5, or 2 times the analysis run, i.e., 25, 37.5, or 50 minutes respectively, before the technician arrives.

If no maintenance would be conducted, 1,738 samples in scenario 1 and 19,913 samples in scenario 2 would expire due to exponential arrival of these blood samples and resulting waiting times for the machine. If the maintenance is conducted at average twice a week as indicated above, the number of expired blood samples increases by 14% respectively 29% for 45 and 60 minutes maintenance duration in scenario 1 (cf. black bars in Fig. 7) and they increase by 13% respectively 41% in scenario 2 (cf. black bars in Fig. 8).

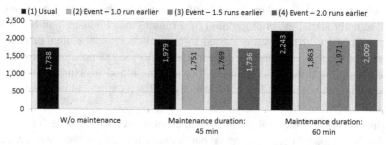

Fig. 7. Scenario 1 – 120 min expiration time: Number of expired blood samples in two years for different simulations

Applying flexible batch adjustments aims at reducing the number of expired blood samples. The recognition of the event indicating the maintenance directly activates all initialized batch clusters by changing the activation rule accordingly (cf. line 4 in Listing 1.2 in Section 5.2). The impact of the batch adjustment rule with respect to the point in time the event is sent is shown by the different gray bars (2)-(4). In 9 of 12 cases, we observe measurable improvements. The highest improvements for the different settings are mostly observed for the light gray bar ((2) Event 1.0 run earlier). It indicates that it is most beneficial for reducing the number of expired blood samples to inform about the maintenance one analysis run before the start of the maintenance. The improvement is at 13% respectively 20% in scenario 1 for 45 respectively 60 minutes maintenance time and at over 3% in scenario 2 (60 minutes maintenance). With these numbers, for scenario 1, we almost compensate for the maintenance.

For scenario 2, shown in Fig. 8, only slight improvements as well as two cases of no improvements are observed. This may be explained as follows: The arriving event enables a batch cluster which is then started for the blood analysis. During the analysis,

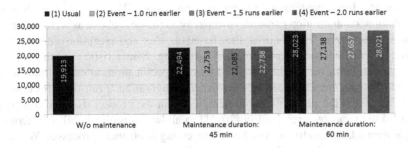

Fig. 8. Scenario 2 – 90 min expiration time: Number of expired blood samples in two years for different simulations

multiple new samples might arrive, but they are not processed before the maintenance as the technician is prioritized. Due to the small expiration time of 90 minutes, there is a good chance that those samples expire. For a maintenance time of 45 minutes, all samples which arrive 5 minutes after the start of the flexibly enabled cluster expire, because they have at least 20 minutes waiting time before the maintenance plus 45 minutes maintenance time plus another 25 minutes analysis time summing up to at least 90 minutes. For 60 minutes maintenance, all samples arriving at least 20 minutes after the start of the flexibly enabled cluster will expire. Thus, if – due to the arrival distribution of the blood samples – many samples arrive within these time frames, also negative results can be observed.

Summarizing above observations, it is important to check the relation between expiration time as well as waiting and maintenance times to decide whether to apply batch adjustments or not. In case, the relations are appropriate as, for instance, in scenario 1, applying batch adjustments provides reasonable and measurable improvements.

The simulation results indicate that the waiting time for the technician slightly increases, in average less than a minute. Due to limited space, the reader is referred to our simulation reports (see footnote 1). If, we take scenario 1, the cost savings due to reductions in expired blood sample will be higher than the technician costs due to small increases in the waiting time.

In most cases, we can observe that the number of zero-waitings increases, because starting an analysis run shortly before the technician arrives, increases the chance that the run is terminated just upon arrival. However, sometimes a run may only be started shortly before the technician's arrival as some other analysis run was still busy. Then, the technician must wait longer resulting in a higher distribution of waiting times and a higher total average waiting time.

7 Related Work

In the business process research domain, few works exists to synchronize the execution of multiple instances. For example in [1,14,23], the integration of batch processing into process models is discussed. These works provide limited parameters to configure the batch execution at design-time, often only the maximum capacity. This also limits opportunities to conduct adjustments at run-time. [23] provides some means for flexible run-time batch control by introducing batch activation by user invocation. Extending the options for batch configuration in business processes, [21] introduces batch activities with three configuration parameters: capacity as the ones above as well, rule-based activation generalizing the user invocation based on rules, and execution order. One step forward, [20] extends the parameters by the grouping characteristic to distinguish process instances. However, all these works focus on specifications at design-time and do not support automatic adjustments of the batch configuration at run-time, for instance, due to changes in the process environment or within the process itself. In this paper, we extend the concepts presented in [20, 21] to allow run-time flexibility in terms of configuration adaptation to improve batch processing in business processes. We utilize events as trigger for taking adjustment actions. These extensions can also be applied to other works for adapting the configuration parameters offered there.

Batch processing flexibility has also been discussed in other domains as, for example, the manufacturing domain [17]. Here, batch scheduling is used to schedule a number of available jobs on a single or on multiple machines for saving set-up costs. Changes of market factors, e.g., a canceled order, or on the operational level, e.g., breakdowns, require a rescheduling functionality. In [17], an overview of suitable algorithms is presented and the need for a framework which combines possibly occurring events with some reschedule action is discussed. The contributions of this paper can be adjusted to offer a first approach in this direction: instead of configuration parameter adjustments, rescheduling action can be used in the batch adjustment rule.

Adoption of process instances during run-time is a widely discovered field. [22] discusses manual ad-hoc changes of single instances, e.g., to insert, delete, or shift activities according a given process model. This provides flexibility for single process executions but this does not provide possibilities to pool several process instances and to work on them as a batch. The CEVICHE framework [9] allows to change process instances automatically during run-time. Similar to this paper, it uses Complex Event Processing (CEP) to detect changes and exceptions which then trigger dynamic adaptation of the BPEL processes. In the same vein, [5] discusses means to integrate CEP with BPMSs on architectural level and shows how to do this for a BPEL engine. [24] introduces an approach to discover deviations of process executions and the underlying process model by using CEP techniques.

In this paper, we use CEP techniques as, for example, described in [7, 15], to create the necessary business and process events. [7] lists definitions for CEP-related terms, e.g., event type, that are used in this paper. Based on these works, a framework for CEP for business processes was introduced [10, 11]. We utilize this framework to allow dynamic batch activation and configuration rule adaptations as presented in Section 5. In this paper, we deal with comparably simple rules to correlate events to each other, to process instances, and to batch clusters. Applying common correlation techniques extends the correlation capability of the presented approach. One of these techniques, the determination of correlation sets based on event attributes, is introduced in [19].

8   Conclusion

In this paper, we showed the necessity to synchronize multiple cases in batch clusters and the requirement of their flexible adjustments during run-time. Therefore, a concept is introduced to apply event processing to batch execution allowing to flexibly adjust batch configuration parameters and batch activation based on run-time changes represented by events. Based on the principle of Event-Condition-Action rules, relevant events are identified and then compared to defined conditions. If the conditions are fulfilled, the configured actions are executed as a batch adjustment for the corresponding batch cluster. Further, an architecture is presented showing details about a technical implementation and the components that are necessary to apply the concept within a process engine. We showed applicability of the introduced concept of batch adjustments during run-time with a real-world use case of a blood analysis in a hospital's laboratory. We simulated two years of work in the laboratory and showed that the application of the presented concept compensates for maintenance interruptions decreasing the blood expiration rate by at most 7%. With integrating more information about the process environment, e.g., the availability of resources, the presented concept can be extended. Further, techniques to ensure that batch adjustments do not lead to inconsistencies should be developed. We will investigate this topic in the future.

References

1. van der Aalst, W., Barthelmess, P., Ellis, C., Wainer, J.: Proclets: A Framework for Lightweight Interacting Workflow Processes. IJCIS 10(4), 443–481 (2001)
2. van der Aalst, W.M.P., ter Hofstede, A.H.M., Kiepuszewski, B., Barros, A.P.: Workflow Patterns. Distributed and Parallel Databases 14(1), 5–51 (2003)
3. Activiti: Activiti BPM Platform, https://www.activiti.org/
4. Bonitasoft: Bonita Process Engine, https://www.bonitasoft.com/
5. Daum, M., Götz, M., Domaschka, J.: Integrating CEP and BPM: How CEP Realizes Functional Requirements of BPM Applications (Industry Article). In: DEBS, pp. 157–166. ACM (2012)
6. Dayal, U.: Active Database Management Systems. In: JCDKB, pp. 150–169 (1988)
7. Etzion, O., Niblett, P.: Event Processing in Action. Manning Publications Co. (2010)
8. University of Hamburg, D.o.C.S.: DesmoJ - A Framework for Discrete-Event Modeling and Simulation, http://desmoj.sourceforge.net/
9. Hermosillo, G., Seinturier, L., Duchien, L.: Using Complex Event Processing for Dynamic Business Process Adaptation. In: SCC, pp. 466–473. IEEE (2010)
10. Herzberg, N., Meyer, A., Weske, M.: An Event Processing Platform for Business Process Management. In: EDOC, pp. 107–116. IEEE (2013)
11. Herzberg, N., Weske, M.: Enriching Raw Events to Enable Process Intelligence - Research Challenges. Tech. Rep. 73, HPI at the University of Potsdam (2013)
12. Knöpfel, A., Gröne, B., Tabeling, P.: Fundamental Modeling Concepts: Effective Communication of IT Systems. Wiley (2005)
13. Lanz, A., Reichert, M., Dadam, P.: Robust and flexible error handling in the aristaFlow BPM suite. In: Soffer, P., Proper, E. (eds.) CAiSE Forum 2010. LNBIP, vol. 72, pp. 174–189. Springer, Heidelberg (2011)
14. Liu, J., Hu, J.: Dynamic Batch Processing in Workflows: Model and Implementation. Future Generation Computer Systems 23(3), 338–347 (2007)
15. Luckham, D.: The Power of Events. Addison-Wesley (2002)
16. Luckham, D., Schulte, R.: Event Processing Glossary - Version 2.0 (July 2011), http://www.complexevents.com/wp-content/uploads/2011/08/EPTS_Event_Processing_Glossary_v2.pdf

17. Méndez, C.A., Cerdá, J., Grossmann, I.E., Harjunkoski, I., Fahl, M.: State-of-the-art review of optimization methods for short-term scheduling of batch processes. Computers & Chemical Engineering 30(6), 913–946 (2006)
18. Meyer, A., Pufahl, L., Fahland, D., Weske, M.: Modeling and Enacting Complex Data Dependencies in Business Processes. In: Daniel, F., Wang, J., Weber, B. (eds.) BPM 2013. LNCS, vol. 8094, pp. 171–186. Springer, Heidelberg (2013)
19. Motahari-Nezhad, H.R., Saint-Paul, R., Casati, F., Benatallah, B.: Event Correlation for Process Discovery from Web Service Interaction Logs. VLDB Journal 20(3), 417–444 (2011)
20. Pufahl, L., Meyer, A., Weske, M.: Batch Regions: Process Instance Synchronization based on Data. In: EDOC. IEEE (2014) (accepted for publication)
21. Pufahl, L., Weske, M.: Batch Activities in Process Modeling and Execution. In: Basu, S., Pautasso, C., Zhang, L., Fu, X. (eds.) ICSOC 2013. LNCS, vol. 8274, pp. 283–297. Springer, Heidelberg (2013)
22. Reichert, M., Dadam, P.: Enabling Adaptive Process-aware Information Systems with ADEPT2. In: Handbook of Research on Business Process Modeling, pp. 173–203. Information Science Reference (2009)
23. Sadiq, S., Orlowska, M., Sadiq, W., Schulz, K.: When Workflows Will Not Deliver: The Case of Contradicting Work Practice. BIS 1, 69–84 (2005)
24. Weidlich, M., Ziekow, H., Mendling, J., Günther, O., Weske, M., Desai, N.: Event-based monitoring of process execution violations. In: Rinderle-Ma, S., Toumani, F., Wolf, K. (eds.) BPM 2011. LNCS, vol. 6896, pp. 182–198. Springer, Heidelberg (2011)
25. Weske, M.: Business Process Management: Concepts, Languages, Architectures. Second Edition, 2nd edn. Springer (2012)

Automatic Generation of Optimized Workflow for Distributed Computations on Large-Scale Matrices

Farida Sabry, Abdelkarim Erradi, Mohamed Nassar, and Qutaibah M. Malluhi

KINDI Center for Computing Research
Qatar University
Doha, Qatar
{faridasabry,erradi,mohamad.nassar,qmalluhi}@qu.edu.qa

Abstract. Efficient evaluation of distributed computation on large-scale data is prominent in modern scientific computation; especially analysis of big data, image processing and data mining applications. This problem is particularly challenging in distributed environments such as campus clusters, grids or clouds on which the basic computation routines are offered as web/cloud services. In this paper, we propose a locality-aware workflow-based solution for evaluation of large-scale matrix expressions in a distributed environment. Our solution is based on automatic generation of BPEL workflows in order to coordinate long running, asynchronous and parallel invocation of services. We optimize the input expression in order to maximize parallel execution of independent operations while reducing the matrix transfer cost to a minimum. Our approach frees the end-user of the system from the burden of writing and debugging lengthy BPEL workflows. We evaluated our solution on realistic mathematical expressions executed on large-scale matrices distributed on multiple clouds.

Keywords: location-aware optimization, distributed computations, BPEL workflows, large-scale matrices.

1 Introduction

Cloud computing offers an attractive alternative to easily and quickly acquire IT services such as storage and computation services. Its adoption continues to grow as companies opt for flexibility, cost savings, performance and scalability. Cloud services such as Elastic MapReduce offer an attractive platform for outsourcing the storage and computations on large scale data because of their optimized algorithmic implementations and access to on-demand large-scale resources. We focus particularly on matrix algebra computations since they are used in many scientific domains; including but not limited to analysis of big data, image processing, computer graphics, information retrieval and data mining applications. The inputs are typically large-scale matrices and performing math operations (e.g. multiply, inverse, transpose, add/subtract, dot product...) on them could be long-running. In this paper, we consider the scenario where several cloud services are offering matrix storage and basic matrix operations with different service characteristics. Based on availability, quality of service (QoS), reliability, security and data locality, the optimal decomposition, task

X. Franch et al. (Eds.): ICSOC 2014, LNCS 8831, pp. 79–92, 2014.
© Springer-Verlag Berlin Heidelberg 2014

scheduling and task assignment of a mathematical expression vary. We propose automated workflow generation and execution in order to optimize the response time of expression evaluation, given the available services and their characteristics, as well the data locality. Our solution improves the productivity of the users by releasing them from the tedious task of manually and timely generating and editing the workflows depending on the input expressions.

The composition could be written using a business workflow language such as BPEL (Business Process Execution Language) [2] or YAWL (Yet Another Workflow Language) [3]. Scientific workflow tools like Taverna [4], Kepler [5], and Pegasus [6] can do similar task; some of them adopt BPEL whereas others use their own language. We choose BPEL because it is a standard XML based language for specifying a Web Services composition. It is also used by some scientific workflow systems. A BPEL process is composed of activities that can be combined through structured operators that specify the control and data flow that govern the ordering of these activities. BPEL constructs include messaging activities (e.g. invoke, receive, reply), sequential execution, conditional branching, structured loops, concurrency constructs (e.g., parallel execution, event-action constructs, correlation sets), exception handling (try-catch blocks). A BPEL engine is responsible for managing the process instances lifecycle, such as process instance creation, termination, and executing according to the process definition. The engine is also responsible for binding the partners to specific Web Services. Many BPEL engines are available as Open Source, such as Apache ODE [7], and commercial engines such as IBM WebSphere Choreographer [8].

Even though workflows can be used to automatically manage the execution of the expression computation, the system is not convenient if the end-users (e.g. researchers, developers) have to manually create a workflow and properly assign the tasks upon the addition of a new expression. Moreover the optimal execution is dependent on the data locality of input matrices and the QoS characteristics of the available matrix computations services. Our system automates the optimization and the generation of a BPEL workflow for the input expression. The resulting workflow is deployed to a BPEL workflow engine for execution.

The rest of the paper is organized as follows. Section 2 overviews related work. Section 3 gives an overview of the proposed method and section 4 presents the details of the transformation from a mathematical expression to a BPEL workflow and the optimization process. Section 5 highlights implementation details. Finally, we conclude and discuss future work in section 6.

2 Related Work

Service composition is closely related to workflow [9]; automatic workflow generation can be considered a subtask from automated web service composition. The latter term is considered more general as it includes an extra step of the automatic service discovery and selection from the set of available services. According to a survey of automated web services composition [10], this can be done using workflow techniques or AI planning. The workflow techniques can be further classified as either static or dynamic [9]. The static techniques mean that the requester should build an abstract process model before the composition planning starts. Only the selection and binding to atomic web services is done automatically. On the other hand, the dynamic composition both creates process model and selects atomic services automatically. This requires the requester to specify several constraints, including the dependency of atomic services, the user's preference and so on. An example for a static workflow generation approach was implemented in ASTRO project [11].

According to [11], one of the phases for the automatic composition of web services is the translation between the external and internal languages used by the service composition system. The external language is used by the service users to express what they can offer or what they want in a relatively easy manner. For example, BPMN (Business Process Modeling Notation) to BPEL translation is presented in [12] where the designer uses BPMN graphical notations to easily describe the process control flow and data flow and then it gets automatically translated to BPEL. This work can also be considered static in the sense that BPMN is describing the control/data flow as input. Similar work was proposed in [13] but using XPDL (XML Process Definition Language) which is a graph-structured language mainly used in internal process modeling. However, in this work the generated outputs are abstract BPEL processes that are not fully executable and deployable and they need some manual editing to be ready for deployment. Also in [12], it is stated that it cannot detect all pattern types and the code produced by this transformation lacks readability.

Our approach for automatic workflow generation presented in this paper is considered dynamic in the sense that the workflow steps and the process model that describes the control flow and data flow are not input by the requester but they are created automatically according to the parsing of the input expression. Additionally the atomic services used for computations are selected based on their functionality and QoS such as accuracy, reliability, performance and security. We assume that developers/researchers are using contract-based web service composition; and they are provided with the WSDLs representing the interfaces of the available services and their characteristics. Our proposed framework depends on the service-oriented architecture where large-scale mathematical computations are offered as services and this differs from other distributed execution engines like MapReduce [23] or DryadLINQ [24].

3   Overview of the Proposed Framework

We can think of the problem of mathematical expression to workflow transformation with analogy to the compilation process [15]. In software compilation, the compiler compiles a program into intermediate form, optimizes intermediate form and generates target code for the running architecture. In hardware compilation, the compiler compiles an HDL model into a sequencing graph, optimizes the sequencing graph and generates gate-level interconnection for a cell library [16].

In our framework of distributed mathematical expression evaluation using services on the web or on the clouds, the end-user (researcher/developer) enters a mathematical expression (e.g. $A * B + C * D$) following a specific grammar such as XPath grammar or JEP (Java Expression Parser) [14]. The expression is then compiled to an intermediate form of a parsed expression tree. This intermediate form is optimized and then the workflow is generated to coordinate the execution of services on the distributed environment. We focus on mathematical expressions but the framework can be extended to more generic computation models.

The main components of our proposed framework are depicted in Fig. 1. First, the developer/researcher inputs the expression and the resources' references corresponding to the aliases of the operands (i.e., the location where each operand is stored). A configuration file specifies additional parameters such as the registry address where the WSDLs of the services are stored. These WSDLs serve as the interface to the external cloud services to be invoked or composed in the generated BPEL process. A parser parses the input mathematical expression into an expression tree. An optimizer then transforms the tree to a more consolidate form based on data locality of operands and identifies independent operations that can be done in parallel. The optimizer also annotates the nodes of the tree based on their types (operands vs. operators). Then the translator traverses the tree and maps the tree parts to corresponding BPEL activities. Attributes of these activities like the partner link to the service to invoke, the values of the input variables to this service and their types are initialized according to the annotations set by the optimizer. The output of the translator is a BPEL process accompanied by a deployment descriptor so that it can be deployed to a BPEL engine for execution. In the next section we present formal definitions and explain in more details the different steps of the automation process.

4   From Expression to BPEL

Before we go through the automation steps in details, it is important to formally define the following key terms: computation services, operations, operands and expression trees.

Definition 1: [*Computation Services*] are defined as a set of services $S = \{s_1, s_2, \ldots s_n\}$, n ≥ 1 where each s_i S is defined by [id, O_{s_i}, QoS_{s_i}] where id is the unique service identifier (e.g. the URL of the service) and O_{s_i} is a set of operations $\{o_{js_i}\}$ provided by s_i. Each $o_{js_i} \in O_{s_i}$ is further defined by its input, output and port type $(X_{o_{js_i}}, Y_{o_{js_i}}, PT_{o_{js_i}})$ where $1 \leq j \leq |O_{s_i}|$. QoS_{s_i} is the set of quality of service parameters for each service s_i: $< P_i, D_i, r_i, a_i >$ where P_i is the set of execution price for all $o_{js_i} \in O_{s_i}$, D_i is the set of expected execution durations for all o_{js_i}, r_i is the reliability and a_i is the availability of the overall service.

In our framework the service definitions are obtained from a local registry by parsing the corresponding WSDL files.

Definition 2: [*Operators*] are the set of predefined tokens representing unary and binary operations on matrices such as addition, subtraction, multiplication, dot product, inverse of a matrix and transpose of a matrix: $O = \{ +, -, *, ., -, {}^{\wedge -1}, {}' \}$.

Definition 3: [*Operands*] are the set of input literals L used in the input mathematical expression, $L = \{ l_1, l_2, \ldots l_m \}$ where each l_k is an alias for a resource matrix M_k with metadata (location, nRows, nCols, datatype). The (l_k, M_k) mapping tuples are stored to a hash map so-called LM.

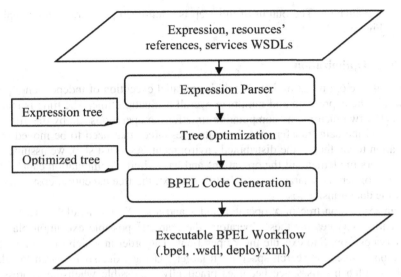

Fig. 1. Mathematical expression to BPEL workflow generation

Definition 4: *[Expression Tree]* is the binary tree obtained from parsing the input string expression and is defined by $(root, N, C)$ where $N = \{n_1, n_2 \dots n_w\}$ is the set of tree nodes, $n_t \in \{O, L\}$, $root \in N$ and $C = \{ (n_u, n_v), (n_u, n_c) \dots \}$ represents the connections between the nodes, where (n_u, n_v) means n_u is a parent of n_v. The following conditions apply:

- *root* is the only node with no parents.
- The leaf nodes must belong to L.
- Internal nodes belong to O, a hash map OS maps each operator node $n_t \in O$ to the service $s_k \in S$ offering this operation and being selected to do the operation according to data locality, concurrency considerations and QoS parameters.
- Each node has at most two direct children.
- Methods $left(n_t)$ and $right(n_t)$ get the left and right child of node n_t.

Given these definitions, we discuss next expression-to-BPEL translation steps in more details.

4.1 Expression Parser

Parsers have undergone significant progress and can now be automatically generated from a simple specification of the language (i.e., BNF grammar). This can be done using one of the existing parser generators like YACC, Bison or ANLTR. There are two main approaches to building parsers that are used in practice: top-down (also known as recursive descent or LL and its variant LL(*) [17] used by ANTLR) and bottom-up (aka shift-reduce, LR and its variant LALR used by YACC and Bison).

In our work, we use the open-source JEP which implements the Shunting-yard algorithm that is considered a bottom-up parser and is used to convert the human-readable infix notation to RPN (Reverse Polish Notation) that is optimized for expression evaluation. The output of this step is a left-deep parse tree, an example is shown in Fig. 2(a).

4.2   Tree Optimization

The goal of tree optimization is to maximize parallel execution of independent operations within the expression and minimize overall evaluation time. The time is mainly composed of two factors: the computation time for the operations run by the different services, and the data transfer time for matrix resources that need to be moved from one location to another in the distributed environment. As a first step, we assume that all the servers implement all the operations and have similar computation capabilities and quality of service characteristics. In this context, the tree execution cost is measured by the data transfer cost.

For an expression tree of x operator nodes and a set S of n available servers all implementing services for these operators, there are n^x possible execution plans to select services from S to execute the x operations. The order in which to invoke these x operations makes the search space even larger. Using exhaustive search to select the optimal plan in this space becomes practically impossible when the expression size increases. We refer to the query optimization problem in distributed databases that have similar conditions to get an optimal query execution plan [19, 20] where projection is done before join and joins of collocated tables are done first to decrease the data to be transferred, cost-optimization techniques are used to choose the optimal execution plan.

We narrow down the search space using the matrix locality information, where we favor operations involving collocated matrices. The basic principle is that matrices that are co-located in storage must be close to each other in the tree whenever it is possible. To do so, we use properties of commutativity, associativity and distributivity of the different operators to identify chains of commutative operators (e.g., matrix addition) and chains of associative operators (e.g., matrix multiplication). We sort the commutative chains based on the data locations. In this way, collocated matrices would be close and put into parenthesis to be operands of the same operator. We also use matrix size as a tie break for associative chains (i.e., we prefer to put together into parenthesis the operands of which the multiplication leads to smaller-size matrices). This problem is the same as the matrix chain multiplication problem [18] and has a well-known dynamic programming solution which we modified its score to favor doing computations for collocated matrices first.

To simplify the explanation of the optimization procedure we consider as example the expression $A + B + C * D * E + F + G$ and the size-location description shown in Table 1. The optimization of this expression is shown in Fig. 2. Fig. 2(a) represents the tree as output by the parser. In Fig. 2(b) we use the associative property of multiplication to do D*E first as matrix D and matrix E both belong to server S1 and must be given priority to decrease data transfer. Similarly the commutative property of addition is used to swap matrix B and matrix F. Indeed matrix A and matrix F both belong to server S1 and can be locally added without additional data transfer.

Note that within the same sub-tree, well known compiler optimization techniques for arithmetic expressions are used to optimize further the execution and identify independent sequences of operations that can be done in parallel. There are a lot of optimization techniques for arithmetic expressions, like tree-height reduction, factorization, expansion and common sub-expression elimination [16, 17]. For example if we assume all the matrices belong to the same location in Fig. 2(a), tree height reduction would recognize that the root node must be changed so the tree height would be 4 instead of 6.

After this step is done we apply the following two-phases-traversal algorithm:

1. The first phase: we identify independent sub-trees that can be run in parallel while traversing down the tree based on the two following conditions:
   - All the nodes of a sub-tree must be hosted by the same server
   - A sub-tree must contain as much nodes as possible. In other words, we expand a tree until no more nodes can be added.
   - Each sub-tree is annotated according to the hosting server where its operations would be invoked so that the generated workflow invokes the services for computations of the sub-trees in parallel e.g. Fig. 2(c).
2. The second phase: going up the tree we generate the main meta-tree representing the final computation steps with annotations added specifying the servers selected to do each operation. Again the goal is to reduce the data transfer volume. So we choose the server where most matrices are located. The metric can be merely the number of matrices but preferably we select the server hosting the maximum sum of the sizes of the operands.

We analyze the transfer cost in terms of the number of matrix elements which is practically reflected in the file size. In this simple example the transfer cost is reduced from 2100100 elements (if re-ordering and optimization algorithm were omitted) to 1001000 elements. This gain is computed given the sizes depicted in Table 1 and assuming dense matrices. Another factor affecting the selection of services and discussed extensively in literature is the QoS parameters. For example, QoS parameters and techniques used in [21] can be applied to choose services with least response time and price. Currently our prototype is based solely on data locality and data size but we intend to extend it to QoS optimization as well. The last step is transforming the optimized tree, along with the annotations of the selected transfer and computation services and obtaining the finally executable BPEL workflow as described next.

Table 1. Example of a distribution of sizes and locations

Matrix ID	A	B	C	D	E	F	G
Size	1000 *1000	1000 *1000	1000 *1	1 *100	100 *1000	1000 *1000	1000 *1000
Location	S1	S2	S2	S1	S1	S1	S2

4.3   BPEL Code Generation

The translation task from the optimized expression tree to BPEL workflow is based on the mapping rules shown in Fig. 3. In the rules, O_u, O_v and O_l represent operator nodes and l_i, l_j represent operand nodes. The rules has for mission to map the expression tree parts to their equivalent BPEL constructs such as assign, invoke, receive, sequence, and flow. BPEL *Assign* activity is used to exchange values between incoming and outgoing message variables. *Invoke* activity is used to do the service invocation. *Receive* activity is to receive an input message or a callback message. *Sequence* activity is to group some activities to be done in sequence. *Flow* activity is used when different sequences are to be done in parallel. Attributes of these activities like the partner link to the service to invoke, values of input variables to the service and their types are initialized according to the annotations values of the nodes (operands and operators: $n_t \in \{O, L\}$).

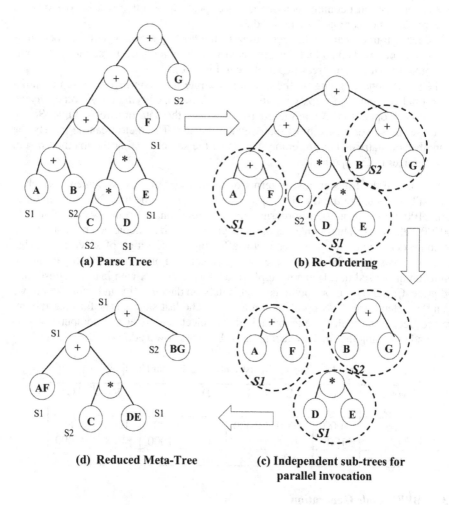

Fig. 2. Simple scenario example for tree optimization for
$$A+B+C*D*E+F+G \rightarrow (A+F) +C*(D*E)+(B+G)$$

The output of this transformation is a BPEL process saved to a ".bpel" file, a workflow interface description saved to a ".wsdl" file. This is because workflow itself is deployed as a web-service. A deployment descriptor saved to "deploy.xml" is also generated so that the workflow can be deployed to a BPEL engine for execution.

The translation algorithm of an expression tree T to executable BPEL code that includes the BPEL constructs to be used and the control flow is shown in Fig. 4. The algorithm is a post-order traversal for the expression tree T with the mapping rules shown in Fig. 3 applied. The rule case (c) in Fig. 3(c) is considered the base case used for the recursive traversal where the tree has an operator $o_u \in O$ as a parent and its two children are operands $\{l_i, l_j\} \in L$ or only left child l_i in case where o_u is a unary operator. In this case, the mapping is a *sequence* activity that includes (*assign, invoke, receive*). The BPEL *assign* activity is for assigning input values for the variable used in the invocation. The *invoke* activity and then the callback *receive* activity are to get the information about the intermediate result location. The attributes of these activities are determined from the computation services definition S and the OS mapping. OS (o_u)is the selected service for operation o_u. The LM (l_k, M_k) mapping is used to get the metadata of the input matrices. Case (a) occurs when the two children are operators which mean that the services in these two paths can be executed in parallel. This corresponds to the BPEL *Flow* construct including two sequences for the mapping of the two children where each child has its own scope. Case (b) occurs when one of the children is an operator o_i and the other is a literal l_j which means that the mapping of o_i and o_u will be a *Sequence* activity. A flow stack is maintained so that during traversal if case (a) is encountered a *Flow* activity is pushed into the stack and the two paths are executed in parallel. The activity is popped out once its left and right children return.

5   Implementation and Experimentation

We made the prototype for Mathematical Expression to BPEL (ME2BPEL) available at https://code.google.com/p/me2bpel/. The objective of the system is to generate a correct, optimized and executable BPEL workflow from the input mathematical expression and resources' references to aliases used in the expression. The inputs are WSDL files representing the interface to different web services on different servers and an expression to be evaluated with metadata about operands used in the expression provided. The whole system operation can be summarized as follows. First, the expression is being parsed using JEP API that uses shunting yard algorithm. Then we detect commutative chains and matrix multiplication chains by traversing the tree. Matrix multiplication chains and their order of execution are determined using the modified dynamic programming approach using data locality as well as matrices sizes. Sorting the commutative chain is done with respect to data locality and the expression tree structure is updated accordingly with annotating operator nodes for collocated operands. The rest of operator nodes are then annotated with the location to execute according to the minimum data transfer criterion. BPEL code generation is done according to the algorithm in Fig. 4. We modified the unified framework package [22] for generation and serialization of BPEL constructs. We used web services using MapReduce for matrix multiplication and addition operations that we used in [1] for testing. These input WSDLs are read and de-serialized using wsdl4j library.

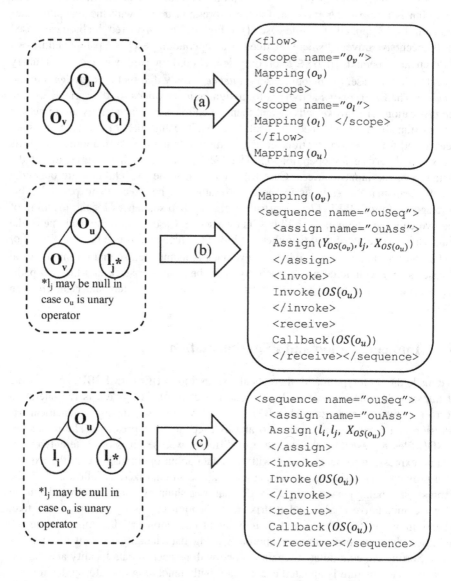

Fig. 3. Mapping expression tree patterns to the corresponding BPEL constructs where Mapping(o_x) is a recursive function with case (c) as the base case

---

(1) **Input:** OptimizedExpressionTree   T,   S,   OS=(o_j, S_i) , $o_j = (X_j, Y_j, PT_j)$ and LM=(l_k, M_k) mapping

(2) **Output:** workflow.bpel, workflow.wsdl, deploy.xml

(3) **Begin**

(4) Workflow W, LastActivity A, FlowStack FS, currentFlow = 0

(5) Initialize W

(6) **Transform T:**

(7) if $left(T) \in L$ AND $(right(T) \in L$ OR $right(L)$ is null) // case Fig. 3(c)

(8)   W ← addMapping(rule in Fig. 3(c)) to currentFlow

(9) W ← connectSequenceToLastFlow(FS)

(10) Update A

(11) LM ← addIntermediateResult($Y_{T,OS(T)}$)

(12)   **Else if** $left(T) \in O$ AND ($right(T) \in L$ OR $right(L)$ is null) // case Fig. 3(b)

(13) **Transform** $left(T)$

(14) W ← addMapping(rule in Fig. 3(b)) to currentFlow

(15) W ← connectSequenceToLastActivity(A)

(16) Update A, Update FS

(17) LM ← addIntermediateResult($Y_{T,OS(T)}$)

(18)   **Else if** $left(T) \in O$ AND $right(T) \in O$ //case Fig. 3(a)

(19) W ← addFlow(), currentFlow= currentFlow+1

(20) W ← connectFlowToLastActivity(A)

(21) Update A, Update FS

(22) **Transform** $left(T)$

(23) **Transform** $right(T)$

(24) Update FS

(25) W ← addMapping(rule in Fig. 3(a)) to currentFlow

(26) W ← connectSequenceToLastActivity(A)

(27) Update A, LM ← addIntermediateResult($Y_{T,OS(T)}$), currentFlow = currentFlow -1

(28) **End Transform**

(29) Serialize W to get workflow.bpel

(30) Generate WSDL from W to get workflow.wsdl

(31) Generate Deployment Descriptor from W to get deploy.xml

Fig. 4. Translation algorithm of expression tree to BPEL workflow

The first experiment is to test for ten different expressions available on the project page as a sample dataset with different number of literals ranging from 4 to 10. The data locality optimization is not taken into consideration in this experiment and it is assumed that the data matrices are stored on the same server offering these web services. Results are shown in Fig. 5 with an average speed-up (Tsequential/Tworkflow) of 1.8. From the results it is clear that the optimized workflow achieve better results for expressions with larger number of literals and which have operations that can be done in parallel.

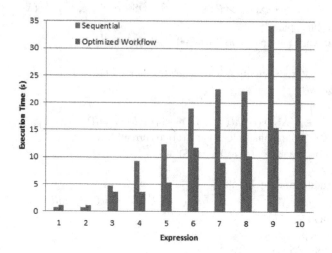

Fig. 5. Optimized workflow execution time vs. the sequential execution time for 10 different expressions

In the second experiment, we assume matrices are stored on different servers and according to the data locality optimization step; a service is chosen to execute a certain operation in an expression tree so that it minimizes the data transfer between servers. So we compare the time taken for data transfer being logged by the web services under test between the optimized workflow with web services selection according to data locality and random web services selection. Fig. 6 shows that for most of the expressions under test, the data transfer time is less when web services are selected according to data locality (expression 8 has all its data stored on the same server, that's why no data transfer time recorded). Some cases show no improvement; this depends on the heterogeneity of the distributed data.

6   Conclusion

Web and cloud-based services evaluating large-scale mathematical operations are typically long running and require the composition of multiple asynchronous computation services. We proposed an automated workflow generation solution in order to coordinate and optimize the execution of these services. We show how to automatically generate workflows for evaluating composed expressions while taking into account the storage location of input matrices and minimizing the data transfer between servers. Our solution optimizes the run-time execution of the services composition by maximizing parallel calls whenever possible. We aim by this contribution to increase the productivity of the system users (researchers or developers) and equipping them with a dynamic workflow generation tool, making the system accessible for non-expert workflow developers.

For future work, we aim to incorporate QoS-based service selection. This feature will allow selecting the most appropriate service among functionally-equivalent computation services having the same score according to data locality and size of input data but offering different QoS guarantees.

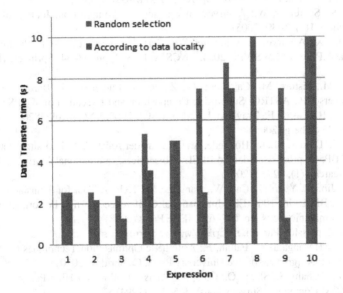

Fig. 6. Data transfer time taken by services selected according to data locality vs. random selection for different expressions

Acknowledgments. This publication was made possible by a grant from the Qatar National Research Fund; award number NPRP 09-622-1-090. Its contents are solely the responsibility of the authors and do not necessarily represent the official views of the Qatar National Research Fund.

References

1. Nassar, M., Erradi, A., Sabri, F., Malluhi, Q.: Secure Outsourcing of Matrix Operations as a Service. In: 6th IEEE International Conference on Cloud Computing, pp. 918–925. IEEE Press (2013)
2. Web Services Business Process Execution Language v2.0, http://docs.oasis-open.org/wsbpel/2.0/OS/wsbpel-v2.0-OS.html
3. Van der Aalst, W.M.P., ter Hofstede, A.: YAWL: Yet Another Workflow Language. Information Systems 30(4), 245–275 (2005)
4. Taverna Workflow Management System, http://www.taverna.org.uk/
5. Altintas, I., Berkley, C., Jaeger, E., Jones, M.: Ludascher. B., Mock, S.: Kepler: an extensible system for design and execution of scientific workflows. In: Scientific and Statistical Database Management International Conference, pp. 423–424 (2004)

6. Sonntag, M., Karastoyanova, D., Deelman, E.: BPEL4Pegasus: Combining Business and Scientific Workflows. In: Maglio, P.P., Weske, M., Yang, J., Fantinato, M. (eds.) ICSOC 2010. LNCS, vol. 6470, pp. 728–729. Springer, Heidelberg (2010)

7. Apache ODE: http://ode.apache.org/

8. WebSphere Application Server Enterprise Process Choreographer, http://www.ibm.com/developerworks/websphere/

9. Dustdar, S., Schreiner, W.: A survey on web services composition. Journal of Web and Grid Services 1(1), 1–30 (2005)

10. Rao, J., Su, X.: A Survey of Automated Web Service Composition Methods. In: Cardoso, J., Sheth, A.P. (eds.) SWSWPC 2004. LNCS, vol. 3387, pp. 43–54. Springer, Heidelberg (2005)

11. Trainotti, M., Pistore, M., Calabrese, G., Zacco, G., Lucchese, G., Barbon, F., Bertoli, P.G., Traverso, P.: ASTRO: Supporting Composition and Execution of Web Services. In: Benatallah, B., Casati, F., Traverso, P. (eds.) ICSOC 2005. LNCS, vol. 3826, pp. 495–501. Springer, Heidelberg (2005)

12. Ouyang, C., Dumas, M., ter Hofstede, A.H.M., van der Aalst, W.M.P.: Pattern-based translation of BPMN process models to BPEL web services. International Journal of Web Services Research 5(1), 42–62 (2007)

13. Yuan, P., Jin, H., Yuan, S., Cao, W., Jiang, L.: WFTXB: A Tool for Translating Between XPDL and BPEL. In: 10th IEEE International Conference on High Performance Computing and Communications, pp. 647–652. IEEE Press (2008)

14. JEP (Java Expression Parser), http://www.singularsys.com/jep

15. Kastner, R., Hosangadi, A., Fallah, F.: Arithmetic Optimization Techniques for Hardware and Software Design. Cambridge University Press, Cambridge (2010)

16. Bacon, D., Graham, S., Sharp, O.: Compiler Transformations for High-Performance Computing. ACM Computing Surveys 26(4), 345–420 (1994)

17. Parr, T., Fisher, K.: LL(*): The Foundation of the ANTLR Parser Generator. In: Programming Language Design and Implementation Conference (PLDI), pp. 425–436 (2011)

18. Cormen, T., Leiserson, C., Rivest, R., Stein, C.: Introduction to Algorithms, 3rd edn., pp. 370–377. MIT Press (2009)

19. Hameurlain, A.: Evolution of Query Optimization Methods: From Centralized Database Systems to Data Grid Systems. In: Bhowmick, S.S., Küng, J., Wagner, R. (eds.) DEXA 2009. LNCS, vol. 5690, pp. 460–470. Springer, Heidelberg (2009)

20. Evrendilke, C., Dogac, A., Nural, S., Ozcan, F.: Multidatabase query optimization. Journal of Distributed and Parallel Databases 5(1), 77–114 (1997)

21. Zeng, L., Benatllah, B., Ngu, A.H.H., Dumas, M., Kalagnanam, J., Chang, H.: QoS-Aware Middleware for Web Services Composition. IEEE Transactions On Software Engineering 30(5), 311–327 (2004)

22. Unify framework package, Software Languages Lab, Vrije Universiteit Brussel, http://soft.vub.ac.be/svn-gen/unify/src/org/unify_framework/

23. Dean, J., Ghemawat, S.: MapReduce: Simplified Data Processing on Large Clusters. Communications of the ACM - 50th anniversary issue 51(1), 107–113 (2008)

24. Yuan, Y., Isard, M., Fetterly, D., Budiu, M., Erlingsson, U., Gunda, P.K., Currey, J.: DryadLINQ: A system for general-purpose distributed data-parallel computing using a high-level language. In: OSDI 2008 Proceedings of the 8th USENIX Symposium on Operating Systems Design and Implementation, pp. 1–14 (2008)

A Dynamic Service Composition Model for Adaptive Systems in Mobile Computing Environments

Nanxi Chen and Siobhán Clarke

Distributed Systems Group, SCSS
Trinity College, Dublin, Ireland
nchen@tcd.ie, Siobhan.Clarke@scss.tcd.ie

Abstract. Service-based applications must be adaptable to cope with the dynamic environments in which they reside. Dynamic service composition is a common solution to achieving adaptation, but it is challenging in mobile ad hoc network (MANET) environments where devices are resource-constrained and mobile. Existing solutions to dynamic service composition predefine the multiple configurations that may be possible, but this requires knowledge of the configurations a-priori. Alternatively, some solutions provide on-demand composition configurations, but they depend on central entities which are inappropriate in MANET environments. We propose a decentralized service composition model, in which a system dynamically adapts its business process by composing its fragments on-demand, as appropriate to the constraints of the service consumer and service providers. Results show a high composition success rate for the service compositions in high mobility environments.

Keywords: Service composition·Distributed·MANET·Overlay networks.

1 Introduction

Extensive use of mobile devices, coupled with advances in wireless technology like Wi-Fi direct, increase the potential for shared ownership applications for mobile ad hoc networks (MANETs) [6]. Devices can employ computational resources in a network to accomplish not only data routing tasks but also a complex user task with value-added services. A widely accepted mechanism to carry out such user tasks is service-based applications (SBAs), in which complex tasks are modelled as loosely-coupled networks of services. A SBA provides appropriate functionalities to consumers by composing cooperating services.

Typical MANET environments are dynamic; mobile SBAs must be adaptable to cope with potential changes in their dynamic operating environments (e.g. topology changes, network disconnections or service failures). Centralized service management for traditional adaptive systems is not applicable to MANETs, as device mobility is likely to be unpredictable, with devices joining and leaving the network at any time. There is, therefore, no guarantee that a suitably resource-rich central node will be available for the duration of a complex service provision.

X. Franch et al. (Eds.): ICSOC 2014, LNCS 8831, pp. 93–107, 2014.

A number of approaches to *distributed service composition* [2], [15], [24], [25] have been proposed. They support the specification of a full composition request as an abstract workflow and distribute it through the network. They can also partition a workflow into independent parts and then assign these parts to corresponding nodes. However, most workflow-based distributed service composition approaches have not addressed adaptation in abstract workflows. Thus, existing systems may fail or have to rediscover service providers, if a service query in such a request is not matched. *Dynamic service compositions* [8], [13], [16], cope with the adaptation problem using task planning algorithms, or graph-theory based techniques. However, graph-theory based techniques have limited support to analyze multiple input/output (I/O) dependencies among services [13]. Moreover, existing task planning algorithms either are constrained to sequential composition or require central knowledge bases.

In this paper, we introduce a service composition algorithm to form and adapt a full business process for a complex user task on-the-fly, without the requirement for a central node. Forming a business process relies on a novel overlay network named Semantic Service Overlay Network (SSON), which clusters semantically similar nodes and semantically dependent nodes for dynamic composition. On SSON networks, a service provider can adapt composition requests and generate potential execution fragments that can be selected to build global execution paths. New service providers may be discovered to replace any that result in composition failures or service outages, composing them into the current execution.

The advantage of this work is that programmers can develop mobile applications structured based on complex user tasks, instead of concretely specifying the possible workflows and configurations in advance. In addition, the approach allows new services not known a-priori to add to the environment at composition as well as execution time, increasing the composition success rate. The approach can be used in application scenarios where service providers are intermittent, or where there are dynamic complex applications with system configurations that cannot be generated a-priori, such as automotive and wearable mobile devices. Taking examples from the automotive domain, systems can benefit from cooperation between vehicles to produce information such as forward collision warning.

The main contribution of this work is a decentralized mechanism to enable service compositions. Our evaluation compares our service composition approach with a dynamic service composition model. The results show that service compositions can be adapted in a decentralized manner and provide a high composition success ratio.

The reminder of this paper is organized as follows. Section 2 introduces the system model. Section 3 illustrates a semantic-based mechanism that supports service composition. Section 4 shows the service composition algorithm and the strategy of service execution management. Section 5 presents the evaluation and result. Section 6 discusses related work. Section 7 summaries this work.

2 System Model Overview

In the service-based environment considered in this paper, a complex user task can be supported with the collaboration of two or more basic services that are composed into a composite service. To enable such collaboration, a service composition can specify complex user tasks as abstract workflows. In much of the existing work that relies on abstract workflows, systems execute ordered service queries individually in a predefined succession [6]. Each of the queries can match with either one basic service, or trigger a process to generate a composite service when there is no service that suffices independently. Such a service matching scheme can be categorized as one-to-N matching (N≥1). This paper investigates a novel, decentralized dynamic L-to-M (L≥1, M≥1) matching scheme for service composition. Instead of matching one service query to N basic service(s), our service composition model matches L service queries to M services, by adapting abstract workflows and their concrete implementation details.

Consider a navigation task as an example. This navigation has a service query list (abstract workflow) including two requirements: a GetLocation service and, a Navigator service that needs the results of a GetLocation service as input. In service composition, if a system can only find a Navigator service that uses both location data and map data as inputs, the system should be able to adapt the original service query list, by adding a requirement for getting map data.

The theory behind this L-to-M scheme is similar to that of semantic-based service compositions [12], but we realize it without needing a centralized reasoning mechanism, and systems can adapt a completed composition during execution. This is a non-trivial challenge as it is based on the assumption that no single node can maintain full knowledge of the network for execution planning. Our approach relies on local nodes receiving a global composition request, and generating the potential fragments of the global execution plan. Network knowledge can be gradually learned through interactions between participating nodes, and each node can adjust a composition request when new knowledge becomes available. Our main hypothesis is that decentralized service compositions can reduce composition failures from mismatched composition requests.

This work is supported by a three-layer composition structure, as illustrated in Fig.1. Specifically, we have defined an overlay network called a Semantic Service Overlay Network (SSON). A SSON can be constructed from service descriptions which are semantically annotated using ontology concepts. We define these concepts using standard taxonomies such as SIC[1] to outline the goal of services. Section 3 elaborates more on how to structure and maintain a SSON.

The lowest layer in the service composition structure is the service layer, which includes services with annotated service descriptions. In particular, we annotate the service with its functionality, inputs and outputs. Naturally, these annotated elements can have different ontology concepts taken from a common standard ontology. For example, an on-line meal order service can capture concepts such as: restaurant meals delivery (functionality), address (input) and price (output),

---

[1] http://www.epa.gov/envirofw/html/sic_lkup.html

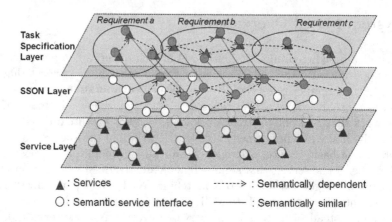

Fig. 1. Overview of Service Composition Model

which are drawn from an online NAICS [2] and Restaurant ontology[3]. The SSON layer is built over the service layer, linking different services based on their semantic similarity and dependency. Services are semantically similar if they provide similar functionalities or they require similar input data and produce outputs with similar types. Two services are semantically dependent if one's output has the same semantic type as the other's input. In other words, it is possible for one to use the others result to execute its own operations. The highest layer is a user task specification layer where a set of composition requirements are defined as a task specification, with the SSON layer aggregating appropriate services for the task specified, as described in Section 4.

For the service model, we describe a service $S =< S_{id}, IN, OUT >$, consisting of a service identification S_{id} and two sets capturing I/O parameters. Semantic annotations for a service are defined in a *Service Annotation Profile* $AP =< S_{id}, AF, AIN, AOUT >$, where AF, AIN, and $AOUT$ are ontology concepts mapped to corresponding functionalities and I/O parameters in a service description. APs inform service compositions about services' logical semantic interfaces, and can be described by semantically rich data models, such as OWL-S and SAWSDL.

3   Semantic Service Overlay Network (SSON)

Research on service composition has explored overlay networks underpinning the service discovery process. There are existing different types of overlay networks to this end, such as service-specific overlay networks [2], service overlay networks [13], and semantic overlay networks (SONs) [5]. SSON is an extension of SONs which were originally explored to improve service discovery performance for Peer-to-Peer (P2P) networks. A SON is a logical network based on similarities between peers shared content, which the network uses to organize peers and improve

---

[2] http://www.census.gov/eos/www/naics/index.html

[3] http://wise.vub.ac.be/ontologies/restaurant.owl

content-based search. The core notion of a SON is to bunch similar peers, making query processes discover bunches instead of individual peers for faster locating. Current research on facilitating distributed service discovery with SONs, like DHT-SON [18] and SDSD [4], shows a SON can be structured at comparable cost to that of producing a normal network by using probe messages.

This proposed SSON supports service composition by introducing the idea of I/O dependencies from service overlay networks [13], [23] which create links between service providers by matching I/O parameters. A SSON combines service overlay networks with normal SON activities. I/O parameters-dependent links can be built as a byproduct of general SONs. A SSON is structured by linking semantically-related services, and the relationship between services can be classified as similarity or dependency. The former represents two service sharing similar functionalities like that defined in traditional SONs; the latter indicates two services with potential I/O data dependencies. Semantic links rely on matchmaking techniques to be established.

3.1   Matchmaking Models

In this work, we introduce a *deductive matchmaking model* (MatchAP), combined with a distributed similarity-based model called ERGOT [19]. ERGOT uses a similarity function $Csim(c_1, c_2) \in [0, 1]$ that returns whether two ontology concepts (c_1 and c_2) are similar. The MatchAP model explores semantic connections (similarity and dependency) between two semantic service interfaces AP_1 and AP_2. It matches the inputs of AP_1 to that of AP_2, as well as matching their outputs and functionalities. It also matches the inputs (respectively, the outputs) of AP_1 to the outputs (respectively, the inputs) of AP_2 to determine any dependency between the two interfaces. We use a matching function [19] between the parameters in two sets X_1 and X_2:

$$ParamSim(X_1, X_2) = \sum_{b \in X_2} \max_{a \in X_1} Csim(a, b) \tag{1}$$

where $AP_1 =< S_1, AF_1, AIN_1, AOUT_1 >$ and $AP_2 =< S_2, AF_2, AIN_2, AOUT_2 >$. The matching function between two APs can then be defined by using of Equation1:

$$MatchAP(AP_1, AP_2) = \alpha ParamSim(AF_1, AF_2)$$
$$+\beta(ParamSim(AIN_1, AIN_2) + ParamSim(AOUT_1, AOUT_2)) \tag{2}$$
$$+\gamma ParamSim(AIN_1, AOUT_2)$$

where the parameters α, β, and γ are used to weight similarity. Depending on values returned by function $MatchAP(AP_1, AP_2)$, we state that if $MatchAP(AP_1, AP_2)$ is larger than a threshold value Θ, a semantic link can be built between the services, and they become semantic neighbours to each other. A semantic link $A \rightarrow B$ can be ranked. We define five different ranks for semantic links that are listed below, taking into account their match types, which extend the definition from a conventional SON [4]:

- *R0_same*: A and B provide the **same functionalities** and ask for the same sets of input data. (e.g. A: Get Location, B: Get Address)
- *R1_reqI*: A provides the same functionalities with B, but asks for **additional input data** with respect to that of B. (e.g. A: Get Location, B: Get Address by Name and Phone Number)
- *R2_share*: A and B have **shared functionalities**. (e.g. A: Navigator, B: Route Planner)
- *R3_dep*: A depends on B's execution result. (e.g. A: Navigator, B: Get Location)
- *R4_in*: A can provide input data to B. (e.g. A: Navigator, B: Route Render)

3.2   SSON Construction

Nodes can join or leave the network over time, so they should be in a position to discover their semantic neighbours. When a peer joins a new network, it advertises its services by initializing a probe service request using the information in the APs of the services and finding its semantic neighbours in the network. The request also includes a threshold value for semantic matchmaking. Such a service request query only operates once when the peer joins the network. As soon as a peer has established semantic links with other peers, other newcomers are able to take advantage of this peers knowledge through their own probe service requests. For example, suppose a Navigator service relies on locations and map data as inputs to generate navigation information between locations. The semantic links Navigator → Get Location service can be created with a rank: *R3_dep* if the latter can provide any of the inputs. Semantic neighbours are neighbouring logically but physically it is also possible that multiple services with semantic relations may be published in the same service provider (peer).

Considering peers' mobility and the dynamic environment in which they reside, overlay management protocols like CYCLON [22] and some stabilization protocols can be used to monitor the neighbours presence and to update the list of semantic neighbours on peers. Updating the list of semantic neighbours can trigger system adaptations that will be illustrated in Section 4.3.

4   Decentralized Service Composition

MANET environments cannot guarantee to provide a single, continuously accessible node to serve a service composition as a central entity because nodes may leave the network, or otherwise fail. This section introduces an alternative based on distributing the processing of service compositions, utilizing semantic links in SSON network.

4.1   Task Model

Complex user tasks are handled by a service composition system that receives the task's specification as an input request and composes value-added services. Our work specifies a task as $SC\_T = <T_{id}, T_{input}, T_{output}, \delta>$, where T_{id} is the request's identification. The end-to-end inputs and outputs are represented as two sets: T_{input} and T_{output}. A set of operations δ is defined that summarise the task's goal, and an operation $Opt_i =< Opt_{id}, IN, OUT >\in \delta$ consists of a specification of operation name (Opt_{id}) and I/O parameters (IN and OUT). A composition request message containing a SC_T can be defined as $SC\_Req =< SC\_T, Log, Comp\_Cache >$, where Log accumulates message-passing history to prevent providers repeatedly processing a request for the same workflow. The $Comp\_Cache$ is used to resolve service composition for a single operation when a service for a requested operation is not found. It caches existing services to discover if a combination from them can match the single operation. In this work, we define a *Composer* role in a service composition process. Task requests can be passed from a composer to its neighbours and adapted by the composer.

Definition 1: A *Composer* is a node in a network who decides to participate in a composition process. It can cooperate with other composers in the network to dynamically generate and maintain the fragments of global execution paths. One node becomes a composer as soon as it successfully matches a received composition request from other nodes. The node resigns this role when the provided services have been executed, or no fragment remains in it.

4.2 Distributed Planning

Logical reasoning algorithms like forward- or backward chaining have previously been used to facilitate semantic-based service composition [12]. General implementation of reasoning forwards and backwards uses decision trees, for which systems require a global view of facts (available services) to build. Our approach leverages a decentralized *backward-chaining* mechanism to create composition plans using local knowledge for user tasks. The core function of this planning process is twofold: a) it aggregates potential providers for a composition request and dynamically adjusts composition requests hop-by-hop based on new local knowledge; b) it allows a potential provider to generate a list of fragments for system configurations. A fragment defines how the potential provider can compose with its semantic neighbours to provide functionalities for the consumer.

Potential Provider Aggregation. When a consumer launches a service composition request, a distributed strategy to devise composition plans for this request, piece by piece, is initiated. Specifically, service consumers initiate a composition request from task specifications. As can be seen in Algorithm 1 (a), an initiator sends the request over the network to discover potential providers who can produce (or partially produce) the set of requested end-to- end outputs. Afterwards, it waits for composers sending tokens to it. Each token represents a discovered plan of a completed execution path, or a completed branch in a parallel execution path. The initiator receives tokens, and starts service execution phases when a complete execution plan emerges (Line 6 in Algorithm 1 (a)).

When a node receives a composition request for the first time, it calls Algorithm 1(b) to decide how its published services could combine to match one or more operations specified in the request's task specification. If an operation is

List 1 : Algorithm 1 (a) - Initiator

1   Send SC_R
2   Set timer T
3   /* Waiting */
4   **if** T expires : the composition fails;
5   Receive a token and store it
6   **if** a complete composition exists : send input data and execute;
7   **else** : back to step 3;

List 2 : Algorithm 1 (b) - Service provider S

Input: Service Composition Request: SC_R

SC_R: $< R_{id}, T_{input}, T_{output}, \delta, Log, Comp\_Cache >, Opt_i \in \delta$

Output: (i) template information and (ii) an updated request

1   /* Listening */
2   S Receives SC_R from Composer Q and log(Log);
3   **if** ComposerMode_S = ON: produceTemplateInfo (SC_R);   **//Output (i)**
4   **else** : **for** each operation Opt[i]{
5   **if** S supports no operation: back to step 1;
6   **else**{ ComposerMode_S := ON
7   **if** S supports Opt[i]'s output type but Opt[i]'s functionality:
8   *Strategy 1*- AddtoComp_Cache (S);
9   **if** S (or S+ Comp_Cache) can provide full functionality for Opt[i]: {
10   eliminate Opt[i]
11   **if** Opt[i] is the last operation in a branch : sendToken(Initiator);
12   **if** S (or S+ Comp_Cache) requires extra input data which
13   is not specified in Opt[i]: *Strategy 2*- create a new operation;
14   produceTemplateInfo (SC_R) }   **//Output (i)**
15   replyToSender(Q)
16   updateTask(SC_R, S)   **//Output (ii)**
17   SendOutList :=getSemanticNeighbours(R3_dep)
18   sendRequest (SC_R, SendOutList) };
19   };

successfully matched, the node becomes a composer. This new composer then stores the received request, eliminates the matched operation of the request and sends out a new request. It also draws up template information for creating configuration fragments. Therefore, the number of operations in a request reduces hop by hop. If the eliminated operation is the last operation of a workflow branch in the request, the composer sends a token to the initiator.

A node has a chance to provide a full service for an operation by combining to other peers in the network when it can only provide a partial service for that operation. To this end, we take into account two situations and apply corresponding two strategies (Line 8 and Line 13 in Algorithm 1 (b)). These strategies allow composers to adapt the abstract workflow on-the-fly. To illustrate such adaptation in our backward planning process, we present a brief example scenario: finding a restaurant and routing to it. Table 1 shows the operations defined in the composition request and the original abstract workflow. It also illustrates available service providers in the example scenario. *We assume there is no provider in the network that can work alone to serve operation o_C.*

Table 1. An example scenario: finding a restaurant and routing to it

Abstract workflow: $o_A \rightarrow o_B \rightarrow o_C$ (deduced from the I&O dependencies)		
Operations Functionality	Input	Output
o_A Restaurant Recommender	Personal profiles (food preferences)	A list of restaurant
o_B Get Location	Names	Addresses
o_C Navigator	Addresses	Audio routing results
Available Functionality Providers	Input	Output
Provider_A Restaurant Recommender	Food preferences	A list of restaurant
Provider_B Get Address	Names	Addresses
Provider_C Navigator	Addresses+Map blocks	Text routing results
Provider_Y Text to Audio	Plain text	Audio stream
Provider_X Map cache	Name of place	Map blocks of the place

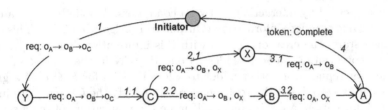

Fig. 2. An example of distributed backward task planning (req: a service composition request. An abstract workflow is implied by the request.)

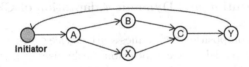

Fig. 3. Concrete workflow from a global perspective

As can be seen in Fig.2, the abstract workflow ($o_A \rightarrow o_B \rightarrow o_C$) is processed backward with the forwarding of composition requests. This process starts from an original composition request sent from the initiator (Arrow 1) to providers that can produce audio streams. Provider_Y receives the request and finds itself cannot support the full functionality of o_C. It applies *Strategy 1*, caching information to indicate its capabilities and forwarding the request to its semantic neighbours. Provider_C gets the request from Provider_Y. As shown in Table 1, Provider_C can fully serve o_C, but requires extra support on input data. Therefore, Provider_C uses *Strategy 2*, eliminating o_C from the request and adding a new operation for discovering the required input data. Afterwards, the updated request will be sent out to match the remainder of the operations. A complete execution path exists after Provider_A applies the requests sending from Provider_X and Provider_B. *During the distributed planning process, the original abstract workflow ($o_A \rightarrow o_B \rightarrow o_C$) is adapted as shown in Fig.3.*

Configuration Fragments Creation. A *configuration fragment* (CF) indicates the possible position of a service in execution paths by defining the pre-conditions and the post-conditions of the service's execution. It is created from template information that is one of the outputs of Algorithm 1(b). Template information includes a CF template that defines how many different pre-conditions and post-conditions the execution of the service has. It also contains a set of CF update instructions (CFUIs) for maintaining the list of CFs. To create CFs we propose two notions: *Pre-Conditional Neighbours (PreCNs)* and *Post-Conditional Neighbours (PostCNs)*. They are both extracted from a potential provider's semantic neighbours. A PreCN or a PostCN has input or output dependence on the potential provider, respectively.

Definition 2: A CF can be described as $CF = < CF_{id}, S\_Pre, S\_Post >$, where S_Pre represents a set of selected PreCNs as the entries of the CF; S_Post represents a set of selected PostCNs as the exits of the CF; and CF_{id} is an identification of the CF. An example of a CF for the scenario illustrated in Table 1 is shown in Fig.4(a).

A CF is created by interactions between composers. A node becomes a composer and gains template information (Output (i) in Algorithm 1(b)). This composer then starts the creation of CFs with this information. The composer regards the composition request sender as one PostCN in the S_Post of a CF and waits for replies from other nodes to select PreCNs for S_Pre. If a group of replies are received and the reply senders can satisfy the CF template in the template information, a CF is created. If more than one group of reply senders are available, a list of CF can be made by repeating the creation step.

4.3   Service Execution and Dynamic Adaptation of CFs

Traditional service composition techniques start service executions only after service binding has completed. The composition mechanism in this paper combines the service binding phase and the execution phase. Our previous work on opportunistic service composition illustrates a distributed execution model [10], [9] that allows systems to bind one service provider, directly executing its provided services, and then forwards the remainder of composition request on to the next node. The bound provider then waits for other providers to reply with messages that include their service functionality information. We apply the distributed execution model in this work with some extensions to discovery mechanisms. Instead of forwarding the rest of the request, the bound provider (composer) selects the best matched CF, sending its execution results to the nodes in the S_Post of the CF.

This paper provides dynamic adaptation mechanisms for systems. Global adaptation is realized by selecting adaptable local CFs hop-by-hop during service execution. The CFs of a composer can be adapted during composition planning phases and service execution phases. Such adaptation is modelled by *a MAPE (Monitor-Analyze-Plan-Execute)* loop, as shown in Fig 4(b). Composers can *monitor* adaptation trigger events with SSON, *analyze* these events when they appear and assign

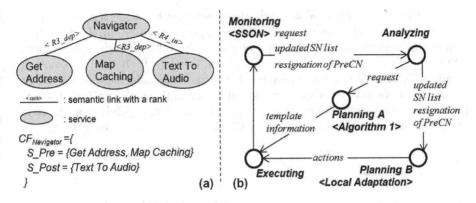

Fig. 4. (a) An example of the CF for Provider_C (Table 1), (b) CFs Adaptation (SN: Semantic Neighbours)

Table 2. Decentralized adaptation rules (Planning B)

Links	Composer's (A) adaptation actions to the new node (B)
R0_same	Action 1: A clones the CFs and the composition request kept in A to B. B becomes a composer.
R1_reqI	Action 2: A clones the composition request kept in A to B. B becomes a composer and calls Algorithm 1(b) to create CFs
R2_share	Action 3: A decides if the functionality it shares with B can support the composition. If so, do Action 1 or Action 2 depending on the required input of B
R3_dep	Action 4: A send the composition request updated by A to B. B calls algorithm 1(b), deciding to take part in the composition or not.

the event information to corresponding *planning* algorithms. These algorithms generate local adaptation plans which are *executed* to adapt CFs.

Adaptation can be triggered by newly arrived composition requests. When an existing composer receives a new request for the same composition, it then analyses the request using its historical data (stored requests and existing template information), and directly generates template information (Planning A in Fig 4(b)). The CFUIs in template information are used to guide the execution of the adaptation. According to different kinds of new requests, we define four CFUIs for adaptation: clone, alter, wait and remove. For example, the Provider_A in our example scenario (as shown in Table 1) receives the request $< req : o_A, o_X >$, and creates a CF ($CF_1 : S\_Pre = \{Initiator\}$, $S\_Post = \{B\}$). When a new request $< req : o_A \to o_B >$ is pushed to Provider_A, this new request will trigger adaptation to alter the CF_1 to $\{S\_Pre = \{Initiator\}, S\_Post = \{B, X\}\}$.

This approach introduces a decentralized adaptation mechanism (Planning B in Fig 4(b)) that deals with *potential node failures* and *recently joined nodes* by adapting the CFs stored in composers. Node failures can be leaded by the selection of invalid CFs during service execution. A CF becomes invalid when the nodes that are recorded in it cannot be reached. If a semantic neighbour of a composer leaves the physical network, this absence of the node can be detected through the management of SSON. The composer removes all the CFs that contain the absent node. If a composer resigns its role, it sends a message to all the PreCN and PostCN nodes, asking them to adapt their CFs by removing invalid CFs. A node can also join the network and engage in the composition at runtime. If a composer finds a new node in its semantic neighbour list, this new node can participate in the composition in different ways depending on the rank of the semantic link established between it and the composer (See Table 2).

5 Evaluation

Our approach maps a composition request to an L-to-M matching scheme to address the problem where a queried service cannot be matched during service composition. Solving one-to-one mis-matching has been investigated by several approaches, for example, discovery algorithms to find more potential providers and dynamic one-to- more composition [2], [13]. Our direction is similar in that it tries to compose a basic service to match a single service query. Thus, we conducted simulations to compare our solution against a Graph-Based (GB) approach [13]. The GB approach assumes a service provider entering a network by broadcasting its service information. The network can rely on a central directory that collects service information and maintains a global service network graph to receive composition requests. The directory finds a consecutive execution path out of the graph based on received requests. We measured the composition success ratio, which is the number of composition requests that are successfully processed with execution paths divided by the total number of requests.

We applied a simulation scenario [2] with services of alphabet converters and joiners. In this scenario, a converter service receives input A and produce output B $(A \rightarrow B)$, and a joiner service receives inputs A and B generating C as an output $(A + B \rightarrow C)$. We employed 7 alphabets to represent I/O parameters in the scenario; therefore, there are 21 different converter services and 35 different joiner services. We used the NS-3 simulator to study the efficiency of our self-adaptive approach and the GB approach. We simulated both approaches with the same limitation of the maximum hops of broadcasting during service publishing. We applied the random walk 2D mobility model, by which we control service density and the proportion of mobile nodes. The service density is the radio scope of a node divided by the whole field where all the nodes are located. This simulation ran 10 rounds with varying numbers for mobile nodes and 9 rounds with different service densities. Each of them is repeated 100 times with random providers' composition requests, and we report the average (see Fig.5). The number of operations in a request is set to 4. We used Self-Adapt to represent our approach in the following simulation study.

Fig.5 shows (a) the success ratio results with different service densities, and (b) the success ratios at 70% service density with the ratio of mobile nodes varying from 20% to 100%. These two studies only employed the converter services since the GB approach cannot model services with multiple I/O parameters.

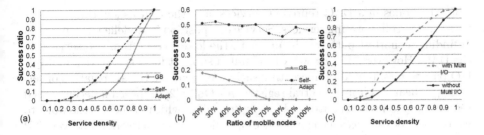

Fig. 5. The result of the study on composition success ratio

The result (a) shows that Self-Adapt has a higher success ratio, especially when the density of services is low, because the SSON network, benefited from its decentralized management, collects and mantains more service information than the service overlay network used in the GB approach. The result (b) suggests that Self-Adapt is more successful than the GB approach in high mobility scenarios. Fig.5(c) illustrates the success ratio with varying service density of services, comparing Self-Adapt using the multiple I/O strategy (see Section 4) with when it does not use this strategy. It shows that the use of the strategy results in a higher success ratio.

6 Related Work

Workflow-based adaptive systems [21] choose, or implement services from a predefined abstract workflow that determines the structure of services. The abstract workflow is implemented as a concrete (executable) workflow by selecting and composing requested services. Adaptation of concrete workflows has been explored in the literature [1], [3]. However, these require central entities for composition and an explicit static abstract workflow, which is usually created manually. Decentralized process management approaches [24], [25] explore distributed mechanisms, like process migration, to manage and update the execution of concrete workflows, which is close to our work in terms of service execution. However, they still need a well- defined system business process at deployment time. In our approach, the partial workflows that composers generate locally, distribute over participating service providers during service discovery phases to gradually devise a global one.

Dynamic service composition can also be reduced to an AI planning problem. Similar to our solution, decentralized planning approaches [7], [11], [20] form a global plan through merging fragments of plans that are created by individual service agents. However, with these approaches, programmers need to provide an explicitly defined goal for planning. The initial plan can become unreliable when the environment changes. Automatic re-planning schemes [12], [14], [17] allow plans to be adapted when matching services are unavailable, but existing approaches depend on central knowledge bases.

Considerable research effort has targeted dynamic service compositions supporting one-to-M ($M > 1$) matching while a matching basic service is not located. They usually define a composition result as a directed acyclic graph [8],

[13]. The nodes in a DAG represent services, and the edges show compositions between the collaborating services. Service composition is modelled as a problem of finding a shortest path (or the one with the lowest cost) from two services in the DAG. However, existing work has limited support for services with multiple I/O parameters. In addition, creating such DAG requires the aggregation of service specifications from a central registry. Al- Oqily [2] proposed a decentralized reasoning system for one-to-M ($M > 1$) matching, which is the closest work to us. It composes services using a Service-Specific Overlay Network built over P2P networks and enables self-organizing through management of the network. However, this approach is based on an assumption that every node in the network knows its geographic location, as service discovery is realized by broadcasting a request over its physical neighbours. Geographic locations usually can be obtained from location services like GIS, but these are not readily accessible for every node in the network. Our approach uses a semantic-based overlay network to discover logical neighbours instead of geographic ones.

7   Conclusion and Future Work

Distributed service composition approaches allow systems to perform complex user tasks without central entities, but do not fit well in dynamic environments. The distributed service composition algorithm proposed in this paper addresses this dynamic problem by adapting workflows during composition planning processes as well as service execution phases. This paper also proposed a SSON network to underpin such adaptation. The presented evaluation result shows an improvement of composition success rate comparing to an influential abstract workflow adaptation scheme for dynamic service composition.

In future work, first, we will investigate the performance of the proposed approach for different application scenarios and varying composition paths like liner, parallel and hybrid composition paths. Although this approach provides a higher success ratio than the GB approach, the cost of maintaining SSON networks and adaptation processes may outweigh the high success ratio benefits in some application scenarios. Second, our future research will include an interesting topic for Quality of Service (QoS)-aware adaptation to not only increase the composition ratio but also provide services with good quality.

References

1. Adams, M., ter Hofstede, A.H.M., Edmond, D., van der Aalst, W.M.P.: Worklets: A service-oriented implementation of dynamic flexibility in workflows. In: Proc. Int. Conf. on On the Move to Meaningful Internet Systems (2006)
2. Al-Oqily, I., Karmouch, A.: A Decentralized Self-Organizing Service Composition for Autonomic Entities. ACM Trans. Auton. and Adapt. Syst. (2011)
3. Ardissono, L., Furnari, R., Goy, A., Petrone, G., Segnan, M.: Context-aware workflow management. In: Proc. 7th Int. Conf. ICWE (2007)

4. Bianchini, D., Antonellis, V.D.: On-the-fly collaboration in distributed systems through service semantic overlay. In: Proc. 10th Int. Conf. Inf. Integr. Web-based Appl. Serv. (2008)
5. Crespo, A., Garcia-Molina, H.: Semantic overlay networks for p2p systems. Agents and Peer-to-Peer Computing (2005)
6. Di Nitto, E., Ghezzi, C., Metzger, A., Papazoglou, M., Pohl, K.: A journey to highly dynamic, self-adaptive service-based applications. Autom. Softw. Eng. 15(3-4), 313–341 (2008)
7. El Falou, M., Bouzid, M., Mouaddib, A.I., Vidal, T.: A Distributed Planning Approach for Web Services Composition. In: 2010 IEEE Int. Conf. Web Serv. (2010)
8. Fujii, K., Suda, T.: Semantics-based dynamic service composition. IEEE Journal on Selected Areas in Communications, 2361–2372 (December 2005)
9. Groba, C., Clarke, S.: Opportunistic service composition in dynamic ad hoc environments. IEEE Trans. Services Computing PP(99), 1 (2014)
10. Groba, C., Clarke, S.: Opportunistic composition of sequentially-connected services in mobile computing environments. In: 2011 IEEE Web Services, ICWS (2011)
11. Helin, H., Klusch, M., Lopes, A., Fernández, A., Schumacher, M., Schuldt, H., Bergenti, F., Kinnunen, A.: CASCOM: Context-aware service co-ordination in mobile P2P environments. In: Eymann, T., Klügl, F., Lamersdorf, W., Klusch, M., Huhns, M.N. (eds.) MATES 2005. LNCS (LNAI), vol. 3550, pp. 242–243. Springer, Heidelberg (2005)
12. Hibner, A., Zielinski, K.: Semantic-based dynamic service composition and adaptation. In: 2007 IEEE Congress on Services, pp. 213–220 (2007)
13. Kalasapur, S., Kumar, M., Shirazi, B.A.: Dynamic Service Composition in Pervasive Computing. In: IEEE Trans. Parallel and Distributed Systems (2007)
14. Klusch, M., Gerber, A.: Semantic web service composition planning with owls-xplan. In: Proc. 1st Int. AAAI Fall Symp. Agents and the Semantic Web (2005)
15. Martin, D., Wutke, D., Leymann, F.: A Novel Approach to Decentralized Workflow Enactment. In: 12th Int.IEEE Enterp. Distrib. Object Comput. Conf. (2008)
16. Mokhtar, S., Liu, J.: QoS-aware dynamic service composition in ambient intelligence environments. In: Proc. IEEE/ACM Int. Conf. Autom. Softw. Eng. (2005)
17. Peer, J.: A pop-based replanning agent for automatic web service composition. In: Proc. 2nd EU Conf. The Semantic Web: Research and Applications (2005)
18. Pirrò, G., Talia, D., Trunfio, P.: A DHT-based semantic overlay network for service discovery. Future Generation Computer Systems 28(4), 689–707 (2012)
19. Pirrò, G., Trunfio, P., Talia, D., Missier, P., Goble, C.: ERGOT: A Semantic-Based System for Service Discovery in Distributed Infrastructures. In: 10th IEEE/ACM Int. Conf. Clust. Cloud Grid Comput. (2010)
20. Poizat, P., Yan, Y.: Adaptive composition of conversational services through graph planning encoding. In: Proc. 4th Int. Conf. Leveraging Apps. of Formal Methods, Verification, and Validation - Volume Part II (2010)
21. Smanchat, S., Ling, S., Indrawan, M.: A survey on context-aware workflow adaptations. In: Proc. 6th Int. Conf. Adv. Mob. Comput. and Multimed. (2008)
22. Voulgaris, S., Gavidia, D., Steen, M.: CYCLON: Inexpensive Membership Management for Unstructured P2P Overlays. J. Netw. Syst. Manag. 13 (2005)
23. Wang, M., Li, B., Li, Z.: sFlow: Towards resource-efficient and agile service federation in service overlay networks. Distributed Computing Systems (2004)
24. Yu, W.: Scalable Services Orchestration with Continuation-Passing Messaging. In: 2009 First Int. Conf. Intensive Applications and Services, pp. 59–64 (April 2009)
25. Zaplata, S., Hamann, K.: Flexible execution of distributed business processes based on process instance migration. J. Syst. Integr. 1(3) (2010)

Optimal and Automatic Transactional Web Service Composition with Dependency Graph and 0-1 Linear Programming

Virginie Gabrel, Maude Manouvrier, and Cécile Murat

PSL Université Paris-Dauphine, LAMSADE UMR CNRS 7243
75775 Paris Cedex 16, France
{gabrel,manouvrier,murat}@lamsade.dauphine.fr

Abstract. In this article, we propose a model based on 0-1 linear programming for automatically determining a transactional composite web service (CWS) from a service dependency graph that optimizes a QoS measure. The QoS measure used in this model can be either a classical weighted sum of QoS criteria or a minmax-type criterion (e.g. response time). The transactional properties are a set of rules that ensures a reliable execution of the resulting CWS. The proposed 0-1 linear program is solved using a standard solver (CPLEX). Our experiments show that this new exact model surpasses two main related approaches: an approximate one based on transactional requirements and an exact one, based on 0-1 linear programming (LP), but not dealing with transactional properties. In a large majority of the test sets used for our experiments, our model finds a better solution more rapidly than both related approaches and is able to guarantee its optimality. Moreover, our model is able to find the optimal solutions of big size test sets, as the ones proposed by the Web Service Challenge 2009.

Keywords: Reliable web service composition, Service dependency graph, Integer Linear Programming model, QoS optimization.

1 Introduction

As explained in surveys [1,2], the management of large number of services in the global Internet creates many open problems, in particular in service composition, which consists in selecting/identifying several existing services and combining them into a composite one to produce value-added process.

Many approaches on QoS-aware web service (WS) composition exist, where QoS represents the quality of the service (e.g. price or response time) – see for example survey [3]. As explained in [4], the inter-operation of distributed software-systems is always affected by failures, dynamic changes, availability of resources, and others. And, as argued by [5], to make service-oriented applications more reliable, web services must be examined from a transactional perspective. The execution of a composite WS is reliable if, in case of a component WS failure, the negative impacts are negligible for the user [6]. A service

X. Franch et al. (Eds.): ICSOC 2014, LNCS 8831, pp. 108–122, 2014.
© Springer-Verlag Berlin Heidelberg 2014

that does not provide a transactional property might be as useless as a service not providing the desired functional results. If the composition considers only functional and QoS requirements, then it is possible that during the execution the whole system becomes inconsistent in presence of failures. WS composition only based on transactional properties ensures a reliable execution, but does not guarantee an optimal QoS composite WS and WS composition only based on QoS does not guarantee a reliable execution of the resulting composite WS. Thus, QoS-aware and transactional-aware should be integrated [7].

In this article, we consider the problem qualified by [8] as the most useful and practical one, which consists in composing services by matching their parameters (input and output attributes) so that the resulting composite service can produce a set of output parameters given a set of input ones. For such problem, the service repository is generally modeled by a Service Dependency Graph (SDG) as defined in [9] and used by example in [7,10,11,12]. The contribution of this article is a new 0-1 linear programming-based optimal approach for QoS and transactional-aware service composition. Experiments show that our model outperforms the two main related approaches: an approximate one [7], based on transactional requirements and an exact one [12], based on 0-1 linear programming, but not dealing with transactional properties.

The rest of the article is structured as follows. Related work is presented in Section 2. Section 3 presents the context and the definitions. Section 4 presents our LP model. Constraints dedicated to transactional properties are separated in a specific Section 5. Section 6 gives experimental results and compare our model to the most related work. Finally, Section 7 concludes.

2   Related Work

Automatic QoS-aware service composition is subject of numerous studies (see for example survey [3]). Two approaches must be distinguished. In the first one, a predefined workflow is supposed to be known. This workflow describes a set of "abstract" tasks to be performed. Moreover, associated to each task, a set of WS with similar functionalities (but different QoS and transactional properties) is also known. The composition problem is then to select one WS per task in order to respect QoS [13,14] and transactional requirements [6,15,16]. In the second approach, the existence of a predefined workflow is not assumed. Available WS are described with a service dependency graph (see for example [7,8,10,11,12,17]) and, the composition problem is to find a sub-graph connecting inputs' query to outputs' query. In this article, we focus on such problem.

Considering QoS-aware composition based on SDG, several methodologies have been proposed: game theory, AI planning (with AND/OR graph and A* algorithm), 0-1 LP (solving with a branch and bound), Petri-Net ... – see a systematic review in [18]. Concerning 0-1 linear programming approach, a model is proposed in [12,19], where a composite WS is decomposed into stages (a stage contains one WS or several WS executed in parallel) and the problem is to select one or several WS per stages. Thus the number of variables and constraints can be huge since it is proportional to the number of WS and data times the number of stages. Moreover, the number of stages is not known; only upper bounds can be chosen (the worst one is to set the number of stages equals to the number of WS). The size of the model does not allow to solve big size test sets: none experimental results are given in [19], while, in [12], computational experiments are performed, for 20 WS and 200 data, taking 200 seconds to find the solution and, for 100 WS and 800 data, taking 900 seconds.

Some approaches extend QoS-aware composition to transactionnal and QoS-based approaches (see for example survey [20]). However, to the best of our knowledge, the approach of [7] is the only one proposing a WS composition algorithm based on service dependency graph integrating both transactional and QoS requirements. In this approach, the dependency graph is represented by a colored Petri Net, where places correspond to the data and transitions to the WS. The proposed algorithm is a greedy-like algorithm locally optimizing the QoS. In order to limit the execution time, the authors proposed to identify the WS which are potentially useful to answer the user query. This identification consists in selecting the transactional paths in the dependency graph, that allow to obtain an output data needed by the user from the inputs of the query. The greedy-algorithm then consists in selecting the solution from a smaller dependency graph, only containing the WS which are potentially useful or relevant to answer the user query.

3   Context and Background Definitions

In this article, the service repository (i.e. the set of available services) is represented by a directed graph $G = (X, U)$. The set of vertices X can be partitioned in two sets: S the set of vertices representing WS and, D the set of vertices representing data. In the following, for all $i \in S$, let us denote by $s(i)$ the WS represented by vertex i and, for all $i \in D$, $d(i)$ denotes the data represented by vertex i. The set of directed edges U represents two kinds of dependency: (1) an edge from $i \in S$ to $j \in D$ represents the fact that WS $s(i)$ produces data $d(j)$ ($d(j)$ is an output of $s(i)$), (2) an edge from $i \in D$ to $j \in S$ represents the fact that WS $s(j)$ needs data $d(i)$ to be executed ($d(i)$ is one intput of $s(j)$). Thus, in this graph representation, there does not exist any directed edge of the form: (i, j) with $i \in S$ and $j \in S$ or, $i \in D$ and $j \in D$. Such graph, generally called a Service Dependency Graph, is used in [7,10,11,12]. An example of SDG is presented in Fig. 1.

The user query is defined by a set I of input data (with $I \subset D$) corresponding to the information that the user provides, and a set O of output data representing the information the user needs (with $O \subset D$). Such query is also used in [7,10,11,12] for example.

A composite WS (CWS) satisfying the user query, characterized by I and O, can be represented by a connected sub-graph if and only if: (a) each $o \in O$ is covered by the sub-graph, (b) in this sub-graph, the only vertices without any predecessor belong to I, (c) if a vertex $i \in S$ is covered by the sub-graph, then all arcs (j, i), with $j \in D$, belong to the sub-graph (indeed each WS $s(i)$ can be executed if and only if all its input data are available) and, (d) this sub-graph does not contain any directed cycle.

For example, given the graph of Fig. 1 and the query described by $I = \{1, 2\}$ and $O = \{7, 8\}$, we can propose different CWS. The CWS $\{s(16), s(18), s(15)\}$ is represented by the following sub-graph: $\{(1, 16), (16, 3), (3, 18), (18, 6), (6, 15),$ $(15, 7), (15, 8)\}$. Let us remark that CWS $\{s(11), s(13), s(15)\}$ is not feasible since it contains the following conflicting situation: to be executed, $s(11)$ needs $d(6)$ as input, and $d(6)$ is obtained by executing $s(13)$ which input $d(4)$ is produced by $s(11)$. In terms of graph, the associated sub-graph $\{(2, 11), (11, 4), (4, 13),$ $(13, 6), (6, 11), (6, 15), (15, 7), (15, 8)\}$ satisfies the aforementioned properties (a), (b) and (c) but does not verify property (d): $(11, 4), (4, 13), (13, 6), (6, 11)$ is a directed cycle.

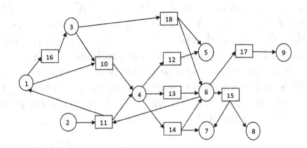

Fig. 1. A service dependency graph with $D = \{1, \ldots, 9\}$ and $S = \{10, \ldots, 18\}$

Given a user query, our problem consists in finding a reliable CWS that optimizes its overall QoS.

4 Linear Programming Model for QoS-Aware Composition

In this article, we model the QoS-aware service composition problem by a 0-1 linear programming model. Decision variables are defined in Subsection 4.1. Subsection 4.2 presents the constraints modeling the I/O of each web service, Subsection 4.3 those implied by the user query, Subsection 4.4 defines the constraints linking decision variables and Subsection 4.5 the constraints eliminating directed cycle. Subsection 4.6 recalls the entire resulting model.

4.1 Decision Variables

We have to introduce three kinds of decision variables:

1. w_i, associated with each $i \in S$: $w_i = 1$ if i is covered by the sub-graph (meaning that $s(i)$ belongs to the composite WS) and 0 otherwise,
2. x_{ij} associated with each directed edge (i,j) of U: $\forall (i,j) \in U$, $x_{ij} = 1$ if the directed edge (i,j) belongs to the sub-graph and 0 otherwise,
3. $t_i \geq 0$ associated with each vertex $i \in X$: t_i represents the topological order of vertex i in the sub-graph.

The objective function is to minimize the following function: $\sum_{i \in S} q_i w_i$, where q_i is the QoS score of WS i. In this article, as in [7,8,12], we use an aggregate QoS score corresponding to a weighted sum of QoS criteria, computed such that the lower the score q_i, the better the service i.

4.2   Constraints Modeling the Input/Output of Each Service

With the previously introduced variables, two constraints, (C_1) and (C_2), modeling the I/O of each service, can be written in a linear form. In the following, for each vertex j, let us denote by $\Gamma^-(j) = \{i \in X : (i,j) \in U\}$ its set of predecessors and, $\Gamma^+(j) = \{i \in X : (j,i) \in U\}$ its set of successors.

For all $j \in S$, a WS $s(j)$ is described by its input and output data: $s(j)$ can be executed if and only if all its input data are available, and $s(j)$ produces a set of output data. In terms of graph, these relations can be described by imposing that an arc (j,k) is in the solution (meaning that output data $d(k)$ is computed by $s(j)$) if and only if all arcs (i,j), with $i \in \Gamma^-(j)$, belong to the solution (meaning that input data for $s(j)$ are available):

$$\forall j \in S, \ \forall k \in \Gamma^+(j), \ \sum_{i \in \Gamma^-(j)} x_{ij} \geq |\Gamma^-(j)| x_{jk} \ (C_1)$$

With such a constraint, if x_{jk} equals to 1, all directed edges entering in vertex j must belong to the solution (ensuring that all input data for $s(j)$ are available). Otherwise, if x_{jk} equals to 0, the constraint is relaxed and plays no role.

Considering the graph of Fig. 1, $s(11)$ produces data $d(1)$ and $d(4)$ and needs data $d(2)$ and $d(6)$ to be executed. Therefore, two constraints must be written for describing inputs and outputs of $s(11)$: (i) considering output $d(1)$, $x_{2,11} + x_{6,11} \geq 2x_{11,1}$ and, (ii) considering output $d(4)$, $x_{2,11} + x_{6,11} \geq 2x_{11,4}$. These constraints imply that $d(1)$ or $d(4)$ can be computed by $s(11)$ if and only if $d(2)$ and $d(6)$ are available as inputs for $s(11)$.

For any data $d(j)$ not provided by the user, $j \in D \setminus I$, $d(j)$ is available when at least one WS computes it. In the associated graph, the set of WS computing $d(j)$ exactly corresponds to $\Gamma^-(j)$ inducing the following constraint:

$$\forall j \in D \setminus I, \ \forall k \in \Gamma^+(j), \ \sum_{i \in \Gamma^-(j)} x_{ij} \geq x_{jk} \ (C_2)$$

This constraint imposes that $d(j)$ can be used by $s(k)$ (inducing that variable x_{jk} is equal to 1) if and only if $d(j)$ has been computed by at least one WS $s(i)$ (leading to $\sum_{i \in \Gamma^-(j)} x_{ij} \geq 1$). When x_{jk} is equal to 0, the constraint plays no role.

Considering the graph of Fig. 1, $d(6)$ is an output of three WS $s(13)$, $s(14)$ and $s(18)$, and is an input of three WS $s(11)$, $s(15)$ and $s(17)$. Thus, three constraints must be written: (i) As input of $s(11)$: $x_{13,6} + x_{14,6} + x_{18,6} \geq x_{6,11}$, (ii) as input of $s(15)$: $x_{13,6} + x_{14,6} + x_{18,6} \geq x_{6,15}$ and, (iii) as input of $s(17)$: $x_{13,6} + x_{14,6} + x_{18,6} \geq x_{6,17}$. Each constraint imposes that $d(6)$ is available if and only if it has been computed by $s(13)$, $s(14)$ and/or $s(18)$.

4.3   Constraints Implied by the User Query

Each data $j \in O$, needed by the user, must be computed by at least one WS:

$$\forall j \in O, \ \sum_{i \in \Gamma^-(j)} x_{ij} \geq 1 \ (C_3)$$

Given the graph of Fig. 1, we consider a user query with $O = \{7,8\}$. $d(7)$ can be computed by $s(14)$ or $s(15)$, and $d(8)$ by $s(15)$ only. Then, we have: $x_{14,7} + x_{15,7} \geq 1$ and $x_{15,8} \geq 1$.

Any data $d(j)$ provided by the user is available, meaning that $\forall j \in I, \forall k \in \Gamma^+(j)$, arc (j,k) can belong to the resulting sub-graph ($x_{jk} \leq 1$). Therefore, input data provided by the user do not introduce any specific constraints in the model.

4.4   Constraints Linking Decision Variables

Given a particular query, constraints (C_1) to (C_3) are sufficient to represent dependency between data and WS. These constraints only concern variables x. Thus, we have to introduce the following additional constraints for linking variables x and w:

$$\forall j \in S, \sum_{k \in \Gamma^+(j)} x_{jk} \leq |\Gamma^+(j)| w_j \ (C_4)$$

This constraint imposes that w_j equals to 1 if at least one directed edge with initial vertex j belongs to the solution. On the contrary, when no edge of the form (j,k) belongs to the solution, constraint plays no role since it becomes $|\Gamma^+(j)| w_j \geq 0$. In this case, w_j can be equal to 1 even if the x values corresponds to a sub-graph which does not cover the vertex j. However, the value of such a solution is strictly greater than the value of the solution with the same x values and $w_j = 0$. Recalling that the objective function is to minimize $\sum_{i \in S} q_i w_i$ ($q_i > 0 \ \forall i$) such a solution cannot be an optimal one.

4.5   Constraints for Eliminating Directed Cycle

The last family of constraints are introduced for eliminating directed cycle in the solution. These constraints are classical (initially proposed in [21]) and are written as follows:

$$t_j - t_i \geq 1 - |X|(1 - x_{ij}) \ \forall (i,j) \in U \qquad (C_5)$$
$$t_i = 0 \qquad\qquad\qquad \forall i \in I \qquad\qquad (C_6)$$
$$0 \leq t_i \leq |X| - 1 \qquad\quad \forall i = 1, \ldots, |X|$$

For all $i \in X$, variable t_i represents the topological order of vertex i in the sub-graph. If x_{ij} equals to 1, arc (i, j) belongs to the sub-graph and constraint (C_5) becomes: $t_j - t_i \geq 1$. This constraint imposes that WS $s(i)$ is executed (or data $d(i)$ is obtained) before producing data $d(j)$ (or executing service $s(j)$). If x_{ij} equals to 0, constraint (C_5) becomes: $t_j - t_i \geq (1 - |X|)$. Since t_i belongs to $[0, |X| - 1]$, constraint (C_5) plays no role even if t_i equals to $(|X| - 1)$.

In graph of Fig. 1, we have previously noticed that CWS $\{s(11), s(13), s(15)\}$ is not a feasible solution. This CWS is described by variables $x_{11,4} = x_{4,13} = x_{13,6} = x_{6,11} = 1$ and constraints (C_5) lead to an unfeasibility: (i) $t_4 - t_{11} \geq 1$, (ii) $t_{13} - t_4 \geq 1$, (iii) $t_6 - t_{13} \geq 1$ and, (iv) $t_{11} - t_6 \geq 1 \implies 0 \geq 4$.

4.6   Resulting Model

The composition problem based on service dependency graph, $G = (X, U)$, can be represented by the following 0-1 linear program:

$$
\begin{cases}
\min \sum_{i \in S} q_i w_i \\
\text{s.t. } \sum_{i \in \Gamma^-(j)} x_{ij} \geq |\Gamma^-(j)| x_{jk} \; \forall j \in S, \; \forall k \in \Gamma^+(j) & (C_1) \\
\sum_{i \in \Gamma^-(j)} x_{ij} \geq x_{jk} & \forall j \in D \setminus I, \; \forall k \in \Gamma^+(j) \; (C_2) \\
\sum_{i \in \Gamma^-(j)} x_{ij} \geq 1 & \forall j \in O & (C_3) \\
\sum_{k \in \Gamma^+(j)} x_{jk} \leq |\Gamma^+(j)| w_j \; \forall j \in S & (C_4) \\
t_j - t_i \geq 1 - |X|(1 - x_{ij}) & \forall (i, j) \in U & (C_5) \\
t_i = 0 & \forall i \in I & (C_6) \\
0 \leq t_i \leq |X| - 1 & \forall i = 1, \dots, |X| \\
w_i \in \{0, 1\} & \forall i \in S \\
x_{ij} \in \{0, 1\} & \forall (i, j) \in U
\end{cases}
$$

This model contains $|S| + |U| + |X|$ variables and $2|U| + |S| + |O|$ constraints.

In this aforementioned model, the QoS is only considered in the objective function. This model can easily be extended for taking into account QoS constraints. For example, let us consider a budget constraint of the form: the cost of the composite WS must be lower than C. This QoS constraint can be easily written as follows: $\sum_{i \in S} c_i w_i \leq C$ with c_i being the cost of WS $s(i)$.

This model does not deal with transactional properties. The next section presents how these properties can be included in our model.

5   Extending Our Model with Transactional Properties

To allow a QoS and transactional WS composition, constraints dealing with WS transactional properties should be added to the model. Subsection 5.1 defines the transactional properties and Subsection 5.2 presents the induced constraints.

5.1   Definitions and Context

In this article, we use the more common transactional properties for a WS (see for example survey [20]): *pivot, retriable* and *compensatable*. A WS is *pivot* (P)

Table 1. Transactional rules of [15]

Transactional property of a WS	Sequential incompatibility	Parallel incompatibility
P	$P \cup C$ (rule 1)	$P \cup C \cup PR$ (rule 2)
PR	$P \cup C$ (rule 3)	$P \cup C$ (rule 4)
C	$\emptyset$	$P \cup PR$ (rule 5)

if once it successfully completes, its effects remain for ever and cannot be semantically undone. If it fails, then it has no effect at all. For example, a service delivering a non refundable and non exchangeable plane ticket is pivot. A WS is *compensatable* (*C*) if it exists another WS, or compensation policies, which can semantically undo its execution. For example, a service allowing to reserve a room in a hotel with extra fees in case of cancellation is compensatable. A WS is *retriable* if it guarantees a successful termination after a finite number of invocations. This property is always combined with the two previous one, defining *pivot retriable* (*PR*) or *compensatable retriable* (*CR*) WS. For example, a payment service may be (pivot or compensatable) retriable in order to guarantee that the payment succeed. The authors of [15] propose transactional rules defining the possible combinations of component WS to obtain a reliable (i.e. a transactional) composite WS. These rules are summarized in Table 1 where the second and the third columns represent the transactional properties of WS which are incompatible in a composition with a WS of transactional property of column 1. For more details about these rules, reader must refer to [15].

Considering the graph $G = (X, U)$ associated to the composition problem, the transactional property of each WS induces a partition of the subset of vertices $S \subset X$ as follows: $S = P \cup C \cup PR \cup CR$ (each subset is denoted by the corresponding transactional property). In the graph of Fig. 1, we set the following partition: $P = \{12, 16, 17\}$, $C = \{10, 13\}$, $PR = \{11, 18\}$, $CR = \{14, 15\}$.

Considering a particular query with given inputs and expected outputs, introducing transactional rules implies that some paths, belonging to the sub-graph, going from an input to an expected output are eliminated (for example paths containing two vertices belonging to P – see line 1 in Table 1). Thus, in terms of our 0-1 linear program, some additional constraints must be introduced in order to eliminate the solutions which do not respect transactional rules. These additional constraints of linear form are presented in the following subsection.

5.2 Constraints Induced by Transactional Requirements

For each vertex $i \in S$ (corresponding to WS $s(i)$), we need to identify the sets of vertices $j \in S$ which can be executed after or in parallel with i. Using a Depth First Search (for DFS algorithm see for example [22]) on $G = (X, U)$, the following sets A_i and L_i can be easily computed. A_i is set of vertices $j \in S$ belonging to the DFS tree with root i. Indeed, if j belongs to the DFS tree rooted by i, then it exists a path in G from i to j meaning that WS $s(j)$ may be executed after WS $s(i)$. L_i is the set of services $j \in S$ that can be executed in parallel of i. L_i contains any vertex $j \in S$ such that it does not exist any path from i to j neither from j to i. We have: $L_i = \{j \notin A_i : i \notin A_j\}$. For example, in graph of Fig. 1, $A_{12} = \emptyset$, $L_{12} = \{13, 14, 15, 17, 18\}$ and, $A_{16} = \{10, 11, 12, 13, 14, 15, 17, 18\}$ and $L_{16} = \emptyset$.

Based on Table 1, we must formulate the following constraints (C_7) to (C_{12}). A transactional composite WS contains at most one pivot:

$$\sum_{i \in P} w_i \leq 1 \ (C_7)$$

For all $i \in P$, if WS $s(i)$ is executed, compensatable WS cannot be executed afterwards (see line 1 of Table 1). The set of compensatable WS that can be executed after WS $s(i)$ is represented by $A_i \cap C$ and the following constraints can be written:

$$\forall i \in P, \ t_i - t_j \geq -|X|(1 - w_i) \ \forall j \in A_i \cap C \ (C_8)$$

Indeed, if the vertex $i \in P$ belongs to the sub-graph, then $w_i = 1$ and the associated constraint becomes $t_i - t_j \geq 0$. Consequently, the order of vertex j is necessarily lower or equal to the order of vertex i implying that WS $s(j)$ cannot be executed after WS $s(i)$ ($s(j)$ may be executed before $s(i)$). If the vertex $i \in P$ is not cover by the sub-graph, then $w_i = 0$ and the associated constraint becomes $t_i - t_j \geq -|X|$. This constraint plays no role. For example, in graph of Fig. 1, vertex 16 represents a pivot WS. Vertex 10 represents a compensatable WS which belongs to A_{16} (since there exists a path from 16 to 10 in G). Thus, we have, for example, the following constraint: $t_{16} - t_{10} \geq -18(1 - w_{16})$ inducing that WS $s(16)$ cannot be executed before WS $s(10)$.

For all $i \in P$, if WS $s(i)$ is executed, compensatable WS and pivot retriable WS cannot be executed in parallel with $s(i)$. The set of vertices representing compensatable WS and pivot retriable WS executing in parallel of WS $s(i)$ is $(C \cup PR) \cap L_i$. Thus the following constraint must be respected:

$$\forall i \in P, \sum_{j \in \{(C \cup PR) \cap L_i\}} w_j \leq |(C \cup PR) \cap L_i|(1 - w_i) \ (C_9)$$

If the vertex $i \in P$ belongs to the sub-graph, then $w_i = 1$ and the associated constraint becomes $\sum_{j \in \{(C \cup PR) \cap L_i\}} w_j \leq 0$. Consequently, vertices belonging to $(C \cup PR) \cap L_i$ cannot be covered by the sub-graph. Otherwise, when $w_i = 0$, the associated constraint plays no role. In graph of Fig. 1, vertex 12 represents a pivot WS. The set of vertices representing WS that can be executed in parallel with WS $s(12)$ is $L_{12} = \{13, 14, 15, 17, 18\}$. Then we have, for example, the following constraint: $w_{13} + w_{18} \leq 2(1 - w_{12})$.

For all $i \in PR$, if WS $s(i)$ is executed, pivot WS and compensatable WS cannot be executed afterwards. The set of pivot or compensatable WS that can be executed after WS $s(i)$ is represented by $A_i \cap (P \cup C)$ and the following constraints can be written:

$$\forall i \in PR, t_i - t_j \geq -|X|(1 - w_i) \ \forall j \in A_i \cap (P \cup C) \ (C_{10})$$

In graph of Fig. 1, vertex 11 represents a pivot retriable WS. Vertex 12 represents pivot WS which belongs to A_{11} (since it exists a path from 11 to 12 in G). Thus, we have the following constraint: $t_{11} - t_{12} \geq -18(1 - w_{11})$.

For all $i \in PR$, if WS $s(i)$ is executed, compensatable WS and pivot WS cannot be executed in parallel. The set of vertices representing pivot or compensatable WS executing in parallel of WS $s(i)$ is $(C \cup P) \cap L_i$. Thus the following constraints must be respected:

$$\forall i \in PR, \sum_{j \in \{L_i \cap (P \cup C)\}} w_j \leq |L_i \cap (P \cup C)|(1 - w_i) \ (C_{11})$$

Finally, for all $i \in C$, only rule 5 must be respected: WS executed in parallel of WS $s(i)$ cannot be a pivot or a pivot retriable one. Thus, the following constraint must be respected:

$$\forall i \in C, \sum_{j \in \{L_i \cap (PR \cup P)\}} w_j \leq |L_i \cap (PR \cup P)|(1 - w_i) \ (C_{12})$$

The number of constraints induced by transactional properties is: $1 + 2 \mid P \mid$ $+ 2 \mid PR \mid + \mid C \mid$, i.e. $O(\mid S \mid)$ constraints.

In the following section, we compare our model to the two main related ones: the linear-programming model of [12] and the approximate approach of [7].

6   Experimental Results

The objectives of our experiments are: without transactional requirements, (i) to compare our model with another recent model based on 0-1 linear programming proposed in [12], and (ii) to test our model on the well-known WS composition benchmark of WS-Challenge 2009 [23], and, with transactional properties, (iii) to measure the difficulty inducing by transactional requirements, and (iv) to compare the optimal solution given by our model to the feasible solution obtained with the approximate algorithm proposed in [7].

6.1   Software Configuration and Test Set Description

The experiments were carried out on a Dell PC with Intel (R) Core TM i7-2760, with 2,4 Ghz processor and 8 Go RAM, under Windows 7, Java 7 and CPLEX solver 12.4.

We have two test sets: (a) the WS repositories and the queries of [7] and (b) the one of WS-Challenge 2009 [23]. In the first test set, there are 10 WS repositories, where the number of WS varies from 100 to 500 (see the first three lines of Table 2), and two repositories containing 1000 WS (not presented in Table 2). The number of data is 20 or 100, representing either sparce (with a small number of data and many dependencies between WS) or non-sparce dependency graphs (with many data and few dependencies between WS). Each WS has between 1 and 5 inputs and between 1 and 3 outputs, randomly generated from an ontology containing 20 generated elements. A transactional property is randomly associated with each WS. On each WS repository, 10 user queries are randomly generated by varying the number of inputs and the number of outputs between 1 and 3 and by randomly generating the QoS score of each WS. The second test set corresponds to the 5 data sets of WS-Challenge[1] 2009 containing 500, 4000, 8000 and 15000 WS (described by their response time and throughoutput QoS values) with respectively 1500, 10000, 15000 or 25000 data.

Each 0-1 linear programming problem is solved with CPLEX solver which uses a branch and bound algorithm to search the optimal solution. We limit the computation time to 3600 seconds for the first test set and to 300 (limit time given by WS-Challenge) for the second one. Thus, two situations can occur: either CPLEX solves the problem in time and, if it exists, the optimal solution is found and otherwise the absence of solution is proved, or CPLEX is disrupted by time out. In this last case, either a solution is proposed but its solution status is unknown (the algorithm cannot prove that this solution is the optimal one because it has not enough time to explore all the feasible solution set), or no solution is founded in time (even if a solution exists).

6.2   Experiments without Transactional Requirements

Table 2. Description of the first test set and LP-based model comparison

1	WS repository	R1	R2	R3	R4	R5	R7	R8	R9	R10	R11
2	Nb of WS	100	200	300	400	500	100	200	300	400	500
3	Nb of data	20	20	20	20	20	100	100	100	100	100
4	Nb of var. in [12]	1840	2920	3730	4840	5760	4280	5240	6190	7090	8130
5	Nb of var. in P_{new}	906	1643	2228	2977	5760	988	1688	2331	2979	3679
6	Nb of const. in [12]	6344	11033	14840	19583	24209	8690	13261	17338	21550	25979
7	Nb of const. in P_{new}	1404	2554	3481	4646	24209	1397	2506	3509	4535	5625
8	Nb of const. in P_{newT}	4609	16490	26064	47206	61241	5064	13165	27953	39422	64483
9	Ratio r	2.8	2.5	2.3	1.1	4	4	2.3	2	2.3	2.14
10	P_{new} comp. time (s)	1.1	12.1	2.3	6.7	21.2	0.06	0.2	0.3	1	9.2
11	P_{newT} comp. time (s)	2	55.6	15.3	80	140.4	0.1	0.6	1.2	7.5	220.7

We first compare our 0-1 linear model, denoted P_{new}, to the one published in [12]. Results are presented in Lines 4 to 7 and in Line 9 of Table 2. In this table, the ratio r (line 9) is equal to the average value (over 10 queries for a given WS repository) of the computational time taken by CPLEX for solving the model of [12] over the one taken for solving P_{new}.

Let us recall that in P_{new}, the variables represent WS execution order, input/output WS and data availability. The 0-1 linear program sizes are reasonable since the numbers of variables and constraints only depend on the dependency graph size (number of vertices and edges). In [12], the model is based on a decomposition in stages (we choose to set a number of stages equal to 10 for all

---

[1] Data sets available at http://www.it-weise.de/documents/files/wsc05-09.zip

experiments) and program sizes are much greater since the number of variables and constraints depends on the dependency graph size times the number of stages (number of constraints and variables are presented in lines 4 to 7 of Table 2).

Consequently, an optimal solution is founded in 3 times faster in average with P_{new}. Moreover, considering big size test sets with 1000 WS and 100 data, CPLEX solves P_{new} at optimality for all the 10 queries (in 266s in average) while it is not the case for the model presented in [12]. More precisely, for 2 queries, model of [12] finds the optimal solution but without proving their optimality status in 3600s, and for one query, it computes a feasible solution with a greater objective function value. For the 7 queries in which both models can find the optimal solution, the problem is solving 7.4 times faster with P_{new}.

These experimental results prove that our 0-1 linear model is the most efficient one. It can find the optimal solution of all the considered 100 queries excepted 2 of them.

Table 3. Experiments of our model on the WS-Challenge 2009 (WSC) test sets

WSC test set	1 (500WS)	2 (4000 WS)	3 (8000 WS)	4 (8000 WS)	5 (15000 WS)
To find optimal sol.	0.35s	3.46s	4.23s	22s	27s
To prove optimality	6.65s	5.8s	6.7s	> 300s	> 300s

We also applied our model on the test sets of WS-Challenge 2009 [23], slightly adapting it by modifying the objective function in order to optimize the response time. The transformations are: (1) adding a fictitious vertex f and the fictitious arcs $(i, f), \forall i \in O$, (2) replacing the objective function by $min\ t_f$, (3) modifying constraints (C_5) that way: $t_j - t_i \geq d_i - T(1 - x_{ij}), \forall (i, j) \in U$, with d_i the response time of each WS i ($i \in 1, \ldots, |X|$) and T an upper bound, and (4) deleting variables w_j and their corresponding constraints C_4 (since they are no more necessary). Our model finds the optimal solution for all the 5 test sets in less than 5 minutes (timeout fixed by the WS-Challenge) – see Table 3. Optimality of the solution can not be proved in 300s for the last two sets. However, the optimal solution finds for the biggest set is better than the solution proposed in WS-Challenge 2009. In terms of quality of the solutions, our model is therefore comparable to the recent related approaches [8,11,17] using the WS-Challenge data for their experiments. We have to notice that, in this article, we do not clean the dependency graph by filtering all services relevant for the query and by discarding the rest as done in the aforementioned approaches. Therefore, our model always finds the optimal solution while other approach [17] can not always find it for the biggest data set without any cleaning process. Moreover, as shown in Section 5.2 and in the next section for experiments, our model can be extended to take into account transactional properties.

6.3   Experiments with Additional Transactional Requirements

We introduce transactional properties into our model, denoted then P_{newT}. Firstly, we analyse the consequences of adding such properties into our model.

Computation times taken to solve the problem at optimality are presented in Lines 10-11 of Table 2. When introducing transactional properties in P_{new}, the number of constraints is multiplied by 6.5 (see Line 8 of Table 2) in average while the computation times are multiplied by 7 in average. The difficulty inducing by transactional requirements is important.

Table 4. Comparison between our model and the approximate approach of [7]

1	WS repository	R1	R2	R3	R4	R5	R7	R8	R9	R10	R11
2	Comp. time (s) of P_{newT}	2	55.6	15.3	80	140.4	0.1	0.6	1.2	7.5	220.7
3	(# Queries solved at optimality)	(9)	(8)	(9)	(9)	(9)	(10)	(10)	(10)	(10)	(10)
4	# Queries with no solution found	1	0	1	0	1	0	0	0	0	0
5	Comp. time (s) of [7]	2	24.9	86.4	287	786.4	0.16	1.45	4.9	12.1	25.5
6	(# Queries with solution found)	(8)	(7)	(10)	(8)	(9)	(7)	(8)	(5)	(6)	(5)
7	Approximate ratio	1.68	1.86	3.53	3	3.3	1	1	1	2.1	1

Secondly, we compare our model with the approximate approach of [7]. When we compute solutions with this approximate algorithm, two possible results can be provided: either a solution is proposed (its solution status is unknown), or no solution is proposed (even if a solution exists). Comparison between our model and the approximate approach is presented in Table 4. Line 2 contains the average computation time (in seconds) taken by CPLEX to solve queries at optimality (the number of these solved queries - at most 10 - is given in parenthesis Line 3). Among queries unsolved at optimality in 3600s, P_{newT} may find a feasible solution or may not find any solution (see Line 4). Lines 5 and 6 show the results obtained with the approximate algorithm. Line 5 corresponds to the average computation time to compute a feasible solution (the number of queries for which the approximate algorithm is able to find a solution is given in parenthesis Line 6). Line 7 presents the average approximate ratio (approximate solution value / optimal solution value). Our experimental results show that, in a large majority of queries, our approach based on the CPLEX branch and bound algorithm computes more rapidly an optimal solution than the approximate algorithm. In only one case over more than 100, the approximate algorithm finds a better solution. The queries on non-sparce SDG ($R7$ to $R11$) are easier to solve at optimality. For $R7$ and $R8$ data sets, computation times are very small: all optimal solutions are found by P_{newT} in less than 1 second. Queries on sparce SDG with 20 data ($R1$ to $R5$) are much more difficult to solve, the computation times are important even if, in average, P_{newT} computes the optimal solution more rapidly (for $R5$, 9 queries are solved at optimality with an average computation time of 140s while the approximate algorithms needs 786s to find a feasible solution with a value equals to 3.3 times the optimal value in average).

Computation times vary a lot with the query. For example, for $R2$ with an average computation times of 55.6, the "harder" query needs 412s to determine the optimal solution while 5 queries take less than 3s and 2 queries around 10s ;

the 2 remaining queries are not solved at optimality: for one query, P_{newT} finds a better solution than one computed by the approximate algorithm (the value is 15% better), and for the other query, P_{newT} finds a feasible solution while the approximate algorithm cannot provide any solution. When no solution can be found by both algorithms, we cannot conclude that no solution exists: either the approximate algorithm cannot find a feasible solution (it often occurs for queries of $R7$ to $R11$), or CPLEX hasn't enough time to find a feasible solution. If we don't impose time limit, P_{newT} should be able to find an optimal solution.

Finally we have experimented our model on two WS repositories containing 1000 WS (data sets $R6$ and $R12$). $R6$ contains 20 data and P_{newT} takes 409s in average to compute the optimal solution of 8 queries. For the two remaining queries, P_{newT} only finds a feasible solution in 3600s for one, and cannot find any solution for the other, because of timeout. $R12$ contains 100 data and P_{newT} takes 525s in average to compute the optimal solution of only 3 queries. It cannot find any solution for 4 queries and a feasible solution for the 3 remaining ones, because of timeout. With this problem size, it becomes hard to solve at optimality with CPLEX.

7   Conclusion

In this article, we present a 0-1 linear program for automatically determining a transactional composite WS optimizing QoS from a service dependency graph. With our model, the QoS and transactional-aware composition problem can be solved at optimality. As far as we know, it is the first time. With consequent experimental results, we show that our model dominates an already recent published one [12], also based on linear programming for solving the QoS-aware composition problem without transactional requirement. Our model also finds all the optimal solutions for the well-known service composition benchmark of WS-Challenge 2009. Then, we compare our approach, with the only related one including transactional requirements [7], which is an approximate approach. Experimental results show that, when an optimal solution exists, our model can find it generally faster than the related work. However, for big size test sets, a standard solver like CPLEX is too long to find optimal solution. Specific resolution methods should be proposed to solve such 0-1 linear programming model. This topic will be the focus of our future research.

References

1. Issarny, V., Georgantas, N., Hachem, S., Zarras, A., et al.: Service-oriented middleware for the Future Internet: state of the art and research directions. J. of Internet Services and App. 2(1), 23–45 (2011)
2. Dustdar, S., Pichler, R., Savenkov, V., Truong, H.L.: Quality-aware Service-oriented Data Integration: Requirements, State of the Art and Open Challenges. SIGMOD Rec. 41(1), 11–19 (2012)
3. Strunk, A.: QoS-Aware Service Composition: A Survey. In: IEEE ECOWS, pp. 67–74 (2010)

4. Liu, A., Li, Q., Huang, L., Xiao, M.: FACTS: A Framework for Fault-Tolerant Composition of Transactional Web Service. IEEE Trans. on Serv. Comp. 3(1), 46–59 (2010)
5. Badr, Y., Benslimane, D., Maamar, Z., Liu, L.: Guest Editorial: Special Section on Transactional Web Services. IEEE Trans. on Serv. Comp. 3(1), 30–31 (2010)
6. Gabrel, V., Manouvrier, M., Megdiche, I., Murat, C.: A new 0-1 linear program for QoS and transactional-aware web service composition. In: IEEE ISCC, pp. 845–850 (2012)
7. Cardinale, Y., Haddad, J.E., Manouvrier, M., Rukoz, M.: CPN-TWS: a coloured petri-net approach for transactional-QoS driven Web Service composition. Int. J. of Web and Grid Services (IJWGS) 7(1), 91–115 (2011)
8. Yan, Y., Chen, M., Yang, Y.: Anytime QoS Optimization over the PlanGraph for Web Service Composition. In: ACM SAC, pp. 1968–1975 (2012)
9. Liang, Q., Su, S.: AND/OR Graph and Search Algorithm for Discovering Composite Web Services. Int. J. Web Service Res. (IJWSR) 2(4), 48–67 (2005)
10. Gu, Z., Li, J., Xu, B.: Automatic Service Composition Based on Enhanced Service Dependency Graph. In: IEEE ICWS, pp. 246–253 (2008)
11. Jiang, W., Zhang, C., Huang, Z., Chen, M., Hu, S., Liu, Z.: QSynth: A Tool for QoS-aware Automatic Service Composition. In: IEEE ICWS, pp. 42–49 (2010)
12. Paganelli, F., Ambra, T., Parlanti, D.: A QoS-aware service composition approach based on semantic annotations and integer programming. Int. J. of Web Info. Sys. (IJWIS) 8(3), 296–321 (2012)
13. Zeng, L., Benatallah, B., Ngu, A., Dumas, M., Kalagnanam, J., Chang, H.: QoS-Aware Middleware for Web Services Composition. IEEE Trans. on Soft. Eng. 30(5), 311–327 (2004)
14. Yu, T., Zhang, Y., Lin, K.J.: Efficient algorithms for Web services selection with end-to-end QoS constraints. ACM Trans. on the Web 1, 1–26 (2007)
15. Haddad, J.E., Manouvrier, M., Rukoz, M.: TQoS: Transactional and QoS-aware selection algorithm for automatic Web service composition. IEEE Trans. on Serv. Comp. 3(1), 73–85 (2010)
16. Syu, Y., FanJiang, Y.Y., Kuo, J.Y., Ma, S.P.: Towards a Genetic Algorithm Approach to Automating Workflow Composition for Web Services with Transactional and QoS-Awareness. In: IEEE SERVICES, pp. 295–302 (2011)
17. Rodriguez-Mier, P., Mucientes, M., Lama, M.: A dynamic qoS-aware semantic web service composition algorithm. In: Liu, C., Ludwig, H., Toumani, F., Yu, Q. (eds.) Service Oriented Computing. LNCS, vol. 7636, pp. 623–630. Springer, Heidelberg (2012)
18. Aleti, A., Buhnova, B., Grunske, L., Koziolek, A., Meedeniya, I.: Software Architecture Optimization Methods: A Systematic Literature Review. IEEE Trans. on Soft. Eng. 39(5), 658–683 (2013)
19. Yoo, J.J.W., Kumara, S., Lee, D., Oh, S.C.: A Web Service Composition Framework Using Integer Programming with Non-functional Objectives and Constraints. In: IEEE CEC/EEE, pp. 347–350 (2008)
20. Cardinale, Y., Haddad, J.E., Manouvrier, M., Rukoz, M.: Transactional-aware Web Service Composition: A Survey. In: Handbook of Research on Non-Functional Prop. for Service-oriented Sys.: Future Directions, pp. 116–142. IGI Global (2011)
21. Miller, C.E., Tucker, A.W., Zemlin, R.A.: Integer Programming Formulation of Traveling Salesman Problems. J. of ACM 7(4), 326–329 (1960)
22. Aho, A.V., Hopcroft, J.E., Ullman, J.: Data Structures and Algorithms, 1st edn. Addison-Wesley Longman Pub. Co., Inc. (1983)
23. Kona, S., Bansal, A., Blake, M.B., Bleul, S., Weise, T.: WSC-2009: A Quality of Service-Oriented Web Services Challenge. In: IEEE CEC, pp. 487–490 (2009)

A Framework for Searching Semantic Data and Services with SPARQL

Mohamed Lamine Mouhoub, Daniela Grigori, and Maude Manouvrier

PSL, Université Paris-Dauphine, 75775 Paris Cedex 16, France
CNRS, LAMSADE UMR 7243
{mohamed.mouhoub,daniela.grigori,maude.manouvrier}@dauphine.fr

Abstract. The last years witnessed the success of Linked Open Data (LOD) project and the growing amount of semantic data sources available on the web. However, there is still a lot of data that will not be published as a fully materialized knowledge base (dynamic data, data with limited acces patterns, etc). Such data is in general available through web api or web services. In this paper, we introduce a SPARQL-driven approach for searching linked data and relevant services. In our framework, a user data query is analyzed and transformed into service requests. The resulting service requests, formatted for different semantic web services languages, are addressed to services repositories. Our system also features automatic web service composition to help finding more answers for user queries. The intended applications for such a framework vary from mashups development to aggregated search.

1 Introduction

The last years witnessed the success of Linked Open Data (LOD) project and the growing amount of semantic data sources available on the web (public sector data published by several government initiatives, scientific data facilitating collaboration, ...). The Linked Open Data cloud, representing a large portion of the semantic web, comprises more then 2000 datasets that are interlinked by RDF links, most of them offering a SPARQL endpoint (according to LODstats[1] as of May 2014) . To exploit these interlinked data sources, federated query processing techniques were proposed ([1]). However, as mentioned in [2] there is still a lot of data that will not be published as a fully materialized knowledge base like:

- dynamic data issued from sensors
- data that is computed on demand depending on a large sets of input data, e.g. the faster public transport connection between two city points
- data with limited access patterns, e.g. prices of hotels may be available for specific requests in order to allow different pricing policies.

Such data is in general available through web API or web services. In order to allow services to be automatically discovered and composed, research works

---

[1] http://stats.lod2.eu/

X. Franch et al. (Eds.): ICSOC 2014, LNCS 8831, pp. 123–138, 2014.
© Springer-Verlag Berlin Heidelberg 2014

in the domain of the semantic web proposed to use machine-readable semantic markup for their description. Semantic web services (SWS) approaches include expressive languages like OWL-S[2], WSMO for complex business services or, more recently, simple vocabularies like MSM to publish various service descriptions as linked data. Most of the SWS description languages are RDF[3]-based (such as OWL-S, MSM) or offer a RDF representation (WSML). Therefore, existing tools for publishing SWS like iServe[4] are basically RDF stores that allow access via SPARQL endpoints and hence, they can be considered also as a part of the LOD.

The integration of LOD data and semantic web services (SWS) offer great opportunities for creating mashups and searching complementary data (data that does not exist on the LOD or that is incomplete or not updated). However, relevant services must be discovered first, and in case they don't exist, composed from atomic services. To achieve such a goal, an user should:

- have an awareness of the existing SWS repositories on the web,
- have a knowledge of the heterogeneous SWS description languages,
- express his needs in terms of the vocabulary used by different repositories
- find relevant services from different repositories and use service composition tools in case a service satisfying his goal does not exist.

As this manual process requires a lot of knowledge and effort for the user, our goal is to provide a framework for searching data and related services on the LOD. We are not aware of other federated approaches able to find data and related services in the LOD. An approach for aggregated search of data and services was proposed in [3], but it requires building global schemas for data and services and lacks a full support for the LOD and for semantic queries.

In this paper we make the following contributions:

- a SPARQL-driven framework to search data and related services in the distributed and dynamic setting characterizing the LOD
- a method to derive a service discovery query from a data query and enrich it in order to increase the number of retrieved services
- a method to find a web service composition on the fly, containing WS from different repositories.

The rest of this paper is structured as follows: In section 2, we highlight the overall functionality of the framework with a motivating scenario and give the important definitions. Section 3 is dedicated to the service discovery. Service composition is explained in section 4. The architecture and implementation details are described in section 5. The last sections are dedicated to the related works and the conclusion.

2   Data and Service Querying

The goal of our framework is to extend a search of linked data with a service discovery/composition to find relevant services that provide complementary data.

---

[2] http://www.w3.org/Submission/OWL-S
[3] http://www.w3.org/RDF/
[4] http://iserve.kmi.open.ac.uk/

Such a search often requires distinct queries: a) data queries to lookup in the LOD to find data b) service requests to discover relevant services in some SWS repositories and c) service composition requests to create relevant service compositions in case no single relevant service is found. Our framework searches for both (data and services) starting from a single query from the user called the data query, i.e. a query intended to search only for data. From this query, it automatically issues service requests and finds relevant services or generates service compositions.

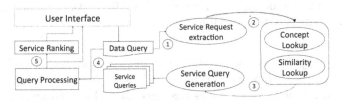

Fig. 1. Process of discovering services with a data query

Figure 1 shows an overview of our approach to search for services in parallel to data. When a SPARQL data query is submitted by a user or an agent, two parallel search processes are launched:

1. Data search process: A process to manage the query answering in the LOD data sources. These sources are distributed and accessible via SPARQL endpoints. Thus, a SPARQL-federation approach along with the appropriate optimization and query rewriting techniques is used for this purpose. This process is out of the scope of this paper.
2. Service search process: A process to discover and possibly compose services that are relevant to the data query. An analysis of the data query is required in order to transform it into one or multiple service requests.

```
SELECT ?person ?book
WHERE {
?person rdf:type     dbpedia-owl:Writer ;
    dbpedia-owl:award     ?prize ;
    dbpedia-owl:birthPlace  dbpedia:Paris .
?book   dbpedia-owl:author   ?person ;
    dbpedia-owl:isbn     ?isbn .}
```

Listing 1.1. Example Data Query Q_D

To explain the motivations and goals of our framework, we consider the following example scenario: A user wants to know all writers born in Paris and holding a Nobel prize as well as the list of all their books. This query is written in SPARQL in listing 1. Answers for this query in the LOD might supposedly find all these writers in DBpedia. However, their published books are not all listed in DBpedia. In this case, data is not complete and might need to be completed with full book listings from services like Amazon API, Google Books API, etc Some of the latter APIs can also provide complementary information on the books such as the prices, ISBN numbers, etc. In addition, there are some other relevant services that allow the user to buy a given book given online. However, if the user wants to buy a given book from a local store, and there is a service that only takes an ISBN number as input to return the available local stores that sell this book, in that case, a service composition can be made to return such information.

2.1 Definitions

To better explain the details of service search we first give the following definitions for the context of the search in this section.

SPARQL Query Overview : A SPARQL query can be seen as a set of one or many graph patterns composed of nodes and edges. Nodes represent variables (prefixed by a '?') or concrete values (resource URIs, Literals) and edges represent properties that link nodes in a pairwise fashion. A subgraph composed of two nodes linked by a property edge is called a triple pattern and is read "subject property object". Multiple group graph patterns in SPARQL refers to queries containing multiple triple blocks separated or contained by UNION, OPTIONAL, brackets, etc. In case there is a single graph pattern, it is called a basic graph pattern.

Nodes and Concepts (n, c_n) : We define a node $n \in N$ in the context of a query as a part of tuple (n, c_n) where c_n is its corresponding concept formally defined by: $(n, c_n) : (n \in N, c_n = Concept(n))$.
A node is either a named variable or a concrete element of a triple pattern (a Literal or a resource URI).
A Concept is the reference rdfs:class that is used to describe the rdf:type of a node in its reference ontology Θ. It is obtained with the function $Concept(n)$.

Data Query (Q_D) : A data query Q_D is a SPARQL query composed of sets of triple patterns and selection variables. It is basically written by the user to fetch data from LOD that match these triples. Listing 1 shows an example of a data query for the provided example above. In this paper, we only consider SELECT queries that have a unique basic graph pattern.

Service Request (R_s) : Given a user SPARQL query Q_D, a service request $R_s = (In_D, Out_D)$ is a couple of two sets In_D, Out_D created by analyzing Q_D in order to extract inputs and outputs that could be considered as parameters of a service request to find relevant services for Q_D. $In_D = \{(n, c_n)\}$ is a set of service inputs provided implicitly by the user in Q_D in form of Literals or URIs in the triple patterns of the WHERE clause. $Out_D = \{(n, c_n)\}$ is a set of service outputs that are explicitly requested by the user in the query in form of variables in the SELECT clause. More details are provided in section 4.1

Service Descriptions (D_s) : In a service collection S, every service s is described by $D_s = (In_S, Out_S)$ where In_S is the set of inputs needed for a service s and Out_S is the set of outputs provided by the service. A service description can be in any known SWS formalism that is RDF/OWL based and that describes the functional and the non-functional features of a service. Currently in our work, we are only interested in the inputs and outputs of a service which are parts of the functional features.

Similar Concepts (e_n) : For a given concept of a node c_n, there exists a set of one or more equivalent (similar) concepts $e_n = Similar(c_n)$ where $Similar(c_n)$ is a function that returns the similar concepts of a given concept defined in its ontology by one of the following rdfs:property predicates: a) `owl:sameAs` b) `owl:equivalentClass` and c) `rdfs:subClassOf` in either directions.

Service Query (Q_s) : Similarly in the Q_D definition above, the service query is a SPARQL query written to select relevant services from their SWS repositories via their SPARQL endpoints . It consists of sets of triple patterns that match the inputs and outputs of R_s with inputs and outputs of a service in S. The triples of Q_s follow the SWS description model used by the repositories to describe services.

3 Service Discovery with SPARQL

To deal with the heterogeneity of the SWS descriptions and the distributed deployments of repositories containing them, we choose to issue service requests in SPARQL queries and adapt them to each description model based on the following assumptions: a) the data in question adheres to the principles of linked data as defined in [4] b) SWS are described by RDF based languages such as OWL-S or MSM[5], c) SWS repositories offer access via SPARQL endpoints to their content.

In addition, existing SWS repositories such as iServe are accessible via SPARQL endpoints. This allows to select SWS and perform explicit RDF entailment on their descriptions to extend the search capabilities. The RDF entailment is done explicitly by rewriting SPARQL queries since the existing implementations SPARQL engines don't offer this feature. Furthermore, using SPARQL allows to deal with the heterogeneous SWS descriptions more effectively without intermediate mapping tools.

We distinguish two kinds of service queries that can be relevant depending on the goal of the discovery. For a given service request R_s extracted from a data query Q_D, the user may want to find one of following kinds of services:

1. Services that provide all the information requested by the user, i.e provide all the requested outputs regardless of the given inputs. However, the more a service consumes the inputs of the request, the more relevant it is. For example, taking into account the location as input returns data that concerns

this location. Such services would be useful as an alternative or an additional data source to the LOD data. They are obtained by applying Strategy#1:

$Strategy\#1(R_s, D_s) : \{\forall o \in Out_D : o \in Out_S\}[\implies (Out_D \subseteq Out_S)]$

A specialization of this strategy, called $Strategy\#1_{exact}$, restricts the relevance on services that, in addition, consume only and only all the given inputs In_D.

$Strategy\#1_{exact}(R_s, D_s) : \{\forall i_d \in In_D, \forall i_s \in In_S, \forall o_d \in Out_D : i_d \in In_S \wedge i_s \in In_D \wedge o_d \in Out_S\}[\implies (In_D = In_S) \wedge (Out_D \supseteq Out_S)]$

2. Services that consume some of the inputs or the outputs of the request, or that return some of the inputs or the outputs of the request. Such services would be useful to: a) provide additional information or services to the data, b) discover candidate services for a mashup or composition of services that fit as providers or consumers in any intermediate step of the composition. The service request for such kind of services is obtained by one of the strategies bellow that satisfy the following:

$Strategy\#2_a(R_s, D_s) : (In_D \cap In_S \neq \phi)$
$Strategy\#2_b(R_s, D_s) : (Out_D \cap In_S \neq \phi)$
$Strategy\#2_c(R_s, D_s) : (Out_D \cap Out_S \neq \phi)$
$Strategy\#2_d(R_s, D_s) : (In_D \cap Out_S \neq \phi)$

3.1   Service Request Extraction

The data query is analyzed to extract elements that can be used as I/O for a service request. Outputs are simply the selected variables of the query. Inputs are the bound values that appear in the triples of the query.

The analysis of the data query Q_D allows to extract the inputs and outputs of Q_D using one of the following rules:

1. Variables in the SELECT *, (selection variables) are considered as outputs $o_d = (n, null) \in Out_D$. Simply because they are explicitly declared as desired outputs of the data query.
2. Bindings of subjects or objects in the WHERE clause of Q_D, i.e literals and RDF resources URIs, are considered as inputs $i_d = (n, null) \in In_D$. This can be explained by the fact that a user providing a specific value for a subject or an object simply wants the final results to depend on that specific value. The same way, a service requiring some inputs returns results that depend on these inputs.

The service request extraction consists of populating In_D and Out_D with the nodes of the elements mentioned above. Algorithm 1 gives an overview of the Service Request Extraction.

The SPARQL operators like OPTIONAL, UNION, FILTER, etc can reveal the preferences of the user for service discovery and composition. For instance, the I/O extracted from an Optional block mean that the user doesn't require services that necessarily provide/consume the optional parts. Therefore, the service request for such a data query is obtained using some of the loose strategies defined in section 4.

Algorithm 1. Service Request Extraction

Input: Q_D
Output: In_D, Out_D
 1: $Out_D.nodes \leftarrow$ GETSELECTVARIABLES(Q_D) ▷ Get the output variables
 2: $triples \leftarrow$ GETALLQUERYTRIPLES(Q_D) ▷ Get all the query triples
 3: **for each** t in $triples$ **do**
 4:     **if** ISCONCRETE(SUBJECT(t)) **then**   ▷ check if URI or literal
 5:        $In_D \leftarrow In_D \cup \{(\text{SUBJECT}(t), null)\}$
 6:     **else if** ISCONCRETE(OBJECT(t)) **then**
 7:        **if** PREDICATE(t) $\neq$ "$rdf : type$" **then**
 8:           $In_D \leftarrow In_D \cup \{(\text{OBJECT}(t), null)\}$
 9:        **end if**
10:     **end if**
11: **end for**

Listing 1.4 shows an example of a service query extracted from Q_D in listing 1.1 using *Strategy#1* to find services that return the same data as the query.

3.2 Semantics Lookup

Once the service request elements are extracted from the query, we try to find the semantic concepts c_n that describe the previously extracted nodes with no concept: $(n, null)$.

Concept Lookup. In general, concepts can either be declared by the user in the data query (as the user probably specifies what he is looking for) or in a graph (set of triples) in an rdf store.

The semantics lookup process starts looking for the concept of a node n in the Q_D triples. The concept is the concrete value given by a URI and linked to n via the property $rdf : type$: i.e. "n $rdf : type$ $conceptURI$". In the example query in listing 1.1, the concept of *?person* is given in Q_D as $dbpedia - owl : Writer$, but the concept of *book* is not given in Q_D

If c_n is not found in Q_D, a concept lookup query q_c is created to look for the concept of n in the ontology in which it is suspected to be.

To generate this concept lookup query q_c, we take all the triples from Q_D in which n is involved as a subject or as an object and then insert them in the WHERE clause of q_c. We add a triple pattern "n $rdf : type$ $?type$" and set the *?type* variable as the SELECT variable of q_c. The URLs of the ontology(ies) in which c_n can be extracted from the namespaces used in Q_D and are added to the From clause of the q_c .

Listing 1.2 shows an example concept lookup query to find the concept of ?book which is not declared in Q_D (listing 1.1).

If no concept is found for a given node (most likely because of a non working namespace URL), then the search space for q_c to find the missing concepts is expanded to the other known sources in the LOD.

```
SELECT  ?bookConcept WHERE {
SERVICE <http://dbpedia.org/sparql>{
?book    dbpedia-owl:author
?person ;
    dbpedia-owl:isbn  ?isbn ;
    rdf:type  ?bookConcept .}}
```

Listing 1.2. An example query of Concept Lookup in the LOD

```
SELECT  ?bookConcept
FROM <http://dbpedia.org/ontology/>
WHERE {
dbpedia-owl:author  rdfs:domain
         ?bookConcept .
}
```

Listing 1.3. An example query of Concept Lookup in Ontology

Similarity Lookup. To extend the service search space, we use the similar concepts e_n of every concept c_n in the service search queries along with the original concepts. To find these similar concepts, we use the rules given by the definition in section 2.1. Based on this definition, we issue a SPARQL query q_e like the one in the concept lookup but slightly different by adding a triple that defines a silimarity link between c_n and a variable *?similar*. The triple pattern has the form c_n *?semanticRelation*   *?similar* where *?semanticRelation* is one of the following properties: a) owl:sameAs, owl:equivalentClass for similar concepts in other ontologies b) rdfs:subClassOf for hierarchically similar concepts within the same ontology.

The similarity lookup query q_e is executed on the sources used in Q_D as well as on the other sources of the LOD because the similar concepts can be found anywhere.

To optimize the search in other sources of the LOD, we use a caching technique to build an index structure on the go of the LOD sources content. The details of this caching is described in section 5.

3.3   Service Query Generation

Once all elements of the service request are gathered, service discovery queries are issued in SPARQL using rewriting templates. Such templates define the structure and the header of the SPARQL service query. There is a single template per SWS description formalism, i.e. OWL-S, MSM, etc. For instance, the OWL-S template defines a header containing triples that match the OWL-S model by specifying that the desired variable is an OWL-S service which has profiles with specific inputs/outputs. Listing 1.4 shows an example of a service query for the example scenario in section 1. It uses an OWL-S template to specify the required input and output concepts according to the OWL-S service model.

To generate the queries, all concepts c_n and their similar concepts e_n for every node $n \in In_D \cup Out_D$ are put together in a basic graph pattern of in a union fashion depending on the chosen selection strategy. More specifically, for every input $i_d \in In_D$ we write triple patterns to match service inputs with variables that have c_n as a concept and accordingly for every output $o_d \in Out_D$.

The service search strategies (c.f. section 3) in the way we define them, describe the how tight(Strategy #1, $\#1_{exact}$) or loose (Strategies $\#2_{a,b,c,d}$)the service selection must be. Therefore, strict strategies require that one or more inputs or outputs are matched at the same time, thus, the query triples will be put in a single basic graph pattern. On the other hand, loose strategies require only partial matching, hence, the query triples are be put in a UNION of multiple graph patterns.

```
SELECT DISTINCT ?service WHERE {
?service a service:Service ; service:presents ?profile .
?profile profile:hasOutput ?output1 ;
         profile:hasOutput ?output2 .
?output1 process:parameterType dbpedia-owl:Writer .
?output2 process:parameterType dbpedia-owl:Book .
OPTIONAL { ?profile profile:hasInput ?intput1 .
           ?input1  process:parameterType dbpedia:Place .}
OPTIONAL { ?profile profile:hasInput ?intput2 .
           ?input2  process:parameterType dbpedia-owl:Award .}}
```

Listing 1.4. Example Service Query Q_S with $Strategy\#1_{exact}$

4 Automatic Service Composition

In the previous section we showed how to make service requests to find relevant individual services for the data query. However, if no such services exist, service composition can create relevant composite services for the matter. In this section we describe our approach to make such compositions automatically.

In the context of our framework, service repositories are part of the LOD as SPARQL endpoints. Therefore, we think that the least expensive way to perform a service discovery and composition is on the fly without any pre-processing. This online composition consists of discovering candidate services at each step of the composition without a need to have a local index or copy of the service repositories. We argue that the approaches based on pre-processing the service repositories often require an expensive maintainability to stay up-to-date. Furthermore, according to [6], the web services are considerably growing and evolving either by getting updated, deprecated or abandoned.

However, some optimization based on caching are described further in section 5 to speed-up this online process for the queries that as already been processed in the past executions.

In this section, we describe our approach for an automatic composition of SWS based on a service dependency graph and an A*-like algorithm. The first subsection is dedicated to the Service Dependency Graph while the second describes the composition algorithm.

4.1 Service Dependency Graph

The Service Dependency Graph (SDG from now on) represents the dependencies between services based on their inputs and outputs. A service depends on another if the later provides some inputs for the former. In our work, we consider that a SDG is specific for each data query because it includes only services related to that query. In other works, the SDG might represent the dependencies for all the services in a repository, but this requires a general pre-processing for the LOD as we stated before.

We use an oriented AND/OR graph structure as in [7] to represent the SDG. Such a graph is composed of AND nodes - that represent services - and OR nodes - that represent data concepts - linked by directed edges. We slightly adapt this representation to include the similarities between concepts of data by : a) Each OR node contains the set of concepts that are similar to each other b) Each edge that links an AND node to an OR node is labeled with the concept that matches the service input/output concept among those in the OR node's concept set. A dummy service N_0 is linked to outputs nodes of Out_D to guarantee that a service composition provides all the requested outputs.

The AND/OR graph representation of the SDG is more adequate for the composition problem than ordinary graphs because the constraints on the inputs of services are explicitly represented by the AND nodes; A service cannot be executed if some of its inputs are not provided; thus, an AND node cannot be accessible unless all of its entering edges are satisfied. Furthermore, this graph has been utilized in a many previous approaches and has proven its efficiency as shown in [7]. However, a classical graph representation can be used to solve the composition problem.

To construct the SDG, we use our service discovery approach to find dependencies for each service in a bottom-up approach starting from the services that provide the final outputs of Q_D. In fact, the SGD construction searches for all services that provide all the unprovided-yet data at one time starting from Out_D nodes. Such a one-time search per iteration allows to reduce the number of service requests that are sent to the SWS repositories, hence, boosting the SDG construction.

For example, to find services that provide O_1 and/or O_2, a service request $R_s(null, \{O_1, O_2\})$ is used by applying $Strategy\#2_b$.

4.2   Service Composition Algorithm

Upon the construction of the SDG, one or many compositions can be found. The aim of the service composition algorithm is to find the optimal composition from the SDG for a given composition request.

For this purpose, we use an A*-like algorithm and adapt it for AND/OR graphs. Starting from the user input In_D nodes, the algorithm finds the optimal path to the target node N_0 (which is linked to the final outputs Out_D). Therefore, an optimal solution is a path that has the least total cost and that respects the AND/OR graph structure.

The total cost of a given path is the aggregation of the costs of each step from a node to another. Generally, the cost at a given step (at an AND node n) in an A* algorithm is given by the aggregation function: $f(n) = g(n) + h(n)$ where $g(n)$ is the total cost of the sub-path from the starting point to n and $h(n)$ is a heuristic that estimates the total cost from the n to the target node N_0.

Since the semantic web services has rich descriptions, the semantics of the Inputs/Outputs can be used for cost calculation to help finding an optimal solution. Therefore, we rely on the sets of similar concepts inside OR nodes and on the labels of the edges in SDG. Therefore, the cost of a move from an AND node n_i to $n_i + 1$ is determined based on the similarity between the labels of the input and the output edges of the two AND nodes respectively. If the two labels (concepts) are the same, then the cost value is null. Otherwise if the two labels are different but similar concepts (sameAs, sub concepts) then the cost value is set to 1. This cost calculation can be resumed by the function: $cost(n_{i+1}) = sim(c_{n_i}, c_{n_{i+1}})$ where c_{n_i} is a concept used by the current service, $c_{n_{i+1}}$ is used by the next one and:

$$sim(c_{n_i}, c_{n_{i+1}}) = \begin{cases} 0 & \text{if } c_{n_i} = c_{n_i+1} \\ 1 & \text{if } c_{n_i} = Similar(c_{n_i+1}) \end{cases} \tag{1}$$

is a function that determines the similarity between two concepts.

From the functions above, the cost of the best known path to the current node subset is given by the following function:

$$g(n) = \sum_{i=0}^{n} cost(n_i) \tag{2}$$

where n_i are all the accessible services for the next step

The heuristic function $h(n)$ calculates the distance between the current node and the target AND node n_0 in the SDG graph. This is justified by the fact that, a better solution is the one that uses less services.

$$h(n) = Distance(n, n_0) \tag{3}$$

5   Implementation and Experiments

In this section, we show briefly the architecture of our framework and some experiments as a proof of concept.

5.1   Framework Architecture

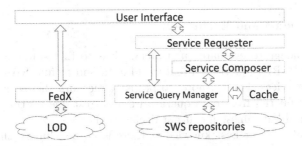

Fig. 2. Framework Architecture

Figure 2 shows an overview of the architecture of our framework. Through an interface, SPARQL queries are submitted to the system to be processed for data search and service search.

The data querying is managed by an external open source SPARQL federator, FedX [1]. FedX uses its own query rewriting to optimize the data querying for each source. Therefore, the LOD is a federation of SPARQL endpoints of different data sources such as DBpedia.

On the service side, queries are processed by the service requester to make service requests or service compositions. The SWS repositories which are SPARQL endpoints as well are considered as a particular part of the LOD. We use our own federation of SPARQL endpoints to query the SWS repositories separately. The reason why we don't simply reuse FedX is because we need specific optimization for service descriptions different than the general purpose optimization offered by FedX. A brief overview of our optimization is described in the next subsection.

We have implemented our framework in Java using Apache Jena[5] framework to manage SPARQL queries and RDF.

5.2   Optimizing Service Discovery with Cache

In order to optimize the service discovery in terms of response time, we use a caching for services and concepts. Such a cache indexes all the concepts and services that has been used in past requests.

We use three different types of cache : a) A cache for similar concepts to decrease the number the similarity lookup requests. b) A cache to index the concepts that have been used in the past and the URIs of services and repositories that use them. c) a local RDF repository to keep in cache the descriptions of services on the go once they are discovered. This later one can be queried directly via a local SPARQL endpoint.

Maintaining the cache costs much less than maintaining a whole index structure of all known SWS repositories and does not require any pre-processing prior to use the framework. Cache maintenance can be scheduled for automatic launch or triggered manually.

5.3   Experiments and Evaluation

Our main challenge to evaluate our framework is to find suitable benchmarks that provide SPARQL queries on real world data and to find SWS repositories of real world services. Furthermore, to properly measure the execution time of writing service queries from data queries, we need test queries that are more or less complex and have missing concept declarations.

Unfortunately, to our best knowledge, there is no benchmark that allows us to fully measure the performance of our framework. Therefore, to prove the feasibility of our approach to search services on the LOD, we have made an implementation as a proof-of-concept and some experiments to measure the execution time of query rewriting from a data query and through semantics lookup

---

[5] https://jena.apache.org/

to write service queries in SPARQL. For experiments we used a set of SPARQL queries that we wrote manually to have missing concepts.

Figure 3 shows a summary of our experiments on a set of queries. This set consists of a 10 queries, each with an increasing amount of undefined variables. We measured separately the total execution time of writing service queries including the execution time of the concept lookup process for each query. The results show that the concept lookup time increases linearly as the number of undefined variables increase.

We performed a partial evaluation for the effectiveness of our service discovery on OWL-S-TC[6] benchmark. Figure 4 show the number of false negatives (<0)and false positives (>0) of the service discovery on a set of 18 OWL-TC queries that have been used for evaluation in [3]. We have rewritten these queries in SPARQL to make them usable within our framework. The results show an overall good error rate. However, in some queries like Q22, some of the I/O parameters are very generic which explains the high number of false positives. In order to avoid such cases, the algorithm must be modified to select services that provide at least a non-generic I/O parameter. For the false negatives like in Q7, the reference matching results in OWLS-TC are set based on other features than I/O parameters such as the textual description of the service, etc.

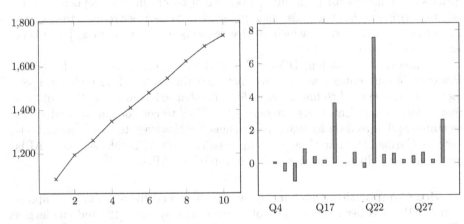

Fig. 3. Average execution Time in MS per number of undefined variables in a random query

Fig. 4. False Negatives and false Positives on OWL-S TC queries

6   Related Works

The motivations and research questions of our work are tackled by many recent works. In fact, our work emerges from a crossing of many research topics in the semantic web and web services. We'll list few of the most recent and relevant works to our paper.

---

[6] http://projects.semwebcentral.org/projects/owls-tc/

SPARQL Query Management. Among the works that tackle the query management in the LOD, SPARQL federation approaches are the most relevant for our context. FedX[1] is one of the most popular works that has good performance results besides the fact that the tool is available in open source. FedX optimizes the query management by performing a cache-based source selection and rewriting queries into sub-queries and running them on the selected sources. Some recent works like [8] introduce some further optimization for FedX and other works by optimizing the source selection. We are actually using FedX as a part of our Framework for answering data queries because, as we stated in section 2, managing data queries is out of the scope of our work in this paper.

Service Discovery. Our context of service discovery involves exclusively the semantic web services. SWS discovery is the topic of interest of many recent works and benchmarks as shown in the survey[9]. The SWS discovery approaches are either semantically based, textual based or hybrid based. The first ones are the most relevant for our context because we operate on linked data which is meant to be properly described and linked. Among the recent works, [10] introduces a repository filtering using SPARQL queries to be used on top of the existing hybrid discovery approaches. However, in our context, SPARQL queries are sufficient for performing a service discovery in SWS repositories. In addition, [10] and the other existing approaches need a service request to operate, in contrast to our work in which service requests are implicit in a data query and have to be extracted first.

For discovery evaluation, OWL-S-TC is the reference benchmark for SWS. However, in our context, we need a benchmark that is based on real-world services because we need to find services for data that exists in the LOD. Unfortunately, for the moment, there are only a few SWS to consider in the real world as stated and agreed on by many researchers [6]. However, there are some tools such as Karma [11] that allow to wrap classical web APIs into semantic APIs and therefore help creating new SWS on top of the APIs.

Service Composition. Similarly to service discovery, the automatic composition of SWS has been the subject of many works, surveys [12] and challenges (WS-Challenge). In general, the automatic composition algorithms The most recent works like [13], [7] still use A*-based algorithms to find composition plans in an SDG graph which is mostly pre-constructed for all known services in a repository. In our paper we use a service composition approach that is very similar to the WSC challenge winner [7] that uses AND/OR graphs. However, we adapted their approach to take advantage of the semantics in cost calculation instead of using a static cost calculation (a fixed cost for all nodes).

Search of Data and Services. Our work is inspired by the work in [3] which aims to look for services that are related to a given query based on keywords comparison between an SQL-like query and a service ontology. This approach uses generated semantics for services to expand the search area.

Another similar work in [14] called ANGIE consists of enriching the LOD from RESTful APIs and SOAP services by discovering, composing and invoking services to answer a user query. However, this work assumes the existence of a global schema for both data and services which is not the case in the LOD. This assumption makes ANGIE domain specific and not suitable for general purpose queries.

Some recent works could complement our work such as [15] which proposes an approach that uses Karma[11] to integrate linked data on-the-fly from static and dynamic sources and to manage the data updates.

7   Conclusion and Perspectives

In this paper we presented a framework for finding data and relevant services in the LOD using a unique SPARQL query. Our framework helps the user to find services that he could exploit to construct mashups or to complement the data found in materialized knowledge bases. We implemented the proposed algorithms and we are evaluating them in terms of efficiency and quality. We plan to enrich the framework by storing and exploiting user actions (selected services and compositions for a given data query) in order to improve the efficiency of the algorithm and the relevance of the retrieved services.

Regarding the previously mentioned issue of lacking real-world SWS, Karma[11] or SmartLink[16] can be used to provide our experiments with SWS from real-world APIs. We plan to use such tools in the future to extend our experiments and have a clear measure of its effectiveness.

References

1. Schwarte, A., Haase, P., Hose, K., Schenkel, R., Schmidt, M.: FedX: Optimization techniques for federated query processing on linked data. In: Aroyo, L., Welty, C., Alani, H., Taylor, J., Bernstein, A., Kagal, L., Noy, N., Blomqvist, E. (eds.) ISWC 2011, Part I. LNCS, vol. 7031, pp. 601–616. Springer, Heidelberg (2011)
2. Speiser, S., Harth, A.: Integrating linked data and services with linked data services. In: Antoniou, G., Grobelnik, M., Simperl, E., Parsia, B., Plexousakis, D., De Leenheer, P., Pan, J. (eds.) ESWC 2011, Part I. LNCS, vol. 6643, pp. 170–184. Springer, Heidelberg (2011)
3. Palmonari, M., Sala, A., Maurino, A., Guerra, F., Pasi, G., Frisoni, G.: Aggregated search of data and services. Information Systems 36(2), 134–150 (2011)
4. Bizer, C., Heath, T., Berners-Lee, T.: Linked data-the story so far. Intl. journal on semantic web and information systems 5(3), 1–22 (2009)
5. Kopecky, J., Gomadam, K., Vitvar, T.: hrests: An html microformat for describing restful web services. In: IEEE/WIC/ACM Intl. Conf. on. Web Intelligence and Intelligent Agent Technology, WI-IAT 2008, vol. 1, pp. 619–625. IEEE (2008)
6. Blthoff, F., Maleshkova, M.: Restful or restless - current state of today's top web apis. In: 11th ESWC 2014 (ESWC 2014) (May 2014)
7. Yan, Y., Xu, B., Gu, Z.: Automatic service composition using and/or graph. In: 2008 10th IEEE Conf. on E-Commerce Technology and the Fifth IEEE Conf. on Enterprise Computing, E-Commerce and E-Services, pp. 335–338. IEEE (2008)

8. Saleem, M., Ngonga Ngomo, A.-C.: HiBISCuS: Hypergraph-based source selection for SPARQL endpoint federation. In: Presutti, V., d'Amato, C., Gandon, F., d'Aquin, M., Staab, S., Tordai, A. (eds.) ESWC 2014. LNCS, vol. 8465, pp. 176–191. Springer, Heidelberg (2014)

9. Ngan, L.D., Kanagasabai, R.: Semantic web service discovery: state-of-the-art and research challenges. Personal and ubiquitous computing 17(8), 1741–1752 (2013)

10. García, J.M., Ruiz, D., Ruiz-Cortés, A.: Improving semantic web services discovery using sparql-based repository filtering. Web Semantics: Science, Services and Agents on the World Wide Web 17, 12–24 (2012)

11. Taheriyan, M., Knoblock, C.A., Szekely, P., Ambite, J.L.: Rapidly integrating services into the linked data cloud. In: Cudré-Mauroux, P., et al. (eds.) ISWC 2012, Part I. LNCS, vol. 7649, pp. 559–574. Springer, Heidelberg (2012)

12. Syu, Y., Ma, S.P., Kuo, J.Y., FanJiang, Y.Y.: A survey on automated service composition methods and related techniques. In: 2012 IEEE Ninth Intl. Conf. on. Services Computing (SCC), pp. 290–297 (June 2012)

13. Rodriguez-Mier, P., Mucientes, M., Vidal, J.C., Lama, M.: An optimal and complete algorithm for automatic web service composition. Intl. Journal of Web Services Research (IJWSR) 9(2), 1–20 (2012)

14. Preda, N., Suchanek, F.M., Kasneci, G., Neumann, T., Ramanath, M., Weikum, G.: Angie: Active knowledge for interactive exploration. Proc. of the VLDB Endowment 2(2), 1570–1573 (2009)

15. Harth, A., Knoblock, C.A., Stadtmüller, S., Studer, R., Szekely, P.: On-the-fly integration of static and dynamic sources. In: Proceedings of the Fourth International Workshop on Consuming Linked Data (COLD 2013) (2013)

16. Dietze, S., Yu, H.Q., Pedrinaci, C., Liu, D., Domingue, J.: SmartLink: A web-based editor and search environment for linked services. In: Antoniou, G., Grobelnik, M., Simperl, E., Parsia, B., Plexousakis, D., De Leenheer, P., Pan, J. (eds.) ESWC 2011, Part II. LNCS, vol. 6644, pp. 436–440. Springer, Heidelberg (2011)

Conformance for DecSerFlow Constraints*

Yutian Sun and Jianwen Su

Department of Computer Science, U C Santa Barbara, USA
{sun,sun}@cs.ucsb.edu

Abstract. DecSerFlow is a declarative language to specify business processes. It consists of a set of temporal predicates that can be translated into LTL but limited to finite sequences. This paper focuses on the "conformance problem": Given a set of DecSerFlow constraints, is there an execution sequence that satisfies all given constraints? This paper provides syntactic characterizations of conformance for several subclasses of DecSerFlow constraints. These characterizations directly lead to efficient (polynomial time) conformance testing. Furthermore, algorithms are developed to generate conforming strings if the set of constraints is conformable. A conformance analyzer is developed based on the syntactic characterizations and the string generating algorithms. Experiments reveal several interesting factors concerning performance and scalability.

1 Introduction

Enterprises rely on business processes to accomplish business goals (handling a loan application, etc.) Business process models are either imperative or declarative [12]. Imperative models typically employ graphs (e.g., automata, Petri Nets) to depict how a process should progress. Declarative models are usually based on constraints [2], they are flexible and easy to change during design time or runtime [18]. A practical problem is whether a given set of constraints allows at least one execution. It is fundamental in business process modeling to test satisfiability of a given set of constraints.

A process execution is a (finite) sequence of activities through time. The declarative language DecSerFlow [2] uses a set of temporal predicates as a process specification, The DECLARE system [11] supports design and execution of DecSerFlow processes. In [14] an orchestrator for a declarative business process called REFlex was developed, where a subset of DecSerFlow can be expressed by REFlex. In this paper, we study the following conformance problem: does there exist an execution that satisfies a given DecSerFlow specification? Clearly efficient conformance testing provides an effective and efficient help to the user of DECLARE and the scheduler of [14]. Temporal predicates in DecSerFlow can be translated into linear temporal logic (LTL) [13] but limited to *finite sequences*. A naive approach to conformance checking is to construct automata representing individual constraints and determine if their cross product accepts a string. Complexity of this approach is exponential in the number of given constraints. This paper aims at efficient comformance checking.

Most DecSerFlow constraints can be categorized into two directions: "response" (*Res*), which specifies that an activity should happen in the future, and "precedence"

---

* Supported in part by a grant from Bosch.

X. Franch et al. (Eds.): ICSOC 2014, LNCS 8831, pp. 139–153, 2014.

(*Pre*), which specifies that an activity should happen in the past. For each direction, there are three types of constraints: (1) An ordering constraint *Res*(*a*, *b*) (or *Pre*(*a*, *b*)) for activities *a* and *b* specifies that if *a* occurs, then *b* should occur in the future (resp. past). As a practical example of a loan application, if activity "loan approval" happens, then in the past a "credit check" activity should have happened. (2) An alternating constraint *aRes*(*a*, *b*) (or *aPre*(*a*, *b*)) specifies that each occurrence of *a* implies a future (resp. past) occurrence of *b* but before (resp. after) the occurrence of *b*, *a* cannot occur again (i.e., between two occurrences of *a*, there should exist an occurrence of *b*). As an example, if a "house evaluation request" activity happens, a "house evaluation feedback" activity should happen in the future and before receiving the feedback, the applicant cannot submit another evaluation request, i.e., "request" and "feedback" should alternate. (3) An immediate constraint *iRes*(*a*, *b*) (or *iPre*(*a*, *b*)) restricts that if *a* occurs, then *b* should immediately follow (resp. occur before). In addition to "response" and "precedence" constraints, there is a special type of "existence" constraints that only require occurrences in any order. An existence constraint *Exi*(*a*, *b*) restricts that if *a* occurs, then *b* should occur either earlier or later. In practice, a common existence constraint can be that a guest can either choose to pay the hotel expense online then check in, or check in first and pay the expense later, i.e., *Exi*("check in", "payment").

In addition to temporal constraints, there may be cardinality requirements on each activity, i.e., an activity should occur at least once. For example, in an online order process, "payment" activity is always required to occur; while "shipping" is not (a customers may pick up the ordered items in a store).

The contributions of this paper are the following: We present a reduction from general DecSerFlow to DecSerFlow "Core" with no existence constraints nor cardinality requirements (Theorem 2.3). For DecSerFlow Core, we formulate syntactic characterizations (sufficient and necessary for conformance) for constraints involving (1) ordering and immediate constraints (Theorem 3.5), (2) ordering and alternating constraints (Theorem 3.9), (3) alternating and immediate constraints (Theorem 3.20), or (4) only precedence (or only response) constraints (Theorem 3.23). For the general case, it remains open whether syntactic characterizations exist. Algorithms are also developed to generate conforming strings when the schema is conformable. Finally, we designed and implemented a conformance analyzer and our experimental evaluation shows that (1) the syntactic condition approach is polynomially scalable (in time) comparing with the exponential-time naive approach using automata, (2) the time complexity of conforming string generation varies from polynomial to exponential complexity, and (3) the increasing number of constraints will increase the time needed of the automata approach exponentially more than the time needed by the syntactic condition approach.

The remainder of the paper is organized as follows. Section 2 defines DecSerFlow constraints studied in this paper. Section 3 focuses on different combinations of constraints together with their conformance checking and conforming string generation. A conformance checker is developed and evaluated in Section 4. Related work and conclusions are provided in Sections 5 and 6, resp. Detailed proofs, some examples, algorithms, and formal definitions are omitted due to space limitation.

2   DecSerFlow Constraints

In this section we introduce DecSerFlow constraints, define the conformance problem, state a straightforward result, and present a reduction to the case of "core" constraints.

Let $\mathcal{A}$ be an infinite set of *activities*, $\mathbb{N}$ the set of natural numbers, and $A \subseteq \mathcal{A}$ a finite subset of $\mathcal{A}$. A *string over A* (or $\mathcal{A}$) is a finite sequence of 0 or more activities in A (resp. $\mathcal{A}$). A^* ($\mathcal{A}^*$) the set of all strings over A (resp. $\mathcal{A}$).

A *subsequence* of $a_1 a_2 ... a_n$ is a string $a_{k_1} a_{k_2} ... a_{k_m}$, where (1) $m \in \mathbb{N}$ and $m \geqslant 1$, (2) $k_i \in [1..n]$ for each $i \in [1..m]$, and (3) $k_i < k_{i+1}$ for each $i \in [1..(m-1)]$; a *substring* is a subsequence $a_{k_1} a_{k_2} ... a_{k_m}$ where for each $i \in [1..(m-1)]$, $k_{i+1} = k_i + 1$.

Let $A \subseteq \mathcal{A}$, $a, b \in A$. A *(sequence) constraint on a, b* is a constraint shown in Fig. 1.

	Response	Precedence
Ordering	$Res(a, b)$: each occurrence of a is followed by an occurrence of b	$Pre(a, b)$: each occurrence of a is preceded by an occurrence of b
Alternating	$aRes(a, b)$: in addition to $Res(a, b)$, a and b alternate	$aPre(a, b)$: in addition to $Pre(a, b)$, a and b alternate
Immediate	$iRes(a, b)$: each occurrence of a is immediately followed by an occurrence of b	$iPre(a, b)$: each occurrence of a is immediately preceded by an occurrence of b
Existence	$Exi(a, b)$: each occurrence of a implies an occurrence of b	

Fig. 1. Summary of Constraints

For ordering precedence constraint $Pre(a, b)$, if "a" occurs in a string, then before "a", there must exist a "b", and between this "b" and "a", all activities are allowed to occur. Similarly, for alternating response constraint $aRes(a, b)$, after an occurrence of "a", no other a's can occur until a "b" occurs. For immediate precedence constraint $iPre(a, b)$, a "b" should occur immediately before "a". The existence constraints have no restrictions on temporal orders. Given a constraint c and a string s, denote $s \models c$ if s satisfies c, for example, $s \models Res(a, b)$, if $s = abcadb$.

Definition 2.1. A *(DecSerFlow) schema* is a triple $S = (A, C, \kappa)$ where $A \subseteq \mathcal{A}$ is a finite set of activities, C a finite set of constraints on activities in A, and κ is a total mapping from A to $\{0, 1\}$, called *cardinality*, to denote that an activity $a \in A$ should occur at least once (if $\kappa(a) = 1$) or no occurrence requirement (if $\kappa(a) = 0$).

Definition 2.2. A finite string s over A *conforms to* schema $S = (A, C, \kappa)$ if s satisfies every constraint in C and for each activity $a \in A$, s should contain a for at least $\kappa(a)$ times. If a string s conforms to S, s is a *conforming string* of S and S is *conformable*.

Conformance Problem: Given a schema S, is S conformable?

A naive approach to solve the conformance problem is to construct an automaton A for each given constraint c (and each cardinality requirement r, i.e., an actvitiy occurring at least 0 or 1 times), such that A can accept all strings that satisfy c (resp. accept all strings that satisfy r) and reject all other strings. Then the conformance problem is reduced to checking if the cross product of all constructed automata accepts a string.

However, the automata approach yields to exponential complexity in the size of the input schema. Our goal is to find syntactic conditions to determine conformity that lead to polynomial complexity.

For notation convenience, given a DecSerFlow schema $S = (A, C, \kappa)$, if for each $a \in A$, $\kappa(a) = 1$, we simply use (A, C) to denote S.

Theorem 2.3. Given $S = (A, C, \kappa)$ as a schema, there exists a schema $S' = (A', C')$ such that S is conformable iff S' is conformable.

Theorem 2.3 shows that conformance of arbitrary schemas can be reduced to conformance of schemas where each activity occurs at least once. If each activity in a given schema occurs at least once, the existence constraints are redundant. In the remainder of this paper, we only focus on schemas with *core* constraints, i.e., from set $\{Res, Pre, aRes, aPre, iRes, iPre\}$ and that each activity occurs at least once.

3 Characterizations for Conformance

3.1 Ordering and Immediate Constraints

This subsection focuses on syntactic characterizations of conformable schemas that only contain ordering and/or immediate constraints.

For each schema $S = (A, C)$, we construct the *causality graph* $\mathcal{G}_S$ of S as a labeled graph $(A, E_{\blacktriangleright}^{or}, E_{\blacktriangleleft}^{or}, E_{\blacktriangleright}^{al}, E_{\blacktriangleleft}^{al}, E_{\blacktriangleright}^{im}, E_{\blacktriangleleft}^{im})$ with the vertex set A and six edge sets where $E_{\blacktriangleright}^{x}$ ($E_{\blacktriangleleft}^{x}$) corresponds to response (resp. precedence) constraints of ordering (x = 'or'), alternating (x = 'al'), or immediate (x = 'im') flavor. Specifically, for all $a, b \in A$, $(a, b) \in E_{\blacktriangleright}^{or}$ iff $Res(a, b)$ is in C, $(a, b) \in E_{\blacktriangleright}^{al}$ iff $aPre(a, b) \in C$, $(a, b) \in E_{\blacktriangleright}^{im}$ iff $iRes(a, b) \in C$, and the other three cases are similar.

Given a causality graph $(A, E_{\blacktriangleright}^{or}, E_{\blacktriangleleft}^{or}, E_{\blacktriangleright}^{al}, E_{\blacktriangleleft}^{al}, E_{\blacktriangleright}^{im}, E_{\blacktriangleleft}^{im})$, if an edge set is empty, we will conveniently omit it; for example, if $E_{\blacktriangleright}^{im} = E_{\blacktriangleleft}^{im} = \varnothing$, we write the causality graph simply as $(A, E_{\blacktriangleright}^{or}, E_{\blacktriangleleft}^{or}, E_{\blacktriangleright}^{al}, E_{\blacktriangleleft}^{al})$.

For technical development, we review some well-known graph notions. Given a (directed) graph (V, E) with vertex set V and edge set $E \subseteq V \times V$, a *path* is a sequence $v_1 v_2 ... v_n$ where $n > 1$, for each $i \in [1..n]$, $v_i \in V$, and for each $i \in [1..(n-1)]$, $(v_i, v_{i+1}) \in E$; n is the *length* of the path $v_1 ... v_n$. A path $v_1 ... v_n$ is *simple* if v_i's are pairwise distinct except that v_1, v_n may be the same node. A (*simple*) *cycle* is a (resp. simple) path $v_1 ... v_n$ where $v_1 = v_n$. A graph is *cyclic* if it contains a cycle, *acyclic* otherwise. Given an acyclic graph (V, E), a *topological order* of (V, E) is an enumeration of V such that for each $(u, v) \in E$, u precedes v in the enumeration. A *subgraph* (V', E') of (V, E) is a graph, such that $V' \subseteq V$ and $E' \subseteq E \cap (V' \times V')$. A graph is *strongly connected* if there is a path from each node in the graph to each other node. Given a graph $G = (V, E)$ and a set $V' \subseteq V$, the *projection* of G on V', $\pi_{V'} G$, is a subgraph (V', E') of G where $E' = E \cap (V' \times V')$. A *strongly connected component* (V', E') of a graph $G = (V, E)$ is a strongly connected subgraph $G' = (V', E')$ of G, such that (1) $G' = \pi_{V'} G$, and (2) for each $v \in V - V'$, $\pi_{V' \cup \{v\}} G$ is not strongly connected.

To obtain the syntactic conditions for deciding the conformance of ordering and immediate constraints, we first present a pre-processing upon a given schema, such that the given schema is conformable if and only if the pre-processed the schema is conformable, and then show the syntactic conditions upon the pre-processed schemas.

Lemma 3.1. Given a schema $S = (A, C)$ and its causality graph $(A, E_{\blacktriangleright}^{or}, E_{\blacktriangleleft}^{or}, E_{\blacktriangleright}^{al}, E_{\blacktriangleleft}^{al}, E_{\blacktriangleright}^{im}, E_{\blacktriangleleft}^{im})$, for each $(u, v) \in E_{\blacktriangleright}^{im} \cup E_{\blacktriangleleft}^{im}$, if there exists $w \in A - \{u\}$, such that $(v, w) \in E_{\blacktriangleleft}^{or}$ (or $E_{\blacktriangleright}^{or}$), then for each conforming string s of S, s satisfies $Pre(u, w)$ (resp. $Res(u, w)$).

Lemma 3.1 is straightforward. Based on Lemma 3.1, we define the following pre-processing given a schema.

Definition 3.2. Given a schema $S = (A, C)$, the *immediate-plus* (or im^+) *schema* of S is a schema (A, C') constructed as follows: 1. Initially $C' = C$. 2. Repeat the following steps while C' is changed: for each distinct $u, v, w \in A$, if (1) $iPre(u, v)$ or $iRes(u, v)$ is in C' and (2) $Pre(v, w) \in C'$ (or $Res(v, w) \in C'$), then add $Pre(u, w)$ (resp. $Res(u, w)$) to C'.

Example 3.3. A schema S has 3 activities, a, b, c, and 4 constraints $iRes(a, c)$, $iRes(b, c)$, $Pre(c, a)$, and $Pre(c, b)$. Let S' be the im^+ schema of S. According to the definition of im^+ schema, in addition to the constraints in S, S' also contains constraints: $Pre(a, b)$ (which is obtained from $iRes(a, c)$ and $Pre(c, b)$) and $Pre(b, a)$. ∎

It is easy to see that for each given schema, its corresponding im^+ schema is unique. The following is a consequence of Lemma 3.1.

Corollary 3.4. A schema is conformable iff its im^+ schema is conformable.

For reading convenience, we introduce the following notations: let x, y, z be one of 'or', 'al', 'im'; we denote $E_{\blacktriangleright}^{x} \cup E_{\blacktriangleright}^{y}$ as $E_{\blacktriangleright}^{x \cup y}$ and use similar notations $E_{\blacktriangleleft}^{x \cup y}$ or $E_{\blacktriangleleft}^{x \cup y \cup z}$.

Theorem 3.5. Given a schema $S = (A, C)$ where C contains only ordering and immediate constraints, the im^+ schema S' of S, and the causality graph $(A, E_{\blacktriangleright}^{or}, E_{\blacktriangleleft}^{or}, E_{\blacktriangleright}^{im}, E_{\blacktriangleleft}^{im})$ of S', S is conformable iff the following conditions all hold.

(1). $(A, E_{\blacktriangleright}^{or \cup im})$ and $(A, E_{\blacktriangleleft}^{or \cup im})$ are both acyclic,

(2). for each $(u, v) \in E_{\blacktriangleright}^{im}$ (or $E_{\blacktriangleleft}^{im}$), there does not exist $w \in A$ such that $w \neq u$ and $(v, w) \in E_{\blacktriangleright}^{im}$ (resp. $E_{\blacktriangleleft}^{im}$), and

(3). for each $(u, v) \in E_{\blacktriangleright}^{im}$ (or $E_{\blacktriangleleft}^{im}$), there does not exist $w \in A$ such that $w \neq v$ and $(u, w) \in E_{\blacktriangleright}^{im}$ (resp. $E_{\blacktriangleleft}^{im}$).

In Theorem 3.5, Condition (1) restricts that the response or precedence direction does not form a loop (a loop of the same direction can lead to infinite execution). Conditions (2) and (3) similarly restrict that the immediate constraints are consistent. For example, it is impossible to satisfy constraints $iRes(a, b)$ and $iRes(a, c)$, where a, b, c are activities. Example 3.6 shows the importance of "pre-processing" to obtain im^+ schemas.

Example 3.6. Let S and S' be as stated in Example 3.3. Note that S satisfies all conditions in Theorem 3.5. However, S' does not, since $Pre(a, b)$ and $Pre(b, a)$ form a cycle in $E_{\blacktriangleleft}^{or \cup im}$, which leads to non-conformability of S. Therefore, a pre-processing to obtain an im^+ is necessary when determining conformability. ∎

Given a conformable schema that contains only ordering and immediate constraints, one question to ask is how to generate a conforming string. To solve this problem, we first introduce a (data) structure, which is also used in the later sections.

For a schema $S = (A, C)$, let $\pi_{im}(S) = (A, C')$ be a schema where C' is the set of all immediate constraints in C. The notation $\pi_{im}(S)$ holds the *projection* of S on immediate constraints. Similarly, let $\pi_{al}(S)$ be the *projection* of S on alternating constraints.

Given a schema $S = (A, C)$, if $\pi_{im}(S)$ satisfies the conditions stated in Theorem 3.5, then for each activity $a \in A$, denote $\bar{s}_{im}(a)$ as a string constructed iteratively as follows:

(i) $\bar{s}_{im}(a) = a$ initially, (ii) for the leftmost (or rightmost) activity u of $\bar{s}_{im}(a)$, if there exists $v \in A$ such that $iPre(u, v) \in C$ (resp. $iRes(u, v) \in C$), then update $\bar{s}_{im}(a)$ to be $v\bar{s}_{im}(a)$ (resp. $\bar{s}_{im}(a)v$), i.e., prepend (resp. append) $\bar{s}_{im}(a)$ with v, and (iii) repeat step (ii) until no more changes can be made. For each $a \in A$, it is easy to see that $\bar{s}_{im}(a)$ is unique and is finite. Let $s_{im}(a)$ be the set of activities that occur in $\bar{s}_{im}(a)$.

Alg. 1 shows the procedure to create a conforming string given a schema with only ordering and immediate constraints. The main idea of Alg. 1 relies on a topological order of both the "precedence" and "response" directions (to satisfy the ordering constraints); then replace each activity a by $\bar{s}_{im}(a)$ (to satisfy the immediate constraints).

Algorithm 1.

Input: A causality graph $(A, E_{\blacktriangleright}^{or}, E_{\blacktriangleleft}^{or}, E_{\blacktriangleright}^{im}, E_{\blacktriangleleft}^{im})$ of an im^+schema of a schema S that satisfies all conditions in Theorem 3.5

Output: A finite string that conforms to S

   A. Let "$a_1 a_2 ... a_n$" and "$b_1 b_2 ... b_n$" be topological sequences of $(A, E_{\blacktriangleright}^{or \cup im})$ and $(A, E_{\blacktriangleleft}^{or \cup im})$, resp.

   B. Return the string "$\bar{s}_{im}(b_n)...\bar{s}_{im}(b_1)\bar{s}_{im}(a_1)...\bar{s}_{im}(a_n)$".

3.2 Ordering and Alternating Constraints

This subsection focuses on syntactic conditions for conformance of schemas that contain ordering and alternating constraints.

We begin with defining "pre-processing" for schemas such that the original schema is conformable if and only if the schema after the pre-processing also is. The preprocessing will also be used in the next subsection.

Definition 3.7. Given a schema $S = (A, C)$ and its causality graph $(A, E_{\blacktriangleright}^{or}, E_{\blacktriangleleft}^{or}, E_{\blacktriangleright}^{al}, E_{\blacktriangleleft}^{al}, E_{\blacktriangleright}^{im}, E_{\blacktriangleleft}^{im})$, the *alternating-plus* (or al^+) *schema* of S is a schema (A, C') where

$$C' = C \cup \{aPre(v, u) \mid (u, v) \in E_{\blacktriangleright}^{al}, u \text{ and } v \text{ are on a common cycle in } (A, E_{\blacktriangleright}^{al} \cup E_{\blacktriangleleft}^{al})\}$$
$$\cup \{aRes(v, u) \mid (u, v) \in E_{\blacktriangleleft}^{al}, u \text{ and } v \text{ are on a common cycle in } (A, E_{\blacktriangleright}^{al} \cup E_{\blacktriangleleft}^{al})\}$$

It is easy to see that for each given schema, its corresponding al^+schema is unique.

Lemma 3.8. A schema is conformable iff its al^+schema is conformable.

Theorem 3.9. Given a schema S that only contains ordering and alternating constraints, let $S' = (A, C)$ be the al^+schema of S and $(A, E_{\blacktriangleright}^{or}, E_{\blacktriangleleft}^{or}, E_{\blacktriangleright}^{al}, E_{\blacktriangleleft}^{al})$ the causality graph of S'. S is conformable iff both $(A, E_{\blacktriangleright}^{or \cup al})$ and $(A, E_{\blacktriangleleft}^{or \cup al})$ are acyclic.

Example 3.10. Consider a schema with 5 activities, a, b, c, d, e, and constraints in the form of a graph $(A, E_{\blacktriangleright}^{or \cup al} \cup E_{\blacktriangleleft}^{or \cup al})$ as shown in Fig. 2, where the edge labels denote constraint types. Note that its al^+schema is itself. The conditions in Theorem 3.9 are satisfied, thus the schema is conformable. A conforming string is *dcebadce*. If we add the constraint $aPre(d, b)$ into the schema, it is no longer conformable since bcd forms a cycle in $(A, E_{\blacktriangleleft}^{or \cup al})$, forcing the subsequence bcd to occur infinitely many times. ∎

Alg. 2 presents the procedure to construct a conforming string given a conformable schema that contains only ordering and alternating constraints. A key step of the Alg. 2 is to first create a topological order of precedence constraints and that of response constraints, then for each violated alternating constraint, insert a string to fix the violation.

Fig. 2. An al$^+$ schema example

Algorithm 2.

Input: The causality graph $(A, E_{\blacktriangleright}^{or}, E_{\blacktriangleleft}^{or}, E_{\blacktriangleright}^{al}, E_{\blacktriangleleft}^{al})$ of an al$^+$ schema S satisfying conditions of Theorem 3.9

Output: A string that conforms to S

  A. Let $s_{\blacktriangleright} = a_1 a_2 \ldots a_n$ be a topological order of $(A, E_{\blacktriangleright}^{or \cup al})$ and $s_{\blacktriangleleft} = b_n b_{n-1} \ldots b_1$ a reversed topological order of $(A, E_{\blacktriangleleft}^{or \cup al})$.

  B. For each $a \in A$, define $R(a)$ as the set of nodes in A reachable from a through edges in $E_{\blacktriangleright}^{al} \cup E_{\blacktriangleleft}^{al}$ (i.e., each $b \in R(a)$ is either a itself or reachable from a in $(A, E_{\blacktriangleright}^{al} \cup E_{\blacktriangleleft}^{al})$), and denote $\bar{R}_{\blacktriangleright}(a)$ and $\bar{R}_{\blacktriangleleft}(a)$ the two enumerations of $R(a)$ such that $\bar{R}_{\blacktriangleright}(a)$ and $\bar{R}_{\blacktriangleleft}(a)$ are subsequences of $s_{\blacktriangleright}$ and $s_{\blacktriangleleft}$, resp.

  C. Let $V_{ns} \subseteq C$ be the set of alternating constraints that are not satisfied by $s_{\blacktriangleleft} s_{\blacktriangleright}$, and $E_{ns} \subseteq V_{ns} \times V_{ns}$ such that an edge $(X(a,b), Y(c,d))$ is in E_{ns} iff $c \in R(b)$, where $X, Y \in \{aRes, aPre\}$ and $a, b, c, d \in A$. Denote $\bar{v}_{ns}$ to be a topological order of (V_{ns}, E_{ns}). (It can be shown that (V_{ns}, E_{ns}) is acyclic)

  D. For each edge $aRes(u, v)$ (or $aPre(u, v)$) in V_{ns} in the order of $\bar{v}_{ns}$, let $s_{\blacktriangleleft} = s_{\blacktriangleleft} \bar{R}_{\blacktriangleleft}(v)$ (resp. $s_{\blacktriangleright} = \bar{R}_{\blacktriangleright}(v) s_{\blacktriangleright}$).

  E. Return $s_{\blacktriangleleft} s_{\blacktriangleright}$.

3.3   Immediate and Alternating Constraints

Before discussing conformity for schemas with alternating and immediate constraints, we define a "pre-processing" for the given al$^+$ schema such that the original al$^+$ schema is conformable if and only if after the pre-processing, the schema is conformable.

Lemma 3.11. Given an al$^+$ schema $S = (A, C)$ that only contains alternating and immediate constraints, the causality graph $(A, E_{\blacktriangleright}^{al}, E_{\blacktriangleleft}^{al}, E_{\blacktriangleright}^{im}, E_{\blacktriangleleft}^{im})$ of S, and two activities $u, v \in A$ such that there is a path from v to u in the graph $(A, E_{\blacktriangleright}^{al \cup im} \cup E_{\blacktriangleleft}^{al \cup im})$, then (1) $iRes(u, v) \in C$ implies if a string s satisfies $iRes(u, v)$, then $s \models iPre(v, u)$, and (2) $iPre(u, v) \in C$ implies if a string s satisfies $iPre(u, v)$, then $s \models iRes(v, u)$

Let u and v be as stated in Lemma 3.11. Note that if u and v satisfy the condition in the lemma, u and v will always "occur together" in a conforming string as if they were one activity. With such an observation, we can then pre-process a given schema by "collapsing" such nodes according to in Lemma 3.11. However, two nodes satisfying Lemma 3.11 does not necessarily mean they are "safe" to be collapsed. For example, if nodes u and v in some schema are eligible to be combined based on Lemma 3.11 and there is a node w in the same schema that has constraint $iRes(w, u)$. The collapsing of u and v implies that $iRes(w, v)$ is also a constraint that should be satisfied. According to Theorem 3.5, the schema is not satisfiable. Thus, in the following definition, we define when two nodes are "safe" to collapse (i.e., "collapsable").

Definition 3.12. Given an al$^+$schema $S = (A, C)$ that contains only alternating and immediate constraints, and its causality graph $(A, E_{\blacktriangleright}^{al}, E_{\blacktriangleleft}^{al}, E_{\blacktriangleright}^{im}, E_{\blacktriangleleft}^{im})$, S is *collapsable* if S satisfies all of the following.

(1). $(A, E_{\blacktriangleright}^{al \cup im})$ and $(A, E_{\blacktriangleleft}^{al \cup im})$ are acyclic,

(2). for each $(u, v) \in E_{\blacktriangleright}^{im}$ (or $E_{\blacktriangleleft}^{im}$), there does not exist $w \in A$ such that $w \neq u$ and $(v, w) \in E_{\blacktriangleleft}^{im}$ (resp. $E_{\blacktriangleright}^{im}$),

(3). for each $(u, v) \in E_{\blacktriangleright}^{im}$ (or $E_{\blacktriangleleft}^{im}$), there does not exist $w \in A$ such that $w \neq v$ and $(u, w) \in E_{\blacktriangleright}^{im}$ (resp. $E_{\blacktriangleleft}^{im}$), and

(4). for each distinct $u, v, w \in A$, if $(u, w), (v, w) \in E_{\blacktriangleright}^{im}$ or $(u, w), (v, w) \in E_{\blacktriangleleft}^{im}$, then there is no path from w to either u or v in graph $(A, E_{\blacktriangleright}^{al \cup im} \cup E_{\blacktriangleleft}^{al \cup im})$.

Note that Conditions (1)–(3) in the above definition are similar to the characterization stated in Theorem 3.5.

Example 3.13. Consider an al$^+$schema with activities a, b, c, d, e, f, and constraints shown in Fig. 3 as $(A, E_{\blacktriangleright}^{al \cup im} \cup E_{\blacktriangleleft}^{al \cup im})$ where the edge labels denote

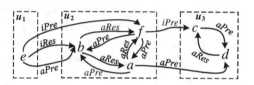

Fig. 3. A collapsed schema example

types of constraints. (Ignore the dashed boxes labeled u_1, u_2, u_3 for now.) The schema is collapsable. However, if constraint $iPre(a, c)$ is added to the schema, Condition (4) (in the collapsability definition) is violated and thus the new schema is not collapsable, since $(f, c), (a, c) \in E_{\blacktriangleleft}^{im}$ and there is a path cda from c to a in $(A, E_{\blacktriangleright}^{al \cup im} \cup E_{\blacktriangleleft}^{al \cup im})$. ∎

Definition 3.14. Given a collapsable schema $S = (A, C)$ with only alternating and immediate constraints, the *collapsed schema* of S is a schema (A', C') constructed as follows:

1. Initially $A' = A$ and $C' = C$.
2. Repeat the following steps while (A', C') is changed:
   i. Let $(A', E_{\blacktriangleright}^{al}, E_{\blacktriangleleft}^{al}, E_{\blacktriangleright}^{im}, E_{\blacktriangleleft}^{im})$ be the corresponding causality graph of (A', C').
   ii. for each $u, v \in A$ on a common cycle in $(A, E_{\blacktriangleright}^{al \cup im} \cup E_{\blacktriangleleft}^{al \cup im})$, If $(u, v) \in E_{\blacktriangleright}^{im}$ or $E_{\blacktriangleleft}^{im}$, then (1) remove each $X(u, v)$ or $X(v, u)$ from C', where X ranges over $aRes$, $aPre$, $iRes$, and $iPre$. (2) Create node w_{uv}; let $A' := A' - \{u, v\} \cup \{w_{uv}\}$, and (3) replace each u and v in C' by w_{uv}.

It is easy to show that given a collapsable al$^+$schema, the corresponding collapsed schema is unique. The following lemma (Lemma 3.15) is easy to verify.

Lemma 3.15. Given a collapsable al$^+$schema S with only alternating and immediate constraints, S is conformable iff its collapsed schema is conformable.

By Corollaries 3.8 and 3.15, conformance checking of a schema that only contains alternating and immediate constraints can be reduced to the checking of its collapsed version. Thus, in the remainder of this subsection, we focus on collapsed schemas.

In order to have a clean statement of the necessary and sufficient condition, we introduce a concept of "gap-free". Essentially, "gap-free" is to deal with a special case of a schema illustrated in the following Example 3.16.

Example 3.16. Continue with Example 3.13; note that the schema in Fig. 3 is a collapsed schema. Consider a schema S^{u_2} that only contains activities a, b, and f, together with the constraints among them shown in Fig. 3 (i.e., a "subschema" bounded by the dashed box labeled as "u_2"). Based on Theorem 3.9, S^{u_2} is conformable and a conforming string is baf. Now consider a schema $S^{u_{1,2}}$ that only contains activities e, a, b, and f, together with the constraints among them shown in Fig. 3 (i.e., a "subschema" bounded by the dashed boxes labeled as "u_1" and "u_2" together with the constraints crossing u_1 and u_2). Due to constraints $iRes(e, b)$ and $iPre(e, f)$, if $S^{u_{1,2}}$ is conformable, then each conforming string of $S^{u_{1,2}}$ must contain substring "feb". This requirement leads to some restriction upon schema S^{u_2}, i.e., if we take out activity "e" from $S^{u_{1,2}}$ and focus on schema S^{u_2} again, one restriction would be: is there a conforming string of S^{u_2} that contains a substring fb? If the answer is negative, then apparently, $S^{u_{1,2}}$ is not conformable, since no substring feb can be formed.   ∎

With the concern shown in Example 3.16, we need a checking mechanism to decide if two activities can occur as a substring (i.e., "gap-free") in some conforming string. More specifically, given $(A, E_{\blacktriangleright}^{al}, E_{\blacktriangleleft}^{al}, E_{\blacktriangleright}^{im}, E_{\blacktriangleleft}^{im})$ as a causality graph of a collapsed schema S, we are more interested in checking if two activities that in the same strongly connected component in $(A, E_{\blacktriangleright}^{al} \cup E_{\blacktriangleleft}^{al})$ can form a substring in a conforming string of S. Note that in Example 3.16, activities a, b, and f are in the same strongly connected component labeled with u_2 in $(A, E_{\blacktriangleright}^{al} \cup E_{\blacktriangleleft}^{al})$.

Definition 3.17. Let $S = (A, C)$ be a schema that only contains alternating constraints and $(A, E_{\blacktriangleright}^{al}, E_{\blacktriangleleft}^{al})$ the causality graph of S, such that $(A, E_{\blacktriangleright}^{al} \cup E_{\blacktriangleleft}^{al})$ is strongly connected. Given two distinct activities $u, v \in A$, u, v are *gap-free* (wrt S) if for each $w, x, y \in A$, the following conditions should all hold wrt graph $(A, E_{\blacktriangleright}^{al})$:

(a). if there is a path p with length greater than 2 from u to v, the following all hold:
   (i). if w is on p, then $(u, v) \notin E_{\blacktriangleright}^{al}$,
   (ii). if there is a path from x to u, then $(x, v) \notin E_{\blacktriangleright}^{al}$,
   (iii). if there is a path from v to y, then $(u, y) \notin E_{\blacktriangleright}^{al}$,
   (iv). if there are paths from x to u and v to y, and then $(x, y) \notin E_{\blacktriangleright}^{al}$, and
(b). if there is a path from v to u, then the following all hold:
   (i). if there is a path from x to v, then $(x, u) \notin E_{\blacktriangleright}^{al}$,
   (ii). if there is a path from u to y, then $(v, y) \notin E_{\blacktriangleright}^{al}$, and
   (iii). if there are paths from x to v and u to y, then $(x, y) \notin E_{\blacktriangleright}^{al}$.

Lemma 3.18. Given a conformable al^+ schema $S = (A, C)$ that only contains alternating constraints, the causality graph $(A, E_{\blacktriangleright}^{al}, E_{\blacktriangleleft}^{al})$ of S, such that $(A, E_{\blacktriangleright}^{al} \cup E_{\blacktriangleleft}^{al})$ is strongly connected, and two activities $u, v \in A$, "uv" can appear as a substring in some a conforming string of S iff u, v are gap-free wrt S.

Given a graph $G = (V, E)$, for each $v \in V$, denote $\text{SV}(v)$ to be the set of all the nodes in the strongly connected component of G that contains v.

Let (A, C) be a collapsed schema and $(A, E_{\blacktriangleright}^{al}, E_{\blacktriangleleft}^{al}, E_{\blacktriangleright}^{im}, E_{\blacktriangleleft}^{im})$ its causality graph. Consider graph $(A, E_{\blacktriangleright}^{al} \cup E_{\blacktriangleleft}^{al} \cup E_{\blacktriangleright}^{im} \cup E_{\blacktriangleleft}^{im})$; given an activity $a \in A$, denote $S(a)$ to be a schema defined as $(\text{SV}(a), \{aRes(u, v) \mid (u, v) \in E_{\blacktriangleright}^{al} \wedge \text{SV}(a) = \text{SV}(u) = \text{SV}(v)\} \cup \{aPre(u, v) \mid (u, v) \in E_{\blacktriangleleft}^{al} \wedge \text{SV}(a) = \text{SV}(u) = \text{SV}(v)\})$.

Example 3.19. Continue with Example 3.13; consider the schema in Fig. 3. Note that the schema is a collapsed schema. $SV(a) = SV(b) = SV(f)$ is the strongly connected component of the graph in Fig. 3 with nodes a, b, and f. Moreover, $S(a) = S(b) = S(f)$ is a schema that only contains activities a, b, and f, together with the constraints among them in Fig. 3. ∎

The following Theorem 3.20 provides a necessary and sufficient condition for conformability of schema with only alternating and immediate constraints.

Theorem 3.20. Given a schema S that only contains alternating and immediate constraints, S is conformable iff the following conditions all hold.

(1). S is collapsable,

(2). $\pi_{al}(\tilde{S})$ is conformable (recall that π_{al} denotes the "projection" only upon alternating constraints), where $\tilde{S}$ is the collapsed schema of S, and

(3). Let $(A, E_{\blacktriangleright}^{al}, E_{\blacktriangleleft}^{al}, E_{\blacktriangleright}^{im}, E_{\blacktriangleleft}^{im})$ be the causality graph of the collapsed schema $\tilde{S}$, for each $u, v, w \in A$, if there is a path from u to w in $(A, E_{\blacktriangleright}^{im})$, there is a path from u to v in $(A, E_{\blacktriangleleft}^{im})$, and $SV(w) = SV(v)$ wrt $(A, E_{\blacktriangleright}^{al \cup im} \cup E_{\blacktriangleleft}^{al \cup im})$, then either (1) v, w are gap-free wrt $S(v)$ if $v \neq w$, or (2) v has no outgoing edge in graph $(A, E_{\blacktriangleright}^{al \cup im} \cup E_{\blacktriangleleft}^{al \cup im})$ if $v = w$.

Example 3.21. Continue with Example 3.19; consider the schema in Fig. 3. The schema satisfies the conditions in Theorem 3.20 and is conformable. A conforming string can be $bdacfebdacf$. ∎

Similar to the previous combinations of constraints, given a schema with only ordering and alternating constraints, an algorithm to construct a conforming string is desired. In this case, the algorithm is rather complicated and thus omitted The main idea is that (1) for each activity a, construct a string that satisfies each constraint "related" to a as well as each alternating constraint with in a strongly connected component, and (2) hierarchically link these constructed strings together. In this paper, we only provide an example of the algorithm.

Example 3.22. Consider the schema shown in Fig. 3. We first construct a string for activity e starting with base $\bar{S}_{im}(e) = cfeb$, where f and b are both in strongly connected component u_2; while c is in u_3. According to the property of gap-free for f and b, there must exist a string that satisfies every constraint in u_2 and has fb as a substring; a possible string could be: $s_1 = \underline{bafbaf}$. Similarly, string $s_2 = \underline{dc}$ satisfies every constraint in u_3 and has c as a substring; then we "glue" the underline parts of s_1 and s_2 to each end of $\bar{S}_{im}(e)$ and have $\underline{badcfebaf}$. Note that this string satisfies every immediate constraint containing e and every alternating constraint within u_1, u_2, and u_3. Further, as there is an alternating precedence constraint from e to b, to satisfy that, we "glue" the topological order of u_2 before $\underline{badcfebaf}$, and have $\hat{s}(e) = \underline{bafbadcfebaf}$. Note that $\hat{s}(e)$ satisfies every constraint containing e and every alternating constraint within u_1, u_2, and u_3. In general, for each activity, a string $\hat{s}(*)$ is constructed. For example $\hat{s}(b) = b$ and $\hat{s}(a) = \underline{dca}$.

The second step is to link these $\hat{s}(*)$ strings together. The way to link them is first constructing a topological order of all the strongly connected components. For example in Fig. 3, a topological order is $u_1u_2u_3$. And within each strongly connected component, the order of activities can be arbitrary, for example $ebafcd$. Then, based on the order $ebafcd$, we first replace each b that occurs in the under line parts in $\hat{s}(e)$ by $\hat{s}(b)$, and we have $baf\underline{b}adcfeba f$. Further, according to the topological order, we replace a that occurs in the under line parts in $ba f\underline{b}adcfeba f$ by $\hat{s}(a)$ and have $bdca f bdcadcf ebdca f$. We repeat these steps and it can be shown that the final string satisfies each constraint. ∎

3.4 Response or Precedence Constraints

In this subsection, we study comformity of either response or precedence constraints but not combined. The following Theorem 3.23 states the syntactic condition for conformity of schemas containing only response constraints or only precedence constraints.

Theorem 3.23. Given a schema $S = (A, C)$ where C contains only response (or only precedence) constraints, and its causality graph $(A, E_\blacktriangleright^{or}, E_\blacktriangleright^{al}, E_\blacktriangleright^{im})$ (resp. $(A, E_\blacktriangleleft^{or}, E_\blacktriangleleft^{al}, E_\blacktriangleleft^{im})$), S is conformable iff the following conditions both hold:

(1). $(A, E_\blacktriangleright^{or \cup al \cup im})$ (resp. $E_\blacktriangleleft^{or \cup al \cup im})$ is acyclic, and

(2). for each $(u, v) \in E_\blacktriangleright^{im}$ (resp. $E_\blacktriangleleft^{im}$), there does not exist any $w \in A$ such that $w \neq v$ and $(u, w) \in E_\blacktriangleright^{im}$ (resp. $E_\blacktriangleleft^{im}$).

Example 3.24. Consider a schema S with 5 activities, a, b, c, d, e, and 6 constraints $iRes(a, b), iRes(c, e), iRes(e, d), aRes(b, c)$ $Res(a, e)$, and $Pre(b, d)$. Based on Theorem 3.23, S satisfies all conditions, thus conformable. A conforming string can be $abced$. However, if constraint $aRes(d, c)$ is added, S will not be conformable as the edge set forms a cycle (violating Condition (1)). ∎

Alg. 3 is used to construct a conforming string from an input schema that satisfies both conditions in Theorem 3.23. The main idea is again to build a topological order based on the causality graph and then fix each violated immediate constraint in the string. Note that the execution of Alg. 3 replies on Theorem 3.23, where Conditions (1) is to ensure the topological order in Step A is achievable, and Condition (2) is to guarantee Step B1 is unique.

Algorithm 3.

Input: A causality graph $(A, E_\blacktriangleright^{or}, E_\blacktriangleright^{al}, E_\blacktriangleright^{im})$ of a schema S that satisfies both conditions in Theorem 3.23
Output: A finite string that conforms to S

    A. Let string s be a topological order of $(A, E_\blacktriangleright^{or \cup al \cup im})$. For each $a \in A$, let $\hat{s}(a)$ be the substring $s^{[k]}s^{[k+1]}...s^{[len(s)]}$ of s such that $s^{[k]} = a$ (clearly $k \in [1..len(s)]$). Let $i = 1$.

    B. While $i \leqslant len(s)$, repeat the following step:

        B1. If $(s^{[i]}, v) \in E_\blacktriangleright^{im}$ for some $v \in A$ and either $i = len(s)$ or $s^{[i+1]} \neq v$, then replace $s^{[i]}$ in s by $s^{[i]}\hat{s}(v)$.

        B2. Increment $i = i + 1$.

    C. Return s.

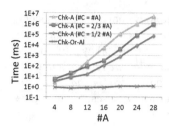 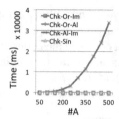 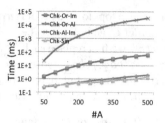

Fig. 4. Automata vs Syn. Cond.   **Fig. 5.** Scalability   **Fig. 6.** Scalability (log)

4   Experimental Evaluations

In this section, several experiments are conducted to evaluate the performance of the syntactic-condition-based conformance checking approaches. Three main types of algorithms are implemented, including: (1) The naive algorithm to check DecSerFlow conformance using automata (denoted as Chk-A), (2) the syntactic-condition-based conformance checking algorithms for all four combinations of predicates (denoted as Chk-Or-Im for ordering and immediate constraints, Chk-Or-Al, Chk-Al-Im, and Chk-Sin for single direction constraints, i.e., either response or precedence), and (3) all four conforming string generation algorithms (denoted as Gen-Or-Im, Gen-Or-Al, Gen-Al-Im, and Gen-Sin). All algorithms are implemented in Java and executed on a computer with 8G RAM and dual 1.7 GHz Intel processors. The data sets (i.e., DecSerFlow schemas) used in experiments are randomly generated. Schema generation uses two parameters: number of activities ($\#A$) and number of constraints ($\#C$), where each constraint is constructed by selecting a DecSerFlow predicate and two activities in a uniform distribution. Each experiment records the time needed for an algorithm to complete on an input schema. In order to collect more accurate results, each experiment is done for 1000 times to obtain an average time result with the same $\#A$ and same $\#C$ for schemas having $\#A < 200$, 100 times for schemas having $\#A \in [200, 400)$, and 10 times for $\#A \in [400, \infty)$. The reason to have less times of experiments for larger $\#A$ is that it takes minutes to hours for a single algorithm execution with large $\#A$, which makes it impractical to run 1000 times. We now report the findings.

The automata approach is exponentially more expensive than syntactic conditions

We compared the time needed for the automata and syntactic condition approaches on checking the same set of schemas that contain only ordering and alternating constraints. (For other three types of combinations of constraints, the results are similar). The input schemas have n activities and either n, $\frac{n}{2}$, or $\frac{2n}{3}$ constraints, where n ranges from 4 to 28. Fig. 4 shows the results (x-axis denotes the number of activities and y-axis denotes the time needed in the log scale). It can be observed that for the automata approach, the time needed is growing exponentially wrt the number of activities/constraints. For a schema with 28 activities and 28 constraints, it takes more than 3 hours to finish the checking. However, the syntactic condition approaches (whose complexity is polynomial) can finish the conformance checking almost instantly. As the times needed for either n, $\frac{n}{2}$, or $\frac{2n}{3}$ constraints are all too close around 1ms, we only use one curve (instead of three) in Fig. 4 to represent the result for the syntactic conditions approach.

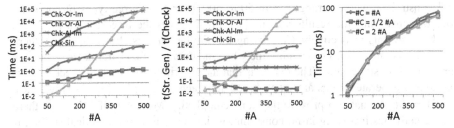

Fig. 7. String Generation   **Fig. 8.** Str. Gen. / Checking   **Fig. 9.** Changing #Constraints

The syntactic conditions approaches have at most a cubic growth rate in the size of the input schemas

We compute the times needed for the syntactic condition approaches for input schemas with n activities and n constraints, n between 50 and 500. Fig. 5 and 6 show the same result with normal and logarithm scales (resp.) of all four combinations of the constraints. From the result, the complexity of the syntactic condition approach for alternating and immediate constraints appears cubic due to the checking of Condition (4) of Definition 3.12 (collapsable); the complexity for ordering and immediate constraints is quadratic due to the pre-processing to form an im^+schema; the complexity for ordering and alternating constraints is linear as the pre-processing (to form an al^+schema by detecting strongly connected components) as well as the acyclicity check of the causality graphs are linear; finally, the complexity for the constraints of a single direction is also linear.

Conforming string generation requires polynomial to exponential times

With the same experiment setting as above, Fig. 7 shows the time to generate a conforming string for a conformable schema. From the results, all string generating approaches are polynomial except for the single direction case (i.e., either response or precedence). According to Alg. 3, the length of a generated string can be as long as 2^n, where n is the number of activities in the given schema. Fig. 8 presents the ratios of the time to generate a conforming string over the time to check conformance of the same schema for conformable schemas. The results indicate that the complexity to generate a string can be polynomially lower (ordering and immediate case), the same (alternating and immediate case), polynomially higher (ordering and alternating case), and exponentially higher (single direction case) than the corresponding complexity to check conformance of the same schema. Note that the curves in Fig. 8 is lower or "smaller" than dividing "Fig. 7" by "Fig. 5" due to the reason that the data shown in Fig. 7 is only for the conformable schemas; while the one in Fig. 5 is for general schemas, where non-conformable schemas can be determined 5 - 15% faster than conformable ones due to the reason that a non-comformable schema fails the checking if it does not satisfy one of the conditions (e.g., in Theorem 3.5, there are three conditions to check); while a comformable schema can pass the check only after all conditions are checked.

Increasing the number of constraints increases more time for the automata approach than syntactic condition approaches

We compute the time needed for the syntactic condition approaches with input schemas containing only ordering and immediate constraints with n activities and either n, $2n$, or $\frac{n}{2}$ constraints, where n ranges from 50 to 500. (For other three types of combinations of constraints, the results are similar). Fig. 9 shows the three curves for n, $2n$, and $\frac{n}{2}$ constraints respectively. Comparing the similar settings shown in Fig. 4, there does not exist an obvious growth in time when the number of constraints grow and the curves are almost the same. The reason is that the algorithms we used to check conformance and generate strings are graph-based approaches. As $\#C \in [\frac{\#A}{2}, 2\#A]$, we have $O(\#C) = O(\#A)$ that can provide the same complexity. Moreover, if $\#C < \frac{\#A}{2}$, there will be activities involving in no constraint, which leads to a non-practical setting; if $\#C > 2\#A$, almost all the randomly generated schemas will be non-confomable based on uniform distribution.

5   Related Work

The work reported here is a part of the study on collaborative systems and choreography languages [16]. The constraint language studied is a part of DecSerFlow [2], whose constraints can be translated to LTL [13].

Original LTL [13] is defined for infinite sequences. [15] proved that LTL satisfiability checking is PSPACE-Complete. A well-know result in [17] shows that LTL is equivalent to Büchi automata; and the LTL satisfiability checking can be translated to language emptiness checking. Several complexity results on satisfiability developed for subsets of LTL. [5] shows that restriction to Horn formulas will not decrease the complexity of satisfiability checking. [6] investigates the complexity of cases restricted by the use of temporal operators, their nesting, and number of variables. [4] and [3] provide upper and lower bounds for different combinations of both temporal and propositional operators. [7] presents the tractability of LTL only with combination of "XOR" clauses.

For the finite semantics, [8] studies the semantics of LTL upon truncated paths. [10] provides an exponential-time algorithm to check if a given LTL formula can be satisfied by a given finite-state model, but the execution is still infinite.

Business process modeling has been studied variously in the last decade ([9,1]). Previous studies of declarative models focus mostly on formal verification of general properties involving data, generally, such verification problems have exponential or higher time complexity (see [9]).

6   Conclusions

This paper studied syntactic characterization of conformance for "core" DecSerFlow constraints that are reduced from general DecSerFlow constraints. We provided characterizations for (1) ordering and immediate constraints, (2) ordering and alternating constraints, (3) alternating and immediate constraints, and (4) ordering, alternating, and immediate constraints with precedence (or response) direction only. The general case for ordering, immediate, and alternating constraints with both precedence and response directions remains as an open problem; furthermore, it is unclear if the conformance problem for DecSerFlow constraints is in PTIME.

References

1. van der Aalst, W.M.P.: Business process management demystified: A tutorial on models, systems and standards for workflow management. In: Desel, J., Reisig, W., Rozenberg, G. (eds.) Lectures on Concurrency and Petri Nets. LNCS, vol. 3098, pp. 1–65. Springer, Heidelberg (2004)
2. van der Aalst, W.M.P., Pesic, M.: DecSerFlow: Towards a Truly Declarative Service Flow Language. In: Bravetti, M., Núñez, M., Zavattaro, G. (eds.) WS-FM 2006. LNCS, vol. 4184, pp. 1–23. Springer, Heidelberg (2006)
3. Artale, A., Kontchakov, R., Ryzhikov, V., Zakharyaschev, M.: The complexity of clausal fragments of LTL. In: McMillan, K., Middeldorp, A., Voronkov, A. (eds.) LPAR-19 2013. LNCS, vol. 8312, pp. 35–52. Springer, Heidelberg (2013)
4. Bauland, M., Schneider, T., Schnoor, H., Schnoor, I., Vollmer, H.: The complexity of generalized satisfiability for linear temporal logic. In: Seidl, H. (ed.) FOSSACS 2007. LNCS, vol. 4423, pp. 48–62. Springer, Heidelberg (2007)
5. Chen, C.C., Lin, I.P.: The computational complexity of satisfiability of temporal horn formulas in propositional linear-time temporal logic. Inf. Proc. Lett. 45(3), 131–136 (1993)
6. Demri, S., Schnoebelen, P., Demri, S.E.: The complexity of propositional linear temporal logics in simple cases. Information and Computation 174, 61–72 (1998)
7. Dixon, C., Fisher, M., Konev, B.: Tractable temporal reasoning. In: Proc. International Joint Conference on Artificial Intelligence (IJCAI). AAAI Press (2007)
8. Eisner, C., Fisman, D., Havlicek, J., Lustig, Y., McIsaac, A., Van Campenhout, D.: Reasoning with temporal logic on truncated paths. In: Hunt Jr., W.A., Somenzi, F. (eds.) CAV 2003. LNCS, vol. 2725, pp. 27–39. Springer, Heidelberg (2003)
9. Hull, R., Su, J., Vaculín, R.: Data management perspectives on business process management: tutorial overview. In: SIGMOD Conference, pp. 943–948 (2013)
10. Lichtenstein, O., Pnueli, A.: Checking that finite state concurrent programs satisfy their linear specification. In: POPL, pp. 97–107 (1985)
11. Pesic, M., Schonenberg, H., van der Aalst, W.M.P.: Declare: Full support for loosely-structured processes. In: EDOC, pp. 287–300 (2007)
12. Pichler, P., Weber, B., Zugal, S., Pinggera, J., Mendling, J., Reijers, H.A.: Imperative versus declarative process modeling languages: An empirical investigation. In: Daniel, F., Barkaoui, K., Dustdar, S. (eds.) BPM Workshops 2011, Part I. LNBIP, vol. 99, pp. 383–394. Springer, Heidelberg (2012)
13. Pnueli, A.: The temporal logic of programs. In: FOCS, pp. 46–57 (1977)
14. Silva, N.C., de Carvalho, R.M., Oliveira, C.A.L., Lima, R.M.F.: REFlex: An efficient web service orchestrator for declarative business processes. In: Basu, S., Pautasso, C., Zhang, L., Fu, X. (eds.) ICSOC 2013. LNCS, vol. 8274, pp. 222–236. Springer, Heidelberg (2013)
15. Sistla, A.P., Clarke, E.M.: The complexity of propositional linear temporal logics. J. ACM 32(3), 733–749 (1985)
16. Sun, Y., Xu, W., Su, J.: Declarative choreographies for artifacts. In: Liu, C., Ludwig, H., Toumani, F., Yu, Q. (eds.) Service Oriented Computing. LNCS, vol. 7636, pp. 420–434. Springer, Heidelberg (2012)
17. Vardi, M.Y., Wolper, P.: An automata-theoretic approach to automatic program verification (preliminary report). In: LICS, pp. 332–344 (1986)
18. Xu, W., Su, J., Yan, Z., Yang, J., Zhang, L.: An Artifact-Centric Approach to Dynamic Modification of Workflow Execution. In: Meersman, R., Dillon, T., Herrero, P., Kumar, A., Reichert, M., Qing, L., Ooi, B.-C., Damiani, E., Schmidt, D.C., White, J., Hauswirth, M., Hitzler, P., Mohania, M. (eds.) OTM 2011, Part I. LNCS, vol. 7044, pp. 256–273. Springer, Heidelberg (2011)

Integrating On-policy Reinforcement Learning with Multi-agent Techniques for Adaptive Service Composition

Hongbing Wang[1], Xin Chen[1], Qin Wu[1], Qi Yu[2], Zibin Zheng[3], and Athman Bouguettaya[4]

[1] School of Computer Science and Engineering, Southeast University, China
hbw@seu.edu.cn, {cyceve,bellawu627}@gmail.com
[2] College of Computing and Information Sciences, Rochester Institute of Tech, USA
qi.yu@rit.edu
[3] Department of Computer Science and Engineering,
The Chinese University of Hong Kong, Hong Kong, China
zbzheng@cse.cuhk.edu.hk
[4] School of Computer Science and Information Technology, RMIT, Australia
athman.bouguettaya@rmit.edu.au

Abstract. In service computing, online services and the Internet environment are evolving over time, which poses a challenge to service composition for adaptivity. In addition, high efficiency should be maintained when faced with massive candidate services. Consequently, this paper presents a new model for large-scale and adaptive service composition based on multi-agent reinforcement learning. The model integrates on-policy reinforcement learning and game theory, where the former is to achieve adaptability in a highly dynamic environment with good online performance, and the latter is to enable multiple agents to work for a common task (i.e., composition). In particular, we propose a multi-agent SARSA (State-Action-Reward-State-Action) algorithm which is expected to achieve better performance compared with the single-agent reinforcement learning methods in our composition framework. The features of our approach are demonstrated by an experimental evaluation.

1   Introduction

As the mainstream paradigm of SOC (Service-oriented Computing), the research on theories of service composition and related technologies for seamless integration of business applications is always the core proposition. However, large-scale service composition faces a multitude of thorny issues, such as, accuracy, interoperability, efficiency and adaptability for practical use, if there exist massive services with similar functionality in a highly-dynamic environment.

Under the premise of validity for service composition, efficiency, adaptability and optimality of composition in large-scale and dynamic scenarios are especially significant. First of all, both the complexity of business flows and the quantity of candidate services may affect the efficiency of the service orchestration. Secondly,

X. Franch et al. (Eds.): ICSOC 2014, LNCS 8831, pp. 154–168, 2014.
© Springer-Verlag Berlin Heidelberg 2014

how to adapt to the services' internal changes and external dynamic environment is a grand challenge. Furthermore, how to achieve the optimal aggregated QoS should also be taken into consideration. Therefore, a novel method should be proposed to obtain a good balance between those objectives.

Previous studies mainly focus on integer programming, graph planning, reinforcement learning (RL) and so on. Ardagna et al. [1] modelled the QoS information of candidate services by a multi-channel framework, and then utilized Mixed Integer Programming (MIP) to obtain the optimal solution. However, this method only performs well for small-scale problems, and the computing resource consumption may become prohibitive when faced with large-scale scenarios. Beauche et al. [2] used a hierarchical planning approach based on graph planning and hierarchical task networks to construct adaptive service composition. However, continuous emergence and demise of services lead to sustained search of viable services for updating the corresponding planning graph, which is not suitable for a highly dynamic environment. Jureta et al. [7] proposed a multi criteria-driven reinforcement learning algorithm to ensure that the system is responsive to the availability changes of Web services. We also [20] proposed an adaptive service composition approach based on reinforcement learning method combined with logic preference. Despite the effectiveness of conventional reinforcement learning in achieving adaptability, such methods can not ensure high efficiency in a large-scale and complex scenario.

As a subdiscipline of distributed artificial intelligence (DAI) [15], multi-agent techniques have arisen as a viable solution for modularity, more computing power, scalability and flexibility required by service composition [16]. Some researchers have already applied multi-agent techniques to service composition. Maamar et al. [11] proposed a web service composition method based on multi agents and context awareness. Gutierrez-Garcia et al. [5] characterized behavior of the services with Colored Petri-net, and exploited multi-agent techniques for services orchestration in the context of cloud computing. Unfortunately, those methods seldom take self-adaptivity into consideration.

In view of superiority from RL and multi-agent technologies, a natural idea to achieve self-adaptability in a dynamic environment and maintain acceptable efficiency when faced with massive candidate services is to combine them together, which has already been discussed in the field of DAI and is called Multi-agent reinforcement learning (MARL) [15]. On the one hand, RL is a commonly used machine learning method for planning and optimization in a dynamic environment [18], which learns by trial-and-error interaction with dynamic environment and thus has good self-adaptability. On the other hand, multi-agent technology can compensate for inefficiencies under large-scale and complex scenarios.

In this paper, we propose a new adaptive model that is built upon MARL. Different from previous work, this new model is based on team Markov Games, which is more mature and generic for service composition in a multi-agent scenario. To tackle the common problems of agent coordination and equilibrium selection emerged in a multi-agent environment, we introduce the coordination equilibrium and fictitious play process to ensure the agents to converge to a unique equilibrium when faced with multiple equilibriums. Finally, we have proposed the multi-agent Sarsa algorithm for our multi-agent service composition. Our contributions are summarized as follows:

- We introduce a *TMG-WSC* model for service composition with massive candidate services in a highly dynamic and complex environment.
- We propose a multi-agent Sarsa algorithm to adapt to the multi-agent service composition scenarios and achieve a better performance.
- We present the concept of multi-agent service composition that caters for the distributed environment and big data era.

The reminder of this paper is organized as follows. Section 2 compares our approach against some related works. Section 3 introduces the problem formulation and basic definitions. Section 4 presents our approach for service composition based on MARL. In section 5, some experimental results are presented for evaluating the proposed approach. Finally, the paper is concluded in Section 6.

2   Related Work

In this section, we review some existing works that are most relevant to our approach, including RL and agent techniques adopted in service composition.

Moustafa et al. [13] proposed a approach to facilitate the QoS-aware service composition problem using multi-objective reinforcement learning, but the method is not very efficient for large-scale service composition scenarios. Our prior work [20] suffer from the same issue with preceding method.

Xu et al. [22] proposed a multi-agent learning model for service composition, based on the Markov game and Q-learning with a hierarchical goal structure to accelerate the searching of states during the learning process. However, their model may not work well when faced with a complicated goal with more mutual dependencies between each sub-goals as their agents are fixed for certain service classes. We proposed a multi-agent learning model [19] based on MDP and knowledge sharing before, however this can not be regarded as a real multi-agent framework as the MDP is designed for a single agent and does not take the potential collaboration between agents into consideration.

MARL has strong connections with game theory [4], because the relation between agents has a great impact on the design of learning dynamics. According to Claus and Boutilier [4], the MARL can be classified into two forms. The first one is independent learners (ILs), which just apply RL methods (Q-learning, Sarsa etc.) and ignore the existence of other agents. The second one is joint action learners (JALs), which learn their actions in conjunction with others via integration of RL with a certain kind of Nash equilibrium, just like the coordination equilibrium [3,4]. Consequently, agents coordination and equilibrium selection are the key issue in MARL for JALs. Wang et al. [21] proposed an algorithm which can ensure to converge to an optimal equilibrium, but its high computational cost has limited its practical use.

In this paper, we integrate on-policy reinforcement learning with multi-agent techniques for services composition. The proposed approach is fundamentally different from existing approaches (e.g., [19,22]) as we exploit the coordination equilibrium and fictitious play process to ensure the agents to converge to a unique equilibrium. We also propose a multi-agent Sarsa algorithm to achieve an optimal or suboptimal solution.

3   Problem Formulation

Defnition 1 (Web Service). *A Web service is modeled as a pair WS=<*
$ID, QoS >$, where ID is the identifier of the Web service. QoS is a n-tuple
$< att_1, ..., att_n >$, where each $att_i(1 \leq i \leq n)$ denotes a QoS attribute value.

As we use Team Markov Games (TMG) to model multi-agent service composition, we first introduce the basis of TMG-based service composition, that is MDP (Markov Decision Process)-based service composition.

Defnition 2 (MDP-based web service composition (MDP-WSC)). *A*
MDP-WSC is a 6-tuple $MDP\text{-}WSC=< S, S_0, S_\tau, A(.), P, R >$, where S is a fi-
nite set of the world states; $S_0 \in S$ is the initial state from which an execution of
the service composition starts; $S_\tau \subset S$ is the set of terminal states, indicating an
end of composition execution when reaching one state $S_\tau^i \in S_\tau$; $A(s)$ represents
the set of services that can be executed in state $s \in S$; P is the probability distribu-
tion. When a web service α is invoked, the world makes a transition from its cur-
rent state s to a succeeding state s'. The probability for this transition is labeled
as $P(s'|s, \alpha)$. R is the immediate reward from the environment after executing
an action.

Fig.1 shows a MDP-WSC graph of a composite service for a vacation plan. It consists of two kinds of nodes, i.e., state nodes and service nodes, which are represented by open circles and solid circles, respectively. s_0 is the initial state node, and nodes with double circles are terminal state nodes, such as s_{10}. A state node can be followed by a number of invoked service nodes, labeled with the transition probability $P(s'|s, \alpha)$. A MDP-WSC transition graph can be created by using some automatic composition approaches, such as an AI planner [14].

With multiple agents in the environment, the fundamental problem of MDP is that the approach treats the other agents as a part of the environment and thus ignores the fact that the decisions of the other agents may influence the environment state. Then how can we extend the single-agent MDP model and adjust it for the multi-agent scenarios? One possible solution is to use the multi-agent Markov decision processes, i.e. Markov games [8].

Defnition 3 (Markov Games). *An n-player involved Markov games is mod-*
eled as a 5-tuple $MG=< a, S, A, T, R >$, where a is the set of agents; S is a
finite environment states set; A $(A_1 \times A_2 \times ... \times A_n)$ is the joint action, $A_i(i =
$1, ..., n$) is a discrete available action set of the ith agent; $T: S \times A \to \prod(S)$
is the transition function, giving for each state and one action from each agent.
A probability distribution $T(s, a_{1,...,}a_n, s')$ is the probability of state transition

from joint state s to s', and each agent $i(1 \le i \le n)$ choose action $a_i \in A_i$; $R_i : S \times A \to \Re$ is the ith agent's reward function, giving the immediate reward gained by the ith agent for each set of available actions.

Markov Games is so called team Markov Games when all agents strive for a common goal and thus share a common reward function. Here we adopt team Markov Games as all agents work for a common service workflow.

However, Markov Games can not directly replace the MDP model for multi-agent service composition, because some differences arises when trying to transfer some concepts in the MDP-WSC model [20] to the new multi-agent environment.

For example, in MDP-WSC, there is only one learning agent, which always starts from the initial state. If it finally reaches the terminal state, it can get a full path from the initial state to the terminal state according to its trajectory.

Unfortunately, it is much more complicated in the multi-agent scenario, as there are a group of learning agents and each one starts from one of the states randomly instead of a fixed initial state in MDP-WSC model. So even someone has reached one of the terminal states, we can not claim that they have completed current learning episode and got the full path, because this "lucky" one may not start from the initial state, and consequently what it has marched is just part of the whole path. In order to handle this problem, we need to introduce some new concepts to fit in the new multi-agent scenario.

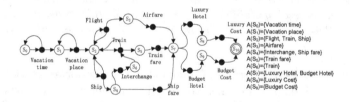

Fig. 1. The MDP-WSC of a Composite Service

Defnition 4 (Candidate   Initial   State).   *The   joint   state $\overline{S_0} = s_1 \times ... \times s_n(s_i, i = 1, ..., n$, is the state of the ith agent in the team) is a candidate initial state iff $s_i = s_0(1 \le i \le n)$, where s_0 is the initial state of the MDP-WSC transition graph.*

Suppose that a 3-agent group is wandering in Fig.1. If agent 1 starts from s_0, agent 2 starts from s_2, and agent 3 starts from s_5, the joint state $\overline{s} = s_0 \times s_2 \times s_5$ is a so-called Candidate Initial State, because it contains the initial state node s_0, which is the initial state in MDP-WSC transition graph. In contrast, a joint state $\overline{s} = s_1 \times s_2 \times s_5$ for Fig.1 can not be regarded as a candidate initial state, because it does not contain any initial state node. Since Candidate Initial State represents the starting points in the Multi-agent scenario, the question is what is the ending state. Hence we introduce the concept of Possible Terminal State.

Defnition 5 (Possible Terminal State). *The joint state $\overline{S_x} = s_1 \times ... \times s_n (s_i, i = 1, ..., n$, is the state of the ith agent) is a possible terminal state iff $s_i = s_\tau (1 \leq i \leq n)$, where s_τ is among terminal states of the MDP-WSC transition graph.*

More specifically, considering Fig. 1 in a 3-agent setting, where agent 1 starts from s_0, agent 2 starts from s_2, and agent 3 starts from s_9. After some steps, agent 3 may reach the terminal state node s_{10}, while agent 1 reaches s_1 and agent 2 reaches s_4. The joint state $\overline{s} = s_1 \times s_4 \times s_{10}$ at this time is obviously a possible terminal state. But it is not a true terminal state for the multi-agent environment, because the three sub-path $s_0 \to s_1$, $s_2 \to s_4$ and $s_9 \to s_{10}$ can not form a full path from the initial state s_0 to the terminal state s_{10}.

Defnition 6 (Passed State Set). *The set S_p is a passed state set iff S_p contains all the states that agents in the team have passed by.*

We can display a back trace from the terminal state and check whether it can stretch back to the initial state using the Passed State Set. Next, we will propose our multi-agent model called TMG-WSC for service composition, which is based on Team Markov Games (TMG) and new concepts mentioned before.

Defnition 7 (TMG-based Web Service Composition(TMG-WSC)). *A TMG-WSC is a 7-tuple=$< a, S, S_0, S_x, A, T, R >$, where a is the set of agents; S is the discrete set of environment states; S_0 is the set containing all the candidate initial state $\overline{S_0}$, and an execution of the composition starts from one state $\overline{S_0}^i \in S_0$; S_x is the set containing all the possible terminal state $\overline{S_x}$, and an execution of the composition has a possibility to terminate upon reaching any state in S_x; $A(\overline{s}) = A_1(s_1) \times A_2(s_2) \times ... \times A_n(s_n)$ is the finite set of joint actions that can be executed in joint state $\overline{s} \in S$, where $A_i(s_i)(i = 1, ..., n)$ is the discrete set of actions available to the ith agent at state S_i; $T:S \times A \times S \rightarrow [0, 1]$ is the transition probability function labeled as $P(\overline{s'} \mid \overline{s}, A(\overline{s}))$, giving for each joint state and each joint action; $R:S \times A \rightarrow \Re$ is the common reward function for all the agents in the team. When the set of services corresponding to the joint action are invoked and the environment has changed into the resulting state $\overline{s'}$, the team will receive an immediate reward $R(\overline{s'} \mid \overline{s}, A(\overline{s}))$ according to the feedback of this execution.*

A TMG-WSC can be visualized as a multi-dimensional transition network based on the MDP-WSC transition graph. Fig.2 shows a part of the TMG-WSC transition graph for vacation plan in a 3-agent scenario, which is constructed based on the MDP-WSC graph in Fig.1.

The solution to a TMG-WSC is a deterministic decision policy, which is defined as a procedure for service selection $ws \in A$ by all agents in every state s. These policies, represented by π, are actually mappings from states to actions, defined as $\pi : S \to A$.

Each deterministic policy can uniquely determine a workflow, and therefore the task of our service composition model is to identify the optimal policy or workflow that offers the best cumulative reward depending on QoS attributes.

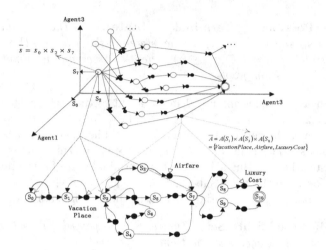

Fig. 2. A Part of the TMG-WSC of a Composite Service

4   Multi-agent On-policy Learning for Composition

The introduced TMG-WSC model allows engineers to integrate multiple alternative services into a single service composition. If the complete information of TMG-WSC is known, the theoretical optimal policy can always be calculated. However, this hypothesis is not true in practice. We may not have complete knowledge about the state transition functions and reward functions.

Moreover, both the state transition functions and the reward functions will change along the time, and the computational cost in a large-scale scenario will inevitably increase to an intolerable point. To solve the above issues, we propose an approach based on Multi-agent techniques and Sarsa algorithm in RL to learn the optimal policy of a TMG-WSC at runtime.

4.1   SARSA

Compared with off-policy learning methods like Q-learning, on-policy learning methods has an advantage in on-line performance, since the estimation policy, that is iteratively improved, is also the policy used to control its behavior [17].

Sarsa is a classic on-policy reinforcement learning method. The task of the learner in Sarsa is to learn a policy that maximizes the expected sum of reward. The cumulative reward starting from an arbitrary state s_t and following a policy π is defined as Eq.1, where r_{t+i} is the expected reward in each step, and γ is a discount factor.

$$V^{\pi}(s_t) = r_t + \gamma * r_{t+1} + \gamma^2 * r_{t+2} + ... = \sum_{i=0}^{\infty} \gamma^i * r_{t+i} \qquad (1)$$

Based on Eq.1, we can deduce the reward of action pair $< s_t, a_t >$, that is, the feedback of executing action a_t at state s_t, which is defined as Eq.2, where s_{t+1}

is the resulting state by executing a_t and $P(s_{t+1}|s_t, a_t)$ is the probability distribution, $r(s_t, a_t)$ represents the immediate reward of taking action a_t at state s_t, which is defined as Eq.3.

$$Q(s_t, a_t) = r(s_t, a_t) + \gamma * \sum_{s_{t+1}} P(s_{t+1}|s_t, a_t) * V^\pi(s_{t+1}) \tag{2}$$

$$r(s_t, a_t) = \sum_{i=1}^{m} w_i * \frac{Att_i^{a_t} - Att_i^{min}}{Att_i^{max} - Att_i^{min}} \tag{3}$$

In Eq.3, $Att_i^{a_t}$ represents the observed value of the ith attribute of the service corresponding to the executed action a_t, and Att_i^{max}, Att_i^{min} represent the maximum and minimum values of Att_i for all services. w_i is the weighting factor. w_i is positive if users prefer Att_i to be high (e.g. reliability). w_i is negative if preferring Att_i to be low (e.g. service fee). m is the number of QoS attributes.

The Q function represents the best possible cumulative reward of executing a_t at s_t. We can run dynamic programming (value iteration) by performing the Bellman back-ups in terms of the Q function as follows:

$$Q(s_t, a_t) = r(s_t, a_t) + \gamma * \sum_{s_{t+1}} P(s_{t+1}|s_t, a_t) * Q(s_{t+1}, a_{t+1}) \tag{4}$$

Further on, we rewrite this recursive formula in a stochastic version:

$$Q(s_t, a_t) \leftarrow (1 - \alpha) * Q(s_t, a_t) + \alpha * [r(s_t, a_t) + \gamma * Q(s_{t+1}, a_{t+1})] \tag{5}$$

$\alpha(0<\alpha<1)$ is the learning ratio, which is an important tuning factor in Sarsa. The stochastic version does not require a priori knowledge of the transition probability distribution P or the reward function R. Eq.5 forms the basis of the Sarsa algorithm, which starts with initial values of $Q(s_t, a_t)$, and updates $Q(s_t, a_t)$ recursively using the actual reward received.

More specifically, $Q(s_t, a_t)$ is initialized to 0 for all s_t and a_t at the beginning. Then, the learning process is performed recursively. The learner starts from the initial state s_0, and takes a sequence of actions following a Boltzmann policy (which is introduced subsequently) in each learning episode. $Q(s_t, a_t)$ is updated by the real feedback of next state-action pair$< s_{t+1}, a_{t+1} >$ rather than the maximum estimation value in Q-learning, which means that it is depending on the engine's on-line execution and performance. However, Eq.5 is just the single-agent version. To incorporating Sarsa with multi-agent techniques, we need to extend Eq.5 for multi-agent scenario.

We first define the reward function in multi-agent framework as follows, which aggregates the reward values of the services invoked by every agent. n is the number of agents, $\bar{s}_t$ is the current joint state, $\bar{a}_t$ is the joint action executed.

$$R(\bar{s}_t, \bar{a}_t) = \sum_{i=1}^{n} \sum_{j=1}^{m} w_{ij} * \frac{Att_{ij}^{\bar{a}_t} - Att_{ij}^{min}}{Att_{ij}^{max} - Att_{ij}^{min}} \tag{6}$$

Based on Eq.6, we can plug this and rewrite Eq.5 in a multi-agent form:

$$Q_{i_1,i_2...i_n}(\bar{s}_t, \bar{a}_t) \leftarrow (1-\alpha) * Q_{i_1,i_2...i_n}(\bar{s}_t, \bar{a}_t) + \alpha * [R(\bar{s}_t, \bar{a}_t) + \gamma * Q_{i_1,i_2...i_n}(\bar{s}_{t+1}, \bar{a}_{t+1})]$$
(7)

4.2   Equilibrium Coordination

For many Markov games, there is no policy that is un-dominated because the performance depends critically on the behavior of the other agents. Then, how can we define a deterministic optimal policy in this case? An natural idea from the game-theory literature is to define an agent's optimal behavior as being its behavior at a Nash equilibrium. Some researchers, like Littman, have already done such work in the field of MARL [6,9,10]. Here we adopt Littman's idea and give the definition of multi-agent optimal policy as follows:

$$\pi^*(s, a_1, ..., a_n) = \sum_{a_1,...,a_n} \pi_1(s, a_1) * ... * \pi_n(s, a_n) * Q(s, a_1, ..., a_n)$$

$$= \max_{a_1,...,a_n} Q(s, a_1, ..., a_n) \quad (8)$$

This definition is based on coordination equilibrium, which means all agents have precisely the same goal and achieve their maximum possible payoff in co-ordination team. It is obvious that the equilibrium of a team Markov game is a Coordination equilibrium as all the players involved strive for a common task.

In view of this, seeking the optimal policy in Team Markov games can be turned into an old question of optimizing the Q-value. To sum up, we can compute an optimal policy by just applying Sarsa in the multi-agent scenario.

However, another important open problem for Markov games is finding a general way of selecting an equilibrium when there exists multiple coordination equilibriums, which is very common in multi-agent scenario [21]. Here we use the indirect coordination methods to solve the problem, which places bias on action selection toward actions that are likely to result in good rewards.

An easy and well-understand indirect coordination method for equilibrium selection in game theory is fictitious play [12]. The key idea of fictitious play is estimating the empirical distribution of others' past actions and thus to help the agents figure out a best response until now. More specially, suppose that $C_{a_j}^j$ is the frequency of agent j invoking action a_j in the past, where a is the set of agents, each $j \in a$ and $a_j \in A_j$ (A_j represents the set of actions available to the jth agent). Then, agent i assumes agent j to play action a_j with the probability as Eq. 9. After each round of playing, agent i will update its $C_{a_j}^j$ according to the actions taken by the others in the last round. In a sense, $C_{a_j}^j$ reflects the beliefs an agent has given the historical choices of others.

$$\Pr_{a_j}^i = \frac{C_{a_j}^j}{\sum_{b_j \in A_j} C_{b_j}^j}$$
(9)

Dov Monderer gives the definition of Fictitious Play Property and also proves the following theorem in his work [12].

Defnition 8 (Fictitious Play Property). *A game has the fictitious play property (FPP) if every fictitious play process converges in beliefs to equilibrium.*

Theorem 1: Every game with identical payoff functions has the fictitious play property.   □

In view of Theorem 1, we can deduce that the team game where the agents have common interests has the fictitious play property. Hence, fictitious play process can be applied in the Team Markov Games and help to converge to a unique equilibrium surely despite the existence of multiple equilibriums.

To improve the efficiency of the fictitious play process, Young [23] proposed an optimized version and proved its validity. Based on it, we construct a new function that combines the Q-value and fictitious play process together for estimating cumulative reward of joint action in TMG-WSC. It is defined as follows, $\frac{K_t^m(A_j)}{k}$ is a probability model for agent i at the joint state $\overline{s}$, based on the fictitious play process. t is the number of times for attending state $\overline{s}$. a_i is the action chosen by the ith agent. m is the length of the queue which stores the reduced joint action $\overline{a_{-i}}$ of agent $i's$ opponents in chronological order. $\Psi(\overline{s}, \overline{a_{-i}})$ is the best response for agent $i's$ opponents' joint action at state $\overline{s}$.

$$WEQ(\overline{s}, a_i) = \sum_{\substack{A_j \in \Psi(\overline{s}, \overline{a_{-i}}) \\ 1 \leq j \leq n, j \neq i}} \frac{K_t^m(A_j)}{k} Q_{i,j}(\overline{s}) \tag{10}$$

Finally, we need a learning policy for the learner to execute the TMG-WSC during the learning. Here we choose the Boltzmann learning policy as it can better characterize our coordination mechanism and equilibrium selection technique. The Boltzmann exploration used here can be depicted as follows, T is temperature parameter, $T = T_0 * (0.999)^c$, T_0 is an initial value, c is the frequency that the learner is in state $\overline{s}_t$.

$$\Pr(\overline{a}_t | \overline{s}_t) = \frac{e^{WEQ(\overline{s}_t, \overline{a}_t)/T}}{\sum_{b \in A} e^{WEQ(\overline{s}_t, \overline{a}_t)/T}} \tag{11}$$

The complete learning process is depicted in Algorithm 1.

5   Simulation Results and Analysis

In this section, we conduct a simulation study to evaluate the properties of our service composition mechanism. We demonstrate the convergence and efficiency of multi-agent Sarsa algorithm. We also compare it with single-agent Sarsa and Q-learning, and analyze the corresponding inherent cause and effect.

Initialization:
$Q_{i1,i2,...,in}(\overline{s}_t, \overline{a}_t)$
repeat
// for each episode
each agent choose an action $a_i(i = 1, 2, ..., n)$ based on Eq.11,
and form the joint action $\overline{a}_t = a_1 \times a_2 \times \cdots \times a_n$;
repeat
// for each step of a episode
1. On-Policy Learning
take joint action $\overline{a}_t$, observe R, $\overline{s}_{t+1}$, each agent choose action a based on
Eq.11, and form the joint action $\overline{a}_{t+1} = a_1 \times a_2 \times \cdots \times a_n$
$Q(\overline{s}_t, \overline{a}_t) \longleftarrow (1 - \alpha) * Q(\overline{s}_t, \overline{a}_t) + \alpha * [R + \gamma * Q(\overline{s}_{t+1}, \overline{a}_{t+1})]$
$\overline{s}_t \longleftarrow \overline{s}_{t+1}$, $\overline{a}_t \longleftarrow \overline{a}_{t+1}$;
2.Terminal condition check
if $\overline{s}_t$ is a possible terminal state, $\overline{s}_t = s_1 \times s_2 \times ... \times s_n$ **then**
Create a set named $Temp$, $Temp = \{\overline{s}_t\}$,
Create a set named $Prev$, $Prev$ contains all the
previously passed states of any element in $Temp$
end if
while $S_p \cap Temp \neq \Phi$ and $s_0 \notin Prev$ **do**
$Temp \leftarrow S_p \cap Temp$
$Prev \leftarrow$ all the previous states of any element in $Temp$
end while
if $Prev$ contains S_0 **then**
This episode is ended
end if
until The current episode is ended
until the cumulative reward matrix converges

Algorithm 1. Multi-agent Sarsa based on TMG-WSC

5.1 Experiment Setting

We randomly generate MDP-WSC transition graphs and use them as the input for the TMG-WSC model, and four QoS attributes are mainly considered as an example for reward assessment, which are *ResponseTime*, *Throughput*, *Availability* and *Reliability* based on the extended QWS Dataset [1]. A number of key parameters are set up for both experiments as follows. The learning rate α of single-agent algorithm is set to 0.6, the discount factor γ is set to 0.9 and the $\epsilon - greedy$ exploration strategy value is set to 0.6. The experiments are conducted on an Intel i3-2120 3.30GHz PC with 4GB RAM.

5.2 Result Analysis

1. Effectiveness and Efficiency

The purpose of the first experiment is to examine the ability of the multi-agent Sarsa algorithm with Boltzmann exploration strategy (abbr. Multi-Sarsa).

---

[1] http://www.uoguelph.ca/~qmahmoud/qws/

We compare the Multi-Sarsa with single-agent Sarsa (abbr.Single-S) and single-agent Q-learning (abbr. Single-Q) in 4-agent scenario with 100 state nodes and 1000 services for each node. As shown in Fig.3 (a), the proposed Multi-Sarsa algorithm yields higher discounted cumulative rewards and efficiency than Single-S algorithm, and is closed to the convergence rate of Single-Q. For instance, Multi-Sarsa converges to the rewards at 17.2, that is higher than Single-S at 15.7. Furthermore, Multi-Sarsa converges at about the 4000th episode, which is closed to Single-Q at about the 3900th episode. However Single-S is slower for converging at about the 4500th episodes. Single-S achieves higher discounted cumulative rewards than Single-Q but performs worse in convergence rate.

Not surprisingly, in Eq.5, the use of a_{t+1} introduces additional variance into the update rule, which may slow convergence rate when compared to Single-Q. However, differing from off-policy Q-learning method, on-policy Sarsa approach has stronger convergence guarantees when combined with function approximation and it has a potential advantage over off-policy methods in its on-line performance. In the light of those characteristics, we propose the Multi-Sarsa algorithm to offset the convergence rate of Single-S by mutual collaboration between each agents and become closer to the optimal convergence simultaneously in which multiple agents explore the learning space adequately.

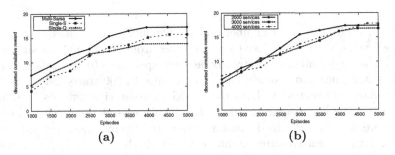

Fig. 3. (a) Effectiveness and Efficiency Comparison   (b) Different number of services

2. Scalability

The purpose of the second experiment set is to assess the scalability of the proposed Multi-Sarsa algorithm. We probe the influence of the service, state and agent number respectively.

Firstly, we vary the number of services for each state node from 2000 to 4000 while fixating the agents number for 4 and state nodes for 100. From Fig.3 (b), we know that the increasing number of candidate services for each state node may postpones the convergence. In 2000-service scenario, the Multi-Sarsa converges at about the 4200th episode, while converging at about the 4500th episode in 3000-service and about the 4700th episode in 4000-service. However, increasing the number of services does not necessarily mean the corresponding improvement of service quality, so the rewards may be higher or lower. In a word, Multi-Sarsa always converge at an acceptable time despite of vast candidate services.

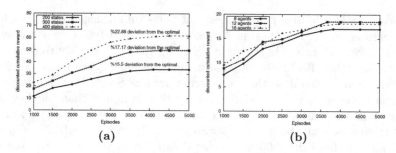

Fig. 4. (a) Different number of state nodes (b) Different number of agents

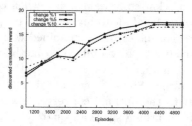

Fig. 5. Adaption Testing

Secondly, we fix the agent number and service number of each state node as 4 and 1000 respectively, and vary the state nodes from 200 to 400. As shown in Fig.4 (a), the bigger number of state nodes corresponds to higher values of the optimal convergence and a slower convergence rate. In 200-state-node scenario, the Multi-Sarsa converges at about the 4100th episode with rewards 33.8, and in 400-state-node, it converges at about the 4500th episode with rewards 61.7. What's more, we calculate the deviation of the current convergence rewards from the optimal convergence rewards in different scenarios by $D = \frac{OPR-CCR}{OPR}$, where D represents deviation degree, OPR indicates the optimal convergence rewards, and CCR is the current convergence rewards. It can be seen from Fig.4 (a), the D is %17.17 in 300 states nodes, and %22.88 in 400 scenario. That is to say, the increasing number of state nodes may aggravate the deviation from the optimality and fall into local optima. Hence, we can conclude that the Multi-Sarsa has the scalability when face with the increment of states nodes.

Finally, we come to the affect of agents number. We set the state nodes for 100, the services number for 1000 to each state node. From Fig.4 (b), we know that the more agents involved, the more adequate space exploration will be done, consequently the discount cumulative rewards is apparently bigger in scenario of 12 and 16 agents. However, the increasing number of agents brings another severe problem, that is, the communication consumption in the process of fictitious play. So, 16-agent does not perform better than 12-agent. In brief, 12-agent may be a compromise for Multi-Sarsa, the increasing number of agents does not necessarily leads to an improvement in efficiency, and the communication consumption between agents must be considered as an important factor.

To sum up, the Multi-Sarsa algorithm can be applied to large-scale service composition scenarios with good scalability.

3. Adaptivity

To simulate the dynamic environment, we randomly change the QoS values of candidate services during the learning process. In order to facilitate comparison, we fixate the number of agent for 4, state nodes for 100, and 1000 services for each node. We also cause QoS fluctuations between the 2000th episode and the 2500th episode. What's more, we allocated the sum of changed QoS values to each candidate services group of each state node averagely. Fig.5 gives clear illustration, no matter how big the volatility of QoS is, the Multi-Sarsa algorithm can converge by learning deterministically, and merely differentiates in convergence time. In short, the changes do not stop the optimization process, and the execution polices are still being optimized when the learning process goes on.

In conclusion, Multi-Sarsa does a good performance in large-scale and highly dynamic environment.

6 Conclusions and Future Directions

In this paper[2], we integrate on-policy reinforcement learning with multi-agent techniques for large-scale and adaptive service composition. First, we propose the new composition model called TMG-WSC, then utilize Multi-Sarsa algorithm in multi-agent scenario to find the optimal solution which is extended from single-agent Sarsa. Additionally, to ensure the convergence of the Multi-Sarsa algorithm, we introduce the fictitious play process which assures the unique equilibrium for equilibrium selection and incorporate it with the Boltzmann learning policy. Our experiments demonstrate that the proposed Multi-Sarsa performs well for large-scale and dynamic service composition.

However, we still have some room for optimizing the proposed framework. Firstly, we do not address the problem of failure services that may lead to entire paralysis of the composition solution. Therefore, reliability prediction or fault-tolerant technologies should be taken into the consideration. Secondly, we just consider the local QoS constraints, while users may only give a global QoS constraints, so how to decompose the global QoS constraints to the local is also a tough challenge. All in all, we will pay more efforts to optimize this framework.

References

1. Ardagna, D., Pernici, B.: Adaptive service composition in flexible processes. IEEE Transactions on Software Engineering 33(6), 369–384 (2007)
2. Beauche, S., Poizat, P.: Automated service composition with adaptive planning. In: Bouguettaya, A., Krueger, I., Margaria, T. (eds.) ICSOC 2008. LNCS, vol. 5364, pp. 530–537. Springer, Heidelberg (2008)

[2] This work is partially supported by NSFC Key Project (No.61232007) and Doctoral Fund of Ministry of Education of China (No.20120092110028).

3. Busoniu, L., Babuska, R., De Schutter, B.: A comprehensive survey of multiagent reinforcement learning. IEEE Transactions on Systems, Man, and Cybernetics, Part C: Applications and Reviews 38(2), 156–172 (2008)
4. Claus, C., Boutilier, C.: The dynamics of reinforcement learning in cooperative multiagent systems. In: AAAI/IAAI, pp. 746–752 (1998)
5. Gutierrez-Garcia, J.O., Sim, K.-M.: Agent-based service composition in cloud computing. In: Kim, T.-h., Yau, S.S., Gervasi, O., Kang, B.-H., Stoica, A., Ślęzak, D. (eds.) GDC and CA 2010. CCIS, vol. 121, pp. 1–10. Springer, Heidelberg (2010)
6. Hu, J., Wellman, M.P.: Multiagent reinforcement learning: theoretical framework and an algorithm. In: ICML, vol. 98, pp. 242–250. Citeseer (1998)
7. Jureta, I.J., Faulkner, S., Achbany, Y., Saerens, M.: Dynamic web service composition within a service-oriented architecture. In: IEEE International Conference on Web Services, ICWS 2007, pp. 304–311. IEEE (2007)
8. Könönen, V.: Asymmetric multiagent reinforcement learning. Web Intelligence and Agent Systems 2(2), 105–121 (2004)
9. Littman, M.L.: Markov games as a framework for multi-agent reinforcement learning. In: ICML, vol. 94, pp. 157–163 (1994)
10. Littman, M.L.: Value-function reinforcement learning in markov games. Cognitive Systems Research 2(1), 55–66 (2001)
11. Maamar, Z., Mostefaoui, S.K., Yahyaoui, H.: Toward an agent-based and context-oriented approach for web services composition. IEEE Transactions on Knowledge and Data Engineering 17(5), 686–697 (2005)
12. Monderer, D., Shapley, L.S.: Fictitious play property for games with identical interests. Journal of Economic Theory 68(1), 258 (1996)
13. Moustafa, A., Zhang, M.: Multi-objective service composition using reinforcement learning. In: Basu, S., Pautasso, C., Zhang, L., Fu, X. (eds.) ICSOC 2013. LNCS, vol. 8274, pp. 298–312. Springer, Heidelberg (2013)
14. Oh, S.C., Lee, D., Kumara, S.R.: Effective web service composition in diverse and large-scale service networks. IEEE Transactions on Services Computing 1(1), 15–32 (2008)
15. Panait, L., Luke, S.: Cooperative multi-agent learning: The state of the art. In: Proceedings of 2005 Autonomous Agents and Multi-Agent Systems(AAMAS), vol. 11(3), pp. 387–434 (November 2005)
16. Papadopoulos, P., Tianfield, H., Moffat, D., Barrie, P.: Decentralized multi-agent service composition. Multiagent and Grid Systems 9(1), 45–100 (2013)
17. Rummery, G.A., Niranjan, M.: On-line Q-learning using connectionist systems. University of Cambridge, Department of Engineering (1994)
18. Sutton, R.S., Barto, A.G.: Reinforcement learning: An introduction, vol. 1. Cambridge Univ. Press (1998)
19. Wang, H., Wang, X.: A novel approach to large-scale services composition. In: Ishikawa, Y., Li, J., Wang, W., Zhang, R., Zhang, W. (eds.) APWeb 2013. LNCS, vol. 7808, pp. 220–227. Springer, Heidelberg (2013)
20. Wang, H., Zhou, X., Zhou, X., Liu, W., Li, W., Bouguettaya, A.: Adaptive service composition based on reinforcement learning. In: Maglio, P.P., Weske, M., Yang, J., Fantinato, M. (eds.) ICSOC 2010. LNCS, vol. 6470, pp. 92–107. Springer, Heidelberg (2010)
21. Wang, X., Sandholm, T.: Reinforcement learning to play an optimal nash equilibrium in team markov games. In: NIPS, vol. 15, pp. 1571–1578 (2002)
22. Xu, W., Cao, J., Zhao, H., Wang, L.: A multi-agent learning model for service composition. In: 2012 IEEE Asia-Pacific Services Computing Conference (APSCC), pp. 70–75. IEEE (2012)
23. Young, H.P.: The evolution of conventions. Econometrica 61(1), 57–84 (1993)

An Agent-Based Service Marketplace for Dynamic and Unreliable Settings

Lina Barakat, Samhar Mahmoud, Simon Miles, Adel Taweel, and Michael Luck

Department of Informatics, King's College London, London, UK
{firstname.surename}@kcl.ac.uk

Abstract. In order to address the unreliable nature of service providers, and the dynamic nature of services (their quality values could change frequently over time due to various factors), this paper proposes a probabilistic, multi-valued quality model for services, capable of capturing uncertainty in their quality values by assigning each quality attribute with multiple potential values (or ranges of values), along with a corresponding probability distribution over these values. The probability distribution indicates the most likely quality value for an attribute at the current time step, but also notifies discovery applications of the possibility of other, possibly worse outcomes, thus ultimately facilitating more reliable service selection and composition via avoiding services with high uncertainty. Such uncertainty-aware, multi-valued quality models of services are maintained via an agent-based service marketplace, where each service is associated with a software agent, capable of learning the time-varying probability distributions of its quality values through applying online learning techniques, based on the service's past performance information. The experiments conducted demonstrate the effectiveness of the proposed approach.

Keywords: quality of service, probabilistic quality model, adaptive learning, dynamic environment, agent based marketplace.

1 Introduction

Service-oriented computing (SOC) is a promising paradigm for the sharing of resources and functionalities in open, distributed environments (e.g., the web and computational Grids). Via exposing such resources and functionalities as *services* [1], and utilising these services as elementary building blocks, this paradigm supports the rapid and economic development of complex, interoperable distributed applications.

Open distributed service-based systems, however, usually exhibit high degrees of dynamism and uncertainty for several reasons, either intentional or unintentional. For example, service providers, being autonomous and self-interested, may choose to act maliciously and announce false quality of service (QoS) capabilities in order to increase their own profit by attracting more customers. Even in cases where the providers are fully cooperative, it might be difficult (or simply

X. Franch et al. (Eds.): ICSOC 2014, LNCS 8831, pp. 169–183, 2014.

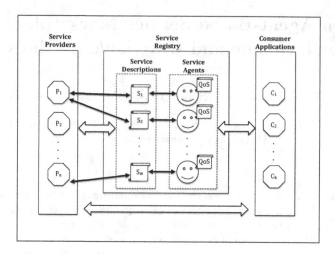

Fig. 1. Agent-augmented service marketplace architecture

not possible) to guarantee specific quality values for a service, because of their dependency on various run-time factors. For instance, the service response time at any particular moment could be significantly affected by the provider load and network traffic at that moment. Such dynamism and uncertainty can lead to highly undesirable situations during service execution (e.g. unfulfilled quality promises), and may demand costly corrective actions.

Consequently, as an attempt to minimise quality deviations of services at execution time, a number of efforts focus on providing more accurate estimation of service quality values, based on the available information regarding their past performance [9–13]. Specifically, assessing a quality attribute for a service is typically performed by applying some aggregation measure (e.g. a time-weighted average) to the previously observed values, which are obtained as feedback from service users, or from service-side monitors. Such a *single-valued* quality estimation model, however, does not capture the uncertainty in the service's quality values, and might produce inaccurate or invalid quality predictions, especially for attributes with high variance in values. For example, assume the values encountered in the past regarding the learning time attribute of a knowledge service are 10, 10, 10, 60, 60, 60 (minutes). Estimating the mean of these values would produce an expected value of 35 minutes, an imprecise indication of the attribute's actual outcome. Moreover, such a model is only limited to quantitative attributes, without the ability to accommodate qualitative cases.

In response, this paper proposes a probabilistic *multi-valued* quality estimation model, applicable to both numeric and categorical attributes. It captures uncertainty in quality values by augmenting these values with reliability scores, allowing more informative reasoning about the various potential quality outcomes of a service, thus enabling more reliable and proactive service selection. The responsibility of instantiating such quality models for services is distributed among a number of learning-enabled software agents, applying online learning techniques to update the models on the availability of new service performance samples, without requiring storage of or iteration over all previous data.

The paper is organised as follows. The proposed agent-based service marketplace is introduced in Section 2. Section 3 and Section 4 present the basic (single-valued) service QoS model [7] and the proposed reliability-aware (multivalued) extension, respectively. Section 5 provides the online quality learning algorithm, while Section 6 evaluates its effectiveness through experimental results. Section 7 discusses related work, and Section 8 concludes the paper.

2 Agent-Augmented Service Marketplace

A basic service marketplace, adopting the classic service-oriented architecture, provides support for the publication, description, discovery, and invocation of services, and involves interaction among three roles, the service provider, service consumer, and service registry. Specifically, a service provider describes its service using a standard format, and publishes this description in a public service registry so that the service can be discovered by potential clients. A service consumer searches the service registry to find a required service, and retrieve its binding details, which are then utilised to locate and invoke the service. Note that such a consumer could be an end-user application, a matchmaker agent (returning services that meet specific criteria), or a service composition engine (aggregating the functionalities of existing services into more sophisticated composite applications in order to fulfil particular high-level goals).

In addition to functional specification, service descriptions could also reference the quality of service (QoS) characteristics of services, indicating their non-functional capabilities. These attributes can be generic, such as price and response time, or domain-dependent, representing specific features and metrics of a particular domain. The QoS characteristics play an important role in differentiating between functionally equivalent services (those overlapping in their functional capabilities, but possibly varying in their QoS levels), and accommodating the different expectations of users (individuals or organisations). Yet, as stated earlier, the features advertised by service providers are not necessarily reliable, due to the untrustworthiness of these providers, and the dynamic nature of service environments, causing the quality values of services to deviate over time as a result of various environmental factors (which might be difficult to anticipate by providers). This could result in unfulfilled quality promises by services, and consequently a number of negative effects on the applications utilising these services, including unsatisfied users, money loss, or interruption in application execution while performing recovery re-planning.

To address this, we propose an extended service registry (see Figure 1), facilitating more reliable and self-adaptive service descriptions via the utilisation of software agents, capable of learning the actual QoS characteristics of services, and adapting their descriptions according to changes. Specifically, a *learning-enabled service agent* resides between a service description published by a provider and any discovery application, and exposes reliability and dynamism aware QoS information of the service to the latter by learning such information based on collected service ratings after each interaction with the service. The ratings can be collected either directly from consumers via feedback interfaces, or automatically via appropriate monitors residing at the service side or over the network. Note that we assume in this paper that the ratings are honest and objective (false ratings can be handled through appropriate filtering and reputation mechanisms [15], but this is out of the scope of this paper).

In what follows, we first outline the traditional QoS model of services (the model corresponding to provider advertisements), and then focus on modelling the service agent, including an improved QoS model, augmenting the traditional model with reliability information, and a learning algorithm.

3 Basic QoS Model

The QoS model of a service registered within a marketplace can be defined as a tuple, $(AN, dom, type, value)$, as detailed below.

AN is the set of quality attributes that characterise the service. For example, $AN = \{\text{price}, \text{response time}, ...\}$.

$dom : AN \rightarrow 2^{AV}$ is an attribute domain function, which maps each quality attribute to its corresponding domain (the possible values of this attribute), where AV is the set of all possible quality attribute values (the union of the domains of all quality attributes). For example, $dom(\text{price}) = \mathbb{R}^+$.

$type : AN \rightarrow \{\text{CTG}, \text{DSC}, \text{CNT}\}$ is an attribute type function, which indicates whether the domain of a quality attribute is categorical (CTG), numeric and discrete (DSC), or numeric and continuous (CNT). For example, $type(\text{price}) = \text{CNT}$.

Finally, $value : AN \rightarrow AV \cup \{\text{undefined}\}$ is an attribute value function, which provides the value offered by the service for each quality attribute, such that $\forall a \in AN$, $value(a) \in dom(a) \cup \{\text{undefined}\}$. For example, $value(\text{price}) = 10$.

Generally, the QoS information of a service can be directly published into public service registries by the service provider, assessed from monitoring previous service performance by specialised proxies, or negotiated with the provider in terms of service level agreements (SLAs).

4 Uncertainty-Aware QoS Model

In order to capture uncertainty in the values that a service might deliver for the quality attributes at a particular time step $t \in T$, the service agent utilises a time-dependent, probabilistic model for describing the QoS features of the service. Specifically, each quality attribute is considered to be a random variable, and is associated with a probability distribution indicating the likelihood of each of its possible values at the current moment. Hence, to reflect this, the static single-valued attribute value function of the basic service model is modified by the service agent, as follows:

$$value_{ag} : AN \times T \rightarrow PROB$$

such that $\forall a \in AN$, $\forall t \in T$, $value_{ag}(a,t) = P(a,t)$ is the probability distribution over the possible outcomes of attribute a at time step t (with $PROB$ denoting the set of all possible probability distributions P). That is,

$$value_{ag}(a,t) = P(a,t) = \{p(a,v,t) \mid v \in dom^d(a)\}$$

with

$$\forall v \in dom^d(a),\ p(a,v,t) \in [0,1]\ \wedge \sum_{v \in dom^d(a)} p(a,v,t) = 1 \tag{1}$$

where $p(a,v,t)$ is the likelihood of attribute a to take on value v at time step t, and $dom^d(a)$ is the discretised domain of attribute a. For categorical and discrete attributes, $a \in AN$ s.t. $type(a) \in \{CTG, DSC\}$, domain $dom^d(a)$ corresponds to the original value space, i.e. $dom^d(a) = dom(a)$. For continuous attributes, $a \in AN$ s.t. $type(a) = CNT$, domain $dom^d(a)$ is obtained via applying an appropriate discretisation algorithm on the original value space $dom(a)$ (a simple example is dividing $dom(a)$ into a number of equal ranges, with values $v \in dom^d(a)$ corresponding to the respective range representatives).

Such a probabilistic, multi-valued modelling of service quality features exposes more accurate and comprehensive details regarding the expected behaviour of the service, facilitating more informative and reliable service selection and accommodating the different needs of discovery applications, as opposed to the single-valued approach, where the discovery application is limited to a single, possibly inaccurate, summary attribute value. In particular, while general indications of the quality features may be sufficient for some discovery applications, others, performing more critical tasks, might favour accounting for the worst case scenario (i.e. selecting services by analysing the least desirable quality values that are probable in their cases). Note that, in the proposed approach, the expected (average) value for a numeric attribute a at time step t, $exp(a,t)$, can be easily derived from probability distribution $P(a,t)$, as follows:

$$exp(a,t) = \sum_{v \in dom^d(a)} v \times p(a,v,t)$$

Example. Consider a content provider, in the e-learning domain, offering a learning object (service) characterised by three quality properties, learning time (LT), difficulty level (DL), and interactivity type (IT), with:

$$type(LT) = CNT\ \wedge\ dom(LT) = [10,60]$$
$$type(DL) = DSC\ \wedge\ dom(DL) = \{1,2,3,4,5\}$$
$$type(IT) = CTG\ \wedge\ dom(IT) = \{active, expositive, mixed\}$$

Figure 2 shows example probabilistic value models for the learning object regarding the three quality properties, illustrating various uncertainty levels at time step t, with the highest uncertainty in value corresponding to attribute DL, where $p(DL,v,t) = 0.2$ for all values $v \in \{1,2,3,4,5\}$.

Note that learning objects meet the conditions of our generic service definition, since they are self-contained, reusable units of instruction, which are made

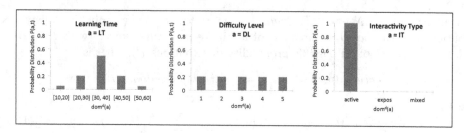

Fig. 2. Probabilistic attribute value function $value_{ag}(a, t)$ for a learning object

available for discovery through dedicated repositories, where their properties are
described using a standard language (e.g. IEEE LOM[1]).

5 Learning Model

The learning problem of the service agent concerns devising a reliable QoS description for the service in the presence of uncertainty in the environment, where
service providers might be untrustworthy, and may change their QoS policies
without notification, either intentionally or unintentionally. Such learning is conducted by observing the behaviour of the service over time, and adapting its
description accordingly. Specifically, the cycle of the service agent involves the
following three steps.

(1) *Observe.* The agent receives new ratings for the service at time step t (e.g.
user feedback after interaction with the service). Let $obs(t) = \{(a, rating(a, t)) \mid a \in AN\}$ denotes such ratings, where function $rating(a, t) \in dom^d(a)$ maps
quality attribute a of the service to the value observed for a at time step t.

(2) *Learn.* The agent utilises the new observation history to update the probability distributions of the quality values of the service, so that the service behaviour is more accurately described for future selection. In other words,

$$value_{ag}(a, t) = P(a, t) = qoslearn(a, OBS_t) \tag{2}$$

where $OBS_t = \{obs(i)\}_{i=1}^{t}$ are the past observations of the service up to time t,
and function $qoslearn$ corresponds to the agent's learning algorithm.

(3) *Expose.* The agent makes the probability distributions, $value_{ag}(a, t)$, of
the service's quality attributes $a \in AN$, available to discovery applications as
the best generalisation of the behaviour of the service at time step t.

Next, we define the properties that need to be satisfied by the learning function
$qoslearn$, followed by a learning algorithm achieving these properties.

5.1 Learner Requirements

Two desirable properties can be identified for a QoS learning algorithm: adaptivity and efficiency.

---

[1] http://ltsc.ieee.org/wg12/

Adaptivity refers to the ability of the learning algorithm to incorporate evolving data over time. It is required in the context of both stationary and non-stationary environments.

In a stationary environment, the underlying probability distributions of the service's quality values remain constant over time, but might not be known in advance due to missing, inaccurate, or untrustworthy QoS descriptions from providers. Hence, since observations of the service's actual behaviour only arrive incrementally (are not available at once), the learning algorithm should be able to increase the accuracy of the predicted quality model with more incoming data.

In a non-stationary environment, the probability distributions of quality values may experience changes over time, and therefore the learning algorithm should be able to accommodate these changes on their occurrence. Generally, probability distribution drifts may follow various patterns. A drift might occur *abruptly*, by suddenly switching from one probability distribution to another at some time step. Examples of such a drift include a significant degradation in a service's availability due to an unexpected network problem, or modification of service characteristics caused by an implementation change (e.g. additional content is added to the learning object, correspondingly affecting its learning time, difficulty level, etc). Alternatively, a drift may happen *gradually*, with the probability distribution exhibiting smaller differences over a longer time period. Examples of such a drift include a slow deterioration or improvement in a service's response time with increasing or decreasing load, respectively, during the day, or a gradual performance degradation of a hardware service due to wearing out with time.

Efficiency refers to the ability of the learning algorithm to operate in a timely and memory-effective manner. Specifically, since the learning is conducted at run time, i.e. while the service is in operation, sensitivity towards time limits becomes a critical feature to ensure that the learning cycle terminates, and consequently the QoS descriptions of the service are updated, prior to the next discovery attempt by a service consumer. Moreover, with the potentially continuous and long-lasting data input (for the duration of service operation), memory consumption is a major concern, and maintaining access to the whole set of past service data is very costly. In the most efficient form (both in terms of memory and processing time), data is discarded once the service's QoS model is updated upon data arrival, with the update being performed using the latest version of the model. That is, function *qoslearn* in Equation 2 should be modified as follows:

$$value_{ag}(a, t) = P(a, t) = qoslearn(a, obs(t), P(a, t-1)) \qquad (3)$$

5.2 Learning Algorithm

For the purpose of instantiating the QoS learning function *qoslearn*, the service agent utilises an algorithm inspired by Policy Hill-Climbing [2], a rational learning algorithm for finding a policy that maximises an accumulative reward perceived from the environment. The idea of the proposed algorithm is as follows. At each learning cycle $t \in T$, and for each quality attribute of the service

---

Algorithm 1. Learning model of a service agent

---

1. Initialise the learning rate δ

2. $\forall a \in AN$, initialise $value_{ag}(a, t_0)$ according to the basic QoS model of the service:

2.1. if $value(a) \neq$ undefined **then**

$$\forall v \in dom^d(a), \quad p(a, v, t_0) = 1 \quad \text{if} \quad v \text{ corresponds to } value(a)$$
$$p(a, v, t_0) = 0 \quad \text{otherwise}$$

2.2. else

$$\forall v \in dom^d(a), \quad p(a, v, t_0) = \frac{1}{|dom^d(a)|}$$

3. Repeat

    3.1. Observe the behaviour of the service, $obs(t) = \{(a, rating(a, t)) \mid a \in AN\}$

    3.2. Learn more accurate QoS policy, $value_{ag}(a, t)$, for each attribute $a \in AN$:

$$\forall v \in dom^d(a), \quad p(a, v, t) = (1 - \delta)p(a, v, t - 1) + \delta \quad \text{if} \quad v = rating(a, t)$$
$$p(a, v, t) = (1 - \delta)p(a, v, t - 1) \quad \text{otherwise}$$

    3.3. Expose $value_{ag}(a, t)$ to discovery applications

$a \in AN$, the currently maintained QoS policy $value_{ag}(a, t - 1)$ is improved according to a learning rate $\delta \in [0, 1]$, increasing the probability of the value with the highest utility (i.e. the value $v \in dom^d(a)$ observed for attribute a) at iteration t. The overall learning model of the service agent is illustrated in Algorithm 1, with the QoS policy re-evaluation rule (i.e. function $qoslearn$) being detailed at Line 3.2. It is easy to see that this rule keeps $value_{ag}(a, t)$ constrained to a legal probability distribution, i.e it satisfies Equation 1.

The agent initialises the QoS policy of each attribute a, $value_{ag}(a, t_0)$, according to provider advertisements, assigning a probability of 1 to the value indicated by the provider (Line 2.1 of Algorithm 1). In the case where an attribute is not instantiated by the provider, equal probabilities are initially assigned to all its possible values (Line 2.2 of Algorithm 1).

The QoS policy adjustment rule clearly satisfies Equation 3, thus fulfilling the *efficiency* requirement, while the choice of the learning factor δ governs the *adaptivity* property. Specifically, factor δ determines the rate at which the past data is forgotten, allowing a gradual discount of the impact of previous information and enabling responsiveness to more recent observations. As δ tends to unity, function $qoslearn$ becomes a greedy function, removing the impact of all previous data up to step $t - 1$, and accounting only for the latest observation. In contrast, lowering the value of δ decreases responsiveness to new data. Also, when factor δ is set to $\frac{1}{t}$ for each learning step t, all old and present observations are considered equally important. That is, in such a case, function $qoslearn$ is equivalent to simply deriving value probabilities from the frequencies of value occurrences over the entire set of observations up to time t, as illustrated below:

$$p(a, v, t) = \frac{\sum_{i=1}^{t} occur(a, v, i)}{t} = \frac{\sum_{i=1}^{t-1} occur(a, v, i) + occur(a, v, t)}{t}$$

$$= (\frac{t-1}{t})p(a, v, t-1) + (\frac{1}{t})occur(a, v, t)$$

where $occur(a, v, i) = 1$ if value v was observed for attribute a at time step i (i.e. $rating(a, i) = v$), and $occur(a, v, i) = 0$, otherwise. Further analysis of the effect of different values for factor δ is provided in Section 6.

6   Experiments and Results

In this section, we present an empirical evaluation of the proposed QoS learning framework, focusing on its performance in terms of producing reliable QoS estimates for services, in marketplaces of varying dynamism and uncertainty. The experiments are conducted on simulated datasets, allowing us to control the QoS policies of providers and their changes, thus facilitating evaluation under different settings.

A simulation run consists of a number of learning episodes (or cycles). At each episode t, the service provider delivers particular values for quality attributes $a \in AN$, which are observed by the service agent as ratings $rating(a, t)$. The generation of these quality values (i.e. the evaluation dataset) is governed by probability distributions $value_{prov}(a, t)$, representing the provider's actual QoS policy for each attribute a at time step t. Table 1 shows two distributions utilised in our experiments for specifying such policies: distribution Q_1 producing a fixed value v_i for attribute a, and normal distribution Q_2 over the possible values. Note that all the results reported are averaged over 100 simulation runs, and among different attribute types (i.e. categorical, discrete, and continuous). For simplicity, we only show the results from the perspective of one service and one quality attribute (other attributes and services exhibit similar trends).

Next, we first outline the strategies to be evaluated (Section 6.1) and the evaluation measure to be utilised (Section 6.2), followed by experimental results (Sections 6.3-6.4) and an overall result summary (Section 6.5).

6.1   Learning Strategies

Throughout the presentation of our experimental results, we refer to the following learning strategies.

Slide Window_w: this is the sliding window learning strategy, a well known way of adapting to potential changes in incoming data and accommodating memory constraints [17]. It is adopted as a memory-based alternative for the purpose of estimating our model, as follows. At each time step, $value_{ag}(a, t)$ is rebuilt on a data window of size w storing the most recent w observations, according to the proportional frequencies of values in this window. Note that, by *Slide Window_all*,

Table 1. Generative models of the provider's actual QoS values

$value_{prov}(a,t)$	Definition	Attribute Type
$Q_1(a,t)$	$q(a,v,t) = \begin{cases} 1 & \text{if } v = v_i \\ 0 & \text{if } v \in dom^d(a) \setminus \{v_i\} \end{cases}$ s.t. $v_i \in dom^d(a)$	$type(a) \in \{\text{CTG}, \text{DSC}\}$
$Q_2(a,t)$	Normal distribution over $dom(a)$, with mean μ and variance σ^2, s.t. $$q(a,v,t) = \frac{1}{\sigma\sqrt{2\pi}} \int_a^b e^{-\frac{(x-\mu)^2}{2\sigma^2}} dx$$ where $v \in dom^d(a)$ corresponds to range $[a,b]$ in $dom(a)$	$type(a) = \text{CNT}$

we refer to re-building the model using *all* the data observed so far, which is utilised as a baseline in our evaluation.

QoSLearn_δ: this is the learning strategy proposed in this paper, utilising a learning rate δ, with no memory requirement.

6.2 Evaluation Measure

In order to assess the reliability of the QoS model estimated by the service agent, we need to compare such a model against the actual QoS model of the provider. In other words, we are interested in quantifying the difference between the agent's estimated probability distribution, $value_{ag}(a,t) = P(a,t)$, and the provider's actual probability distribution, $value_{prov}(a,t) = Q(a,t)$, over the values of attribute a, at any time step t. For this purpose, we adopt the Hellinger Distance measure [3], which computes the distance, denoted $h(P,Q)$, between probability distribution $P(a,t) = \{p(a,v,t) \mid v \in dom^d(a)\}$, and probability distribution $Q(a,t) = \{q(a,v,t) \mid v \in dom^d(a)\}$, as follows:

$$h(P,Q) = \sqrt{\frac{1}{2} \sum_{v \in dom^d(a)} (\sqrt{p(a,v,t)} - \sqrt{q(a,v,t)})^2} \in [0, \sqrt{2}]$$

When $h(P,Q) = 0$, probability distributions P and Q are identical, whereas $h(P,Q) = \sqrt{2}$ corresponds to the maximum divergence between P and Q. Note that the Hellinger Distance measure is symmetric, i.e. $h(P,Q) = h(Q,P)$. Other probability distribution distances, e.g. the earth mover's distance (EMD), could also be utilised here.

6.3 Stationary Marketplace

In a stationary environment, the QoS policy of the service provider for attribute a remains static over time. Such an environment is simulated by generating

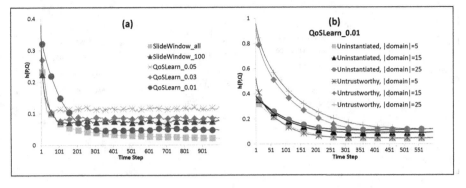

Fig. 3. Evaluation results in a stationary environment

the observations $rating(a, t)$, for all the time steps t, according to the same probability distribution $value_{prov}(a, t_0) = Q(a, t_0)$, s.t. $\forall t$, $Q(a, t) = Q(a, t_0)$ (i.e. value v_i and mean μ for distributions Q_1 and Q_2, respectively, remain fixed for all time steps). Here, we are interested in testing the ability of the proposed approach to learn probability distribution $Q(a, t_0)$, in the following two settings: *Untrustworthy Provider*, where the provider acts maliciously and advertises false capability $value(a)$ for attribute a, i.e. $value(a)$ does not correspond to v_i in the case of actual distribution Q_1 (see Table 1), and $value(a)$ differs significantly from μ in the case of actual distribution Q_2 (see Table 1); and *Uninstantiated Attribute*, where no performance indication regarding attribute a is available by the provider, i.e. $value(a) = $ undefined.

Figure 3(a) reports the results of the considered learning strategies. As expected, *Slide Window_all* is the best performing strategy, with smaller window sizes achieving lower accuracy due to excluding relevant observations (all observations remain relevant in a static environment). By setting the learning rate δ to a small value of 0.01, the proposed learning strategy, *QoSLearn_0.01*, keeps the effect of older observations without necessitating their storage, and manages to approximate the performance of *Slide Window_all*. However, such a small learning rate causes slower learning at the beginning, achieving an accuracy of about 0.2 only after 60 observations, compared to *Slide Window_all* that achieves similar accuracy after just 15 observations. This initial learning period is further highlighted in Figure 3(b), distinguishing the two cases of *Untrustworthy Provider* and *Uninstantiated Attribute*, and varying the size of the attribute's domain dom^d. As can be seen, the effect of misleading providers generally takes longer to overcome, especially for a larger domain size, requiring a larger number of samples to accurately learn the actual underlying distribution.

6.4 Non-stationary Marketplace

In a non-stationary environment, the QoS policy of the service provider for attribute a changes over time. Two cases are distinguished depending on the change type, as detailed below.

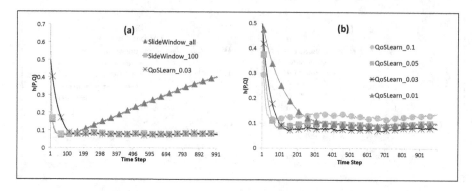

Fig. 4. Evaluation results in a dynamic environment (gradual change)

Gradual Change. Here, the generative model of the quality observations, $value_{prov}(a, t) = Q(a, t)$, changes slowly at each time step. For distribution Q_1, this is simulated by slightly decreasing the probability of value v_i, and correspondingly increasing the probability of another value $v_j \in dom^d(a) \setminus \{v_i\}$. For distribution Q_2, this is achieved by a slight repositioning of the mean μ.

Figure 4(a) shows the corresponding results of the considered learning strategies. As can be seen, the performance of *SlideWindow_all* slowly deteriorates with time as older observations become less relevant. Better prediction accuracy is obtained when the outdated data is gradually forgotten, favouring more recent observations, with well-performing strategies corresponding to settings *SlideWindow_100* and *QoSLearn_0.03* (note that Figure 4(a) only reports these settings for reasons of clarity). The effect of different learning rates for the proposed learning strategy is further studied in Figure 4(b), which demonstrates that setting δ to lower and higher values (in comparison with 0.03) would increase the prediction error due to intensifying the effect of irrelevant data and the lack of sufficient samples, respectively.

Abrupt Change. Here, the generative model of observations, $value_{prov}(a, t) = Q(a, t)$, experiences a considerable change every 200 time steps. Such a change is simulated by assigning probability 0 to value v_i and probability 1 to another value $v_j \in dom^d(a) \setminus \{v_i\}$ in the case of distribution Q_1, and switching to a significantly different mean μ in the case of distribution Q_2.

As depicted in Figure 5(a), strategy *QoSLearn_0.05* (as well as *SlideWindow_50*) achieves a good tradeoff between reactivity and stability, allowing fast adaptation to a change ($h(P, Q)$ falls below 0.2 in less than 15 time steps) while assuring high accuracy ($h(P, Q) < 0.1$) in times of stability. *SlideWindow_all*, on the other hand, suffers from poor performance, especially after a change occurrence, where the learned model mostly reflects irrelevant observations. Figure 5(b) provides further analysis of the performance of strategy *QoSLearn_δ* between consecutive change points, for various learning rates δ. Clearly, the larger the learning rate, the quicker the observations are forgotten, resulting in

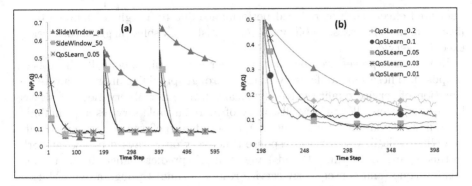

Fig. 5. Evaluation results in a dynamic environment (abrupt change)

faster reactivity after a change, but lower performance in stable periods. In contrast, smaller learning rates improve the accuracy of the learner due to capturing enough samples to reflect the current distribution, yet causes slower adaptation to a change since irrelevant data takes longer to be forgotten.

6.5 Result Summary

The results above demonstrated that, for both *SlideWindow_w* and *QoSLearn_δ*, appropriate parameter setting plays an important role for achieving accurate learning of the probability distributions of quality values, and depends on the environment dynamism. Moreover, the learning-rate-based strategy performs almost as good as the memory-based one, while achieving considerable saving in terms of storage and computation, especially with the increasing dimensionality and number of services in the marketplace. For instance, given a marketplace with 1000 services, each with 10 quality attributes, applying *QoSLearn_δ*, as compared to *SlideWindow_100*, in a gradually changing environment eliminates the need for storing and iterating over 100×10^4 quality ratings at each time step, with the gain increasing in static environments (which require larger window sizes).

7 Related Work

The dynamism and uncertainty of open distributed service-based systems, where the QoS features of the comprising services are unreliable and may exhibit high volatility, have been recognised by many researchers. Existing approaches in this regard can be categorised into reactive approaches and preventive approaches.

Reactive approaches aim at fault-tolerance during QoS-based service selection [8] or application execution [4–6], via performing appropriate corrective actions (e.g. service re-planning) that are triggered in reaction to a change or erroneous behaviour of a service. Such approaches, however, may suffer from undesired effects such as reduced performance due to a high re-planning over-head, and in some cases, inability to find a satisfactory solution given the already executed services.

In response, preventive approaches (under which this paper falls) have been proposed. These aim at fault-avoidance through providing more accurate estimation of service quality values (typically from prior observations of service behaviour), thus allowing the discovery of more suitable services and minimising quality deviations at run time. A number of such efforts are concerned with modelling volatility in service response time, very often caused by the network. In this regard, Dai et al. [11] and Yang et al [12] predict changes in data transmission time (and consequently service response time) through a Semi-Markov Process. Aschoff et al. [10] model the response time of a service as a random variable, changing as a result of various factors related to the network and system resources (e.g. request queuing time). The exponentially weighted moving average is utilised for estimating the expected value of this variable at a particular time step, according to historical data. Similarly, time series modelling based on ARIMA (AutoRegressive Integrated Moving Average) has been proposed by Amin et al. [9] for the purpose of QoS forecasting. These approaches, however, mostly produce a single-valued quantification per quality attribute, and hence may suffer from inaccurate predictions, do not support reasoning about attribute value uncertainty, and are not suitable for categorical attributes.

Trust and reputation mechanisms have also been considered for the purpose of accurate quality predictions [13,14,16]. In particular, prior to an interaction with a service, an assessment of its overall trustworthiness [14,16] or the trustworthiness of each of its QoS dimensions [13] is undertaken, to avoid selecting services that may not honour their promises. Typically, such an assessment is performed by producing reputation scores for the service based on feedback collected from its users (e.g. calculating a time-weighted average of past service ratings). Again, the reputation measures in these approaches are summarised by single aggregative values, thus suffering form similar limitations as above.

In contrast, we propose a probabilistic, multi-valued estimation model, which predicts multiple potential outcomes per quality attribute, and augments such outcomes with uncertainty degrees, thus facilitating more informative reasoning and reliable service selection. Moreover, it is applicable to both numeric and categorical attribute types.

8   Conclusion

The paper presented a probabilistic QoS learning model, tailored towards dynamic and untrustworthy service environments, where each service is associated with a software agent, able to learn, based on past performance information, the uncertainty degrees regarding the service's quality outcomes in the form of probability distributions over such outcomes. The learning is both efficient and adaptable to various degrees of environment dynamism via an appropriate choice of the learning rate, which is demonstrated through experimental results.

Future work involves investigating more complex stochastic models for the dynamic adjustment of the learning rate during the learning process when environment dynamics change over time, as well as accommodating the addition of new quality characteristics. Moreover, we intend to explore the social ability of software agents (e.g. collaboration among those monitoring services for the same provider) to improve QoS predictions in the proposed marketplace architecture, where the role of agents has been limited so far to individual learning.

References

1. Papazoglou, M.P., Traverso, P., Dustdar, S., Leymann, F.: Service-oriented Computing: State of the Art and Research Challenges. Computer 40, 38–45 (2007)
2. Bowling, M., Veloso, M.: Rational and Convergent Learning in Stochastic Games. In: 17th Int. Joint Conf. on Artificial Intelligence, pp. 1021–1026 (2001)
3. Simpson, D.G.: Hellinger Deviance Tests: Efficiency, Breakdown Points, and Examples. Journal of the American Statistical Association 84, 107–113 (1989)
4. Zeng, L., Benatallah, B., Ngu, A.H.H., Dumas, M., Kalagnanam, J., Chang, H.: QoS-aware Middleware for Web Services Composition. IEEE Trans. Softw. Eng. 30, 311–327 (2004)
5. Ardagna, D., Pernici, B.: Adaptive Service Composition in Flexible Processes. IEEE Trans. Softw. Eng. 33, 369–384 (2007)
6. Canfora, G., Penta, M.D., Esposito, R., Villani, M.L.: QoS-Aware Replanning of Composite Web Services. In: IEEE Int. Conf. on Web Services, pp. 121–129 (2005)
7. Barakat, L., Miles, S., Poernomo, I., Luck, M.: Efficient Multi-granularity Service Composition. In: IEEE Int. Conf. on Web Services, pp. 227–234 (2011)
8. Barakat, L., Miles, S., Luck, M.: Efficient Adaptive QoS-based Service Selection. Service Oriented Computing and Applications (2013), doi:10.1007/s11761-013-0149-z
9. Amin, A., Colman, A., Grunske, L.: An Approach to Forecasting QoS Attributes of Web Services Based on ARIMA and GARCH Models. In: IEEE Int. Conf. on Web Services, pp. 74–81 (2012)
10. Aschoff, R., Zisman, A.: QoS-driven proactive adaptation of service composition. In: Kappel, G., Maamar, Z., Motahari-Nezhad, H.R. (eds.) Service Oriented Computing. LNCS, vol. 7084, pp. 421–435. Springer, Heidelberg (2011)
11. Dai, Y., Yang, L., Zhang, B.: QoS-driven Self-healing Web Service Composition Based on Performance Prediction. Journal of Computer Science and Technology 24, 250–261 (2009)
12. Yang, L., Dai, Y., Zhang, B.: Performance Prediction Based EX-QoS Driven Approach for Adaptive Service Composition. Information Science and Engineering 25, 345–362 (2009)
13. Maximilien, E.M., Singh, M.P.: Agent-based Trust Model Involving Multiple Qualities. In: 4th Int. Joint Conf. on Autonomous Agents and Multiagent Systems, pp. 519–526 (2005)
14. Xu, Z., Martin, P., Powley, W., Zulkernine, F.: Reputation-Enhanced QoS-based Web Services Discovery. In: IEEE Int. Conf. on Web Services, pp. 249–256 (2007)
15. Vu, L., Hauswirth, M., Aberer, K.: QoS-based Service Selection and Ranking with Trust and Reputation Management. In: The Cooperative Information System Conference, pp. 446–483 (2005)
16. Malik, Z., Bouguettaya, A.: RATEWeb: Reputation Assessment for Trust Establishment among Web Services. The VLDB Journal 18, 885–911 (2009)
17. Gama, J., Žliobaitė, I., Bifet, A., Pechenizkiy, M., Bouchachia, A.: A Survey on Concept Drift Adaptation. ACM Computing Surveys 46, 1–37 (2014)

Architecture-Centric Design of Complex Message-Based Service Systems

Christoph Dorn, Philipp Waibel, and Schahram Dustdar

Distributed Systems Group, Vienna University of Technology, Austria
{dorn,dustdar}@infosys.tuwien.ac.at, philipp.waibel@gmail.com

Abstract. Complex, message-based service systems discourage central execution control, require extremely loose coupling, have to cope with unpredictable availability of individual (composite) services, and may experience a dynamically changing number of service instances. At the topmost level, the architecture of such a complex system often follows a messaging style most naturally. A major problem during the design of these systems is achieving an overall consistent configuration (i.e, ensuring intended message routing across producers, consumers, and brokers). While orchestration or choreography-based approaches support the design of individual composite services along a workflow-centric paradigm, they are an awkward fit for specifying a message-centric architecture. In this paper, we present an architecture-centric approach to designing complex service systems. Specifically we propose modeling the system's high-level architecture with an architecture description language (ADL). The ADL captures the message-centric configuration which subsequently allows for consistency checking. An architecture-to-configuration transformation ensures that the individual deployed services follow the architecture without having to rely on a central coordinator at runtime. Utilizing our provided tool support, we demonstrate the successful application of our methodology on a real world service system.

Keywords: Decentralized Composite Services, Architecture Description Language, Consistency Checking, Message-based Style.

1 Introduction

The last two decades have witnessed the emergence of various techniques for composing complex service systems. Composition approaches based on orchestration languages such as BPEL [12] and YAWL [1] or those based on choreography languages such as WS-CDL[1] share a common assumption on the underlying system architecture: namely workflow-like control and data flow among services. Not all application scenarios, however, fit this workflow-centric scheme and hence existing approaches are cumbersome to apply. A publish-subscribe architecture is a better match for a complex service system which (i) discourages centralized

---

[1] Web Services Choreography Description Language
http://www.w3.org/TR/ws-cdl-10/

X. Franch et al. (Eds.): ICSOC 2014, LNCS 8831, pp. 184–198, 2014.
© Springer-Verlag Berlin Heidelberg 2014

execution control, (ii) consumes and provides data rather than method invocations, (iii) experiences unpredictable service availability, and (iv) must support a dynamically changing number of service instances.

In this paper we address challenges emerging from the design and configuration efforts of such decentralized, highly decoupled, event-based (composite) services. A system architect following a naive approach would specify the individual (composite) services and wire them up in an ad-hoc manner via message queues. The resulting message flow might be documented somewhere but the overall consistency of the ultimately developed services and the deployed message brokers cannot be guaranteed. The ground truth message flow remains implicit in the configuration of individual services and the utilized message-oriented middleware (MOM). It is only a matter of time and complexity before the design and configuration of such a composite system becomes inconsistent. An engineer engaging in example tasks such as restructuring the message flow, integrating additional services, deploying additional instances, or adapting services has little means to ensure that a particular change leaves the updated system in a coherent state. Enterprise Application Integration (EAI) patterns [10] guide the architect in how to structure the overall system but cannot guarantee correct implementation. Consequently high costs occur in terms of time and invested resources when attempting to maintain consistency, as well as for detecting and repairing inconsistencies.

We propose to address this problem through a combination of architecture-centric composite service specification, separation of message routing aspects from local invocation-centric message processing, and architecture-to-configuration transformation. Specifically, our approach applies a component and connector view for describing the high-level, overall complex service system's architecture. The components represent individual, composite services while the connectors represent message brokers. The resulting centralized system architecture serves as the authoritative source for configuring the MOM and each service's publish/subscribe endpoints. Individual services leverage the advantages of proven technologies such as Enterprise Service Buses (ESB) and workflow engines for processing messages locally. This cleanly separates the responsibility of designing the overall, distributed architecture from designing its constituent components. Constraint checks ensure that the architecture itself is consistent. Ultimately transformations derive the actual technology configuration automatically from the architecture description and thus guarantee consistency.

In support of this approach, our contribution in this paper is four-fold. We provide (i) an message-centric extension for the Architecture Description Language xADL [5] (Sec. 5.2), (ii) message-centric architecture consistency checking (Sec. 5.3), (iii) tool support through extension of ArchStudio4 [4] (Sec. 6), and (iv) proof-of-concept architecture-to-configuration transformations for the ActiveMQ JMS server and the Mule ESB (Sec. 6.1). We applied our approach and techniques to an industry case study, demonstrating that our methodology is not only feasible, but also easily applicable in real world situations (Sec. 7).

2   Motivating Scenario

A parking management system consists of a high number of distributed services. Figure 1 depicts a simplified, typical system configuration. Data services at parking sites provide primarily static and highly dynamic information about the parking sites structure (e.g., structure layout, spots per vehicle type), properties (e.g., location, typical occupation level at a given time), the current capacity, and reserved spots. Filter services obtain these details and bring all messages to a uniform format for structural data and dynamic change events (i.e., EAI message translator pattern and the normalizer pattern). Aggregator services maintain a coherent, property-specific view on the parking structures. For example, one aggregator provides details on all parking structures in a particular region, another specializes on caravan parking. Ultimately, Point-of-Sales (POS) services serve particular business cases such as hotels, airports, train stations, rental-car companies, or car-sharing initiatives for reserving parking spots. These POS services obtain the structural data, and changes thereof from aggregator services but receive dynamic updates from filter services directly.

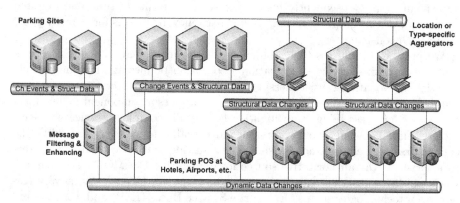

Fig. 1. Parking Management Complex Service System comprising, Data Services, Filter Services, Aggregator Services, and POS Services, as well as message brokers. (Note that icons are meant to depict services and not servers.)

   This scenario reflects the challenges from the introduction. The overall system relies primarily on asynchronous message exchange. There is no single service that would logically serve as a central point of control. Individual service participants may be disconnected or briefly overloaded and thus temporarily unavailable. New services may be introduced anytime but must not affect the remaining service participants' interaction nor require their extensive reconfiguration. Our approach aims at preventing (respectively detecting) following example problems: a Data service publishing its updates to the wrong topic, respectively a Filter service reading from the wrong topic; an Aggregator service expecting an incompatible message type from a filter. Multiple POS services using a single, shared reply queue for asynchronous requests, or a POS service connecting to a non-existing request topic.

3 Related Work

Choreography and Orchestration are the two main contemporary paradigms for addressing design and configuration of complex service systems. Orchestration languages such as BPEL [12], JOpera [13], or YAWL [1] represent centralized approaches and thus need a single coordinating entity (i.e., the workflow engine) at runtime. Decentralized orchestration approaches (e.g.,[11,16]) mitigate this shortcoming through distributing control flow among the participating services. While orchestration takes on a single process view including all participating services, choreography specification languages such as *BPEL4Chor* [6], *Let's Dance* [17], or *MAP* [3], on the other hand, aim at a holistic, overarching system view. Both choreography and orchestration, however, presume a workflow-like system style, with services playing fixed roles, and being highly available (respectively easily replaceable on the fly). It is rather cumbersome to model complex service systems that experience dynamically fluctuating service instances, multiple (a-priori unknown) instances of the same service type, and temporal unavailability with the languages and approaches outlined above. Our work caters predominately to systems that more naturally rely on one-way events and less on request/reply style information exchange. In addition, our approach offers more flexibility on where to locate and manage coordinating elements by strictly separating them from services concerned with business logic as well as modeling them as first class entities. Enterprise Application Integration patterns (EAI) [10] demonstrate the benefits of message-centric service interaction. Scheibler et al. [14] provide a framework for executing EAI-centric configurations; however, by means of a central workflow engine.

At no point are we suggesting that our approach is superior to any of these existing approaches, methodologies, or technologies. We rather see our work as focusing on different service system characteristics. We believe that integrating these existing technologies are well worth investigating as part of future work. This holds also true for existing research efforts that focus on other qualities than high-level architectural consistency. Work on integrating QoS or resource allocation is highly relevant but currently not applicable to our scenarios. Such approaches [7] typically rely on centralized control and/or exclusively employ the request/reply invocation pattern.

Our work takes inspiration from significant contributions in the software architecture domain. Zheng and Taylor couple architecture-implementation conformance with change management in their 1.x mapping methodology [18]. 1.x mapping focuses primarily on maintaining consistency between an architecture specification and its underlying Java implementation and how changes are propagated from the architect to the software developer. We follow a similar procedure by separating high-level architectural design and configuration decisions from the engineers that implement the actual (composite) services.

Garcia et al. investigate the issues of architecture-centric consistency bottom-up [9]. In contrast to our top-down specification of event handling, Garcia et al. identify message flows from source code of event-based systems implemented in Java or Scala. Their technique appears also very suitable for recovering the messaging architecture of an already existing complex service system.

Baresi et al. model publish/subscribe systems for rigorous verification [2]. Their approach requires modeling of a component's internal publishing/subscribing behavior in order to evaluate message reliability, ordering, filtering, priorities, and delays. On the one hand, we do not assume knowledge of precise service internal behavior at the architectural level, and on the other hand, such analysis is significantly more fine-grained than required for our purpose.

The SASSY framework [8] targets service system specification by domain experts through the Service Activity Schema (SAS) language. Inspired by BPMN, SAS provides OR, XOR, AND gateways, loops, activities, input/output elements, and external services for specifying the system's data and control flow. The resulting specification lacks first class connectors and primarily lends itself to workflow-style systems.

4   Approach

Our approach to designing and configuring a complex service system consists of four phases (depicted in Figure 2). First, a high-level architectural component and connector view identifies the main (composite) services (architecture-level components), and their interactions via messages (architecture-level interfaces). Explicit message channels (architecture-level connectors) enable the clear separation of interaction concerns from (service) logic concerns [15]. An architect may model connector-specific properties, configurations, simplify N:M links (become N:1:M), interaction monitoring, etc when connectors become first class model elements. In our specific context, the high-level architecture also separates the responsibility of the overall service system architect from engineers tasked with the internal design and wiring of the individual services (incl. applied tools such as ESBs). We apply an existing extensible Architecture Description Language (xADL) [5] for expressing the high-level architecture. Subsection 5.1 below provides a short introduction of xADL and its main modeling elements.

At any stage in the architecture modeling, the architect may choose to specify messaging-specific configuration properties. For connectors, these properties define messaging middleware-specific details such as channel name, applicable protocol, or deployment host. For interfaces, these properties include messaging endpoint related details such as reply channel references, event-centric request endpoint references, as well as framework-centric properties.

Upon triggering consistency checking, our algorithm iterates through all components, connectors, and links that exhibit messaging-specific configurations. It verifies allowed link cardinalities, missing configuration values, and matching interface details. For a detailed description of constraints see Subsection 5.3.

For all elements that passed these constraint checks, the system architect may then trigger architecture-to-configuration transformations. Distinct tool-centric transformations exist for connectors and components. Connectors plus messaging-centric configuration become a message broker configuration; in our case a set of ActiveMQ configurations. Components plus messaging-centric configuration translate into Mule workflow skeletons (see Subsection 6.1).

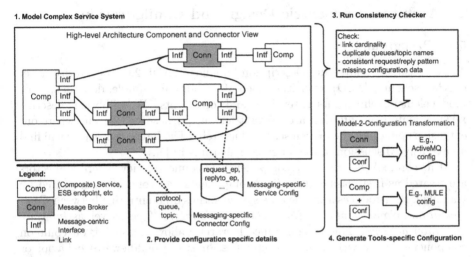

Fig. 2. A methodology for designing and configuring complex service systems

Figure 2 displays the four phases in a sequential manner. The system architect and her co-worker, however, will typically progress through these phases in an iterative manner. An initial configuration may sufficiently serve for checking overall consistency and for identifying core individual services. This approach addresses the four properties of complex service systems outlined earlier in the introduction:

No centralized execution control. The high-level system architecture constitutes a central, authoritative specification only at design-time. The top-down specification of message infrastructure and message-centric service endpoints ensures that the decentralized elements remain true to the architecture at runtime.

Publish/Subscribe interaction. The high-level composite services in this system are primarily concerned with their business logic and not how many sources they receive information from or how many destination in turn are interested in their processed information. Hence, an event-driven interaction style best reflects this loose coupling.

Unpredictable service availability. The message-oriented architecture enables reasoning on the effect of unavailable services. As a durable subscriber, individual services may process at their own pace without affecting simultaneous subscribers. Explicit connector modeling also enable reasoning on where to host which channels, further decoupling message routing from processing.

Dynamically fluctuating service instances the system architect may specify in the architecture that there may exist multiple instances of particular composite service types, and control their impact on the overall system through selection of publish-subscribe versus point-to-point channel connectors.

5 Architecture-Centric Design and Configuration

5.1 Background

The extensible Architecture Description Language xADL 2.0 [5] comprises a set of XML schemas (XSD) explicitly aimed at encouraging simple, domain-specific model element refinements, extensions, and constraints.[2] We will briefly describe xADL's main elements that are relevant for our purpose and outline where our extensions plug into the overall schema hierarchy. The interested reader will find an extensive discussion of the language's features in [5].

At its core, xADL provides a component and connector view where connectors are treated as first class entities (i.e., components and connectors are wired up via links). It introduces a simple type systems, thus differentiating between *Component* and *ComponentType*, *Connector* and *ConnectorType*, as well as *Interface* and *InterfaceType*. This type-instance hierarchy allows reasoning on common component (i.e. service) and connector (i.e., message middleware) behavior or implementation. For our purpose, within the scope of the xADL *types* schema, the architect defines general publish-subscribe and point-to-point channel connector types in addition to all the various component types foreseen in the complex service system. *ComponentTypes* and *ConnectorTypes* expose *Signatures* which in turn may refer to interface types. It is thus possible to distinguish between provided and required interfaces. A messaging connector type typically exhibits a signature for sending messages and a signature for retrieving messages, both according to the same interface type. The xADL *structure* schema subsequently exhibits all the component and connector instances including their specific wiring. Type inheritance is optional.

A second set of schemas target the specification of implementation details. The *abstract implementation* schema identifies the plug-in locations where concrete implementations subsequently provide technology specific details. Natively xADL provides only modeling constructs for Java-based implementations deployed on a single JVM. Figure 3 depicts the xADL modeling constructs, their relations, and our extensions.

5.2 Message-Centric ADL Extension

The main architecture modeling concerns in a message-centric complex service system are configuration of the messaging middleware, definition of message channels, direction and type of messages, message request/reply correlation beyond generic one-way messages, and messaging middleware access properties.

---

[2] Throughout this paper any reference to xADL always implies xADL version 2.0.

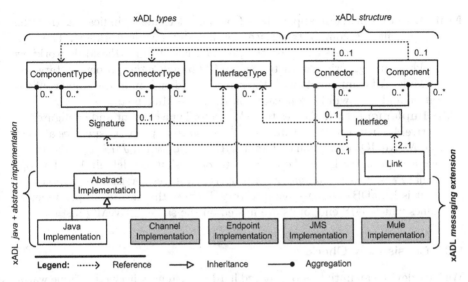

Fig. 3. Simplified xADL schema excerpt including the messaging extensions (dark grey)

To this end, we provide a set of four implementation extensions (see also Figure 3 bottom). The schemas for *Channel Implementation* and *Endpoint Implementation* provide general messaging properties, while *Mule Implementation* and *JMS Implementation* express technology specific properties for Mule and ActiveMQ respectively. The separation into four schemas also reflect the fact that each schema applies only to a particular core architecture element.

Channel Implementation (aka EAI message channel pattern) applies to a Connector element and specifies whether the Connector behaves as a publish-subscribe channel or point-to-point channel and provides the respective name.

Endpoint Implementation (aka EAI message adapter pattern) applies to an Interface element associated with a Component (and will be ignored when the Interface is associated with a Connector). The *Durable_ Name* properties identifies the subscriber of a durable subscription towards the channel connector. When a component dispatches a message for which is expects a reply, its sending interface must identify the point-to-point channel where it expects to eventually receive the reply message from via the *Reply_ To_ Queue* property. To completely specify a request/reply pattern, the requesting component exhibits a receiving interface that signals its role via the *Connection_ To_ Request_ Endpoint* property. A component may thus exhibit multiple, unambiguously defined request/reply interface pairs. On the replying component (within a request/reply pattern), the receiving *in* interface points to the replying *out* interface via the *Reply_ To_ Queue* property, which in turn completes the bi-directional references via the *Connection_ To_ Request_ Endpoint* property. The *Endpoint_ Position_ No* property allows for specifying an ordering of interfaces.

Mule Implementation applies to a Component element, indicating that the component is a composite service, specified by a Mule workflow. The configuration properties comprise the *file_ id* where to save the Mule workflow skeleton and generic parameter/value *AdditionalConfig* properties targeted at Mule. All components with the same *file_ id* end up in the same configuration and thus will be collocated on the same Mule instance.

JMS Implementation applies to a ConnectorType element and configures an ActiveMQ instance. The *Transport_ Configuration* property specifies at least one ActiveMQ connection endpoint URL. The optional *JMS_ Specification_ Version* property holds the JMS protocol version, by default 1.1. The optional *Persistence_ Configuration* property captures persistence adapter (default is kahaDB) and storage directory. Finally, the *file_ id* property determines which JMS endpoints are hosted on the same ActiveMQ instance.

5.3   Consistency Checks

We have devised an initial set of soft and hard consistency checks that issue warnings and recommendations on how to mitigate the inconsistency. The checks are restricted to Component, Connectors, ConnectorTypes, and Interfaces refined with our xADL extensions. Basic checks such as interface direction and type compatibility are already available in the ArchStudio4 (see Sec. 6).

Most messaging-centric checks apply at the architecture level. We detect when there exists a link directly between two components or two connectors. Two connector instances of the same connector type cannot share the same channel name. Subscriber and publishers would otherwise share the same channel which is in conflict with the architecture-prescribed distinct channels. Every component interface can only link to a single connector interface as the interface represents the message channel at the service side. We recommend that every connector has exactly one *in* and one *out* interface. The use of *inout* interfaces is discouraged. Instead a set of separate request and reply queues, thus implying separate *in* and *out* interfaces, unambiguously document the intent of the *inout* direction. Our checks warn when multiple message consumers link to the out interface of a point-to-point channel. Only one nondeterministic subscriber will be able to obtain the message. We also warn when a publish-subscribe channel (rather than a point-to-point channel) is used within the scope of a request/reply pattern. With multiple subscribers to the request topic, multiple responses may occur.

Complementary component level checks ensure the proper use of the message-centric request/response pattern. A response endpoint (interface) must refer to its respective, initiating request endpoint (interface), both must exist, reside on the same component, and may not be identical. Additional tool-centric checks ensure that the architect provided all required information for transforming the model to message broker and ESB configuration (see following section 6).

6 Tool Support

6.1 Architecture-to-Configuration Transformation

For the purpose of this paper, we focused on two architecture-to-configuration transformations. As example for configuring a message-oriented middleware, we generate the XML-based ActiveMQ Server configuration. A ConnectorType's JMS implementation is sufficient for deriving a server's configuration which consists of two parts. The *Persistence_ Configuration* determines the *persistenceAdapter* and all *Transport_ Configurations* determine the set of available *transportConnectors*. The transformation also ensures traceability by adding the connector type's id as a comment to the configuration files *broker* element. Note that the transformation ignores any connectors and thus doesn't specify what queues or topics the server will eventually manage as ActiveMQ creates these on the fly. Ultimately, every connector type with a JMS implementation results in a separate *transportConnector* element. Configurations for connector types that share a *file_ id* are aggregated into a single configuration file and subsequently end up collocated on the same ActiveMQ server instance.

As example for configuring a service endpoint, we provide the complete message specification for a Mule workflow, i.e., a workflow designer may neglect any message-broker related details and can focus purely on the local message processing. The Mule workflow configuration captures components, interfaces, and their wiring to the various connectors, while the ActiveMQ service configuration represents only the connector types in complex service system's architecture. Each component results in a separate mule workflow specification. The transformation places all workflow specifications from component with the same *file_ id* in the same file, and thus collocates them on the same Mule ESB instance. To this end, the transformation first retrieves all connectors (with channel implementation) and obtains the JMS configuration from the corresponding connector type. Each distinct connector type becomes an *activemq-connector* element. For each interface, a new *[inbound/outbound]-endpoint* element obtains the configuration properties from the endpoint implementation, the channel name from the linked connector's channel implementation, and the respective *connector-ref* to the *activemq-connector*. Our transformation treats two interfaces coupled via a *Connection_ To_ Request_ Endpoint* property and *Reply_ To_ Queue* property differently depending on whether they represent the requesting component or the replying component. In case of the former, the respective two mule endpoints become wrapped in a *request-reply* element and a preceding *message-properties-transformer* element. In case of the latter, the receiving interface becomes a *inbound-endpoint* with an *exchange-pattern="request-response"* property while the outgoing interface is ignored. The respective reply endpoint information arrives embedded in the request message at runtime.

6.2 ArchStudio Integration

We realized our approach as a prototype on top of ArchStudio 4 [4], a visual, Eclipse-based IDE for editing xADL documents. ArchStudio comes with two

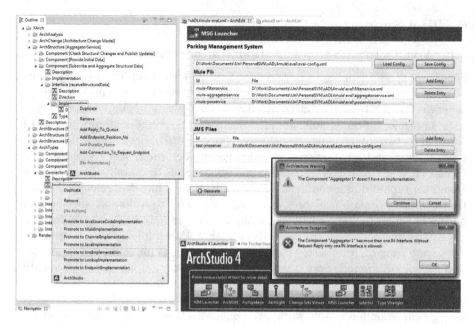

Fig. 4. ArchStudio extension screenshot: schema extension (left), transformation configuration file mapping (top), exemplary inconsistency alerts (inset)

main editors: *ArchEdit* provides access to the underlying xADL document (including all extensions) as a tree, while *Archipelago* offers a drag-and-drop, point-and-click interface for placing and wiring up components and connectors. ArchStudio foresees the integration of additional functionality through extensions.

Schema Extensions. For the purpose of our approach, it proved sufficient to extend xADL at the implementation schema level. The additional elements (recall subsection 5.2) blend in smoothly with the existing user interface, merely appearing as new implementation options (see Figure 4 left). An existing ArchStudio 4 user won't have to learn any new steps for utilizing our schema extensions. Under the hood, ArchStudio applies its *Apigen* tool for creating a data binding library for each xADL schema. *ArchEdit* and *Apigen*'s limitations combined result in configuration properties being limited to strings, references, and complex data structures thereof.

Consistency Checking. We implemented the consistency checker as a dedicated component within ArchStudio. The checker raises warnings and errors during execution, depending on the consistency rule severity. The user may decide to ignore warnings and still continue to configuration transformation later on. Transformation is disabled, however, in the presence of consistency errors (see Figure 4 inset). In general, consistency checking is cheap. The consistency algorithm's runtime complexity is $\Theta(comp + l)$ for architecture components (*comp*) and links (*l*) as rules are either local (e.g., interface properties, interface link cardinality) or access only a link's two referenced elements (e.g., compatible interface direction). Checking the uniqueness of channel names of connectors deriving from the same connector type is slightly less efficient: the algorithm's complexity is $\Theta(n\ log\ n)$ in the number of connectors.

Transformation. As mentioned above, the actual transformation component becomes only available after passing all consistency checks. The only user interaction with the transformation consists of mapping a component's and connector type's file id to an actual file location (see Figure 4 top).

We are currently in the process of open-sourcing our tool as an ArchStudio4 add-on and will update this paper with a link to the tool website as soon as we have put together sufficient installation documentation. For now, the extending xADL schema documents, example architecture model, and corresponding generated configuration files are available as Supporting Online Material (SOM) at `http://wp.me/P1xPeS-5H`.

7   Proof-of-Concept Case Study

We utilized our prototype tool support for developing a parking management complex service system. The system is similar to the one introduced in the motivating scenario but for reasons of confidentiality we cannot disclose the actual system architecture. Any depicted and described architecture excerpts, hence, closely match the system in structure but exhibit generalized element names and properties. We briefly report on the development process and respective application of our approach to demonstrate not only feasibility but also actual benefit in a representative, real-world development environment.

Our approach and tool support allows for an iteratively refining system design methodology. As the architecture goes through various iterations, the architect gradually assigns implementation elements to components, connectors, and interfaces. Mule workflow developers pick the various components and generated workflow specification and implement the internal composite service behavior. Specification and changes need not necessarily flow only from architecture to configuration. Due to page constraints, we are unable to describe our additional tool capabilities such as generating the messaging endpoints within pre-existing Mule workflows (rather than from-scratch workflow generation), non-destructive change propagation of architecture updates into workflow configurations, and consistency checking upon changing message-centric elements conducted within the mule workflow editor. These aspects are subject to future publications. The architect runs consistency checks in any development phase, after any update to the architecture or Mule workflow and thus can guarantee that inconsistencies are immediately detected, respectively that the prescribed architecture and system are in a consistent configuration.

Ultimately, the architect arrives at a model similar to the excerpt in Figure 5. It contains one composite Filter Service, Aggregator Service, and POS Service each (for a total of eight Mule workflows), along with the five intermediate message queues/topics. The Filter Service comprises of two components: one Mule workflow for filtering and enhancing dynamic changes events from parking sites

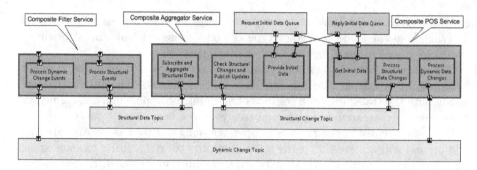

Fig. 5. Evaluation system architecture except: depicting composite service components (dark/blue) and message broker connectors (light/beige) - ArchStudio screenshot (colors online)

(not shown), and one workflow processing structural events. The composite Aggregator Service comprises three workflows: one for obtaining structural data (typically provided by more than one Filter Service), one for checking the structural data for changes relevant to POS services and dispatching those changes, and one for providing POS services with initial complete state information. A generic POS Service contains at minimum flows for (i) obtaining initial data (in this case, the POS service is aware from which Aggregator Service it receives such initial information), for (ii) receiving structural updates and for (iii) dynamic data updates. Further locally relevant flows which contain the actual business logic are irrelevant at this architectural level. Similarly, shared databases serving multiple flows within a single Mule instance need not be configured at this level but instead are within the scope of a Mule configuration file. Note also that the architectural substructures are included for sake of better understanding. Collocation of mule workflows depends solely on specifying the same implementation file id property.

Tool supported consistency checking pays of even for this small architecture excerpt. A single execution of the all consistency checks outlined in Section 5.3 on the architecture in Figure 5 results in four architecture-level checks, four link-specific checks, three connector checks, one connector type check, and six component checks (including respective interfaces). Remember that an architecture would need to conduct many more checks when conducting the same analysis on Mule and ActiveMQ files alone. The ActiveMQ configuration is void of any topic and queues definitions, thus there exists no authoritative, explicit connector element. Observing a simple example such as ensuring that a queue has only a single receiver or that queue/topic names are unique: the architect needs to traverse the Mule configuration for each queue and topic definition first to the corresponding Mule messaging endpoint definitions (requiring a detailed understanding of the configuration file) and then pairwise compare this information across all included mule workflows (i.e., $n * (n - 1)/2$ comparisons, thus 45x for our use case's 10 connected component interfaces); a tedious and error-prone task, especially for larger systems.

Discussion and Limitations

Complex service systems do not necessarily need to exhibit all the challenging properties listed in the introduction: prohibiting centralized execution control, consuming and providing data rather than invocations, experiencing unpredictable service availability, and supporting a dynamically changing number of service instances. Systems that encounter only a subset will equally benefit from our approach and tools.

Currently, our architecture-to-configuration transformation produces only Mule workflows and ActiveMQ configurations. The underlying real world development project underlying our evaluation scenario identified these technologies as sufficient and providing a good balance between a light-weight messaging framework and the expressive and extensible Mule workflows for composite service design. Our approach remains valid for other messaging protocols or frameworks as well as for other service design methodologies. The architecture-level consistency checking mechanism remain applicable. Ultimately, supporting other runtime frameworks does not necessarily require adapting our ArchStudio add-on. For small deviating tasks, such as generating an OpenJMS server configuration, access to the architecture model via *Apigen*'s data binding libraries, or directly via the xADL XML file will be sufficient.

8   Conclusions

We made the case for architecture-centric design of complex, message-based service systems. Our approach targets the specification of systems comprising dynamically fluctuating instances of message-driven, highly decoupled composite services with uncertain availability. Our extension to xADL provides the basis for central specification and consistency checking at design-time, subsequently achieving consistent run-time configuration without having to rely on a central coordinator. Our prototypical tool integrated with ArchStudio4 produces configurations for the ActiveMQ message broker and Mule workflow endpoints.

Our future work focuses on following two aspects: on the one hand, we plan to extend the set of supported protocols and tools (e.g., the advanced message queue protocol AMQP or WS-Notification). It will be especially worthwhile evaluating how the EAI patterns (currently modeled internally in Mule) may be explicitly supported by our ADL and subsequently mapped to EAI frameworks such as Apache Camel. On the other hand, we will investigate additional analysis aspects such as optimal channel allocation across message-broker instances and their location in proximity to the various services.

Acknowledgment. This work is partially supported by the European Union within the SIMPLI-CITY FP7-ICT project (Grant agreement no. 318201).

References

1. van der Aalst, W., Hofstede, A.H.M.T.: Yawl: Yet another workflow language. Information Systems 30, 245–275 (2003)
2. Baresi, L., Ghezzi, C., Mottola, L.: On accurate automatic verification of publish-subscribe architectures. In: Proc. of the 29th International Conference on Software Engineering, ICSE 2007, pp. 199–208. IEEE Computer Society, Washington, DC (2007)
3. Barker, A., Walton, C., Robertson, D.: Choreographing web services. IEEE Transactions on Services Computing 2(2), 152–166 (2009)
4. Dashofy, E., Asuncion, H., Hendrickson, S., Suryanarayana, G., Georgas, J., Taylor, R.: Archstudio 4: An architecture-based meta-modeling environment. In: Companion to the Proc. of the 29th International Conference on Software Engineering, pp. 67–68. IEEE Computer Society, Washington, DC (2007)
5. Dashofy, E.M., Van der Hoek, A., Taylor, R.N.: A highly-extensible, xml-based architecture description language. In: Proceedings of the Working IEEE/IFIP Conference on Software Architecture, pp. 103–112. IEEE (2001)
6. Decker, G., Kopp, O., Leymann, F., Weske, M.: Bpel4chor: Extending bpel for modeling choreographies. In: IEEE 20th International Conference on Web Services, pp. 296–303. IEEE Computer Society, Los Alamitos (2007)
7. Dustdar, S., Schreiner, W.: A survey on web services composition. Int. J. Web Grid Serv. 1(1), 1–30 (2005)
8. Esfahani, N., Malek, S., Sousa, J.P., Gomaa, H., Menascé, D.A.: A modeling language for activity-oriented composition of service-oriented software systems. In: Schürr, A., Selic, B. (eds.) MODELS 2009. LNCS, vol. 5795, pp. 591–605. Springer, Heidelberg (2009)
9. Garcia, J., Popescu, D., Safi, G., Halfond, W.G.J., Medvidovic, N.: Identifying message flow in distributed event-based systems. In: Proceedings of the 2013 9th Joint Meeting on Foundations of Software Engineering, ESEC/FSE 2013, pp. 367–377. ACM, New York (2013)
10. Hohpe, G., Woolf, B.: Enterprise Integration Patterns: Designing, Building, and Deploying Messaging Solutions. Addison-Wesley, Reading (2003)
11. Nanda, M.G., Chandra, S., Sarkar, V.: Decentralizing execution of composite web services. SIGPLAN Not 39(10), 170–187 (2004)
12. Organization for the Advancement of Structured Information Standards (OASIS): Web Services Business Process Execution Language (WS-BPEL) Version 2.0 (April 2007), http://docs.oasis-open.org/wsbpel/2.0/OS/wsbpel-v2.0-OS.html
13. Pautasso, C., Heinis, T., Alonso, G.: Jopera: Autonomic service orchestration. IEEE Data Eng. Bull. 29(3), 32–39 (2006)
14. Scheibler, T., Leymann, F.: A framework for executable enterprise application integration patterns. In: Mertins, K., Ruggaber, R., Popplewell, K., Xu, X. (eds.) Enterprise Interoperability III, pp. 485–497. Springer, London (2008)
15. Taylor, R.N., Medvidovic, N., Dashofy, E.M.: Software Architecture: Foundations, Theory, and Practice. Wiley (2009)
16. Yildiz, U., Godart, C.: Information flow control with decentralized service compositions. In: IEEE Int. Conf. on Web Services, pp. 9–17 (July 2007)
17. Zaha, J.M., Barros, A., Dumas, M., ter Hofstede, A.: Let's dance: A language for service behavior modeling. In: Meersman, R., Tari, Z. (eds.) OTM 2006. LNCS, vol. 4275, pp. 145–162. Springer, Heidelberg (2006)
18. Zheng, Y., Taylor, R.N.: Enhancing architecture-implementation conformance with change management and support for behavioral mapping. In: Proc. of the 34th Int. Conf. on Software Engineering, ICSE 2012, pp. 628–638. IEEE Press, Piscataway (2012)

Managing Expectations: Runtime Negotiation of Information Quality Requirements in Event-Based Systems

Sebastian Frischbier[1], Peter Pietzuch[2], and Alejandro Buchmann[1]

[1] Technische Universität Darmstadt, Darmstadt, Germany
{frischbier,buchmann}@dvs.tu-darmstadt.de
[2] Imperial College London, London, United Kingdom
p.pietzuch@imperial.ac.uk

Abstract. Interconnected smart devices in the Internet of Things (IoT) provide fine-granular data about real-world events, leveraged by service-based systems using the paradigm of event-based systems (EBS) for invocation. Depending on the capabilities and state of the system, the information propagated in EBS differs in content but also in properties like precision, rate and freshness. At runtime, consumers have different dynamic requirements about those properties that constitute quality of information (QoI) for them. Current approaches to support quality-related requirements in EBS are either domain-specific or limited in terms of expressiveness, flexibility and scope as they do not allow participants to adapt their behavior. We introduce the generic concept of **expectations** to express, negotiate and enforce arbitrary requirements about information quality in EBS at runtime. In this paper, we present the model of expectations, capabilities and feedback based on generic properties. Participants express requirements and define individual tradeoffs between them as expectations while system features are expressed as capabilities. We discuss the algorithms to (i) negotiate requirements at runtime in the middleware by matching expectations to capabilities and (ii) adapt participants as well as the middleware. We illustrate the architecture for runtime-support in industry-strength systems by describing prototypes implemented within a centralized and a decentralized EBS.

Keywords: event-based systems, quality of information, self-adaptive systems, runtime negotiation, malleability.

1 Motivation

Having information of adequate quality available at the right time in the right place is vital for software systems to react to situations or support decisions. Supply chain management based on the Internet of Things (IoT) and data centre monitoring are just two examples of reactive systems where information provided by data sources has to be interpreted and where false alarms, missed events or otherwise information of inadequate quality carries a cost [18]. Event-based systems (EBS) and service-oriented architectures (SOA) complement each other

X. Franch et al. (Eds.): ICSOC 2014, LNCS 8831, pp. 199–213, 2014.

well to leverage those streams of dynamic real-time information in enterprise software systems and react on meaningful events in a timely manner: software components can be exposed as services for direct communication while also acting as participants of an EBS to follow an indirect communication model [8,10]. EBS are anonymous, information-centric systems with many-to-many communication: loosely-coupled software components (publishers) publish notifications about events they are confident to have detected (e.g., critical workload at node) as messages which are pushed to interested components (subscribers) by a middleware. Information exchanged in EBS is characterized by type (e.g., *temperatureEvent*), content (e.g., *temperatureCelsius*=50) and quality-related properties (e.g., rate of publication, confidence, precision, trustworthiness) [14].

Subscribers in EBS require information with sufficient quality of information (QoI) to decide whether to react or not: being notified too late or causelessly due to false positive can have severe consequences [18]. Whether some QoI is sufficient depends on the information's properties fitting the purpose it is intended to be used for; this is application-specific and dynamic as it depends on the context of each subscriber [6]. For example, monitoring data about a virtual machine delivered at a given rate and confidence might be (i) sufficient for the purpose of one subscriber while another subscriber might need the same type of data at a higher rate but would tolerate less confidence; (ii) sufficient for a subscriber as long as there is no indication of malfunction at the monitored entity - in case of anomalies the same data is required at high rate for root cause analysis [18].

QoI in EBS depends on the system satisfying individual requirements about quality-related properties at runtime [4]. Subscribers have to be able to (i) define requirements about arbitrary quality-related properties of information they want to consume; (ii) expose individual tradeoffs between those requirements if they are willing to accept degradations in exchange for getting other requirements satisfied; (iii) adapt requirements at runtime to reflect changes to their current situation; and (iv) get feedback about the state of their requirements to decide if their needs are satisfied or if they have to adapt. At the same time, delivering information with specific properties comes at a cost for the system as it depends on the current configuration of available publishers and the middleware [3]. Thus, the system has to decide at runtime *how* to satisfy *which* requirements.

Runtime support for quality-related properties in EBS is currently limited in terms of expressivity, extensibility and scope; feedback is not provided at runtime [2,11]. Requirements about quality-related properties in EBS can be implicitly supported by publishers either by using types that encode quality-related properties in their name (e.g., CpuUsage_rate50_confidence70), or by adding metadata to the content of each published message (e.g., *rate=50, confidence=70*). Subscribers can express their requirements by subscribing to the type they are interested in using the common API of EBS [22]. However, this restricts the set of available properties to those determinable by publishers at design-time, excluding important runtime properties like latency and reliability that are provided by the middleware. For encoded types, it would also result in an unmanageable growth of available types for different combinations of

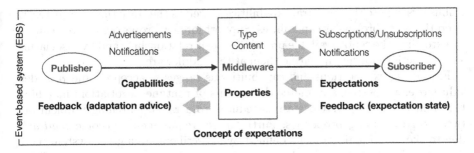

Fig. 1. Our concept extends the model of EBS (top) with capabilities, expectations and bidirectional feedback for runtime adaptation (bottom, bold)

quality-properties, as well as, traffic overhead as the same information has to be processed for multiple encoded types [9]. Systems providing explicit support for quality-related properties like IndiQoS [9], Adamant [15] or Harmony [28] focus on a fixed set of middleware-related properties at a low level of abstraction. They try to satisfy requirements by adapting the middleware on the transport proto-col level and do not enforce requirements about properties that would require publishers to adapt at runtime, limiting the scope of runtime flexibility.

In this paper, we propose the concept of **expectations** as a generic approach to support QoI in EBS as a first-class citizen and enable participants to adapt at runtime. Fig. 1 shows how our approach complements the paradigm of EBS.

Our key idea is to define quality-related properties like *rate*, *confidence* or *latency* in a generic way together with actions that define how those properties can be adjusted at runtime. Requirements (*expectations*) and the system state (*capabilities*) defined as ranges over such properties can be efficiently matched in the middleware at runtime to identify the extent to which the system would have to adapt to satisfy requirements. Based on this assessment, requirements can be declined or satisfied by adapting the system using platform-specific instantiations of the associated actions. Subscribers receive feedback about the state of their requirements while publishers get feedback about the usage of their capabilities, including advice to adapt if necessary.

For example, application M has to monitor the temperature of a chemical process during manufacturing to detect anomalies and trigger a dedicated workflow. In terms of QoI, M subscribes to notifications for temperatureEvent with an expectation about *rate* and *confidence*: it requires notifications to be of 75-95% confidence (minimizing false-positives/negatives) while they could be published at a low rate of 5-10 events/minute. A temperature sensor P, currently publishing 2 events/minute with 90% confidence, is able to publish up to 60 events/minute with a maximum confidence of 80%, expressing this as capabilities for *rate* and *confidence*. Matching M's expectation to available capabilities, the middleware realizes that P is suitable but has to adapt, advising it to do so.

Subscribers can express requirements and individual tradeoffs between them as expectations in a consistent and information-centric way over arbitrary properties.

Publishers expose their general capabilities as well as the state they are currently operating at to brokers as capabilities. Support for new properties can be realized by extending the set of available properties, their relationships and by associating suitable actions for manipulating them at the middleware.

Expressing expectations and capabilities as ranges of accepted and provided values over properties automates the process of runtime negotiation: matching requirements to the system state is reduced to a range matching problem between corresponding properties. Furthermore, requirements become *malleable* due to the individual tradeoffs defined by subscribers, giving the system more degrees of freedom when deciding on the extent of adaptation necessary. Feedback enables participants to adapt their behavior at runtime and extends the scope of supported properties to those influenced by publishers.

The concept of expectations complementary extends the paradigm of EBS without compromising the model of indirect many-to-many communication, making it backward compatible. As shown in Fig. 1, expectations and capabilities can be defined independently of advertisements, notifications or subscriptions. They are matched only at the middleware, preserving the anonymity of the associated participants necessary for scalability in EBS. Bidirectional feedback enables participants to assess their current situation and adapt their behavior at runtime if necessary. Our concept encompasses related approaches by treating them as dedicated actions for enforcing requirements for specific properties.

This paper makes the following contributions to support QoI in EBS:

1. a generic model to express malleable requirements and capabilities for arbitrary quality-related properties in EBS at runtime (Sec. 2);
2. algorithms for negotiating requirements at runtime in the middleware by (i) matching expectations and capabilities to identify satisfied, satisfiable and unsatisfiable requirements; (ii) deciding on the requirements to satisfy based on strategies for optimization and load balancing; (iii) enforcing those requirements by adapting participants, the middleware or both (Sec. 3); and
3. runtime support in industry-strength systems illustrated by prototypes implemented in Java within the centralized ActiveMQ JMS messaging broker and the decentralized REDS middleware (Sec. 4).

Related work is discussed in Sec. 5 before Sec. 6 concludes with final remarks.

2   Expectations: Support for QoI in EBS

This section describes the challenges supporting QoI in EBS at runtime and our proposed solution using expectations, capabilities and feedback.

2.1   Background: Event-Based Systems in a Nutshell

Participants in EBS are independent but cooperative software components with different roles that communicate indirectly using notifications: publishers send *advertisements* once before they *publish* notifications to announce the type of event to be provided. Different kinds of data sources can act as publishers: sensors, services or other software components. Subscribers are components that express interest about notifications with a specific type or content by registering *subscriptions* at the middleware. Subscribers and publishers are fully decoupled by the middleware. It matches subscriptions to advertisements and processes notifications from publishers to subscribers based on routing trees, following a many-to-many communication pattern. The middleware can consist of a single, centralized message broker or a distributed network of brokers. Brokers perform efficient en-route filtering and selective forwarding of notifications based on their content. As the message flow is unidirectional, from publishers to subscribers, subscribers are anonymous to publishers, and vice versa.

2.2   Challenges Supporting QoI in EBS at Runtime

Support for QoI means to deliver information with specific quality-related properties that satisfy individual, sometimes vague, requirements while balancing the costs for provisioning against it [3,18]. EBS are designed for heterogeneous and dynamic populations: publishers and subscribers can join, leave or change at runtime. Multiple publishers can provide information of the same type and content but with different quality-related properties as those depend on each publisher's configuration (e.g., available hardware, setup) and can change dynamically based on a publisher's current context (e.g., enforced energy-saving mode for battery-powered sensors). Information is only propagated by the middleware in a many-to-many fashion, preventing direct negotiation.

2.3   The Model of Expectations and Capabilities

The basic building blocks of our approach are *properties* that characterize information in addition to its content or type. Examples for properties are *precision, rate, transport latency, trustworthiness, order,* or *confidence* [20]. Properties do not have to be comparable (e.g., *trustworthiness* vs. *order*) but they can be conflicting due to system constraints (e.g., *rate* vs. *latency* vs. bandwidth). Every property can be modeled over a range or a set of values that apply a total order (ordinal scale) depending on the semantics of the property. For example, *trust* can be modeled over the set {none, low, medium, high}, with none < low < medium < high; *confidence* can be modeled using the range [0%; 100%]; *transport latency* can be modeled as the number of milliseconds elapsed since publication using the range [0; ∞]. Each property can be *improved* by either maximizing or minimizing it, depending on the semantics of the property (e.g., improve latency by minimizing it). A value *dominates* another value of the same property if it improves it (e.g., a confidence of 88% dominates a confidence of 25%, a latency of 300ms dominates a latency of 700ms).

Expectations to express QoI requirements. The context of a subscriber might change at runtime, affecting requirements about quality-related properties of notifications but not those about content or type as expressed in the subscription (c.f. Sec. 1). We introduce the notion of *expectations* to encapsulate quality-related requirements, enabling subscribers to manage their requirements about quality-related properties at runtime.

Definition 1 (expectation). *An expectation describes a malleable set of requirements that a subscriber has about quality-related properties of information it has subscribed to. Each expectation $\mathcal{X}_i^e$ consists of a set of tuples (p_e, lb, ub) as well as a utility value $\mathcal{X}_i^e.u$ which reflects the individual importance of this expectation for the subscriber and allows a ranking.*

Each tuple in $\mathcal{X}_i^e$ refers to a requirement about a property like *rate, confidence* or *latency*: it is defined as a range of values $[p_e.lb; p_e.ub]$ that a subscriber would accept for property p_e and the associated event e. By combining different requirements in a single expectation, each subscriber defines a tradeoff between the ranges of those properties, making the requirements malleable. For example, subscriber M with expectation $\mathcal{X}_1^e = \{(rate, 5, 10), (confidence, 75, 95)\}$ accepts notifications with $\{rate = 7, confidence = 90\}$ as well as notifications with $\{rate = 10, confidence = 80\}$. A subscriber can associate multiple expectations with the same subscription to allow for alternative configurations, ranked by their utility values [27,13]. For example, M needs highly reliable information $(\mathcal{X}_1^e)$ but could alternatively do with less reliable information at a higher rate to compensate false-positives/negatives: $\mathcal{X}_2^e = \{(rate, 30, 45), (confidence, 50, 60)\}$.

Each expectation has a lifecycle that starts with *registering* it at the broker, making the system aware of the described requirements. Changes in the context of the subscriber can be reflected by changing the lifecycle of a registered expectation by *updating, suspending/resuming* or *revoking* it. Registered expectations are active unless they are suspended or revoked. When unsubscribing, all associated expectations are treated as revoked by the broker.

Capabilities to express the system state. In EBS, the system state regarding QoI depends on the extent to which properties are provided by publishers and supported by brokers. We introduce *capabilities* to describe this.

Definition 2 (capability). *A capability describes the extent to which publisher j supports property p_e. Each capability $\mathcal{C}_j^e$ is a tuple $(p_e, lb, ub, cv, cost_{p_e}(x))$ that defines (a) the range of values $[C_j^e.lb; C_j^e.ub]$ publisher j in principle is capable of providing; (b) the value $C_j^e.cv$ within this range that publisher j is currently operating at; and (c) the cost function $cost_{p_e}(x)$ for operating at x.*

A capability describes the current support for a property by a publisher as well as the realizable spectrum of values. Providing p_e at a specific quality comes at a cost [3], captured in $cost_{p_e}()$. A publisher can provide multiple capabilities while the same capability can be provided by multiple publishers with different ranges or costs. Capabilities for some properties like *confidence* are provided only by publishers, others depend on assessment and enforcement by the middleware or a cooperation of publishers and the middleware at runtime (e.g., to support *latency, reliability, order*). A *capability profile* bundles all capabilities of a publisher for a given event.

Definition 3 (capability profile). *A capability profile CP_j^e is a set of capabilities $\{C_1^e, \ldots, C_k^e\}$ associated with publisher j for events of type e. It consists of capabilities determined by the publisher itself and those determined by the broker.*

A capability profile reflects the full set of capabilities available from a specific publisher for a given event type and can be matched against expectations. Capabilities determinable only by the broker are added at runtime. Capability profiles for the same type of event (CP^e) but associated with different publishers can be heterogenous in terms of the (i) set of properties (e.g., $CP_2^e = \{rate \wedge latency\} \subset CP_1^e = \{rate \wedge latency \wedge confidence\}$), (ii) ranges, and (iii) current values.

A capability profile's lifecycle starts with *registering* it at the broker and ends with *revoking* it. During runtime, the situation of a publisher might change in a way that requires *updating* registered capability profiles without changing the advertisement. For example, a battery powered sensor runs low on energy and has to switch to an energy-saving mode, decreasing the *rate* of publication; or new resources become available at runtime, improving or adding capabilities (e.g., higher *confidence* due to better contextual information [16]).

Feedback to subscribers and publishers. At runtime, publishers and subscribers are able and willing to adapt their behavior if they get feedback about their actions and the system state. As traditional EBS do not give such feedback at runtime, participants cannot assess if and how they would have to adapt [11]. We introduce *bidirectional* feedback from the middleware to participants to provide them with additional information about their actions and support adaptation at runtime. Subscribers get feedback about the state of their active expectations (*satisfied* or *unsatisfied*). They are informed about the *reason* if an expectation cannot be satisfied by the system at the time. Reasons are expressed as tuples $(\mathcal{X}_i^e, p_e, \alpha)$, describing the value currently provided by the system for each property that is not satisfied. As soon as the expectation can be satisfied, the subscriber is notified about the new state. Publishers receive feedback about each active capability profile's usage together with advice to adapt their publications if necessary. This includes the list of capabilities to adapt together with the required target values, expressed as tuples (CP_j^e, C^e, β). We consider publishers to be able to adapt automatically at runtime if notified as we show in [13].

3   Negotiating Requirements for QoI in EBS

Using expectations to model requirements about QoI and capabilities to describe the corresponding system state, requirements negotiation in EBS can be done automatically at runtime inside the middleware. For every active expectation associated with a subscription, the middleware has to check if it could deliver information with quality-related properties that satisfies the expectation and the associated subscription. This can be possible already with the current state of the system or after adaptation, depending on the capabilities of publishers providing notifications that match the subscription in type or content. In some cases, however, a requirement cannot be satisfied even after adapting due to limitations of the system or cost constraints and has to be declined. The remainder of this section describes the algorithm for matching expectations to capabilities, outlines how to decide about *satisfiable* expectations and illustrates how suitable reactions are selected at runtime by the middleware.

3.1   Matching Expectations to Capabilities

As publishers are described by their capability profile in terms of QoI, the whole decision problem is reduced to first a *set-* and then a *range-*matching problem between an expectation $\mathcal{X}_i^e$ and available capability profiles. The result is either a set of publishers with capability profiles already satisfying $\mathcal{X}_i^e$ ($\text{CAND}_{\mathcal{X}_i^e}$) or a set of publishers that are capable but would have to adapt ($\overline{\text{CAND}}_{\mathcal{X}_i^e}$).

The algorithms for matching an expectation $\mathcal{X}_i^e$ to a set of capability profiles $\{\mathcal{CP}_1^e, \ldots, \mathcal{CP}_l^e\}$ are shown in Fig. 3. The whole process is performed for a single expectation at a time. It can be triggered by a subscriber registering/updating an active expectation or by changes to capability profiles. A changed capability profile requires checking all expectations affected by it.

We define the following terms and relationships for a property p_e of an expectation $\mathcal{X}_i^e$ and a matching capability $\mathcal{C}_j^e$ of a capability profile $\mathcal{CP}_j^e$:

Covered property. A property of an expectation is *covered* if its range overlaps with the range of a matching capability (i.e., $C_j^e.lb \leq p_e.lb \vee C_j^e.ub \geq p_e.ub$) (c.f., Fig. 2 (a)). A property is *fully covered* if its range is enclosed or improved by the range of $\mathcal{C}_j^e$ (i.e., $C_j^e.lb \geq p_e.ub$ for maximization).

Dominated property. A property of an expectation is *dominated* if a matching capability's current value dominates the lower or upper bound of the property. A property that is dominated is also covered whereas a covered property is not necessarily dominated (c.f., Fig. 2 (b)).

Satisfiable expectation. An expectation is *satisfiable* if all its properties are covered by matching capabilities of at least one capability profile.

Satisfied expectation. An expectation is *satisfied* if all its properties are dominated by capabilities of a matching capability profile (c.f., Fig. 2 (c)).

Unsatisfied expectation. An expectation is *unsatisfied* if no matching set of capabilities exists (i.e., $\mathcal{CP}_j^e \subset \mathcal{X}_i^e \vee \mathcal{CP}_j^e \bigcap \mathcal{X}_i^e = \emptyset$) or if at least one property is not dominated by any matching capability (c.f., Fig. 2 (d)).

Deciding *if* an expectation is satisfied, satisfiable or unsatisfied does not require the middleware to compare it with every known capability profile but only with the most promising ones. Thus, each broker B maintains a *SuperSet* $\mathcal{S}_B^e$ per event type e that represents the *skyline* [7] of capabilities available at this broker: For every set of capabilities in $\mathcal{CP}^e$ it contains those capability profiles that are as good or better than all other capability profiles known at this broker in all capabilities and dominating in at least one capability as illustrated in Fig. 4. The *SuperSet* is updated with every change to a capability profile.

An expectation $\mathcal{X}_i^e$ is satisfied ($\mathcal{X}_i^e \in \text{SAT}$) if it is dominated by the *SuperSet*, satisfiable ($\mathcal{X}_i^e \in \overline{\text{SAT}}$) if covered by it and unsatisfiable ($\mathcal{X}_i^e \in \underline{\text{SAT}}$) if not.

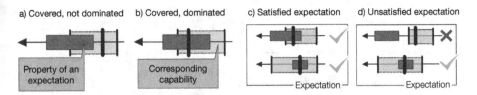

Fig. 2. Relationship between properties and corresponding capabilities

global: $\text{SAT}, \overline{\text{SAT}}, \underline{\text{SAT}}, \text{CAND}, \overline{\text{CAND}}$

function MATCH($\mathcal{X}_i^e, \mathcal{CP}_1^e, \ldots, \mathcal{CP}_l^e$)
  $State \leftarrow$ unsatisfied
  for all $\mathcal{CP}_j^e \in \{\mathcal{CP}_1^e, \ldots, \mathcal{CP}_l^e\}$ **do**
    $tS \leftarrow$ CHECKSTATE($\mathcal{X}_i^e, \mathcal{CP}_j^e$)
    switch tS **do**
      case satisfiable
        $\overline{\text{CAND}}_{\mathcal{X}_i^e}.add(\mathcal{CP}_j^e)$
        $State \leftarrow$ satisfiable
      case satisfied
        $\text{CAND}_{\mathcal{X}_i^e}.add(\mathcal{CP}_j^e)$
        $State \leftarrow$ satisfied
    end switch
  end for

  switch State **do**
    case satisfied: $\text{SAT}.add(\mathcal{X}_i^e)$
    case satisfiable: $\overline{\text{SAT}}.add(\mathcal{X}_i^e)$
    case unsatisfied: $\underline{\text{SAT}}.add(\mathcal{X}_i^e)$
  end switch
end function

function CHECKSTATE($\mathcal{X}_i^e, \mathcal{CP}_j^e$)
  $\text{SAT}_{p_e}, \overline{\text{SAT}}_{p_e}, \underline{\text{SAT}}_{p_e} \leftarrow \emptyset$
  for all $p_e \in \mathcal{X}_i^e$ **do**
    if SATISFIES($\mathcal{C}_j^e.cv, p_e$) **then**
      $\text{SAT}_{p_e}.add(p_e)$
    else if COVERS($\mathcal{C}_j^e, p_e$) **then**
      $\overline{\text{SAT}}_{p_e}.add(p_e)$
    else $\underline{\text{SAT}}_{p_e}.add(p_e)$
  end for

  if $\underline{\text{SAT}}_{p_e} \neq \emptyset$ **then return** unsatisfied
  else if $\text{SAT}_{p_e} = \mathcal{X}_i^e$ **then return** satisfied
  else return satisfiable
end function

function SATISFIES(v, p_e)
  if p_e.minimize **then**
    if $v \leq p_e.ub$ **then return** true
  if p_e.maximize **then**
    if $v \geq p_e.lb$ **then return** true
  return false
end function

Fig. 3. Algorithms in pseudocode for matching expectations to capabilities; function COVERS (checking if p_e is covered) is omitted due to space limitation

In a distributed setup, each broker forwards its *SuperSet* to its directly connected neighbors along the routing tree after modifying it: each contained capability profile is associated with the forwarding broker, masking the identity of the locally known provider (i.e., $\mathcal{CP}_j^e \rightarrow \mathcal{CP}_{b_k}^e$). Broker-related capabilities like *latency* have to be updated as well. Forwarded *SuperSets* are handled like capability profiles registered by local clients at each neighboring broker, starting an iterative update that generates a global skyline at the edge brokers.

Example: Matching in distributed EBS. Consider a distributed EBS with an acyclic routing topology as shown in Fig. 4 (top), consisting of brokers B and C, five publishers and four subscribers for events of type e. Expectations and capabilities are defined over properties p_a and p_b (improvable by minimization). Publishers $P_1 \rightarrow \{\mathcal{CP}_1^e\}, P_2 \rightarrow \{\mathcal{CP}_2^e\}, P_3 \rightarrow \{\mathcal{CP}_3^e\}$ register their capability profiles at broker B (c.f. Fig.. 4 (bottom left)), $P_4 \rightarrow \{\mathcal{CP}_4^e\}$ and $P_5 \rightarrow \{\mathcal{CP}_5^e\}$ at broker C. Broker B forwards its *SuperSet* $\mathcal{S}_B^e = \{\mathcal{CP}_1^e, \mathcal{CP}_2^e\}$ to broker C, masking the identity of P_1 and P_2. Note that $\mathcal{S}_C^e = \mathcal{S}_B^e$ as $\mathcal{S}_B^e$ dominates all other local capability profiles at broker C. At broker C, the sequentially registered

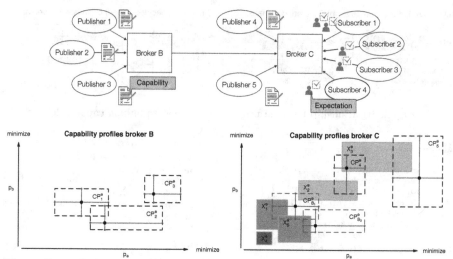

Fig. 4. Example for matching expectations to capabilities in a distributed broker network (top): Broker B forwards the *SuperSet* of its capability profiles (bottom left) to broker C where it is merged with the capability profiles of local publishers ($\mathcal{CP}_4^e, \mathcal{CP}_5^e$) and matched to expectations $\mathcal{X}_4^e$ (not satisfied), $\mathcal{X}_2^e$ & $\mathcal{X}_3^e$ (satisfied), and $\mathcal{X}_1^e$ & $\mathcal{X}_5^e$ (satisfiable), (bottom right). Axes show improvement direction.

expectations ($S_1 \to \{\mathcal{X}_3^e, \mathcal{X}_1^e\}, S_2 \to \{\mathcal{X}_2^e\}, S_3 \to \{\mathcal{X}_5^e\}, S_4 \to \{\mathcal{X}_4^e\}$) are each matched against $\mathcal{S}_C^e$ (c.f., Fig. 4 (bottom right)) using $\text{MATCH}(\mathcal{X}_i^e, \mathcal{S}_C^e)$ (c.f., Fig. 3). This results in: $\text{SAT} = \{\mathcal{X}_3^e, \mathcal{X}_2^e\}$ (satisfied), $\overline{\text{SAT}} = \{\mathcal{X}_1^e, \mathcal{X}_5^e\}$ (satisfiable) and $\underline{\text{SAT}} = \{\mathcal{X}_4^e\}$ (not satisfiable as it is not covered by any capability profile).

3.2 Deciding on Satisfiable Expectations

The matching algorithm marks an expectation as *satisfiable* if the system could satisfy it by self-adaptation. As this comes at a cost, the middleware has to assess if the expectation should be satisfied or declined. Different optimization strategies can be applied to such a decision problem [21]. For example, we can apply a strategy aiming at pareto-optimal states for subscribers: we decline an adaptation to satisfy $\mathcal{X}_i^e \in \overline{\text{SAT}}$ for subscriber i only if another expectation $\mathcal{X'}_i^e$ is already satisfied for subscriber i (i.e., $\mathcal{X'}_i^e \in \text{SAT}$) and satisfying $\mathcal{X}_i^e$ would be more expensive than the current state; we decide to adapt in all other cases. Referring to the example in Fig. 4, we assume S_1 to register $\mathcal{X}_1^e$ after $\mathcal{X}_3^e$ has been satisfied. The middleware would approve satisfying $\mathcal{X}_1^e$ by adapting publisher P_1 if $\sum_{p_e}^{\mathcal{X}_1^e} \mathcal{CP}_1^e.cost_{p_e}(p_e.ub) < \sum_{p_e}^{\mathcal{X}_3^e} \mathcal{CP}_1^e.cost_{p_e}(p_e.lb)$

3.3 Select Suitable Adaptations

The last step of the runtime negotiation process is to adapt the system and give feedback to subscribers. While system adaptation is limited to routing adjustments based on load-balancing strategies for *satisfied* expectations, approved *satisfiable* expectations require further adaptation. In this paper, we focus on runtime adaptation to satisfy an expectation $\mathcal{X}_i^e \in \overline{\text{SAT}}$; adaptation to free up resources or optimize system costs is part of future work.

The system adapts to increase ($\uparrow$) or decrease ($\downarrow$) properties to turn a suitable capability profile $\mathcal{C}_j^e$ into one satisfying $\mathcal{X}_i^e$. This can be achieved by adapting the middleware itself or by using feedback to advise the publisher associated with $\mathcal{C}_j^e$ to adapt. *Actions* define dedicated activities such as adaptPublisher. They are associated with properties as tuples $(p_e, \uparrow \vee \downarrow, action, costs_{action})$. Please note that sequences of actions can be defined as a new action. Alternative actions can be defined by associating multiple tuples for a property. They can have different costs but we assume $costs_{action} = 0$ if there is no alternative action available. For example, *rate* can be decreased by adapting a publisher or by applying a filter at the broker before delivering notifications to the subscriber [13]. This can be modeled in our concept by associating two tuples: $(rate, \downarrow, adaptPublisher, costs_{adaptPublisher})$ and $(rate, \downarrow, applyFilter, costs_{applyFilter})$.

We are currently selecting the least expensive action for a property to apply. Using other selection strategies at runtime is out of scope of this paper.

4   Implementation

Runtime support for QoI in EBS using expectations and capabilities is realized by extending the middleware with an ExpectationController and providing additional handlers to participants as shown in Fig. 5. We have implemented two prototypes in Java, extending the ActiveMQ JMS messaging broker[1] and the distributed REDS middleware[2]. We chose these two platforms for their different features: ActiveMQ is representative of an industrial-strength messaging system focussing on high performance, while the modular REDS systems allows us to exploit routing strategies and broker topologies for adaption. Both systems are easy to extend without affecting existing code. We use our prototypes to support QoI at runtime within the open-source monitoring system Ganglia[3] [13]. In this paper, we focus on describing the key components for a single broker setup.

4.1   Broker Extension: ExpectationController

We require access to the broker state for monitoring the system and to apply broker-related reactions like filtering messages or routing adaptation [12,13]. Thus, we provide ExpectationController as a plugin using BrokerPluginSupport on ActiveMQ and as an extended NodeDescriptor class defining a new broker type on REDS. Other components are implemented in an platform-agnostic way while platform-specific messages are used to communicate with participants. An ExpectationController consists of five key components (c.f. Fig. 5 (centre)):

[1] https://activemq.apache.org
[2] http://zeus.ws.dei.polimi.it/reds/
[3] http://ganglia.sourceforge.net/

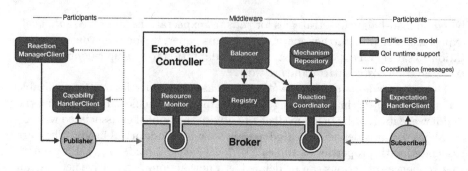

Fig. 5. Runtime support for QoI in EBS with expectations and capabilities showing additional components (dark gray) for participants and middleware (gray)

RessourceMonitor monitors the broker's state and the system's population, reporting changes to the Registry.

Registry stores all expectations and capabilities registered at this broker with the definitions of available properties and their matching. Changes trigger a negotiation of requirements at the Balancer.

Balancer matches expectations to capabilities (c.f., Sec. 3) while applying different optimization strategies. Triggers ReactionCoordinator upon completion.

ReactionCoordinator selects applicable actions from the MechanismRepository and coordinates their execution by adapting the broker, advising selected publishers to adapt using feedback or notifying subscribers.

MechanismRepository stores available actions for specific properties (c.f., Sec. 3.3). Actions are objects implementing generic or platform-specific activities.

4.2   Handlers for Participants

We provide participants with handlers to deal with feedback by the middleware and use platform-agnostic APIs for managing the lifecycle of expectations and capabilities: ExpectationHandlerClient allows subscribers to store, load, register, revoke, update, suspend or resume expectations. CapabilityHandlerClient enables publishers to store, load, register, revoke or update capabilities and access their usage statistics; publishers can register to be triggered by adaptation advices. Otherwise, an optional ReactionManagerClient adapts its associated publisher if advised by the ReactionCoordinator. For example, within our Ganglia scenario we implemented it as a wrapper that changes the configuration of each gmond publisher on the fly before restarting it, realizing adaptation within 26ms.

Expectations and capabilities are stored in XML while property definitions are separately stored using a key-value syntax. We chose these open formats for maximum portability. We provide a parser to process instances of expectations and capabilities with their property definitions in Java as well as a graphical editor to support the user.

5   Related Work

Work done by Keeton et al. [18] on general considerations about information quality and by Wilkes [27] on balancing requirements with consumers' utility has highly influenced our work; Behnel et al. [4] and Appel et al. [1] identify a basic set of quality guarantees and the levels of abstractions specific to EBS.

Our model has been inspired by complementary work on specifying and categorizing QoI for sensor networks: Perera et al. [20] support users in searching for sensor data sources using ontologies while the CommonSens middleware for assisted living by Soberg et al. [26] automatically selects sensors based on their domain-specific capabilities. Hossain et al. [16] and Bahjat et al. [3] propose frameworks to quantify QoI in IoT applications focussing on properties like uncertainty, precision, integrity or timeliness of detection. Bisdikian et al. [6] try to separate inherent quality attributes from application-specific ones as do Sachidananda et al. [23]. Our concept generalizes these application- and domain-specific properties, allowing requirements and capabilities to be expressed in a consistent and information-centric way.

We see most approaches proposed in the domain of EBS as complementary to our concept as they provide mechanisms to enforce dedicated quality-related properties that we can model using expectations: several systems address the issue of quality of service (QoS), focussing on network-specific properties like latency or jitter. We refer to [5] for an extensive overview and a more detailed discussion. Directly related to our work are the reactive middleware systems IndiQoS, as proposed by Carvalho et al. [9], Adamant by Hoffert [15] and Harmony by Yang et al. [28]. They support requirements about latency, reliability and bandwidth but focus on a closed set of requirements that is resolved on the transport protocol level only and omit enforcing publisher-related properties. We expand the scope of runtime support to include the enforcement of publisher-related properties by runtime adaptation based on feedback and allow subscribers to expose individual tradeoffs between requirements.

Related topics actively researched on in the area of (cloud-based) SOA are concepts for service selection as well as the negotiation of quality requirements and service-level agreements at runtime. We refer to [19,25] for a detailed discussion due to space limitations and would like to focus on two related contributions: Kattepur et al. [17] define a QoS metric similar to properties in expectations. However, they focus on interactions in heterogeneous SOA choreographies while expectations are information-centric; Pernici et al. [21] use fuzzy parameters for deciding on web service adaptation. Those approaches, however, are based on direct contracts between service providers and service consumers, often assuming the existence of explicitly modeled workflows or a central authority for coordination. They are not directly applicable to the indirect communication model of anonymous EBS. Integrating them with our concept is part of ongoing work.

6   Conclusion, Ongoing and Future Work

Event-based systems (EBS) complement SOA and enable enterprises to react to meaningful events in a timely manner. While quality of information (QoI) is crucial in these information-centric systems, it is supported only to a limited degree in today's EBS. We introduce the concept of **expectations** as a generic model to express, negotiate and enforce requirements about QoI in EBS at runtime. Instead of providing a fixed set of supported properties, our solution enables participants to define and manage requirements about arbitrary quality-related properties while exposing individual tradeoffs. Requirements are negotiated and enforced at the middleware by adapting data sources and brokers based on different optimization strategies and platform-specific mechanisms. Ongoing work focusses on evaluating our prototypic implementations in terms of performance and scalability using SPEC Research FINCoS[4] and the jms2009-PS benchmark [24]. Future work investigates interdependent and conflicting properties (e.g., adapting the system to support *order* for satisfying one expectation might lead to increased *latency*, violating other expectations). We also plan to extend our model to handle *composite properties* of expectations and capabilities such as *alternatives* [4] (i.e., notifications have to be provided by a number of different publishers all supporting a specific set of properties). Security and privacy aspects are important but orthogonal to our approach and currently out of scope.

Acknowledgements. We thank Stefan Appel, John Wilkes and Kimberly Keeton for their feedback on our work; Pascal Kleber and Erman Turan for their support in building the prototypes. Funding by German Federal Ministry of Education and Research (BMBF) under research grants 01|C12S01V and 01|S12054.

References

1. Appel, S., Sachs, K., Buchmann, A.: Quality of service in event-based systems. In: 22nd GI-Workshop on Foundations of Databases, GvD (2010)
2. Araujo, F., Rodrigues, L.: On QoS-aware publish-subscribe. In: ICDCSW (2002)
3. Bahjat, A., Jiang, Y., Cook, T., La Porta, T.: Quality of information functions for networked applications. In: PERCOM Workshops (2012)
4. Behnel, S., Fiege, L., Mühl, G.: On quality-of-service and publish-subscribe. In: ICDCS Distributed Computing Systems Workshops (2006)
5. Bellavista, P., Corradi, A., Reale, A.: Quality of service in wide scale publish/subscribe systems. IEEE Communications Surveys & Tutorials (99), 1–26 (2014)
6. Bisdikian, C., Kaplan, L., Srivastava, M.: On the quality and value of information in sensor networks. ACM Transactions on Sensor Networks 9(4), 39 (2010)
7. Borzsony, S., Kossmann, D., Stocker, K.: The skyline operator. In: ICDE (2001)
8. Buchmann, A., Appel, S., Freudenreich, T., Frischbier, S., Guerrero, P.E.: From calls to events: Architecting future BPM systems. In: Barros, A., Gal, A., Kindler, E. (eds.) BPM 2012. LNCS, vol. 7481, pp. 17–32. Springer, Heidelberg (2012)

---

[4] http://research.spec.org/tools/overview/fincos.html

9. Carvalho, N., Araujo, F., Rodrigues, L.: Scalable QoS-based event routing in publish-subscribe systems. In: Network Computing and Applications (2005)
10. Frischbier, S., Gesmann, M., Mayer, D., Roth, A., Webel, C.: Emergence as competitive advantage - engineering tomorrow's enterprise software systems. In: ICEIS (2012)
11. Frischbier, S., Margara, A., Freudenreich, T., Eugster, P., Eyers, D., Pietzuch, P.: ASIA: application-specific integrated aggregation for publish/subscribe middleware. In: Middleware 2012 Posters and Demos Track (2012)
12. Frischbier, S., Margara, A., Freudenreich, T., Eugster, P., Eyers, D., Pietzuch, P.: Aggregation for implicit invocations. In: AOSD (2013)
13. Frischbier, S., Margara, A., Freundenreich, T., Eugster, P., Eyers, D., Pietzuch, P.: McCAT: Multi-cloud Cost-aware Transport. In: EuroSys Poster Track (2014)
14. Hinze, A., Sachs, K., Buchmann, A.: Event-based applications and enabling technologies. In: DEBS (2009)
15. Hoffert, J., Schmidt, D.: Maintaining QoS for publish/subscribe middleware in dynamic environments. In: DEBS (2009)
16. Hossain, M.A., Atrey, P.K., Saddik, A.E.: Context-aware QoI computation in multisensor systems. In: MASS (2008)
17. Kattepur, A., Georgantas, N., Issarny, V.: QoS analysis in heterogeneous choreography interactions. In: Basu, S., Pautasso, C., Zhang, L., Fu, X. (eds.) ICSOC 2013. LNCS, vol. 8274, pp. 23–38. Springer, Heidelberg (2013)
18. Keeton, K., Mehra, P., Wilkes, J.: Do you know your IQ? A research agenda for information quality in systems. ACM SIGMETRICS Performance Evaluation Review 37(3), 26–31 (2010)
19. Kritikos, K., Pernici, B., Plebani, P., Cappiello, C., Comuzzi, M., Benrernou, S., Brandic, I., Kertész, A., Parkin, M., Carro, M.: A survey on service quality description. ACM Computing Surveys 46(1), 1 (2013)
20. Perera, C., Zaslavsky, A., Christen, P., Compton, M., Georgakopoulos, D.: Context-aware sensor search, selection and ranking model for internet of things middleware. In: Mobile Data Management (2013)
21. Pernici, B., Siadat, S.H.: Adaptation of web services based on qoS satisfaction. In: Maximilien, E.M., Rossi, G., Yuan, S.-T., Ludwig, H., Fantinato, M. (eds.) ICSOC 2010. LNCS, vol. 6568, pp. 65–75. Springer, Heidelberg (2011)
22. Pietzuch, P., Eyers, D., Kounev, S., Shand, B.: Towards a common API for publish/subscribe. In: DEBS (2007)
23. Sachidananda, V., Khelil, A., Suri, N.: Quality of information in wireless sensor networks: a survey survey. In: ICIQ (2010)
24. Sachs, K., Appel, S., Kounev, S., Buchmann, A.: Benchmarking publish/subscribe-based messaging systems. In: Database Systems for Advanced Applications: DASFAA 2010 International Workshops: BenchmarX 2010 (2010)
25. Shi, Y., Chen, X.: A survey on QoS-aware web service composition. In: Multimedia Information Networking and Security (2011)
26. Soberg, J., Goebel, V., Plagemann, T.: CommonSens: personalisation of complex event processing in automated homecare. In: ISSNIP (2010)
27. Wilkes, J.: Utility functions, prices, and negotiation. HP Labs HPL-2008-81 (2008)
28. Yang, H., Kim, M., Karenos, K., Ye, F., Lei, H.: Message-oriented middleware with qoS awareness. In: Baresi, L., Chi, C.-H., Suzuki, J. (eds.) ICSOC-ServiceWave 2009. LNCS, vol. 5900, pp. 331–345. Springer, Heidelberg (2009)

C2P: Co-operative Caching
in Distributed Storage Systems

Shripad J. Nadgowda[1], Ravella C. Sreenivas[2], Sanchit Gupta[3], Neha Gupta[4],
and Akshat Verma[1]

[1] IBM Research, India
{nadgowdas,akshatverma}@in.ibm.com
[2] IIT Kharagpur, India
chaitanya.sreenivas@cse.iitkgp.ernet.in
[3] IIT Kanpur, India
sanchitg@iitk.ac.in
[4] IIT Delhi, India
cs1100230@cse.iitd.ac.in

Abstract. Distributed storage systems (e.g. clustered filesystems - HDFS, GPFS
and Object Stores - Openstack swift) often partition sequential data across storage systems for performance (*data striping*) or protection (*Erasure-Coding*) .
This partitioning leads to logically correlated data being stored on different physical storage devices, which operate autonomously. This un-coordinated operation may lead to inefficient caching, where different devices may cache segments
that belong to different working sets. From an application perspective, caching
is effective only if all segments needed by it at a given point in time are cached
and a single missing segment may lead to high application latency. In this work,
we present C2P: a middleware for co-operative caching in distributed storage.
C2P uses an event-based architecture to co-ordinate caching across the storage
devices and ensures that all devices cache correlated segments. We have implemented C2P as a caching middleware for hosted Openstack Swift Object Store.
Our experiments show 4-6% improved cache hit and 3-5% reduced disk IO with
minimal resource overheads.

1 Introduction

Distributed storage systems often partition sequential data across storage systems for
performance (*data striping*) or protection (*Erasure-Coding*) . *Data striping* [5][4] is a
technique in which logically sequential data is partitioned into segments and each segment is stored on different physical storage device(HDD). This helps improve aggregate
I/O performance by allowing multiple I/O requests to be serviced in parallel from different devices. Striping has been used in practice by storage controllers to manage HDD
storage arrays for improved performance for more than a decade (e.g., *RAID 0* [15])
. Most of the popular enterprise cluster/distributed filesystems IBM GPFS[13], EMC
Isilon OneFS[14], Luster[17] etc. support data striping. Also, popular blob-storage like
Amazon S3[2], Openstack Swift[20], Microsoft Azure[18], Google Cloud Storage[11]
support segmented blob uploads.

X. Franch et al. (Eds.): ICSOC 2014, LNCS 8831, pp. 214–229, 2014.
© Springer-Verlag Berlin Heidelberg 2014

Logically correlated data in storage systems also gets partitioned due to new data protection techniques like Erasure-Coding (*EC*)[3][12][24], which deliver higher mean time between data loss (MTBDL) as compared to RAID. For example, with 9:3 *EC* data protection policy, when a new data is written, it is first partitioned into 9 equal-sized segments. Next, 3 additional code segments are computed from the data segments. These 12 segments are then stored on different storage nodes. Any 9 of these 12 segments then can be used to satisfy subsequent read requests for the data.This provides availability of the data for maximum up to 3 disk failures. Thus, either for performance or for redundancy, we are increasingly seeing data segmentation in distributed storage systems today.

1.1 Our Contributions

In this work, we specifically study and analyze cache efficiency for distributed storage systems. Typically, the placement policy in these systems is to store each segment on a different storage device/node, which operate autonomously with their own cache management policies. This leads to inefficient caching across all nodes, where different devices may cache segments that belong to different working sets. From an application perspective, caching is effective only if all segments needed by it at a given point in time are cached and a single missing segment may lead to high application latency.

We build the *C2P* system, which implements co-operative caching for distributed storage. *C2P* implements a reliable communication protocol between the cache controllers of individual storage nodes. Through this protocol, each controller communicates *relevant* local cache events (not the data) to the peer nodes. Each node leverages their local cache events and events communicated from peer nodes to implement a *co-ordinated caching policy*, which ensures that all the logically co-related segments of data will remain in the cache. We have implemented *C2P* for Openstack Swift, which is one of the most popular object stores. Our experiments show that *C2P* improves cache hit for objects by 4-6% and allows 5% of the additional requests to be serve from cache, with minimal resource overheads.

1.2 Paper Overview

The rest of this paper is organized as follows. We provide some background and motivate our problem and solution in Section 2. We also discuss the main challenges we faced, describe the architecture of *C2P*, and discuss certain key design choices. Section 3 describes our implementation of *C2P* and certain optimizations we performed. We evaluate *C2P* and report the results in Section 4. Section 5 discusses related work, and Section 6 highlights the limitations and other potential applications of *C2P*. We finally conclude this paper in Section 7.

2 Design

In this section, we first motivate the need for co-operative caching in distributed storage systems. We discuss few key design challenges for *C2P* and our approach.

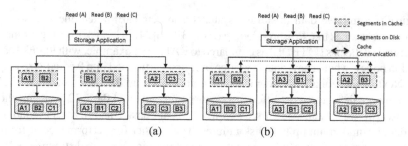

Fig. 1. Distributed Systems with (a) Independent and (b) Co-operative Caches

2.1   Motivation

Let's consider a distributed storage application with 3 storage nodes as shown in Fig.1. Each node has a cache capacity to host only 2 segments. We store 3 objects - *A, B, C* in this storage system. Each object is segmented into *3* partitions and placed on different storage nodes as shown. Also, consider the latency to access a segment from cache to be $50ms$ compared to the *disk latency* of $200ms$. We identify an *object access* as complete only when all its segments are read. Hence, *access latency* is defined as the maximum time taken to read any segment for the object. *Disk IO* is measured as the total segments read from disk across all storage nodes.

Fig.1 (a) shows the cache state at some point in time of a traditional system without any cache co-ordination and (b) shows the cache state of a co-operative co-ordinated cache system. At this stage if objects *A, B and C* are accessed from application, then we can observe the system characteristics as shown in Tab.1. As we can see, for both traditional and *C2P* system total segments hit (6) and miss (3) in the cache are same. Also, number of disk IOs (3) are same. However, applications experience very different access latency with the two systems. In the traditional system without any cache co-ordination, each of the object suffers disk latency (200 ms) in their access. On the other hand, in a co-operative cache system with co-ordination, we are able to reduce the access latency for 2 objects (*A, B*) to cache latency (50 ms) and only 1 object (*C*) incurs disk latency. Hence, if all cache controllers are able to achieve a distributed consensus on the segments to cache, this can lead to improved response time for served objects.

Table 1. Comparison between (a) Independent and (b) Co-operative Caches

	Traditional System				C2P System			
	Cache Hits	cache Miss	Access latency	Disk IO	Cache Hits	Cache Miss	Access latency	Disk IO
read(A)	2	1	200	1	3	0	50	0
read(B)	2	1	200	1	3	0	50	0
read(C)	2	1	200	1	0	3	200	3
Total	6	3	-	3	6	3	-	3

2.2   Design Challenges and Approach

A key appeal of distributed storage systems is their scale and reliability as there are no single points of contention or failure. A co-operative caching system needs to ensure that core distributed nature of the systems is not impacted. Hence, our design space is restricted to peer-based caching, where caching decision on each node is made in a completely distributed manner in contrast to a central controller that makes caching decisions. Each cache controller will implement an identical algorithm and the only change from classical independent cache controller is that each cache controller in *C2P* has access to relevant cache events from all peers. This kind of peer-based co-operative caching poses the following key challenges.

- **Distributed Consensus for Cache Management**: Each node in the *C2P* will have 2 sets of cache information - namely **Local Cache Metadata or LMD** and **Remote Cache Metadata or RMD**. LMD on a node is the repository of the cache events generated by that node while RMD is the repository of the cache events received from the peer nodes. In an ideal situation, all cache controllers need to arrive at a consensus on the objects to be cached in a fully distributed manner. Designing a distributed consensus is challenging and we address this problem by defining global metrics based on the local metrics and remote metrics. Our defined metrics lead to consistent values for objects across all storage nodes in a probabilistic sense. This ensures that even though each cache controller executes a cache eviction policy in isolation, all of them converge to the same object ordering in most cases.
- **Identifying Relevant Events**: Every data operation (READ/WRITE/DELETE) has associated one or more cache event(s). Moreover, same data operation can create different cache events. E.g. READ request for some data might cause <cache miss >or <cache hit >event. It is important to snoop these events very efficiently without adding any overhead to the data path. These captured events then need to be classified into predefined categories. These categories then help implement cache management policies in *C2P* system. E.g. prefetching policy would need <cache miss >category.
- **Peer node discovery**: A set of nodes are identified as **peer** if they are hosting the segments for the same objects. Set of peer nodes is different for each object. Peers are created dynamically and need to be identified quickly to ensure that *relevant* cache events are quickly communicated to peer. We had two design choices here: 1) each node broadcast their events to all nodes but only peer nodes will match and process those events. 2) each node send the events only to its peer nodes. The former option clearly had the downside of overloading the network. Consider, a storage system with 100 nodes where an object with 2 segments is stored will generate 200 events on the network (100 by each node) for each object access. Later option would certainly minimize this overhead. But it has challenge on how a node will discover it's peers for a given object. Storage applications typically decide on the placement of segments for an object dynamically and also stores this mapping. Thus, we could have an *application-tailored* peer node discovery for this purpose. In *C2P* we selected the latter option.
- **Load-proportional Communication Overhead**: Peak load in storage systems are co-related with high number of cache activities (reads, evictions, writes). Hence, more cache activities across nodes generate large number of cache events in the system. As a consequence, the network may become a bottleneck during high load and lead to inefficient caching. We address this problem by implementing an aggregation scheme, which ensures a communication overhead that is almost oblivious to application I/O load. In **aggregation**, cache events are buffered for short duration

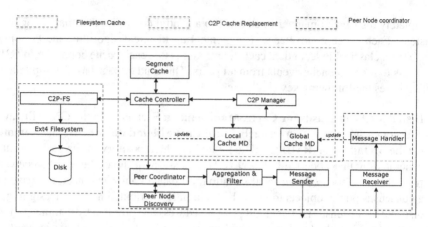

Fig. 2. Architecture of *C2P*

before transmitting and multiple cache events to the same peer node are coalesced together. We also use **filtering** to prioritize and drop low priority events.

3   Implementation

The design for *C2P* in itself can be implemented as an extension to any distributed storage system that supports data segmentation. As a concrete implementation, we have implemented *C2P* into a filesystem cache for open-sourced and widely accepted Openstack Swift - a highly available, distributed, eventually consistent object/blob store. We next discuss the implementation details.

3.1   Filesystem Cache

- **Filesystem:** For implementing *C2P* into a filesystem cache, we decided to use *Filesystem in user space (FUSE)* [10]. FUSE allows us to develop a fully functional filesystem in user's space with simple API library, and it has a proven track record of stability. We call our filesystem implementation C2P-FS. In C2P-FS we have primarily extended read() and write() API calls and other calls are simply redirected to the lower filesystem.
- **Cache:** Similar to "page cache" in traditional filesystem, we have defined "segment cache" in C2P-FS. We have implemented cache using a fixed-size shared memory. Based on size of the workload used during the experiments and heuristics derived from real world scenarios, we configured cache size to be *128 MB* on each storage node. Further, cache line size is changed from page size to segment size i.e. from 4KB to 1 MB. Thus, C2P-FS cache can hold maximum of 128 segments. This change in the cache line size is motivated by three facts: 1) swift application is going to be used for storing/accessing segmented dynamic large objects with segment size of 1 MB 2) partial object access is not available in swift 3) Thus, any object IO (GET/PUT) in swift will cause file IOs (read/write) on C2P-FS on each storage node in the unit of 1 MB. And, having a cache line aligned with the size of IO request is going to boost the performance for any storage system.

Table 2. C2P Data Structures

Event ID	Definition
1	(cache replace) data flushed from the cache
2	(cache add) new data added to cache
3	(cache miss) data is read from disk and added to cache
4	(cache hit) data read from the cache
5	(cache delete) data is deleted from disk and cache

(a) Cache Event Classification

MD field	Definition
path	local filepath of the segment
timestamp	local access time of segment
hitcount	local hit count of segment

(b) Local cache Metadata (LMD)

MD field	Definiition
path	local filepath of the segment
timestamp	global access time of an object
hitcount	global hit count of an object
Object in Cache (OiC)	fraction of object's all segments present in the cache

(c) Global Cache Metadata (GMD)

3.2 Peer Nodes Co-ordination

– **Cache Events:** We first identified and classified the important cache operations that needs to be communicated to the peer nodes as shown in Tab.2(a). For each file IO request in C2P-FS there are going to be one or more cache operations in cache controller. E.g. if the cache is full and there is a read request for data which is not present in the cache, then there will be *cache miss* and *cache replacement* operations in cache controller. For each operation, cache controller then generates a *cache event* and asynchronously sends it for communication. Cache event is a tuple with <event id, file path, timestamp>and size less than 100 bytes. Cache controller also adds this cache event to the *Local Cache MD* (discussed below).

– **Peer nodes discovery:** In object stores, data has different namespaces in storage application (like swift) and filesystem on storage node where it is stored. When user uploads a data, it is identified as "/<container(s)>/<objectid>" by swift. And when it is stored on filesystem is has a filepath like <objectid>/ <timestamp>/ <size>/ . E.g. for uploading 5 MB data with 1MB segment size user will have command like "swift upload mycontainer myfile" and say on storage nodes node1, node2,...node5 these segments gets stored with filepaths like my-file /1401080357/ 1000000/ 01, myfile/ 1401080357/ 1000000/ 02 ,../05. Since, we have a cache implemented at filesystem, in cache events we can only get filepath for segments. For finding the peer nodes storing the segments for the same objects we made following two changes: 1) inverse lookup for object path from filepath, we changed swift-client to add an extra header "X-Obj-Name:<objpath >" for each segment. This header gets stored as an xattr of the segment file, which we can read to get an object path for a segment. 2) We have developed a new swift service called "swift-discovery" implementing the same protocol as a swift's ring service. Given an object path this discovery service returns a list of peer nodes storing the segments for the same objects and the local filepaths of those segments on the respective storage nodes. For example, calling discovery service on node1 with filepath my-file/../01, will return a peer nodes map as node2:myfile/../02, node3:myfile/../03,....

– **Message Broker:** We use RabbitMQ [22] as a message broker for communicating cache events between storage nodes. We create one message queue per node. Then, for a given cache event and list of peer nodes, it publishes each event in queue of respective peer node. To minimize the network overhead, we implemented

'Aggregation and Filter' policy. In aggregation, before publishing the cache event, we buffer them for short duration of 200 ms. And during this time, if there are more cache events for the same node, then they are aggregated which reduces the payload size. While aggregation is an optimization policy, filtering is a throttling policy. In an overloaded system filtering essentially prioritize and drop some events.

3.3 C2P for Cache Replacement

– **Local cache MD:** Local cache MD (LMD) is the metadata about the segments which are currently present in the segment cache. This MD is maintained in a separate segment of a shared-memory. Each storage node will have their own LMD. The metadata primarily contains 3 fields as shown in Tab.2(b). When a new segment is added to the cache (for cache add/miss) a tuple with <path, current time, 1> is added into this MD. Them for every segment read (cache hit) from the cache this tuple is updated with <current time, hitcount++>. Finally, when a segment is removed from the cache (cache delete/replaced) the MD is removed. In the absence of any co-operation between the storage nodes, cache controller on each node can use this LMD to implement *Least Recently Used (LRU)* replacement policy as described in Algo 1.

Algorithm 1. LRU Comparator

1: **procedure** LRU-COMPARE(candidate a, candidate b)
2:      $affinity_{th} \leftarrow temporal - affinity - threshold$
3:      **if** $(|a.timestamp - b.timestamp|) < affinity_{th}$ **then**
4:          **if** $a.timestmap > b.ttimestamp$ **then**
5:              **return** 1
6:          **else** $a.timestamp < b.timestamp$
7:              **return** -1
8:          **end if**
9:      **end if**
10:     **if** $a.hitcount > b.hitcount$ **then**
11:         **return** 1
12:     **else** $a.hitcount < b.hitcount$
13:         **return** -1
14:     **end if**
15:     **return** 0
16: **end procedure**

– **Global cache MD:** Global cache MD (GMD) on a given storage node is the metadata about segments hosted on that storage node and which is communicated from the peer storage nodes. Note that, the segments in this GMD not necessarily be in present in the cache but it could also be on the disk as well. Fields of the GMD are shown in Tab.2(c). When an object is read, all it's segments will be accessed generating an cache event for their peer nodes. Also, each node will receive cache event from all peer nodes for a given segment. <timestamp> is the latest timestamp received from cache event for a segment. <hitcount>for a segment is incremented for each cache event received. Thus, when an object is accessed, each node hosting the segments will have *Local hitcount = 1* and *Global hitcount = 5*. We normalise *Global hitcount* w.r.t *Local hitcount* to determine an *object size* i.e. number of segments for an object. E.g. For *Global hitcount = 5 and Local hitcount = 1* object size = Global hitcount / Local hitcount = 5. Finally, *Object in Cache (OiC)* is the most critical field from the GMD and is being used to implement C2P cache replacement policy. OiC is defined as the fraction of all segments of an object available in cache across all peer nodes. Considering that with swift, there won't be any partial object access, *OiC* is reset to 1 for any *cache add or cache miss* event. And it is recomputed as follows: first *segeval* is computed as (1/object size) which is the fractional value for each segment of an object. Then, for every *cache replace* event OiC is decremented as (OiC = OiC - segeval). Fig.3 shows along a timeline, few sample cache events and how those are reflected into GMD state on one of the storage node for one segment

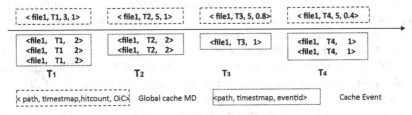

Fig. 3. GMD State Transition

- **Hitcount Decay:** We have defined exponentially decay function on hitcount of an object. If an object is not accessed recently (not within last 60 secs, which is a heuristically derived period) then, we decrement the current hitcount by factor of 0.8. This decay ensures cache-fairness through normalization of hitcount for objects which are popular for short period (gets high hitcount in short time).

- **C2P Cache Replacement:** To demonstrate the effectiveness of co-ordinated caching in distributed storage systems, we have designed and implemented a cache replacement policy on C2P system named *C2P-CR*. We have also implemented the *LRU* replacement policy to simulate the one in traditional systems. In *LRU* we sort all the candidate cache MDs using an LRU-Comparator function as described in Algo. 1. In this function, we first measure the *temporal affinity* between the two candidates, which is essentially difference between their timestamps. If the affinity is less than a (heuristically derived) threshold, then they are sorted based on their timestamps. Otherwise, they are sorted from their hitcount. For *C2P* we have defined a C2P-Comparator for sorting candidates to be selected for cache replacement as described in Algo.2. In this we leverage both LMD as well as GMD to select the segment(s) to be replaced from cache. First *Object in Cache*(OiC) is computed from GMD as discussed earlier and candidates are compared based on OiC. If the candidates have same OiC, then those candidates are sorted using LRU-Comparator. Thus, *C2P-CR* is essentially built on top of *LRU*.

Algorithm 2. C2P CR Comparator

1: **procedure** C2P-COMPARE(candidate a, candidate b)
2:     **if** $a.OiC > b.OiC$ **then**
3:         **return** 1
4:     **else** $a.OiC < b.OiC$
5:         **return** -1
6:     **end if**
7:     **return** LRU-Compare(a,b)
8: **end procedure**

---

4   Evaluation

We evaluate *C2P* with Openstack Swift Object store. Swift was deployed on a set of 8 VMs running Ubuntu 12.04 LTS. The VMs were hosted on 2 servers each with 24-core 3:07GHz Xeon(R) processor and 64GB memory. Each VM was configured with 2 vC-PUs, 2 GB memory and a 50 GB disk formatted with ext4 filesystem. We configured 128 MB cache size for C2P-FS on each VM. This cache size was decided based on heuristics and size of our workloads. We have defined two configurable modes of cache management for C2P-FS - namely C:ON and C:OFF. C:ON indicates that co-operative caching policy is ON for cache replacement on all storage nodes while C:OFF indicates that each node implements default *LRU* cache replacement policy. We evaluate *C2P* based on several metrics. First, in the *baseline experiments*, we measured the overhead of our cache implementation by comparing the performance with native implementation of fuse. Then, in the *case study* experiment we specifically measured the cache efficiency with *C2P* cache replacement policy against traditional *LRU: Least recently used*.

We tag all the data access (read) on each of the individual storage node either as a *segment hit* or a *segment miss*. *segment hit* indicates that the data is read from the cache while the later indicates that data is read from the disk. More importantly we also tag each object access. When each segment of an object is a *segment hit* we identify it as an *Object hit*. If there is a *segment miss* for even a single segment, it is an *Object miss*. We further decompose *Object miss* into *Object miss complete* and *Object miss partial* to indicate whether there is a *segment miss* for all the segments or some segments respectively . We define *comm latency* as the delay between the times when a cache event is published by any storage node and when it is delivered to peer nodes. We also measured *comm overhead* as the number of messages (cache events) generated per second. Finally, we measured *object throughput* as size of object (in MB) read per second.

4.1   Baseline Experiment

In this section, we discuss baseline experiments that we conducted to evaluate the performance overhead of our cache implementation with fuse [10] filesystem. We conducted these experiments in two phases. In the first phase, we used standard swift deployment wherein each storage node had ext4 filesystem with it's native *LRU* cache replacement policy. In the second phase, we deployed swift with our C2P-FS in C:OFF mode i.e.cache

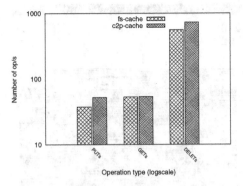

Fig. 4. Swiftbench Evaluation

co-operation is disabled and default *LRU* cache replacement policy is used on storage nodes to match standard setup. We used *Swift-bench* [21] which is a standard benchmarking tool for Openstack Swift. We chose three common IO workloads on any object store - namely PUT, GET and DELETE for these experiments. We further define the workload profile with 500 PUTs, 2000 (random) GETs and 500 DELETEs for object size of *1 MB*. Then, we ran this same workload profile in both phases and measured operation throughput as shown in Fig.4. As we can see, C2P-FS achieves almost the same throughput as with the standard filesystem deployment for all three kinds of workloads. Thus through these baseline experiment we established that our C2P-FS cache implementation does not incur any performance overhead over a standard swift deployment. Hence, in the case study experiments below we used C2P-FS in C:OFF mode as a reference system implementing *LRU*. Then we compared and contrasted the metric measurements of *C2P* system against it.

4.2   Case Study

In case study experiment, we try to motivate application of *C2P* for distributed storage system hosting a segmented or striped data for improved cache efficiency.

Data Store: We first uploaded 500 objects of size *5 MB* each. During upload, we split the object with *1 MB* segment size using swift's support for dynamic large object. Ideally, we would expect each segment to be stored on different storage node. But, swift uses a ring service for placement which does not guarantee this segment isolation for a given object. We captured segment placements for all the objects across 8 storage nodes in a heatmap shown in Fig.5. As we can see for some objects maximum of 4 segments are stored on a same storage node. We also measured total number of segments stored on each storage node. Fig.6(b) shows the distribution of all (500 x 5 = 2500) segments across 8 storage nodes. The distribution is not even across the nodes, and this is typically true for all the distributed systems.

Access pattern: We used powerlaw to generate a long tail distribution series with 2000 numbers in the range [0:500] which would mimic a real-world application access pattern. Such series typically identifies a workset which contains few popular objects that are accessed more frequently as shown in Fig.6(a). We numbered all objects from the data store from 1-500 and then used this series to identify the object number to

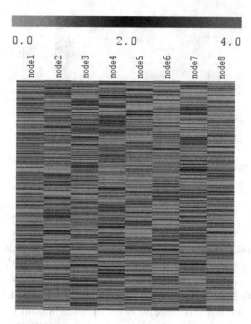

Fig. 5. Segment Placement heatmap for objects

access. When we access an object, we access it completely i.e. all 5 segments. But, even for partial access *C2P* efficiency will be the same. We also measured total segments accessed across all storage nodes as shown in Fig.6(b). As we can see, there is a large variation in the access load across storage nodes which is again mostly true for all distributed storage systems.

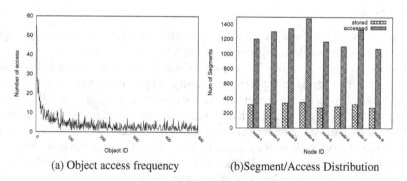

(a) Object access frequency   (b)Segment/Access Distribution

Fig. 6. Data Store and Access pattern

Thus, this un-even segment distribution compounded with variant access load creates an erratic data pressure across storage nodes in distributed storage systems. Thus, there is a greater need of co-operation to enable highly utilized nodes to mantain their cache states in consistent with their peer nodes which are less utilized.

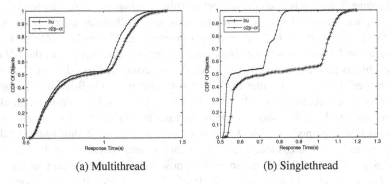

(a) Multithread   (b) Singlethread

Fig. 7. Response Time CDF

Single-threaded Run. In single-threaded run we used a single swift client which would read objects from the data store following an access pattern. In the results, first we analyze the most important aspect from application's point of view i.e. *Object hit* ratio. As shown in Fig.8(a) for C2P systems we get almost 6.7% more *Object hit* in the cache. Amongst object misses, we measured around 50% reduction for *Object miss partial* and 4% increase for *Object miss complete*. Putting these numbers in perspective, we note that for applications storing segmented objects, C2P system can help achieve better cache efficiency at object level to reduce an application latency. In Fig.7(b), we also plot cdf of number of objects against their response time. This is an important measure which can be translated into SLA assurance of a storage system. For example, for SLA of *response time <0.8 sec C2P* system has about 6% more objects satisfying the SLA than the one implementing *LRU*. Another interesting observation we made here is that, for cache missed objects response time for *C2P* is between $0.7s$ to $0.9s$ while that for *LRU* is between $0.7s$ to $1.2s$. We conjecture that this increased latency for *LRU* for cache missed objects is attributed to the increased disk queue length for missed segments. Fig.8(b) shows the *object throughput* measured for each object access. It shows for *C2P*, most of the objects have either high throughput around $9\ MBps$ (Object hit) or low throughput around around $4\ MBps$(Object miss complete). While for *LRU* there are many objects with throughput in between (Object miss partial). As mentioned earlier, for *C2P* we increases *Object miss complete*, but that does not necessarily means disk IO is also increased. To elaborate on this, for each object accessed we also traced *segment hit* ratio on each storage node. As shown in Fig.8(c) on each individual storage node we get more *segment hits*. In effect, we reduces disk IO on each storage node and overall we observed about 5% reduced disk IO across all storage nodes which is a very critical measure for any storage system. Finally, Fig.10 shows the Rabbit MQ's monitored state of the message queue. As we can see, C2P system requires around 20 messages/s to cache event co-ordination and *comm latency* less than 200 ms. And considering size of each message is less than 100 Bytes, the network overhead is very minimal.

Multi-threaded Run. In multi-threaded run we used 4 swift clients. We split the access pattern of 2000 objects into 4 access patterns of 500. Then, we ran all the 4 clients in parallel requesting objects from the respective split-access pattern. Similar to Single-threaded run, we measured system characteristics across different metrics. Fig.9(a) shows 4.5% improved *Object hit*, and amongst object misses 43% reduced *Object miss partial* and around 4% increases for *Object miss complete*. Fig.7(a) shows the cdf of number of objects against their response time. Again, compared to *LRU* in *C2P* we measured larger % of objects under any given response time. Fig.9(b) shows *object throughput* for object access across all 4 clients. We observe similar pattern to that of a singlethread run. And Fig.9(c) shows *segment hit* distribution across all storage nodes. Again, on each storage node we observe better cache hits for C2P, thus reducing the disk IO by around 3.5% across all nodes. Fig.11 shows *comm overhead* in the order of 70 messages/s (7KBps) still very minimal. But, now we get *comm latency* in around 1 second. *Comm overhead* and *latency* are observed to be higher than the respective numbers in the single-threaded run. This is because in multithreaded run, object request rate is higher being coming from 4 clients in parallel which in turn increases the rate of cache activities on individual storage nodes, thus cache events are published at a higher rate. We observed, *Object hit* for C2P system in this run is slightly less than that in the single threaded run. This is attributed to the higher *comm latency* which increases the delay between cache co-ordination across storage nodes. In out future work, we will try to minimize this effect of latency on cache efficiency.

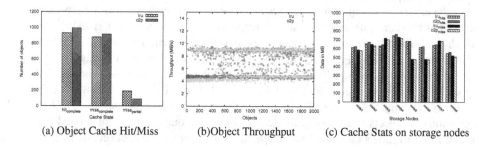

(a) Object Cache Hit/Miss   (b)Object Throughput   (c) Cache Stats on storage nodes

Fig. 8. Single Threaded Data Access Evaluation

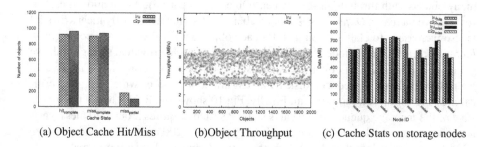

(a) Object Cache Hit/Miss   (b)Object Throughput   (c) Cache Stats on storage nodes

Fig. 9. Multi Threaded Data Access Evaluation

 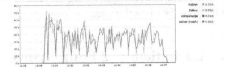

Fig. 10. Singlethread run overhead   **Fig. 11.** Multithread run overhead

The maximum value of *comm latency* for optimal performance of C2P system, is a function of size of cache on each storage node. Although, it is important to note here that effectiveness of C2P systems is not limited by *comm latency* of less than a second. But, since we had a small cache size on storage nodes,

To summarize the case study results we note: 1) compare to traditional *LRU* cache replacement policy, C2P achieves 4-6% increase in the object hits thus reducing the access latency for more objects. 2) In C2P systems, on each of the comprising storage nodes cache hits are improved reducing the disk IO by around 3-5%. And 3) event-based architecture to co-ordinate caching incurs a very minimal network overhead.

5   Related Work

Distributed systems and cache coordination techniques in such systems has been around for a long time[1][23][7][6][16]. But cache cooperation traditionally been applied in contexts like scaling or disk IO optimization. To our best knowledge *C2P* is the first system designed to maximize cache efficiency of distributed storage hosting segmented data.

Scale: Memcached[9] is a general-purpose distributed memory caching system. For a large scale cache requirements, hundreds of nodes are setup. And these nodes then leverages their memory through memcached to build a large in-memory key-value store for small chunks of arbitrary data. Facebook probably is the world's largest user of memcached[19].

Disk IO optimization: CCM[8] probably is closet to our work. For cluster-based servers, CCM keeps an accounting information for multiple copies of the same data (blocks) available in the cache across all nodes. Then, this information is used to forward IO requests between nodes to ensure cache hit. Essentially, they increase network communication to reduce disk access. Similarly in [1], technique of split caching is used to avoid disk reads by using the combined memory of the clients as a cooperative cache. DSC[16] describes the problems of the exposition of one nodes resources to others. As they state, cache state interactions and the adoption of a common scheme for cache management policies are two primary reasons behind the problem. [6] mentions interesting techniques for data prefetching with Co-Operative Caching. The bottomline in all these prior work is that - a cache cooperation will happen between the nodes only if they contains the same data.

In *C2P*, the primary distinction is that cache cooperation is designed for *logically related* data e.g. different segments of the same object. Also, there is no resource exposition between the nodes in the cluster i.e. each node will serve the ONLY IO requests for which it is actually hosting the data. Thus, IO requests are not forwarded between the nodes, but just the cache events are communicated.

6   Limitations and Future Work

C2P design presented in this paper caters to the distributed systems storing segmented data and ensures better cache efficiency for them. In our current implementation we have exploited this cache cooperation only for *cache replacement* policy. We also plan to implement and exercise *cache prefetching* for *C2P*, wherein we can prefetch segments based on cache events from the peer nodes. We believe such prefetching will further improve the cache efficiency.

One of the data property we haven't considered in *C2P* is - *replication*. For storage systems, data striping and replication can be applied simulteneously. Here, first we need to understand placement and access characteristics of such data. Then for these scenarios, through cache cooperation we can ensure only one copy of the data segment remains in the cache across all nodes. And these segments in cache might belong to different replica copy of the data.

Finally, we plan to deploy *C2P* in some production distributed system and measure the scalability, overhead for live data.

7   Conclusion

In this paper we present *C2P*: a coperative caching policy for distributed stoarge systems. *C2P* implements a coordination protocol wherein each node communicates their local cache events to peers. Then based on these additional cache state information of peers, each node implements a co-ordinated caching policy for *cache replacement* and *cache prefetching*. These policies in turn ensures a consistent caching across nodes for segments of the data which are logically related. Thus, we can reduce the access latency for the data and improve the overall performance of the system.

References

1. Adya, A., Castro, M., Liskov, B., Maheshwari, U., Shrira, L.: Fragment reconstruction: Providing global cache coherence in a transactional storage system. In: Proceedings of the 17th International Conference on Distributed Computing Systems, pp. 2–11. IEEE (1997)
2. Amazon: Amazon S3, http://aws.amazon.com/s3/
3. Bloemer, J., Kalfane, M., Karp, R., Karpinski, M., Luby, M., Zuckerman, D.: An xor-based erasure-resilient coding scheme (1995)
4. Cabrera, L.F., Long, D.: Using data striping in a local area network (1992)
5. Cabrera, L.F., Long, D.D.E.: Swift: Using distributed disk striping to provide high i/o data rates. Computing Systems 4(4), 405–436 (1991)
6. Chi, C.H., Lau, S.: Data prefetching with co-operative caching. In: 5th International Conference on High Performance Computing, HIPC 1998, pp. 25–32. IEEE (1998)
7. Clarke, K.J., Gittins, R., McPolin, S., Rang, A.: Distributed storage cache coherency system and method, US Patent 7,017,012 (March 21, 2006)

8. Cuenca-Acuna, F.M., Nguyen, T.D.: Cooperative caching middleware for cluster-based servers. In: Proceedings of the 10th IEEE International Symposium on High Performance Distributed Computing, pp. 303–314. IEEE (2001)

9. Fitzpatrick, B.: Distributed caching with memcached. Linux Journal 2004(124), 5 (2004)

10. Fuse: Filesystem in Userspace, http://fuse.sourceforge.net/

11. Google: Google Cloud Storage, http://cloud.google.com/Storage

12. Huang, C., Simitci, H., Xu, Y., Ogus, A., Calder, B., Gopalan, P., Li, J., Yekhanin, S., et al.: Erasure coding in windows azure storage. In: USENIX ATC, vol. 12 (2012)

13. IBM: Introduction to GPFS 3.5 - IBM. RedBook (2012)

14. Isilon, E.: EMC Isilon OneFS: A Technical Overview. White paper (2013)

15. LACIE: RAID Technology. White paper

16. Laoutaris, N., Smaragdakis, G., Bestavros, A., Matta, I., Stavrakakis, I.: Distributed selfish caching. IEEE Transactions on Parallel and Distributed Systems 18(10), 1361–1376 (2007)

17. Luster: Lustre Filesystem, http://wiki.lustre.org

18. Microsoft: Microsoft Azure, http://azure.microsoft.com

19. Nishtala, R., Fugal, H., Grimm, S., Kwiatkowski, M., Lee, H., Li, H.C., McElroy, R., Paleczny, M., Peek, D., Saab, P.: et al.: Scaling memcache at facebook. In: Proceedings of the 10th USENIX conference on Networked Systems Design and Implementation, pp. 385–398. USENIX Association (2013)

20. Openstack: Openstack Swift, http://swift.openstack.org

21. Openstack: Swiftbench. https://launchpad.net/swift-bench

22. RabbitMQ: RabbitMQ., https://www.rabbitmq.com/

23. Sarkar, P., Hartman, J.H.: Hint-based cooperative caching. ACM Transactions on Computer Systems (TOCS) 18(4), 387–419 (2000)

24. Weatherspoon, H., Kubiatowicz, J.D.: Erasure coding vs. replication: A quantitative comparison. In: Druschel, P., Kaashoek, M.F., Rowstron, A. (eds.) IPTPS 2002. LNCS, vol. 2429, pp. 328–337. Springer, Heidelberg (2002)

Detection of REST Patterns and Antipatterns: A Heuristics-Based Approach

Francis Palma[1,2], Johann Dubois[1,3], Naouel Moha[1],
and Yann-Gaël Guéhéneuc[2]

[1] Département d'informatique, Université du Québec à Montréal, Canada
moha.naouel@uqam.ca
[2] Ptidej Team, DGIGL, École Polytechnique de Montréal, Canada
{francis.palma,yann-gael.gueheneuc}@polymtl.ca
[3] École supérieure d'informatique, eXia.Cesi, France
johann.dubois@viacesi.fr

Abstract. REST (REpresentational State Transfer), relying on *resources* as its architectural unit, is currently a popular architectural choice for building Web-based applications. It is shown that *design patterns*—good solutions to recurring design problems—improve the design quality and facilitate maintenance and evolution of software systems. *Antipatterns*, on the other hand, are poor and counter-productive solutions. Therefore, the detection of REST (anti)patterns is essential for improving the maintenance and evolution of RESTful systems. Until now, however, no approach has been proposed. In this paper, we propose SODA-R (Service Oriented Detection for Antipatterns in REST), a heuristics-based approach to detect (anti)patterns in RESTful systems. We define detection heuristics for eight REST antipatterns and five patterns, and perform their detection on a set of 12 widely-used REST APIs including BestBuy, Facebook, and DropBox. The results show that SODA-R can perform the detection of REST (anti)patterns with high accuracy. We also found that Twitter and DropBox are not well-designed, *i.e.*, contain more antipatterns. In contrast, Facebook and BestBuy are well-designed, *i.e.*, contain more patterns and less antipatterns.

Keywords: REST, Antipatterns, Patterns, Design, Heuristics, Detection.

1 Introduction

Over the last decade, there is a paradigmatic shift from the traditional stand-alone software solutions towards the service-oriented paradigm to design, develop, and deploy software systems [1]. REST (REpresentational State Transfer) [7] architectural style is simpler and more efficient than the traditional SOAP-based (Simple Object Access Protocol) Web services in publishing and consuming services [18]. Thus, RESTful services are gaining an increased attention. Facebook, YouTube, Twitter, and many more companies leverage REST.

However, the increased usage of REST for designing and developing Web-based applications confronts common software engineering challenges. In fact, likewise

X. Franch et al. (Eds.): ICSOC 2014, LNCS 8831, pp. 230–244, 2014.
© Springer-Verlag Berlin Heidelberg 2014

any software system, RESTful systems must evolve to handle new web entities and resources, *i.e.*, meet new business requirements. Even, the changes in underlying technologies or protocols may force the REST APIs to change. All these changes may degrade the design of REST APIs, which may cause the introduction of common poor solutions to recurring design problems—*antipatterns*—in opposition to *design patterns*, which are good solutions to the problems that software engineers face while designing and developing RESTful systems. Anti(patterns) might be introduced even in the early design phase of RESTful systems. Antipatterns in RESTful systems not only degrade their design but also make their maintenance and evolution difficult, whereas design patterns facilitate them [3,5,6].

Forgetting Hypermedia [16] is a common REST antipattern that corresponds to the absence of *hypermedia*, *i.e.*, links within resource representations. The absence of such links hinders the state transition of RESTful systems and limits the runtime communication between clients and servers. In contrast, *Entity Linking* [6]—the corresponding design pattern—promotes runtime communication via links provided by the servers within resource representations. By using such hyper-links, the services and consumers can be more autonomous and loosely coupled. For REST APIs, the automatic detection of such (anti)patterns is an important activity by assessing their design (1) to ease their maintenance and evolution and (2) to improve their design quality.

REST (anti)patterns require a concrete detection approach, to support their rigorous analysis, which is still lacking. Despite the presence of several technology-specific approaches in SCA (Service Component Architecture) and Web services (*e.g.*, [3,9–11,13]), they are not applicable for detecting (anti)patterns in REST. Indeed, the key differences between REST architecture and other SOA standards prevents the application of these approaches because: (1) traditional service-orientation is operations-centric, whereas REST is resources-centric, (2) RESTful services are on top of JSON (or XML) over HTTP, whereas traditional Web services are on top of SOAP over HTTP or JMS (Java Message Service), (3) Web services use WSDL (Web Service Definition Language) as their formal contracts; REST has no standardised contract except the human-readable documentations, (4) traditional services are the set of self-contained software artefacts where operations are denoted using verbs; resources in REST are denoted by nouns and are directly-accessible objects via URIs, and (5) REST clients use the standard HTTP methods to interact with resources; Web services clients implement separate client-stubs to consume services.

Among many others, the differences discussed above motivate us to propose a new approach, SODA-R (Service Oriented Detection for Antipatterns in REST) to detect (anti)patterns in RESTful systems. SODA-R is supported by an underlying framework, SOFA (Service Oriented Framework for Antipatterns) [9] that supports static and dynamic analyses of service-based systems.

To validate SODA-R, first, we perform a thorough analysis of REST (anti)patterns from the literature [2,5,6,8,12,16] and define their detection heuristics. A detection heuristic provides an indication for the presence of certain design issues. For instance, a heuristic "*servers should provide entity links in their responses*", suggests that REST developers need to provide *entity links* in the responses that REST clients can use. For such case, we define a detection heuristic to check if the response header or body contains any resource location or entity links. Following the defined heuristics, we implement their concrete detection algorithms, apply them on widely used REST APIs, and get the list of REST services detected as (anti)patterns. Our detection results show the effectiveness and accuracy of SODA-R: it can detect five REST patterns and eight REST antipatterns with an average precision and recall of more than of 75% on 12 REST APIs including BestBuy, Facebook, and DropBox.

Thus, the main contributions in this paper are: (1) the definition of detection heuristics for 13 REST (anti)patterns from the literature, namely [2, 5, 6, 8, 12, 16], (2) the extension of SOFA framework from its early version [9] to allow the detection of REST (anti)patterns, and, finally, (3) the thorough validation of SODA-R approach with 13 REST (anti)patterns on a set of 12 REST APIs by invoking 115 REST methods from them.

The reminder of the paper is organised as follows. Section 2 briefly describes the contributions from the literature on the specification and detection of SOA (anti)patterns. Section 3 presents our approach SODA-R, while Section 4 presents its validation along with detailed discussions. Finally, Section 5 concludes the paper and sketches the future work.

2   Related Work

It is important to design REST (REpresentational State Transfer) APIs of quality for building well-maintainable and evolvable RESTful systems. In the literature, the concept of (anti)patterns are well-recognised as the means to evaluate various design concerns in terms of quality. Despite of the presence of some REST (anti)patterns defined recently by the SOA (Service Oriented Architecture) community, the methods and techniques for their detection are yet to propose.

Indeed, there are few books [2, 5, 6] that discuss a number of REST patterns. In addition, a number of online resources [8, 12, 16] by REST practitioners provide a high-level overview of REST (anti)patterns and discuss how they are introduced by developers at design-time. Beyond those contributions, however, the detection of (anti)patterns require a concrete approach, to support their rigorous analysis, which is still lacking in the current literature.

For instance, Erl in his book [5] discussed 85 SOA patterns related to service design and composition. Erl *et al.* [6] also explained the REST and RESTful service-orientation, and discussed seven new REST patterns, thus in total, the catalog defines 92 SOA patterns. Daigneau [2] introduced 25 design patterns for SOAP (Simple Object Access Protocol) and RESTful services related to the service interaction, implementation, and evolution. Moreover, various online resources [8, 12, 16] defined a limited number of REST antipatterns related to API design with simple examples. All those books and online resources discussed (1) the solutions to recurring design problems (*i.e.*, patterns) or (2) the bad design practices (*i.e.*, antipatterns), but none of them discussed their detection.

A few contributions are available on the detection of SOA (anti)patterns for various SOA standards, *e.g.*, SCA (Service Component Architecture) [3, 9–11] and Web services [13]. To the best of our knowledge, the detection of REST (anti)patterns, in the literature deserves yet to receive attention. As a continuous effort to investigate diverse SOA technologies with the goal of detecting REST (anti)patterns, we focus, in this paper, on analysing the REST APIs, both statically and dynamically.

3 The SODA-R Approach

We propose the SODA-R approach (Service Oriented Detection for Antipatterns in REST) for the detection of REST (anti)patterns. The steps in SODA-R include:

Step 1. Analysis of Patterns and Antipatterns: This manual step involves analysing the description of REST (anti)patterns to identify the relevant properties that characterise them. We use these properties to define detection heuristics.

Step 2. Detection of Patterns and Antipatterns: This semi-automatic step involves the implementation of detection algorithms based on the heuristics defined in the previous step. Later, we automatically apply these detection algorithms on a set of REST APIs, which return detected (anti)patterns.

The next sections detail the analysis of REST (anti)patterns, the implementation of detection algorithms, and the application of the detection algorithms on REST APIs. The validation of SODA-R is discussed in Section 4.

3.1 Analysis of Patterns and Antipatterns

For the definition of heuristics, we perform a thorough analysis of REST (anti)patterns by studying their descriptions and examples in the literature [6, 12, 16, 17]. This analysis helps us to identify the static and dynamic properties relevant to each REST (anti)pattern. A static property is a property that is defined on a RESTful service and is obtained statically, *i.e.*, before invoking the REST methods.

A dynamic property, on the other hand, is obtained after making a service call to access a resource and can be found in the request/response headers and bodies, at runtime. For instance, the HTTP request headers Accept and Cache-Control and their corresponding values, respectively used to set the resource formats requested by the clients and to set the caching preferences, correspond to dynamic properties. Similarly, the HTTP response headers Location and Status and their corresponding values, respectively used to set the new location by servers and to indicate the current context and status of the action performed by the server on a client request, also correspond to dynamic properties. Table 1 shows the relevant static and dynamic properties for each (anti)pattern, which we use and combine in the following section to define detection heuristics.

Table 1. Relevant properties of patterns and antipatterns

REST Antipatterns	REST Patterns	Properties
Breaking Self-descriptiveness	–	*request-header fields; response-header fields*
Forgetting Hypermedia	Entity Linking	*http-methods; entity-links;* Location
Ignoring Caching	Response Caching	Cache-Control; Cache-Control; ETag
Ignoring MIME Types	Content Negotiation	Accept; Content-Type
Ignoring Status Code	–	*http-methods; status; status-code*
Misusing Cookies	–	Cookie; Set-Cookie
Tunnelling Through GET	–	*http-method; request-uri*
Tunnelling Through POST	–	*http-method; request-uri*
–	End-point Redirection	Location; *status-code*
–	Entity Endpoint	*end-points; http-methods*

Detection Heuristics of REST Antipatterns and Patterns: Using the static and dynamic properties, we define detection heuristics of REST (anti)patterns. Figures 1 and 2 show the detection heuristics defined for the *Forgetting Hypermedia* antipattern and the corresponding *Entity Linking* pattern, respectively.

```
1: FORGET-HYPER-MEDIA(response-header, response-body, http-method)
2:    body-links[] ← EXTRACT-ENTITY-LINKS(response-body)
3:    header-link ← response-header.getValue("Link")
4:    if(http-method = GET and (length(body-links[]) = 0 or header-link = NIL)) or
5:    (http-method = POST and ("Location:" ∉ response-header.getKeys() and
6:    length(body-links[]) = 0))) then
7:       print "Forgetting Hypermedia detected"
8:    end if
```

Fig. 1. Heuristic of *Forgetting Hypermedia* antipattern

Forgetting Hypermedia [16] is a REST antipattern that identifies the absence of *entity links* in the response body or header. In general, for the HTTP GET requests, the *entity links* are provided in the response body or header, hence, checking for the absence of links in the response body (*i.e.*, the size of the array containing the entity-links is zero) or the absence of link in the response header is sufficient (line 4, Figure 1). As for the HTTP POST requests, usually the server provides a *location* in the response header or *links* in the response body. Therefore, it is sufficient to look for the absence of Location in the response header (line 5, Figure 1) or the absence of links in the response body (line 6, Figure 1) to detect *Forgetting Hypermedia* antipattern. The corresponding pattern, *Entity Linking* [6] (Figure 2) refers to a REST service that provides entity links to follow in their response bodies or headers. We put the detection heuristics for the seven other REST antipatterns and four REST patterns on our web site[1].

Heuristics are more suitable, in particular for the detection of REST (anti)patterns, because they are more intuitive. Moreover, the engineer's knowledge and experience on REST (anti)patterns play a key role in defining heuristics.

3.2   Detection of Patterns and Antipatterns

In this section, we detail the detection of REST (anti)patterns. We show the different implementation and application steps in Figure 3.

---

[1] http://sofa.uqam.ca/soda-r/

```
1: ENTITY-LINKING(response-header, response-body, http-method)
2:     body-links[] ← EXTRACT-ENTITY-LINKS(response-body)
3:     header-link ← response-header.getValue("Link")
4:     if(http-method = GET and (length(body-links[]) ≥ 1 or header-link ≠ NIL)) or
5:        (http-method = POST and ("Location:" ∈ response-header.getKeys() or
6:        length(body-links[]) ≥ 1))) then
7:           print "Entity Linking detected"
8:     end if
```

Fig. 2. Heuristic of *Entity Linking* pattern

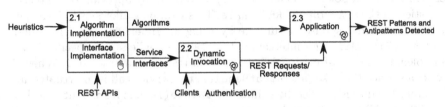

Fig. 3. Steps of the detection of REST (anti)patterns

Step 2.1: Implementation - From the heuristics defined in the previous step (in Section 3.1), we manually implement their corresponding detection algorithms. These algorithms are thus conform to detection heuristics that use and combine static and dynamic properties. We implement also the service interfaces for invoking REST services, and later to analyse their static and dynamic properties. These interfaces written in JAVA contain a set of methods mapped to respective HTTP requests for all REST APIs from their online documentations (see Table 4). The REST API online documentations comprise of (1) a list of resources, (2) a list of actions to perform on these resources, (3) the HTTP requests with entity end-points, and (4) a list of parameters for each HTTP request.

Step 2.2: Dynamic Invocation - After we have JAVA interfaces for REST APIs, we implement the REST clients to invoke each service by providing the correct parameter lists. The REST clients must conform to the API documentations. During the detection time, we dynamically invoke the methods of service interfaces. From REST point of view, invocation of a method refers to performing an action on a *resource* or on an *entity*. For some method invocations, clients require to authenticate themselves to the servers. For each authentication process, we need to have a user account to ask for the developer credentials to the server. The server then supplies the user with the authentication details to use every time to make a signed HTTP request. For instance, YouTube and DropBox support OAuth 2.0 authentication protocol to authenticate their clients. At the end of this step, we gather all the requests and responses.

Step 2.3: Application - For the application, we rely on the underlying framework SOFA (Service Oriented Framework for Antipatterns) [9] that enables the analysis of static and dynamic properties specific to REST (anti)patterns. We automatically apply the heuristics in the form of detection algorithms on the requests from the clients and responses from the servers, gathered in the previous step. In the end, we obtain a list of detected REST (anti)patterns.

From its initial version in [9], we further developed the SOFA framework to support the detection of REST (anti)patterns. SOFA itself is developed based on the SCA (Service Component Architecture) standard [4] and is composed of several SCA components. SOFA framework uses FraSCAti [15] as its runtime support. We added a new *REST Handler* SCA component in the framework. The *REST Handler* component supports the detection of REST (anti)patterns by (1) wrapping each REST API with an SCA component and (2) automatically applying the detection heuristics on the SCA-wrapped REST APIs. This wrapping allows us to introspect each request and response at runtime by using an IntentHandler. The intent handler in FraSCAti is an interceptor that can be applied on a specific service to implement the non-functional features, *e.g.*, transaction or logging. When we invoke a service that uses an IntentHandler, the service call is interrupted and the intent handler is notified by calling the invoke(IntentJoinPoint) method. This interruption of call enables us to introspect the requests and responses of an invoked REST service.

4 Validation

In this section, we want to show the robustness of SODA-R approach, accuracy of our detection heuristics, and performance of the implemented algorithms.

4.1 Hypotheses

We define three hypotheses to assess the effectiveness of our SODA-R approach.

H_1. **Robustness:** *The SODA-R approach is robust.* This hypothesis claims that our SODA-R approach is assessed rigorously on a large set of REST APIs and with a set of different REST patterns and antipatterns.

H_2. **Accuracy:** *The detection heuristics have an average precision of more than 75% and a recall of 100%, i.e., more than three-quarters of detected (anti)patterns are true positive and we do not miss any existing (anti)patterns.* Having a trade-off between precision and recall, we presume that 75% precision is acceptable while our objective is to detect all existing (anti)patterns, *i.e.*, 100% recall. This hypothesis claims the accuracy of the defined detection heuristics and the implemented detection algorithms.

H_3. **Performance:** *The implemented algorithms perform with considerably a low detection times, i.e., on an average in the order of seconds.* Through this assumption, we support the performance of the implemented detection algorithms.

4.2 Subjects and Objects

We define heuristics for eight different REST antipatterns and five REST patterns from the literature. Tables 2 and 3 list those REST antipatterns and patterns

Table 2. List of eight REST antipatterns

Breaking Self-descriptiveness: REST developers tend to ignore the *standardised headers, formats,* or *protocols* and use their own customised ones. This practice shatters the self-descriptiveness or containment of a message header. Breaking the self-descriptiveness also limits the *reusability* and *adaptability* of REST resources [16].

Forgetting Hypermedia: The *lack* of *hypermedia, i.e., not linking resources,* hinders the state transition for REST applications. One possible indication of this antipattern is the *absence* of URL *links* in the *resource representation,* which typically restricts clients to follow the links, *i.e.,* limits the dynamic communication between clients and servers [16].

Ignoring Caching: REST clients and server-side developers tend to *avoid* the caching capability due to its complexity to implement. However, caching capability is one of the principle REST constraints. The developers ignore caching by setting *Cache-Control: no-cache* or *no-store* and by not providing an *ETag* in the *response header* [16].

Ignoring MIME Types: The server should represent *resources* in various formats, *e.g., xml, json, pdf,* etc., which may allow clients, developed in diverse languages, a more flexible service consumption. However, the server side *developers* often intend to have a *single representation* of resources or rely on their *own formats,* which limits the resource (or service) *accessibility* and *reusability* [16].

Ignoring Status Code: Despite of a rich set of defined *application-level status codes* suitable for various contexts, REST developers tend to *avoid* them, *i.e., rely* only on *common ones,* namely 200, 404, and 500, or even use the *wrong or no* status *codes.* The correct use of status codes from the classes *2xx, 3xx, 4xx, and 5xx* helps clients and servers to communicate in a more semantic manner [16].

Misusing Cookies: Statelessness is another REST principle to adhere—*session state* in the server side is *disallowed* and any *cookies violate* RESTfulness [7]. Sending *keys* or *tokens* in the *Set-Cookie* or *Cookie* header field to server-side session is an example of misusing cookies, which concerns both *security* and *privacy* [16].

Tunnelling Through GET: Being the most fundamental HTTP method in REST, the *GET* method *retrieves* a resource identified by a URI. However, very often the developers *rely only* on *GET* method to perform any kind of actions or operations including *creating, deleting,* or even for *updating* a resource. Nevertheless, HTTP GET is an inappropriate method for any actions other than *accessing* a *resource,* and does not match its *semantic purpose,* if improperly used [16].

Tunnelling Through POST: This anti-pattern is very similar to the previous one, except that in addition to the URI the *body* of the HTTP POST request may *embody operations* and *parameters* to apply on the resource. The *developers* tend to *depend* only on HTTP POST method for *sending any* types of *requests* to the server including *accessing, updating,* or *deleting* a resource. In general, the proper use of HTTP POST is to *create* a server-side resource [16].

collected from the literature, mainly [6, 8, 12, 16, 17]. In Tables 2 and 3, we put the relevant properties for each antipattern and pattern in *bold-italics*.

As for the objects in our experiment, we use some widely-used and popular REST APIs for which their underlying HTTP methods, service end-points, and authentication details are well documented online. Large companies like Facebook or YouTube provide self-contained documentations with good example sets. Table 4 lists the 12 REST APIs that we analysed in our experiment.

4.3 Validation Process

Through the implemented clients, we invoked a total set of 115 methods from the service interfaces to access resources and received the responses from servers. Then, we applied the detection algorithms on the REST requests and responses and reported any existing patterns or antipatterns using our SOFA framework. We manually validated the detection results to identify the true positives and

Table 3. List of five REST patterns

Content Negotiation: This pattern supports *alternative resource representations*, *e.g.*, in *json*, *xml*, *pdf*, etc. so that the service consuming becomes more flexible with *high reusability*. Servers can provide resources in *any standard format* requested by the clients. This pattern is applied via standard HTTP *media types* and adhere to *service loose coupling* principle. If not applied at all, this turns into *Ignoring MIME Types* antipattern [6].

End-point Redirection: The *redirection* feature over the Web is supported by this pattern, which also plays a role as the means of *service composition*. To redirect clients, servers send a new *location* to follow with one of the *status code* among *301*, *302*, *307*, or *308*. The main benefit of this pattern is—an *alternative service* remains *active* even if the requested service end-point is not sound [6].

Entity Linking: This pattern enables *runtime communication* via *links* provided by the server in the *response body* or via *Location:* in the *response header*. By using *hyper-links*, the servers and clients can be *loosely coupled*, and the clients can *automatically find* the *related entities* at *runtime*. If not properly applied, this pattern turns into *Forgetting Hypermedia* antipattern [6].

Entity Endpoint: Services with single *end-points* are too coarse-grained. Usually, a client requires at least *two identifiers*: (1) a *global* for the *service* itself and (2) a *local* for the *resource or entity* managed by the service. By applying this pattern, *i.e.*, using *multiple end-points*, each *entity (or resource)* of the incorporating service can be *uniquely identified* and *addressed* globally [12].

Response Caching: Response caching is a good practice to *avoid sending duplicate requests* and *responses* by caching all response messages in the *local* client machine. In opposed to *Ignoring Caching* antipattern, the *Cache-Control:* is set to any value other than *no-cache* and *no-store*, or an *ETag* is used along with the *status code 304* [6].

Table 4. List of 12 REST APIs and their online documentations.

REST APIs	Online Documentations
Alchemy	alchemyapi.com/api/
BestBuy	bbyopen.com/developer/
Bitly	dev.bitly.com/api.html
CharlieHarvey	charlieharvey.org.uk/about/api/
DropBox	dropbox.com/developers/core/docs/
Facebook	developers.facebook.com/docs/graph-api/
Musicgraph	developer.musicgraph.com/api-docs/overview/
Ohloh	github.com/blackducksw/ohloh_api/
TeamViewer	integrate.teamviewer.com/en/develop/documentation/
Twitter	dev.twitter.com/docs/api/
YouTube	developers.google.com/youtube/v3/
Zappos	developer.zappos.com/docs/api-documentation/

to find false negatives. The validation was performed by two professionals who have knowledge on REST and were not part of the implementation and experiment. We provided them the descriptions of REST (anti)patterns and the sets of all requests and responses collected during the service invocations. We used precision and recall to measure our detection accuracy. Precision concerns the ratio between the true detected (anti)patterns and all detected (anti)patterns. Recall is the ratio between the true detected (anti)patterns and all existing true (anti)patterns.

4.4 Results

Table 5 presents detailed detection results for the eight REST antipatterns and five REST patterns. The table reports the (anti)patterns in the first column followed

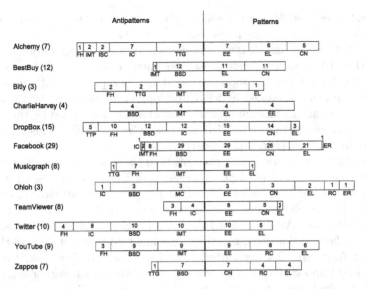

Fig. 4. Bar-plots of the detection results for eight antipatterns and five patterns. (APIs are followed by the number of method invocations in parentheses. The acronyms correspond to the (anti)pattern name abbreviation and the numbers represent their detected instances.)

by the analysed REST APIs in the following twelve columns. For each REST API and for each (anti)pattern, we report: (1) the total number of validated true positives with respect to the total detected (anti)patterns by our algorithms, *i.e.*, the precision, in the first row and (2) the total number of detected true positives with respect to the total existing true positives, *i.e.*, the recall, in the following row. The last two columns show, for all APIs, the average precision-recall and the total detection time for each (anti)pattern. The detailed results on all the test cases, *e.g.*, 115 methods from 12 REST APIs, are available on our web site[1].

4.5   Overview on the Results

Figure 4 shows the bar-plots of the detection results for the eight antipatterns and five patterns on the 12 REST APIs.

REST developers are most likely to use their own header fields, data formats, and protocols, which limit the comprehension and reusability of REST APIs. For example, among more than 80 instances of detected *Breaking Self-descriptiveness* (BSD) antipattern: Facebook (29 instances), DropBox (12 instances), and Best-Buy (12 instances) were mostly using customised header fields, data formats, and protocols. Also, *Forgetting Hypermedia* (FH) antipattern was detected in Facebook (8 instances) and DropBox (10 instances) APIs. Moreover, *Ignoring MIME Types* (IMT) antipattern was detected in Twitter (10 instances) and YouTube (9 instances) APIs. Among the less frequent antipatterns, *Ignoring Status Code*

(ISC, 2 instances) and *Misusing Cookies* (MC, 3 instances) were not significantly observed among the 115 tested methods.

As for REST patterns, *Content Negotiation* (CN, 70 instances) and *Entity Linking* (EL, 62 instances) were most frequently applied by REST developers. *Content Negotiation* pattern supports the ability to represent REST resources in diverse formats (implemented by REST developers) as requested by the clients. *Entity Linking* pattern facilitates clients to follow links provided by the servers. Furthermore, some APIs also applied *Response Cashing* (RC, 13 instances) and *End-point Redirection* (ER, 2 instances) patterns.

Overall, REST APIs that follow patterns tend to avoid corresponding antipatterns and *vice-versa*. For example: BestBuy and Facebook are found involved respectively in 0 and 8 instances of *Forgetting Hypermedia* antipattern; however, these APIs are involved in 11 and 21 corresponding *Entity Linking* pattern. Moreover, DropBox, Alchemy, YouTube, and Twitter APIs had 27 instances of *Ignoring Caching* antipattern, but they were involved in 8 instances of the corresponding *Response Cashing* pattern. Finally, we found Facebook, DropBox, BestBuy, and Zappos APIs involved in only 3 instances of *Ignoring MIME Types* antipattern, which conversely are involved in more than 55 instances of corresponding *Content Negotiation* pattern.

In general, among the 12 analysed REST APIs with 115 methods tested and eight antipatterns, we found Twitter (32 instances of four antipatterns), DropBox (40 instances of four antipatterns), and Alchemy (19 instances of five antipatterns) are more problematic, *i.e.*, contain more antipatterns than others (see Figure 4). On the other hand, considering the five REST patterns, we found Facebook (49 instances of four patterns), BestBuy (22 instances of two patterns), and YouTube (15 instances of three patterns) are well designed, *i.e.*, involve more patterns than others (see Figure 4).

4.6   Details of the Results

In this section, we discuss three detection results in detail, obtained in our experiment as presented in Table 5.

REST developers tend to rely on their own customised headers, formats, and protocols, and thus introduce *Breaking Self-descriptiveness* antipattern. The analysis on the 12 REST APIs shows that developers used non-standard header fields and protocols in most APIs including BestBuy, DropBox, Facebook, and Twitter. For example, Facebook used `x-fb-debug` and `x-fb-rev` header fields, which are mainly used to track a request id for their internal bug management purpose. Similarly, we found DropBox using the `x-dropbox-request-id` and Twitter using `x-tfe-logging-request-*` and `x-xss-protection` header fields. In general, the designers and implementers often distinguish the standardised and non-standardised header members by prefixing their names with "x-" (a.k.a. *eXperimental*). Indeed, the "x-" convention was highly discouraged by the Internet Society in RFC822 [14]. The manual validation reveals that all our detection was true positives and we reported all existing non-standard header fields and protocols, except two in DropBox where the manual validation considered

Table 5. Detection results of the eight REST antipatterns and five REST patterns obtained by applying detection algorithms on the 12 REST APIs (numbers in the parentheses show total test methods for each API).

REST API	(7)Alchemy	(12)BestBuy	(3)Bitly	(4)CharlieHarvey	(15)DropBox	(29)Facebook	(8)Musicgraph	(3)Ohloh	(8)TeamViewer	(10)Twitter	(9)YouTube	(7)Zappos	precision-recall	(115)Total	Average Precision-Recall	Detection Time
REST Antipatterns																
Breaking Self-	0/0	12/12	0/0	4/4	12/12	29/29	0/0	3/3	0/0	10/10	9/9	7/7	p	86/86	100%	21.31s
descriptiveness	0/0	12/12	0/0	4/4	12/14	29/29	0/0	3/3	0/0	10/10	9/9	7/7	r	86/88	98.21%	
Forgetting	1/1	0/0	2/2	0/0	9/10	8/8	7/7	0/0	3/3	4/4	2/3	0/0	p	36/38	94.58%	19.54s
Hypermedia	1/1	0/0	2/2	0/0	9/9	8/8	7/7	0/0	3/3	4/4	2/2	0/0	r	36/36	100%	
Ignoring	7/7	0/0	0/0	0/0	12/12	1/1	0/0	1/1	4/4	8/8	0/0	0/0	p	33/33	100%	18.99s
Caching	7/7	0/0	0/0	0/0	12/12	1/1	0/0	1/1	4/4	8/8	0/0	0/0	r	33/33	100%	
Ignoring	2/2	1/1	3/3	4/4	0/0	2/2	8/8	0/0	0/0	10/10	9/9	0/0	p	39/39	100%	19.39s
MIME Types	2/2	1/1	3/3	4/4	0/0	2/2	8/8	0/0	0/0	10/10	9/9	0/0	r	39/39	100%	
Ignoring	1/2	0/0	0/0	0/0	0/0	0/0	0/0	0/0	0/0	0/0	0/0	0/0	p	1/2	50%	21.22s
Status Code	1/2	0/0	0/0	0/0	0/0	0/0	0/0	0/0	0/0	0/0	0/0	0/0	r	1/3	25%	
Misusing	0/0	0/0	0/0	0/0	0/0	0/0	0/0	3/3	0/0	0/0	0/0	0/0	p	3/3	100%	19.1s
Cookies	0/0	0/0	0/1	0/0	0/0	0/0	0/0	3/3	0/0	0/0	0/0	0/0	r	3/3	100%	
Tunnelling	5/7	0/0	0/2	0/0	0/0	0/0	0/1	0/0	0/0	0/0	0/0	0/1	p	5/11	17.86%	28.26s
Through GET	5/5	0/0	0/0	0/0	0/0	0/0	0/0	0/0	0/0	0/0	0/0	0/0	r	5/5	100%	
Tunnelling	0/0	0/0	0/0	0/0	5/5	0/0	0/0	0/0	0/0	0/0	0/0	0/0	p	5/5	100%	28.64s
Through POST	0/0	0/0	0/0	0/0	5/5	0/0	0/0	0/0	0/0	0/0	0/0	0/0	r	5/5	100%	
REST Patterns																
Content	5/5	11/11	0/0	0/0	14/14	26/26	0/0	3/3	5/5	0/0	0/0	7/7	p	71/71	100%	19.63s
Negotiation	5/5	11/11	0/0	0/0	14/14	26/26	0/0	3/3	5/5	0/0	0/0	7/7	r	71/71	100%	
Entity	6/6	11/11	1/1	4/4	3/3	21/21	1/1	2/2	1/1	5/5	6/6	4/4	p	65/65	100%	19.90s
Linking	6/6	11/11	1/1	4/4	3/3	21/21	1/1	2/2	1/1	5/5	6/7	4/4	r	65/66	98.81%	
End-point	0/0	0/0	0/0	0/0	0/0	1/1	0/0	1/1	0/0	0/0	0/0	0/0	p	2/2	100%	20.36s
Redirection	0/0	0/0	0/0	0/0	0/0	1/1	0/0	1/1	0/0	0/0	0/0	0/0	r	2/2	100%	
Entity	1/1	0/0	1/1	1/1	1/1	1/1	1/1	1/1	1/1	1/1	1/1	0/0	p	10/10	100%	23.06s
Endpoint	1/1	0/0	1/1	1/1	1/1	1/1	1/1	1/1	1/1	1/1	1/1	0/0	r	10/10	100%	
Response	0/0	0/0	0/0	0/0	0/0	0/0	0/0	1/1	0/0	0/0	8/8	4/4	p	13/13	100%	19.23s
Caching	0/0	0/0	0/0	0/0	0/0	0/0	0/0	1/1	0/0	0/0	8/8	4/4	r	13/13	100%	
Average													p	369/378	89.42%	21.43s
													r	369/374	94%	

them as non-standard practice. This leads to the precision of 100% and the recall of 98.21% for this detection.

Any RESTful interaction is driven by *hypermedia*—by which clients interact with application servers via URL links provided by servers in resource representations [7]. The absence of such interaction pattern is known as *Forgetting Hypermedia* antipattern [16], which was detected in eight APIs, namely Bitly, DropBox, Facebook, and so on (see Table 5). Among the 115 methods tested, we found 38 instances of this antipattern. Moreover, REST APIs that do not have this antipattern well applied the corresponding *Entity Linking* pattern [6], *e.g.*, Alchemy, BestBuy, and Ohloh, which is a good practice. This observation suggests that, in practice, developers sometimes do not provide hyper-links in resource representations. As for the validation, 36 instances of *Forgetting Hypermedia* antipattern were manually validated; therefore, we have an average precision of 94.58% and a recall of 100%. For *Entity Linking* pattern, the manual validation confirmed 66 instances whereas we detected a total of 65 instances, all of which were true positives. Thus, we had an average precision of 100% and a recall of 98.81%.

Caching helps developers implementing high-performance and scalable REST services by limiting repetitive interactions, which if not properly applied violates one of the six REST principles [7]. REST developers widely ignore the caching capability by using *Pragma: no-cache* or *Cache-Control: no-cache* header in the requests, which forces the application to retrieve duplicate responses from servers. This bad practice is known as *Ignoring Caching* antipattern [16]. In contrast, the corresponding pattern, *Response Caching* [6] supports response cacheability. We detected six REST APIs that explicitly avoid caching capability, namely Alchemy, DropBox, Ohloh, and so on (see Table 5). On the other hand, cacheability is supported by YouTube and Zappos, which were detected as *Response Caching* patterns. The manual analysis of requests and responses also confirmed these detections, and we had an average precision and recall of 100%.

4.7   Discussion on the Hypotheses

In this section, we discuss the hypotheses defined in Section 4.1.

H_1. **Robustness:** To validate the SODA-R approach, we performed experiment on 12 REST APIs including well-known Facebook, BestBuy, DropBox, Twitter, and YouTube. We analysed 115 methods in the form of HTTP requests from these APIs and applied detection algorithms of eight common REST antipatterns and five REST patterns on them. For each request among 115, we analysed individual request headers and bodies, and the corresponding response headers and bodies. With such an extensive evaluation and validation, we support our first hypothesis on the robustness of our SODA-R approach.

H_2. **Accuracy:** As shown in Table 5, we obtained an average recall of 94% and an average precision of 89.42% on all REST APIs and for all test methods. The precision ranges from 17.86% to 100%, while we obtained a recall between 25% and 100% for all REST (anti)patterns. Thus, with an average precision of 89.42% and a recall of 94%, we can positively support our second hypothesis on the accuracy of our defined heuristics and implemented detection algorithms.

H_3. **Performance:** The total required time includes: (i) the execution time, *i.e.*, sending REST requests and receiving REST responses (ranges from 19.1s to 24.55s) and (ii) the time required to apply and run the detection algorithms on the requests and responses (ranges from 0.004s to 4.312s). Each row in Table 5 (last column) reports the total required detection time for a pattern or an antipattern, which varies from 19.1s to 28.64s. We performed our experiments on an Intel Core-i7 with a processor speed of 2.50GHz and 6GB of memory. The detection time is comparatively very low (on an average 3% of the total required time) than the execution time. With a low average detection time of 21.43s, we can positively support our third hypothesis on performance.

4.8   Threats to Validity

As future work, we plan to generalise our findings to other REST APIs. However, we tried to minimise the threat to the *external validity* of our results by performing experiments on 12 REST APIs by invoking and testing 115 methods from them. The detection results may vary based on the heuristics defined for the REST (anti)patterns. To minimise the threats to the *Internal validity*, we made sure that every invocation receives responses from servers with the correct request URI, and the client authentication done while necessary. Moreover, we tested all the major HTTP methods in REST, *i.e.*, GET, DELETE, PUT, and POST on resources to minimise the threat to the internal validity. Engineers may have different views and different levels of expertise on REST (anti)patterns, which may affect the definition of heuristics. We attempted to lessen the threat to *construct validity* by defining the heuristics after a thorough review of existing literature on the REST (anti)patterns. We also involved two professionals in the intensive validation of the results. Finally, the threats to *reliability validity* concerns the possibility of replicating this study. To minimise this threat, we provide all the details required to replicate the study, including the heuristics, client requests, and server responses on our web site[1].

5   Conclusion and Future Work

REST (REpresentational State Transfer) is now a popular architectural style for building Web-based applications. REST developers may apply design patterns or introduce antipatterns. These REST patterns and antipatterns may respectively: (1) facilitate and hinder semantically richer communications between clients and servers, or (2) ease and cause difficult maintenance and evolution.

This paper presented the SODA-R approach (Service Oriented Detection for Antipatterns in REST) to define detection heuristics and detect REST (anti)patterns in REST APIs. The detection of (anti)patterns in REST APIs requires an in-depth analysis of their design, invocation, and authentication. We applied SODA-R to define the detection heuristics of five common REST patterns and eight REST antipatterns. Using an extended SOFA framework (Service Oriented Framework for Antipatterns), we performed an extensive validation with 13 REST (anti)patterns. We analysed 12 REST APIs and tested 115 methods, and showed the accuracy of SODA-R with an average precision of 89.42% and recall of 94%.

In future work, we want to replicate SODA-R on other REST APIs and methods with more REST (anti)patterns. We also intend to enrich the catalog of antipatterns and patterns by thoroughly investigating a large set of REST APIs.

Acknowledgements. The authors thank Abir Dilou for initiating the study. This study is supported by NSERC (Natural Sciences and Engineering Research Council of Canada) and FRQNT research grants.

References

1. Bennett, K., Layzell, P., Budgen, D., Brereton, P., Macaulay, L., Munro, M.: Service-based Software: The Future for Flexible Software. In: Proceedings of Seventh Asia-Pacific Software Engineering Conference, pp. 214–221 (2000)
2. Daigneau, R.: Service Design Patterns: Fundamental Design Solutions for SOAP/WSDL and RESTful Web Services. Addison-Wesley (November 2011)
3. Demange, A., Moha, N., Tremblay, G.: Detection of SOA Patterns. In: Basu, S., Pautasso, C., Zhang, L., Fu, X. (eds.) ICSOC 2013. LNCS, vol. 8274, pp. 114–130. Springer, Heidelberg (2013)
4. Edwards, M.: Service Component Architecture (SCA). OASIS, USA (April 2011)
5. Erl, T.: SOA Design Patterns. Prentice Hall PTR (January 2009)
6. Erl, T., Carlyle, B., Pautasso, C., Balasubramanian, R.: SOA with REST: Principles, Patterns & Constraints for Building Enterprise Solutions with REST. The Prentice Hall Service Technology Series from Thomas Erl. (2012)
7. Fielding, R.T.: Architectural Styles and the Design of Network-based Software Architectures. PhD thesis (2000)
8. Fredrich, T.: RESTful Service Best Practices: Recommendations for Creating Web Services (May 2012)
9. Moha, N., Palma, F., Nayrolles, M., Conseil, B.J., Guéhéneuc, Y.-G., Baudry, B., Jézéquel, J.-M.: Specification and Detection of SOA Antipatterns. In: Liu, C., Ludwig, H., Toumani, F., Yu, Q. (eds.) Service Oriented Computing. LNCS, vol. 7636, pp. 1–16. Springer, Heidelberg (2012)
10. Nayrolles, M., Moha, N., Valtchev, P.: Improving SOA Antipatterns Detection in Service Based Systems by Mining Execution Traces. In: 20th Working Conference on Reverse Engineering, pp. 321–330 (October 2013)
11. Palma, F., Nayrolles, M., Moha, N., Guéhéneuc, Y.G., Baudry, B., Jézéquel, J.M.: SOA Antipatterns: An Approach for their Specification and Detection. International Journal of Cooperative Information Systems 22(04) (2013)
12. Pautasso, C.: Some REST Design Patterns (and Anti-Patterns) (October 2009), http://www.jopera.org/node/442
13. Penta, M.D., Santone, A., Villani, M.L.: Discovery of SOA Patterns via Model Checking. In: 2nd International Workshop on Service Oriented Software Engineering: In Conjunction with the 6th ESEC/FSE Joint Meeting, IW-SOSWE 2007, pp. 8–14. ACM, New York (2007)
14. RFC2822: Internet Message Format by Internet Engineering Task Force. Technical report (2001)
15. Seinturier, L., Merle, P., Rouvoy, R., Romero, D., Schiavoni, V., Stefani, J.B.: A Component-Based Middleware Platform for Reconfigurable Service-Oriented Architectures. Software: Practice and Experience 42(5), 559–583 (2012)
16. Tilkov, S.: REST Anti-Patterns (July 2008), http://www.infoq.com/articles/rest-anti-patterns
17. Tilkov, S.: RESTful Design: Intro, Patterns, Anti-Patterns (December 2008), http://www.devoxx.com/
18. Vinoski, S.: Serendipitous Reuse. IEEE Internet Computing 12(1), 84–87 (2008)

How Do Developers React
to RESTful API Evolution?

Shaohua Wang, Iman Keivanloo, and Ying Zou

Queen's University, Kingston, Ontario, Canada
shaohua@cs.queensu.ca, {iman.keivanloo,ying.zou}@queensu.ca

Abstract. With the rapid adoption of REpresentational State Transfer (REST), more software organizations expose their applications as RESTful web APIs and client code developers integrate RESTful APIs into their applications. When web APIs evolve, the client code developers have to update their applications to incorporate the API changes accordingly. However client code developers often encounter challenges during the migration and API providers have little knowledge of how client code developers react to the API changes. In this paper, we investigate the changes among subsequent versions of APIs and classify the identified changes to understand how the RESTful web APIs evolve. We study the on-line discussion from developers to the API changes by analyzing the StackOverflow questions. Through an empirical study, we identify 21 change types and 7 of them are new compared with existing studies. We find that a larger portion of RESTful web API elements are changed between versions compared with Java APIs and WSDL services. Moreover, our results show that *adding new methods* in the new version causes more questions and views from developers. However the *deleted methods* draw more relevant discussions. In general, our results provide valuable insights of RESTful web API evolution and help service providers understand how their consumers react to the API changes in order to improve the practice of evolving the service APIs.

Keywords: REST API, API Evolution, StackOverflow, Social Media.

1 Introduction

Nowadays, on-line users can conduct various tasks such as posting text on Twitter[1] through web applications or services. With the rapid emergence of REpresentational State Transfer (REST) and high demand of engaging on-line experience from end-users, software organizations such as Twitter are willing to open their applications as RESTful web service APIs described in plain HTML pages [7]. Client code developers often integrate the web APIs into their applications or services to accelerate their development or stay away from low level programming tasks [4]. Typically web API providers (*e.g.*, Twitter) evolve their APIs for various reasons, such as adding new functionality [10]. Client code developers have no control of web API evolution and have to evolve their

---

[1] https://twitter.com/

X. Franch et al. (Eds.): ICSOC 2014, LNCS 8831, pp. 245–259, 2014.

client applications or services to incorporate the changes of new versions of web APIs [4][10]. It causes difficulties to developers to migrate client applications, since the API client code developers have no knowledge of how the web APIs evolve [2]. Moreover, API providers are not aware of how client code developers react to web API evolution. Therefore analyzing and understanding client code developers' on-line discussion related to API changes is essential for service providers to improve API evolution practices. The communication gap between API providers and client developers should be resolved.

Recently, several research studies have explored the impact of API evolution. For example, Espinha *et al.* [4] conduct semi-structured interviews with web API client developers and mine source code changes of client applications. Li *et al.* [10] conduct an empirical study on classifying the changes of web API evolution, without studying the developers' reactions to the changes. Understanding all of the possible types of changes can help developers have a better preparation for migration. Recently, crowd-sourced resources such as StackOverflow is getting popular among developers. When studying the new changes of web APIs or solving a specific software development problem, client code developers start posting questions or development experience on these crowd-sourced resources instead of mailing lists or project-specific forums [9][12]. Therefore, crowd-sourced social media platforms become an excellent source for studying developers' discussion. Linares-Vásquez *et al.* [11] investigate how developers react to the Andorid API instability in StackOverflow[2], a question & answer website for developers to share experience on software development. They study which types of changes trigger more questions and more discussion in StackOverflow.

In this paper, we conduct an empirical study on API changes between subsequent versions of web APIs to explore all of the possible types of changes during API evolution. Since web API source code is usually not publicly available, we compare web API documentation (*i.e.*, migration guides or reference documents), and identify changes between subsequent versions of each API. We further categorize the changes into different change types. Compared with the change types identified in [10], we identify 7 more types of changes in web API evolution. Moreover, we explore how client code developers react to identified types of changes by analyzing developers' online discussion regarding API changes. We adopt the analysis approach in [11] for analyzing StackOverflow posts related to RESTful APIs. To the best of our knowledge, we are the first to link the analysis of developer discussion in StackOverflow with web API changes.

We conduct our empirical study on 11 web APIs from 9 application domains and address the following three research questions:

RQ1. What are the change types of web API evolution?
Identifying and understanding all of the possible types of changes of RESTful web APIs is useful for client code developers to have a better preparation for migrating their code. We manually compare the API documentation of a web API to identify the changes [10][3]. We classify the identified changes into 21 change types and count the number of changes for each change type. Compared with existing research work, we identify new unreported change types. Our empirical results

---

[2] http://stackoverflow.com/

show that the change type of *Adding New Methods* has the highest percentage of the number of total changes (*i.e.*, 41.52% of total changes belongs to *Adding New Methods*).

RQ2. Which types of changes trigger more questions from client code developers?
To understand the difficulties of developers to adopt different types of API changes, the first step is to identify which types of changes trigger a larger volume of discussion (*i.e.*, in terms of the number of questions) regarding the changes from client code developers. We extract the question posts related to change types of web API evolution in StackOverflow, an online platform for developers to share software development experience. We investigate the differences between change types in terms of the average number of question posts per change from developers. Our empirical results show that the change type of *Adding New Methods* attracts more question than other change types do.

RQ3. Which types of changes bring discussion on posted questions from developers?
When a question post attracts developers' attention and is worth discussing, the post starts receiving more answers, comments and views from developers. Analyzing such question posts regarding API changes is helpful to understand on which type of problems the developers are stuck. We use the number of answers, the number of views from developers received by a question and its score as measurements of the more discussed questions for developers. In RQ2, the impact of API changes on the volume of discussion is explored. In this question, we investigate the impact of API changes on the quality of discussion. Our empirical results show that *Deleted Methods* generates most discussed questions in the developer community, and the type of change *Adding New Methods* draws the questions with more view counts from developers.

The rest of this paper is organized as follows. Section 2 presents the background of this study. Section 3 introduces the empirical study setup and research questions. Section 4 discusses threats to validity. Section 5 summarizes the related literature. Finally, Section 6 concludes the paper and outlines some avenues for future work.

2   Background

In this section, we introduce the basic structure of web APIs and Question & Answer websites.

2.1   Web APIs

The software organizations open their resources (*e.g.*, services or data) by defining application programming interfaces (APIs) to a request-response message system [15]. The resources can be data or services provided by the organizations. The web APIs are usually described in plain HTML web pages. Client applications access the resources via direct HTTP requests and responses. The format of the requests and responses can be defined in various protocols, such as

XML-RPC. A RESTful HTTP request must be associated with one of four standard HTTP methods: GET, PUT, POST and DELETE. A typical RESTful HTTP request includes 1) a HTTP method (*e.g.*, GET); 2) a domain address of API server; 3) a name of RESTful API method; 4) a format of return data; 5) a set of parameters of the method. The (domain + method name) can also be referred as *resource URL*. For example, a Twitter RESTful request of retrieving the 2 most recent mentions is listed as follows:

GET https://api.twitter.com/1.1/statuses/mentions_timeline.json?count=2

GET is the standard HTTP method. *api.twitter.com/1.1* is the address of the API server. *statuses/mentions_timeline* is the method name. *json* is the format of return data. *count* is a parameter specifying the number of tweets to be retrieved.

2.2   Question and Answer Websites

Recently, developers have started posting on Question&Answer (Q&A) websites, such as StackOverflow, to share their experience in software development or search for solutions regarding software development. Such Q&A websites has become an excellent data source for analyzing developers.

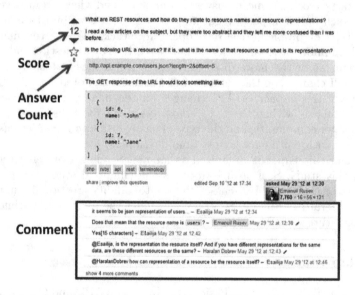

Fig. 1. A labeled screen shot of a question titled "What are REST resources?" in StackOverflow

StackOverflow is one of the top Q&A websites, allows developers to ask a new question or answer any existing questions, as well as to make a comment on other developers' posts. There are three types of posts: question, answer and comment. Developers can "vote" a post (*i.e.*, a question or answer) up or down. Every question post has the number of answers received by the question, possible comments and a score which equals the number of up votes minus the number of down votes. Fig. 1 illustrates a sample post with the number of answers, comments and a score. StackOverflow opens its dataset on-line through StackExchange Data Explorer[3]. In this paper, we extract developers' posts in StackOverflow through StackExchange Data Explorer for analyzing developers' discussions regarding the evolution of RESTful services.

3   Empirical Study

In this section, we first introduce the setup. Then we discuss the research questions of our study. For each question, we introduce the motivation of the question, analysis approach and the findings.

3.1   Study Setup

We conduct our study on public web APIs and StackOverflow posts.

Table 1. Subject Web APIs

API Name	Category	Versions Studied
Twitter	Social Network	V1, V1.1
Blogger	Blogging	V1, V2, V3
Bitly API	Service	V2, V3
MusicBrainz	Music	V1, V2
Friendfeed	Social Network	V1, V2
Tumblr	Social Network	V1, V2
Sunlight Congress	Government	V1, V2
OpenStreetMap (OSM)	Mapping	V0.3, V0.4, V0.5, V0.6
Groupon	Shopping	V1, V2
Yelp	Recommendation	V1, V2
New York Times Article Search (NYT)	News	V1, V2

Table 2. Number of Posts of Each Web API in StackOverflow

API Name	Keyword	Number of Posts Retrieved
Twitter	twitter	46,646
Blogger	blogger	982
Bitly API	bit.ly	146
MusicBrainz	musicbrainz	39
Friendfeed	friendfeed	11
Tumblr	tumblr	1,372
Sunlight Congress	sunlight	0
OpenStreetMap (OSM)	openstreetmap	1,072
Groupon	groupon	21
Yelp	yelp	108
New York Times Article Search (NYT)	newyork	0

---

[3] https://data.stackexchange.com/

Data Collection

Collecting web APIs: To study web API changes, we need different versions of a web API. We extracted the list of most popular APIs in ProgrammableWeb[4] and use them as the candidates of our study. Then, we use the following criteria to choose web APIs as the subject APIs in our study: 1) The web APIs have at least two versions, and the API documentation of each version is available on-line; 2) The web APIs are from different application domains; 3) The web APIs are from different companies, since we aim to study the various change types of different development teams. For each selected web API, we study all of the publicly available versions of the API. We identify the types of web API changes by comparing the differences between subsequent versions of each API. We downloaded the web pages describing the web API methods for comparison. Table 1 shows the information of our subject web APIs.

Collecting the developers' on-line discussion on web API changes in Stack-Overflow: We composed SQL scripts and ran these scripts to retrieve posts related to web APIs through StackExchange Data Explorer[5]. For each web API, we defined a keyword and conducted a wild-card search to mine all of the posts tagged with labels including the keyword [11]. We considered only posts with the matching labels to exclude possible irrelevant posts. For example, we retrieved 46,646 posts with labels including the "twitter" keyword (*e.g.*, twitter, twitter-api). Table 2 shows the keywords used and the number of posts retrieved for each API. All of the posts were retrieved on May 1st, 2014.

3.2   Research Questions

In this sub-section, we present our three research questions. For each research question, we introduce the motivation of the research question, analysis approach and findings of the question.

RQ1. What are the change types of web APIs during evolution?
Motivation. Usually, the web API providers conduct various changes on their APIs between two subsequent versions such as adding new functionality or fixing bugs [10]. The API client developers have to study the API changes and incorporate the client applications with the changes accordingly. Understanding the types of changes is useful to help client code developers to conduct a code migration [10]. In this question, we explore the change types during API evolution.

Analysis Approach. To answer this question, we conduct the following steps: *Step 1:* We first identify API changes among subsequent versions of web APIs. We manually compare API documentation, such as migration guides or reference documents, of subsequent versions of an API. We process two versions of a web API in the following steps:

1. We cross-reference two versions of the API and identify any changes made for all of the API methods. Such changes are considered as *API-level changes.*

---

[4] http://www.programmableweb.com/
[5] https://data.stackexchange.com/

Table 3. Summary of API-level Change Types.

Change Type	Explanation
Change Response Format	1) Entire Format Change: *e.g.*, from XML to JSON 2) Structure Change: add, remove or reorganize XML tags 3) Slight Modification: change XML tag or attribute name *e.g.*, OpenStreetMap API conducted practices 2) and 3).
Change Resource URL	Replace the old version number with new one in URLs *e.g.*, The domain name of Twitter changed from api.twitter.com/1 to api.twitter.com/1.1.
Change Authentication Model	Update existing authN model with new one *e.g.*, Twitter API v1.1 requires every request to be authenticated and client applications must use OAuth.
Change Rate Limit	1) Change Limit Window: change the length of window 2) New Headers and Resp Codes: update messages showing limit exceeded or status
Delete Response Format	Unsupport a format: *e.g.*, XML is not supported in Twitter API v1.1.
Add Response Format	Support a new format in new version: *e.g.*, NYT Article Search API added JSONP in Version 2.
Add Authentication Model	Support a new model but keep old ones: *e.g.*, MusicBrainz and Blogger API added more models.

2. We focus on changes made on methods such as changing a method name, adding a new method or deleting a method. Such changes are considered as *method-level changes*.
3. We identify any changes made on parameters. Such changes are considered as *parameter-level changes*.

Step 2: We summarize and classify the identified changes in *Step 1*. Then, in order to identify new change types, we compare the summarized change types of web APIs with the ones of Web APIs [10], JAVA APIs [3] and WSDL service [5][6].
Step 3: We summarize and count the frequency of each change type to identify the common practices.

Findings. In total, we identify 21 change types on the eleven studied web APIs. We divide them into three groups: 1) the API-level change types made on all of the methods; 2) the method-level change types made on specific methods; 3) the parameter-level change types made on parameters of methods.

Table 3 shows our summary of change types at API-level. All of the change types in Table 3 are observed based on the comparison of subsequent versions of a web API. However API providers can support several versions and make changes on all of the running versions at the same time. For example, on Nov. 2nd, 2012, Twitter changed the format of "withheld_in_countries" field from a comma-separated JSON string to an array of uppercase strings [14], which is a breaking change applicable to all of the versions of Twitter.

Table 4 shows our summary of change types at method-level and Table 5 shows our summarized change types at parameter-level. We found that the functionality of several API methods was merged into the functionality of one method, or the functionality of a method was divided into several methods in the newer

Table 4. Summary of Method-level Change Types.

Change Type	Explanation
Change Method Name	*e.g.*, We observed this practice from Twitter, Blogger MusicBranz, FriendFeed, Yelp and NYT Article Search.
Change Response Format	The return format of a method can be changed, such as returning more values *e.g.*, Twitter method "GET friendships/lookup"
Change Rate Limit	A limit is usually set up on the number of data units can be retrieved per request. The rate limit can be changed.
Change Authentication Model	Different authentication models are set up for different methods. *e.g.*, to protect critical data, they update the authN model on methods modifying databases. *e.g.*, OpenStreetMap and MusicBrainz practiced this.
Change Domain URL	It is different from "Resource URL change" on, API level, because it is only applicable to very few methods. *e.g.*, the domain name of Twitter method "POST statuses/update_with_media" is changed from upload.twitter to api.twitter.com.
Delete Method	Unsupported methods in new version: *e.g.*, we observe every API practiced this, except for Blogger (v1 to v2), Yelp and NYT search
Add Method	Support new methods: *e.g.*, we observe every API practiced this, except for Blogger (v1 to v2) and NYT search
Add Error Code	Add more error codes to specific methods: *e.g.*, Twitter Blogger and OpenStreetMap.

version of API [10][3][5]. The web APIs follow a long deprecate-replace-remove cycle to preserve backward compatibility on "Deprecated" methods. Because we compare subsequent versions of APIs, the deprecated methods are removed and new methods are added. Therefore, our way of dealing these three scenarios is similar to the way in [5], we consider a merged, divided or deprecated method in older version as a deleted method, and the method replacing them in new version as an added method in new version. In addition, we observed that some APIs, such as OpenStreetMap, are added with more resource types and each resource is associated with a set of methods. In this scenario, we consider the set of methods as new methods.

We compare our identified change types with the ones of web APIs [10], Java API [3], and WSDL services [5][6], we found that:

> The unique API-level change types are Delete Response Format, Add Response Format and Change Resource URL. The unique method-level types are Change Response Format, Change Domain URL, Add Error Code. The unique parameter-level change type is Change Require Type.

Table 6 shows that the average proportion of changed elements (*i.e.*, Methods and Parameters) between two consecutive versions of a web API is 82%. However only 30% of JAVA API elements and 41% of WSDL service elements (*i.e.*, Types and Operations) are changed compared with two consecutive versions [3][6].

Table 5. Summary of Parameter-level Change Types Made on Parameters

Change Type	Explanation
Change	Rename parameters with a self-explanatory names
Change Format or Type	The return format of using a parameter can be changed. NYT Article Search practiced.
Change Rate Limit	The limit can be raised up or reduced. *e.g.*, OpenStreetMap raised up a limit.
Change Require Type	*e.g.*, require type of "cursor" of "GET friends/ids" is changed from optional to semi-optional.
Delete Parameter	Unsupported some functionalities of a method
Add Parameter	Support new functionalities of a method

Table 6. Total Number of Elements Changed Between subsequent Versions

API Name	Versions	# of Elements in Latter Version	# of Elements Changed	Proportion(%)
Twitter	v1-v1.1	109	51	47
Blogger	v1-v2	12	5	29
Blogger	v2-v3	33	33	100
Bitly API	v2-v3	74	74	100
MusicBrainz	v1-v2	36	36	100
Friendfeed	v1-v2	23	17	74
Tumblr	v1-v2	21	21	100
Sunlight Congress	v1-v2	12	12	100
OpenStreetMap	v0.3-v0.4	23	12	52
OpenStreetMap	v0.4-v0.5	35	20	57
OpenStreetMap	v0.5-v0.6	52	51	91
Groupon	v1-v2	8	8	100
Yelp	v1-v2	2	2	100
New York Times Article Search	v1-v2	1	1	100
Average				82

> *RESTful web APIs are more change-prone than JAVA APIs and WSDL services during API evolution.*

Table 7 summarizes the number of changes of each change type. The most four common practices are: *Add Method, Delete Method, Change Method Name* and *Add Parameter*. In total, we identify 460 changes and 191 changes (*i.e.*, 41.52%) of them belong to *Add Method*. The API-level change types are not included in the frequency counting, since they are typically applicable to all of the methods and including the frequency of API level change types will skew the results.

> *The change type of Add Method makes up the largest proportion (i.e., 41.52%) of total changes in the studied RESTful services*

Table 7. Frequency of Change Types. Prop. stands for Proportion.

Category	Method Level			Parameter Level		
	Type	Count	Prop.(%)	Type	Count	Prop.(%)
Change	Method Name	53	11.52	Parameter Name	32	6.96
	Response Format	7	1.52	Format or Type	13	2.83
	Rate Limit	7	1.52	Rate Limit	1	**0.22**
	Authentication Model	10	2.18	Require Type	4	0.87
	Domain URL	2	0.43			
Delete	Method	72	15.65	Parameter	21	4.57
Add	New Method	191	**41.52**	New Parameter	51	11.09
	New Error Code	2	0.43			

RQ2. Which types of changes trigger more questions from client code developers?

Motivation. When encountering problems in software development, developers start using crowd-sourced resources such as StackOverflow instead of using mailing lists or project-specific forums [11]. Therefore, analyzing on-line discussion regarding API changes in StackOverflow is useful to understand the developers' difficulties in dealing with different types of API changes. The first step of understanding the developer's challenges is to identify the change types drawing more discussion (*i.e.*, in terms of the number of questions) than others in StackOverflow. By knowing the change types triggering more discussion, RESTful API providers can arrange their resources to approach such change types carefully to help client code developers during the client code migration.

Analysis Approach. To answer this question, we analyze the StackOverflow question posts from Twitter, Blogger, Tumblr and OpenStreetMap, because they relatively have more posts than the other APIs in our dataset in Section 3.1. To identify which change types trigger more questions from developers, we conduct the following steps:

Step 1: we link API changes with StackOverflow posts in the following steps: 1) we obtain a mapping from method-level and parameter-level changes to API HTTP methods from **RQ1**. We search for API-related posts containing the API method names; 2) we remove any special characters such as "/" in a method name; 3) some methods can be linked with several change types. In this case, we cannot identify the change types with which StackOverflow posts belong to. Instead of introducing bias in our results, we remove such methods from our analysis (*i.e.*, we only have very few such methods). We obtain a mapping chain: a change type— a set of API methods—a set of Posts.

Step 2: we compute the average number of questions concerning each method. In this question, we only study the method and parameter level change types, because such types of changes can be linked with StackOverflow posts through API method names and introduce less noise in our data than API-level changes.

Step 3: we compute the Mann-Whitney Test and the Cliff's Delta, a nonparametric effect size measure [8], to compare the distribution of questions for different types of changes (*i.e.*, only change types at method and parameter level) in our study. We follow the guidelines in [8] to interpret the effect size

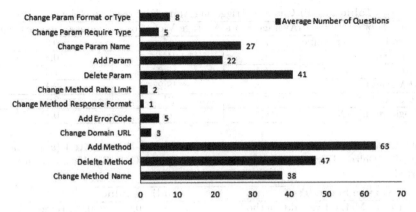

Fig. 2. Average Number of Questions Per Methods with Different Change Types

Table 8. Questions per Method of Change Types: Manny-Whitney Test (adj. p-value) and Cliff's Delta (d) Between Different Change Types. Only Significant Results and Major Change Types are reported.

Test	adj. p-value	d
Add Method vs Delete Parameter	< 0.01	-0.12 (Small)
Add Method vs Change Method Name	< 0.01	0.15 (Small)
Add Method vs Add Parameter	< 0.01	-0.57 (Large)
Add Method vs Change Parameter Name	< 0.01	-0.48 (Large)
Add Method vs Delete Method	< 0.01	0.07 (Small)
Delete Method vs Add Parameter	< 0.01	-0.39 (Medium)
Delete Method vs Change Parameter Name	< 0.01	-0.36 (Medium)
Delete Parameter vs Add Parameter	< 0.01	-0.33 (Medium)
Delete Parameter vs Change Parameter Name	< 0.01	-0.29 (Medium)

values: small for $d < 0.33$ (positive as well as negative values), medium for $0.33 \leq d < 0.474$ and large for $d \geq 0.474$.

Findings. Fig. 2 shows that the change type of *Add Method* draws average 63 questions per change which is higher than other change types. *Add Method* draw 1.3 times more questions than *Delete Method*, with a statistically significant difference (p-value< 0.01) shown in Table 8. Furthermore, the method-level change types trigger more questions that parameter-level change types. Summarizing results in Fig. 2 and Table 8, we find that

> *Add Method draws more questions than other change types.*

RQ3. Which types of changes bring discussion on posted questions from developers?
Motivation. When a question is worth discussing and attracting developers' attention due to various reasons (*e.g.*, the question is hard to be solved), the question post starts receiving more answers, comments and views from developers. Identifying the change types drawing such questions is helpful to understand which change types are more related to developers. In RQ2, the impact of change

Table 9. API Changes Triggering More Discussed Questions

Change Type	Average Score	Average View Count	Average Answer Count
Change Parameter Name	2.4	15	0.5
Add Parameter	1.2	21.4	0.8
Delete Parameter	4.1	15.6	1.4
Add Method	5.8	48.2	2.1
Delete Method	7.8	31	3.1
Change Method Name	4.9	18	0.8

Table 10. Discussed Questions of Change Types: Manny-Whitney Test (adj. p-value) and Cliff's Delta (d) Between Different Change Types. Only Significant Results are reported.

Average Score Test	adj. p-value	d
Delete Method vs Add Method	<0.01	-0.92. (large)
Delete Method vs Add Parameter	<0.01	-3.41 (large)
Delete Method vs Change Parameter Name	<0.01	-2.44 (large)
Add Method vs Add Parameter	<0.01	-2.93 (large)
Average View Count Test	adj. p-value	d
Add Method vs Delete Method	<0.01	-1.21 (large)
Add Method vs Add Parameter	<0.01	-2.37 (large)
Add Method vs Change Method Name	<0.01	-2.62 (large)
Delete Method vs Delete Parameter	<0.01	-1.83 (large)
Average Answer Count Test	adj. p-value	d
Delete Method vs Add Method	<0.01	-1.01 (large)
Delete Method vs Add Parameter	<0.01	-3.73 (large)
Delete Method vs Change Method Name	<0.01	-3.86 (large)
Delete Method vs Delete Parameter	<0.01	-1.82 (large)
Add Method vs Change Method Name	<0.01	-2.32 (large)
Add Method vs Add Parameter	<0.01	-2.22 (large)

types on the volume of discussion regarding API changes is investigated. In this question, we analyze the quality of discussion.

Analysis Approach. We compute metrics for each question. We use similar metrics in [11] for measuring the discussion quality of a question:

- *Score:* is the difference between up-votes and down-votes.
- *View Count:* is the number of times the question has been viewed.
- *Answer Count:* is the number of answers for the question.

Each question post has 3 values and each change type is associated with a set of questions. Second, based on the results in **RQ2**, we study 6 change types causing more questions than other change types: *Change Method Name, Delete Method, Add Method, Delete Parameter, Add Parameter and Change Parameter Name.* We compute the average score, average view count, average answer count for each change type. Third, to check whether there are significant differences between the sets of questions associated with different change types, we run Mann-Whitney test (adj. p-Value) and Cliff's Delta (d) on the sets of questions.

Findings. Table 9 shows that the questions of *Delete Method* receive a higher score and more answers than those related to other change types, questions of

Add Method have a higher view count than those related to the other types. Table 10 shows that statistical tests confirm the above three findings. The results suggest that when dealing with the change type of *Delete Method*, developers can have more various solutions and more communication with other developers. However, when learning new methods in the newer version, developers experience a hard time to find a solution. Our study supports the fact that since deleted methods can break client applications, client code developers feel the pressure to update their client applications and start searching for a solution intensively.

> *Questions related to Delete Method are most relevant and discussed in terms of higher score values and more answers.*

4 Threats to Validity

This section discusses the threats to validity of our study following the guidelines for case study research [16].

Construct validity threats concern the relation between theory and observation. In this paper, the construct validity threats are mainly from the human judgment involved in identification and categorization of API changes during web API evolution. Many research studies (*e.g.*, [3][10]) have conducted manual analysis of API changes. We set guidelines before we conduct manual study and we paid attention not to violate any guidelines to avoid the big fluctuation of results with a change of the experiment conductor.

External validity threats concern the generalization of our findings. In this paper, we only analyze the dataset from StackOverflow. Although StackOverflow is one of the top Questions&Answer websites for developers and many research studies (*e.g.*, [11][1]) have been conducted on only StackOverflow, further analysis is desired to claim that our findings of reactions of developers are generalized well for different Questions&Answer websites, different developer population and other forums for programming.

Reliability validity threats concern the possibility of replicating this study. We attempt to provide all the necessary details to replicate our study. The posts from developers are publicly available on Stack Exchange Data Explorer[6]. All the documentation of our subject web APIs are available on-line.

5 Related Work

In this section, we summarize the related work on API changes and developer discussion in StackOverflow.

Analysis of evolution of Java APIs, WSDL services, and web APIs
Several studies (*e.g.*, [10][3][5]) have studied the API evolution. Li *et al.* [10] conduct an empirical study on classifying web API changes. They identify 16 API change patterns. This study is the most similar one to our analysis in research question 1. However our study is based on more web APIs and identifies 7 more change types. Although Li *et al.* [10] discuss the potential troubles from

---

[6] https://data.stackexchange.com/

developers during the migration, they do not conduct any empirical study on the developers reactions to the changes. Dig *et al.* [3] conduct a manual analysis on classification of API changes of Java API evolution. They mainly focus on breaking changes due to the refactoring during the evolution. Fokaefs *et al.* [5] conduct an empirical study on the changes, potentially affecting client applications, of WSDL web service interface evolution using VTracker to differentiate XML schema by comparing different versions of web service. Furthermore, Fokaefs *et al.* [6] introduce a domain-specific differencing method called WSDarwin to compare interfaces of web services described in WSDL or WADL. Romano *et al.* [13] propose a tool called WSDLDiff analyzing fine-grained changes by comparing the versions of WSDL interfaces. However all of the above studies do not analyze changes of web API evolution and how developers react to the API evolution.

Analysis of Developer Reactions

Espinha *et al.* [4] explore the impact of common change practices of API evolution on the client applications by conducting semi-structured interviews with client developers and mining source code changes of client applications, however their focus is not on identifying change types of web APIs. Linares-Vásquez *et al.* investigate how developers react to the Andorid API instability on Stack-Overflow[7] and suggest practices to both API providers and client developers. A survey [2] conducted among 130 web API clients was published online about the integration pain from API evolution, and reports some practices (*e.g.*, bad documentation and randomly change without warnings) causing troubles to developers. Barua *et al.* [1] explore the hot topics of software development on StackOverflow as well as their relationships and trends over time using topic modeling techniques. The topics of the posts from developers reflect developers' reactions on specific technologies. In our study, we mostly study the discussions on the Stack Overflow to know the impact of API changes on developers.

6   Conclusion and Future Work

API changes affect client applications, however it is unclear how the web APIs evolve and how developers react to the evolution. In this paper, we conduct an empirical study on identifying and categorizing API changes. We identify 21 change types, and 7 of them (*e.g.*, Add Response Format) are newly discovered compared with existing research studies. In total, we identify 460 changes of 21 change types, and 41.52% of 460 changes belong to the change type *Add Method*, which makes the change type of *Add Method* the most common API change practice. Furthermore, our empirical results show that the change type *Delete Method* draws more discussed and relevant questions from developers in the community, and the change type *Add Method* receives more questions and views from developers. The identified change types of web API evolution are useful for client developers to understand the API changes and reduce troubles during client application migration. Furthermore, understanding the developers' discussion regarding change types is useful for API providers to conduct better practices on releasing new versions to reduce the negative effect of API evolution on client code developers.

---

[7] http://stackoverflow.com/

In the future, we plan to include more web APIs in our analysis. Furthermore, we want to conduct fine-grained analysis on source code changes of client applications.

Acknowledgments. The authors would like to thank Pang Pei and Nasir Ali for their valuable comments on this work.

References

1. Barua, A., Thomas, S.W., Hassan, A.E.: What are developers talking about? an analysis of topics and trends in stack overflow. Empirical Software Engineering 19(3), 619–654 (2014)
2. Blank, S.: API integration pain survey results (2014), https://www.yourtrove.com/blog/2011/08/11/api-integration-pain-survey-results (accessed on May 18, 2014)
3. Dig, D., Johnson, R.: How do apis evolve? a story of refactoring. Journal of software maintenance and evolution: Research and Practice 18(2), 83–107 (2006)
4. Espinha, T., Zaidman, A., Gross, H.G.: Web api growing pains: Stories from client developers and their code. In: 2014 Software Evolution Week-IEEE Conference on Software Maintenance, Reengineering and Reverse Engineering (CSMR-WCRE), pp. 84–93. IEEE (2014)
5. Fokaefs, M., Mikhaiel, R., Tsantalis, N., Stroulia, E., Lau, A.: An empirical study on web service evolution. In: 2011 IEEE International Conference on Web Services (ICWS), pp. 49–56. IEEE (2011)
6. Fokaefs, M., Stroulia, E.: Wsdarwin: Studying the evolution of web service systems. In: Advanced Web Services, pp. 199–223. Springer (2014)
7. Gomadam, K., Ranabahu, A., Nagarajan, M., Sheth, A.P., Verma, K.: A faceted classification based approach to search and rank web apis. In: IEEE International Conference on Web Services, ICWS 2008, pp. 177–184. IEEE (2008)
8. Grissom, R.J., Kim, J.J.: Effect sizes for research: A broad practical approach. Lawrence Erlbaum Associates Publishers (2005)
9. Li, H., Xing, Z., Peng, X., Zhao, W.: What help do developers seek, when and how? In: 2013 20th Working Conference on Reverse Engineering (WCRE), pp. 142–151. IEEE (2013)
10. Li, J., Xiong, Y., Liu, X., Zhang, L.: How does web service api evolution affect clients? In: 2013 IEEE 20th International Conference on Web Services (ICWS), pp. 300–307. IEEE (2013)
11. Linares-Vásquez, M., Bavota, G., Di Penta, M., Oliveto, R., Poshyvanyk, D.: How do api changes trigger stack overflow discussions? a study on the android sdk. In: Proceedings of the 22nd International Conference on Program Comprehension, pp. 83–94. ACM (2014)
12. Mamykina, L., Manoim, B., Mittal, M., Hripcsak, G., Hartmann, B.: Design lessons from the fastest q&a site in the west. In: Proceedings of the SIGCHI Conference on Human Factors in Computing Systems, pp. 2857–2866. ACM (2011)
13. Romano, D., Pinzger, M.: Analyzing the evolution of web services using fine-grained changes. In: 2012 IEEE 19th International Conference on Web Services (ICWS), pp. 392–399. IEEE (2012)
14. Twitter: Changes to withheld content fields (2014), https://blog.twitter.com/2012/changes-withheld-content-fields (accessed on May 1, 2014)
15. Wikipedia: Web API (2014), http://en.wikipedia.org/wiki/Web_API (accessed on May 19, 2014)
16. Yin, R.K.: Case study research: Design and methods. Sage Publications (2014)

How to Enable Multiple Skill Learning in a SLA Constrained Service System?

Sumit Kalra[1], Shivali Agarwal[2], and Gargi Dasgupta[2]

[1] Indian Institute of Technology, Kanpur, India
sumitk@cse.iitk.ac.in
[2] IBM Research, Bengaluru, India
{shivaaga,gaargidasgupta}@in.ibm.com

Abstract. In a knowledge based service system like IT services, the requirements of skills to service customer requests keep changing with time. The service workers are expected to learn the required skills very quickly and become productive. Due to high attrition rate and demand, service workers are given basic class room training and then rest of the training is carried out on-job. When a service worker learns multiple skills simultaneously, learning slows down due to factors like forgetting and interference. At the same time, the organization needs to meet service level agreements (SLA). We have developed a model for on-job training which extends the business process for IT service delivery. The key idea is to model learning, forgetting and interference in service time estimation to get realistic service times. Accurate estimation of service time taken by a service worker to resolve the service tickets helps in resource allocation and planning decisions for achieving the desired objectives of upskilling and SLA success. The simulation of execution of the augmented business process provides insights into what kind of planning and dispatch policies should be practiced for achieving the desired goals of multi-skill learning and SLA success.

1 Introduction

A *Service System (SS)* is an organization composed of (a) the human resources who perform work, and (b) the processes that drive service interactions so that the outcomes meet customer expectations [22]. Typically, a *service worker (SW)* represents a unit of human resource and a *service request (SR)* represents a unit of service work that (s)he is assigned. Hence, management of the SWs in service provider organizations is crucial. Over the past years, business and education groups have issued a series of reports indicating that due to rapid technological changes and increasing global competition, the skill demands of work are continually rising. Economists studying the changing workplace skill demands, have found that technological change is "skill-biased" thereby increasing the demand for people who have multiple skills. Many businesses are asking employees to assume multiple roles and because of this shift, hiring has become difficult in countries in spite of steady unemployment rates.

X. Franch et al. (Eds.): ICSOC 2014, LNCS 8831, pp. 260–274, 2014.

This need for multi-faceted workers entails not only retaining the right skills, but also transforming the skills of the workers as dictated by the changing business requirements. For example, in the IT services domain, it may so happen that due to a transformation in the customer's environment, a provider has to quickly upskill his team. The current team of 10 people who only had expertise in the Solaris operating system needs to be transformed to a team where both the operating systems of Windows and Solaris need to be supported. While one option for the provider is to replace some of the Solaris personnel with new hires having Windows skills, a better option is to impart new skills to existing SWs such that they collectively meet the target skill requirements.

There are several approaches for imparting new skills: (a) class room training, where SWs dedicate training time for a certain duration and incur costs, (b) shadowing, where SWs observe the work of skilled SWs and learn, or (c) on-job training, where SWs pick up skills while actually doing the work. The nature of work in services involves substantial interactions not only with the customer but also with colleagues. Also, carrying out a task is far more difficult than simply knowing how to carry out a task. Hence, on-job training following minimal classroom training is the approach commonly adopted by service providers. As of today, very little understanding exists on how the on-job training should be carried out. For example, how does the skill of a SW evolve when one or multiple new learnings are imparted ? Does this evolution of target skills change when (s)he already has some existing skills ? How do multiple learnings interfere with each other ? Can parallel learnings also reinforce ? How should the on-job training be planned and carried out such that impact to customer service in terms of service level agreement (SLA) is minimized ?

We have addressed the problem of incorporating on-job training in IT business process in this paper. This internalizes many of the questions raised above for on-job training. Our main contributions are:

1) We have developed an on-job training model based on the Dreyfus model of skill acquisition [10], the Learn-Forget-Curve-Model(LFCM)[15] and theory of interference in learning [19]. This model can be used to create a standalone training process or embedded into existing business processes. **The main components of the model are service time estimation model, skill distribution policies and finally the dispatch heuristics.**
2) The on-job training model has been woven into the IT incident management(ITIM) business process as a case study.
3) We have carried out an evaluation of the proposed model using discrete event simulation.

The evaluation focuses on understanding (i) the role of interference and skill multiplicity while imparting training for multiple skills simultaneously and (ii) how do dispatch(work assignment) policies influence learning. The rest of the paper is organized as follows. Section 2 describes the learning model based on service times during on-job training. Section 3 explains the skill distribution and dispatch heuristics components. Section 4 explains how the on-job training components get integrated into a business process. The evaluation of the training model as a part of business process is presented in section 4.1 and 4.2. Related work is discussed in section 5 and we conclude in section 6.

2   Learning Curve and Skill Progression Model

On-job training seems to be an effective way to bridge the gaps between the new and existing skills. In this scenario, a service worker gets to work on tasks which require the specific new skills (s)he is expected to be upskilled on and improvement in service times is the main observable measure to quantify learning. While initially the tasks will take longer to complete, as (s)he works on them the service time to complete tasks become smaller. In specific, authors in [15] have shown that the reduction in service time with experience follows the power-law [1]. However if there exists breaks between the new-skill tasks assigned to a worker, forgetting may happen. Also if multiple new skills are being learnt by a worker, learning interference may creep in among the multiple skills. Both forgetting and interference slow down the learning process and affect the service time. Keeping this in mind, the service time model has been designed drawing upon the existing work on learning and skill acquisition namely, LFCM and Dreyfus model respectively. We briefly explain the factors that play a role in the service time estimation below.

Learning Effect on Service Time: During on-job training, when people initially take-on new skill work, service times are longer. Assuming the difference between skills could be mapped to a gap function, we state that larger the gap between the skills, longer becomes the service times. This is modeled as gap learning factor or *glf.*

Forgetting Effect on Service Time: Time gaps between task executions [15]cause forgetting, which in turn has the effect of longer service times. Forgetting is proportional to the time gap [13].

Interference Effect on Service Time: When a service worker works on multiple new skills within the same span of time, the learning of these new skills interfere with each other. This interference results in lower recall accuracy of other skills [19] and hence in longer service times.

Skill Level Gap Effect on Service Time: Dreyfus model [10] of skill acquisition models the progression levels as Novice, Advanced beginner, Competent, Proficient and Expert. The interpretation of each level has been provided in terms of qualitative translation of each level to the task performance. This model is very appropriate for on-job training. The service times are least at the expert level and highest at the beginner's level. The time taken by a SW at any level to complete an SR is stochastic and is shown [1] to follow a lognormal distribution for a single skill.

---

[1] While this is true for manufacturing, the same principle can be applied to any industry where there is rhythmic and repeatable work, for example, IT service management.

We now present a service time model that takes into account the above factors. This represents the skill progression model of a worker as multiple new learnings are imparted to her.

Let T_s be the service time required by a SW for a SR with particular skill requirement while working for n^{th} , $n > 1$, time on the same skill where the SW is working on the skill after a time gap. T_{BS} is the base service time which denotes the time taken by service worker when working on the skill for the first time. T_{BS} is defined for each SW skill level. Let $dist$ be the gap between required skill level of the SR and the current skill level possessed by SW. If the latter is higher or equal, $dist$ is 0. The base service time is computed as $T_{BS}(1 + \log(1 + dist))$. Equations 1, 2 and 3 show the learning model while factoring in the time gap [13] only. The $timeGap$ is the time spent on resolving SRs with other skills and the $timeUsed$ is the time spent on resolving SRs with relevant skill. The learning factor (lf) is a constant [15] which depends the learning pace of the SW. The gap learning factor (glf) incorporates the lf and γ, $0 \le \gamma < 1$, which is function of $timeGap$ and $timeUsed$.

$$\gamma = \frac{\log(1 + timeGap/timeUsed)}{\log n} \tag{1}$$

$$glf = lf * (1 - \gamma) \tag{2}$$

$$T_s = T_{BS} * n^{-glf} \tag{3}$$

There has been sufficient evidence in the literature to indicate that interference also causes forgetting. To include the interference in this model, we assumed that the effect of interference is equivalent to stretched time gap. To include the interference in this model, we used the results from [7] that show that the effect of interference is equivalent to stretched time gap and modify the Equation 1 as Equation 4.

$$\gamma = \frac{\log(1 + \frac{(timeGap + interferenceMeter)}{timeUsed})}{\log n} \tag{4}$$

$InterferenceMeter$ keeps the track of number of times the SW has worked on other interfering skills since last worked on the current skill. Each increment denotes a unit of time. This meter is reset to zero every time when SW works on the skill. If a SW works on the interfered skill less often, then the effect of interfering skills are more and vice-versa. However, as n increases, the impact of forgetting and interference reduces.

The quantitative model for skill progression corresponding to the Dreyfus qualitative model is obtained using time and motion studies. These studies provide a threshold on quantum of work to be done for being eligible to move to next skill level. We assume in this work that the SWs are provided basic classroom training for skills that they have never worked on before to make on-job training feasible. We shall now describe how to carry out on-job training.

3   How Is On-job Training Performed?

A SS has an existing set of skills according to the current requirements of clients. The SS periodically updates the target set of skills required based on changes in existing clients' requirements and IT infrastructure of new clients. The target skills may have only a partial overlap with the existing skills in the system. On-job training is used for transforming the existing skill profiles to the target skill profiles. We assume, w.l.o.g., that the total workforce remains same and the transition does not entail hiring. Given this setup, the training problem is solved in two phases. The first phase is the skill distribution phase that determines the skills for each SW on which she will be trained. This is a one time decision process based on heuristics as described in 3.1. The second phase is the dispatch of an incoming request to a SW as and when it arrives. This phase involves a continuous decision making process so that SS can achieve the training targets and ensure SLA success. The first phase fixes the target skills for each SW and this information is used for the dispatch of SRs upon arrival in the second phase. The two phases are explained next.

3.1   Skill Distribution

The decision of skill distribution is a preliminary step in carrying out the training. Table 1 shows the input to the distribution problem. It states the current skills possessed by three SWs with id SW_1, SW_2 and SW_3. They have 2 skills each. Last two columns in the table show the new skills required and the required number of SWs respectively. Here we can see that the skill id 5 is already present in the current skill profile while others are not. The skill distribution is carried out by adopting one of the following strategies i) *Balance skill load*, that is, balance the number of new skills to be learned per worker, ii) *Balance interference*, that is, balance the number of new skills to be learned in terms of interference. We explain both the strategies with the example input of table 1 . Let us assume that the pair of skills $\{5, 7\}$ is highly interfering and other pairs are not interfering. The output based on strategy (i), where target skills are distributed in such a manner that each SW gets a chance to learn equal number of new skill, is shown in second column of Table 2. The output provides the distribution of target skills per SW. Here, each SW requires to learn two new skills. However, the output looks different if we distribute using strategy (ii) where target skills are distributed by minimizing the interference among skills to be learned by a SW. Third column in the Table 2 shows one such possible distribution where no SW receives any interfering skill pair. We can observe that in strategy (i), the SW_3 has received skill 7 which is interfering with his existing skill 5, whereas in strategy (ii), SW_3 only gets one new skill to learn as he already knows skill 5 which is not interfering with existing skills.

We would like to add that there can be other heuristics as well for doing skill distribution. For the purpose of this work, we assume that the skill distribution is done using one of the strategies. We do not delve deep into the details of the algorithm as they are straightforward.

Table 1. SWs Current Profile and Target Requirements

Current Profiles		Target Requirements	
SW Id	Skill Ids	Skill Id	Requirement
SW_1	1,2	5	1
SW_2	2,3	6	3
SW_3	4,5	7	2

Table 2. Skill Distribution Strategies

	Balance New Skills	Balance Interfering Skills
SW Id	Skill Ids	Skill Ids
SW1	5,6	6,7
SW2	6, 7	6,7
SW3	6,7	5,6

3.2 Dispatching

The task of carrying out on-job training is equivalent to multiple sequential invocations of the task of assigning incoming SR to appropriate SW such that the SLA target is met and up-skilling of all the service worker is maximized. We have designed two different heuristics(policies) for selection of SW for an incoming SR which along with the naive policy of SLA Priority can handle different types of SS's goals. Simulations can be run for a real life SS to learn which is the best dispatch policy for the fore-casted demand. We describe the different policies next but before that, we briefly explain the interpretation of SLA in terms of timestamps.

SLA is specified by the customers for each incoming SR in terms of expected date and time of resolution. This is modeled in SS using timestamps according to the Equation 5.

$$SLA_{remain} = SR_{SLATime} - SR_{compTime} \qquad (5)$$

$SR_{SLATime}$ denotes the timestamp by which the SR should be completed in order to meet SLA, $SR_{compTime}$ denotes the timestamp when the SR got completed and SLA_{remain} denotes the time remaining to meet the specified SLA.The positive value of SLA_{remain} indicates an SLA success otherwise SLA miss.The $SR_{compTime}$ is dependent on the expected service time of the SW who is working on it.

Skill-Level Priority Policy: Skill-Level Priority policy aims to maximize the SLA success, based on the observation that service worker w having matching skill level with least load, denoted by $minLoad$, is able to quickly complete the assigned SR, hence maximizing the SLA success. Each SR in the SW's queue contributes to load proportional to the skill level gap between incoming SR and the SW. A threshold on the queue load determines if a SW is overloaded.

Algorithm 1 formally describes the Skill-Level Priority policy for assigning a service request SR to assign appropriate service worker w among the pool of available service workers $SWList$. Initially Skill-Level Priority policy checks for all the service workers which have same skill level as required by the SR, are not overloaded and can meet SLA based on expected service time. Among them, it finds the least loaded service worker w. The load due to pending SRs in the queue is denoted by $SRPendingQueueLoad$. If all the service workers with equal skill level as required by SR are overloaded or not available, then the policy looks for the service workers having the same skill required by the SR with one level lower and higher which are not overloaded and so on. As we have finite skill levels, the algorithm terminates. If it does not find anyone, then the least loaded SW is chosen. Amongst the shortlisted SWs, it then computes γ to find who has the maximum learning potential.

Input: $SR, SWList$
Output: SW_{id}
$id = \phi$
$minLoad = 150$
$diff = 0$
while $id = \phi$ AND $diff < 4$ **do**
   for each $w_i \epsilon$ SWList **do**
      if $abs(SR_{SkillLevel} - w_i.SkillLevel) = diff$ AND $w_i.overload = false$
      then
         if $minLoad > w_i.SRPendingQueueLoad$ **then**
            $id = w_i.id$
            $minLoad = w_i.SRPendingQueueLoad$
         end
      end
   end
   if $id == \phi$ **then**
      $diff = diff + 1$
   end
   else
      break
   end
end
return id

Algorithm 1. SKILL-LEVEL PRIORITY POLICY OUTLINE

Learning Priority Policy: Learning Priority policy gives more chances to the service workers with lower skill levels in order to assign them more service requests and increase their experience and learning. This policy looks at all the service workers which can complete the SR and meet SLA by calculating the expected service time and check if it is less than the remaining SLA time. Since this policy always prefers the service worker with maximum worst case service time $maxWorstServiceTime$ who can complete the SR within SLA, there are higher chances of increasing the skill level of the service worker at the cost of increasing the probability of missing SLA.

Algorithm 2 formally describes the Learning Priority policy for assigning a service request SR to assign appropriate service worker w among the pool of available service workers $SWList$. Initially Learning Priority policys checks for all the service workers which have expected service time less than remaining service time and not overloaded. Among them, it finds the least loaded service worker w with highest value of worst case service time $maxWorstServiceTime$.

Input: $SR, SWList$
Output: SW_{id}
$id = \phi$
$minLoad = 150$
$maxWorstServiceTime = 0$
for each $w_i \epsilon SWList$ **do**
   if $w_i.expectedServiceTime < SR.SLA_{remain}$ AND $w_i.overload = false$
   then
      if $minLoad > w_i.SRPendingQueueLoad$ AND
      $maxWorstServiceTime < w_i.worstServiceTime$ **then**
         $id = w_i.id$
         $minLoad = w_i.SRPendingQueueLoad$
         $maxWorstServiceTime = w_i.worstServiceTime$
      end
   end
end
return id

Algorithm 2. LEARNING PRIORITY POLICY OUTLINE

SLA Priority Policy: The work dispatch based on SLA priority policy mimics on ground reality of existing service systems. It basically dispatches the SR to the first available SW who has skills to carry out the work. There is no other consideration like skill level, learning progress etc. Note that SLA Priority policy does not compute expected service time according to the learning curve model of section 2 while choosing the SW as is done by Skill-Level or Learning Priority policy thus differing from them in a crucial way.

4 Case Study - IT Incident Management

ITIM process is one of the main candidates for on-job training use case in SS, hence, we chose it for the case study. The IT incident management process extended with tasks for on-job training is illustrated in Fig. 1. We have built upon the ITIM process studied in [18] which is revisited briefly as follows. A problem or issue faced by a business user is reported to a help desk. The help desk personnel opens an incident ticket in a ticketing tool and records the description of the issue. Then the incident is assigned to a specific work group based on the problem described by the user. The incident, once assigned to a work group, is picked up by an available resource within the work group who then updates the assignment information indicating the ownership of the incident. The incident enters the resolution stage. The resource further analyzes the problem in the ticket, communicates to the business user for more input on the problem, and resolves the problem. Once an incident is resolved, the resource restores the functionality of the system as required by the business user. The business user validates and confirms the service provided by the resource. Once confirmed by the business user, the incident is closed.

The extension to the existing ITIM process for training is primarily in the dispatch task. The incident, once assigned to a group, is assessed by a dispatch engine for the skills that it requires and the load on the SWs that have been identified to work on those skills. Subsequently, the expected service time for the shortlisted SWs is computed according to the model in section 2. Then, after considering the SLA requirements, the engine selects an incident owner following one of the proposed policies and the incident is dispatched. Once the incident is resolved, the parameters that track the learning of the SWs are updated and so is the SLA measurement. The process to initiate the closure of the incident is also initiated in parallel.

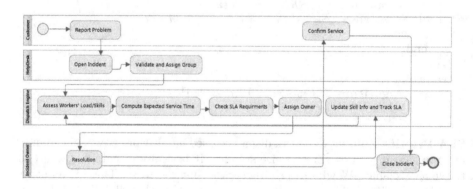

Fig. 1. IT Incident Management Process Extended with On-Job Training Tasks

4.1   Simulation Framework Overview of Enhanced ITIM Process

A discrete event simulation [1] of the ITIM process augmented with training has been used to gain insights into the proposed training model. A service request(SR) arrives in the system and is redirected to a service worker (SW) who resolves it. A valid set of states for a SR is *inqueue* (default), *pending*, *inservice*, *rework* or *completed* and similarly, set of valid state of service worker is defined as {Available, NotAvailable}. For each SW, we also maintain information such as existing skills, new skills being learned, working hours shift availability, overload status. The expected service time of a SR for each SW is computed using the learning curve described in section 2. SLA requirements for all customers are assumed to be: *as long as a provider completes 95% of all SRs received every month within specified hours*, the quality of service is deemed adequate. We also assume that each SR requires single skill like unix, windows, db2 etc. The main components are described below.

Global Queue: A global queue is maintained which accepts all the incoming SRs with different priority and different skill requirement. For every SR, we maintain the information such as priority, SLA deadline, skill and corresponding level requirement and status as *inqueue* (default), *pending*, *inservice*, *rework* or *completed*. This global queue serves as the input to the dispatching module.

Dispatch Module: The dispatching module accepts SRs from global queue one by one and uses list of all the SWs in order to search for the most suitable SW for the current SR based on a policy described in section 3. A policy remains in force for the period of simulation (say, a month). After identifying the SW, SR is sent to its queue and the status of the SR is changed from *inqueue* to *pending*. The $SRPendingQueueLoad$ is updated as described in equation 6.

Service Workers' Queue: A service worker's queue can have SRs of skill levels different than his current level. The load value in such a situation is normalized by having more complex SRs contribute more to the load than the lower level ones. We assume the normal load of a SR for SW is equal to 20 and the Equation 6 is used to calculate the load due to different levels.

$$weight = 20 + (SR_{skill-level} - SW_{skill-level}) \times 5 \qquad (6)$$

Let *curload* of a SW denote the load due to pending SRs in the queue. We calculate whether a SW is overloaded or not as follows:

$$overloaded = \begin{cases} yes & \text{if } curload \geq 100 \\ no & \text{otherwise} \end{cases}$$

Once SR is assigned to a SW, it remains in *pending* state in the queue of the SW till all the SRs which arrived before it are resolved. When SW works on the SR, the status is updated to *inservice*. To introduce some failure cases in the simulation model, where a SW fails to resolve the SR as per requirements, every SR with 0.01% prbability sent for rework. If the SR being sent for rework, it is status is updated to *rework* and placed on the global queue along with recently arrived SRs. Otherwise, the status is updated to *completed*.

Learning Parameters and Interference Meter: For simulation purpose, we set the learning factor lf to 0.1 and $timeGap$ is captured in unit of work hours. We start an interferenceMeter for each skill for every SW with value 0. Whenever a SW works on a particular skill, the value of interferenceMeter of skills being interfered by current skill is incremented. It is reset to 0 for a skill for SW when he works on that skill.

Statistical data collection and Skill Progression: The framework continuously collects data such as skill level progression rate, SLA success rate. Skill level is upgraded after sufficient experience for the skill. In our simulation model, we assume that after working on 500 SRs of the same skill, SWs skill level is incremented by 1 with minimum value 1 and maximum value 4. These skill level from 1 to 4 represents the proficiency of SW as Basic, Developed, Advanced and Expert respectively. We have adopted a simplified model of skill levels as proposed in [10].

Workload Generation: Diverse workloads for the simulation are generated as described below. Given the average inter-arrival time, assuming Poisson distribution, the workload is generated for a specified number of weeks. For each arrival, there are associated parameters of priority, skill and skill-level required to resolve the SR. Here we assume that a SR is assigned to only one SW and that SWs can have multiple SRs with a limit upto 5 SRs with skill gap 0, pending in its queue at any given instance of time during simulation. For a particular skill, the number of current and required SWs is specified as illustrated in table 1. Dispatch simulation is performed on different combinations of skill distributions arising out of the two strategies. Under uniform skill load distribution, each SW gets equal number of skills where as in left (right) skewed skill load distribution, most of the SWs get less (more) number of skills. Analogously, the workload consists of left skewed and right skewed distribution of interference load.

Note: It is possible that one skill pair is more interfering than the other pair. Interference can also be unidirectional. However, there is no quantitative model for this yet in the literature. In the absence of any quantitative model for interference load, we consider only presence or absence of interference between two skills and assume symmetric interference. The value for Interference load is 10 if two skills are not interfering as oppose to value 90, which denotes that the pair of skills are interfering. The interference load is computed as a summation of pairwise interference when more than two skills are being learned.

4.2   Simulation Experiments and Results

The training process is simulated under different workloads and policies to understand the tradeoffs that exist in adopting such a process while delivering services. The key insights obtained from the experiments are listed below.

Observation 1 (On Skill Load vs. Interference): Skill load and interference are equally strong deterrents in learning. We carried out experiments with a target skill profile having high number of skills to be learned uniformly such that the skills do not interfere (Table 3 Scheme S-2) and compared the learning time with a target profile where the skills to be learned do not exceed *two* but these skills interfere with each other (Table 3 Scheme S-3). In both scenarios, we find the similar pattern of skill level progression. In Scheme S-1, we kept both the skill load and interference load to low. The entries in the table show the percentage of SWs at the levels L1 to L4 at starting of weeks 1, 10, 20 and 40. These numbers are of Learning First Policy. However, the observation holds in the other two policies also.

Observation 2 (On Learning Pace): Learning Priority policy aids in uniform learning while Skill-Level Priority policy aids in greedy learning. Fig. 2

Table 3. Effect of Skill Load/Interferene Load on skill progression

	S-1				S-2				S-3			
	L1	L2	L3	L4	L1	L2	L3	L4	L1	L2	L3	L4
1	100	0	0	0	100	0	0	0	100	0	0	0
10	5	80	15	0	100	0	0	0	100	0	0	0
20	0	35	45	20	58	42	0	0	67	33	0	0
40	0	0	25	75	38	55	7	0	36	51	13	0

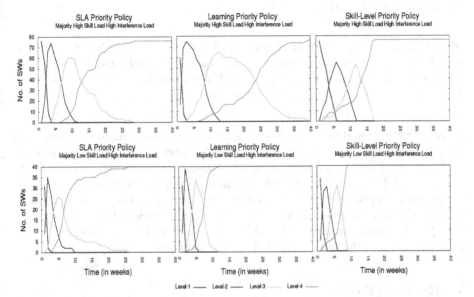

Fig. 2. Skill progression: High/Low skill load and high/low interference load

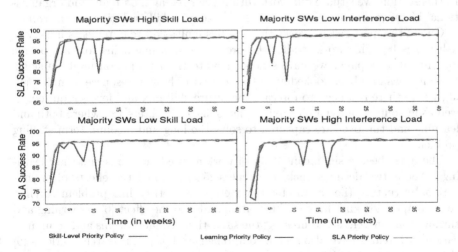

Fig. 3. SLA Success Rate Comparison

demonstrates this for two types of workloads. It can be seen in Learning Priority policy that at any given time more than 90% SWs are distributed at two consecutive levels but this is not so for the other policies. This is indicative of uniform learning where the level gap between SWs is not too much at any given point in time. Skill-Level Priority, however, follows non-uniform learning and SWs reach the highest level faster compared to the other policies. SLA Priority is neither uniform nor greedy. The simulations were run for all combinations of workload and the same trends were observed. We have presented results only for two distributions for sake of brevity.

Observation 3 (On SLA success): An interesting insight that we got was that if the dispatch policy tries to prioritize on exact match of skill levels as in Skill Level Priority, then sharp dips in SLA success rate are likely as shown in Fig. 3. This happens due to longer SR pending queue.

Applying the Insights: The insights obtained above from simulation runs can be applied in practice by SSs to achieve desired behavior. We summarize some of the important practical considerations that emerged from the experiments: i) SS should adopt Learning Priority policy if uniform learning is more desirable, ii) If the goal is to promote a competitive environment, Skill-Level Priority policy is most advisable provided SLAs are relaxed, iii) For efficient learning, the new skills to be learned per worker should be minimized; and an attempt should be made to minimize the interfering skills to be learnt per worker.

5   Related Work

In this section, we situate our work within prior research on team and organizational learning theories, resource planning, human skill evolution and learning.

One of the most recent works that studies multi-skill requirements in service delivery is [8]. This work studies the problem of optimal skills to train people on while in this paper we have studied how to train people on multiple skills. Learning has also been looked at in the context of human resource planning [4], [3], where there is a need to forecast the future skill mix and levels required, as well as in context of dynamic environments like call centers[12], where both and learning and turnover are captured to solve the long and medium term staffing problem.

There has been a significant body of work focused on teams and their learnings. About two decades back researchers[25,11] studied the effects of organizational structure (i.e. hierarchy, team etc.) on metrics like problem solving, cost, competition and drive for innovation and also the effect [6] of learning and turnover on different structures. At the same time, collaborations and communication with teams have also seen a comprehensive body of research. Carley's [5] theory of group stability postulates a relationship between individual's current knowledge and her behavior. She also found that a group's interaction increases as commonality across knowledge dimensions increases. Very recently [17] presented the notion of synergy in human teams or *how well* they work together. In context of skill evolution, Dibbern et. al [9] captures the dependencies of expertise, task complexity, support information and learning tasks on learning effectiveness during Knowledge Transfer. Imparting knowledge with on-the-job training has also been another popular method for imparting skills. Work in labor economic theory [2] has attempted to assess how much on-the-job training is needed for a specific worker, based on his current expertise and learning ability.

In the domain of learning, authors [16] talks about accelerating learning of agents via human feedback. It is also shown that [24] optimizing skills in isolation does not necessarily benefit their combined operation. According to authors, how much an individual learns when challenged, depends on the skill level of the performer and the task complexity. Apart from the learning and forgetting models ([15,14,20,21]) presented in Section 1, recent work [23] presents interesting results on how memory consolidation and forgetting processes regulate the memory capacity, and can mutually improve the effectiveness of learning.

6 Conclusions

We conclude that distribution and dispatch policies play a crucial role in balancing SLA success and upskilling when performing on-job training. The presence of interference slows down the learning rate and so does the number of skills to be learned. As part of future work, we plan to formalize interference model and study semantic facilitation during training. We also plan to study the training method in context of other business processes where on-job training is practiced.

References

1. Banerjee, D., Dasgupta, G., Desai, N.: Simulation-based evaluation of dispatching policies in service systems. In: Winter Simulation Conference (2011)
2. Barron, J., Black, D.A., Loewenstein, M.A.: Job matching and on-the-job training. Journal of Labor Economics 7(1), 1–19 (1989)
3. Bordoloi, S.: A control rule for recruitment planning in engineering consultancy. Journal of Productivity Analysis 26(2), 147–163 (2006)
4. Bordoloi, S.K., Matsuo, H.: Human resource planning in knowledge-intensive operations: A model for learning with stochastic turnover. European Journal of Operational Research 130(1), 169–189 (2001)
5. Carley, K.: A Theory of Group Stability. American Sociological Review 56, 331–354 (1991)
6. Carley, K.M.: Organizational learning and personnel turnover. Organization Science 3, 20–46 (1992)
7. Das, A., Stuerzlinger, W.: Unified modeling of proactive interference and memorization effort: A new mathematical perspective within act-r theory. In: Proceedings of the Annual Meeting of the Cognitive Science Society, COGSCI 2013, pp. 358–363 (2013)

8. Dasgupta, G.B., Sindhgatta, R., Agarwal, S.: Behavioral analysis of service delivery models. In: Proceedings of the Service-Oriented Computing - 11th International Conference, ICSOC 2013, Berlin, Germany, December 2-5, pp. 652–666 (2013)

9. Dibbern, J., Krancher, O.: Individual knowledge transfer in the transition phase of outsourced softwaremaintenance projects. In: ISB-IBM Service Science Workshop (2012)

10. Dreyfus, S.E., Dreyfus, H.L.: A Five-Stage Model of the Mental Activities Involved in Directed Skill Acquisition. Tech. rep. (February 1980), http://stinet.dtic.mil/cgi-bin/GetTRDoc?AD=ADA084551&Location=U2&doc=GetTRDoc.pdf

11. Jablin, F.M., Putnam, L.L., Roberts, K.H., Porter, L.W. (eds.): Handbook of Organizational Communication: An Interdisciplinary Perspective. Sage (1986)

12. Gans, N., Zhou, Y.P.: Managing learning and turnover in employee staffing. Oper. Res. 50(6) (2002)

13. Jaber, M.Y., Bonney, M.: Production breaks and the learning curve: The forgetting phenomenon. Applied Mathematical Modelling 20(2), 162–169 (1996), http://www.sciencedirect.com/science/article/pii/0307904X9500157F

14. Jaber, M.Y., Kher, H.V., Davis, D.J.: Countering forgetting through training and deployment. International Journal of Production Economics 85, 33–46 (2003)

15. Jaber, M.Y., Sikstrom, S.: A numerical comparison of three potential learning and forgetting models. International Journal of Production Economics 92(3) (2004)

16. Knox, W.B., Stone, P.: Reinforcement learning from simultaneous human and mdp reward. In: Proceedings of the 11th International Conference on Autonomous Agents and Multiagent Systems, AAMAS 2012, vol. 1 (2012)

17. Liemhetcharat, S., Veloso, M.: Modeling and learning synergy for team formation with heterogeneous agents. In: Proceedings of the 11th International Conference on Autonomous Agents and Multiagent Systems, AAMAS 2012, vol. 1, pp. 365–374 (2012)

18. Liu, R., Agarwal, S., Sindhgatta, R.R., Lee, J.: Accelerating collaboration in task assignment using a socially enhanced resource model. In: Daniel, F., Wang, J., Weber, B. (eds.) BPM 2013. LNCS, vol. 8094, pp. 251–258. Springer, Heidelberg (2013)

19. Jan Mensink, G., Raaijmakers, J.G.W.: A model for interference and forgetting. Psychological Review, 434–455 (1988)

20. Nembhard, D.A., Uzumeri, M.V.: Experiential learning and forgetting for manual and cognitive tasks. International Journal of Industrial Ergonomics 25, 315–326 (2000)

21. Sikstrom, S., Jaber, M.Y.: The power integration diffusion (pid) model for production breaks. Journal of Experimental Psychology 8, 118–126 (2002)

22. Spohrer, J., Maglio, P., Bailey, J., Gruhl, D.: Steps toward a science of service systems. Computer 40(1), 71–77 (2007)

23. Subagdja, B., Wang, W., Tan, A.H., Tan, Y.S., Teow, L.N.: Memory formation, consolidation, and forgetting in learning agents. In: Proceedings of the 11th International Conference on Autonomous Agents and Multiagent Systems, AAMAS 2012, vol. 2 (2012)

24. Urieli, D., MacAlpine, P., Kalyanakrishnan, S., Bentor, Y., Stone, P.: On optimizing interdependent skills: A case study in simulated 3d humanoid robot soccer. In: Proc. of 10th Int. Conf. on Autonomous Agents and Multiagent Systems (AAMAS 2011) (May 2011)

25. Williamson, O.E.: The economics of organization: The transaction cost approach. American Journal of Sociology (1981)

ADVISE – A Framework for Evaluating Cloud Service Elasticity Behavior*

Georgiana Copil[1], Demetris Trihinas[2], Hong-Linh Truong[1], Daniel Moldovan[1], George Pallis[2], Schahram Dustdar[1], and Marios Dikaiakos[2]

[1] Distributed Systems Group, Vienna University of Technology
{e.copil,d.moldovan,truong,dustdar}@dsg.tuwien.ac.at
[2] Computer Science Department, University of Cyprus
{trihinas,gpallis,mdd}@cs.ucy.ac.cy

Abstract. Complex cloud services rely on different elasticity control processes to deal with dynamic requirement changes and workloads. However, enforcing an elasticity control process to a cloud service does not always lead to an optimal gain in terms of quality or cost, due to the complexity of service structures, deployment strategies, and underlying infrastructure dynamics. Therefore, being able, a priori, to estimate and evaluate the relation between cloud service elasticity behavior and elasticity control processes is crucial for runtime choices of appropriate elasticity control processes. In this paper we present ADVISE, a framework for estimating and evaluating cloud service elasticity behavior. ADVISE gathers service structure, deployment, service runtime, control processes, and cloud infrastructure information. Based on this information, ADVISE utilizes clustering techniques to identify cloud elasticity behavior produced by elasticity control. Our experiments show that ADVISE can estimate the expected elasticity behavior, in time, for different cloud services thus being a useful tool to elasticity controllers for improving the quality of runtime elasticity control decisions.

1 Introduction

One of the key features driving the popularity of cloud computing is elasticity, that is, the ability of cloud services to acquire and release resources on-demand, in response to runtime fluctuating workloads. From customer perspective, resource auto-scaling could minimize task execution time, without exceeding a given budget. From cloud provider perspective, elasticity provisioning contributes to maximizing their financial gain while keeping their customers satisfied and reducing administrative costs. However, automatic elasticity provisioning is not a trivial task.

A common approach, employed by many elasticity controllers [1, 2] is to monitor the cloud service and (de-)provision virtual instances when a metric threshold is violated. This approach may be sufficient for simple service models

---

* This work was supported by the European Commission in terms of the CELAR FP7 project (FP7-ICT-2011-8 #317790).

X. Franch et al. (Eds.): ICSOC 2014, LNCS 8831, pp. 275–290, 2014.

but, when considering large-scale distributed cloud services with various inter-dependencies, a much deeper understanding of its elasticity behavior is required. For this reason, existing work [2,3] has identified a number of elasticity control processes to improve the performance and quality of cloud services, while additionally attempting to minimize cost. However, a crucial question still remains unanswered: *which elasticity control processes are the most appropriate for a cloud service in a particular situation at runtime?* Both cloud customers and providers can benefit from insightful information such as *how the addition of a new instance to a cloud service will affect the throughput of the overall deployment and individually of each part of the cloud service.* Thus, cloud service elasticity behavior knowledge under various controls and workloads is of paramount importance to elasticity controllers for improving runtime decision making.

To this end, a wide range of approaches relying on service profiling or learning from historic information [3–5] have been proposed. However, these approaches limit their decisions to evaluating only low-level VM metrics (e.g., CPU and memory usage) and do not support elasticity decisions based on cloud service behavior at multiple levels (e.g., per node, tier, entire service). Additionally, current approaches only evaluate resource utilization, without considering elasticity as a multi-dimensional property composed of three dimensions (cost, quality, and resource elasticity). Finally, existing approaches do not consider the outcome of a control process on the overall service, where often enforcing a control process to the wrong part of the cloud service, can lead to side effects, such as increasing the cost or decreasing performance of the overall service. In our previous work, we focused on modeling current and previous behavior with the concepts of elasticity space and pathway [6], or using different algorithms to determine enforcement times in observed behavior (e.g., with change-point detection), but without modeling expected behavior of different service parts, in time.

In this paper, we focus on addressing the limitations above by introducing the ADVISE (*evAluating clouD serVIce elaSticity bEhavior*) framework, which estimates cloud service elasticity behavior by utilizing different types of information, such as service structure, deployment strategies, and underlying infrastructure dynamics, when applying different external stimuli (e.g., elasticity control processes). At the core of ADVISE is a clustering-based evaluation process which uses these types of information for computing expected elasticity behavior, in time, for various service parts. To evaluate ADVISE effectiveness, experiments were conducted on a public cloud platform with a testbed comprised of two different cloud services. Results show that ADVISE outputs the expected elasticity behavior, in time, for different services with a low estimation error rate. ADVISE can be integrated by cloud providers alongside their elasticity controllers to improve their decision quality, or used by cloud service providers to evaluate and understand how different elasticity control processes impact their services.

The rest of this paper is structured as follows: in section 2 we model relevant information regarding cloud services. In section 3, we present the elasticity behavior evaluation process. In section 4, we evaluate ADVISE framework effectiveness. In section 5 we discuss related work. Section 6 concludes this paper.

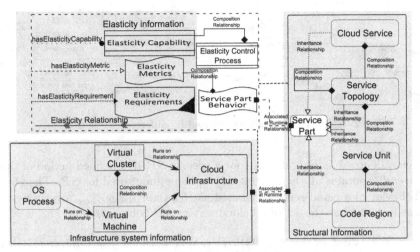

Fig. 1. Elasticity capabilities exposed by different elastic objects

2 Cloud Service Structural and Runtime Information

2.1 Cloud Service Information

To follow existing common service descriptions [7], we refer to a cloud application in our study as a *cloud service*. A cloud service can be decomposed into *service topologies* (e.g., a business tier, or a part of a workflow) which represent a group of semantically connected service units. A *service unit* (e.g., a web service) represents a module offering computation or data capabilities. In order to refer to these cloud service structures globally, we use the term *Service Parts (SP)*.

We extend the conceptual cloud service representation model proposed in [8] with a rich set of information types for determining cloud elasticity behavior. Fig. 1 depicts the extensions we made (white background) to include *elasticity control processes*, *service part behaviors* and *service parts*. Overall, this representation contains: (i) *Structural Information*, describing the architectural structure of the application to be deployed on the cloud, (ii) *Infrastructure System Information*, describing runtime information regarding resources allocated by the cloud service from the underlying cloud platform, and (iii) *Elasticity Information*, which is associated with both structural and infrastructure system information for describing elasticity *metrics*, *requirements*, and *capabilities*.

Elasticity information is composed of elasticity metrics, elasticity requirements, and elasticity capabilities, each of them being associated to different *SPs* or infrastructure resources. *Elasticity Capabilities* are grouped together as *Elasticity Control Processes (ECPs)*, as described in the next subsection, and inflict specific elasticity behaviors upon enforcement on different *SPs*, which we model as *Service Part Behaviors*. We model *SP* behaviors, since controllers must determine the effect of enforcing an *ECP* at different levels (e.g., before allocating a new database node, the effect at the database service topology and at the entire cloud service level should also be determined). Conceptually, a *Service Part*

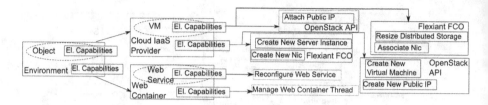

Fig. 2. Elasticity capabilities exposed by different elastic objects

Behavior, denoted as $Behavior_{SP_i}$, for a specific SP_i in a defined period of time $[start, end]$, contains all the metrics, $M_a^{SP_i}$, being monitored for SP_i. Therefore, the behavior of a cloud service, denoted as $Behavior_{CloudService}$, over a period of time is defined as the set of all cloud service SP behaviors:

$$M_a^{SP_i}[start, end] = \{M_a(t_j)|SP_i \in ServiceParts, j = \overline{start, end}\} \quad (1)$$

$$Behavior_{SP_i}[start, end] = \{M_a^{SP_i}[start, end]|M^a \in Metrics(SP_i)\} \quad (2)$$

$$Behavior_{CloudService}[start, end] = \{Behavior_{SP_i}[start, end]|SP_i \in$$
$$ServiceParts(CloudService)\} \quad (3)$$

The above information is captured and managed at runtime through an *Elasticity Dependency Graph*, which has as nodes instances of concepts from the model presented in Fig. 1 (e.g., Virtual Machine), and relationships (e.g., Elasticity Relationship) as edges. The elasticity dependency graph is populated and continuously updated with (i) *pre-deployment* information, such as service topology descriptions (e.g., TOSCA [7]) or profiling information; and (ii) *runtime* information such as metric values from monitoring tools or allocated resources information from cloud provider APIs.

2.2 Elasticity Control Processes

Elasticity capabilities (*ECs*) are the set of actions associated with a cloud service, which a cloud service stakeholder (e.g., an elasticity controller) may invoke, and which affect the behavior of a cloud service. Such capabilities can be exposed by: (i) different SPs, (ii) cloud providers, or (iii) resources which are supplied by cloud providers. An EC can be considered as the abstract representation of API calls, which differ amongst providers and cloud services. Fig. 2 depicts the different subsets of ECs provided for an exemplary web application when deployed on two different cloud platforms (e.g., Flexiant, and Openstack private cloud), as well as the ECs exposed by the cloud service and the installed software. In each of the two aforementioned cloud platforms, the cloud service needs to run on a specific environment (e.g., Apache Tomcat web server), and all these capabilities, when enforced by an elasticity controller, will have an effect on various parts of the cloud service. For instance, even if not evident at first sight, elasticity capabilities of a web server topology of the cloud service could also affect the performance of its database backend.

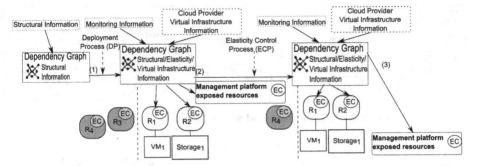

Fig. 3. Elastic cloud service evolution

Elasticity Control Processes (ECP) are sequences of elasticity capabilities $ECP_i = [EC_{i_1} \rightarrow EC_{i_2} \rightarrow ... \rightarrow EC_{i_n}]$, which can be abstracted into higher level capabilities having predictable effects on the cloud service. An *ECP* causes a change in the elasticity dependency graph and in the virtual infrastructure related information (e.g., change in *ECP* properties or in the properties of the VM). For example, in the case of a distributed database backend which is composed of multiple nodes, a scale out *ECP*, with certain parameters, can apply for both a Cassandra and an HBase database, with the following *ECs*: (i) add a new node, (ii) configure node properties and (iii) subscribe node to the cluster.

2.3 Cloud Service Elasticity during Runtime

To be able to estimate the effects of *ECPs* upon *SPs*, we rely on the elasticity dependency graph which captures all the variables that contribute to cloud service elasticity behavior evolution. Fig. 3 depicts on the left-hand side the cloud service at a pre-deployment time, where automatic elasticity controllers know about it only from structural information provided by different sources (e.g., TOSCA service description). After enforcing a Deployment Process (e.g., create machine x, and configure software z), the elasticity dependency graph will additionally contain infrastructure-related information obtained from the cloud provider, and elasticity information, obtained from monitoring services showing the metrics evolution for different *SPs*. This information is continually updated during runtime (step 3 in Fig. 3), while for estimating the behavior we make the assumption that we have complete information (i.e., no information missing).

Infrastructure resources, as mentioned previously, have associated elasticity capabilities (*EC* in Fig. 3), that describe the change(s) to be enforced and the mechanisms for triggering them (e.g., API call assigned to the *EC*). In addition, a cloud platform exposes *ECs* in order to create new resources or instantiate new services (e.g., increase memory is an *EC* exposed by a VM, while create new VM is an *EC* exposed by the cloud platform). In this context, for being able to discover the effects that an *ECP* produces in time, for each *SP*, taking into account correlations between metrics, we use the elasticity dependency graph. We analyze this information to determine the effect of an *ECP* for all *SPs*,

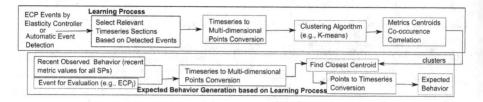

Fig. 4. Modeling cloud service behavior process

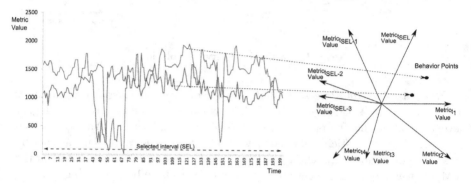

Fig. 5. Relevant timeseries sections to points

regardless on whether the ECP is application specific, or it does not have any apparent link to other SPs. In fact, as we show in Section 4, the impact of various $ECPs$ over different SPs and over the entire cloud service is quite interesting.

3   Evaluating Cloud Service Elasticity Behavior

Existing behavior learning solutions [4,5] learn discrete metric models, without correlating them with the multiple variables which affect cloud service behavior. As opposed to them, we are learning the behavior of different cloud service parts, and their relation to different $ECPs$, not only with directly linked ones, and estimating the effect of an ECP, *in time*, considering the correlations among several metrics and among several service parts. The *Learning Process* used to determine cloud service part behavior is depicted in Fig. 4, and is executed continuously, refining the previously gathered knowledge base.

3.1   Learning Process

Processing input data. Our learning process takes as input each metric's evolution, in time, $M_a^{SP_i}[start, current]$ (see Equation 3) from the beginning of the service execution on the current cloud platform. To evaluate the expected evolution of metrics in response to enforcing a specific ECP, we select for each monitored metric, of each service part, a *Relevant Timeseries Section* (RTS), in order to compare it with previously encountered $M_a^{SP_i}[start, current]$. The RTS size strongly depends on the average time needed to enforce an ECP

(see Section 4.3). Consequently, a metric RTS is a sub-sequence of the $M_a^{SP_i}$, from before enforcing an ECP until after the enforcement is over:

$$RTS_{M_a}^{SP_i} = M_a^{SP_i}[x - \frac{\delta + ECP_{time}}{2}, x + \frac{\delta + ECP_{time}}{2}], \quad (4)$$

$$[ECP_{startTime}, ECP_{endTime}] \subset [x - \frac{\delta + ECP_{time}}{2}, x + \frac{\delta + ECP_{time}}{2}]$$

, where x is the ECP index and δ is the length of the period we aim to evaluate.

As part of the input pre-processing phase, we represent $\delta + ECP_{time}$ as multi-dimensional points, BP in Equation 5, in the n-dimensional Euclidian space (see Fig. 5), where the value for dimension $t(j)$ is the timestamp j of current RTS.

$$BP_a^{SP_i}[j] = RTS_{M_a}^{SP_i}[t(j)], j = 0, ..., n, BP : M^{SP} \mapsto R^n, n = \delta + ECP_{time} \quad (5)$$

Clustering process. To detect the expected behavior, as a possible result of enforcing an ECP, we construct clusters of behavioral points $Cluster_{SP_i}$ for all SPs and each ECP based on the distance between behavior points as defined in Equation 6. We do not limit our approach to only considering $ECPs$ available for the current SP_i since, as previously mentioned, enforcing an ECP to a specific SP may affect the behavior of another SP or the overall cloud service. The objective function of this process is finding the multi-dimensional behavior point $C(\Theta^*)$, which minimizes the distance among points belonging to the same cluster $Cluster_k$ (see Equation 7). Since the focus of this paper is not to evaluate the quality of different clustering algorithms, we choose to use the K-means algorithm, following the practice where the number of clusters is $K = \sqrt{N/2}$, N being the number of objects. However, as shown in Section 4, even with a simple K-means algorithm, our approach outputs the expected elasticity behavior with a low estimation error rate.

$$dist(BP_a^x, BP_a^y) = \sqrt{\sum_i (BP_a^x[i] - BP_a^y[i])^2} \quad (6)$$

$$\Theta^* = \arg\min \sum_{k=0}^{K} \sum_{i=0}^{N} \theta_{i,k} dist(Cluster_k, BP_i), \quad \theta_{i,k} = \begin{cases} 1 & BP_i \in Cluster_k \\ 0 & BP_i \notin Cluster_k \end{cases} \quad (7)$$

After obtaining $\delta + ECP_{time}$-dimensional point clusters, we construct for each SP_i a correlation matrix, $CM_{SP_i}[C_x, C_y]$, where C_x is the centroid of $Cluster_x$, giving the probability, for all metrics, of clusters from different metrics to appear together (e.g., increase in data reliability is usually correlated with increase in cost). An item in the CM represents a ratio between the number of times the behavior points C_x and C_y were encountered together towards the total number of behavior points. This matrix is continuously updated when behavior points move from one cluster to another, or when new $ECPs$ are enforced, thus, increasing the knowledge base.

3.2 Determining the Expected Elasticity Behavior

In the *Expected Behavior Generation based on Learning Process* step in Fig. 4, we select latest metrics values for each SP_i, $M_a^{SP_i}[current - \delta, current]$, and the ECP_ξ which the controller is considering for enforcement, or for which the user would like to know the effects. We find the *ExpectedBehavior* (see Equation 8) which consists of a tuple of cluster centroids from the clusters constructed during the *Learning Process* that are the closest to the current metrics behavior for the part of the cloud service we are focusing on, and which have appeared together throughout the execution of the cloud service. The result of this step is, for each metric of SP_i, a list of expected values from the enforcement of ECP_ξ (e.g., expected values for each metrics for the case the user would like to deploy one new web service of type x in the same web application container).

$$ExpectedBehavior[SP_i, Behavior_{SP_i}[current - \delta, current], ECP_\xi] =$$
$$\{C_{i_{a^1}}^{M_{a^1}}, ..., C_{i_{a^m}}^{M_{a^m}} | M_{a^m} \in Metrics(SP_i)\} \quad (8)$$

The above process is executed continuously, as shown in Fig. 4, by refining clusters, re-computing cluster centroids with the time and with the enforcement of new $ECPs$. This process is highly flexible and configurable, as we can use different manners of detecting $ECPs$ (e.g., sent by the elasticity controller), or other clustering algorithms which lead to different solutions.

4 Experiments

To evaluate the effectiveness of the proposed approach, we have developed the ADVISE framework[1] which incorporates the previously described concepts. Current ADVISE version gathers various types of information to populate the elasticity dependency graph, such as: (i) *Structural information*, from TOSCA service descriptions; (ii) *Infrastructure and application performance information* from JCatascopia [9] and MELA [6] monitoring systems; (iii) *Elasticity information* regarding ECPs from the rSYBL [8] elasticity controller where we developed an enforcement plugin to randomly enforce ECPs on cloud services. To evaluate the functionality of the ADVISE framework, we established a testbed comprised of two services deployed on the Flexiant public cloud. On both cloud services, we enforce random $ECPs$ exposed by different SPs. We do not use a rational controller, since we are interested in estimating the elasticity behavior for all SPs as a result of enforcing both good and bad elasticity control decisions.

ADVISE currently receives monitoring information in two formats: (i) as simple *.csv files, or (ii) automatically pulling monitoring information from MELA. ADVISE can be used both in service profiling/pre-deployment phase or during runtime, for various service types, whenever monitoring information and enforced $ECPs$ are available for generating estimations for various metrics of service parts.

---

[1] Code & documents: http://tuwiendsg.github.io/ADVISE

Table 1. Elasticity control processes available for the two cloud services

Cloud Service	ECP Id	Action Sequence
Video Service	ECP_1	*Scale In Application Server Tier:* (i) stop the video streaming service, (ii) remove instance from HAProxy, (iii) restart HAProxy, (iv) stop JCatascopia Monitoring Agent, (v) delete instance
	ECP_2	*Scale Out Application Server Tier:* (i) create new network interface, (ii) instantiate new virtual machine, (ii) deploy and configure video streaming service, (iv) deploy and start JCatascopia Monitoring Agent, (v) add instance IP to HAProxy, (vi) restart HAProxy
	ECP_3	*Scale In Distributed Video Storage Backend:* (i) select instance to remove, (ii) decommission instance data to other nodes (using Cassandra nodetool API), (iii) stop JCatascopia Monitoring Agent, (iv) delete instance
	ECP_4	*Scale Out Distributed Video Storage Backend:* (i) create new network interface, (ii) instantiate new instance, (iii) deploy and configure Cassandra (e.g., assign token to node), (iv) deploy and start JCatascopia Monitoring Agent, (v) start Cassandra
M2M DaaS	ECP_5	*Scale In Event Processing Service Unit:* (i) remove service from HAProxy, (ii) restart HAProxy, (iii) remove recursively virtual machine
	ECP_6	*Scale Out Event Processing Service Unit:* (i) create new network interface, (ii) create new virtual machine, (iii) add service IP to HAProxy configuration file
	ECP_7	*Scale In Data Node Service Unit:* (i) decommision node (copy data from virtual machine to be removed), (ii) remove recursively virtual machine
	ECP_8	*Scale Out Data Node Service Unit:* (i) create new network interface, (ii) create virtual machine, (iii) set ports, (iv) assign token to node, (v) set cluster controller, (vi) start Cassandra

4.1 Experimental Services

The first cloud service is a three-tier web application providing video streaming services to online users, comprised of: (i) an *HAProxy Load Balancer* which distributes client requests (i.e., download, or upload video) across application servers; (ii) An *Application Server Tier*, where each application server is an Apache Tomcat server containing the video streaming web service; (iii) A Cassandra *NoSQL Distributed Data Storage Backend* from where the necessary video content is retrieved. We have evaluated the ADVISE framework by generating client requests under a stable rate, where the load depends on the type of the requests and the size of the requested video, as shown in the workload pattern in Fig.6.

The second service in our evaluation is a Machine-to-Machine (M2M) DaaS which processes information originating from several different types of data sensors (e.g., temperature, atmospheric pressure, or pollution). Specifically, the M2M DaaS is comprised of an *Event Processing Service Topology* and a *Data End Service Topology*. Each service topology consists of two service units, one with a processing goal, and the other acting as the balancer/controller. To stress this cloud service we generate random sensor event information (see Fig. 6) which is processed by the *Event Processing Service Topology*, and stored/retrieved from

Table 2. Elasticity metrics for different service parts

Cloud Service	SP Name	Metrics
Video Service	Application Server Tier	cost, busy thread number, memory utilization, request throughput
	Distributed Video Storage Backend	cost, CPU usage, memory usage, query latency
M2M DaaS	Cloud Service	cost per client per hour (Cost/Client/h)
	Event Processing Service Topology	cost, response time, throughput, number of clients
	Data End Service Topology	cost, latency, CPU usage

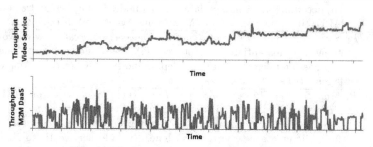

Fig. 6. Workload applied on the two services

the *Data End Service Topology*. Tables 1 and 2 list the *ECPs* associated to each *SP* and the monitoring metrics analyzed for the two cloud services respectively.

4.2   Elasticity Behavior Estimation

Online Video Streaming Service. Fig. 7 depicts both the *observed* and the *estimated behavior* for the Application Server Tier of the cloud service when a *remove application server from tier* ECP occurs (ECP_1). At first, we observe that the average request throughput per application server is decreasing. This is due to two possible cases: (i) the video storage backend is under-provisioned and cannot satisfy the current number of requests which, in turn, results in requests being queued; (ii) there is a sudden drop in client requests which indicates that the application servers are not utilized efficiently. We observe that after the scale in action occurs, the average request throughput and busy thread number rises which denotes that this behavior corresponds to the second case where resources are now efficiently utilized. ADVISE revealed an insightful correlation between two metrics to consider when deciding which *ECP* to enforce for this behavior.

Similarly, in Fig. 8 we depict both the *observed* and the *estimated behavior* for the Distributed Video Storage Backend when a scale out action occurs (add Cassandra node to ring) due to high CPU utilization. We observe that after the scale out action occurs, the actual CPU utilization decreases to a normal value as also indicated by the estimation. Finally, from Fig. 7 and 8,

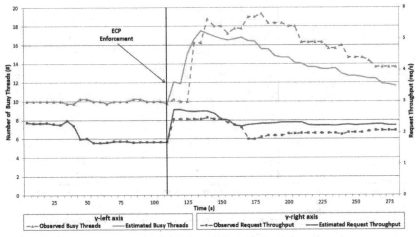

Fig. 7. Effect of ECP_1 on the application server tier

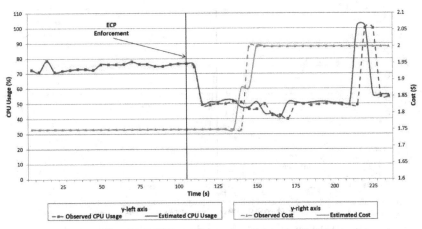

Fig. 8. Effect of ECP_4 on the entire video streaming service

we conclude that the ADVISE estimation successfully follows the actual behavior pattern and that in both cases, as time passes, the curves tend to converge.

M2M DaaS. Fig. 9 shows how an ECP targeting a service unit affects the entire cloud service. The Cost/Client/h is a complex metric (see Table 2) which depicts how profitable is the service deployment in comparison to the current number of users. Although Cost/Client/h is not accurately estimated, due to the high fluctuation in number of clients, our approach approximates how the cloud service would behave in terms of *expected time* and *expected metric fluctuations*. This information is important for elasticity controllers to improve their decisions when enforcing this ECP by knowing how the Cost/Client/h for the entire cloud service would be affected. Although the CPU usage is not estimated perfectly, since it is a highly oscillating metric, and it depends on the

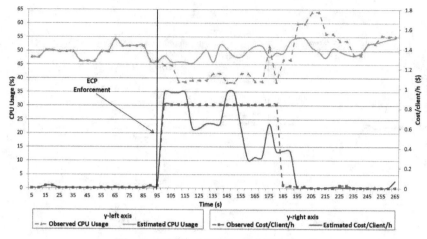

Fig. 9. Effect of ECP_7 on M2M DaaS

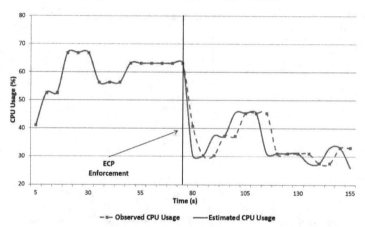

Fig. 10. Effect of ECP_8 on the data controller service unit

CPU usage at each service unit level, knowing the baseline of this metric can also help in deciding whether this ECP is appropriate (e.g., for some applications CPU usage above 90% for a period of time might be inadmissible).

ADVISE can estimate the effect of an ECP of a SP, on a different SP, even if apparently unrelated. Fig. 10 depicts an estimation on how the Data Controller Service Unit is impacted by the data transferred at the enforcement of ECP_8. In this case, the controller CPU usage drops, since the new node is added to the ring, and a lot of effort goes for transferring data to the new node, then it raises due to the fact that reconfigurations are also necessary on the controller, following a slight decrease and stabilization. Therefore, even in circumstances of random workload, ADVISE can give useful insights on how different SPs behave when enforcing $ECPs$ exposed by other SPs.

Table 3. Elasticity control processes time statistics

	ECP	Standard Deviation	Average ECP Time (s)
Video Service	ECP1	0	65
	ECP2	0	15
	ECP3	0	25
	ECP4	1.414	150
M2M Service	ECP1	4.5	45
	ECP2	1.4	20
	ECP3	0	20
	ECP4	1	75

4.3 ECP Temporal Effect

Table 3 presents the *average time* required for an ECP to be completed. This application-specific information is of high importance and affects the decision-making process of the elasticity controller since it is an indicator of the *grace period* which it should await until effects of the resizing actions are noticeable. Thus, it defines the time granularity of which resizing actions should be taken into consideration. For example, we observe that the process of adding and configuring a new instance to the video service's storage backend requires an average time interval of 150 seconds which is mainly the time required to receive and store data from other nodes of the ring. If decisions are taken in smaller intervals, the effects of the previous action will not be part of the current decision process.

4.4 Quality of Results

ADVISE is able to estimate, in time, the elasticity behavior of different SPs by considering the correlations amongst metrics and the $ECPs$ which are enforced. To evaluate the quality of our results, we have considered the fact that existing tools do not produce continuous-time estimations. Thus, we choose to evaluate ADVISE by computing the variance Var and standard deviation $StdDev$ (Equation 9), over 100 estimations as the result differs little afterwise.

$$Var_{metric_i} = \frac{\sum (estMetric_i - obsMetric_i)^2}{nbEstimations - 1}, StdDev_{metric_i} = \sqrt{Var_{metric_i}} \quad (9)$$

Table 4 presents the accuracy of our results. When comparing the two services, the Video Service achieves a higher accuracy (smaller standard deviation), since the imposed workload is considerably stable. Focusing on the M2M DaaS estimation accuracy, we observe that it depends on the granularity at which the estimation is calculated, and on the ECP. Moreover, the standard deviation depends on the metrics monitored for the different parts of the cloud service. For instance, in the case of the M2M Service, the number of clients metric can be hardly predicted, since we have sensors sending error or alarm-related information. This is evident for the Event Processing Service Topology, where the maximum variance for the number of clients is 4.9.

Table 4. ECPs effect estimation quality statistics

Cloud Service	Observed Cloud Service Part	Elasticity Control Process	Average Standard Deviation	Maximum Variance	Minimum Variance
Video Service	Video Service	ECP_3	0.23	0.09	0.03
		ECP_4	0.61	0.99	0.23'
	Distributed Video Storage Backend	ECP_3	0.28	0.14	0.034
		ECP_4	0.2	0.042	0.04
	Application Server	ECP_1	0.43	0.4	0.06
		ECP_2	0.31	0.47	0.01
M2M Service	Cloud Service	ECP_5	0.9	6.65	0.24
	Data End Service Topology	ECP_5	0.23	0.35	7.44E-05
	Event Processing Service Topology	ECP_7	1.1	4.9	0.046
		ECP_8	0.76	2.46	0.027
	Data Controller Service Unit	ECP_6	0.12	0.25	0
		ECP_8	0.22	0.41	0
	Data Node Service Unit	ECP_5	0.572	0.68	0.32
		ECP_6	0.573	1.4	0.07
	Event Processing Service Unit	ECP_7	1.08	3.59	0.11
		ECP_8	0.77	1.9	0.14

Overall, even in random cloud service load situations, the ADVISE framework analyses and provides accurate information for elasticity controllers, allowing them to improve the quality of control decisions, with regard to the evolution of monitored metrics at the different cloud service levels. Without this kind of estimation, elasticity controllers would need to use VM-level profiling information, while they have to control complex cloud services. This information, for each SP, is valuable for controlling elasticity of complex cloud services, which expose complex control mechanisms.

5   Related Work

Verma et al. [3] study the impact of reconfiguration actions on system performance. They observe infrastructure level reconfiguration actions, with actions on live migration, and observe that the VM live migration is affected by the CPU usage of the source virtual machine, both in terms of the migration duration and application performance. The authors conclude with a list of recommendations on dynamic resource allocation. Kaviani et al. [10] propose profiling as a service, to be offered to other cloud customers, trying to find tradeoffs between profiling accuracy, performance overhead, and costs incurred. Zhang et al. [4] propose algorithms for performance tracking of dynamic cloud applications, predicting metrics values like throughput or response time. Shen et al. [5] propose the CloudScale framework which uses resource prediction for automating resource allocation according to service level objectives (SLOs) with minimum cost. Based on resource allocation prediction, CloudScale uses predictive migration for solving scaling conflicts (i.e. there are not enough resources for accommodating scale-up requirements) and CPU voltage and frequency for saving energy with minimum SLOs impact. Compared with this research work, we construct our model considering multiple levels of metrics, depending on the application structure for which the behavior is learned. Moreover, the stress factors considered are also adapted to the application structure and the elasticity capabilities (i.e. action types) enabled for that application type. Juve et al. [11] propose a system which helps at automating the provisioning process for cloud-based applications. They consider two application models, one workflow application and one data storage case, and show how for these cases the applications can be deployed and configured automatically. Li et al. [12] propose CloudProphet framework, which uses resource events and dependencies among them for predicting web application performance on the cloud.

Compared with presented research work, we focus not only on estimating the effect of an elasticity control process on the service part with which it is associated, but on different other parts of the cloud service. Moreover, we estimate and evaluate the elasticity behavior of different cloud service parts, in time, because we are not only interested in the effect after a predetermined period, but also with the pattern of the effect that the respective ECP introduces.

6 Conclusions and Future Work

We have presented ADVISE framework, which is able to estimate the behavior of cloud service parts, in time, when enforcing various $ECPs$, by taking into consideration different types of information represented through the elasticity dependency graph. Based on results from two different cloud services, we show that ADVISE framework is indeed able to *advise* elasticity controllers about cloud service behavior, contributing towards improving cloud service elasticity.

As future work, we intend to integrate ADVISE with the rSYBL elasticity controller [8] and develop new decision mechanisms that take continuous ECP effects as inputs, taking decisions based on the expected behavior of each SP.

References

1. Al-Shishtawy, A., Vlassov, V.: Elastman: Autonomic elasticity manager for cloud-based key-value stores. In: Proceedings of the 22nd International Symposium on High-Performance Parallel and Distributed Computing, HPDC 2013, pp. 115–116. ACM, New York (2013)
2. Wang, W., Li, B., Liang, B.: To reserve or not to reserve: Optimal online multi-instance acquisition in IaaS clouds. Presented as part of the 10th International Conference on Autonomic Computing, Berkeley, CA, USENIX, pp. 13–22 (2013)
3. Verma, A., Kumar, G., Koller, R.: The cost of reconfiguration in a cloud. In: Proceedings of the 11th International Middleware Conference Industrial Track. Middleware Industrial Track 2010, pp. 11–16. ACM, New York (2010)
4. Zhang, L., Meng, X., Meng, S., Tan, J.: K-scope: Online performance tracking for dynamic cloud applications. Presented as part of the 10th International Conference on Autonomic Computing, Berkeley, CA, USENIX, pp. 29–32 (2013)

5. Shen, Z., Subbiah, S., Gu, X., Wilkes, J.: Cloudscale: elastic resource scaling for multi-tenant cloud systems. In: Proceedings of the 2nd ACM Symposium on Cloud Computing, SOCC 2011, pp. 5:1–5:14. ACM, New York (2011)
6. Moldovan, D., Copil, G., Truong, H.L., Dustdar, S.: Mela: Monitoring and analyzing elasticity of cloud services. In: 2013 IEEE Fifth International Conference on Cloud Computing Technology and Science, CloudCom (2013)
7. OASIS Committee Specification Draft 01: Topology and Orchestration Specification for Cloud Applications Version 1.0 (2012)
8. Copil, G., Moldovan, D., Truong, H.-L., Dustdar, S.: Multi-level Elasticity Control of Cloud Services. In: Basu, S., Pautasso, C., Zhang, L., Fu, X. (eds.) ICSOC 2013. LNCS, vol. 8274, pp. 429–436. Springer, Heidelberg (2013)
9. Trihinas, D., Pallis, G., Dikaiakos, M.D.: JCatascopia: Monitoring Elastically Adaptive Applications in the Cloud. In: 14th IEEE/ACM International Symposium on Cluster, Cloud and Grid Computing (2014)
10. Kaviani, N., Wohlstadter, E., Lea, R.: Profiling-as-a-service: Adaptive scalable resource profiling for the cloud in the cloud. In: Kappel, G., Maamar, Z., Motahari-Nezhad, H.R. (eds.) Service Oriented Computing. LNCS, vol. 7084, pp. 157–171. Springer, Heidelberg (2011)
11. Juve, G., Deelman, E.: Automating application deployment in infrastructure clouds. In: Proceedings of the 2011 IEEE Third International Conference on Cloud Computing Technology and Science, CLOUDCOM 2011, pp. 658–665. IEEE Computer Society, Washington, DC (2011)
12. Li, A., Zong, X., Kandula, S., Yang, X., Zhang, M.: Cloudprophet: towards application performance prediction in cloud. In: Proceedings of the ACM SIGCOMM 2011 Conference, SIGCOMM 2011. ACM, New York (2011)

Transforming Service Compositions into Cloud-Friendly Actor Networks *

Dragan Ivanović[1] and Manuel Carro[1,2]

[1] IMDEA Software Institute, Spain
[2] School of Computer Science, T. University of Madrid (UPM), Spain
{dragan.ivanovic,manuel.carro}@imdea.org

Abstract. While conversion of atomic and back-end services from centralized servers to cloud platforms has been largely successful, the composition layer, which gives the service-oriented architecture its flexibility and versatility, often remains a bottleneck. The latter can be re-engineered for horizontal and vertical scalability by moving away from coarser concurrency model that uses transactional databases for keeping and maintaining composition internal state, towards a finer-grained model of concurrency and distribution based on actors, state messaging, and non-blocking write-only state persistence. In this paper we present a scheme for automatically transforming the traditional (orchestration-style) service compositions into Cloud-friendly actor networks, which can benefit from high performance, location transparency, clustering, load balancing, and integration capabilities of modern actor systems, such as Akka. We show how such actor networks can be monitored and automatically made persistent while avoiding transactional state update bottlenecks, and that the same networks can be used for both executing compositions and their testing and simulation.

Keywords: Service Composition, Actor Systems, Cloud Service Provision.

1 Introduction

In recent years, the use of private and public clouds for providing services to users has proliferated as organizations of all sizes embraced the Cloud as an increasingly technically mature and economically viable way to reach markets and meet quality requirements on the global scale. This is especially true for simple (atomic and back-end) services that perform individually small units of work. Such services can be distributed on different cloud nodes, and the requests are routed to different instances based on node availability and load balancing. The key enablers here are distributed databases, which offer high availability and distribution at the price of limited, eventual consistency [7].

Service compositions typically need to store their internal state (point of execution and state variables) along with the domain-specific user data on which they operate. That is needed because service compositions may be long-running and may involve

---

* The research leading to these results has received funding from the EU FP 7 2007-2013 programme under agreement 610686 POLCA, from the Madrid Regional Government under CM project S2013/ICE-2731 (N-Greens), and from the Spanish Ministry of Economy and Competitiveness under projects TIN-2008-05624 DOVES and TIN2011-39391-C04-03 StrongSoft.

X. Franch et al. (Eds.): ICSOC 2014, LNCS 8831, pp. 291–305, 2014.
© Springer-Verlag Berlin Heidelberg 2014

many internal steps, so that it would be inefficient to let them occupy the scarce server resources (such as threads and database connections) for the whole duration of their execution, most of which is typically spent waiting for responses from other services. Besides, saving the composition state in a persistent store allows resumption after server restarts or network failures. This leads to an essentially event-driven implementation of most composition engines, where incoming events (messages or timeouts) either create new composition instances or wake up dormant ones, which perform a short burst of processing and then either terminate or go to sleep until the next wake-up event.

However, even when eventual consistency on user data is permitted, any inconsistency in the saved internal state of an executing composition may lead to wrong or unpredictable behavior, and must be avoided. That is why most service composition engines, such as Apache ODE [5], Yawl [1], and Orchestra [17], rely on a transactional database to ensure state consistency of long-running processes. This presents a problem for scaling the SOA's composition layer in the Cloud, as concurrent processing of events within the same composition instance implicitly requires access synchronization, transactional isolation, and locking or conflict detection on a central database.

In this paper, we argue that SOA's service composition layer can more successfully exploit the advantages offered by the Cloud if it is based on state messaging rather than mutable shared state kept in a database. This means basing the design of composition engines on well-defined, fine-grained, and Cloud-friendly parallelism and distribution formalisms, rather than "hacking" the existing centralized implementations.

In Section 2, we motivate our approach and outline it in Section 3. Section 4 presents the details of the approach, and Section 5 gives some implementation notes and presents an experimental validation of the approach. We close with conclusions in Section 6.

2   Motivation

According to the *Reactive Manifesto* [4], the ability to react to events, load fluctuations, failures, and user requirements is the distinguishing mark of reactive software components, defined as being readily responsive to stimuli. In this paper, we try to facilitate some of those capabilities in service compositions, starting with service orchestrations with centralized control flow.

Take, for instance, an example currency exchange composition whose pseudo-code is shown in Figure 1. (The syntax and semantics of a sample composition language is given in Section 4.1.) This composition takes a list of amounts in different currencies (*in*), and tries to find the maximal amount of Euros to which they can be converted, using two external currency conversion services, P and Q. Each amount/currency pair ($\mathsf{head}(in)$) is sent to P and Q in parallel, and the responses (x and y) add to the result (r) before continuing with the rest of the input list ($\mathsf{tail}(in)$). Finally, the result is sent to the caller.

```
r := 0;
while ¬empty(in) do begin
  join begin
    send head(in) to P;
    receive x from P
  end and begin
    send head(in) to Q;
    receive y from Q
  end;
  r := r + max(x,y);
  in := tail(in)
end;
send r to caller
```

Fig. 1. Sample composition

To allow the sample composition to scale both up and out, we need to surpass the limits posed by the shared state store architecture. One way to achieve that is to turn

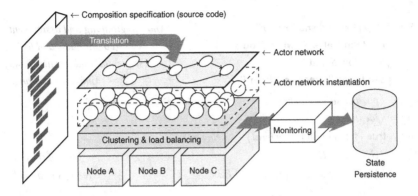

Fig. 2. Outline of the approach

the logical flow of control within the composition into a message flow, by transforming the composition into a network of interconnected stateless, reactive components, each performing a small unit of work, and forwarding results down the logical control flow. Ideally, slower components would be automatically pooled and load-balanced in order to enhance throughput, and/or spread between different nodes in a cluster, depending on available cloud resources. Instead of being kept in a shared data store, the composition state would be reconstructed from observed messages and pushed to a persistent store in a write-only, non-blocking manner.

A major challenge – and the main contribution of this paper – is to find a method for automatically and transparently transforming compositions into such networks of readily scalable reactive components. The transformation needs to hide the underlying implementation details and preserve semantics of state variables, complex control constructs (loops and parallel flows), operations on a rich data model, and message interchange with external services.

We therefore address a similar problem as the concept of Liquid Service Architecture [8], but targeting specific issues in the composition layer, based on formal models of composition semantics and semantically correct transformations.

3 Outline of the Approach

Figure 2 shows the outline of the proposed approach. The starting point is a specification of a composition, expressed in some composition language. This source code is translated into an actor network, which expresses the behavior of the composition as a (statically inferred) collection of stateless, reactive components that perform individually small units of processing. The translation ensures that the behavior of the actor network is consistent with the original semantics of the composition.

We use actor systems [12,13,2,3] as the underlying model of concurrent and distributed computing. Along with π-calculus [16], join-calculus [10], and ambient-calculus [9], actor systems are one of well known approaches to modeling and reasoning about concurrent and distributed computations. However, their component and open asynchronous messaging model makes actor systems closer to the conventional

$$
\begin{aligned}
S ::= &\ \textbf{skip} \mid \textbf{begin}\ S\ \textbf{end} \mid x := E &&(\textit{no-op, grouping and assignment})\\
&\mid \textbf{if}\ C\ \textbf{then}\ S\ \textbf{else}\ S \mid \textbf{while}\ C\ \textbf{do}\ S &&(\textit{conditionals and loops})\\
&\mid S;S \mid \textbf{join}\ S\ \textbf{and}\ S &&(\textit{sequential and parallel flows})\\
&\mid \textbf{send}\ E\ \textbf{to}\ P \mid \textbf{receive}\ x\ \textbf{from}\ P &&(\textit{message exchange})
\end{aligned}
$$

$$
\begin{aligned}
P ::= &\ \langle \textit{partner service name} \rangle\\
x ::= &\ \langle \textit{identifier} \rangle\\
C,E ::= &\ \textbf{true} \mid \textbf{false} \mid \textbf{null} \mid \langle \textit{numeral} \rangle \mid \langle \textit{string} \rangle \mid x\\
&\mid f(E,...,E) \mid E \circ E &&(f, \circ \in \text{Builtins})\\
&\mid \{\} \mid \{x:E[,x:E]^*\} \mid E\{x:E\} \mid E.x &&(\textit{records and fields})
\end{aligned}
$$

Fig. 3. Abstract syntax of a sample composition language

(e.g., object-oriented and functional) programming languages and facilitates efficient implementation (cf. Section 5).

At run-time, the actor network is used as a blueprint to instantiate sets of actors that implement the behavior specified by the network. The instantiated network is deployed into an actor system, where it can benefit from clustering, load balancing, integration and other capabilities of the state-of-the-art actor systems. Being stateless and reactive, the instantiated actors can be scaled both vertically (by organizing them in pools), and horizontally (by distributing them among different interconnected nodes).

The internal state of the executing compositions is not stored in a database, but is kept in messages sent and received by the communicating actors. By monitoring these messages, it is possible to keep an up-to-date snapshot of the state of each executing composition instance, and to record it to a persistent store.

4   Translating Compositions into Actor Networks

4.1   Sample Composition Language

Figure 3 shows the abstract syntax of a composition language fragment. Our intention here is not to "invent" a new composition language, but to present a fragment containing some of the most common control and data handling constructs (found in actual languages like BPEL) whose semantics – control flow, data operations, and messaging – can be formally specified. Such a formal specification of semantics is crucial for reasoning about the correctness of our approach.

The composition language fragment includes state updates (assignments), sequential constructs (such as conditionals and loops), messaging primitives (**send** and **receive**), and **join-and** parallel flows which wait for both branches to complete. The language is based on a rich data model that features Boolean, numeric and string literals, the special **null** value, as well as records. Expressions include literals, composition state variables, record constructors, record field accesses, and a set of arithmetic, logical and string built-ins (always terminating).

Records can be used to represent many other data structures. For instance, a list $[A|B]$ with the first element A and the remainder B can be modeled with $\{\textsf{cons}: \textbf{true}, \textsf{head}:$

$$\frac{\{C \wedge \phi \mid \pi\} S_1 \{\phi' \mid \pi'\} \quad \{\neg C \wedge \phi \mid \pi\} S_2 \{\phi' \mid \pi'\}}{\{\phi \mid \pi\} \text{ if } C \text{ then } S_1 \text{ else } S_2 \{\phi' \mid \pi'\}} \text{ COND} \qquad \frac{}{\{\phi \mid \pi\} \text{ skip } \{\phi \mid \pi\}} \text{ SKIP}$$

$$\frac{\{C \wedge \phi \mid \pi\} S \{\phi \mid \pi'\}}{\{\phi \mid \pi'\} \text{ while } C \text{ do } S \{\neg C \wedge \phi \mid \pi'\}} \text{ LOOP} \qquad \frac{\{\phi \mid \pi\} S_1 \{\phi' \mid \pi'\} \quad \{\phi' \mid \pi'\} S_2 \{\phi'' \mid \pi''\}}{\{\phi \mid \pi\} S_1 ; S_2 \{\phi'' \mid \pi''\}} \text{ SEQ}$$

$$\frac{}{\{\phi[x \backslash E] \mid \pi\} x := E \{\phi \mid \pi\}} \text{ STATE} \qquad \frac{\{\phi \mid \pi\} S_1 \{\phi' \mid \pi'\} \quad \{\phi \mid \pi\} S_2 \{\phi' \mid \pi'\}}{\{\phi \mid \pi\} \text{ join } S_1 \text{ and } S_2 \{\phi' \mid \pi'\}} \text{ JOIN}$$

$$\frac{\pi' \text{ contains no } (\_ \leftarrow P) \quad \pi'' \text{ contains no } (\_ \leftarrow\!\!+ P)}{\{\phi[x \backslash u] \mid \pi'(u \leftarrow P)\pi''\} \text{ receive } x \text{ from } P \{\phi \mid \pi'(u \leftarrow\!\!+ P)\pi''\}} \text{ RECV}$$

$$\frac{\phi \vdash E = u \quad \pi'' \text{ contains no } (\_ \rightarrow P) \text{ or } (\_ \leftarrow\!\!+ P)}{\{\phi \mid \pi'\pi''\} \text{ send } E \text{ to } P \{\phi \mid \pi'(u \rightarrow P)\pi''\}} \text{ SEND}$$

Fig. 4. Abstract semantics of a fragment of the composition language

A, tail : B}, and the empty list [] with {cons : **false**}. In turn, records and lists can represent JSON and XML documents. In examples, we use sans serif font to distinguish field, built-in and other global names from local names in cursive.

We use a form of axiomatic semantics to specify the meaning of control constructs, data operations, and message exchanges for the language fragment, with the inference rules (axiom schemes) shown in Figure 4. The pre- and post-conditions are expressed in the form $\{\phi \mid \pi\}$, where logic formula ϕ characterizes the composition state as in the classic Hoare Logic [14,6], and π is a chronological sequence of outgoing messages $(u \rightarrow P)$, incoming unread messages $(u \leftarrow P)$, and incoming read messages $(u \leftarrow\!\!+ P)$, where u is a datum. The consequence rule, which states that pre-conditions can always be strengthened as well as post-conditions weakened, is implicit. Condition $\{\phi' \mid \pi'\}$ is stronger than $\{\phi \mid \pi\}$ iff ϕ' logically implies ϕ (in the data domain theory), and π is a (possibly non-contiguous) sub-sequence of π'.

Rules COND, SKIP, LOOP, SEQ, and STATE are direct analogues of the classical Hoare Logic rules for sequential programs. The abstract semantics of parallel and-join flow is given in rule JOIN. The parallel branches are started together, and race conditions on state variables and partner services are forbidden: variables modified by one branch cannot be read of modified by the other, and the branches cannot send or receive messages to or from a same partner service.

In rule RECV, the conditions on π' and π'' ensure that messages are read in the order in which they are received, and the condition on π'' in rule SEND ensures the chronological ordering of outgoing messages. The underscores here denote arbitrary data. The message exchange is asynchronous, and thus the relative ordering of messages to/from a partner matters more than the absolute ordering of all messages.

4.2 Actor Language

The abstract syntax of a functional actor language is given in Fig. 5, along the lines of Aga et al. [3] and Varela [18], with some syntactic modifications. Its domain of values (V) is the same as in the sample composition language, with addition of actor references (A) used for addressing messages. The expressions (E) extend expressions in the composition language with functional and actor-specific constructs.

$$E ::= L \mid x \mid \lambda x \to E \mid E(E) \mid \mathbf{rec}(E) \qquad \textit{(standard } \lambda\textit{-calculus constructs)}$$
$$\mid f(E, ..., E) \mid E \circ E \qquad (f, \circ \in \text{Builtins})$$
$$\mid R_E \mid E\{x : E\} \qquad \textit{(record of expressions, update)}$$
$$\mid \mathbf{match}\ E\ \mathbf{with}\ T \to E[; T \to E]^*\ \mathbf{end} \qquad \textit{(pattern matching)}$$
$$\mid \mathbf{new}(E) \mid \mathbf{stop} \qquad \textit{(actor creation \& termination)}$$
$$\mid \mathbf{ready}(E) \mid \mathbf{send}(E, E) \qquad \textit{(message reception \& dispatch)}$$
$$L ::= \mathbf{true} \mid \mathbf{false} \mid \mathbf{null} \mid \langle \textit{numeral} \rangle \mid \langle \textit{string} \rangle \qquad \textit{(primitive value)}$$
$$V ::= L \mid A \mid R_V \qquad \textit{(value)}$$
$$R_\Phi ::= \{\} \mid \{x : \Phi[, x : \Phi]^*\} \qquad \textit{(record structure)}$$
$$T ::= x \mid \_ \mid L \mid R_T \qquad \textit{(pattern)}$$
$$x ::= \langle \textit{identifier} \rangle \qquad A ::= \langle \textit{actor reference} \rangle$$

Fig. 5. The basic actor language

Function abstractions and applications from λ-calculus are included together with the special recursion operator **rec**. The **match** construct searches for the first clause $T \to E$ where pattern T matches a given value, and then executes E to the right of "$\to$". At least one match must be found. Variables in patterns capture matched values, and each underscore stands for a fresh anonymous variable. The order of fields in record patterns is not significant, and matched records may contain other, unlisted fields. Several common derived syntactic forms are shown in Table 1.

Construct **new** creates a new actor with the given behavior, and returns its reference. An actor behavior is a function that is applied to an incoming message. Construct **ready** makes the same actor wait for a new message with the given behavior. Construct **send** sends the message given by its second argument to the agent reference to which the first argument evaluates. Finally, **stop** terminates the actor.

Fig. 6 shows two simple examples of actor behaviors. The sink behavior simply accepts a message (m) without doing anything about it, and repeats itself. The cell behavior models a mutable cell with content x. On a 'get' message, the current cell value x is sent to the designated recipient a, and the same behavior is repeated. On a 'set' message, the cell forgets the current value x and repeats the same behavior with the new value y. Note how in both cases the construct **rec** allows the behavior to refer to itself via b.

$$\text{sink} \equiv \mathbf{rec}(\lambda b \to \lambda m \to \mathbf{ready}(b))$$

$$\text{cell} \equiv \mathbf{rec}(\lambda b \to \lambda x \to \lambda m \to$$
$$\mathbf{match}\ m\ \mathbf{with}$$
$$\{\text{get}: a\} \to \mathbf{do\ send}(a, x)\ \mathbf{then\ ready}(b(x));$$
$$\{\text{set}: y\} \to \mathbf{ready}(b(y))$$
$$\mathbf{end})$$

Fig. 6. Two simple actor behaviors

Table 1. The derived actor language constructs and abbreviations

Abbreviation	Basic construct
let $x = E_1$ **in** E_2	**match** E_1 **with** $x \to E_2$ **end**
do E_1 **then** E_2	**match** E_1 **with** $\_ \to E_2$ **end**
if E_1 **then** E_2 **else** E_3	**match** E_1 **with true** $\to E_2$; $\_ \to E_3$ **end**
$E.x$	**match** E **with** $\{x : y\} \to y$; $\_ \to$ **null end**

The operational semantics of actor systems is expressed in terms of transitions between actor configurations. Each actor configuration $\langle\!\langle\, \alpha \parallel \mu \,\rangle\!\rangle$ consists of a set of actors α and a bag (multiset) μ of messages in transit. Elements of α are written as $[E]_a$, denoting an actor with the unique address (actor reference) $a \in A$ and behavior E. Elements of μ are written as $(a \Leftarrow v)$, denoting a value v sent to an actor whose reference is a. In rules, both α and μ are written as unordered sequences without repetition of elements.

We first frame the actor expressions in terms of redexes and reduction contexts, shown in Figure 7. It can be shown that any actor expression E can be uniquely framed in the form $E_\square \triangleright e \triangleleft$, where $E_\square$ is a reduction context which contains exactly one hole ($\square$) which is filled by redex e. A redex is the next sub-expression to be evaluated (and replaced with the evaluation result, if any) in the left-to-right call-by-value evaluation strategy. The exceptions are stand-alone values (V) and function abstractions ($\lambda x \to E$), which are syntactically valid, but do not denote any meaningful actor behavior.

The transitions defining the operational semantics of the actor language are given in Figure 8. The purely functional redexes follow the relation "$\longrightarrow_\lambda$" and are reduced locally within an actor under rule FUN. For instance, APP is β-reduction from λ-calculus, REC defines the behavior of the recursion operator, UPD defines record updates, and BI the application of built-ins. Rule MATCH₁ fires if there exists a substitution θ of variables from pattern T which makes $T\theta$ identical to the value v that is matched; in that case, the **match** expression reduces to the expression $E\theta$, i.e., E to the right of "$\to$" with these variable substitutions applied. Rule MATCH₂ throws away the first pattern if a matching substitution cannot be found, and continues with the rest.

The actor redexes are regulated by rules other than FUN. In STOP, any actor that encounters **stop** is immediately terminated. Rule NEW creates a new actor which becomes **ready** to execute behavior w given by **new**, and returns its address a' to the creating actor. Rule READY says that whenever an actor executes construct **ready**, it blocks if necessary until there is a message v sent to it, and then starts from the scratch by applying the behavior w given by **ready** to the message. Finally, rule SEND creates a new message for the receiver, and returns **null** on the sender side.

An important characteristic of the actor system semantics is fairness, in the sense that all enabled transitions eventually fire. In particular, this means that every message sent to an actor is eventually received, unless the actor is terminated, halted by an error, or caught in an infinite loop while processing an earlier message.

$W ::= V \mid \lambda x \to E$

$e ::= W(W) \mid x \mid f(W,\ldots,W) \mid W \circ W \mid \mathbf{rec}(W) \mid R_W \mid W\{x:W\}$
$\quad \mid \mathbf{match}\ W\ \mathbf{with}\ T \to E\, [; T \to E]^* \ \mathbf{end} \mid \mathbf{new}(W) \mid \mathbf{stop} \mid \mathbf{ready}(W) \mid \mathbf{send}(W,W)$

$E_\square ::= \square \mid W(E_\square) \mid E_\square(E) \mid f(W,\ldots,W,E_\square,E,\ldots,E) \mid W \circ E_\square \mid E_\square \circ E$
$\quad \mid \mathbf{rec}(E_\square) \mid \{x:W,\ldots,x:W,x:E_\square,x:E,\ldots,x:E\} \mid W\{x:E_\square\} \mid E_\square\{x:E\}$
$\quad \mid \mathbf{match}\ E_\square\ \mathbf{with}\ T \to E\,[; T \to E]^* \ \mathbf{end} \mid \mathbf{new}(E_\square) \mid \mathbf{ready}(E_\square) \mid \mathbf{send}(W,E_\square) \mid \mathbf{send}(E_\square,E)$

Fig. 7. Reduction contexts and redexes

$$\frac{w \in W}{(\lambda x \to E)(w) \longrightarrow_\lambda E[x \backslash w]} \text{ APP} \qquad \frac{e \equiv \mathsf{rec}(\lambda x \to E)}{e \longrightarrow_\lambda E[x \backslash e]} \text{ REC} \qquad \frac{r \equiv \{x : \_, \varphi\} \quad v \in V}{r\{x : v\} \longrightarrow_\lambda \{x : v, \varphi\}} \text{ UPD}$$

$$\frac{f^n \in \text{Builtins} \quad n \geq 0 \quad [\![f^n]\!] : V^n \to V}{f^n(v_1, \ldots, v_n) \longrightarrow_\lambda [\![f^n]\!](v_1, \ldots, v_n)} \text{ BI} \qquad \frac{v \in V \quad \exists \theta \cdot v \equiv T\theta}{(\mathsf{match}\ v\ \mathsf{with}\ T \to E[; \tau]\ \mathsf{end}) \longrightarrow_\lambda E\theta} \text{ MATCH}_1$$

$$\frac{v \in V \quad \nexists \theta \cdot v \equiv T\theta}{(\mathsf{match}\ v\ \mathsf{with}\ T \to E; \tau\ \mathsf{end}) \longrightarrow_\lambda (\mathsf{match}\ v\ \mathsf{with}\ \tau\ \mathsf{end})} \text{ MATCH}_2$$

$$\frac{e \longrightarrow_\lambda e'}{\langle\!\langle \alpha, [E_\square \triangleright e \triangleleft]_a \parallel \mu \rangle\!\rangle \longrightarrow \langle\!\langle \alpha, [E_\square \triangleright e' \triangleleft]_a \parallel \mu \rangle\!\rangle} \text{ FUN} \qquad \frac{}{\langle\!\langle \alpha, [E_\square \triangleright \mathsf{stop} \triangleleft]_a \parallel \mu \rangle\!\rangle \longrightarrow \langle\!\langle \alpha \parallel \mu \rangle\!\rangle} \text{ STOP}$$

$$\frac{w \in W \quad a' \in A \text{ fresh}}{\langle\!\langle \alpha, [E_\square \triangleright \mathsf{new}(w) \triangleleft]_a \parallel \mu \rangle\!\rangle \longrightarrow \langle\!\langle \alpha, [E_\square \triangleright a' \triangleleft]_a, [\mathsf{ready}(w)]_{a'} \parallel \mu \rangle\!\rangle} \text{ NEW}$$

$$\frac{w \in W}{\langle\!\langle \alpha, [E_\square \triangleright \mathsf{ready}(w) \triangleleft]_a \parallel \mu, (a \Leftarrow v) \rangle\!\rangle \longrightarrow \langle\!\langle \alpha, [w(v)]_a \parallel \mu \rangle\!\rangle} \text{ READY}$$

$$\frac{a' \in A \quad v \in V}{\langle\!\langle \alpha, [E_\square \triangleright \mathsf{send}(a', v) \triangleleft]_a \parallel \mu \rangle\!\rangle \longrightarrow \langle\!\langle \alpha, [E_\square \triangleright \mathsf{null} \triangleleft]_a \parallel \mu, (a' \Leftarrow v) \rangle\!\rangle} \text{ SEND}$$

Fig. 8. Operational semantics of the actor language

4.3 Translating Compositions into Actor Networks

After explaining the syntax and semantics of the sample composition language and the actor language, we now proceed with the crucial step in our approach: the transformation of a service composition into an actor network.

An actor network is a statically generated set of actor message handling expressions that correspond to different sub-constructs in a composition. At run-time, actor networks are instantiated into a set of reactive, stateless actors, which accept, process and route information to other actors in the network, so that the operational behavior of the instantiated network is correct with respect to the abstract semantics of the composition language. The stateless behavior of the actors in an instantiated network enables their replacement, pooling, distribution, and load-balancing.

For a composition S, by $\mathscr{A}[\![S]\!]$ we denote its translation into an actor network, as a set whose elements have the form $\ell_i : E_i$ or $\ell_i \mapsto \ell_j$. Here, ℓ_i and ℓ_j are (distinct) code location labels, which are either 0 (denoting composition start), 1 (denoting composition finish), or are hierarchically structured as $\ell.d$, where d is a single decimal digit (denoting a child of ℓ). Element $\ell_i : E$ means that the behavior of the construct at ℓ_i is realized with actor behavior E over input message m. Element $\ell_i \mapsto \ell_j$ means that ℓ_i is an alias for ℓ_j. Alias $\ell_i \mapsto \ell_j$ is sound iff $\mathscr{A}[\![S]\!]$ contains either $\ell_j : E_j$ or $\ell_i \mapsto \ell_k$ such that $\ell_k \mapsto \ell_j$ is sound. Unsound or circular aliases are not permitted.

$\mathscr{A}[\![S]\!]$ is derived from the structure of S, by decomposing it into simpler constructs. Figure 9 shows the translations $\mathscr{A}[\![S']\!]_\ell^{\ell'}$ for each construct S' located at ℓ, and immediately followed by a construct at ℓ'. For the whole composition, $\mathscr{A}[\![S]\!] = \mathscr{A}[\![S]\!]_0^1$. Items P, ℓ, ℓ', $\ell.1$, $\ell.2$, etc. are treated as string literals in actor expressions.

The translation of **skip** simply maps the behavior of location ℓ to that of ℓ', without introducing new actors. For other constructs, the structure of the incoming message m is relevant: $m.\mathsf{inst}$ holds the unique ID of the composition instance; $m.\mathsf{loc}$ maps location labels to actor addresses (discussed below); $m.\mathsf{env}$ is a record whose fields are the

$$\mathscr{A}[\![\, \mathbf{skip}\,]\!]_\ell^{\ell'} = \{\ell \mapsto \ell'\}$$

$$\mathscr{A}[\![\, x := E\,]\!]_\ell^{\ell'} = \{\ell : (\mathbf{send}(\mathsf{fget}(m.\mathsf{loc}, \ell'), m\{\mathsf{env}.x : \bar{E}\}\{\mathsf{from} : \ell\}))\}$$

$$\mathscr{A}[\![\, \mathbf{if}\ C\ \mathbf{then}\ S_1\ \mathbf{else}\ S_2\,]\!]_\ell^{\ell'} = \{\ell : (\mathbf{send}(\mathsf{fget}(m.\mathsf{loc}, \mathbf{if}\ \bar{C}\ \mathbf{then}\ \ell.1\ \mathbf{else}\ \ell.2), m\{\mathsf{from} : \ell\}))\}$$
$$\cup\, \mathscr{A}[\![\, S_1\,]\!]_{\ell.1}^{\ell'} \cup \mathscr{A}[\![\, S_2\,]\!]_{\ell.2}^{\ell'}$$

$$\mathscr{A}[\![\, \mathbf{while}\ C\ \mathbf{then}\ S\,]\!]_\ell^{\ell'} = \{\ell : (\mathbf{send}(\mathsf{fget}(m.\mathsf{loc}, \mathbf{if}\ \bar{C}\ \mathbf{then}\ \ell.1\ \mathbf{else}\ \ell'), m\{\mathsf{from} : \ell\}))\} \cup \mathscr{A}[\![\, S\,]\!]_{\ell.1}^{\ell}$$

$$\mathscr{A}[\![\, S_1 ; S_2\,]\!]_\ell^{\ell'} = \{\ell \mapsto \ell.1\} \cup \mathscr{A}[\![\, S_1\,]\!]_{\ell.1}^{\ell.2} \cup \mathscr{A}[\![\, S_2\,]\!]_{\ell.2}^{\ell'}$$

$$\mathscr{A}[\![\, \mathbf{send}\ E\ \mathbf{to}\ P\,]\!]_\ell^{\ell'} = \{\ell : (\mathbf{do}\ \mathsf{send}(\mathsf{fget}(m.\mathsf{link}, P), m\{\mathsf{out} : \bar{E}\})\ \mathbf{then}$$
$$\mathsf{send}(\mathsf{fget}(m.\mathsf{loc}, \ell'), m\{\mathsf{from} : \ell\}))\}$$

$$\mathscr{A}[\![\, \mathbf{receive}\ x\ \mathbf{from}\ P\,]\!]_\ell^{\ell'} = \{\ell : (\mathbf{send}(\mathsf{fget}(m.\mathsf{link}, P), m\{\mathsf{in} : \text{"}x\text{"}\}\{\mathsf{from} : \ell\}\{\mathsf{to} : \ell'\}))\}$$

$$\mathscr{A}[\![\, \mathbf{join}\ S_1\ \mathbf{and}\ S_2\,]\!]_\ell^{\ell'} = \{\ell : (\mathbf{let}\ m_2 = m\{\mathsf{from} : \ell\}\{\mathsf{loc} : \mathsf{fset}(m.\mathsf{loc}, \ell.2, \mathbf{new}(\mathscr{J}[\![\, S_1, S_2\,]\!]_\ell^{\ell'}(m)))\}$$
$$\mathbf{in}\ \mathbf{do}\ \mathsf{send}(\mathsf{fget}(m.\mathsf{loc}, \ell.1.1), m_2)\ \mathbf{then}\ \mathsf{send}(\mathsf{fget}(m.\mathsf{loc}, \ell.1.2), m_2))\}$$
$$\cup\, \mathscr{A}[\![\, S_1\,]\!]_{\ell.1.1}^{\ell.2} \cup \mathscr{A}[\![\, S_2\,]\!]_{\ell.1.2}^{\ell.2}$$

$$\mathscr{J}[\![\, S_1, S_2\,]\!]_\ell^{\ell'} \equiv \lambda m \to \lambda m_1 \to \mathbf{ready}(\lambda m_2 \to \mathbf{do}\ \mathsf{send}(\mathsf{fget}(m.\mathsf{loc}, \ell'),$$
$(S_2\ writes\ \bar{z})$ (if $m_1.\mathsf{from} \geq \ell.1.1$ then $m\{\mathsf{env} : m_1.\mathsf{env}\overline{\{z : m_2.\mathsf{env}.z\}}\}$
$(S_1\ writes\ \bar{y})$ else $m\{\mathsf{env} : m_2.\mathsf{env}\overline{\{y : m_1.\mathsf{env}.y\}}\}\{\mathsf{from} : \ell.2\})\ \mathbf{then}\ \mathbf{stop}$

Fig. 9. Translation of composition constructs as actor networks

composition state variables with their current values; and $m.\mathsf{link}$ is a map from available partner service names to references of the actors which serve as their mailbox interfaces. The initial content of m is set up upon the reception of the initiating message with which the composition is started. For simplicity, we assume that $m.\mathsf{env}.in$ holds the input message, and that the initiating party is by convention called caller.

The translation of an assignment uses the built-in fget to fetch the value of $m.\mathsf{loc}$ associated with ℓ' (as a string literal). That value is the reference of the next actor in the flow, to which a message is sent with the modified value of the assigned variable x. With $\bar{E}$ we denote the result of replacing each state variable name y encountered in E with $m.\mathsf{env}.y$. Here, as in other translations, we additionally modify the from field in m to hold the location from which the message is sent.

The translation of the conditional creates two sub-locations, $\ell.1$ and $\ell.2$ to which it translates the then- and the else-part, respectively. Then, at run-time the incoming message is routed down one branch or another, depending on the value of the condition $\bar{C}$ (which is rewritten from C in the same way as $\bar{E}$ from E in assignment). The translation of the **while** loop is analogous to that of the conditional. When a sequence is translated, two sub-locations $\ell.1$ and $\ell.2$ are created and chained in a sequence.

The translations of the messaging primitives rely on partner links in $m.\mathsf{link}$. For **send**, the outgoing message is asynchronously sent to the partner link, wrapped in $m.\mathsf{out}$, and then the incoming message is forwarded to the next location in the flow. For **receive**, the partner mailbox is asked to forward m to ℓ' when the incoming message becomes available, by placing it in $m.\mathsf{env}$ under the name of the receiving variable.

The most complex behavior is for the **join** construct, which needs to create a transient join node (at $\ell.2$) which collects and aggregates the results of both parallel branches before forwarding it to ℓ'. The branches are translated at $\ell.1.1$ and $\ell.1.2$. The branches receive message m_2 whose $m_2.\mathsf{loc}$ is modified (using the built-in fset) to point to the transient join node under $\ell.2$. Its behavior of is defined by $\mathscr{J}[\![\, S1, S2\,]\!]_\ell^{\ell'}$: m is the

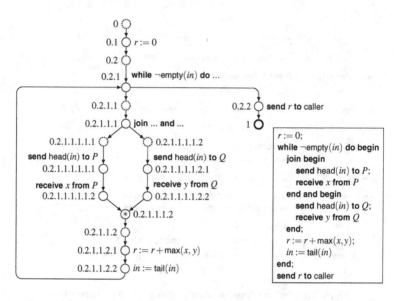

Fig. 10. Deployment of the example composition between $\ell = 0$ and $\ell' = 1$

original incoming message, and m_1 and m_2 are messages received from the branches. The outgoing message is based on m, and inherits env from the first branch to terminate, with the added modifications from the other one: the value of each state variable z written by S_2 (or state variable y written by S_1) is copied into the resulting environment.

Figure 10 shows the topology of the actor network resulting from the translation of the our example composition, annotated with location labels and the corresponding composition constructs, with the message flow indicated with arrows. The transient node is marked with an asterisk, and the dotted nodes correspond to the sequences and are aliased to the next node in the flow.

4.4 Actor Network Instantiation and Semantic Correctness

An instantiation of an actor network $\mathscr{A}[\![S]\!]$ is a pair $\langle \Lambda, \alpha \rangle$, where Λ is a (partial) mapping from locations to actor references, and α a minimal set of actors such that (a) for each $\ell : E \in \mathscr{A}[\![S]\!]$, there is $[\mathbf{ready}(\mathbf{rec}(\lambda b \to m \to \mathbf{do}\ E\ \mathbf{then\ ready}(b)))]_{\Lambda(\ell)} \in \alpha$; and (b) for each $\ell_1 \mapsto \ell_2 \in \mathscr{A}[\![S]\!]$, $\Lambda(\ell_1) = \Lambda(\ell_2)$. When a new composition instance is created, its $m.\mathsf{loc}$ is set to Λ.

The following theorem is central to validating the correctness of the approach:

Theorem 1. *The operational behavior of any instantiation* $\langle \Lambda, \alpha \rangle$ *of* $\mathscr{A}[\![S]\!]$ *is correct with respect to the abstract semantics of S.*

The correctness criteria applies to any valid triplet $\{\phi \mid \pi\}\ S\ \{\phi' \mid \pi\pi'\}$ that can be inferred from the rules in Figure 4 (with the implicit consequence rule), and any instantiation $\langle \Lambda, \alpha \rangle$ of $\mathscr{A}[\![S]\!]$. It requires that whenever S terminates and ϕ holds on the input message received at location 0: (i) exactly one output message (of the same

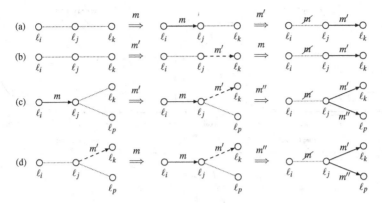

Fig. 11. Example updates of an instance snapshot

instance) is sent to location 1; (ii) ϕ' holds on the output message; and (iii) the messages sent to and received from the external service mailboxes are compatible with π'.

The proof of this theorem is based on structural induction of correctness on the building blocks of S. For each building block, the operational semantics of the actors in α (augmented with partner mailbox actors) is validated against the pre- and post-conditions defined in the abstract semantics of the composition language, applied to the content and the circulation of messages that belong to a same composition instance.

Note that the behavior $\mathbf{rec}(\lambda b \to m \to \mathbf{do}\ E\ \mathbf{then}\ \mathbf{ready}(b))$ with which new actors are created is fully stateless and repetitive, and thus a single actor can be seamlessly replaced with a load-balanced and possibly dynamically resizable pool of its replicas attached to the same location, without affecting the semantics of the instantiation.

4.5   Composition State Persistence

By observing all messages sent between actors in the instantiated actor network (with the addition of partner service mailbox actors), a monitor can keep the current snapshot of the execution state for each executing instance, distinguished by m.inst. The snapshot can be represented as a tuple $\langle \sigma, \varsigma \rangle$, where σ is the stable, and ς the unstable set of observed messages. The two sets are needed because messages can arrive out of order.

For example, part (a) of Figure 11 treats the case of location ℓ_j which needs one incoming, and produces one outgoing message. When messages come in order, the incoming message m from ℓ_i is placed in σ and is subsequently replaced with the outgoing message m'. It may, however, happen, as in Figure 11(b), that the outgoing message m' is observed first. In that case, it is placed in ς (indicated by the dashed line). When the incoming message m is observed, it is discarded, and m' is moved from ς to σ. Two analogous cases for a location corresponding to a parallel split node, which sends two outgoing messages, is shown in Figure 11(c)-(d). In these examples, we tacitly merge the aliased locations together, and include the partner service mailboxes.

After each observation, the stable set of observed messages σ can be written to a persistent data store, and used for reviving the execution of the instance in case of a system stop or crash, simply by replaying the messages from σ. This may cause

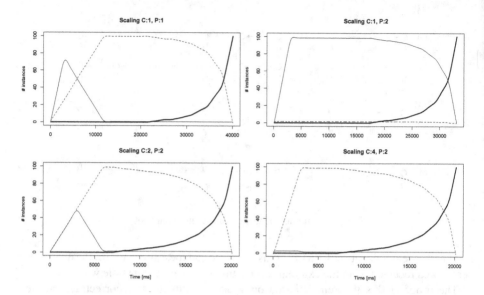

Fig. 12. Dynamic behavior of the sample composition deployed as an actor network

repetition of some steps (including the external service invocations), whose completion has not been observed when the last stable set was committed to the persistent store, but the messages in σ always represent a complete and consistent instance snapshot.

4.6   Use for Testing and Simulation

The presented actor network translation and instantiation scheme, which aims at executing compositions in a production environment, can also serve as a basis for service testing and simulation. Service composition can be tested by observing the messages between the locations in the actor network to verify pre- and post-conditions at various points in the composition code. For that purpose, the syntax of composition statements (S) in Figure 3 can be extended with assertions that express conditions on state variables and external messages. A testing monitor can then check the conditions at run-time and compute code and path coverage of the tests.

In a simulation mode, external service mailboxes can be replaced with mock-ups, and the translation scheme in Figure 9 can be slightly extended to include a new message field m.time that represents the simulated time. Such a simulation could be used to study the behavior of the system under different load scenarios, and would have the advantage of correctly modeling its state, logic, and control flow.

5   Implementation Notes and Experimental Validation

We base our implementation of the proposed approach on Akka [11], a toolkit and runtime for building concurrent, distributed, and fault tolerant event-driven applications on the JVM platform. Among other capabilities, Akka enables transparent remote actor creation, supervision and communication between different network nodes, as well as easily configurable actor pooling and load balancing. Akka also easily integrates with Apache Camel [15], a versatile integration framework which allows actor systems to interface with external services and systems using a large number of standard protocols.

To evaluate the potential benefits of the proposed approach with respect to the performance of service compositions, we have implemented the sample currency conversion composition from Figures 1 and 10 as an actor network, which was then instantiated with different scaling factors, where the composition scaling factor n means that each logical actor from the actor network is instantiated as a pool of n load-balanced actors. The external service invoked within the loop has also been implemented in a scalable manner, with a scaling factor of its own, and with a round-trip invocation time (of a solitary request in a quiescent system) between 12 ms and 18 ms. In each experimental run, the composition was fed with 100 input requests (at intervals of 10 ms) with input lists of size 10, and the messages within the actor network were monitored to reveal the number of instances awaiting or undergoing processing at different locations in the network.[1]

The top-left graph in Figure 12 shows the results for the base configuration, where the scaling factor for both the composition (C) and the external service (P) is 1, which means that each actor in C, as well as P, could process one request at a time. The thick solid rising line gives the number of finished instances over time (i.e., the number of messages reaching location $\ell' = 1$ in Figure 10). It takes approx. 40 s for the entire train of 100 input requests to be served. The dashed line shows the backlog of invocations to P, and the thin solid line shows the backlog of all internal operations in the composition, such as the control constructs and assignments. As the requests arrive, the backlog of internal operations quickly builds up, and then recedes as more and more instances block waiting on P.

Since P represents an obvious bottleneck, a common-sense approach would be to scale it up. The top-right graph in Figure 12 shows the behavior of a configuration where the scaling factor for C is kept at 1, and that of P increased to 2. However, it turns out that in spite of modest performance improvements (cutting the overall execution time by 17.5% from 40 s to approx. 33 s), C cannot significantly exploit the benefits of scaling up P without scaling up itself. In fact, the graph shows that the backlog of P now almost disappears, while the backlog of the internal operations in C now dominates the dynamics of the system. In this case, the reason for such highly non-linear aggregate behavior is the effective halving (on the average) of P's request-response time, which now becomes shorter than the interval between incoming requests.

The bottom-left graph in Figure 12 shows the case when both C and P have scaling factor 2. In this case, the composition performance of the system is practically doubled, with the overall execution time cut from 40 s to approx. 20 s. The bottom-right graph in Figure 12 suggests that scaling C more than P does not yield significant performance improvements: an appropriate scaling strategy seems to be using the same scaling factor for both C and P. Note that in our approach the scaling factor for C can be configured at will at run-time, without affecting the transformation.

---

[1] The experiment was performed on a Mac Airbook computer with 1.7 GHz Intel Core i5 and 4 GB of RAM, running Mac OS X 10.9.2, Oracle Java 1.7_55, and Akka 2.3.2.

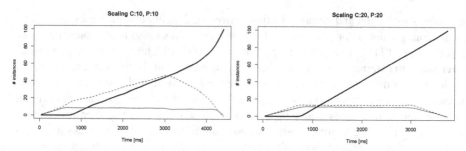

Fig. 13. Limits of performance improvements when increasing the scaling factor

Figure 13 shows how the effects on performance degrade as the common scaling factor increases. While scaling factors $n = 2$, $n = 4$ and $n = 10$ reduce the overall execution time almost proportionally by factors 1.993, 3.937, and 9.097, respectively, for $15 \le n \le 20$ the reduction factor remains close to 10.7.

6   Conclusions and Future Work

In this paper we presented an approach for ensuring scalability of service compositions (focusing on orchestrations with centralized control flow) – with rich control structure (involving branches, loops and parallel flows), state and data operations – by translating them in a network of actor behaviors which behaves correctly with respect to the semantics of the composition specification. Such a network can be instantiated and automatically scaled up/out by the underlying actor platform (in this case Akka on JVM) whose remoting and clustering capabilities facilitate deployment in the Cloud.

The experimental results indicate that using this approach the composition can be easily scaled (in this case vertically) to match the elasticity of the external services and to yield significant performance improvements. We have also shown how the state of an executing composition instance can be monitored and pushed to a persistent store in a non-blocking manner to allow for restoring and continuing a stopped instance. The same monitoring mechanism can be used for testing the composition on a fine-grained level against pre- and post-conditions on the composition as a whole and individual constructs from which it is built, and for computing code and path coverage of a test suite. Additionally, the scheme can be easily adapted for simulation of service behavior against different load scenarios.

There are several directions for expanding on the work presented in this paper. The authors are currently working on expanding the prototype implementation into a system which allows drop-in of composition definitions and their compilation into actor specifications, which is parametric with respect to the syntax of the composition language. Our plan is to support not only orchestration languages based on the procedural, but also on logical and functional programming paradigms. This can be followed with an elaboration of a testing framework that integrates automatic generation of test cases and performance analysis. Another direction would be creating, on the common basis, of an offline simulation platform that can be complemented with online data to provide forecasts of system performance under different load scenarios. Additionally, the underlying actor formalism into which compositions are translated can be used for reasoning about safety and liveness properties of choreographies involving several orchestrations.

References

1. van der Aalst, W.M.P., ter Hofstede, A.H.M.: YAWL: Yet Another Workflow Language. Information Systems 30(4), 245–275 (2005)
2. Agha, G.: Actors: A Model of Concurrent Computation in Distributed Systems. MIT Press, Cambridge (1986)
3. Agha, G., Mason, I.A., Smith, S.F., Talcott, C.L.: A foundation for actor computation. Journal of Functional Programming 7(1), 1–72 (1997)
4. et al., M.D.D.: The reactive manifesto. Web (September 2013), http://www.reactivemanifesto.org/
5. Apache Software Foundation: Apache ODE Documentation (2013), https://ode.apache.org/
6. Apt, K.R., De Boer, F.S., Olderog, E.R.: Verification of sequential and concurrent programs. Springer (2010)
7. Bailis, P., Ghodsi, A.: Eventual consistency today: Limitations, extensions, and beyond. Commun. ACM 56(5), 55–63 (2013), http://doi.acm.org/10.1145/2447976.2447992
8. Bonetta, D., Pautasso, C.: An architectural style for liquid web services. In: 2011 9th Working IEEE/IFIP Conference on Software Architecture (WICSA), pp. 232–241 (June 2011)
9. Cardelli, L., Gordon, A.D.: Mobile ambients. Theoretical Computer Science 240(1), 177–213 (2000)
10. Fournet, C., Gonthier, G.: The join calculus: A language for distributed mobile programming. In: Barthe, G., Dybjer, P., Pinto, L., Saraiva, J. (eds.) APPSEM 2000. LNCS, vol. 2395, pp. 268–332. Springer, Heidelberg (2002)
11. Gupta, M.: Akka Essentials. Packt Publishing Ltd. (2012)
12. Hewitt, C.: A universal, modular actor formalism for artificial intelligence. In: IJCAI 1973. IJCAI (1973)
13. Hewitt, C.: Viewing control structures as patterns of passing messages. Artificial Intelligence 8(3), 323–364 (1977)
14. Hoare, C.A.R.: An axiomatic basis for computer programming. Communications of the ACM 12(10) (1969)
15. Ibsen, C., Anstey, J.: Camel in Action, 1st edn. Manning Publications Co., Greenwich (2010)
16. Milner, R.: Communicating and mobile systems: The pi calculus. Cambridge University Press (1999)
17. Team, O.: Orchestra User Guide. Bull-SAS OW2 Consortium (October 2011), http://orchestra.ow2.org/
18. Varela, C.A.: Programming Distributed Computing Systems: A Foundational Approach. MIT Press (2013)

A Runtime Model Approach for Data Geo-location Checks of Cloud Services

Eric Schmieders, Andreas Metzger, and Klaus Pohl

paluno (The Ruhr Institute for Software Technology)
University of Duisburg-Essen, Essen, Germany
{eric.schmieders,andreas.metzger,klaus.pohl}@paluno.uni-due.de

Abstract. Organizations have to comply with geo-location policies that prescribe geographical locations at which personal data may be stored or processed. When using cloud services, checking data geo-location policies during design-time is no longer possible - data geo-location policies need to be checked during run-time. Cloud elasticity mechanisms dynamically replicate and migrate virtual machines and services among data centers, thereby affecting the geo-location of data. Due to the dynamic nature of such replications and migrations, the actual, concrete changes to the deployment of cloud services and thus to the data geo-locations are not known. We propose a policy checking approach utilizing runtime models that reflect the deployment and interaction structure of cloud services and components. By expressing privacy policy checks as an st-connectivity problem, potential data transfers that violate the geo-location policies can be rapidly determined. We experimentally evaluate our approach with respect to applicability and performance using an SOA-version of the CoCoME case study.

Keywords: Privacy, Cloud Service Management, Service Governance, Runtime Checking.

1 Introduction

Privacy regulations such as the EU Data Protection Directive[1] constrain the geographical location of personal data. Therefore, organizations have to comply with data geo-location policies when storing or processing personal data. For instance, the EU Data Protection Directive permits organizations to transfer personal data within the EU only or to such non-EU countries that guarantee sufficient data protection mechanisms.

In case personal data is stored or processed using cloud services, compliance with geo-location policies cannot be checked during design-time, it has to be continuously monitored and checked at runtime. Cloud infrastructures apply replication as well as migration to databases and data processing services in order to scale resources on demand and to accomplish performance, availability, and

---

[1] http://eur-lex.europa.eu/

X. Franch et al. (Eds.): ICSOC 2014, LNCS 8831, pp. 306–320, 2014.

cost goals [5, 23]. These elasticity mechanisms replicate and migrate virtual machines and services among data centers, which may lead to dynamic re-locations of personal data. During design-time, changes to service deployments and consequently to geo-locations of data are unknown and have to be checked during runtime. For instance, two interacting services process personal data and are initially deployed on cloud data centers within the EU. For performance reasons, one service is migrated to a cloud data center located outside the EU. When both services interact after the migration, they exchange personal data across the EU-borders and thus violate data geo-location policies.

Privacy checking approaches such as host geo-location [8, 13] consider the cloud as a black box. These approaches are agnostic to migrations and replications that may occur behind service interfaces. Approaches on access control mechanisms [7, 17] neither consider changes of data geo-locations imposed by migration or replication nor transitive data transfers. In summary, existing approaches are limited in detecting privacy violations that arise from the combination of cloud elasticity and service interactions.

In this paper, we systematically analyze cloud service elasticity in combination with service interactions towards potential policy violations. We propose a novel policy checking approach based on runtime models that covers the identified cases of policy violations. The proposed runtime models reflect the deployment and interaction of cloud services and components. The models are updated when migrations or replications are applied to the reflected cloud applications. By expressing the privacy policy checks as an st-connectivity problem on the runtime models, potential data transfers that violate the geo-location policies can be rapidly determined. The empirical evaluation indicates that the approach is both effective and performant.

The remainder of the paper is structured as follows. Sec. 2 systematically analyzes the changes in the cloud infrastructure that need to be considered to identify data geo-location violations. Sec. 3 discusses the related work. Sec. 4 introduces our policy checking approach. In Sec. 5 we evaluate our approach concerning its effectiveness and performance using the CoCoMe case study. Sec. 6 concludes the paper and provides an outlook to future work.

2   Cloud Changes impacting on Data Geo-location Policies

In this section, we systematically analyze the changes in cloud infrastructures that need to be covered in order to detect data geo-location violations. In order to illustrate the different changes, we use the CoCoMe case study.

2.1   CoCoME Case Study

The CoCoME case study [18] describes a typical trading application run by a supermarket chain. CoCoME has been used in various empirical evaluations of, e.g., performance predictions and model transformations approaches[2]. We

---

[2] http://sourceforge.net/apps/trac/cocome/

employ a variant of CoCoME that has been adapted to the cloud (within a working group of the DFG Priority Programme "Design For Future"[3] described in, e.g., [14]). This variant collects shopping transactions of customers in order to offer payback discounts, thereby involving the storage and processing of personal data. In the following, we describe the CoCoMe case study in terms of service and component interactions, the characterization of data, and the definition of data geo-location policies.

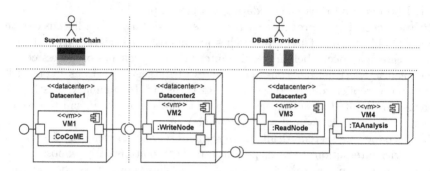

Fig. 1. Initial deployment of the CoCoME application

:CoCoME is the core component of the trading application. It is deployed on virtual machine *VM1*. *:CoCoME* provides its features as a service (via an interface) to a web shop as well as to the local stores of the supermarket chain. The trading application uses a data-base as a service (*DBaaS*) provided by a cloud provider located in Italy. The database is vertically fragmented and distributed among a write node and a read node (further read nodes may be added on demand). The *:WriteNode* stores personal sales data and the *:ReadNode* stores anonymized sales data. *VM4* executes the transaction analysis component *:TAAnalysis*. *:TAAnalysis* accesses the WriteNode and collects all log files of the connected data bases for logging and analysis reasons. Due to the EU-DPD, the supermarket chain decides that neither personal identifiable data nor anonymized data (as it may be de-anonymized) shall leave the EU and specifies a corresponding set of policies.

The initial deployment of the virtual machines is shown in Fig. 1. In the following subsection, we use the case study to illustrate situations in which the deployment is changed by replication and migration. The changes lead to violations of data geo-location policies.

2.2   Data Re-location in the Cloud

A virtual machine stores data, receives data from other virtual machines, or transfers data to them. Further, a virtual machine can be migrated or replicated.

---

[3] http://www.dfg-spp1593.de

Based on these characteristics, cloud elasticity influences data geo-locations (i) when a virtual machine stores personal data and this virtual machine is migrated or replicated to a new geo-location (case 1) and (ii) when data is transferred to a virtual machine by service interactions after migrating or replicating the virtual machine to a new geo-location. Data may be transferred to the new location by directly interacting components and services (case 2) or by indirectly interacting components and services (case 3).

In the following, we examine these three cases that have to be covered to detect potential violations. This allows us to systematically identify the information required to perform geo-location checks at runtime (labelled $R1$ to $R8$):

- Case 1: A virtual machine that stores personal data is migrated or replicated across data centers.
  In this case, personal data is transferred inside a virtual machine to a remote location, which may violate data geo-location policies. In our case study, $VM3$ is migrated to $Datacenter4$ located in the US. The migration of the data base that contains personal data violates the imposed data geo-location policy for personal sales data. Information required for detecting this case: information on components storing data ($R2$) of certain types ($R3$), information on component deployments to physical resources ($R4$), and information on the geo-location information of physical resources ($R5$).
- Case 2: A component A stores personal data and interacts with a component B. The virtual machine executing B is migrated to a remote data center.
  Personal data might be transferred to the remote location, after B has been migrated or replicated. Both cases 2 and 3 allow the derivation of data transfers, which potentially violate geo-location policies. In our case study, $VM4$ is migrated to a data center located in the US. Personal sales data stored at $VM2$ will be transferred to the $:TAAnalysis$ component located in the US after the migration. The transfer of personal data to the US violates the data geo-location policy. Information required for detecting this case: information $R2$-5 is required as in case 1. Furthermore, information about the interaction of the two components is required ($R1$).
- Case 3: A component A stores personal data and interacts transitively with a component C. The virtual machine executing C is replicated or migrated to a remote data center.
  Components may transitively interact among several intermediate components offered by different providers. Once personal data is transferred to a third-party service this service may distribute the data to providers not being aware of the policies applicable to the data. In our case study, $VM4$ is transferred to a remote data center located in Ireland (other than case 2). $VM4$ executes the $:TAAnalysis$ component, which logs personal data accessed from $VM2$. The data center is connected to a back up service from a third party (such as Glacier[4]). The service distributes backup data (including

---

[4] https://aws.amazon.com/glacier/

the personal data) among data centers outside the EU, which violates geo-location policies. Information required for detecting this case: information *R1-5* is required as in case 2. Furthermore, explicit or implicit information about transitive data transfers among components is required (*R6*).

Checks covering the three cases have to access the relevant information summarized in Tab. 1.

Table 1. Required information

#	Required information to carry out runtime checks
R1	Interactions of two components
R2	Access of components to locally stored files
R3	Meta-information of stored or processed data
R4	Information on component deployments on physical resources
R5	Geo-location information of physical resources
R6	Explicit or implicit information on transitive data transfers

3   Related Work

In the related work, we analyze whether existing privacy checking approaches cover the three data re-location cases. Furthermore, we examine if current runtime models provide the required information summarized in Tab. 1.

3.1   Privacy Checks during Runtime

Three major directions of checking geo-location policies during runtime have been investigated in the literature: geo-locating data centers, employing access control mechanisms, and enforcing elasticity rules. Approaches for checking data geo-locations based on service interface locations have been proposed in [8,13,19]. Round-trip times of pings sent to the service interfaces are correlated to geographical information in order to determine the geo-location of data centers. This allows to determine, whether service interfaces reside at specific geo-locations. However, the software components behind the service interfaces might be migrated or replicated, while the service interface remains at the same geo-location. For instance, Hadoop data nodes might be replicated to different locations while the request handling node is not migrated. Thus, the concept of using round-trip times of service endpoints to determine data geo-location is not able to cover the cases 1-3 (Sec. 2.2).

Approaches on access control mechanisms [7,17] equip cloud services with mechanisms that permit or grant data access after matching the client characteristics with the data policies. However, access control mechanisms do not consider changes of data geo-locations imposed by migration or replication of the service storing the data (case 1). Moreover, data transfers between the client services and further services are not covered. Transitive data transfers (case 3) that may lead to policy violations thus remain undetected.

Rules for controlling cloud elasticity have been proposed in [21] as well as in the MODAClouds[5] and Optimis[6] projects. Those elasticity rules are defined during design time. They are utilized to achieve quality goals, such as response time, energy consumption, cost, and reliability during runtime. However, rules that implement data geo-location policies have to be defined considering the data stored by a virtual machine (case 1) as well as the data, which may be transferred to it (case 2 and 3). Yet, this information is not available during design time (see Sec. 2.2), and thus defining geo-location rules during design-time is not feasible.

To summarize, none of the existing approaches cover the cases 1-3. The approaches in [7,17] cover case 2, but fall short in detecting policy violations resulting from transitive data accesses and cloud elasticity.

3.2 Runtime Models

Work on runtime models utilizes sequence-models [15], workflow models [12,20], Markov-chains [6], and state machines [1]. These behavioral models include activities, interactions, and states of reflected applications. Concerning the required information described in Sec. 2 the utilized runtime models lack information on data access ($R2$), meta-information of data ($R3$), deployment of components to physical resources ($R4$), and the geo-location of physical resources ($R5$).

Architectural runtime models, such as proposed in [2,10,11,16], combine behavioral aspects of the system with structural information. The utilized runtime models reflect components, workflows executed within the components, and the deployment of components to physical resources. Concerning the required information, the proposed models lack information on data access ($R2$), meta-information of data ($R3$), and the geo-location of physical resources ($R5$).

To summarize, current runtime models do not provide the required information $R1$-6 to run checks covering cases 1-3.

4   Runtime Model-Based Policy Checks

In order to address the limitations of current privacy checking approaches, our approach utilizes runtime models that reflect the deployment and communication structure of cloud services and components. A data geo-location policy p codifies which types of data are forbidden to be stored or processed at specified geographical locations. During runtime, the runtime model G is updated in case of cloud migration or replication automatically. In turn, such model update triggers a check of the model against the data geo-location policies, i.e. $G \models p$.

Below we describe the concepts (meta-model) of the runtime models (Sec. 4.1), the formalization of geo-location policies (Sec. 4.2), and the implementation of

---

[5] http://www.modaclouds.eu
[6] http://www.optimis-project.eu

the policy checks as an st-connectivity problem, and discuss how this covers cases 1-3 (Sec. 4.3).

4.1   Runtime Model

The concepts for the runtime models underlying our approach are shown in Fig. 2. The concepts *Datacenter*, *VM*, *Component*, and the relations between them provide the information on components and their deployments required to run the policy check (see *R4* in Sec. 2). One *GeoLocation* references several *Datacenter* (*R5*). Modeling this relation is important to facilitate the runtime check (to be discussed in Sec. 4.3). The *Component* concept subsumes both traditional components and services. Components execute processes (*Process*) that may interact across components (*R1*) and data centers. The meta-model allows defining components that access data through further components and can represent direct or transitive data transfers (*R6*). From this relation potential data transfers are derived.

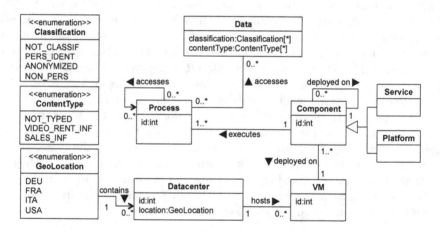

Fig. 2. Relevant concepts of the runtime model

Processes access data that is stored in the component executing the process (*R2*). Anonymized data can potentially be de-anonymized [24]. Furthermore, accidental or intentional disclosure of different content types is attached to diverse severities and penalties as stipulated, e.g., in the Video Privacy Protection Act[7] and the Health Insurance Portability and Accountability Act[8]. Consequently, data may be treated differently with respect to its classification and content. To support a flexible definition, we enrich the modeled *Data* entity with a *Classification* and a *ContentType* (*R3*).

---

[7] http://www.law.cornell.edu/
[8] http://www.cms.gov/

The runtime model may be created manually during the software design phase or may be generated from software artifacts (source code, deployment descriptors etc.) as part of a model-driven engineering process. During runtime, whenever replication or migration changes the deployment or composition of the reflected application, the model has to be updated. Due to space limitations we focus on the presentation and evaluation of the policy checking approach in this paper and examine the monitoring-driven update of the runtime model structure in our future work. However, a comprehensive survey on updating runtime models based on monitoring data can be found in [22].

4.2 Data Geo-location Policy

In approaches such as [8] data geo-location policies are defined in natural language. However, we need a formal specification of data geo-location policies in order to run automized checks. To this end, we define a data geo-location policy $p \in P$ as triple $p = (S, T, L)$, with data classifications S, data content types T, and geo-locations L (in correspondence to classifications, content types, and geo-locations specified in the runtime model). A policy p specifies that every combination $S \times T \times L$ is forbidden. Using sets S, T, and L rather than single elements is a design decision helping to reduce the amount of policies to be specified.

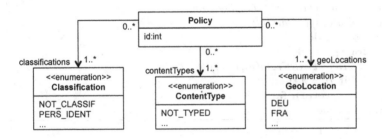

Fig. 3. Relevant concepts for data geo-location policies

In order to implement the geo-location policy concept, existing technologies and languages may be used. The elasticity rules presented in [21] specify the exchange of resources but do not reflect data classifications and content types. Approaches for specifying data access, e.g., work based on XACML[9] and [7], do not provide entities for specifying data types and geo-location constraints. However, more generic languages such as WS-Policy[10] or WS-Agreement[11] do not provide dedicated expressions to specify data geo-location constraints but may be extended to formalize the policy concepts described above, such as in [9].

---

[9] http://docs.oasis-open.org/xacml/
[10] http://www.w3.org/TR/ws-policy/
[11] http://www.ogf.org/documents/GFD.107.pdf

4.3 Policy Check

The approach specifies the geo-location policy check as an st-connectivity problem on the runtime model. Solving the st-connectivity problem answers the question whether a target node is reachable from a source node in a graph.

To check the reachability, the algorithm selects a subset of geo-location nodes from the runtime model specified in the policy to be checked. The same is performed for the data nodes. After defining both subsets the algorithm checks if there is any path from the subset of geo-locations to the subset of data nodes in the runtime model. If a path exists, it indicates that a potential data transfer violates the checked policy (as defined by the *access* semantics of the model).

As an example, Fig. 4 shows a simplified version of the runtime model reflecting case 2 (*VM4* has been migrated to the US, see Sec. 2.1). There exists a path with *geoLocation(usa)* as start node v_s and *Data*(1, [*PERS_IDENT*], [*HEALTH_INF*]) as target node v_t, i.e. personal data may flow into the US. The existence of this path indicates the violation of the policy described in the case study ("storing or processing personal data in the USA is forbidden").

The algorithm of the policy check is shown in Alg. 1.

Algorithm 1. Policy Checking Algorithm

1: **function** CHECK(G, p)
2:     $V_s \leftarrow GeoLocation(p) \cap GeoLocation(G)$
3:     $V_t \leftarrow Data(p) \cap Data(G)$
4:     **for** $v_s \in V_s$ **do**
5:         **for** $v_t \in V_t$ **do**
6:             $H \leftarrow PathFrom(v_s, v_t, G)$
7:             **if** $H \neq \emptyset$ **then**
8:                 **return false**
9:     **return true**

We choose st-connectivity over generic model checking approaches because st-connectivity is sufficient to solve the checking problem. Due to their generality, model checkers have a wide scope of application but also may impose high performance needs. Thus, runtime checking approaches (such as [3,12,20]) typically propose tailored concepts for solving specific problems. Furthermore, the st-connectivity problem is NL-complete and thus solvable within polynomial time (analyzed in Sec. 5). In the following, we describe the foundation of the geo-location check.

Definition 1. *Let G be a directed graph $G = (V, E)$ (as depicted in the example in Fig. 4). Vertices V are the entities of the runtime model. Edges E are the relations of the runtime model. Let policy p be defined as triple $p = (S, T, L)$ with data classifications S, content types T, and geo-locations L.*

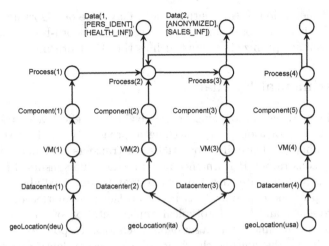

Fig. 4. Runtime model instance of case 2

Definition 2. *Let V_s be the intersection from geo-locations in G and p with $V_s = \{v | v \in V \wedge GeoLocation(v) \in L\}$ serving as start nodes. Let V_t be the subset of data nodes from G specified in p with $V_t = \{v | v \in V \wedge Classification(v) \in S \wedge ContentType(v) \in T\}$. Let $H_{v_s,v_t} = (v_s, ..., v_t)$ be a path in G with $v_s \in V_s$ and $v_t \in V_t$.*

With Def. 1 we define the runtime model as graph G and with Def. 2 we define a path H in G. When searching path H in graph G, modeling the relation between *GeoLocation* and *Datacenter* is important. Based on this, the runtime model can be transversed from *GeoLocation* entities V_s to data nodes V_t, which allows defining the policy check as st-connectivity problem with Def. 3.

Definition 3. *Given a graph G and a policy p, we define the model check $G \models p$ as function $f(G,p) : G \times \{p\} \to \{true, false\}$*

$$f(G,p) = \begin{cases} true & : \quad \neg(\exists v_s \exists v_t : H_{v_s,v_t}, with\ v_s \in V_t \wedge v_t \in V_t) \\ false & : \quad else \end{cases}$$

where "true" means the checked equation holds and "false" means the policy is violated.

The checking approach covers the data re-location cases 1-3 introduced in Sec. 2:

- **Case 1** is covered when both v_t and the host where the data reside are at geo-location v_s.
- **Case 2** is covered when a component executed at geo-location v_s directly accesses v_t from a remote component.
- **Case 3** is covered when a component at geo-location v_s accesses v_t from a remote component transitively through further components.

The implementation of the runtime check may base on algorithms for graph traversal. For instance, basic breadth-first search or depth-first search may be applied as well as optimized variants such as the A^* algorithm.

5 Experimental Evaluation

The experimental evaluation aims for analyzing the effectiveness and performance of the geo-location policy checking approach. Here, effectiveness refers to the capability of identifying potential data transfers that may violate data geo-location constraints. Performance refers to the time consumed for checking the violations and indicates how timely one may be informed about violations.

The set up of the experiments is based on the combination of a simulated cloud environment and the prototypical implementation of our approach. The set up includes a runtime model, a set of data geo-location policies, a prototypical implementation of the runtime checking approach using depth first search, and a simulator that simulates replication and migration of virtual machines. We implemented the runtime and policy meta models as Ecore instances[12]. The runtime model reflects the SOA-version of CoCoME (see Sec. 2.1) and includes 22 data centers distributed among five countries, four virtual machines, seven components, and six processes accessing two different types of personal data. The simulation environment allows us to run controlled, reproducible functional tests and to examine policy checking performance without provider limitations or side effects.

5.1 Experiment on Effectiveness

To determine the effectiveness of our approach, we investigate "*whether the proposed approach correctly identifies potential data transfers that may violate data geo-location constraints?*" To evaluate the expressiveness, we modeled the functionalities of two CoCoME use cases (use case 1 and 7 from the CoCoME-specification[13]). In use case 1, a web shop customer adds products to the shopping cart. In use case 7, the sales manager changes the price of a product. Use case 1 serves as a positive example that includes potential policy violations. Use case 7 serves as a counterexample as it does not include any policy violation. We create six equivalence partitions to test the effectiveness of the checking approach systematically. The six partitions result from defining positive and negative tests for each of the three data re-location cases (see Sec. 2.2). For each partition, we define up to three test cases in which we provide the policy checker with input that corresponds to the specified equivalence partition. For instance, a valid positive test case of data re-location case 3 includes (i) a runtime model that reflects the transitive transfer of anonymized sales data into the USA, (ii) a policy that forbids to store or process anonymized sales data in the USA, and (iii) the detected policy violation as the expected test result.

---

[12] http://www.eclipse.org/modeling/emf/
[13] http://sourceforge.net/projects/cocome/

Our approach passes the functional tests and thus correctly identifies all three cases of policy violations. Of course, the generalizability (external validity) of these findings is limited by the fact that we examined the expressiveness by means of a single case study. Although CoCoME is used in a multitude of empirical studies, we thus plan to apply our approach to further applications in our future work.

5.2   Experiment on Performance

In order to explore the performance, we examine *"how the runtime model complexity impacts on the response time of the proposed approach?"* To this end, we stepwise increase the complexity of the runtime model (independent variable) and measure the response times of the policy checks (dependent variable).

The complexity of a graph with respect to the time consumption of depth first searches is determined by the numbers of edges within a graph (the runtime model), which we use as a complexity metric. To stepwise increase the complexity of the initial model, we iteratively replicate virtual machines and insert new interactions (reflected in the model). To give an example: the model complexity of 1000 results from the edges of 68 virtual machines and 119 modeled processes. We stop the experiment at the complexity of 135183, which results from the edges of 814 virtual machines and 1414 processes. We execute the Java-based prototype (SDK 1.6) on a 2,3 GHz Quad-Core i7 machine running OS X 10.

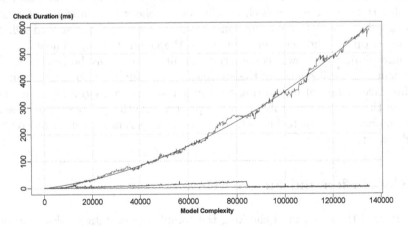

Fig. 5. Measured response times of policy checks

We measure three different situations of runtime policy checking: "best case", "worst case", and "typical case". Fig. 5 shows the measured time consumption (y-axis) over the model complexity (x-axis). We observed the following:

- In the "best case" (green flat graph), personal data is stored at a geo-location and this storage relation is forbidden by one of the policies. The search depth is low and the checks stop at $t_b \leq 1$ *ms*.

- In the "worst case" (red graph) the search algorithm has to traverse every possible path entirely to detect the policy violation. The measured growth in checking durations of worst cases is of polynomial time as the upper bound can be described by a quadratic expression (black curve in the figure), i.e. $t_w = 1.112 \times 10^{-3} * x + 2.460 \times 10^{-8} \times x^2$ with x as model complexity (expression estimated by non-linear regression). This indicates that the growth indeed maps to the analytical complexity of the st-connectivity problem.
- The "typical case" experiment is repeated several times with different seed values. We observe that the checking durations increase according to t_w (all paths are explored) until a violation occurs. After this, the checking durations increase linear or remain constant. Durations of the "typical case" are within $[t_b, t_w]$. Fig. 5 shows one example run (blue bouncing graph). First, the run duration increases according to t_w until the complexity of 12275 at which the checked model exhibits a policy violation. After the violation occurs, the number of visited nodes required for detecting the violation grows linear due to replication adding each step up to one node to the search path. At a complexity of 83847, a service interaction is randomly inserted. The interaction connects a service located at the excluded geo-location to a service that processes personal data. This almost reduces the time checking duration to t_b. Further runs of the "typical case" show similar behaviors.

An amount of more than 800 virtual machines is realistic for large applications as, for instance, Hadoop-clusters typically utilize several hundreds of data nodes (see [4]). However, our approach is still able to check the worst case for large cloud applications (> 500 virtual machines) in less than one second (cf. t_b). Of course, due to the decision to simulate the cloud, the experimental design may have limitations towards construct validity. There may be further factors influencing the performance of the approach in a productive cloud environment. For instance, delays of monitoring data may result from geographical distances between the monitoring probes and the place where the policy checker resides. These limitations have to be tackled in future experiments conducted on real cloud infrastructures.

6   Conclusion and Future Work

We analyzed the problem of checking the compliance of data geo-location policies for cloud services. We identified and described three cases that may violate data geo-location policies. These cases result from changes in service interactions in combination with cloud elasticity. In contrast to existing policy checks, the proposed approach considers direct and indirect data transfers resulting from service interactions. Initial experimental evidence indicates that the proposed approach is able to correctly identify violations and that it may do so - even for large cloud settings - with very fast response times. As a part of future work, we plan to apply our approach to other application types as well. Further, we aim for investigating the approach's effectiveness in realistic cloud environments.

To this end, we will investigate its violation detection capabilities with respect to precision, recall, and further evaluation metrics. In addition, we will complement our approach by leveraging cloud monitoring data to update the proposed runtime models.

Acknowledgements. This work was partially supported by the DFG (German Research Foundation) under the Priority Programme "SPP1593: Design For Future – Managed Software Evolution" (grant PO 607/3-1).

References

1. van der Aalst, W., Schonenberg, M., Song, M.: Time prediction based on process mining. Information Systems 36(2) (Apr 2011)
2. Brosig, F., Huber, N., Kounev, S.: Automated extraction of architecture-level performance models of distributed component-based systems. In: 2011 26th IEEE/ACM International Conference on Automated Software Engineering, ASE (2011)
3. Canfora, G., Di Penta, M., Esposito, R., Villani, M.L.: A framework for QoS-aware binding and re-binding of composite web services. Journal of Systems and Software 81(10) (2008)
4. Chen, Y., Alspaugh, S., Katz, R.: Interactive analytical processing in big data systems: A cross-industry study of MapReduce workloads. Proc. VLDB Endow. 5(12) (August 2012)
5. Copil, G., Moldovan, D., Truong, H.-L., Dustdar, S.: Multi-level elasticity control of cloud services. In: Basu, S., Pautasso, C., Zhang, L., Fu, X. (eds.) ICSOC 2013. LNCS, vol. 8274, pp. 429–436. Springer, Heidelberg (2013)
6. Epifani, I., Ghezzi, C., Mirandola, R., Tamburrelli, G.: Model evolution by runtime parameter adaptation. In: 31st Internal Conference on Software Engineering (ICSE) (2009)
7. e-Ghazia, U., Masood, R., Shibli, M.A.: Comparative analysis of access control systems on cloud. In: 2012 13th ACIS International Conference on Software Engineering, Artificial Intelligence, Networking and Parallel Distributed Computing (SNPD) (2012)
8. Gondree, M., Peterson, Z.N.: Geolocation of data in the cloud. In: Proceedings of the Third ACM Conference on Data and Application Security and Privacy, CODASPY 2013. ACM, New York (2013)
9. Gutiérrez, A.M., Cassales Marquezan, C., Resinas, M., Metzger, A., Ruiz-Cortés, A., Pohl, K.: Extending WS-Agreement to support automated conformity check on transport and logistics service agreements. In: Basu, S., Pautasso, C., Zhang, L., Fu, X. (eds.) ICSOC 2013. LNCS, vol. 8274, pp. 567–574. Springer, Heidelberg (2013)
10. van Hoorn, A., Rohr, M., Hasselbring, W.: Engineering and continuously operating self-adaptive software systems: Required design decisions. In: Engels, G., Reussner, R.H., Momm, C., Stefan, S. (eds.) Design for Future 2009, Karlsruhe, Germany (November 2009)
11. Huber, N., Brosig, F., Kounev, S.: Modeling dynamic virtualized resource landscapes. In: Proceedings of the 8th International ACM SIGSOFT Conference on Quality of Software Architectures (2012)

12. Ivanović, D., Carro, M., Hermenegildo, M.: Constraint-based runtime prediction of sla violations in service orchestrations. In: Kappel, G., Maamar, Z., Motahari-Nezhad, H.R. (eds.) Service Oriented Computing. LNCS, vol. 7084, pp. 62–76. Springer, Heidelberg (2011)

13. Juels, A., Oprea, A.: New approaches to security and availability for cloud data. Commun. ACM 56(2) (February 2013)

14. Jung, R., Heinrich, R., Schmieders, E.: Model-driven instrumentation with kieker and palladio to forecast dynamic applications. In: Symposium on Software Performance: Joint Kieker/Palladio Days 2013. CEUR (2013)

15. Maoz, S.: Using model-based traces as runtime models. Computer 42(10) (2009)

16. von Massow, R., van Hoorn, A., Hasselbring, W.: Performance simulation of runtime reconfigurable component-based software architectures. In: Crnkovic, I., Gruhn, V., Book, M. (eds.) ECSA 2011. LNCS, vol. 6903, pp. 43–58. Springer, Heidelberg (2011)

17. Park, S., Chung, S.: Privacy-preserving attribute distribution mechanism for access control in a grid. In: 21st International Conference on Tools with Artificial Intelligence (2009)

18. Rausch, A., Reussner, R., Mirandola, R., Plášil, F. (eds.): The Common Component Modeling Example. LNCS, vol. 5153. Springer, Heidelberg (2008)

19. Ries, T., Fusenig, V., Vilbois, C., Engel, T.: Verification of data location in cloud networking. IEEE (December 2011)

20. Schmieders, E., Metzger, A.: Preventing performance violations of service compositions using assumption-based run-time verification. In: Abramowicz, W., Llorente, I.M., Surridge, M., Zisman, A., Vayssière, J. (eds.) ServiceWave 2011. LNCS, vol. 6994, pp. 194–205. Springer, Heidelberg (2011)

21. Suleiman, B., Venugopal, S.: Modeling performance of elasticity rules for cloud-based applications. In: 2013 17th IEEE International Enterprise Distributed Object Computing Conference (EDOC) (September 2013)

22. Szvetits, M., Zdun, U.: Systematic literature review of the objectives, techniques, kinds, and architectures of models at runtime. Software & Systems Modeling (December 2013)

23. Vaquero, L.M., Rodero-Merino, L., Buyya, R.: Dynamically scaling applications in the cloud. ACM SIGCOMM Computer Communication Review 41(1) (2011)

24. Zang, H., Bolot, J.: Anonymization of location data does not work: A large-scale measurement study. In: Proceedings of the 17th Annual International Conference on Mobile Computing and Networking. ACM, New York (2011)

Heuristic Approaches
for Robust Cloud Monitor Placement

Melanie Siebenhaar, Dieter Schuller, Olga Wenge, and Ralf Steinmetz

Technische Universität Darmstadt, Multimedia Communications Lab (KOM),
Rundeturmstr. 10, 64283 Darmstadt, Germany
{firstname.lastname}@KOM.tu-darmstadt.de

Abstract. When utilizing cloud-based services, consumers obtain high
configurable resources with minimal management effort and eliminate
large up-front IT investments. However, this shift in responsibility to
the cloud provider is accompanied by a loss of control for the cloud consumer. By offering SLAs and corresponding monitoring solutions, cloud
providers already try to address this issue, but these solutions are not
considered as sufficient from a consumer's perspective. Therefore, we developed an approach that allows to verify compliance with SLAs from
a consumer's perspective in our former work. Since the monitoring infrastructure itself may fail, this approach was enhanced in one of our
subsequent works in order to account for reliability. We introduced the
Robust Cloud Monitor Placement Problem and a formal optimization
model. In this paper, we propose corresponding solution approaches and
evaluate their practical applicability, since the problem is NP-complete.

Keywords: Cloud Computing, Monitoring, Placement, Performance.

1 Introduction

Utilizing services from the cloud, consumers gain a very high level of flexibility.
Configurable computing resources are provided on-demand in a similar manner
like electricity or water [4] at a minimal amount of management effort. However,
this shift in responsibility to the cloud provider bears several risks for the cloud
consumer. Amongst these risks is a loss of control concerning aspects like performance, availability, and security. Quality guarantees in the form of so-called
Service Level Agreements (SLAs) offered by cloud providers aim at lowering this
risk in favor for cloud consumers. Basically, an SLA represents a contract between
a cloud provider and a cloud consumer and defines certain quality levels (e.g.,
lower bounds for performance parameters such as availability) to be maintained
by the cloud provider. In addition, such a contract specifies some penalties for
the cloud provider in case of SLA violations. Nevertheless, the cloud consumers'
perception still is that providers do not sufficiently measure performance against
SLAs [5]. Furthermore, cloud providers often assign the task of violation reporting to their customers [11]. But even despite the fact that some cloud providers
also offer consumers corresponding monitoring solutions, these solutions cannot

X. Franch et al. (Eds.): ICSOC 2014, LNCS 8831, pp. 321–335, 2014.

be perceived as an independent evidence base for the detection and documentation of SLA violations from a consumer's perspective.

Our previous works ([15], [14]) addressed this issue. We proposed a hybrid monitoring approach in order to provide reliable means to verify adherence with SLAs from a consumer's perspective. This approach focuses on the consumer-side verification of availability of cloud applications and comprises the placement of monitoring units on provider and consumer side. Furthermore, we argue that not only the monitoring quality of such an approach has to be taken into account, but also the reliability of the monitoring infrastructure itself. This view was emphasized by our evaluation which revealed the sensitivity of our approach to network impairments. Therefore, we extended our approach and explored the placement of monitoring units with respect to current network reliability. As result, we introduced the *Robust Cloud Monitor Placement Problem* (RCMPP) as a new research problem along with a corresponding formal optimization model. Since the RCMPP is a nonlinear, multi-objective optimization problem, we further proposed transformations in order to turn the problem into a linear, single-objective optimization problem and thus, laying the foundation to exactly solve the problem using off-the-shelf optimization algorithms.

In this paper, we investigate the applicability of such exact optimization algorithms and also propose new heuristic solution approaches. Due to the fact that the RCMPP is NP-complete, exact optimization algorithms are very likely to be inapplicable for real-world scenarios exhibiting large-scale data center infrastructures. Hence, we compare the computation time and solution quality of an exact, ILP-based approach against heuristic solution approaches in order to derive recommendations for their applicability in practice. Furthermore, we extend our approach to a broker-based scenario and propose the concept of *Monitoring Level Agreements* (MLAs). In doing so, our extended approach permits an advanced performance control for cloud consumers.

The remainder of this paper is structured as follows: Section 2 gives an overview of related work. Section 3 briefly describes our extended approach and gives an overview of our former work. In Section 4, we propose exact and heuristic solution approaches for the RCMPP and present a corresponding evaluation in Section 5. In Section 6, the paper closes with a summary and future work.

2   Related Work

Only a few approaches exist which consider a reliable placement of monitoring units. A distribution of sensor pods on each cloud node in order to enable tenants to monitor the connectivity between their allocated nodes is proposed by [12]. The authors in [2] follow a different approach and focus on relocatable VMs in the presence of up to k host failures. For this purpose, the authors propose different optimization algorithms in order to determine k independent paths from the monitoring nodes to all other nodes in the network. Concerning networks in general, [10] aim at minimizing the number of monitoring locations while taking a maximum of k node/edge failures into account. A related problem also exists in the field of Operations Research. The fault-tolerant facility location problem, first studied by [8], tries to connect each city with at least a certain number of distinct facilities in order to account for failures. However, none of the related approaches addresses robust monitor placement by jointly considering current network reliability, monitor redundancy, and resource as well as location constraints.

3 Performance Control for Cloud Consumers

In this section, we give an overview of our extended approach and align our former work as well as our new contributions in the context of a broker-based scenario. Our former work is briefly described in the next sections followed by a detailed description of our new contributions.

This paper focuses on a broker-based scenario that is based on a cloud market model. In such a cloud market, cloud consumers submit their functional and non-functional requirements for their desired cloud services to brokers, which constitute mediators between cloud consumers and providers [4]. The brokers are capable to determine the most suitable cloud providers by querying a service registry residing in the market. Furthermore, such a broker enables consumers to negotiate SLAs to be provided by the cloud provider. For this purpose, a broker acts on behalf of a cloud consumer and conducts SLA negotiations with cloud providers. Now, in order to be able to verify compliance with SLAs from a consumer's perspective later on, the broker can also act on behalf of consumers and apply our proposed monitoring approach during runtime. The advantage of a broker-based perspective for our approach is the exploitation of global knowledge. In case that SLA violations are detected, a broker is aware of the adherence to SLAs of other cloud providers and thus, is able to recommend alternative cloud providers. In addition, the monitoring information gained at runtime can be used to initiate SLA re-negotiations or to adapt the properties of the monitoring approach in order to improve monitoring quality or monitoring infrastructure reliability.

In the following, we focus on an enterprise cloud consumer utilizing a set of applications running in different data centers of a cloud provider. In order to verify the performance guarantees in the form of SLAs obtained from the cloud provider, the enterprise cloud consumer entrusts the broker which conducted the SLA negotiations before with the monitoring of the running cloud applications. As part of such a monitoring service order, we propose the definition of *Monitoring Level Agreements* (MLAs) specifying the properties of the monitoring tasks for each application (cf. Section 3.1 for details). The broker then applies our hybrid monitoring approach and places monitoring units for each cloud application on provider- as well as on broker-side. Besides the provider-side monitoring, the broker-side monitoring permits an assessment of the status of a cloud application from a consumer's perspective. In order to obtain a robust monitor placement, the broker can select one of our proposed monitor placement algorithms according to our investigation in Section 4.

3.1   Hybrid Monitoring Approach and Monitoring Level Agreements

Our hybrid monitoring approach introduced in our former work in [15] focuses on verifying the availability of cloud applications from a consumer's perspective, since availability is one of the very few performance parameters contained in current cloud SLAs. Nevertheless, other performance parameters can be easily incorporated in our monitoring approach as well. In order to allow for an independent assessment of the status of a cloud application and visibility of the end-to-end performance of cloud applications, we proposed a hybrid monitoring approach with placements of monitoring units on provider and consumer side. The latter are now replaced by broker-side placements. Furthermore, such a hybrid approach permits to differentiate between downtimes caused by issues on broker and provider side and thus, enables a broker to filter downtimes that relate to cloud provider SLAs. In our hybrid monitoring approach, each monitoring unit observes predefined services of a cloud application as well as processes of the underlying VM. For each cloud application, the set of services to be invoked by a monitoring unit can be defined in advance. Same applies for the system processes to be observed on VM level. For this purpose, MLAs can specify the consumer's requirements concerning all the cloud applications to be monitored. Besides the services and processes, an amount of redundant monitoring units to be placed for each application can be defined. Higher numbers of redundant monitoring units are reasonable for business critical applications, since the probability that all redundant monitors fail decreases. We also follow this assumption in our monitor placement approach described in the next section.

3.2   Robust Cloud Monitor Placement

As already stated before, our approach must not only consider monitoring quality, but also has to account for downtimes of the monitoring infrastructure itself. Therefore, the monitoring units have to be placed by a broker in the data centers on provider- and broker-side in such a way that maximizes the robustness of the monitoring infrastructure. We introduced this problem, denoted as *Robust Cloud Monitor Placement Problem* (RCMPP), in our former work in [14]. The corresponding formal model is briefly described in the following. Table 1 shows the basic entities (upper part) and parameters (lower part) used in the formal model. Each instance of the RCMPP consists of a set $S = \{1, ..., n\}$ of data center sites comprising the set $S'' = \{1, ..., d\}$ of data center sites on broker side and the set $S' = \{d+1, ..., n\}$ of data center sites on cloud provider side. On each data center site $s \in S$ on provider and broker side, a set $V_s = \{1, ..., i\}$ of VMs is running which constitute candidates for monitor placement. A set of cloud applications $C_{s'v'} = \{1, ..., j\}$ to be monitored is running on each VM $v' \in V_{s'}$ located on a data center site $s' \in S'$ on provider side. A set of links $L = \{l(sv \rightleftharpoons s'v')\}$ interconnects the VMs $v \in V_s$ constituting placement candidates with the VMs $v' \in V_{s'}$ of the cloud applications $C_{s'v'}$. Each cloud application $c \in C_{s'v'}$ has certain requirements concerning the corresponding monitoring units. These requirements comprise a specific resource demand of $rd_{s'v'cr} \in \mathbb{R}^+$ for a specific

Table 1. Used symbols in the formal model

Symbol	Description
$S = \{1, ..., n\}$	set of n data center sites
$S'' = \{1, ..., d\}$	consumer sites, $S'' \subset S$
$S' = \{d + 1, ..., n\}$	provider sites, $S' \subset S$
$V_s = \{1, ..., i\}$	VM candidates for monitor placement on site $s \in S$
$C_{s'v'} = \{1, ..., j\}$	cloud applications to monitor on VM $v' \in V_{s'}, s' \in S'$
$L = \{l(sv \rightleftharpoons s'v')\}$	links interconnecting VM monitor candidates V_s and VMs of applications $C_{s'v'}$
$R = \{1, ..., k\}$	set of k considered VM resource types
$rd_{s'v'cr} \in \mathbb{R}^+$	resource demand for monitoring application $c \in C_{s'v'}$ for resource $r \in R$
$rs_{svr} \in \mathbb{R}^+$	resource supply of VM $v \in V_s$ for resource $r \in R$
$rf_{s'v'c} \in \mathbb{N}_{>1}$	redundancy factor for monitoring application $c \in C_{s'v'}$
$p_{l(sv \rightleftharpoons s'v')} \in \mathbb{R}^+$	observed reliability for each link $l \in L$
$p_{sv} \in \mathbb{R}^+$	observed reliability for each VM $v \in V_s$

resource type $r \in R = \{1, ..., k\}$ such as CPU power or memory, and a redundancy factor $rf_{s'v'c} \in \mathbb{N}_{>1}$, indicating that the cloud application c has to be monitored by $rf_{s'v'c}$ different monitoring units. In order to account for the reliability of the monitoring infrastructure, it has to be noted that the broker is not aware of the underlying network topologies of the cloud provider and the Internet service provider. However, we assume that the broker is able to utilize traditional network measurement tools in order to estimate the end-to-end performance between any pair of VMs that are represented by a given link $l \in L$ in order to determine the observed reliability $p_{l(sv \rightleftharpoons s'v')} \in \mathbb{R}^+$ for a given link $l \in L$. Furthermore, we assume that the broker can also utilize such measurement tools in order to estimate the reliability $p_{sv} \in \mathbb{R}^+$ of a given VM $v \in V_s$ on a site $s \in S$. Finally, our model must also consider the respective resource supply of $rs_{svr} \in \mathbb{R}^+$ each VM $v \in V_s$ on a site $s \in S$ is able to provide. The objective of the RCMPP now is to assign $rf_{s'v'c}$ monitoring units for each cloud application to be monitored on broker and provider side, while maximizing the reliability of the whole monitoring infrastructure. Hereby, we express the reliability by the probability that at least one of the monitoring units for each cloud application is working properly. In doing so, the resource constraints of the VMs must not be exceeded and all monitoring units must be placed. Furthermore, we incorporate a set of placement restrictions for the monitoring units. First of all, no monitoring unit is allowed to be placed on the VM of the cloud application to be monitored and second, one monitoring unit must be placed on broker and provider side, respectively. Both restrictions directly follow from our hybrid monitoring approach. Third, for reasons of fault-tolerance, each monitoring unit to be placed for a single application must be placed on a different site.

3.3   Formal Model

The corresponding optimization model for the RCMPP is depicted in Model 1 and serves as a starting point for the development of solution algorithms. The RCMPP constitutes a multi-objective optimization problem, since we want to maximize the reliability of the monitoring units for each cloud application, simultaneously (cf. Equation 1). Each of these potentially conflicting objective functions expresses the probability $p_{s'v'c}^{mon}(x)$, that at least one monitoring unit

---

Model 1. Robust Cloud Monitor Placement Problem

$$Maximize \quad \{p_{s'v'c}^{mon}(x)|s' \in S', v' \in V_{s'}, c \in C_{s'v'}\} \tag{1}$$

$$p_{s'v'c}^{mon}(x) = 1 - \prod_{s \in S, v \in V_s} (q_{svs'v'}^{path})^{x_{svs'v'c}} \tag{2}$$

$$q_{svs'v'}^{path} = [(1 - p_{sv}) + (1 - p_{l(sv \rightleftharpoons s'v')}) \tag{3}$$
$$- (1 - p_{sv})\,(1 - p_{l(sv \rightleftharpoons s'v')})]$$

subject to

$$\sum_{s \in S, v \in V_s} x_{svs'v'c} = rf_{s'v'c} \tag{4}$$

$$\forall s' \in S', v' \in V_{s'}, c \in C_{s'v'}, rf_{s'v'c} \geq 2$$

$$\sum_{s' \in S', v' \in V_{s'}, c \in C_{s'v'}} rd_{s'v'cr}\, x_{svs'v'c} \leq rs_{svr} \tag{5}$$

$$\forall s \in S, v \in V_s, r \in R$$

$$\sum_{v \in V_s} x_{svs'v'c} \leq 1 \tag{6}$$

$$\forall s \in S, s' \in S', v' \in V_{s'}, c \in C_{s'v'}$$

$$\sum_{s \in S, v \in V_s} x_{svs'v'c} \geq 1 \tag{7}$$

$$\forall s' \in S', v' \in V_{s'}, c \in C_{s'v'}, s = \{d+1, ..., n\}$$

$$\sum_{s \in S, v \in V_s} x_{svs'v'c} \geq 1 \tag{8}$$

$$\forall s' \in S', v' \in V_{s'}, c \in C_{s'v'}, s = \{1, ..., d\}$$

$$x_{svs'v'c} = 0 \tag{9}$$
$$\forall c \in C_{s'v'}, \ s = s' \ and \ v = v'$$

$$x_{svs'v'c} \in \{0, 1\} \tag{10}$$
$$\forall s \in S, v \in V_s, s' \in S', v' \in V_{s'}, c \in C_{s'v'}$$

---

for the respective application does not fail. Equation 2 represents this probability by 1 minus the probability that all monitors for a specific cloud application $c \in C_{s'v'}$ fail. Equation 3 determines the probability to fail ($q^{path}_{svs'v'}$) for a given monitoring unit of a specific cloud application $c \in C_{s'v'}$. Hereby, the reliability of the VM $v \in V_s$ where the monitoring unit is placed as well as the reliability of the link between this VM and the VM where the cloud application is running on are considered. Equation 10 defines a set $x_{svs'v'c}$ of binary decision variables indicating whether a monitoring unit for a cloud application $c \in C_{s'v'}$ running on VM $v' \in V_{s'}$ on site $s' \in S'$ is placed on VM $v \in V_s$ running on site $s \in S$. The vector x in Equation 1 represents all decision variables $x_{svs'v'c}$. In order to ensure that $rf_{s'v'c}$ redundant monitoring units monitor the corresponding cloud application, Equation 4 has been added to the model. Equations 7 and 8 account for the hybrid monitoring approach and specify that at least one monitoring unit has to be placed on broker and provider side, respectively. Equation 5 prevents the exceeding of the resource supplies of each VM $v \in V_s$ and Equation 6 ensures that each monitoring unit for a given application $c \in C_{s'v'}$ is placed on a different data center site. Last, but not least, a monitoring unit is not allowed to be placed on the VM where the corresponding application is running (cf. Equation 9).

The RCMPP is a multi-objective optimization problem, hence, no unique solution can be obtained. Furthermore, as can be seen from Equation 2 in Model 1, it also constitutes a nonlinear problem. Although approaches exist for solving multi-objective optimization problems, these approaches only yield pareto-optimal solutions and typically require some kind of preference structure concerning the set of solutions as input. Since defining a preference structure, e.g., in the form of a lexicographic preference order with regard to all applications to be monitored, is very exhausting on a large data center scale, we aim for a solution approach focusing on a single-objective.

4 Exact and Heuristic Solution Approaches

This section describes an exact ILP-based solution approach as well as two heuristics in order to solve the RCMPP. The heuristic algorithms are partly inspired from existing solution approaches (e.g., [6], [9]) for the related generalized assignment problem and its bottleneck version. A direct application of existing heuristics is not feasible, since no full mapping exists from the RCMPP to an existing optimization problem. Furthermore, since the RCMPP is NP-complete, ILP-based algorithms will also not be able to find solutions for large-scale problems. Therefore, the development of new heuristics is required. Our heuristics consist of an opening procedure (Greedy), which aims to find a first feasible solution, and an improvement procedure (TSearch) aiming to improve an initial solution. Hence, we obtain two different heuristics in total: Greedy and Greedy+TSearch (denoted as GTSearch).

Model 2. Robust Cloud Monitor Placement Problem after Transformation

$$Minimize \quad z \tag{11}$$

subject to

$$q^{log}_{s'v'c}(x) \leq z \tag{12}$$
$$\forall s' \in S', v' \in V_{s'}, c \in C_{s'v'}, z \in \mathbb{R}$$

$$q^{log}_{s'v'c}(x) = \sum_{s \in S, v \in V_s} x_{svs'v'c} \, log(q^{path}_{svs'v'}) \tag{13}$$

$$q^{path}_{svs'v'} = [(1 - p_{sv}) + (1 - p_{l(sv \rightleftharpoons s'v')}) \tag{14}$$
$$-(1 - p_{sv}) \, (1 - p_{l(sv \rightleftharpoons s'v')})]$$

$$q^{path}_{svs'v'} > 0 \; \forall s \in S, v \in V_s, s' \in S', v' \in V_{s'} \tag{15}$$

4.1 Integer Linear Programming (ILP)-Based Approach

In order to turn the RCMPP into a linear, single-objective optimization problem, we proposed a set of transformations in our former work in [14]. The transformations are briefly summarized in the following.

First of all, the maximization problem is turned into a minimization problem. This can be achieved by considering the complementary objectives of the former Model 1, i.e., the probability $q^{mon}_{s'v'c}(x)$ that all monitors fail for each cloud application. The first step enables a subsequent linearization of the problem by taking the logarithm of both sides (this approach is also followed by [1]). Our last step is based on a worst-case analysis, where we aim to minimize the worst possible outcome. For this purpose, we apply a so-called *minimax strategy* [7], which turns the initial set of objective functions into a single objective function that aims to minimize the maximum probability of all $q^{mon}_{s'v'c}(x)$. In doing so, a new decision variable $z \in \mathbb{R}$ expressing this maximum value is introduced. In addition, $|C_{s'v'}|$ new constraints $\forall s' \in S', v' \in V_{s'}$ are added to the constraints of our former Model 1. The resulting linear, single-objective optimization problem is depicted in Model 2. Please note, that the initial constraints have been neglected due to lack of space. Furthermore, we assume $q^{path}_{svs'v'} > 0$, since no system is without failure. The resulting problem represents a mixed-integer linear programming problem that can be solved exactly using off-the-shelf algorithms such as branch-and-bound [6].

4.2 Greedy Algorithm

Algorithm 3 describes our opening procedure. This algorithm is inspired by the *steepest ascent approach* (cf. [6]), which is typically applied in local search procedures. However, although local search algorithms belong to the group of improvement procedures, the idea behind our Greedy algorithm is very similar.

Algorithm 3. Greedy Heuristic

---

input: *connections C, vm capacities V, application monitor requirements R*
output: *monitor placements P*
1: **procedure** GREEDY(C, V, R)
2:     $P \leftarrow \{\}$
3:     SORTDESCREL(C)
4:     **for all** $c \in C$ **do**
5:         $app \leftarrow app(c)$
6:         $sourcevm \leftarrow source(c)$
7:         $targetvm \leftarrow target(c)$
8:         **if** $app \in R$ **then**
9:             $violation \leftarrow$ CHECKCONSTRAINTS($app, sourcevm, targetvm, V, R, P$)
10:            **if** $violation \neq TRUE$ **then**
11:                $P = P \cup \{c\}$
12:                UPDATE($app, sourcevm, targetvm, V, R$)
13:            **end if**
14:            $n \leftarrow remunits(app, R)$
15:            **if** $n = 0$ **then**
16:                $R \leftarrow R/\{app\}$
17:            **end if**
18:        **end if**
19:    **end for**
20:    $l \leftarrow size(R)$
21:    **if** $l > 0$ **then**
22:        $P \leftarrow NULL$ ▷ no feasible solution could be found
23:    **end if**
24:    **return** P
25: **end procedure**

In each step, the Greedy algorithm tries to improve the partial solution obtained so far to a maximum extent. For this purpose, the set of connections between each VM (sourcevm) where a cloud application (app) to be monitored is running and each VM (targetvm) constituting a candidate for monitor placement is sorted according to decreasing reliability values (line 3). Afterwards, we explore the connections in descending order (line 4). In each step, if all redundant monitoring units for each application have not been placed so far (line 8), we examine, whether we can place a monitoring unit on the targetvm of the current connection. For this purpose, we check, whether any constraints of the RCMPP are violated when the placement is realized. In case that no violation is detected (line 10), we can add the current connection to the result set of final placements (line 11) and update the auxiliary data structures (line 12). If all redundant monitoring units have been placed for a given application, this application is removed from the set R of monitor requirements (line 16). The Greedy algorithm continues to explore further connections until all monitoring units have been placed for each application (line 21).

Algorithm 4. Tabu Search Algorithm

---

input: *initial solution S, iteration limit max, connections C, vm capacities V,
application monitor requirements R*
output: *monitor placements P*
1: **procedure** TSEARCH(S, C, V, R)
2:     $T \leftarrow \{\}$, $mp \leftarrow FALSE$, $r \leftarrow 1$
3:     $bestobjval \leftarrow$ COMPOBJVAL(S, C)
4:     **while** $r <= max$ **do**
5:         UPDATE(T)
6:         **if** $mp = TRUE$ **then**
7:             $i \leftarrow 0$
8:         **else**
9:             $i \leftarrow i + 1$
10:         **end if**
11:         **if** $i < size(R)$ **then**
12:             $b \leftarrow$ BOTTLENECKAPP(i, S, C)
13:         **else**
14:             **return** P ▷ no improvement can be found anymore
15:         **end if**
16:         $AM \leftarrow \{\}$
17:         $PM \leftarrow$ PLACEDMONITORS(b)
18:         **for all** $pm \in PM$ **do**
19:             $NB_{SWAP} \leftarrow$ SWAPNEIGHBOURHOOD(pm)
20:             $NB_{SHIFT} \leftarrow$ SHIFTNEIGHBOURHOOD(pm)
21:             $N \leftarrow NB_{SWAP} \cup NB_{SHIFT}$
22:             $AM \leftarrow$ ADMISSIBLEMOVES(pm, N, V, R, P)
23:         **end for**
24:         SORTDESCOBJVAL(AM)
25:         **for all** $am \in AM$ **do**
26:             **if** $(am \notin T) or (objval(am) > bestobjval)$ **then**
27:                 DOMOVE(am)
28:                 $T \leftarrow T \cup \{am\}$
29:                 **if** $(objval(am) > bestobjval)$ **then**
30:                     $bestobjval \leftarrow objval(am)$
31:                 **end if**
32:                 $mp \leftarrow TRUE$
33:                 **break**
34:             **end if**
35:         **end for**
36:         $r \leftarrow r + 1$
37:     **end while**
38:     **return** P
39: **end procedure**

4.3   Tabu Search Algorithm

Our tabu search algorithm is depicted in Algorithm 4 and is inspired by the work
from Karsu and Azizoglu [9], who proposed a tabu search-based algorithm for

the multi-resource agent bottleneck generalised assignment problem. However, the problem they consider deals with workload balancing over a set of agents over multiple periods.

The TSearch algorithm constitutes an improvement procedure, hence, requires an initial solution S as starting point. Our Greedy algorithm can be applied for this purpose. The TSearch algorithm then tries to improve the initial solution over a number of iterations until a predefined number of iterations is reached (line 4). In each iteration, the TSearch algorithm determines a so-called neighbourhood based on the current solution. Basically, a neighbourhood of a given solution is a set of solutions that can be obtained by performing so-called moves. Thereby, a move typically consists of dropping and adding one or more parts (monitor placements in this case) of the current solution. In the TSearch algorithm, we make use of a combined shift and swap neighbourhood (lines 20 and 19). That is, each move either constitutes in shifting a monitoring unit to a different VM or two monitoring units swapping places. For the determination of the neighbourhoods, the TSearch algorithm starts from the cloud application exhibiting the worst total reliability for its monitoring units placed (line 12) and thus, having a pivotal role for the calculation of the lower bound z in our optimization model. We denote this cloud application as *bottleneck application*. However, in case that no shift or swap of at least one of the monitoring units of the bottleneck application is feasible during an iteration, we select the cloud application with the second worst total reliability for its monitoring units placed in the next iteration (line 9). At the end of each iteration, we determine the set of admissible moves with respect to the constraints of the RCMPP among the solutions in the neighbourhood (line 22). From the set of admissible moves, we then either select the move with the highest improvement or lowest decrease with respect to the objective value of the current solution. For this purpose, the list of admissible moves is sorted in decreasing order of objective values (line 24). This is a typical approach when following a tabu search-based procedure. Also a decrease is accepted in order to obtain a different solution, so that the algorithm does not get stuck in a local optimum. However, in order to prevent that the algorithm is running in circles, a global tabu list is maintained (line 2) that forbids the last moves to be performed again for a predefined number of subsequent iterations. Only in case that a move that is currently part of the tabu list would yield a better solution than the current best solution found so far, this move is performed despite being part of the tabu list (line 26).

5 Performance Evaluation

We have implemented our solution approaches in Java and conducted an evaluation in order to assess their applicability for real-world scenarios. For the implementation and evaluation of the ILP-based approach, we used the JavaILP framework[1] and the commercial solver framework IBM ILOG CPLEX[2].

---

[1] http://javailp.sourceforge.net/

[2] http://www.ibm.com/software/integration/optimization/cplex-optimizer

Table 2. Independent variables and values used in the evaluation

Independent Variable	Symbol and Values
Number of sites:	$|S'|, |S''| \in \{2, \underline{3}, 4\}$
Number of VMs:	$|V_s| \in \{4, \underline{5}, 6, 7, 8\}$
Number of applications:	$|C_{s'v'}| \in \{1, \underline{2}, 3\}$
Redundancy factor:	$rf_{s'v'c} \in \{2, \underline{3}, 4\}$

5.1 Evaluation Methodology

In order to assess the practical applicability of our approaches, we examine the two *dependent variables* computation time and solution quality. Solution quality is expressed by the objective value achieved by a solution approach being transformed into the corresponding downtime in seconds on a yearly basis. Furthermore, we consider four *independent variables*, namely, the total number of data center sites on broker and provider side, the number of VMs on each site, the number of cloud applications concurrently running on each VM, and the redundancy factor for the placement of the monitoring units. As evaluation methodology, we follow a fractional factorial design [3]. That is, at each point in time, we only vary one independent variable while keeping the other independent variables fixed. Hence, the impact of each independent variable on the two dependent variables is measured separately. In total, the evaluation consists of 14 test cases depicted in Table 2, each comprising 100 randomly generated problems. For the generation of the problems, we incorporate realistic data including VM capacities and availability guarantees from the specifications of Amazons EC2 VM offers[3], as well as packet loss statistics from the PingER project[4] to model link reliability. In addition, we consider only one resource type, CPU, since our early experiments have shown that CPU is the primary determinant for placing the monitoring units. Furthermore, we choose each application out of three application types, each exhibiting different CPU requirements for the monitoring units to be placed. We also obtained the CPU requirements from our early experiments. Synthetic VM workloads based on the work by [13] are used to determine the remaining VM resource supplies. Each problem was solved using our three solution approaches. In addition, we added a random solution approach, which conducts a random placement of the monitoring units, while only considering adherence with all constraints. For the solution of each problem and each optimization approach, we set a timeout of 5 minutes, which can be perceived as a realistic value in the context of our broker-based scenario and on-demand cloud service provisioning. For the GTSearch heuristic, we set the maximum number of iterations to 1000 and the tabu tenure to 50 based on [9].

---

[3] http://aws.amazon.com/ec2/

[4] http://www-iepm.slac.stanford.edu/pinger/

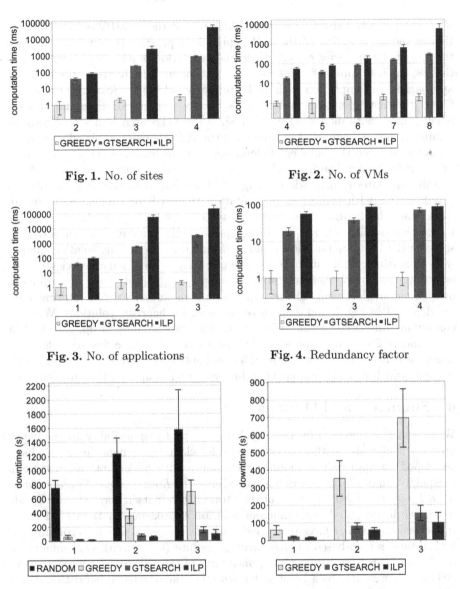

Fig. 1. No. of sites

Fig. 2. No. of VMs

Fig. 3. No. of applications

Fig. 4. Redundancy factor

Fig. 5. No. of applications

Fig. 6. No. of applications (magnified view)

5.2 Simulation Results

Figures 1 to 6 depict selected results of the evaluation. Please note the logarithmic scale in the first four figures.

When using the ILP approach, the computation time shows an exponential growth with increasing problem size, e.g., 100ms up to 10000ms in Fig. 1. However, this effect is considerably less when increasing the redundancy factor. All in all, the exponential growth underlines the fact that the RCMPP is NP-complete. Hence, the applicability of the ILP approach in practice is very limited, since the size of the problems considered in the evaluation is relatively small. Nevertheless, the ILP approach can serve as a baseline in order to assess the heuristic approaches. In comparison to the ILP approach and the GTSearch heuristic, the Greedy heuristic performs best with respect to computation time and yields a linear growth with increasing problem size. The GTSearch heuristic also shows smaller values in computation time than the ILP approach. This effect is most pronounced when the number of cloud applications increases (cf. Fig. 3). However, the GTSearch heuristic exhibits no linear growth with respect to problem size like the Greedy heuristic (cf. Fig. 2). Therefore, a further improvement of this heuristic with respect to computation time will be considered in future work, since this heuristic performs best, besides the ILP approach, with respect to solution quality (cf. Fig. 5). In comparison, the Greedy heuristic although showing the best computation times performs worse regarding solution quality with increasing complexity of the problem (cf. Fig. 6 for a magnified view). Nevertheless, the Greedy heuristic still achieves a considerably large improvement over a random placement. The results of a random placement of monitoring units are depicted in Fig. 5 and emphasize the need for heuristic solutions. Without conducting any optimization, the monitoring units would end up, e.g., with a downtime of 25 minutes (on a yearly basis) in contrast to a few seconds when using the other approaches in case of 3 cloud applications deployed on each VM. A result which is unacceptable when business critical applications are utilized.

6 Summary and Outlook

When using resources from the cloud, the shift of responsibility to the cloud provider is attended with a loss of control for cloud consumers. Hence, we have developed an approach to monitor compliance with SLAs from a consumer's perspective in our former work and introduced the *Robust Cloud Monitor Placement Problem* (RCMPP), since the monitoring system itself may also fail. In this paper, we investigated three different solution approaches for the RCMPP: an ILP-based approach, a Greedy heuristic, and the Greedy heuristic in conjunction with a tabu search-based improvement procedure (GTSearch). Our simulation results confirmed the practical inapplicability of the ILP-based approach. Nevertheless, it was used as a baseline for assessing the developed heuristics. All in all, only the GTSearch heuristic is able to achieve near optimal results, but exhibits no linear growth in computation time in contrast to the Greedy heuristic. Therefore, we will explore the improvement of our heuristics in future work.

Acknowledgments. This work was supported in part by the German Federal Ministry of Education and Research (BMBF) under grant no. "01|C12S01V" in the context of the Software-Cluster project SINNODIUM (www.software-cluster. org), the German Research Foundation (DFG) in the Collaborative Research Center (SFB) 1053 – MAKI, and the E-Finance Lab Frankfurt am Main e.V. (http:// www.efinancelab.com).

References

1. Andreas, A.K., Smith, J.C.: Mathematical Programming Algorithms for Two-Path Routing Problems with Reliability Considerations. INFORMS Journal on Computing 20(4), 553–564 (2008)
2. Bin, E., Biran, O., Boni, O., Hadad, E., Kolodner, E., Moatti, Y., Lorenz, D.: Guaranteeing High Availability Goals for Virtual Machine Placement. In: 31st International Conference on Distributed Computing Systems (ICDCS), pp. 700–709 (2011)
3. Box, G.E.P., Hunter, J.S., Hunter, W.G.: Wiley, 2nd edn. (2005)
4. Buyya, R., Yeo, C.S., Venugopal, S., Broberg, J., Brandic, I.: Cloud Computing and Emerging IT Platforms: Vision, Hype, and Reality for Delivering Computing as the 5th Utility. Future Generation Computer Systems 25(6), 599–616 (2009)
5. CSA, ISACA: Cloud Computing Market Maturity. Study Results. Cloud Security Alliance and ISACA (2012), http://www.isaca.org/Knowledge-Center/Research/ResearchDeliverables/Pages/2012-Cloud-Computing-Market-Maturity-Study-Results.aspx (last access: May 30, 2014)
6. Hillier, F.S., Liebermann, G.J.: Inroduction to Operations Research, 8th edn. McGraw-Hill (2005)
7. Jensen, P.A., Bard, J.F.: Appendix A: Equivalent Linear pROGRAMS. In: Supplements to Operations Research Models and Methods. John Wiley and Sons (2003), http://www.me.utexas.edu/~jensen/ORMM/supplements/units/lp_models/equivalent.pdf (last access: May 30, 2014)
8. Kamal, J., Vazirani, V.V.: An Approximation Algorithm for the Fault Tolerant Metric Facility Location Problem. In: Jansen, K., Khuller, S. (eds.) APPROX 2000. LNCS, vol. 1913, pp. 177–182. Springer, Heidelberg (2000)
9. Karsua, Z., Azizoglua, M.: The Multi-Resource Agent Bottleneck Generalised Assignment Problem. International Journal of Production Research 50(2), 309–324 (2012)
10. Natu, M., Sethi, A.S.: Probe Station Placement for Robust Monitoring of Networks. Journal of Network and Systems Management 16(4), 351–374 (2008)
11. Patel, P., Ranabahu, A., Sheth, A.: Service Level Agreement in Cloud Computing. Tech. rep., Knoesis Center, Wright State University, USA (2009)
12. Sharma, P., Chatterjee, S., Sharma, D.: CloudView: Enabling Tenants to Monitor and Control their Cloud Instantiations. In: 2013 IFIP/IEEE International Symposium on Integrated Network Management (IM 2013), pp. 443–449 (2013)
13. Shrivastava, V., Zerfos, P., Lee, K.W., Jamjoom, H., Liu, Y.H., Banerjee, S.: Application-aware Virtual Machine Migration in Data Centers. In: Proceedings of the 30th IEEE International Conference on Computer Communications (INFOCOM 2011), pp. 66–70 (April 2011)
14. Siebenhaar, M., Lampe, U., Schuller, D., Steinmetz, R.: Robust Cloud Monitor Placement for Availability Verification. In: Helfert, M., Desprez, F., Ferguson, D., Leymann, F., Muoz, V.M. (eds.) Proceedings of the 4th International Conference on Cloud Computing and Services Science (CLOSER 2014), pp. 193–198. SciTe Press (April 2014)
15. Siebenhaar, M., Wenge, O., Hans, R., Tercan, H., Steinmetz, R.: Verifying the Availability of Cloud Applications. In: Jarke, M., Helfert, M. (eds.) Proceedings of the 3rd International Conference on Cloud Computing and Services Science (CLOSER 2013), pp. 489–494. SciTe Press (May 2013)

Compensation-Based vs. Convergent Deployment Automation for Services Operated in the Cloud

Johannes Wettinger, Uwe Breitenbücher, and Frank Leymann

Institute of Architecture of Application Systems, University of Stuttgart, Stuttgart,
Germany
{wettinger,breitenbuecher,leymann}@iaas.uni-stuttgart.de

Abstract. Leading paradigms to develop and operate applications such
as continuous delivery, configuration management, and the merge of development and operations (DevOps) are the foundation for various techniques and tools to implement automated deployment. To expose such
applications as services (SaaS) to users and customers these approaches
are typically used in conjunction with Cloud computing to automatically
provision and manage underlying resources such as storage or virtual machines. A major class of these automation approaches follows the idea of
converging toward a desired state of a resource (e.g., a middleware component deployed on a virtual machine). This is achieved by repeatedly
executing idempotent scripts until the desired state is reached. Because
of major drawbacks of this approach, we present an alternative deployment automation approach based on compensation and fine-grained snapshots using container virtualization. We further perform an evaluation
comparing both approaches in terms of difficulties at design time and
performance at runtime.

Keywords: Compensation, Snapshot, Convergence, Deployment Automation, DevOps, Cloud Computing.

1 Introduction

Cloud computing [10,21,7] can be used in different setups such as public, private,
and hybrid Cloud environments to efficiently run a variety of kinds of applications, exposed as services (SaaS). Prominent examples are Web applications,
back-ends for mobile applications, and applications in the field of the "internet
of things", e.g., to process large amounts of sensor data. Users of such services
based on Cloud applications expect high availability and low latency when interacting with a service. Consequently, the applications need to scale rapidly and
dynamically to serve thousands or even millions of users properly. To implement
scaling in a cost-efficient way the application has to be elastic, which means that
application instances are provisioned and decommissioned rapidly and automatically based on the current load. Cloud providers offer on-demand self-service
capabilities, e.g., by providing corresponding APIs to provision and manage resources such as virtual machines, databases, and runtime environments. These

X. Franch et al. (Eds.): ICSOC 2014, LNCS 8831, pp. 336–350, 2014.
© Springer-Verlag Berlin Heidelberg 2014

capabilities are the foundation for scaling applications and implementing elasticity mechanisms to run them efficiently in terms of costs. Moreover, users of services operated in the Cloud expect fast responses to their changing and growing requirements as well as fixes of issues that occur. Thus, underlying applications need to be redeployed frequently to production, e.g., several times a week. Development and operations need to be tightly coupled to enable such frequent redeployments. *DevOps* [5,3] aims to eliminate the split between developers and operations to automate the complete deployment process from the source code in version control to the production environment. Today, the DevOps community follows a leading paradigm to automate the deployment, namely to implement *idempotent* scripts to *converge* resources toward a desired state. Because this approach has some major drawbacks we propose an alternative approach based on compensation. Our major contributions are presented in this paper:

- We present the fundamentals of state-of-the-art deployment automation approaches and point out existing deficiencies and difficulties
- We propose an alternative approach to implement deployment automation based on compensation on different levels of granularity to improve the efficiency and robustness of script execution
- We further show how compensation actions can be automatically derived at runtime to ease the implementation of compensation based on snapshots
- We evaluate the compensation-based deployment automation approach based on different kinds of applications operated in the Cloud and exposed as services

The remainder of this paper is structured as follows: based on the fundamentals showing state-of-the-art deployment automation approaches (Sect. 2), focusing on convergent deployment automation, we present the problem statement in Sect. 3. To tackle the resulting challenges, Sect. 4 presents approaches to implement compensation-based deployment automation. Our evaluation of compensation-based deployment automation is presented and discussed in Sect. 5 and Sect. 6. Finally, Sect. 7 presents related work and Sect. 8 concludes this paper.

2   Fundamentals

The automated deployment of middleware and application components can be implemented using general-purpose scripting languages such as Perl, Python, or Unix shell scripts. This is what system administrators and operations personnel were primarily using before the advent of DevOps tools providing domain-specific languages [2] to create scripts for deployment automation purposes. We stick to the following definition 1 for a script to be used for automating operations, especially considering deployment automation:

Definition 1 (Operations Script). *An operations script (in short script) is an arbitrary executable to deploy and operate middleware and application components by modifying the state of resources such as virtual machines. Such a state* *modification could be the installation of a software package, the configuration of a middleware component, etc. A script consists of a sequence of actions such as command statements that implement state modifications.*

Technically, a script can be implemented imperatively (e.g., using general-purpose scripting languages) or declaratively (e.g., using domain-specific languages [2]). In case of using a declarative language, the concrete imperative command statements and their sequential ordering has to be derived in a pre-processing step before the actual execution. As an alternative to scripts, compiled programs could be used, based on portable general-purpose programming languages such as Java. However, this would decrease the flexibility and may have performance impact, because the source code has to be compiled after each change.

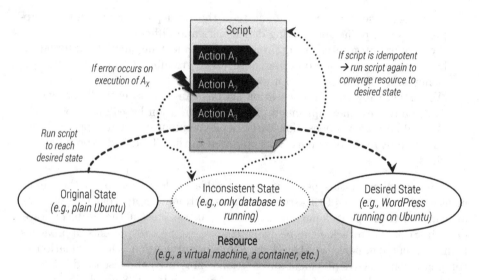

Fig. 1. Script to transfer or converge a resource toward a desired state

Fig. 1 shows the basic usage of scripts: several actions A_x are specified in the script that are command statements (install package "mysql", create directory "cache", etc.) to transfer a particular resource such as a virtual machine (VM) or a container [15,17] into a desired state. For instance, the original state of the virtual machine could be a plain Ubuntu operating system (OS) that is installed, whereas the desired state is a VM that runs a WordPress blog[1] on the Ubuntu OS. Consequently, a script needs to execute commands required to install and configure all components (Apache HTTP server, MySQL database server, etc.) that are necessary to run WordPress on the VM.

This is a straightforward implementation of deployment automation. However, this approach has a major drawback: in case an error occurs during the execution

---

[1] WordPress: http://www.wordpress.org

of the script, the resource is in an unknown, most probably inconsistent state. For instance, the MySQL database server is installed and running, but the installation of Apache HTTP server broke, so the application is not usable. Thus, either manual intervention is required or the whole resource has to be dropped and a new resource has to be provisioned (e.g., create a new instance of a VM image) to execute the script again. This is even more difficult in case the *original state* is not captured, e.g., using a VM snapshot. In this case manual intervention is required to restore the original state. This is error-prone, time-consuming, costly, and most importantly even impossible in cases where the original state is not documented or captured. Since errors definitely occur in Cloud environments, e.g., if the network connection breaks during the retrieval of a software package, it is a serious challenge to implement full and robust deployment automation.

This is why the DevOps community provides techniques and tools to implement *convergent deployment automation:* its foundation is the implementation of *idempotent* scripts [4], meaning the script execution on a particular resource such as a VM can be repeated arbitrarily, always leading to the same result if no error occurs; if an error occurs during execution and the desired state is not reached (i.e., resource is in an unknown state) the script is executed again and again until the desired state is reached. Thus, idempotent scripts can be used to *converge* a particular resource toward a desired state without dropping the resource as shown in Fig. 1. With this approach the resource does not get stuck in an inconsistent state. DevOps tools such as Chef [11] provide a declarative domain-specific language to define idempotent actions (e.g., Chef resources[2]) that are translated to imperative command statements at runtime, depending on the underlying operating system. For instance, the declarative statement "ensure that package `apache2` is installed" is translated to the following command on an Ubuntu OS: `apt-get -y install apache2`; on a Red Hat OS, the same declarative statement is translated to `yum -y install apache2`. Imperative command statements can also be expressed in an idempotent manner. For instance, a simple command to install the Apache HTTP server on Ubuntu (`apt-get -y install apache2`) is automatically idempotent because if the package `apache2` is already installed, the command will still complete successfully without doing anything. Other command statements need to be adapted such as a command to retrieve the content of a remote Git[3] repository: `git clone http://gitserver/my_repo`. This command would fail when executing it for a second time because the directory `my_repo` already exists. To make the command statement idempotent a minor extension is required that preventively deletes the `my_repo` directory: `rm -rf my_repo && git clone http://gitserver/my_repo`.

---

[2] Chef resources: `http://docs.opscode.com/resource.html`
[3] Git: `http://git-scm.com`

3   Problem Statement

As discussed in Sect. 2, convergent deployment automation makes the execution of scripts more robust. However, it may not be the most efficient approach to repeatedly execute the whole script in case of errors until the desired state is reached. Furthermore, this approach only works in conjunction with idempotent scripts. While in most cases it is possible to implement idempotent actions, it can be challenging and sophisticated to implement fully idempotent scripts without holding specific state information for each action that was executed. Typical examples include:

- An action to create a database or another external entity by name, so the second execution results in an error such as "the database already exists".
- An action that sends a non-idempotent request to an external service (e.g., a POST request to a RESTful API), so the second request most probably produces a different result.
- An action to clone a Git repository, so the second execution fails because the directory for the repository already exists in the local filesystem.

Consequently, major efforts need to be invested to create and test idempotent scripts to ensure their robustness. Moreover, issues may occur, preventing a resource from converging toward the desired state, so the resource hangs in an unknown state. As an example, Ubuntu's apt package manager[4] may crash during the installation of software packages (e.g., in case of a dropped network connection or a memory bottleneck), so the lock file (ensuring that apt is not running multiple times in parallel) was not removed. In this case the lock file needs to be removed manually; otherwise all subsequent executions of apt fail. Sophisticated monitoring is required to detect such issues at runtime.

In the following Sect. 4 we present *compensation-based deployment automation* on the level of scripts and actions as an alternative to the leading convergent deployment automation approach. Our goal is to increase efficiency and robustness without additional overhead. Moreover, our approach aims to reduce the complexity of creating scripts by allowing arbitrary non-idempotent actions in it.

4   Compensation-Based Deployment Automation

The main idea of *compensation* is to implement an *undo* strategy that is run in case an error occurs during the execution of a particular script or action. Depending on the level of implementing compensation, either *compensation scripts* can be implemented to roll back the work performed by a particular script or *compensation actions* can be implemented to undo a single action. In the following Sect. 4.1 and Sect. 4.2, we discuss how compensation can be implemented on these two different levels. Moreover, Sect. 4.3 presents an approach to automatically derive compensation actions at runtime based on fine-grained snapshots.

---

[4] Ubuntu's apt package manager: http://packages.ubuntu.com/trusty/apt

4.1   Compensation on the Level of Scripts

To implement compensation on the level of scripts, a *compensation script* has to be implemented for each script to compensate the work performed by the script itself. For instance, if the script has installed parts of the WordPress application, the compensation script needs to uninstall these parts in case an error occurs during the installation. Then, the script runs again. Obviously, a proper retry strategy needs to be implemented such as defining the maximum number of retries to deal with situations where a certain issue persists. If the maximum number of retries is reached the compensation script is executed for the last time and the error gets escalated to the invoker of the script, e.g., a deployment plan implemented as a workflow [20].

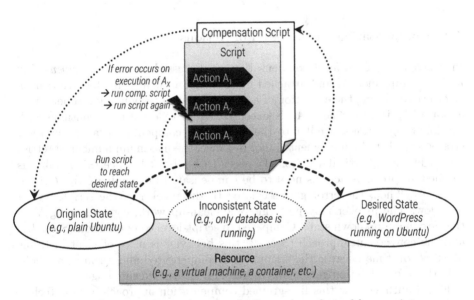

Fig. 2. Compensation script to undo the work performed by a script

Fig. 2 outlines how this coarse-grained way of implementing compensation works, considering a script as an atomic entity in terms of compensation. As an example, the following listing shows an extract of a Unix shell script to create a database and to retrieve the content of a Git repository:

```
1  #!/bin/sh
2
3  ...
4
5  echo "CREATE DATABASE $DBNAME" | mysql -u $USER
6
7  git clone http://gitserver/my_repo
```

The following extract of a Unix shell script shows how a corresponding compensation script could be implemented:

```
1  #!/bin/sh
2
3  echo "DROP DATABASE $DBNAME" | mysql -u $USER
4
5  rm -rf my_repo
6
7  ...
```

The challenge of implementing a compensation script is that the current state of the corresponding resource is unknown, depending on the point in time the error occurred during script execution. Consequently, the compensation script has to consider a lot of potential problems that may occur. This makes a compensation script hard to implement and to maintain. Thus, the following Sect. 4.2 presents a more fine-grained approach to implement compensation on the level of actions.

4.2   Compensation on the Level of Actions

In contrast to script-level compensation as discussed before, a *compensation action* is implemented and attached to each action defined in the script: if an error occurs during the execution of action A_x, the corresponding compensation action CA_x is run. Then, A_x is executed again to eventually continue with the following actions. Similar to the script-level compensation a proper retry strategy needs to be implemented. For instance, the maximum number of retries for rerunning a particular action A_x needs to be defined. Once this number is reached all previous actions need to be compensated by running CA_x, CA_{x-1}, ..., CA_1. Then, the error gets escalated to the invoker of the script, e.g., a workflow. The invoker may perform some clean-up work, e.g., removing VMs that are in an unknown state. Compared to script-level compensation (Sect. 4.1) and the convergent approach (Sect. 2) this behavior is more efficient in terms of execution time because the script is not compensated and rerun as a whole; only the affected action gets compensated and is then executed again.

Fig. 3 outlines how this fine-grained compensation approach works. Technically, compensation actions CA_x can be defined and attached on the level of command statements. For instance, the compensation action CA_3 attached to action A_3 that clones a Git repository (`git clone http://gitserver/my_repo`) could be the following to remove the cloned repository from the filesystem: `rm -rf my_repo`. Another example is sending a PUT request to a RESTful API to create a resource. For instance, the compensation action may have to send one or several DELETE requests to the API to remove the created resource and maybe other resources that were created as a result of the original PUT request. The following extract of an extended Dockerfile[5] (sequence of Unix shell commands) shows how compensation actions (`COMPENSATE` statements) can be defined and attached to actions (`RUN` statements) using cURL[6], a simple command-line HTTP client.

---

[5] Dockerfile reference: `http://docs.docker.io/reference/builder`
[6] cURL: http://curl.haxx.se

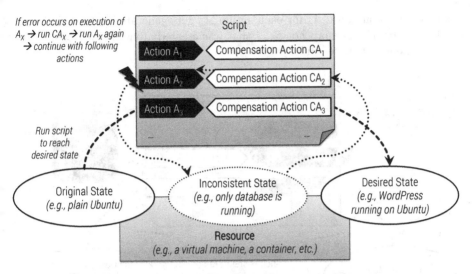

Fig. 3. Compensation actions to undo the work of individual actions

```
1   ...
2
3   RUN  curl  -H  'Content-Type:  application/json'  -X  PUT  --data  '@$ID.json'
        -u  $USER:$PASSWORD  http://.../ entries/$ID
4
5       COMPENSATE  curl  -X  DELETE  -u  $USER:$PASSWORD  http://.../ entries/
            $ID
6
7   RUN  ...
8       COMPENSATE  ...
```

Compared to compensation scripts, compensation actions are easier to implement because only the scope of one particular command statement needs to be considered. However, it may be tedious to manually implement compensation actions for each particular action defined in a script. Thus, the following Sect. 4.3 presents a compensation approach to dynamically generate compensation actions at runtime based on fine-grained snapshots.

4.3   Snapshot-Based Compensation

Action-level compensation as discussed before provides some advantages over script-level compensation because only the scope of a single action has to be considered when implementing the compensation logic. However, for scripts with a huge number of actions, many individual compensation actions have to be implemented and attached to the script. Because their creation is time-consuming and error-prone, plus they are hard to maintain, we need a means to automatically generate compensation actions. Fig. 4 shows how fine-grained snapshots can be used to capture and restore an arbitrary state of a resource. This technique can be used to create a snapshot S_0 of the original state and an additional snapshot $S_1, S_2, \ldots$ for each action $A_1, A_2, \ldots$ that was executed successfully. Moreover, a compensation action CA_x for each action A_x gets generated automatically at runtime to restore the snapshot S_{x-1} that was created after the previous action has been executed successfully.

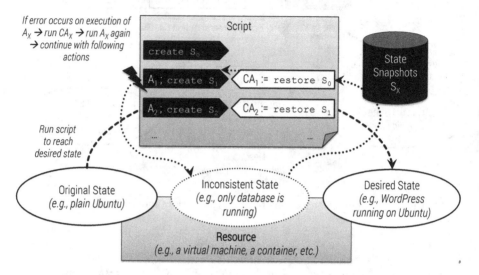

Fig. 4. Snapshot-based compensation of individual actions

Of course, the snapshot-based compensation approach can also be implemented on the level of scripts as discussed in Sect. 4.1. However, this is only feasible if all actions of a script can be compensated using snapshots and do not need custom compensation logic such as sending specific requests to external resources. In this case custom compensation actions have to be attached to the affected actions. Consequently, the snapshot-based compensation approach can be used as a fallback to generate compensation actions at runtime for all actions that do not have a custom compensation action attached. This speeds up the development of scripts because compensation actions have to be implemented only for actions that cannot rely on the snapshot-based approach to compensate their work.

5   Evaluation

Conceptually, we discussed multiple variants of compensation-based deployment automation in Sect. 4. Our evaluation compares the compensation-based approach with convergent deployment automation in terms of performance impact at runtime and difficulties at design time. We implemented the automated deployment of three different kinds of open-source Web applications, covering a set of wide-spread technologies and middleware to implement such applications.

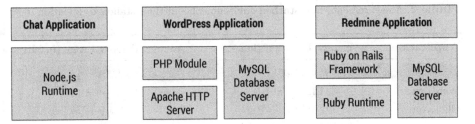

Fig. 5. Architectures of three Web applications

Fig. 5 outlines the architectures of the applications, namely a simple Chat Application[7] based on Node.js, the Ruby-based project management and bug-tracking tool Redmine[8], and WordPress[9] to run blogs based on PHP. Each application is deployed on a clean VM (1 virtual CPU clocked at 2.8 GHz, 2 GB of memory) on top of the VirtualBox hypervisor[10], running a minimalist installation of the Ubuntu OS, version 14.04.

Table 1. Measurements in clean environment and their standard deviation σ

Application	Average Duration (in sec.)	Average Memory Usage (in MB)
Clean Deployments Using Chef:		
WordPress	211 $(\sigma = 114)$	333 $(\sigma = 2)$
Chat App	265 $(\sigma = 37)$	248 $(\sigma = 1)$
Redmine	1756 $(\sigma = 191)$	1479 $(\sigma = 4)$
Clean Deployments Using Docker:		
WordPress	71 $(\sigma = 10)$	548 $(\sigma = 1)$
Chat App	249 $(\sigma = 7)$	478 $(\sigma = 2)$
Redmine	741 $(\sigma = 17)$	583 $(\sigma = 5)$

Technically, we use Chef solo[11] version 11.12.4 as a configuration management solution to implement convergent deployment automation for all three applications based on idempotent scripts (Chef cookbooks). Furthermore, we use Docker[12] version 0.9.1 as a container virtualization solution to implement action-level compensation based on fine-grained container snapshots. Consequently, we

---

[7] Chat Application: http://github.com/geekuillaume/Node.js-Chat
[8] Redmine: http://www.redmine.org
[9] WordPress: http://www.wordpress.org
[10] VirtualBox: http://www.virtualbox.org
[11] Chef solo: http://docs.opscode.com/chef_solo.html
[12] Docker: http://www.docker.io

Table 2. Measurements in disturbed environment and their standard deviation σ

Application	Average Duration (in sec.)	Average Memory Usage (in MB)
Disturbed Deployments Using Chef:		
WordPress	182 $(\sigma = 84)$	334 $(\sigma = 3)$
Chat App	394 $(\sigma = 78)$	237 $(\sigma = 5)$
Redmine	1948 $(\sigma = 262)$	1479 $(\sigma = 2)$
Disturbed Deployments Using Docker:		
WordPress	74 $(\sigma = 6)$	779 $(\sigma = 1)$
Chat App	258 $(\sigma = 36)$	576 $(\sigma = 59)$
Redmine	991 $(\sigma = 120)$	1260 $(\sigma = 268)$

implemented scripts as Dockerfiles (sequence of Unix shell commands) that do exactly the same as the Chef cookbooks created before, but without being idempotent. Based on these implementations we run the deployment process of each application using both Chef and Docker in two different environments: the *clean* environment allows the deployment process to run without any errors; the *disturbed* environment emulates networking issues and memory bottlenecks by blocking TCP connections and killing system processes. We run each of the 24 combinations five times, so table 1 and table 2 present the average duration, the average memory usage, and their standard deviation. Each run is triggered using the same setup without any pre-cached container images or beneficial preparations. In the following Sect. 6 we discuss the results of our evaluation based on the measurements presented in table 1 and table 2 as well as the experience we gained during the implementation of the scripts following different deployment automation approaches.

6   Discussion

By analyzing the measurements presented in Sect. 5 we see that the compensation-based deployment automation approach with snapshots on the level of actions based on Docker consistently has a better performance in terms of deployment duration than the convergent approach based on Chef. This shows that repetitively executing an idempotent script to reach the desired state is more time-consuming than using a compensation-based approach on the level of actions. Moreover, the convergent approach may require more resources because declarative configuration definitions such as Chef cookbooks need to be compiled to imperative command statements at runtime. However, especially for deployment processes that have a shorter duration the memory consumption for convergent deployment automation is less compared to the compensation-based approach. This manifests the overhead of a snapshot-based approach where fine-grained, incremental snapshots are cached to quickly restore the state captured after the last successfully executed action. This happens preventively, even in case the snapshots are not used, e.g., if no error occurs (clean environment). For longer-running deployment processes with more memory consumption in general such as the one of Redmine this overhead becomes less relevant, so in some cases such as the Docker-based deployment of Redmine the memory usage is even less compared to the corresponding Chef-based deployment.

In a disturbed environment that may be similar to an error-prone Cloud environment, where network issues appear and memory bottlenecks occur, the gap between the compensation-based and the convergent approach is significantly larger in terms of deployment duration. In this case compensation clearly outperforms convergence. Considering the design and implementation of scripts the compensation-based scripts and actions are easier to implement because they do not have to be idempotent as in the convergent approach. Moreover, most compensation actions can be automatically generated at runtime based on snapshots, so the implementation of custom compensation actions is not necessary for most actions. Fine-grained snapshots are also a convenient tool when developing, testing, and debugging scripts: snapshots can be created at any point in time to capture a working state and build upon this state, always having the possibility to quickly restore this state. Without using snapshots the whole script has to be executed for each test run. This can be time-consuming in case of more complex scripts that do not terminate after a few seconds already.

7   Related Work

Today, compensation techniques for deploying and managing infrastructure resources, middleware, and application components are mainly used by workflows on the orchestration level: workflows or plans based on standardized languages such as BPMN [14] or BPEL [12] are used on a higher level to coordinate the execution of scripts, API calls etc. [1,6,20]. Fig. 6 provides an overview of a possible interrelation between higher-level plans (e.g., BPEL workflows) defining the overarching flow of activities and the scripts SCR_y that actually manage the states ST_n of the underlying resources R_m that are involved. Compensation activities can be defined to compensate the work of another activity in case an error occurs [9,18,8]. In this example the *install* activity triggers the execution of script SCR_1 on R_1. If an error occurs, e.g., during the execution of the *install* activity, the attached *compensate* activity is triggered to run script SCR_2, which could be some kind of compensation script.

As an alternative to workflows, model-based approaches such as application topology models can be used to orchestrate scripts in a declarative manner. The Topology and Orchestration Specification for Cloud Applications (TOSCA) [13] is an emerging standard to specify such models. Moreover, there are provider- and tooling-specific approaches to build topology templates such as Amazon's

CloudFormation[13], OpenStack Heat[14], and Juju bundles[15]. All these approaches utilize scripts for lower-level tasks such as installing and configuring packages on VMs. Thus, the compensation-based deployment automation approaches presented in this paper can be combined with any of these higher-level approaches to ease the development of underlying scripts and to enhance the overall efficiency and robustness at runtime. Previous work [19,20] shows how to implement separation of concerns for plans that invoke and orchestrate scripts and services.

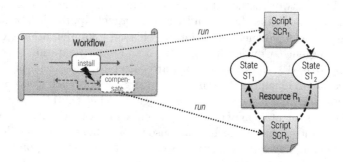

Fig. 6. Activities and compensation activities in workflows

8   Conclusions

Convergent deployment automation based on idempotent scripts is the leading paradigm implemented by wide-spread DevOps tools such as Puppet [16] and Chef [11]. We discussed the issues and deficiencies of this approach that occur at design time and at runtime: idempotent scripts are hard to test and to implement; due to their repetitive execution to converge a resource toward a desired state, the scripts' efficiency and robustness is not ideal. Based on these deficiencies we presented compensation-based deployment automation as an alternative to the convergent approach. We discussed how to implement compensation on the level of scripts and on the level of individual actions. Moreover, we showed how action-level compensation can be implemented using fine-grained snapshots to minimize the effort of implementing custom compensation actions. Our evaluation of compensation-based deployment automation compared to the convergent approach showed:

- Compensation is more robust, preventing a resource such as a VM from hanging in an inconsistent state without converging toward the desired state anymore

---

[13] Amazon CloudFormation: http://aws.amazon.com/cloudformation
[14] OpenStack Heat: http://wiki.openstack.org/wiki/Heat
[15] Juju bundles: http://juju.ubuntu.com/docs/charms-bundles.html

- Action-level compensation is always more efficient in terms of deployment duration
- Compensation may consume slightly more memory in some cases
- Compensation is easier to implement because scripts and actions do not have to be idempotent
- Snapshot-based compensation eases the development of scripts because compensation actions such as *restore snapshot S_x* can be automatically generated at runtime for most actions defined in a script

Currently, one major drawback of the compensation-based approach is its minimalist tooling support. We were using Docker as a container virtualization solution and Dockerfiles (construction plans for Docker containers) as scripts that can be compensated based on fine-grained container snapshots. In terms of future work we plan to extend existing domain-specific languages such as the ones used by Chef, Puppet, and Docker to seamlessly integrate the compensation approaches discussed in this paper. For instance, Chef can be extended to capture and restore fine-grained container snapshots automatically in the background, moving away from the inefficient strategy of running the whole script again and again. Another approach would be to automatically generate Dockerfiles from Chef scripts and then use Docker to execute them based on Docker's compensation and snapshot capabilities. In addition to deployment we plan to extend the scope of our research to cover further lifecycle operations that are relevant after the deployment phase. Existing approaches such as Cloud Foundry[16] centered around the platform-as-a-service model may be the technical foundation to consider these lifecycle operations such as scaling certain application components. Furthermore, we plan to extend our evaluation, including additional measurements such as the disk storage used for storing snapshots.

Acknowledgments. This work was partially funded by the BMWi project CloudCycle (01MD11023).

References

1. Breitenbücher, U., Binz, T., Kopp, O., Leymann, F.: Pattern-based Runtime Management of Composite Cloud Applications. In: Proceedings of the 3rd International Conference on Cloud Computing and Services Science. SciTePress (2013)
2. Günther, S., Haupt, M., Splieth, M.: Utilizing Internal Domain-Specific Languages for Deployment and Maintenance of IT Infrastructures. Tech. rep., Very Large Business Applications Lab Magdeburg, Fakultät für Informatik, Otto-von-Guericke-Universität Magdeburg (2010)
3. Humble, J., Molesky, J.: Why Enterprises Must Adopt Devops to Enable Continuous Delivery. Cutter IT Journal 24 (2011)
4. Hummer, W., Rosenberg, F., Oliveira, F., Eilam, T.: Testing Idempotence for Infrastructure as Code. In: Eyers, D., Schwan, K. (eds.) Middleware 2013. LNCS, vol. 8275, pp. 368–388. Springer, Heidelberg (2013)

---

[16] Cloud Foundry: http://cloudfoundry.org

5. Hüttermann, M.: DevOps for Developers. Apress (2012)
6. Kopp, O., Binz, T., Breitenbücher, U., Leymann, F.: BPMN4TOSCA: A Domain-Specific Language to Model Management Plans for Composite Applications. In: Mendling, J., Weidlich, M. (eds.) BPMN 2012. LNBIP, vol. 125, pp. 38–52. Springer, Heidelberg (2012)
7. Leymann, F.: Cloud Computing: The Next Revolution in IT. In: Photogrammetric Week 2009. Wichmann Verlag (2009)
8. Liu, F., Danciu, V.A., Kerestey, P.: A Framework for Automated Fault Recovery Planning in Large-Scale Virtualized Infrastructures. In: Brennan, R., Fleck II, J., van der Meer, S. (eds.) MACE 2010. LNCS, vol. 6473, pp. 113–123. Springer, Heidelberg (2010)
9. Machado, G.S., Daitx, F.F., da Costa Cordeiro, W.L., Both, C.B., Gaspary, L.P., Granville, L.Z., Bartolini, C., Sahai, A., Trastour, D., Saikoski, K.: Enabling Rollback Support in IT Change Management Systems. In: IEEE Network Operations and Management Symposium, NOMS 2008, pp. 347–354. IEEE (2008)
10. Mell, P., Grance, T.: The NIST Definition of Cloud Computing. National Institute of Standards and Technology (2011)
11. Nelson-Smith, S.: Test-Driven Infrastructure with Chef. O'Reilly Media, Inc. (2013)
12. OASIS: Web Services Business Process Execution Language (BPEL) Version 2.0 (2007)
13. OASIS: Topology and Orchestration Specification for Cloud Applications (TOSCA) Version 1.0, Committee Specification 01 (2013), http://docs.oasis-open.org/tosca/TOSCA/v1.0/cs01/TOSCA-v1.0-cs01.html
14. OMG: Business Process Model and Notation (BPMN) Version 2.0 (2011)
15. Soltesz, S., Pötzl, H., Fiuczynski, M.E., Bavier, A., Peterson, L.: Container-based Operating System Virtualization: A Scalable, High-Performance Alternative to Hypervisors. ACM SIGOPS Operating Systems Review 41, 275–287 (2007)
16. Turnbull, J., McCune, J.: Pro Puppet. Apress (2011)
17. Vaughan-Nichols, S.J.: New Approach to Virtualization is a Lightweight. Computer 39(11), 12–14 (2006)
18. Weber, I., Wada, H., Fekete, A., Liu, A., Bass, L.: Automatic Undo for Cloud Management via AI Planning. In: Proceedings of the Workshop on Hot Topics in System Dependability (2012)
19. Wettinger, J., Behrendt, M., Binz, T., Breitenbücher, U., Breiter, G., Leymann, F., Moser, S., Schwertle, I., Spatzier, T.: Integrating Configuration Management with Model-Driven Cloud Management Based on TOSCA. In: Proceedings of the 3rd International Conference on Cloud Computing and Services Science. SciTePress (2013)
20. Wettinger, J., Binz, T., Breitenbücher, U., Kopp, O., Leymann, F., Zimmermann, M.: Unified Invocation of Scripts and Services for Provisioning, Deployment, and Management of Cloud Applications Based on TOSCA. In: Proceedings of the 4th International Conference on Cloud Computing and Services Science. SciTePress (2014)
21. Wilder, B.: Cloud Architecture Patterns. O'Reilly Media, Inc. (2012)

On Enabling Time-Aware Consistency of Collaborative Cross-Organisational Business Processes

Saoussen Cheikhrouhou[1], Slim Kallel[1],
Nawal Guermouche[2,3], and Mohamed Jmaiel[1]

[1] ReDCAD Laboratory, University of Sfax, Tunisia
saoussen.cheikhrouhou@redcad.org, slim.kallel@fsegs.rnu.tn,
mohamed.jmaiel@enis.rnu.tn
[2] CNRS-LAAS, 7 avenue du colonel Roche, F-31400 Toulouse, France
[3] Univ de Toulouse, INSA, LAAS, F-31400 Toulouse, France
nawal.guermouche@laas.fr

Abstract. Collaborative Inter-Organisational Business Processes (IOBPs) are a major step in automating and supporting collaborations of organisations. In this context, collaborative IOBP are usually constrained by hard timing requirements. This paper proposes an approach for analyzing *temporal consistency* of collaborative IOBPs. The aim is to verify temporal consistency of IOBP and to provide the enactment service with largest intervals as starting time windows of the processes. The proposed approach enables organisations to detect, early on, temporal inconsistencies that may constitute obstacles towards their interaction. Indeed, it provides an enactment service, which provides each partner with information about temporal restrictions to respect by its own processes in accordance with the overall temporal constraints of all involved processes.

Keywords: Temporal Constraints, Collaborative Inter-organisational Business Process (IOBP), Temporal Consistency analysis.

1 Introduction

In today's organisations, business entities often operate across organisational boundaries giving rise to inter-organisational collaborations, which have received a great deal of attention during the last years. The reduction of commercial barriers helps organisations to create value by combining processes, increasing speed to market and reaching a bigger market share. On the basis of these expectations, we can find among others, the following factor: *to maximize the ability to offer competitive products or services within restrictive deadlines.*

In the context of such extended collaborations, collaborative inter-organisational business processes, or *IOBP* for short, are becoming one of the dominant elements in designing and implementing complex inter-organisational

X. Franch et al. (Eds.): ICSOC 2014, LNCS 8831, pp. 351–358, 2014.

business applications. IOBP are typically subject to conflicting temporal constraints of the involved organisations. Hence, *temporal consistency* of business processes are one of the important and critical ingredients to consider.

Temporal consistency analysis of IOBP aims at verifying the capability of a set of processes to interact by exchanging messages in a successful way so that all the temporal constraints are respected. Among research works which have investigated the temporal consistency analysis problem, we mention the work detailed in [1,2] which deals with a collaboration constituted by only two processes. Moreover, theses works assume that all the processes must start at the same time. This is very restrictive and does not correspond to real life scenario applications where processes can belong to different organisations with different geographic and time zones.

In this paper we tackle the problem of analyzing the temporal consistency of IOBP. Our purpose is to provide an approach enabling organisations to detect, early on, temporal inconsistencies that may constitute obstacles towards their interaction. In case of temporal inconsistencies, our approach provides an enactment service, which allows to define automatically temporal constraints so that the formed collaborative IOBP will carry out successful timed collaborations.

This paper is organized as follows. A motivating example is introduced in Section 2. Section 3 presents a brief description of the timed model we consider and exhibits the proposed consistency analysis approach. A review of related literature is given in Section 4. Finally, Section 5 concludes.

2   Motivating Example

To illustrate the features of the proposed approach, we introduce a Web shopping scenario inspired by Amazon [3]. The booking process can be described as follows : When ordering books on-line, a collaboration between a customer, a seller company like Amazon and a shipper company like FedEx is established. Fig. 1 shows such a collaboration with the help of an excerpt of an IOBP involving the processes of different partners. The BPMN 2.0 standard, is used for the depiction of the IOBP. This latter represents a simple scenario in which the customer sends an order to the seller, makes payment and expects to receive the items from a shipper.

As shown in Fig. 1, different temporal constraints can be assigned to business processes. Theses constraints include duration of activities (e.g., the duration of the activity *Ship products* is 24 *hours*) and deadlines (e.g., $D_{Seller} = 35$ *hours* to denote that the execution of the *Seller* process takes no longer than 35 *hours*).

Additionally, dashed lines between activities depict message exchange. For instance, there is a message exchange between activities *Send order* of the *Customer* and *Receive order* of the *Seller*. In spite each business process is consistent against its temporal constraints, the IOBP does not intrinsically guarantee the satisfaction of the whole temporal constraints such as those related to deadlines. We see significant potential in proposing a consistency analysis approach. Indeed, it is clear that considering temporal constraints of the example while respecting process deadlines is a fastidious and error prone task.

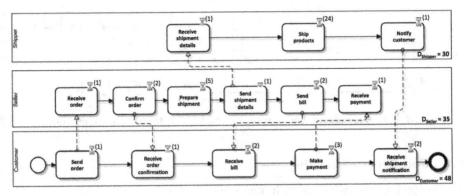

Fig. 1. Web shopping collaboration

3 Consistency Analysis of Inter-Organisational Business Processes

Given the problem description in terms of an IOBP; a set of communicating processes; enriched with a set of temporal constraints, the aim of the consistency analysis approach proposed in this paper is to verify temporal consistency of IOBP. We first describe the formalism of timed graphs, then we present the consistency checking steps that we propose.

3.1 Timed Business Process Modelling

As the basic modeling formalism we use *timed graphs* proposed in [1,2]. Fig. 2 shows the representation of a node with its duration, its earliest possible start and latest allowed end values.

Activity Name (Ai)	Activity Duration (Ai.d)
Earliest Possible Start (Ai.eps)	Latest Allowed End (Ai.lae)

Fig. 2. An activity node in the timed graph

In the sequel of the paper, we refer to activities of the motivating example with abbreviations using first letters' name of activities (eg. RSD to denote *Receive shipment details*). Fig. 3 exhibits the timed graphs of the processes of different partners involved in the motivating example, namely the *Shipper* (P_{Ship}), the *Seller* (P_{Sel}) and the *Customer* (P_{Cust}) processes. For more details about the calculation of the timed graph, we refer the reader to [1,2].

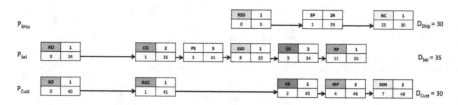

Fig. 3. Timed graphs of the *Shipper*, the *Seller* and the *Customer* processes

3.2 Consistency Checking Steps

The proposed approach consists in two steps.

-Analysing consistency of pairwise processes (Step 1) In order to check if **two processes** are temporally consistent, it must be checked if the execution intervals of both communicating activities overlap [2]. Hence, in order to check the temporal consistency of two communicating activities it must be checked if there is any temporal interval in which both activities can execute. In this context, we assume that the communication time is very small, thus, it is negligible.

$P_i \leftrightarrow P_j{}^1$ denotes that P_i and P_j are two processes exchanging at least one message, say between activities A_i and A_j. From the calcultaed timed graphs of both processes, we can deduce $A_i.[A_i.eps, A_i.lae]$ and $A_j.[A_j.eps, A_j.lae]$. In order to ensure that both P_i and P_j are consistent, we should ensure that the execution interval of all communicating activities, for instance A_i and A_j overlap [2].

Consider now clock C_i which is reset on the starting time of process P_i. Consequently, according to C_i, P_j should start executing on a time lag $x \in P_{j/C_i}$. P_{j/C_i} denotes the interval delimiting the starting time of process P_j according to clock C_i while considering only direct communications between P_i and P_j. This time lag will shift the execution window of the communicating activity,A_j to be $A_j.[A_j.eps + x, A_j.lae + x]$. The condition of consistency is :

$$[A_j.eps + x, A_j.lae + x] \bigcap [A_i.eps, A_i.lae] \neq \emptyset \quad (1)$$

Let $x \in P_{j/C_i}$ be the set of solutions satisfying the consistency condition (Eq.1).

$$P_{j/C_i} = \begin{cases} [min_{ji}, max_{ji}] = [A_i.eps - A_j.lae, A_i.lae - A_j.eps] \neq \emptyset & (2.a) \\ \emptyset & (2.b) \end{cases}$$

If there is an overlap of the execution interval of communicating activities, namely A_i and A_j, those activities are temporally consistent (Eq. 2.a). Otherwise, A_i and A_j are temporally inconsistent (Eq. 2.b). Namely, in order to decide if processes P_i and P_j are temporally consistent, all pairs of communicating activities, must be temporally consistent[2].

Conversely, if we consider C_j which is reset on the starting time of process P_j. We should find the following :

---

[1] Equivalent to $P_j \leftrightarrow P_i$ because $\leftrightarrow$ is commutative.

$$P_{i/C_j} = \begin{cases} [min_{ij}, max_{ij}] = [-max_{ji}, -min_{ji}] & \text{if } P_{j/C_i} \neq \emptyset \text{ (3)} \\ \emptyset & \text{otherwise.} \end{cases}$$

Starting from a set of processes, namely three processes P_i, P_j, and P_k. The output of *step 1* consists in bringing out the starting time bounds of each pairwise communicating timed processes. as follows :

$$\forall \{l, m\} \subset \{i, j, k\}, P_{l/C_m} \text{ is computed.}$$

Step 1 is considered to be *completed successfully* iff $\forall \{l, m\} \subset \{i, j, k\}, P_{l/C_m} \neq \emptyset$ and *not completed successfully* otherwise.

As an example, let's consider the timed graphs of the shipper (P_{Ship}), the seller (P_{Sel}), and the customer (P_{Cust}) processes of the motivating example as depicted in Fig. 3. We are mainly interested in communicating activities, namely activities that are sender or receiver of the same message e.g. activities "Send order" (SO) of customer and "receive order" (RO) of seller (denoted $(SO \leftrightarrow RO)$) In the following, we apply Step 1 of the approach on pairwise communicating processes of the motivating example.

– $P_{Cust} \leftrightarrow P_{Sel}$:
$(SO \leftrightarrow RO) : SO.[0 + x, 40 + x] \cap RO.[0, 24] \neq \emptyset$ then $x \in [-40, 24]$
$(ROC \leftrightarrow CO) : ROC.[1 + x, 41 + x] \cap CO.[1, 26] \neq \emptyset$ then $x \in [-40, 25]$
$(SB \leftrightarrow RB) : RB.[2 + x, 43 + x] \cap SB.[9, 34] \neq \emptyset$ then $x \in [-34, 32]$
$(MP \leftrightarrow RP): MP.[4 + x, 46 + x] \cap RP.[11, 35] \neq \emptyset$ then $x \in [-35, 31]$
Hence, $P_{Cust/C_{Sel}} = [-34, 24]$ (i.e. $[-40, 24] \cap [-40, 25] \cap [-34, 32] \cap [-35, 31]$)
– the same applies to $P_{Ship} \leftrightarrow P_{Sel} = [3, 32]$ and $P_{Ship} \leftrightarrow P_{Cust} = [-23, 23]$.

For example, the interval $P_{Cust/C_{Sel}} = [-34, 24]$ limits the starting time of the Customer process P_{Cust} to start not earlier than 34 hours before and no later than 24 hours after the starting time of the Seller process P_{Sel}. Assume then that the process P_{Sel} starts at time point 0 and P_{Cust} starts at time point - 21 which means that this latter starts execution 21 hours before the process P_{Sel} starts. Since $-21 \in [-34, 24]$, the two processes suceed all their communication and hence they are consistent. Indeed, considering these latter starting times, we have $RO.[0, 24] \cap SO.[-21, 19] \neq \emptyset$, $CO.[1, 26] \cap ROC.[-20, 20] \neq \emptyset$, $SB.[9, 34] \cap RB.[-19, 13] \neq \emptyset$, and $RP.[11, 35] \cap MP.[-17, 25] \neq \emptyset$. Nevertheless, if the process P_{Cust} begins 26 hours after the starting time of process P_{Sel}, we obtain, $RO.[0, 24]$ and $SO.[26, 66]$. It is clear that $[0, 24] \cap [26, 66] = \emptyset$, and the two processes are not consistent since $26 \notin P_{Cust/C_{Sel}} = [-34, 24]$.
Step 1 is considered to be *completed successfully* since $\forall \{l, m\} \subset \{Ship, Sel, Cust\}$, $P_{l/C_m} \neq \emptyset$ (see Eq. 3).

Step 1 of our consistency approach considers only direct communication links between processes. For instance, given direct comminications between processes P_j and P_i one the one hand and between P_k and P_i on the other. *Step 1* computes the starting times of P_j (P_{j/C_i}) and P_k (resp. P_{k/C_i}) related to the starting time of P_i. In such a way, we have not yet considered the indirect communication between P_j and P_k; for the calculation of both P_{j/C_i} and P_{k/C_i}. Supposing at least one communication between processes P_j and P_k, additional calculations must be performed in order to adjust the intervals P_{j/C_i} and P_{k/C_i} accordingly; which will be the main focus of *Step 2*.

- **Analyzing consistency of multiple processes (Step 2)**

The aim of *Step 2* is to gather solutions for temporal inconsistencies while considering all involved processes in the IOBP (i.e. all communications between the processes). Indeed, it provides a set of constraints on the starting time of processes such that if each process satisfies the constraint, the whole collaboration is still possible to be successfully carried out. *Step 2* requires that *Step 1* be *completed successfully*.

In an inter-organisational business process, we can deduce implicit temporal relations beyond those resulting from direct communications between P_j and P_i. We argue that the communication between processes P_j and P_k, has an impact on both time intervals P_{j/C_i} and P_{k/C_i}.

In our approach, the transitivity behavior of the temporal relationships introduced by Allen in [4] helps to deduce a new interval P'_{j/C_i} from the two intervals P_{j/C_k} and P_{k/C_i} (the result of Step1). P'_{j/C_i} denotes the interval delimiting the starting time of process P_j related to the start of process P_i (related to clock C_i) while considering **indirect communication links** between processes P_i and P_j (precisely, the communication between P_j and P_k and between P_k and P_i). Given $P_{j/C_k} = [min_{jk}, max_{jk}]$ and $P_{k/C_i} = [min_{ki}, max_{ki}]$, P'_{j/C_i} is calculated as follows: $P'_{j/C_i} = [min_{jk} + min_{ki}, max_{jk} + max_{ki}]$.

As a result, we introduce P_{j/C_i}^{IOBP} to denote the resulting interval delimiting the starting time of process P_j regarding the starting time of process P_i while considering **both direct and indirect communication links** as follows :

$$P_{j/C_i}^{IOBP} = P_{j/C_i} \cap P'_{j/C_i} \quad (4)$$

Given processes P_i, P_j, and P_k on which we have already conducted *Step 1* of the approach. The output of *step 2* of our algorithm consists in bringing out the starting time bounds of each process P_l regarding another process P_m while considering all communication links between P_i, P_j, and P_k as follows :

$$\forall \{l, m\} \subset \{i, j, k\}, P_{l/C_m}^{IOBP} \text{ is computed.}$$

Consider again the timed graphs of the shipper (P_{Ship}), the seller (P_{Sel}), and the customer (P_{Cust}) processes of the motivating example as depicted in Fig. 3. Provided also with the starting time intervals resulting from *Step 1* of our approach, namely, $P_{Ship/C_{Sel}} = [3, 32]$, $P_{Cust/C_{Sel}} = [-34, 24]$, and $P_{Ship/C_{Cust}} = [-23, 23]$. Let's conduct now *Step 2* of the approach.
$P_{Ship}^{IOBP}{}_{/C_{Sel}} = P_{Ship/C_{Sel}} \cap P'_{Ship/C_{Sel}} = [3, 32] \cap [-57, 47] = [3, 32]$. (
$P'_{Ship/C_{Sel}} = [-57, 47] = [-23-34, 23+24]$ deduced from $P_{Ship/C_{Cust}} = [-23, 23]$
and $P_{Cust/C_{Sel}} = [-34, 24]$). The same applies to $P_{Cust/C_{Sel}}^{IOBP} = [-20, 24]$.

Step 2 of the proposed approach has tightened the intervals $P_{Cust/C_{Sel}}$ = $[-34, 24]$ to be $P^{IOBP}_{Cust}{}_{/C_{Sel}}$ = $[-20, 24]$ and has no impact on $P_{Ship/C_{Sel}}$ since $P^{IOBP}_{Ship}{}_{/C_{Sel}}$ = $[3, 32]$. The aim behind Step 2 is to omit some starting time points leading to consistent pairwise processes while considering only direct communication links between processes but fail to ensure consistent IOBP. Let's analyze the consistency of the IOBP after conducting Step 2 on the motivating example for the same starting time points presented above (suppose that P_{Sel} starts at time point 0 and P_{Cust} starts at time point -21). As argued in Step 1, P_{Sel} and P_{Cust} are consistent since all execution intervals of their communicating activities overlap. Neverthless, these starting times fail eventual communications between P_{Ship} and P_{Cust}. Given $P^{IOBP}_{Ship}{}_{/C_{Sel}}$ = $[3, 32]$, the execution time window of the activity *Notify Customer* (NC) balance between NC.[28, 33] (for the starting time 3) and NC.[57, 62] (for the starting time 32) and there is no eventual overlap with RSN.[-14, 27]. Hence, we can conclude that P_{Ship} and P_{Cust} are not consistent and the IOBP is not consistent anymore. If we consider now the intervals resulting from Step2, the proposed approach ensures that it exists starting time points leading to consistent inter-organisational business process. For instance, P_{Sel} starts at time point 0, P_{Ship} starts at time point 4, and P_{Cust} starts at time point -15. Indeed, all execution intervals of all communicating activities of the IOBP overlap.

4 Related Work

The approach of Bettini et al. [5] provides temporal constraints reasoning and management tool offering the consistency checking of temporal requirements in workflows systems. Second, it monitors workflow activities and predicts their starting and ending time. Finally it provides the enactment service with useful temporal information for activity scheduling. Reluctantly, consistency algorithms have only been defined for activities of a single process and does not consider collaborative processes exchanging messages.

In [6,7,8,9,10], the authors use temporal properties in order to analyse the timed compatibility in Web service compositions. Several temporal conflicts are identified in asynchronous web service interactions. In this approach, the focus has been on the construction of a correct Web service composition using mediators. Nevertheless, the scope of this approach is limited to the verification of time constraints only caused by message interaction between services of the process.

In [11], Du et al. present a Petri net-based method to compose Web services by adding a mediation net to deal with message mismatches. Their approach implements both timed compatibility checking by generating modular timed state graphs. Compared to our work, they can only work at service level, and have limitation to cover the temporal dependencies of involved services in a business collaboration.

The approach proposed by Eder in [1,2] is closely related to ours since it uses the concept of timed graphs while analysing the consistency issue in inter-organisational collaborations. Nevertheless, this work is too restrictive since it assumes that both processes begin at the same time. Furthermore, only the case with two partners is considered.

5 Conclusion

In this paper, we proposed an approach aiming at discovering temporal inconsistencies that may constitute obstacles towards the interaction of business processes. Additionally, it gathers for solutions to resolve the temporal inconsistencies by providing each partner with temporal restrictions about the starting time of its processes in accordance with the overall temporal constraints of all involved processes. Consequently, as long as each process starts executing within the specified time period, the overall temporal constraints of the IOBP will be satisfied. Currently, we are working on a tool support for the proposed approach based on the Eclipse BPMN2 modeler.

References

1. Eder, J., Panagos, E., Rabinovich, M.I.: Time Constraints in Workflow Systems. In: Jarke, M., Oberweis, A. (eds.) CAiSE 1999. LNCS, vol. 1626, pp. 286–300. Springer, Heidelberg (1999)
2. Eder, J., Tahamtan, A.: Temporal Consistency of View Based Interorganizational Workflows. In: Kaschek, R., Kop, C., Steinberger, C., Fliedl, G. (eds.) Synchronization Techniques for Chaotic Commun. Syst. LNBIP, vol. 5, pp. 96–107. Springer, Heidelberg (2008)
3. van der Aalst, W.M.P., Weske, M.: The P2P Approach to Interorganizational Workflows. In: Dittrich, K.R., Geppert, A., Norrie, M. C. (eds.) CAiSE 2001. LNCS, vol. 2068, pp. 140–156. Springer, Heidelberg (2001)
4. Allen, J.F.: Maintaining knowledge about temporal intervals. Communications of the ACM 26(11), 832–843 (1983)
5. Bettini, C., Wang, X.S., Jajodia, S.: Temporal Reasoning in Workflow Systems. Distributed and Parallel Databases (2002)
6. Guermouche, N., Godart, C.: Timed Conversational Protocol Based Approach for Web Services Analysis. In: Maglio, P.P., Weske, M., Yang, J., Fantinato, M. (eds.) ICSOC 2010. LNCS, vol. 6470, pp. 603–611. Springer, Heidelberg (2010)
7. Guermouche, N., Godart, C.: Timed model checking based approach for web services analysis. In: ICWS. IEEE CS (2009)
8. Cheikhrouhou, S., Kallel, S., Guermouche, N., Jmaiel, M.: Enhancing Formal Specification and Verification of Temporal Constraints in Business Processes. In: Proceedings of the 11th IEEE International Conference on Services Computing (SCC). IEEE Computer Society (2014)
9. Kallel, S., Charfi, A., Dinkelaker, T., Mezini, M., Jmaiel, M.: Specifying and Monitoring Temporal Properties in Web Services Compositions. In: ECOWS. IEEE CS (2009)
10. Guidara, I., Guermouche, N., Chaari, T., Tazi, S., Jmaiel, M.: Pruning Based Service Selection Approach under Qos and Temporal Constraints. In: ICWS. IEEE CS (2014)
11. Du, Y., Tan, W., Zhou, M.: Timed compatibility analysis of web service composition: A modular approach based on petri nets. IEEE Transaction on Automation Science and Engineering (2014)

Weak Conformance between
Process Models and Synchronized Object Life Cycles

Andreas Meyer and Mathias Weske

Hasso Plattner Institute at the University of Potsdam
{Andreas.Meyer,Mathias.Weske}@hpi.de

Abstract. Process models specify behavioral execution constraints between activities as well as between activities and data objects. A data object is characterized by its states and state transitions represented as object life cycle. For process
execution, all behavioral execution constraints must be correct. Correctness can
be verified via soundness checking which currently only considers control flow
information. For data correctness, conformance between a process model and its
object life cycles is checked. Current approaches abstract from dependencies between multiple data objects and require fully specified process models although,
in real-world process repositories, often underspecified models are found. Coping
with these issues, we apply the notion of weak conformance to process models
to tell whether each time an activity needs to access a data object in a particular
state, it is guaranteed that the data object is in or can reach the expected state.
Further, we introduce an algorithm for an integrated verification of control flow
correctness and weak data conformance using soundness checking.

1 Introduction

Business process management allows organizations to specify their processes struc-
turally by means of process models, which are then used for process execution. Process
models comprise multiple perspectives with two of them receiving the most attention
in recent years: control flow and data [22]. These describe behavioral execution constraints between activities as well as between activities and data objects. It is usually
accepted that control flow drives execution of a process model. While checking control
flow correctness using soundness [1] is an accepted method, correctness regarding data
and control flow is not addressed in sufficient detail. In this paper, we describe a formalism to integrate control flow and data perspectives that is used to check for correctness.

In order to achieve safe execution of a process model, it must be ensured that every
time an activity attempts to access a data object, the data object is in a certain expected
data state or is able to reach the expected data state from the current one, i.e., data specification within a process model must conform to relevant object life cycles, where each
describes the allowed behavior of a distinct class of data objects. Otherwise, the execution of a process model may deadlock. To check for deadlock-free execution in terms
of data constraints, the notion of object life cycle conformance [9, 20] is used. This approach has some restrictions with respect to data constraint specification, because each
single change of a data object as specified in the object life cycle, we refer to as data
state transition, must be performed by some activity. [21] relaxes this limitation such

X. Franch et al. (Eds.): ICSOC 2014, LNCS 8831, pp. 359–367, 2014.

that several state changes can be subsumed within one activity. However, gaps within the data constraints specification, i.e., implicit data state transitions, are not allowed although some other process may be responsible of performing a state change of an object, i.e., these approaches can only check whether an object is in a certain expected state. We assume that implicit data state transitions get realized by an external entity or by detailed implementations of process model activities. In real world process repositories, usually many of those *underspecified* process models exist, which motivates the introduction of the notion of weak conformance [13]. It allows to also check underspecified models.

Additionally, in real world, often dependencies between multiple data objects exist; e.g., an order may only be shipped to the customer after the payment is recognized. Non of above approaches supports this. Thus, we utilize the concept of synchronized object life cycles that allows to specify dependencies between data states as well as state transitions of different object life cycles [16]. Based thereon, we extend the notion of weak conformance and describe how to compute it for a given process model and the corresponding object life cycles including synchronizations. We utilize the well established method of soundness checking [1] to check for process model correctness. For mapping a process model to a Petri net, we utilize an extension covering data constraints [16] to a widely-used control flow mapping [4] to enable an integrated checking of control flow and data correctness. Further, fundamentals and preliminaries required in the scope of this paper are discussed in Section 2 of our report [16].

The remainder is structured as follows. First, we discuss weak conformance in general and compare it to existing conformance notions in Section 2 before we introduce the extended notion of weak conformance in Section 3. Afterwards, we discuss the procedure for integrated correctness checking in Section 4. Section 5 is devoted to related work before we conclude the paper in Section 6.

2   Weak Conformance

The notion of weak conformance has been initially proposed in [13] as extension to the notion of object life cycle conformance [9, 20] to allow the support of underspecified process models. A fully specified process model contains all reads and writes of data nodes by all activities. Additionally, each activity reads and writes at least one data node except for the first and last activities, which may lack reading respectively writing a data node in case they only create respectively consume a data node.

In contrast, underspecified process models may lack some reads or writes of data nodes such that they are implicit, performed by some other process, or they are hidden in aggregated activities changing the state multiple times with respect to the object life cycle. Though, full support of underspecified process models requires that the process model may omit state changes of data nodes although they are specified in the object life cycle.

Table 1. Applicability and time complexity of data conformance computation algorithms

Attribute	[9, 20]	[21]	[13]	this
Full specification	+	+	+	+
Underspecification	-	o	+	+
Synchronization	-	-	-	+
Complexity	exp.	poly.	–	exp.

In this paper, we extend the notion of weak conformance to also support object life cycle synchronization. First, we compare different approaches to check for conformance between a process model and object life cycles. Table 1 lists the applicability and specifies the time complexity of the computation algorithms for approaches described in [9, 20], [21], [13], and this paper. The notion from [9, 20] requires fully specified process models and abstracts from inter-dependencies between object life cycles by not considering them for conformance checking in case they are modeled. Conformance computation is done in polynomial time. In [21], underspecification of process models is partly supported, because a single activity may change multiple data states at once (aggregated activity). Though, full support of underspecified process models would require that the process model may omit data state changes completely although they are specified in the object life cycle. Synchronization between object life cycles is not considered in that approach and complexity-wise, it requires exponential time. [13] supports fully and underspecified process models but lacks support for object life cycle synchronization, which is then solved by the extension described in this section. For [13], no computation algorithm is given such that no complexity can be derived. The solution presented in this paper requires exponential time through the Petri net mapping and subsequent soundness checking as described in Section 4. However, state space reduction techniques may help to reduce the computation time for soundness checking [6]. The choice of using soundness checking to verify weak conformance allows to check for control flow soundness as well as weak conformance in one analysis and still allows to distinguish occurring violations caused by control flow or data flow.

3   The Notion of Weak Conformance

Weak conformance is checked for a process model with respect to the object life cycles referring to data classes used within the process model. To such concept, we refer as *process scenario* $h = (m, \mathcal{L}, C)$, where m is the process model, $\mathcal{L}$ is the synchronized object life cycle, and C is the set of data classes. Next, we define several notions for convenience considerations before we introduce the notion of weak conformance. Let $f \in \mathfrak{F}_m$ be a data flow edge of process model m indicating either a data object read or write. With f_A and f_D, we denote the activity (A) and data node (D) component of f, respectively. For instance, if f is equal to (a, d), a read, or to (d, a), a write, then (in both cases) $f_A = a$ and $f_D = d$. With $\vartheta(f)$, we denote the data state r_d involved in a read $(f = (d, a) \in \mathfrak{F})$ or write $(f = (a, d) \in \mathfrak{F})$ operation. We denote the set of synchronization edges having data state r_d as target data state with SE_r. Further, $a \Rightarrow_m a'$ denotes that there exists a path in process model m which executes activity $a \in A_m$ before activity $a' \in A_m$. Analogously, $s \Rightarrow_{l_c} s'$ denotes that there exists a path in the object life cycle l_c of data class c which reaches state $s \in S_c$ before state $s' \in S_c$. Thereby, we assume trace semantics. Due to space limitations, details about the concepts utilized throughout this paper and especially in this section can be found in [16], where we introduce the corresponding fundamentals.

Definition 1 (Weak Data Class Conformance). Given process scenario $h = (m, \mathcal{L}, C)$, $m = (N, D, Q, \mathfrak{C}, \mathfrak{F}, type, \mu, \varphi)$ and $\mathcal{L} = (L, SE)$, process model m satisfies *weak conformance* with respect to data class $c \in C$ if for all $f, f' \in \mathfrak{F}$ such that $f_D = d = f'_D$

with d referring to c holds (i) $f_A \Rightarrow_m f'_A$ implies $\vartheta(f) \Rightarrow_{l_c} \vartheta(f')$, (ii) $\forall se \in SE_{\vartheta(f')}$ originating from the same object life cycle $l \in L : \exists \xi(se) == true$, and (iii) $f_A = f'_A$ implies f represents a read and f' represents a write operation of the same activity. ◇

Given a process scenario, we say that it satisfies *weak conformance*, if the process model satisfies weak conformance with respect to each of the used data classes. Weak data class conformance is satisfied, (i),(iii) if for the data states of each two directly succeeding data nodes referring to the same data class in a process model there exists a path from the first to the second data state in the corresponding object life cycle and (ii) if the dependencies specified by synchronization edges with a target state matching the state of the second data node of the two succeeding ones hold such that all dependency conjunctions and disjunctions are fulfilled. Two data nodes of the same class are directly succeeding in the process model, if either (1) they are accessed by the same activity with one being read and one being written or (2) there exists a path in the process model in which two different activities access data nodes of the same class in two data states with no further access to a node of this data class in-between.

4   Computation of Weak Conformance via Soundness Checking

A given process scenario $h = (m, \mathcal{L}, C)$ can be checked for weak conformance by applying the following four steps in sequence:

1. Map the process model m and the synchronized object life cycle $\mathcal{L}$ to Petri nets,
2. integrate both Petri nets,
3. post-process the integrated Petri net and transform it to a workflow net system, and
4. apply soundness checking to identify violations within the process scenario h.

Before we discuss these four steps, we recall the notions of preset and postset. A preset of a transition t respectively a place p denotes the set of all places respectively transitions directly preceding t respectively p. A postset of a transition t respectively a place p denotes the set of all places respectively transitions directly succeeding t respectively p.

1—Petri Net Mapping: The process model is mapped to a Petri net following the rules described in [4] for the control flow and in [16] for the data flow. The mapping of the synchronized object life cycle is split. First, each single object life cycle $l \in L$ is mapped to a Petri net, which than secondly are integrated utilizing the set of synchronization edges. The mapping of single object life cycles utilizes the fact that Petri nets are state machines, if and only if each transition has exactly one preceding and one succeeding place [2]. Thus, each state of an object life cycle is mapped to a Petri net place and each data state transition connecting two states is mapped to a Petri net transition connecting the corresponding places.

For each typed synchronization edge, one place is added to the Petri net. If two typed synchronization edges have the same source and the same dependency type, target the same object life cycle, and if the corresponding target states each have exactly one incoming synchronization edge, both places are merged to one. Similarly, two places are merged, if two typed synchronization edges have the same target, the same dependency type, and origin from the same object life cycle. The preset of an added place comprises all transitions directly preceding the places representing the source and the target data states of the corresponding synchronization edge. The postset of an added place comprises all transitions directly preceding the place representing the target state of the synchronization edge. For currently typed edges, the postset additionally comprises the set of all transitions directly succeeding the place representing the source state.

For each untyped synchronization edge, one transition is added to the Petri net. If $\bigcap_{se_T}\{src \cup tgt\} \neq \emptyset$ for two untyped synchronization edges, i.e., they share one data state, then both transitions are merged. The preset and postset of each transition comprise newly added places; one for each (transitively) involved synchronization edge for the preset and the postset respectively. Such preset place directly succeeds the transitions that in turn are part of the preset of the place representing the data state from which the data state transition origins. Such postset place directly precedes the transition representing the corresponding source or target transition of the typed synchronization edge.

2—Petri Net Integration: First, data states occurring in the object life cycles but not in the process model need to be handled to ensure deadlock free integration of both Petri nets. We add one place p to the Petri net, which handles all not occurring states, i.e., avoids execution of these paths. Let each q_i be a place representing such not occurring data state. Then, the preset of each transition t_j being part of the preset of q_i is extended with place p, if the preset of t_j contains a data state which postset comprises more than one transition in the original Petri net mapped from the synchronized object life cycle.

Each data state represented as place in the Petri net mapped from the process model consists of a control flow and a data flow component as visualized in Fig. 1 with C and D. Within the integrated Petri net, the control flow component is responsible for the flow of the object life cycle and the data flow component is responsible for the data flow in the process model. The integration of both Petri nets follows three rules, distinguishable with respect to read and write operations. The rules use the data flow component of data state places.

Fig. 1. Internal places for a place representing a data state

(IR-1) A place p from the object life cycle Petri net representing a data state of a data class to be read by some activity in the process model is added to the preset of the transition stating that this data node (object) is read in this specific state, e.g., the preset of transition *Read O in data state s* is extended with the place representing data state s of class O, and (IR-2) a new place q is added to the integrated Petri net, which extends the postset of the transition stating that the data node (object) is read in the specific state and which extends the preset of each transition being part of the postset of place p, e.g., the place connecting transition *Read O in data state s* and the two transitions succeeding the place labeled $O.s$. (IR-3) Let v be a place from the object life cycle Petri net representing a data state of a class to be written by some activity in the process model. Then a new place w is added to the integrated Petri net, which extends the preset of each transition being part of the preset of w and which extends the postset of the transition stating that the data node (object) is written in the specific state. the Petri net derived from the process model stating this write.

3—Workflow Net System: Soundness checking has been introduced for workflow net systems [1,12]. Workflow nets are Petri nets with a single source and a single sink place and they are strongly connected after adding a transition connecting the sink place with the source place [1]. The integrated Petri net needs to be post-processed towards these properties by adding *enabler* and *collector* fragments. The enabler fragment consists of the single source place directly succeeded by a transition y. The postset of y comprises all places representing an initial data state of some object life cycle and the source place of the process model Petri net. The preset of each place is adapted accordingly.

The collector fragment first consists of a transition t preceding the single sink node. For each distinct data class of the process scenario, one place p_i and one place q_i are added to the collector. Each place p_i has transition t as postset[1]. Then, for each final data state of some object life cycle, a transition u_i is added to the collector. Each transition u_i has as preset the place representing the corresponding data state and some place q_i referring to the same data class. The postset of a transition u_i is the corresponding place p_i also referring to the same data class. Additionally, a transition z succeeded by one place is added to the collector. The place's postset is transition t. The preset of z is the sink place of the process model Petri net. The postset of z is extended with each place q_i.

Next, the synchronization places need to be considered. If a typed synchronization edge involves the initial state of some object life cycle as source, then the corresponding place is added to the postset of transition y of the enabler fragment. For all synchronization edges typed previously, the postset of the corresponding place is extended with transition t of the collector. If a currently typed synchronization edge involves a final state of some object life cycle as source, then the corresponding place is added to the postset of the corresponding transition u_i of the collector fragment. Finally, the semaphore places need to be integrated. Therefore, for each semaphore place, the preset is extended with transition y from the enabler and the postset is extended with transition t from the collector fragments. Now, connecting sink and source node, the workflow net is strongly connected. A workflow net system consists of a workflow net and some initial marking. The workflow net is given above and the initial marking puts a token into the single source place and nowhere else.

4—Soundness Checking: Assuming control flow correctness, if the workflow net system satisfies the soundness property [1], no contradictions between the process model and the object life cycles exist and all data states presented in all object life cycles are implicitly or explicitly utilized in the process model, i.e., all paths in the object life cycles may be taken. If it satisfies the weak soundness property [12], no contradictions between the process model and the object life cycles exist but some of the data states are never reached during execution of the process model. In case, control flow inconsistencies would appear, places and transitions representing the control flow would cause the violation allowing to distinguish between control flow and data conformance issues.

Validation. The described approach reliably decides about weak conformance of a process scenario. It takes sound Petri net fragments as input and combines them with

---

[1] Generally, we assume that addition of one element a to the preset of another element b implies the addition of b to the postset of a and vice versa.

respect to specified data dependencies. Single source and sink places are achieved through the addition of elements either marking the original source places or collecting tokens from the original final places. Thus, they do not change the behavior of the process model and the object life cycles, i.e., they do not influence the result.

5 Related Work

The increasing interest in the development of process models for execution has shifted the focus from control flow to data flow perspective leading to integrated scenarios providing control as well as data flow views. One step in this regard are object-centric processes [3,17,23] that connect data classes with the control flow of process models by specifying object life cycles. [8] introduces the essential requirements of this modeling paradigm. [9, 20] present an approach, which connects object life cycles with process models by determining commonalities between both representations and transforming one into the other. Covering one direction of the integration, [10] derives object life cycles from process models. Tackling the integration of control flow and data, [14, 15] enable to model data constraints and to enforce them during process execution directly from the model. Similar to the mentioned approaches, we concentrate on integrated scenarios incorporating process models and object life cycles removing the assumption that both representations must completely correspond to each other. Instead, we set a synchronized object life cycle as reference that describes data manipulations allowed in a traditional, i.e., activity-driven, modeled process scenario, e.g., with BPMN [18].

The field of compliance checking focuses on control flow aspects using predefined rule sets containing, for instance, business policies. However, some works do consider data. [11] applies compliance checking to object-centric processes by creating process models following this paradigm from a set of rules. However, these rules most often specify control flow requirements. [7] provides a technique to check for conformance of object-centric processes containing multiple data classes by mapping to an interaction conformance problem, which can be solved by decomposition into smaller sub-problems, which in turn are solved by using classical conformance checking techniques. [23] introduces a framework that ensures consistent specialization of object-centric processes, i.e., it ensures consistency between two object life cycles. In contrast, we check for consistency between a traditional process model and an object life cycle. Eshuis [5] uses a symbolic model checker to verify conformance of UML activity diagrams [19] considering control and data flow perspectives while data states are not considered in his approach. [9] introduces compliance between a process model and an object life cycle as the combination of object life cycle conformance (all data state transitions induced in the process model must occur in the object life cycle) and coverage (opposite containment relation). [21] introduces conformance checking between process models and product life cycles, which in fact are object life cycles, because a product life cycle determines for a product the states and the allowed state transitions. Compared to the notion of weak conformance, both notions do not support data synchronization and both set restrictions with respect to data constraints specification in the process model.

6 Conclusion

In this paper, we presented an approach for the integrated verification of control flow correctness and weak data conformance using soundness checking considering dependencies between multiple data classes, e.g., an order is only allowed to be shipped after the payment was received but needs to be shipped with a confirmed invoice in one package. Therefore, we utilized the concept of synchronized object life cycles. For checking data correctness, we use the notion of weak conformance and extended it with means for object life cycle synchronization. Additionally, we utilized a mapping of a process model with data constraints to a Petri net and described a mapping of a synchronized object life cycle to a Petri net. Both resulting Petri nets are combined for an integrated control flow and data conformance check based on the soundness criterion. With respect to the places or transitions causing soundness violations, we can distinguish between control flow and data flow issues and therefore, we can verify the notion of weak conformance. Revealed violations can be highlighted in the process model and the synchronized object life cycle to support correction. In this paper, we focused on the violation identification such that correction is subject to future work.

References

1. van der Aalst, W.M.P.: Verification of Workflow Nets. In: Azéma, P., Balbo, G. (eds.) ICATPN 1997. LNCS, vol. 1248, pp. 407–426. Springer, Heidelberg (1997)
2. van der Aalst, W.M.P.: Workflow Verification: Finding Control-Flow Errors Using Petri-Net-Based Techniques. In: van der Aalst, W.M.P., Desel, J., Oberweis, A. (eds.) Business Process Management. LNCS, vol. 1806, pp. 161–183. Springer, Heidelberg (2000)
3. Cohn, D., Hull, R.: Business Artifacts: A Data-centric Approach to Modeling Business Operations and Processes. IEEE Data Engineering Bulletin 32(3), 3–9 (2009)
4. Dijkman, R.M., Dumas, M., Ouyang, C.: Semantics and Analysis of Business Process Models in BPMN. Information & Software Technology 50(12), 1281–1294 (2008)
5. Eshuis, R.: Symbolic Model Checking of UML Activity Diagrams. ACM Transactions on Software Engineering and Methodology (TOSEM) 15(1), 1–38 (2006)
6. Fahland, D., Favre, C., Jobstmann, B., Koehler, J., Lohmann, N., Völzer, H., Wolf, K.: Instantaneous Soundness Checking of Industrial Business Process Models. In: Dayal, U., Eder, J., Koehler, J., Reijers, H.A. (eds.) BPM 2009. LNCS, vol. 5701, pp. 278–293. Springer, Heidelberg (2009)
7. Fahland, D., de Leoni, M., van Dongen, B.F., van der Aalst, W.M.P.: Conformance Checking of Interacting Processes with Overlapping Instances. In: Rinderle-Ma, S., Toumani, F., Wolf, K. (eds.) BPM 2011. LNCS, vol. 6896, pp. 345–361. Springer, Heidelberg (2011)
8. Künzle, V., Weber, B., Reichert, M.: Object-aware Business Processes: Fundamental Requirements and their Support in Existing Approaches. IJISMD 2(2), 19–46 (2011)
9. Küster, J.M., Ryndina, K., Gall, H.C.: Generation of Business Process Models for Object Life Cycle Compliance. In: Alonso, G., Dadam, P., Rosemann, M. (eds.) BPM 2007. LNCS, vol. 4714, pp. 165–181. Springer, Heidelberg (2007)
10. Liu, R., Wu, F.Y., Kumaran, S.: Transforming Activity-Centric Business Process Models into Information-Centric Models for SOA Solutions. J. Database Manag. 21(4), 14–34 (2010)
11. Lohmann, N.: Compliance by design for artifact-centric business processes. In: Rinderle-Ma, S., Toumani, F., Wolf, K. (eds.) BPM 2011. LNCS, vol. 6896, pp. 99–115. Springer, Heidelberg (2011)

12. Martens, A.: On Usability of Web Services. In: Web Information Systems Engineering Workshops, pp. 182–190. IEEE (2003)
13. Meyer, A., Polyvyanyy, A., Weske, M.: Weak Conformance of Process Models with respect to Data Objects. In: Services and their Composition (ZEUS), pp. 74–80 (2012)
14. Meyer, A., Pufahl, L., Batoulis, K., Kruse, S., Lindhauer, T., Stoff, T., Fahland, D., Weske, M.: Automating Data Exchange in Process Choreographies. In: Jarke, M., Mylopoulos, J., Quix, C., Rolland, C., Manolopoulos, Y., Mouratidis, H., Horkoff, J. (eds.) CAiSE 2014. LNCS, vol. 8484, pp. 316–331. Springer, Heidelberg (2014)
15. Meyer, A., Pufahl, L., Fahland, D., Weske, M.: Modeling and Enacting Complex Data Dependencies in Business Processes. In: Daniel, F., Wang, J., Weber, B. (eds.) BPM 2013. LNCS, vol. 8094, pp. 171–186. Springer, Heidelberg (2013)
16. Meyer, A., Weske, M.: Weak Conformance between Process Models and Object Life Cycles. Tech. rep., Hasso Plattner Institute at the University of Potsdam (2014)
17. Nigam, A., Caswell, N.S.: Business artifacts: An approach to operational specification. IBM Systems Journal 42(3), 428–445 (2003)
18. OMG: Business Process Model and Notation (BPMN), Version 2.0 (January 2011)
19. OMG: Unified Modeling Language (UML), Version 2.4.1 (August 2011)
20. Ryndina, K., Küster, J.M., Gall, H.C.: Consistency of Business Process Models and Object Life Cycles. In: Kühne, T. (ed.) MoDELS 2006. LNCS, vol. 4364, pp. 80–90. Springer, Heidelberg (2007)
21. Wang, Z., ter Hofstede, A.H.M., Ouyang, C., Wynn, M., Wang, J., Zhu, X.: How to Guarantee Compliance between Workflows and Product Lifecycles? Tech. rep., BPM Center Report BPM-11-10 (2011)
22. Weske, M.: Business Process Management: Concepts, Languages, Architectures, 2nd edn. Springer (2012)
23. Yongchareon, S., Liu, C., Zhao, X.: A Framework for Behavior-Consistent Specialization of Artifact-Centric Business Processes. In: Barros, A., Gal, A., Kindler, E. (eds.) BPM 2012. LNCS, vol. 7481, pp. 285–301. Springer, Heidelberg (2012)

Failure-Proof Spatio-temporal Composition of Sensor Cloud Services

Azadeh Ghari Neiat, Athman Bouguettaya, Timos Sellis, and Hai Dong

School of Computer Science and Information Technology, RMIT, Australia
{azadeh.gharineiat,athman.bouguettaya,timos.sellis,
hai.dong}@rmit.edu.au

Abstract. We propose a new failure-proof composition model for Sensor-Cloud services based on dynamic features such as spatio-temporal aspects. To evaluate Sensor-Cloud services, a novel spatio-temporal quality model is introduced. We present a new failure-proof composition algorithm based on D* Lite to handle QoS changes of Sensor-Cloud services at run-time. Analytical and simulation results are presented to show the performance of the proposed approach.

Keywords: Spatio-temporal Sensor-Cloud service, spatio-temporal composition, Sensor-Cloud service composition, spatio-temporal QoS, service re-composition.

1 Introduction

The large amount of real-time sensor data streaming from Wireless Sensor Networks (WSNs) is a challenging issue because of storage capacity, processing power and data management constraints [1]. Cloud computing is a promising technology to support the storage and processing of the ever increasing amount of data [2]. The integration of WSNs with the cloud (i.e., Sensor-Cloud) [3] provides unique capabilities and opportunities, particularly for the use of data service-centric applications. Sensor-Cloud is a potential key enabler for large-scale data sharing and cooperation among different users and applications.

A main challenge in Sensor-Cloud is the efficient and real-time delivery of sensor data to end users. The preferred technology to enable delivery is services [4], i.e., sensor data made available as a service (i.e. Sensor-Cloud service) to different clients over a Sensor-Cloud infrastructure. The service paradigm is a powerful abstraction hiding data-specific information focusing on how data is to be used. In this regard, sensor data on the cloud is abstracted as Sensor-Cloud services easily accessible irrespective of the distribution of sensor data sources. In this paper, we propose a service-oriented Sensor-Cloud architecture that provides an integrated view of the sensor data shared on the cloud and delivered as services.

The *"position"* and *"time"* of sensed data are of paramount importance reflecting the spatio-temporal characteristics. Spatio-temporal features are fundamental to the functional aspect of the Sensor-Cloud. In this regard, we focus on spatio-temporal aspects as key parameters to query the Sensor-Cloud.

Composition provides a means to aggregate Sensor-Cloud services. In a highly dynamic environment such as those found in sensed environments, the non-functional

X. Franch et al. (Eds.): ICSOC 2014, LNCS 8831, pp. 368–377, 2014.
© Springer-Verlag Berlin Heidelberg 2014

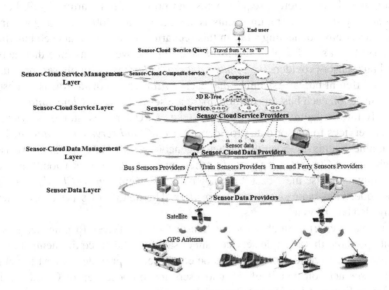

Fig. 1. The Public Transport Motivation Scenario

properties (QoS) of Sensor-Cloud services may fluctuate [5]. For example, a participant service may no longer be available or its QoS constraint has been fluctuated at runtime. As a result, the service may no longer provide the required QoS and fail. Therefore, the initial composition plan may become non-optimal and needs to be replanned to deal with the changing conditions of such environments.

This paper focuses on providing an efficient failure-proof spatio-temporal composition model for Sensor-Cloud services. In particular, new spatio-temporal QoS attributes to evaluate Sensor-Cloud services based on spatio-temporal properties of the services are proposed. We propose a failure-proof spatio-temporal combinatorial search algorithm to deal with the affecting component Sensor-Cloud services based on D* Lite algorithm [6] which is an incremental version of A* algorithm. D* Lite algorithm is efficient at repairing the plan when the new information about the environment is received [10]. Our proposed approach continually improves its initial composition plan and find the best composition plan from a given source-point to a given destination point while QoS constraints change.

The rest of the paper is structured as follows: Section 2 presents the proposed spatio-temporal model for Sensor-Cloud services. Section 3 illustrates the spatio-temporal QoS model. Section 4 elaborates the details of the proposed failure-proof composition approach. Section 5 evaluates the approach and shows the experiment results. Section 6 concludes the paper and highlights some future work.

Motivating Scenario

We use a typical scenario from public transport as our motivating scenario. Suppose Sarah is planning to travel from 'A' to 'B'. She wants to get information about the travel services (i.e., buses, trams, trains and ferries) in the city to plan her journey. Different users may have different requirements and preferences regarding QoS. For example, Sarah may specify her requirements as maximum walk 300 meters and waiting time 10 minutes at any connecting stop. In this scenario, we assume that each bus (tram / train / ferry) has a set of deployed sensors (see Fig. 1). We also assume that there are several bus sensor providers (i.e., *sensor data providers*) who supply sensor data collected from different buses. Assuming that each *sensor data provider* owns a subset of a set of sensors on each bus. In addition, there are several *Sensor-Cloud data providers* who supply Infrastructure as a Service (IaaS), i.e., CPU services, storage services, and network services to sensor data providers. *Sensor-Cloud service providers* make services available that may query multiple heterogeneous *sensor data providers*. We assume that each *Sensor-Cloud service provider* offers one or more Sensor-Cloud services to help commuters devise the " best " journey plan. Different *Sensor-Cloud service providers* may query the same *sensor data providers*. The quality of services that they provide may also be different.

In our scenario, Sarah uses the Sensor-Cloud services to plan her journey. It is quite possible that a single service cannot satisfy Sarah's requirements. In such cases, Sensor-Cloud services may need to be composed to provide the best travel plan. *The composer* acts on behalf of the end users to compose Sensor-Cloud services from different *Sensor-Cloud service providers*.

2   Spatio-temporal Model for Sensor-Cloud Service

To model and access spatio-temporal Sensor-Cloud services, we consider spatio-temporal dependency constraints between different Sensor-Cloud service operations. We propose a new formal spatio-temporal model for a Sensor-Cloud service and Sensor-Cloud service composition.

2.1   Spatio-temporal Model for Atomic Sensor-Cloud Service

We introduce the notion of Sensor-Cloud service based on spatio-temporal aspects. We discuss the key concepts to model a Sensor-Cloud service in terms of spatio-temporal features. The Sensor-Cloud service model is formally defined as follows:

- *Definition 1:* Sensor *sen*. A sensor sen_i is a tuple of $< id, (loc_i, ts_i)>$ where
  - id is a unique sensor ID,
  - (loc_i, ts_i) shows the latest recorded location of sensor sen_i and timestamp ts_i is the latest time in which sensor data related to Sensor-Cloud service is collected from sensor sen_i.
- *Definition 2:* Sensor-Cloud Service S. A Sensor-Cloud service S_i is a tuple of $< id, IS_i, FS_i, d_i, F_i, Q_i, SEN_i >$ where
  - id is a unique service ID,
  - IS_i (Initial State) is a tuple $< P_s, t_s >$, where
    * P_s is a GPS start-point of S_i ,
    * t_s is a start-time of S_i.

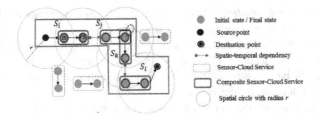

Fig. 2. Spatio-Temporal Composite Sensor-Cloud Service Model

- FS_i (Final State) is a tuple $< P_e, t_e >$, where
  * P_e is a GPS end-point of S_i,
  * t_e is an end-time of S_i.
- d_i represents the intra-dependency between two states from S_i meaning that FS_i is invoked after IS_i,
- F_i describes a set of functions offered by S_i,
- Q_i is a tuple $< q_1, q_2, ..., q_n >$, where each q_i denotes a QoS property of S_i,
- $SEN_i = \{sen_i | 1 \leqslant i \leqslant m\}$ represents a finite set of sensors sen_i collecting sensor data related to S_i.

For example, the function of a bus service S_{65} (F_{65}) can be defined as travelling from stop 4 at 5:10 pm (i.e., $IS_{65} = < stop\ 4\ ,\ 5 : 10pm >$) to stop 54 (i.e., $FS_{65} = < stop\ 54\ ,\ 5 : 22pm >$) by bus.

2.2 Spatio-temporal Model for Sensor-Cloud Service Composition

In some instances, an atomic Sensor-Cloud service may not fully meet user's requirements. In this case, a composition of services may be required. The main idea for composing Sensor-Cloud services is spatio-temporal dependencies among services. We represent a composite Sensor-Cloud service as a directed acyclic graph in which the nodes are service states (i.e., IS or FS) provided by component services and edges denote spatio-temporal dependencies among services (Fig. 2).

- *Definition 3:* Composite Sensor-Cloud Service CS. A composite Sensor-Cloud service CS is defined as a tuple $< SCS, r, t, D, \varsigma, \xi >$
  - $SCS = \{S_i | 1 \leqslant i \leqslant n\}$ represents a set of component services in which n is the total number of component services of CS,
  - r and t are user-defined spatial radius and time interval, respectively.
  - $D = \{< S_k, S_l > | 1 \leqslant k \leqslant n \wedge 1 \leqslant l \leqslant n \wedge k \neq l\}$ represents spatio-temporal neighbour dependencies between two component services S_k and S_l. A spatio-temporal neighbour dependency consists of two types of dependencies:
    * *spatial dependency:* two services S_k and S_l have spatial dependency if $S_l . P_s$ is located inside the spatial circle centred at $S_k . P_e$ with a geographic radius r. For example, the bus stop 4 of bus service 65 has the spatial dependency with the tram stop 13 of tram service 8 supporting a walk of 300 meters (i.e., $r = 300$) between the bus stop and tram station.

∗ *temporal dependency*: two services S_k and S_l have temporal dependency if S_l will be executed in a time window t of S_k, i.e., $S_k.t_e \leq S_l.t_s + t$. For example, the bus service 65 arrives in the bus stop 4 within 10 min ($t = 10$) before departing the tram service 8 from the tram stop 13. S_k and S_l have spatio-temporal neighbour dependency, if they are both spatially and temporally dependent.

• ς and ξ are a source-point and a destination-point, respectively.

In the remainder of the paper, the service and composite service are used to refer to a Sensor-Cloud service and composite Sensor-Cloud service, respectively.

3   Spatio-temporal Quality Model for Sensor-Cloud Service

Multiple Sensor-Cloud providers may offer similar services at varying quality levels. Given the diversity of service offerings, an important challenge for users is to discover the 'right' service satisfying their requirements. We introduce novel QoS attributes for services that focus on the spatio-temporal aspects. The proposed quality model is extensible. For the sake of clarity, we use a limited number of QoS.

3.1   Spatio-temporal Quality Model for Atomic Sensor-Cloud Service

We propose to use spatio-temporal quality criteria which is part of describing the non-functional aspects of services:

– *Service time (st):* Given an atomic service S, the service time q_{st}(S) measures the expected time in minutes between the start and destination points. The value of q_{st}(S) is computed as follows:

$$q_{st}(S) = S.t_e - S.t_s \qquad (1)$$

– *Currency (cur):* Currency indicates the temporal accuracy of a service. Given an atomic service S, currency q_{cur}(S) is computed using the expression $(currenttime - timestamp(S))$. Since each service consists of a set of sensors $\{sen_1, ..., sen_n\}$, $timestamp(S)$ will be computed as follows:

$$timestamp(S) = Avg(ts_i) \qquad (2)$$

– *Accuracy (acc):* Accuracy reflects how a service is *assured*. For example, a smaller value of accuracy shows the fewer sensors contribute to the results of the service. Given an atomic service S, the accuracy q_{acc}(S) is the number of operating sensors covering the specific spatial area related to S. The value of the q_{acc}(S) is computed as follows:

$$0 \leqslant \frac{N_{sen}(S)}{T_c} \leqslant 1 \qquad (3)$$

where $N_{sen}(S)$ is the expected number of operating sensors in S and T_c is the total number of sensors covering the spatial area related to S. $N_{sen}(S)$ can be estimated based on the number of sen in S. We assume that T_c is known. It is also assumed that all sensors have the same functionalities and accuracy. For example, sensor data related to the bus service S_{65} is collected from 4 sensors ($N_{sen} = 4$) from 20 sensors ($T_c = 20$) deployed on a bus where is the spatial area related to S_{65}.

3.2 Spatio-temporal Quality Model for Composite Sensor-Cloud Service

The quality criteria defined above are in the context of atomic services. Aggregation functions are used to compute the QoS of the composite service. Table 1 presents these aggregation functions:

- *Service time:* The service time of a composite service is the sum of the service time of all its component services in addition to the transition time *trans* between two component services. The transition time is computed as follows:

$$trans = \sum_{j=1}^{n-1}(S_{(j+1)}.start\text{-}time - S_j.end\text{-}time) \qquad (4)$$

where S_j and S_{j+1} are two subsequent component services and $S_1.end\text{-}time$ is the start time of a query Q_t.
- *Currency:* The currency value of a composite service is the average of the currency of all the selected services.
- *Accuracy:* The accuracy value for a composite service is the product of the accuracy of all its component services.

Table 1. QoS Aggregation Functions

QoS attribute	Service Time	Currency	Accuracy
Aggregation Function	$\sum_{i=1}^{m} q_{st}(S_i) + trans$	$\dfrac{\sum_{i=1}^{m} q_{cur}(S_i)}{m}$	$\prod_{i=1}^{m} q_{acc}(S_i)$

4 Failure-Proof Spatio-temporal Composition Approach

When a service experiences significant quality fluctuation at runtime, an established composition plan may no longer be optimal. There are two situations in which a composition may become non-optimal. First, when QoS constraints of a component service violate or a component service may no longer be available at runtime and the composition may fail. Second, when a component service may provide better QoS and a more optimal composition plan may be provided. In such situations, all compositions that include the affecting service should adapt to the fluctuation.

We propose a heuristic algorithm called Spatio-Temporal A* (*STA**) algorithm [7] which is a variation of A* offering an optimal composition plan. *STA** differs on *neighbour* and *search cost* functions. In [7], we present a new spatio-temporal index data structure based on a 3D R-tree [8] to organize and access services. The nodes of the 3D R-tree represent actual services. We define a new *neighbour* function to find spatio-temporal neighbour services (i.e. candidate services) of a service, called *Spatio-TemporalSearch* algorithm, based on a 3D R-tree [7]. We also define the *search cost* function *f-score* as follows:

$$f\text{-}score[S] = g\text{-}score[S] + h\text{-}score[S] \qquad (5)$$

where g-*score* calculates the QoS utility score [9] of selected services from the source-point ς to the current service and heuristic function h-*score* estimates the Euclidean distance between the end-point of candidate service S and the destination-point ξ.

In this section, we propose a novel failure-proof service composition approach based on spatio-temporal aspects of services to support real-time response to fluctuation of QoS attributes. We introduce a new heuristic algorithm based on D* Lite, called *STD*Lite*. D* Lite is a dynamic shortest path finding algorithm that has been extensively applied in mobile robot and autonomous vehicle navigation. D* Lite is capable of efficiently replanning paths in changing environment [10]. Whenever the QoS values of component services in the initial composition plan significantly change at runtime, *STD*Lite* recomputes a new optimal composition plan from its current position to the destination. Without loss of generality, we only consider temporal QoS fluctuations in service time q_{st}. In our approach, the existence of a temporal QoS change is ascertained by measuring the value of difference τ between the measured q_{st} of a service at runtime and its promised q_{st}. If τ is more than a defined threshold ϵ, a QoS change has occurred.

*STD*Lite* algorithm , like *STA**, maintains an estimate g-*score* for each service S in the composition plan. Since *STD*Lite* searches backward from the destination-point to the source-point, g-*score* estimates the QoS utility score of the optimal path from S to the destination. It also maintains a second kind of estimates called rhs value which is one step lookahead of g-*score*. Therefore, it is better informed than g-*score* and computed as follows:

$$rhs(S) = \begin{cases} 0 & S.P_e = \xi \\ min_{S' \in SuccNeighboursList(S)}(trans(S', S) + g\text{-}score(S')) & S.P_e \neq \xi \end{cases} \quad (6)$$

where $trans(S', S)$ is the transition time between S' and S and $SuccNeighboursList$ is the set of *successor* neighbours of the service S. The rationale of using neighbours is that the optimal plan from S to the destination must pass through one of the neighbours of S. Therefore, if we can identify the optimal plans from any of the neighbours to the destination, we can compute the optimal plan for S. The successor neighbours of a service S are identified through *Spatio-TemporalSearch* algorithm in [7].

By comparing g-*score* and rhs, the algorithm identifies all affecting, called inconsistent, component services. A service is called locally consistent iff its rhs value equals to its g-*score* value, otherwise it is called locally inconsistent. A locally inconsistent service falls into two categories: *underconsistent* (if g-*score*$(S) < rhs(S)$) and *overconsistent* (if g-*score*$(S) > rhs(S)$). A service is called *underconsistent* if its QoS values degrades. In such a situation, the QoS values of affecting services should be updated and the composition plan should adapt to the violations. Moreover, a service is called *overconsistent* if its QoS values become better. An overconsistent service implies that a more optimal plan can be found from the current service. When a service is inconsistent, the algorithm updates all of it's neighbours and itself again. Updating services makes them consistent.

Algorithm 1 presents the details of *STD*Lite* algorithm. The algorithm generates an optimal initial composition plan like a *backward STA** search {Line 33-42}. If the QoS values of component services change after generating the initial composition plan, *STD*Lite* updates the inconsistent (i.e., affecting) component services and expands the services to recompute a new optimal composition plan {43-47}. All inconsistent services are then inserted in a priority queue *CandidateQueue* to be updated and made consistent. *STD*Lite* avoids redundant updates through updating only the inconsistent services which are necessary to modify, while A* updates all of the plan. The priority of an inconsistent service in *CandidateQueue* is determined by *key value* as follows:

$$key(S) = [k_1(S), k_2(S)]$$
$$= [min(g\text{-}score(S), rhs(S)) + h\text{-}score(S_{start}, S), min(g\text{-}score(S), rhs(S))] \quad (7)$$

The keys are compared in a lexicographical order. The priority of $key(S) < key(S')$, iff $k_1(S) < k_1(S')$ or $k_1(S) = k_1(S')$ and $k_2(S) < k_2(S')$. The heuristics in k_1 serves in the same way as $f\text{-}score$ in *STA**. The algorithm applies this heuristic to ensure that only the services either newly overconsistent or newly underconsistent that are relevant to repairing the current plan are processed. The inconsistent services are selected in the order of increasing priority which implies that the services which are closer to the S_{start} (i.e. less $h\text{-}score$ value) should be processed first. Note that as the algorithm tracks the execution of the composition plan, the start service S_{start} becomes the current running service of the plan. Therefore, when a QoS value fluctuates, a new optimal plan is computed from the original destination to the new start service (i.e. current service).

The algorithm finally recompute a new optimal plan by calling *ComputePlan()* function {48}. *ComputePlan()* expands the local inconsistent services on *CandidateQueue* and updates $g\text{-}score$ and rhs values and add them to or remove them from *Candidate-Queue* with their corresponding keys by calling *UpdateService()* function {4-15}.

When *ComputePlan()* expands an overconsistent service, it sets $g\text{-}score$ value of the service equals to its rhs value to make it locally consistent {20}. Since rhs values of predecessor neighbours of a service are computed based on the $g\text{-}score$ value of the service, any changes of its $g\text{-}score$ value can effect the local consistency of its predecessor neighbours. As a result, predecessor neighbours {19} of an inconsistent service should be updated {21-23}.

When *ComputePlan()* expands an underconsistent service, it sets $g\text{-}score$ value of the service to infinity to make it either overconsistent or consistent {25}. The predecessor neighbour services of the service need also to be updated {26-28}. *ComputePlan()* expands the services until the key value of the next service to expand is not less than the key value of S_{start} and S_{start} is locally consistent {17}.

5   Experiments Results

We conduct a set of experiments to assess the effectiveness of the proposed approach over different QoS fluctuation ratio. We run our experiments on a 3.40 GHZ Intel Core i7 processor and 8 GB RAM under Windows 7. To the best of our knowledge, there is no spatio-temporal service test case to be used for experimental purposes. Therefore, we focus on evaluating the proposed approach using synthetic spatio-temporal services.

In our simulation, 1000 nodes are randomly distributed in a 30 *km* × 30 *km* region. The radius for neighbour search r as 0.5% of the specified region. All experiments are conducted 1000 times and the average results are computed. Each experiment starts from a different source and destination which are randomly generated. Two spatio-temporal QoS attributes of the syntactic service instances are randomly generated with

---

Algorithm 1. STD*Lite [basic version]

1: **procedure** CALCULATEKEY(S)
2:     **return**   [$min(g\text{-}score(S), rhs(S))$
    $+h\text{-}score(S_{start}, S), min(g\text{-}score(S), rhs(S))$]
3: **end procedure**
4: **procedure** UPDATESERVICE(S)
5:     **if** $S.P_e \neq \xi$ **then**
6:         SuccNeighboursList = Spatio-TemporalSearch(G,
    RT, $S.p_e$, $S.t_e$, r, t)
7:         rhs(S)   = $min_{S' \in SuccNeighboursList}$
    (trans(S',S)+ g-score(S'))
8:     **end if**
9:     **if** S ∈ CandidateQueue **then**
10:        CandidateQueue.remove(S)
11:    **end if**
12:    **if** g-score(S) $\neq$ rhs(S) **then**
13:        CandidateQueue.insert(S,CalculateKey(S))
14:    **end if**
15: **end procedure**
16: **procedure** COMPUTEPLAN( )
17:    **while** $min_{S \in CandidateQueue}$(key(S))<
    key(S_{start}) or rhs(S_{start}) $\neq$ g-score(S_{start}) **do**
18:        CandidateQueue.remove(S with minimum key)
19:        PredNeighboursList = Spatio-TemporalSearch(G,
    RT, $S.p_s$, $S.t_s$-t, r, t)
20:        **if** g-score(S) > rhs(S) **then** g-score(S) = rhs(S)
21:        **for all** S' ∈ PredNeighboursList **do**
22:            UpdateService(S)
23:        **end for**
24:        **else**
25:            g-score(S) = ∞
26:            **for all** S' ∈ PredNeighboursList ∪ S **do**
27:                UpdateService(S)
28:            **end for**
29:        **end if**
30:    **end while**
31: **end procedure**
32: **procedure** MAIN( )
33:    CandidateQueue = ∅
34:    **for all** services S **do**
35:        g-score(S) = rhs(S) = ∞
36:    **end for**
37:    rhs($S_{destination}$) = 0
38:    CandidateQueue.insert($S_{destination}$,
    CalculateKey($S_{destination}$))
39:    ComputePlan()
40:    **if** g-score(S_{start}) = ∞ **then**
41:        print "there is no plan"
42:    **end if**
43:    **while** $S_{start} \neq S_{destination}$ **do**
44:        Runtime monitoring to find the affecting ser-
    vices
45:        **for all** affecting services S **do**
46:            UpdateService(S)
47:        **end for**
48:        ComputePlan()
49:    **end while**
50: **end procedure**

---

a uniform distribution from the following intervals: $q_{acc} \in [0, 1]$ and $q_{cur} \in [60, 1440]$. The q_{st} is assigned based on the distance between P_s and P_e considering a fixed speed. The remaining parameters are also randomly generated using a uniform distribution.

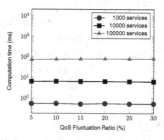

Fig. 3. Computation time vs. fluctuation ratio

We test the performance of *STD*Lite* in terms of computation time with the number of services varying from among 1000, 10000 and 100000. For each group of services, we also vary the QoS fluctuation ratio from 5 to 30 %. The QoS fluctuation ratio indicates that the ratio of the number of affecting services over the total number of services. For example, a fluctuation ratio of 10% denotes that the service time of 10% of the total number of services change at runtime. Fig. 3 shows *STD*Lite* performs very efficiently on a large number of services (i.e., less than 100 *ms* on 100000 services). The computation time increases along with the number of services, which is an expected result. It can be seen that the similar computation time is achieved regardless of the QoS fluctuation ratio. The slight difference (i.e., less than 10 ms over 100000 services) shows the relative stability of our approach when QoS is highly violated.

6 Conclusion

This paper proposes a novel approach for failure-proof composition of Sensor-Cloud services in terms of spatio-temporal aspects. We introduce a new failure-proof spatio-temporal combinatorial search algorithm based on D* Lite to replan a composition plan in case of QoS changes. We conduct preliminary experiments to illustrate the performance of our approach. Future work includes implementing a prototype and test it with real-world applications with focusing on building Sensor-Clouds for public transport.

References

1. Hossain, M.A.: A survey on sensor-cloud: architecture, applications, and approaches. International Journal of Distributed Sensor Networks (2013)
2. Lee, K., Murray, D., Hughes, D., Joosen, W.: Extending sensor networks into the cloud using amazon web services. In: 2010 IEEE International Conference on Networked Embedded Systems for Enterprise Applications (NESEA), pp. 1–7. IEEE Press (2010)
3. Rajesh, V., Gnanasekar, J., Ponmagal, R., Anbalagan, P.: Integration of wireless sensor network with cloud. In: 2010 International Conference on Recent Trends in Information, Telecommunication and Computing (ITC), pp. 321–323. IEEE Press (2010)
4. Carey, M.J., Onose, N., Petropoulos, M.: Data services. Communications of the ACM 55(6), 86–97 (2012)
5. Ben Mabrouk, N., Beauche, S., Kuznetsova, E., Georgantas, N., Issarny, V.: Qos-aware service composition in dynamic service oriented environments. In: Bacon, J.M., Cooper, B.F. (eds.) Middleware 2009. LNCS, vol. 5896, pp. 123–142. Springer, Heidelberg (2009)
6. Koenig, S., Likhachev, M.: D* lite. In: AAAI/IAAI, pp. 476–483 (2002)
7. Ghari Neiat, A., Bouguettaya, A., Sellis, T., Ye, Z.: Spatio-temporal composition of sensor cloud services. In: 21th IEEE International Conference on Web Services (ICWS), pp. 241–248. IEEE Press (2014)
8. Theoderidis, Y., Vazirgiannis, M., Sellis, T.: Spatio-temporal indexing for large multimedia applications. In: Proceedings of the Third IEEE International Conference on Multimedia Computing and Systems, pp. 441–448. IEEE Press (1996)
9. Zeng, L., Benatallah, B., Ngu, A.H.H., Dumas, M., Kalagnanam, J., Chang, H.: Qos-aware middleware for web services composition. IEEE Transactions on Software Engineering 30(5), 311–327 (2004)
10. Koenig, S., Likhachev, M.: Improved fast replanning for robot navigation in unknown terrain. In: IEEE International Conference on Robotics and Automation, pp. 968–975 (2002)

Probabilistic Prediction of the QoS of Service Orchestrations: A Truly Compositional Approach*

Leonardo Bartoloni, Antonio Brogi, and Ahmad Ibrahim

Department of Computer Science, University of Pisa, Italy
{bartolon,brogi,ahmad}@di.unipi.it

Abstract. The ability to a priori predict the QoS of a service orchestration is of pivotal importance for both the design of service compositions and the definition of their SLAs. QoS prediction is challenging because the results of service invocations is not known a priori. In this paper we present an algorithm to probabilistically predict the QoS of a WS-BPEL service orchestration. Our algorithm employs Monte Carlo simulations and it improves previous approaches by coping with complex dependency structures, unbound loops, fault handling, and unresponded service invocations.

Keywords: QoS prediction, service orchestration, WS-BPEL, Monte Carlo method.

1 Introduction

Quality of Service (QoS) of a service orchestration depend on the QoS of services it invokes. When selecting and composing various services together, the designer of an orchestrator has to consider whether the desired composition yields an overall QoS level which is acceptable for the application. In order to predict QoS two characteristics of service orchestration must be considered:

- *Different results of service invocations.* Each invoked service can return a successful reply, a fault notification, or even no reply at all. If a fault is returned, a fault handling routine will be executed instead of the normal control flow. If no reply is received, the orchestrator may wait forever for a reply (unless some parallel branch throws a fault). In either case, the resulting QoS of the composition differs from the case of successful invocation.
- *Non-determinism in the workflow.* Different runs of the same application can have different QoS values just because the orchestration control flow is non-deterministic due to two reasons. Firstly, different runs of the orchestration can get different service invocation results (success/fault/no reply). It is worth noting that a service is not always faulty or successful, rather it has a certain probability of being successful (as guaranteed in its SLA). Secondly,

---

* Work partly supported by the EU-FP7-ICT-610531 SeaClouds project.

X. Franch et al. (Eds.): ICSOC 2014, LNCS 8831, pp. 378–385, 2014.

alternative and iterative control flow structures (if/else and loops) depend on input data which may differ in different runs. This leads, for instance, to different numbers of loop iterations or to different branches executed in a if/else structure. Moreover certain QoS properties of invoked services can vary from one run to another (e.g., response time).

The objective of this paper is to present an algorithm to probabilistically predict the QoS of a workflow defining a service orchestration. The inputs of the algorithm are a WS-BPEL [1] workflow, and probability distributions for the QoS properties of the services used as well as for branch guard evaluations. The output of the algorithm is a probability distribution for the QoS properties of the orchestration. We represent distributions (both input and output) as *sampling functions* due to which not only we can compute average/expected values but also many other statistical properties (e.g., standard deviation or the probability of QoS not respecting a target SLA) by using the Monte Carlo method [2]. Our method provides a more accurate representation than traditional sequential and parallel decomposition, by using a different pair of basic composition functions which can model more suitably arbitrary dependency structures, unbound loops and fault handling in a compositional way. Furthermore, our method improves previous work by providing more accurate predictions by modeling a certain degree of correlation between parallel branches.

2   Related Work

Various approaches (e.g., [3–9]) have been proposed to determine the QoS of service compositions.

Cardoso [3] presented a mathematical model and an algorithm to compute the QoS of a workflow composition. He iteratively reduces the workflow by removing parallel, sequence, alternative and looping structures according to a set of reduction rules, until only one activity remains. However, some workflow complex dependencies cannot be decomposed into parallel or sequence, as shown in [9]. This kind of approach has been adopted also by others [5, 7, 8], some of whom (e.g., [4]) tried to overcome such limitation by defining more reduction patterns.

Mukherjee et al. [6,9] presented a algorithm to estimate the QoS of WS-BPEL compositions. They convert a WS-BPEL workflow into an activity dependency graph, and assign probabilities of being executed to each activity. In their framework it is possible to treat any arbitrary complex dependency structure as well as *fault* driven flow control. However, they do not consider correlation between activities which do not have a direct dependency, and this in some cases can yield a wrong result.

Zheng et al. [8] focused on QoS estimation for compositions represented by service graphs. In their approach however they only marginally deal with parallelism, by not considering arbitrary synchronization links (i.e., they restrict to cases in which is possible to decompose *flow*-like structures into parallel and sequences, as in [3]), and they do not take into account fault handling. Moreover, they need to fix an upper bound to the number of iterations for cycles, in order to allow decomposition into acyclic graph. They also assume that service invocations are deterministic, namely services are always successful and their QoS is not changing from one run to another.

To the best of our knowledge all previous approaches require to know a priori the exact number of iterations, or at least an upper bound for each loop in order to estimate QoS values. Also, other approaches rarely take fault handling into account, and never deal with non-responding services.

3 Determine the QoS of a Service Orchestration

In this section we introduce our algorithm to provide a QoS estimate for a service orchestration based on the QoS of the services it invokes. Our input workflows can contain any arbitrary dependency structure (i.e., not only for parallel and sequential execution patterns), fault handling, unbound loops and can preserves correlation, for example in diamond dependencies.

Our algorithm uses a structural recursive function that associates each WS-BPEL activity with a *cost* structure. This cost structure is a tuple of metadata chosen accordingly to the QoS values we want to compute. The *cost* structure has to carry enough information to allow computation of QoS values and allow composing it with other costs using the standard WS-BPEL constructs, i.e. it needs to have a composition function for each WS-BPEL construct. Later we will show that it is possible to write a composition function for most of WS-BPEL composition constructs by only requiring two basic operations on the *cost* data type. The first is the compositor for independent parallel execution of two activities. Suppose we have two activities A and B, we assume to be able to compute the cost of executing both in parallel only knowing the cost of those activities, by using a given function Both. The second compositor is the one we use to resolve dependency. If a WS-BPEL construct of A and B introduces some dependency/synchronization between the two activities, namely we suppose that it forces the activity B to start after completion of A, we will need to adjust the cost of B to take into account the dependence introduced by the composition structure, and we suppose to be able to do it from the costs of A and B by using a given operation Delay[1]. For example in our model the Sequence(A,B) construct is decomposed into a parallel execution of the independent activity A and the activity B synchronized after A, as such its cost can be written, in absence of faults, as:

$$\frac{\mathrm{Cost}(A) = cA \quad \mathrm{Cost}(B) = cB}{\mathrm{Cost}(\mathrm{Sequence}(A,B)) = \mathrm{Both}(cA, \mathrm{Delay}(cB, cA))}$$

This is similar to what has been done in previous approaches (e.g., [3]) in which the Flow dependency graph is decomposed into parallel and sequence

---

[1] We use Delay as function name because in most cases this affects only time-based properties of the dependent activity, such as completion time.

compositions. By choosing `Both` and `Delay` as basic composition operators however we can define cost composition functions for any dependence structure, while the parallel and sequence decomposition fails for a significantly wide range of dependency graph allowed by the WS-BPEL `Flow` construct [9].

Because of the definition it can be verified that functions `Both` and `Delay` need to respect the following properties:

- `Both` is commutative, i.e. $\forall a, b.\,\mathrm{Both}(a, b) = \mathrm{Both}(b, a)$
- `Both` is associative, i.e. $\forall a, b, c.\,\mathrm{Both}(a, \mathrm{Both}(b, c)) = \mathrm{Both}(\mathrm{Both}(a, b), c)$
- `Delay` is associative, i.e. $\forall a, b, c.\,\mathrm{Delay}(a, \mathrm{Delay}(b, c)) = \mathrm{Delay}(\mathrm{Delay}(a, b), c)$
- `Delay` is right-distributive over `Both`, i.e. $\forall a, b, c.\,\mathrm{Delay}(\mathrm{Both}(a, b), c)) = \mathrm{Both}(\mathrm{Delay}(a, c), \mathrm{Delay}(b, c))$

We also explicitly name a neutral element `Zero` (i.e. : `Both(A,Zero) = A` and `Delay(A,Zero) = A`) which can be useful for example to define the `All` function, which extend the `Both` function to any number of parameters:

$$\frac{}{\mathrm{All}([\,]) = \mathrm{Zero}} \qquad \frac{\mathrm{All}(t) = tc}{\mathrm{All}(h :: t) = \mathrm{Both}(h, tc)}$$

3.1   Control Flow Trimming

In WS-BPEL there are two control flow mechanism that will ultimately result in some activities not being executed: Explicit control flow (`IfThenElse` statements, iterations, and synchronization `<link>` status) and faults management. To effectively resolve such control flow structures and exclude from computation costs of activities which are not executed, we require to associate additional metadata to an activity:

- To resolve explicit control flow we assume an *environment* holding the synchronization `<link>` status and variable values. We restrict to Boolean variables in order to keep the size of the environment finite, and thus computable.
- To resolve fault handling we compute also the *outcome* of an activity, i.e., whether an activity is successfully executed or not. We identify three different outcomes for an activity: the `Success` outcome, which result in execution of consequent activities and skipping eventual *fault handlers*, the `Fault` outcome, which on the opposite will result in skipping consequent activities but executing *fault handlers*, the `Stuck` outcome is assigned to activities where the orchestrator waits for a service which failed to provide a response.

3.2   Statistical Non-determinism

It is not possible to define a deterministic function that given an activity and an input *environment* yields its *outcome*, its *cost* and the modified *environment* because:

- Outcome and cost of `Invoke` activities are in general non-deterministic, because they depend on external services.

- Data dependent control flow can not be evaluated exactly, because data values are unknown.

We can however define an `Eval` function which computes a distribution on the *outcome, cost* and output *environment* for a given activity and a given status of input *environment*. Many models can be chosen to represent a distribution. For simplicity we choose sampling functions for this purpose. Sampling functions are algorithm that extracts random values according to the distribution being represented, which can be used in a Monte Carlo simulation to retrieve probabilities and expected values. A structural recursive definition of such `Eval` function can be given by exploiting the monadic property of distributions, i.e., if an expression contains some variable whose distribution is known the distribution for the value of the expression can be computed (by integrating the variable). For sampling functions this means that it is possible to generate samples for an expression that contains a random variable for which a sampling function is available, which can be done by sampling the variable first then replacing its value inside the expression.

To give a grasp of the algorithm we give an example of the `Eval` function for the `Scope` construct (written using F# [10] programming language). As the expression depends on two subactivities, it recursively compute the sampling function for needed subactivities, then evaluate it when needed. Here the `Scope(A,H)` expression represents a scope activity with inner activity A and fault handler H, and generator is an entropy source to be used for sampling:

```
let Eval (Scope(A,H)) env =
    fun generator ->
        let aSamplingFun = Eval A env
        let newEnv,outcome,cost = asamplingFun generator
        if outcome = Fault then
            let hSamplingFun = Eval newEnv H
            let newerEnv,outcome, newCost = hSamplingFun generator
            newerEnv,outcome,Both(cost,Delay(newCost,cost))
        else
            newEnv,outcome,cost
```

From the flow analysis point of view the `Scope` activity is very similar to a `Sequence`, except that while `Sequence` executes the second activity only if the first is successful, in `Scope` the fault handler is executed only when the first yields a `Fault`. For external invocations we expect to have a sampling function describing the service, which can be written according to the service's QoS. Note that if the service has a WS-BPEL description, its sampling function can be computed in the same way with this algorithm.

```
let Eval (Invoke(s)) env =
    s.getSamplingFunction()
```

As explicit control flow construct, we implemented deterministic `IfThenElse`, whose sampling function evaluates the guard on the environment and then delegates sampling to either of branches. The transition/join conditions in the `Flow` model are implemented in a similar fashion. For the `While` loop construct the body is sampled until either the guard yields false for the output environment or a `Fault` or `Stuck` result are reached. In this case too we assume the guard evaluation to be deterministic. Since we do not allow random branching we introduce random Boolean variable assignment (OpaqueAssign). A random branching can be emulated by replacing it with a Sequence of random variable assignment followed by the branch instruction. We purposely do not allow random branching and random transition/join condition evaluation for two reasons: first it simplifies the model by keeping only one construct which introduces randomness, secondly it makes clear to the user when-conditions are correlated and when they are not. We also allow a deterministic Assign instruction to perform evaluation of Boolean expressions which are not immediately bound to a branch instruction.

For Flow we sort all activities according to the link dependencies, then for each of them we recursively compute sampling functions and generate samples for each activity outcome, cost and output environment. We store the outcome and the cost delayed by the cost of all dependencies, evaluate transition conditions, which are deterministic, and store link statuses. This allow us to skip all activities where one of the dependencies has a Stuck or Fault outcome, or whose join condition is not satisfied. We assume that there is no race condition on variables, i.e. if the same variable is used by two activities the two activities have a dependency relation (i.e. one depends on the other or vice versa), thus we only keep track of one environment. The Flow activity *outcome* will be successful if all activities inside it are successful, will be a Fault if at least one of the activities is faulty, Stuck otherwise. The *cost* is computed by merging together all delayed costs for inner activities using Both/All, since the Flow construct encodes parallel execution. The *environment* is the one resulting after executing all activities.

4 Example

To illustrate our approach, we consider a bank customer loan request example (Figure 1), which is variation of the well-known WS-BPEL loan example [1]. We want to estimate values for the Reliability, amortized expense for successful execution and average response time of this composition. Let us assume for the loan example the distribution of variable assignments and invoked services QoS shown in Table 1.

Table 1. Input distributions

	True	False
bigAmount	50%	50%
highRisk	60%	40%

	Success	Fault	Stuck
0.1$, 1 sec	79%	-	-
0.1$, 2 sec	20%	-	-
0.1$, 0 sec	-	-	1%

	Success	Fault	Stuck
5$, 10 min	30%	-	-
10$, 20 min	35%	-	-
15$, 30 min	20%	-	-
0$, 5 min	-	15%	-

   (a) Control Flow   **(b)** Risk Assessment   **(c)** Approval

The algorithm will start by evaluating the *cost* and *outcome* for the outermost Flow activity and computes *delayed costs* for the activities in the flow, and then sums them with the All compositor. Table 2 summarizes six runs of the Eval

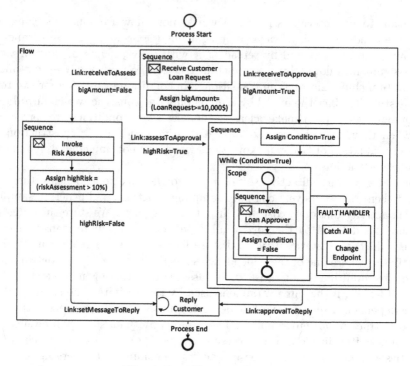

Fig. 1. Loan Request Example

function on the loan request example. To estimate the required QoS properties, we will perform a Monte Carlo sampling. Reliability can be determined by
computing the expectation of `successCount`. *Amortized expense* and *average
response time* are divided by reliability to normalize them with respect to the
number of successful executions.

Table 2. Total cost for different runs of the loan example

bigAmount	highRisk	Risk Assessment	Approval(s)	Composition
True		Success (Zero)	Fault (0$, 5 min); Success (5$, 10 min)	Success (5$, 15 min)
False	False	Success (0.1$, 2 sec)		Success (0.1$, 2 sec)
False	True	Success (0.1$, 1 sec)	Success (15$, 30 min)	Success (15.1$, 181 sec)
True		Success (Zero)	Fault (0$, 5 min); Success (10$, 20 min)	Success (10$, 25 min)
True		Success (Zero)	Success (15$, 30 min)	Success (15$, 30 min)
False		Stuck (0.1$, 0)		Stuck (0.1$, 0)

By computing the above values for the samples of Table 2 we get:

```
expectedSuccessfulTime = 1/6 · (15 · 60 + 2 + 181 + 25 · 60 + 30 · 60 + 0) = 6003/6  sec
expectedExpense = 1/6 · (5 + 0.1 + 15.1 + 10 + 15 + 0.1) = 45.3/6 $
reliability = 5/6 = 83%
amortizedExpense = 45.3/5 = 9.06$
averageResponseTime = 6003/5 = 1200.6 sec = 20 min 0.6 sec
```

5 Conclusions

In this paper we have presented a novel approach to probabilistically predict the QoS of service orchestrations. Our algorithm improves previous approaches by coping with complex dependency structures, unbound loops, fault handling, and unresponded service invocations. Our algorithm can be fruitfully exploited both to probabilistically predict QoS values before defining the SLA of an orchestration and to compare the effect of substituting one or more endpoints (viz., remote services).

We see different possible directions for future work. One of them is to extend our approach to model some other WS-BPEL constructs that we have not discussed in this paper, like `Pick` and `EventHandlers`. Another possible extension could be to allow for cases in which *no information at all* (not even a branch execution probability) is available for flow control structures. Similarly the *uncorrelated samples* restriction imposed on invocations and assignments should be relaxed. We would also like to be able to specify some degree of correlation between consecutive samples (e.g., if a service invocations yields a fault because it is "down for maintenance" we should increase the probability of getting the same fault in the next invocation).

References

1. Jordan, D., Evdemon, J., Alves, A., Arkin, A., Askary, S., Barreto, C., Bloch, B., Curbera, F., Ford, M., Goland, Y., et al.: Web services business process execution language version 2.0. OASIS standard 11 (2007)
2. Dunn, W.L., Shultis, J.K.: Exploring Monte Carlo Methods. Elsevier (2011)
3. Cardoso, A.J.S.: Quality of service and semantic composition of workflows. PhD thesis, Univ. of Georgia (2002)
4. Jaeger, M., Rojec-Goldmann, G., Muhl, G.: QoS aggregation for web service composition using workflow patterns. In: Proceedings of the Eighth IEEE International Enterprise Distributed Object Computing Conference, EDOC, pp. 149–159 (2004)
5. Ben Mabrouk, N., Beauche, S., Kuznetsova, E., Georgantas, N., Issarny, V.: QoS-Aware service composition in dynamic service oriented environments. In: Bacon, J.M., Cooper, B.F. (eds.) Middleware 2009. LNCS, vol. 5896, pp. 123–142. Springer, Heidelberg (2009)
6. Mukherjee, D., Jalote, P., Gowri Nanda, M.: Determining QoS of WS-BPEL compositions. In: Bouguettaya, A., Krueger, I., Margaria, T. (eds.) ICSOC 2008. LNCS, vol. 5364, pp. 378–393. Springer, Heidelberg (2008)
7. Wang, H., Sun, H., Yu, Q.: Reliable service composition via automatic QoS prediction. In: IEEE International Conference on Services Computing (SCC), pp. 200–207 (2013)
8. Zheng, H., Zhao, W., Yang, J., Bouguettaya, A.: Qos analysis for web service compositions with complex structures. IEEE Transactions on Services Computing 6, 373–386 (2013)
9. Mukherjee, D.: QOS IN WS-BPEL PROCESSES. Master's thesis, Indian Institute of Technology, Delhi (2008)
10. Syme, D., Granicz, A., Cisternino, A.: Expert F# 3.0, 3rd edn. Apress, Berkeley (2012)

QoS-Aware Complex Event Service Composition and Optimization Using Genetic Algorithms*

Feng Gao[1], Edward Curry[1], Muhammad Intizar Ali[1],
Sami Bhiri[2], and Alessandra Mileo[1]

[1] INSIGHT Centre,
NUI, Gawaly, Ireland
firstname.lastname@insight-centre.org
[2] Computer Science Department,
TELECOM SudParis, France
sami.bhiri@telecom-sudparis.eu

Abstract. The proliferation of sensor devices and services along with
the advances in event processing brings many new opportunities as well
as challenges. It is now possible to provide, analyze and react upon real-
time, complex events about physical or social environments. When existing event services do not provide such complex events directly, an event
service composition maybe required. However, it is difficult to determine
which compositions best suit users' quality-of-service requirements. In
this paper, we address this issue by first providing a quality-of-service
aggregation schema for event service compositions and then developing
a genetic algorithm to efficiently create optimal compositions.

Keywords: event service composition, genetic algorithm, quality-of-
service.

1 Introduction

Recent developments in the Internet-of-Things (IoT) services envision "Smart
Cities", which promise in improving urban performances in terms of sustainability, high quality of life and wiser management of natural resources. Complex
Event Processing (CEP) and event-based systems are important enabling technologies for smart cities [4], due to the need for integrating and processing high
volumes of real-time physical and social events. However, with the multitude
of heterogeneous event sources to be discovered and integrated [3], it is crucial
to determine which event services should be used and how to compose them
to match non-functional requirements from users or applications. Indeed, non-
functional properties, e.g.: quality-of-service (QoS) properties, can play a pivotal
role in service composition [7].

* This research has been partially supported by Science Foundation Ireland (SFI)
under grant No. SFI/12/RC/2289 and EU FP7 CityPulse Project under grant
No.603095. http://www.ict-citypulse.eu

X. Franch et al. (Eds.): ICSOC 2014, LNCS 8831, pp. 386–393, 2014.

In this paper, we extend the work in [2], which aims to provide CEP applications as reusable services and the reusability of those event services is determined by examining complex event patterns and primitive event types. This paper aims to enable a QoS-aware event service composition and optimization. In order to facilitate QoS-aware complex event service composition, two issues should be considered: QoS aggregation and composition efficiency. The QoS aggregation for a complex event service relies on how its member events are correlated. The aggregation rules are inherently different to conventional web services. Efficiency becomes an issue when the complex event consists of many primitive events, and each primitive event detection task can be achieved by multiple event services. This paper addresses both issues by: 1) creating QoS aggregation rules and utility functions to estimate and assess QoS for event service compositions, and 2) enabling efficient event service compositions and optimization with regard to QoS constraints and preferences based on Genetic Algorithms.

The remainder of the paper is organized as follows: Section 2 discusses related works in QoS-aware service planning; Section 3 presents the QoS model we use and the QoS aggregation rules we define; Section 4 presents the heuristic algorithm we use to achieve global optimization for event service compositions based on Genetic Algorithms (GA); Section 5 evaluates the proposed approach; conclusions and future work are discussed in Section 6.

2   Related Work

The first step of solving the QoS-aware service composition problem is to define a QoS model, a set of QoS aggregation rules and a utility function. Existing works have discussed these topics extensively [5,7]. In this paper we extract typical QoS properties from existing works and define a similar utility function based on *Simple Additive Weighting* (SAW). However, the aggregation rules in existing works focus on conventional web services rather than complex event services, which has a different QoS aggregation schema. For example, event engines also has an impact on QoS aggregation, which is not considered in conventional service QoS aggregation. Also, the aggregation rules for some QoS properties based on event composition patterns are different to those based on workflow patterns (as in [5]), which we will explain in details in Section 3.1.

As a second step, different concrete service compositions are created and compared with regard to their QoS utilities to determine the optimal choice. To achieve this efficiently, various GA-based approaches are developed [8,1,6]. The above GA-based approaches can only evaluate service composition plans with fixed sets of service tasks (abstract services) and cannot evaluate composition plans which are semantically equivalent, but consist of different service tasks, i.e., service tasks on different granularity levels. A more recent work in [7] addresses this issue by developing a GA based on Generalized Component Services. Results in [7] indicate that up to a 10% utility enhancement can be obtained by expanding the search space. Composing events on different granularity levels is also a desired feature for complex event service composition. However, [7]

Table 1. QoS aggregation rules based on composition patterns

Dimensions	Root Node Event Operators			
	Repetition	Sequence	And	Or
$P(\mathcal{E}), E(\mathcal{E}) =$	$\sum P(e), \sum E(e)$, where $e \in \mathcal{E}_{ice}$			
$Ava(\mathcal{E}) =$	$\prod Ava(e)$, where $e \in \mathcal{E}_{ice}$			
$S(\mathcal{E}) =$	$min\{S(e), e \in \mathcal{E}_{ice}\}$			
$L(\mathcal{E}) =$	$L(e), e$ is the last event in $\mathcal{E}_{dst}$			$avg\{L(e), e \in \mathcal{E}_{dst}\}$
$C(\mathcal{E}) =$	$\dfrac{min\{C(e) \cdot f(e), e \in \mathcal{E}_{dst}\}}{card(\mathcal{E}) \cdot f(\mathcal{E})}$			$\dfrac{max\{C(e) \cdot f(e), e \in \mathcal{E}_{dst}\}}{f(\mathcal{E})}$
$Acc(\mathcal{E}) =$	$\dfrac{card(\mathcal{E}) \cdot f(\mathcal{E})}{min\{Acc(e)^{-1} \cdot f(e), e \in \mathcal{E}_{dst}\}}$			$\dfrac{f(\mathcal{E})}{max\{Acc(e)^{-1} \cdot f(e), e \in \mathcal{E}_{dst}\}}$

only caters for *Input, Output, Precondition* and *Effect* based service compositions. Complex event service composition requires an *event pattern* based reuse mechanism [2].

3 QoS Model and Aggregation Schema

In this section, a QoS aggregation schema is presented to estimate the QoS properties for event service composition. A utility function is introduced to evaluate the QoS utility under constraints and preferences.

3.1 QoS Aggregation

In this paper, some typical QoS attributes are investigated, including: latency, price, bandwidth consumption, availability, completeness, accuracy and security. A numerical quality vector $Q =< L, P, E, B, Ava, C, Acc, S >$ is used to specify the QoS measures of an event service with regard to these dimensions. The *Composition Plan* is a key factor in aggregating quality vectors for event service compositions. As in [2], a composition plan contains an event pattern correlating event services with event operators. Event patterns are modeled as event syntax trees. In this paper, a step-wise transformation of event syntax tree is adopted to aggregate QoS properties. Aggregation rules for different QoS dimensions can be event operator dependent or independent, as shown in Table 1. In Table 1, $\mathcal{E}$ denotes an event service composition. $P(\mathcal{E}), E(\mathcal{E})$ etc. denote QoS values of $\mathcal{E}$. $\mathcal{E}_{ice}$ and $\mathcal{E}_{dst}$ denotes the set of Immediately Composed Event services and Direct Sub-Trees the syntax tree of $\mathcal{E}$, respectively. $f(\mathcal{E})$ gives the frequency of $\mathcal{E}$, $card(\mathcal{E})$ gives the repetition cardinality of the root node in $\mathcal{E}$.

3.2 Event QoS Utility Function

Given a quality vector Q representing the QoS capability of an event service (composition), we denote $q \in Q$ as a quality value in the vector, $O(q)$ as the theoretical optimum of q, $C(q)$ as the user-defined hard constraint on q and

$0 \le W(q) \le 1$ as the weight of q representing users' preferences. Further, we distinguish between QoS properties with the positive or negative tendency: $Q = Q_+ \cup Q_-$, where $Q_+ = \{Ava, R, Acc, S\}$ is the set of properties with the positive tendency (bigger values the better), and $Q_- = \{L, P, E, B\}$ is the properties with the negative tendency (smaller values the better). QoS utility U is given by:

$$U = \sum \frac{W(q_i) \cdot (q_i - C(q_i))}{O(q_i) - C(q_i)} - \sum \frac{W(q_j) \cdot (q_j - O(q_j))}{C(q_j) - O(q_j)} \tag{1}$$

where $q_i \in Q_+, q_j \in Q_-$. U should be maximized for the best candidate.

4   Genetic Algorithm for QoS-Aware Event Service Composition Optimization

We propose a heuristic method based on *Genetic Algorithms* (GA) to derive global optimizations for event service compositions, In our approach, the "fitness" of each solution can be evaluated by the QoS utility function in Equation (1). Compared to traditional GA-based optimizations for service compositions (where a composite service is accomplished by a fixed set of service tasks), event service compositions can have variable sets of sub-event detection tasks. Determining which event services are reusable to the event service request is resolved with hierarchies of reusable event services, called an Event Reusability Forest (ERF) [2]. In this section we elaborate how we utilize the ERF in the genetic algorithm for optimizing event service composition.

4.1   Population Initialization

Given an complex event service request expressed as a *canonical* event pattern *ep*, we consider the initialization of the population consists of three steps. First, enumerate all *Abstract Composition Plans* (ACPs) of *ep*. An ACP is a composition plan without concrete service bindings. Second, pick randomly a set of ACPs. Third, for each chosen ACP, pick randomly one concrete event service binding for each sub event involved. Then, a set of random *Concrete Composition Plans* (CCPs) is obtained. To create ACPs, we mark the *reusable nodes* of the event patterns in ERF. A reusable node is denoted N_r: $N_r \subseteq f_{canonical}(ep) \wedge \forall n \in N_r, \exists ep' \in ERF$, ep' is reusable to *ep* on *n*, as depicted in Figure 1. The ACPs for any *ep* can be enumerated by listing all possible combinations of the ACPs of their *immediate* reusable sub-patterns. By recursively aggregating those combinations, we derive the ACPs for *ep*.

4.2   Genetic Encodings for Event Syntax Trees

Given a CCP, we first assign global identifiers for the nodes in the event pattern *ep* of the CCP. Then we encode each leaf node in *ep* with its identifier, a service identifier referring to the service it represents and a string of identifiers indicating the path of the ancestor nodes of the leaf node, as shown in Figure 2.

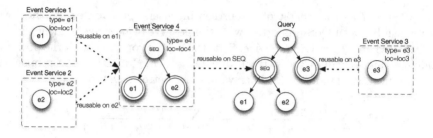

Fig. 1. Marking the reusable nodes

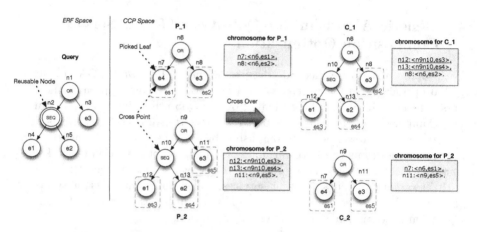

Fig. 2. Example of genetic encoding and crossover operation

4.3 Crossover and Mutation Operations

Given two genetically encoded parent CCPs P_1 and P_2, the event pattern specified in the query Q and the event reusability forest ERF, the crossover algorithm
takes the following steps to produce the children (see example in Figure 2):

1. Pick randomly a leaf node l_1 from P_1, query the reusable relations stored in
   ERF to find the relevant reusable node n_r in Q.
2. Starting from l_1, search backwards along the prefix of l_1 and locate node
   $n_1 \in P_1$, such that the event pattern represented by $T(n_1) \subseteq P_1$[1] is a
   substitute to $T(n_r) \subseteq Q$, then mark node n_1 as the cross point for P_1.
3. For all leaf nodes in P_2, denoted L_2, find $l_2 \in L_2$ which are also reusable to
   Q on n_r, or on n_r' which is a descendant of n_r, then, mark the cross point
   $n_2 \in P_2$.
4. If $L_2 = \emptyset$, it means the sub event pattern $T(n_r) \in Q$ is not implemented
   locally in P_2, so there must be at least one leaf node $l_2 \in L_2$, such that the
   event pattern represented by $T(l_1) \subseteq P_1$ is reusable to the one represented

---

[1] Given $n \in P$ is a node in pattern P, we denote $T(n) \subseteq P$ the sub-tree/sub-pattern
of P with n as its root.

Table 2. Brute-force enumeration vs. genetic algorithm

Test No.	CCP Size	Time (ms)	Avg. Utility	Max. Utility
BF-4	8004	5676	0.62	1.336
BF-5	27005	15429	0.624	1.771
BF-6	74074	37702	0.646	1.529
Init. Population			Init. Avg. Utility	
GA-4	200	353	0.413	1.121
GA-5	200	649	0.442	1.324
GA-6	200	757	0.473	1.252
GA-50	200	1270	0.403	1.303

by $T(l_2) \subseteq P_2$. For each such l_2, mark the relevant reusable node in Q as the new n_r, and try to find n_1 in the prefix of l_1 such that $T(n_1) \subseteq P_1$ is a substitute to $T(n_r) \subseteq Q$. If such n_1 is found, mark it as the new crossover point for P_1, similarly, mark the new cross point $n_2 \in P_2$.

5. If n_1 or n_2 is the root node, do nothing but keep the parents along with the new generations and give them a 100% chance of selection next time. Otherwise, swap the sub-trees in P_1, P_2 whose roots are n_1, n_2 (and therefore the relevant genes), resulting in two new CCPs.

The mutation operation changes the composition plan for a leaf node in a CCP. To do that we select a random leaf node n in a CCP P, and treat the event pattern of n (possibly a primitive event) as an event query to be composed, then we use the same random CCP creation process specified in the population initialization (Section 4.1) to alter its implementation.

5   Evaluation

In this section we present the experimental results of the proposed approaches based on simulated datasets. The weights of QoS metrics in the preference vector are equally set to 1.0, and a loose constraint is defined in the query which do not reject any event service compositions to enlarge the search space.

5.1   Brute-Force Enumeration vs. Genetic Algorithm

In the first experiment, we compare our genetic algorithm with brute-force enumerations in terms of the maximum QoS utility obtained and execution time required. We test both methods over three random event service repositories with different sizes. The results are shown in Table 2 ("BF" and "GA" indicate the test for brute-force enumeration and genetic algorithm, receptively. The number after the dash is the number of candidate event services for each sub-event detection task). From the results in Table 2, we can see that GA based approach

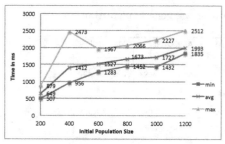

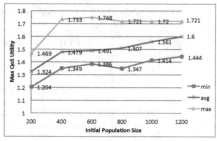

(a) Convergence time under various population size

(b) Max QoS utility under various population size

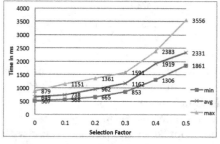

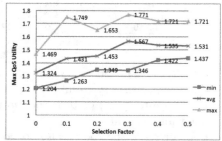

(c) Convergence time under different selection factor

(d) Max QoS utility under different selection factor

Fig. 3. Performances under different population sizes and selection factors

produces about 79% optimal results in much a shorter time, compared with the brute-force enumerations.

5.2   Convergence Time vs. Degree of Optimization

There are two ways to increase the utility in the GA results: increase the size of the initial population or the selection probability for the individuals in each generation. To evaluate the influence of the initial population size and selection probability, we execute the genetic evolutions with different population sizes and selection probabilities over the second dataset (BF-5) in Table 2.

Figure 3(a) and Figure 3(b) show the growth of execution time and best QoS utility retrieved using from 200 to 1200 CCPs as the initial populations. From the results we can see that the growth of evolution time is (almost) linear to the size of the initial population. In total, increasing the initial population from 200 to 1200 gains an additional 0.276 (15.6%) QoS utility with the cost of 1344 milliseconds of execution time.

In the tests above, we adopt the *Roullete Wheel* selection policy with *elites*. However, this selection policy results in early extinction of the population. To produce more generations, we simply increase the selection probability with a constant $0 \leq F \leq 1$, we call the additional F the *selection factor*. Figure 3(c) and Figure 3(d) show the execution time and best evolution results with different selection factors from 0 to 0.5.

6 Conclusions and Future Work

In this paper a QoS aggregation schema and utility function is proposed to calculate QoS vectors for event services (compositions) and rank them based on user-defined constraints and preferences. Then, a genetic algorithm is developed and evaluated to efficiently create optimal event service compositions. The experimental results show that the genetic algorithm is scalable, and by leveraging the trade-off between convergence time and degree of optimization, the algorithm gives 79% to 97% optimized results. As future work, we plan to validate our approach based on real-world datasets. We also plan to enable adaptive event compositions based on the GA developed in this paper.

References

1. Canfora, G., Di Penta, M., Esposito, R., Villani, M.L.: A lightweight approach for qos-aware service composition. In: Proceedings of 2nd International Conference on Service Oriented Computing, ICSOC 2004 (2004)
2. Gao, F., Curry, E., Bhiri, S.: Complex Event Service Provision and Composition based on Event Pattern Matchmaking. In: Proceedings of the 8th ACM International Conference on Distributed Event-Based Systems. ACM, Mumbai (2014)
3. Hasan, S., Curry, E.: Approximate Semantic Matching of Events for The Internet of Things. ACM Transactions on Internet Technology, TOIT (2014)
4. Hinze, A., Sachs, K., Buchmann, A.: Event-based applications and enabling technologies. In: Proceedings of the Third ACM International Conference on Distributed Event-Based Systems, DEBS 2009, pp. 1:1–1:15. ACM, New York (2009)
5. Jaeger, M., Rojec-Goldmann, G., Muhl, G.: Qos aggregation for web service composition using workflow patterns. In: Proceedings of the Eighth IEEE International Enterprise Distributed Object Computing Conference, EDOC 2004, pp. 149–159 (2004)
6. Karatas, F., Kesdogan, D.: An approach for compliance-aware service selection with genetic algorithms. In: Basu, S., Pautasso, C., Zhang, L., Fu, X. (eds.) ICSOC 2013. LNCS, vol. 8274, pp. 465–473. Springer, Heidelberg (2013)
7. Wu, Q., Zhu, Q., Jian, X.: Qos-aware multi-granularity service composition based on generalized component services. In: Basu, S., Pautasso, C., Zhang, L., Fu, X. (eds.) ICSOC 2013. LNCS, vol. 8274, pp. 446–455. Springer, Heidelberg (2013)
8. Zhang, L.J., Li, B.: Requirements driven dynamic services composition for web services and grid solutions. Journal of Grid Computing 2(2), 121–140 (2004)

Towards QoS Prediction Based on Composition Structure Analysis and Probabilistic Models[*]

Dragan Ivanović[1], Manuel Carro[1,2], and Peerachai Kaowichakorn[2]

[1] IMDEA Software Institute, Spain
[2] School of Computer Science, U. Politécnica de Madrid (UPM), Spain
dragan.ivanovic@imdea.org, mcarro@fi.upm.es

Abstract. The quality of service (QoS) of complex software systems, built by composing many components, is essential to determine their usability. Since the QoS of each component usually has some degree of uncertainty, the QoS of the composite system also exhibits stochastic behavior. We propose to compute probability distributions of the QoS of a service composition using its structure and the probability distributions of the QoS of the components. We experimentally evaluate our approach on services deployed in a real setting using a tool to predict probability distributions for the composition QoS and comparing them with those obtained from actual executions.

1 Introduction

Analyzing and predicting QoS of service compositions during the design phase makes it possible to explore design decisions under different environment conditions and can greatly reduce the amount and cost of maintenance, help the adaptation of software architectures, and increase overall software quality.

The QoS of a service composition depends both on the QoS of the individual components and on the structure of the composition. The effects of the execution environment also impact the observed QoS, which exhibits a stochastic variability due (among others) to changes in network traffic, machine load, cache behavior, database accesses at a given moment, etc. QoS prediction is notoriously challenging when, as in the case of service-oriented systems, boundaries and behavior are not fully specified.

```
Input: transport
if transport == "train"
    call SearchTrain
else
    call SearchFlight
end
```

Fig. 1. Simple orchestration

Fig. 1 shows a fragment of a service composition. Let us assume that we are interested on execution time and that we know (e.g., from observations) the probability distribution functions for the response times of the two services invoked in it (Fig. 2 (a) and (b)), whose averages are 5 and 3 seconds, respectively. The average response time for Fig. 1 may actually be seldom observed, as executions cluster around 3 and 5

[*] The research leading to these results has received funding from the EU FP 7 2007-2013 program under agreement 610686 POLCA, from the Madrid Regional Government under CM project S2013/ICE-2731 (N-Greens), and from the Spanish Ministry of Economy and Competitiveness under projects TIN-2008-05624 DOVES and TIN2011-39391-C04-03 StrongSoft.

X. Franch et al. (Eds.): ICSOC 2014, LNCS 8831, pp. 394–402, 2014.
© Springer-Verlag Berlin Heidelberg 2014

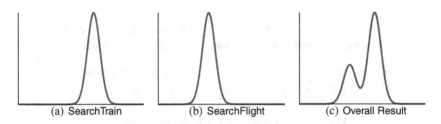

(a) SearchTrain   (b) SearchFlight   (c) Overall Result

Fig. 2. Statistical profiles for Fig. 1

seconds. Moreover, this average is not useful to answer questions such as *what is the probability that the answer time is less than 4 seconds*, which is interesting to, for example, negotiate penalties to compensate for SLA deviations.

If we know the probability that train / plane trips are requested (e.g., 0.3 and 0.7, respectively), we can construct the probability distribution of the QoS of the composition (Fig. 2 (c)). This result gives much more information and insight on the expected QoS of the composition, and makes it possible to answer the question presented above.

2 Related Work

The basis for the classical approach to the analysis of QoS for service compositions [2,1,4] is *QoS aggregation*. Most approaches focus on the control structure without considering data operations, and return expected values as result. This falls short to describe the composition behavior. More recent approaches infer upper and lower bounds of QoS based on input data and environmental factors [5]. However, bounds often need to be too large, since services often exhibit a "long-tail" behavior, and bounds do not capture the shape of the distribution of values, which limits the usefulness of the description.

Recent proposals [7] work directly with statistical distributions of QoS, but use a very abstract composition model that is far from existing implementation languages and does not take into account internal compositions of data and operations, which is bound to give less accurate results. The work in [6] uses probability distributions to drive SLA negotiation and optimization. While its focus is complementary to ours, it does not take into account the relationships between the internal state and data operations of the composition (including the initial inputs) and its QoS.

3 Probabilistic Interpretation of Compositions

Our method interprets control structures and data operations (Fig. 3) in a probabilistic domain by computing with discrete probability distributions rather than just with representative data points. For each (tuple of) variable(s) there is a mapping ρ which assigns a probability to each value / tuple. These represent the uncertainty in the QoS of services, the values of data items, and the resulting QoS of the composition. The mapping initially assigns a separate probability distribution for the domain of each variable (including QoS metrics). When variables are used together in an expression or a branch condition, their values may become related and joint probabilities need to be used. The

$$C ::= \langle \text{variable} \rangle := E \quad | \text{ call } \langle \text{service} \rangle \quad | \text{ if } B \text{ then } C \text{ else } C \quad | \text{ while } B \text{ do } C$$
$$| \text{ begin } C[; \ C]^* \text{ end } | \text{ or } C[; \ C]^* \text{ end } | \text{ and } C[; \ C]^* \text{ end } | \text{ skip}$$

$$E ::= \langle \text{numeral} \rangle \mid \langle \text{variable} \rangle \mid E \circ E \qquad (\circ \in \{+, -, *, \textbf{div}, \textbf{mod}\})$$
$$B ::= E \, \delta \, E \mid B \wedge B \mid B \vee B \mid \neg B \qquad (\delta \in \{>, \geq, =, \neq, <, \leq\})$$

Fig. 3. Abstract syntax for composition constructs

interpretation of every construct starts with a distribution ρ before the construct is executed and produces a ρ' after it is executed. ρ' describes all possible executions (and only those) that are consistent with the distribution ρ before the execution.

Let us assume variables $x, y \in \{1, 2\}$ and their probability distributions in Fig. 4 and the code in Fig. 5. At the beginning, all the combinations of these two values are equally probable. The question is what are the probabilities of the possible values of x and y at the end of the if–then–else; let us call these values x' and y'. Since whether x or y are updated depends on their concrete values, not all combinations of $x + 10$ and $y + 10$ are possible. If $x' = 1$, it must be $y' = 11$, but $y' = 12$ is not possible: y cannot be incremented if $x = 1, y = 2$. The only valid combinations are $(x', y') \in \{(1, 11), (11, 2), (2, 11), (2, 12)\}$ with probability 0.25 each. Then, the values of x and y have become entangled and need to be described as a joint probability distribution.

3.1   Elements of the Model

The elements that make up our model are: composition structure (to describe control constructs / data operations), the composition data (including input data and internal variables), the QoS attributes of interest, and statistical data on the services used in the composition. The QoS attributes may include execution time, amount of data sent / received, number of general / specific operations executed, availability, etc. as long as it can be numerically quantified. Our proposal is parametric on the QoS attribute: we only require probability distributions for each service and an aggregation operator.

Integer random variables are used to represent both the state of internal variables (discretized after an abstraction process, if necessary) and of the QoS attribute of interest. Random variables are categorized in three types:

- $\mathbf{X} = X_1 X_2 X_3 \ldots X_n$ represents variables in the composition.
- $\mathbf{S} = S_1 S_2 S_3 \ldots S_m$ represents the QoS attributes for each service in the composition.
- Q models the behavior of the selected QoS attribute for the composition.

We represent the values of the random variables in the set $Q\mathbf{XS}$ of $N = 1 + n + m$ variables with a *discrete joint probability distribution* $\rho : \mathbb{Z}^N \to [0, 1]$ such that

Var.	Val. $\mapsto$ Prob.	Val. $\mapsto$ Prob.
x	$1 \mapsto 0.5$	$2 \mapsto 0.5$
y	$1 \mapsto 0.5$	$2 \mapsto 0.5$

Fig. 4. Probability distributions

if x < y then x = x + 10 else y = y + 10 end

Fig. 5. Code to be interpreted in a probabilistic domain

$\sum_{\mathbf{v} \in \mathbb{Z}^N} \rho(\mathbf{v}) = 1$. If $Y_1, Y_2, \ldots, Y_k$ are distinct variables from $Q\mathbf{XS}$ which we want to highlight and $\mathbf{V}$ is the ordered set of the $N - k$ remaining variables from $Q\mathbf{XS}$, we write

$$\rho(Y_1 = y_1, Y_2 = y_2, \ldots, Y_k = y_k, \mathbf{V} = \mathbf{v}) \tag{1}$$

to denote the probability that $Y_1, Y_2, \ldots, Y_k$ and $\mathbf{V}$ have exactly the values $y_1, y_2, \ldots y_k \in \mathbb{Z}$ and $\mathbf{v} \in \mathbb{Z}^{N-k}$, respectively. When it is clear from the context we write (1) simply as $\rho(y_1, y_2, \ldots, y_k, \mathbf{v})$. When it is precisely known that $Q = q$, $\mathbf{X} = \mathbf{x}$ and $\mathbf{S} = \mathbf{s}$ for some $(q, \mathbf{x}, \mathbf{s}) \in \mathbb{Z}^N$, then $\rho(q, \mathbf{x}, \mathbf{s}) = 1$, and for all other arguments ρ gives zero.

3.2 Initial Conditions and Independence

The interpretation starts with an initial distribution ρ. We do not enforce independence (non-entanglement) in this ρ, but we assume it here to simplify the presentation. For each state variable X_i and service S_j, $\rho_{X_i} : \mathbb{Z} \to [0,1]$ and $\rho_{S_j} : \mathbb{Z} \to [0,1]$ describe resp. their initial distributions of values and of QoS. $\rho_Q : \mathbb{Z} \to [0,1]$ describes the initial value for the composition QoS, Q, normally initialized to zero. The aggregate distribution $\rho_{\mathbf{X}} : \mathbb{Z}^n \to [0,1]$ (and similarly for $\rho_{\mathbf{S}} : \mathbb{Z}^m \to [0,1]$) is computed as

$$\rho_{\mathbf{X}}(x_1, x_2, \ldots, x_n) = \rho_{X_1}(x_1) \times \rho_{X_2}(x_2) \times \cdots \times \rho_{X_n}(x_n) \tag{2}$$

3.3 Assignments and Arithmetic

In an assignment $X := E$, E may involve any number of variables from $\mathbf{X}$, including X. The *after* distribution ρ' needs to satisfy the condition $\rho'(x, \mathbf{v}) = \sum \{\rho(u, \mathbf{v}) \mid x = E[u, \mathbf{v}]\}$ where $E[u, \mathbf{v}]$ represents the result of E for $X = u$ and $\mathbf{V} = \mathbf{v}$. The probability for $(x, \mathbf{v})$ in ρ' aggregates the probabilities of all tuples $(u, \mathbf{v})$ from ρ where the expression E evaluates to x. For all other tuples, ρ' gives zero.

Assignments make the variable to the left of ":=" depend on the variables in E. E.g., for $X_1 := X_2 + X_3$, the independent $\rho_{X_1}(x_1)$ from (2) is replaced with $\rho'_{X_1|X_2,X_3}(x_1 \mid x_2, x_3)$ which gives the probability of $X_1 = x_1$ given $X_2 = x_2$ and $X_3 = x_3$. Fig. 6 shows *before* and *after* distributions for the same example of assignment. The *after* state distribution ρ'_{X_1,X_2,X_3} is then computed as $\rho'_{X_1|X_2,X_3} \times \rho_{X_2} \times \rho_{X_3}$.

3.4 Service Invocation

A service invocation **call** s_i updates the expected QoS Q by composing its initial distribution with the random variable S_i representing the QoS of service s_i. For the case of execution time it amounts to adding random variables: $Q := Q + S_i$.

x_1	ρ_{X_1}
0	1.0

x_3	ρ_{X_3}
0	0.4
1	0.6

x_2	ρ_{X_2}
1	0.3
2	0.5
4	0.2

x_1	x_2	x_3	$\rho'_{X_1|X_2,X_3}$
1	1	0	1.0
2	1	1	1.0
2	2	0	1.0
3	2	1	1.0
4	4	0	1.0
5	4	1	1.0

x_1	x_2	x_3	ρ'_{X_1,X_2,X_3}
1	1	0	0.12
2	1	1	0.18
2	2	0	0.20
3	2	1	0.30
4	4	0	0.08
5	4	1	0.12

Fig. 6. Sample probabilities for $X_1 := X_2 + X_3$

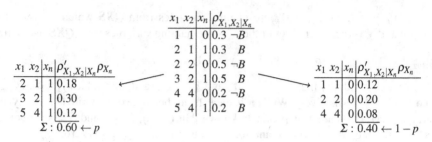

Fig. 7. Grouping and splitting under $X_2 > X_1$

Other QoS attributes will need specific aggregation operators. For example, availability will need to be aggregated with $\times$ instead of $+$. If the invoked service gives value to some variable X, its result value will have to be replaced in the after ρ'_X.

We assume that the QoS and results of s_i do not depend on its input data. In our framework, taking this into account would require to include probability of outputs given inputs. Although doable, in practice this is a challenge for which we still do not have a satisfactory solution other than assuming a uniform distribution.

3.5 Sequential Composition

In a sequential composition **begin** C_1; C_2; $\ldots$; C_k **end** the interpretation of each C_i computes ρ'_i from $\rho_i = \rho'_{i-1}$, and the sequence computes then $\rho' = \rho'_k$ from $\rho = \rho_0$.

3.6 Conditionals

In the construct **if** B **then** C_1 **else** C_2, we need to determine the probability of each branch. If $\mathbf{v}$ represents the value of all random variables from $Q\mathbf{XS}$, the probability of executing the **then** part is:

$$p = \sum \{\rho(\mathbf{v}) \mid B[\mathbf{v}]\} \tag{3}$$

where $B[\mathbf{v}]$ represents the truth value of B. If $p = 1$ or $p = 0$, we continue interpreting C_1 or C_2, resp. Otherwise, we interpret independently C_1 and C_2 with initial distributions ρ_1 and ρ_2, respectively, which are adjusted so that $\sum_{\mathbf{v} \in \mathbb{Z}^N} \rho_1(\mathbf{v}) = 1$ (resp. for ρ_2) according to the probability that B holds:

$$\rho_1(x, \mathbf{v}) = \rho(x, \mathbf{v})/p \quad (4) \qquad\qquad \rho_2(x, \mathbf{v}) = \rho(x, \mathbf{v})/(1 - p) \quad (5)$$

If ρ'_1 and ρ'_2 are the probabilistic interpretations of C_1 and C_2, the result for the whole construct will be $\rho' = p \times \rho'_1 + (1 - p) \times \rho'_2$. ρ_1 and ρ_2 are generated by splitting the values of the variables in the condition B. Rather than filtering ρ in a straightforward implementation of (3), (4) and (5), we can group and split only the values of the random variables from $\mathbf{X}$ that appear in B. Fig. 7 shows the process using the same variables as in Fig. 6 for $B \equiv X_1 > X_2$. In the central table the probabilities for the **then** and **else** branches are normalized according to the probabilities of B and $\neg B$, and later split into two tables according to these two cases.

3.7 Loops

We restrict ourselves to terminating loops. Loop constructs (Eq. (6)) are unfolded into a conditional, treated according to Section 3.6, and a loop (Eq. (7)):

while B **do** C_1 (6)   **if** B **then begin** C_1; **while** B **do** C_1 **end else skip**   (7)

Termination ensures that the unfolding is finitary. Existing techniques [3] can decide termination for many cases.

3.8 Or-Split and And-Split

For conciseness, we will not detail here the and- and or-split rules. We model them similarly to the sequential composition with two differences:

- The distributions for internal data are not carried over from C_i to C_{i+1}. The forked activities are assumed to work in independent environments.
- QoS aggregation differs. In the case of execution time, for the or-split, the total execution time is the minimum of the C_i; resp. maximum for the and-split.

3.9 Interpreting the Results

Let us recall that we want to answer questions such as what is the value $\Pr[Q \leq a]$. This can be computed from the final ρ' as $\Pr[Q \leq a] = \sum_{q \leq a} \sum_{\mathbf{v}} \rho'(q, \mathbf{v})$, where $\mathbf{v}$ is a tuple of values for all random variables from **XS**. Questions such as *"what is the probability that the process finishes in (exactly) 3 seconds"* are not useful, as it can be argued that the answer tends to zero. Questions such as *"what is the probability that the process finishes in 2.95 to 3.05 seconds?"* are more interesting; the answer can be computed as $\Pr[a \leq Q \leq b] = \Pr[Q \leq b] - \Pr[Q \leq a]$ for some a, b.

4 Experimental Validation

The experimental validation focused on execution time and was conducted on fully-deployed services. We compared actual execution times, obtained from a large number of repeated executions, with the distribution predicted by a tool.

4.1 Tool Implementation Notes

A fully-functional prototype of the tool has been implemented in Prolog, which gives excellent capabilities for symbolic representation and manipulation (for the abstract syntax and the probability distributions) and automatic memory management. The prototype receives the composition code, the values of the observed QoS for the services, and the expected values of the input variables; it interprets the program in a domain of probability distributions, and gives as result the expected QoS (time, in our examples) and, if requested, the distribution of the values of internal variables.

The services were implemented in Java and deployed on *Google App Engine*. The orchestration is a client-side Java application that connects to the services. The composition and the individual services were executed several hundred times to obtain a distribution ρ_E of the composition and the distributions ρ_{s_i} of the services. The distribution

ρ_P of the predicted execution time is produced from a single run of the interpreter. In order to find out the network impact on our results, we measured time both on the client and on the service to derive:

1. Total (round-trip) execution time (t_a), as measured on the client side.
2. Service execution time (t_e), measured by the service implementation and passed to the client. This excludes network transmission time.
3. Network transmission time $t_n = t_a - t_e$.

4.2 Experiment One: Matrix Multiplication

This service performs matrix multiplication. It receives two matrices from the orchestration (Fig. 8) and returns their product. Large square matrices (dimensions 500×500) are used to ensure meaningful execution times.

The multiplication service is called 500 times, recording t_a, t_e, and t_n for each invocation. The composition is executed 500 times.

```
begin
  x := 0;
  while x < 5 do begin
    call MatrixMultiplicationService;
    x := x + 1
  end
end
```

Fig. 8. Matrix multiplication

4.3 Experiment Two: Sorting

Implementations of *BubbleSort* and the *QuickSort* algorithms were deployed. Both services receive an array of integers and return a sorted array. The client-side composition creates ten 1000-element arrays of integers and invokes the services. To generate service time distributions for the analyzer, each service is invoked 500 times.

Fig. 9 sketches the composition. BubbleSort is invoked 20% of the times, QuickSort 30% of the time, and a mix of both 50% of the time.

```
Input: n from 0 to 9
// Sort depending on the mode
if n < 2 then // bubble sort
  repeat 10 times:
    call BubbleSortService;
else if n < 5 then // quick sort
  repeat 10 times:
    call QuickSortService;
else // mix sort
  repeat 5 times:
    call BubbleSortService;
  repeat 5 times:
    call QuickSortService;
end
```

Fig. 9. Experiment two: composition structure

4.4 Experimental Results

Fig. 10 displays, for both experiments, the accumulated predicted and actual probability, i.e. $\Pr[T_P < t]$ and $\Pr[T_E < t]$ for the service execution times. Both lines are so close that it is difficult to distinguish them. While this suggests that the prediction is very accurate, it does not allow drawing clear conclusions about the prediction accuracy. Therefore we resorted to a numerical comparison using the *Mean Square Error* (MSE):

$$MSE = \frac{1}{t_{\max} - t_{\min}} \sum_{t = t_{\min}}^{t_{\max}} (\Pr[T_P < t] - \Pr[T_E < t])^2 \qquad (8)$$

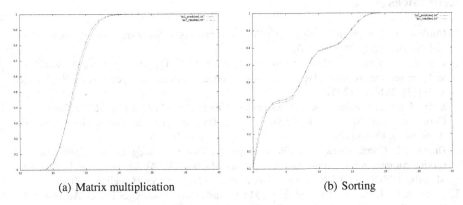

(a) Matrix multiplication   (b) Sorting

Fig. 10. Comparisons for $\Pr[T_{Pn} < t]$ against $\Pr[T_{En} < t]$

Table 1. Mean Square Error

Measurement	Observed Probability	Uniform Probability	Constant Probability
Experiment 1			
$\Pr[T_{Pa} < t]$	0.070	0.383	0.577
$\Pr[T_{Pn} < t]$	0.012	0.310	0.434
$\Pr[T_{Pe} < t]$	0.0003	0.138	0.537
Experiment 2			
$\Pr[T_{Pa} < t]$	0.006	0.388	0.494
$\Pr[T_{Pn} < t]$	0.010	0.306	0.383
$\Pr[T_{Pe} < t]$	0.0001	0.126	0.488

The smaller the MSE, the more accurate the prediction is. However, the MSE is just a number whose magnitude we need to put in context to decide how good is the fitness we obtain — for example, comparing this number with the fitness obtained with other prediction techniques. This is not easy due to to the difficulty of installing and running tools implementing existing proposals.

Therefore we repeated the predictions using as input probability distributions to characterize external services either a single point (for the average approach) or a uniform distribution ranging from the observed lower to upper bound (for the bounds approach). We termed these scenarios *Constant Probability* and *Uniform Probability*, resp. Table 1 shows the evaluation results. From them it is clear that using the observed probability distribution produces much more accurate (for orders of magnitude) predictions. Most of the prediction errors come from the network characteristics, which are difficult to control. If the network issues are excluded ($\Pr[T_{Pe} < t]$), the predictions show very promising results with very small MSE.

References

1. Cardoso, J.: Complexity analysis of BPEL web processes. Software Process: Improvement and Practice 12(1), 35–49 (2007)
2. Cardoso, J., Sheth, A., Miller, J., Arnold, J., Kochut, K.: Quality of service for workflows and web service processes. Web Semantics: Science, Services and Agents on the World Wide Web 1(3), 281–308 (2004),
   http://www.sciencedirect.com/science/article/pii/S157082680400006X
3. Cook, B., Podelski, A., Rybalchenko, A.: Proving program termination. Commun. ACM 54(5), 88–98 (2011)
4. Dumas, M., García-Bañuelos, L., Polyvyanyy, A., Yang, Y., Zhang, L.: Aggregate quality of service computation for composite services. In: Maglio, P.P., Weske, M., Yang, J., Fantinato, M. (eds.) ICSOC 2010. LNCS, vol. 6470, pp. 213–227. Springer, Heidelberg (2010)
5. Ivanović, D., Carro, M., Hermenegildo, M.: Towards Data-Aware QoS-Driven Adaptation for Service Orchestrations. In: Proceedings of the 2010 IEEE International Conference on Web Services (ICWS 2010), Miami, FL, USA, July 5-10, pp. 107–114. IEEE (2010)
6. Kattepur, A., Benveniste, A., Jard, C.: Negotiation strategies for probabilistic contracts in web services orchestrations. In: ICWS, pp. 106–113 (2012)
7. Zheng, H., Yang, J., Zhao, W., Bouguettaya, A.: QoS Analysis for Web Service Compositions Based on Probabilistic QoS. In: Kappel, G., Maamar, Z., Motahari-Nezhad, H.R. (eds.) Service Oriented Computing. LNCS, vol. 7084, pp. 47–61. Springer, Heidelberg (2011)

Orchestrating SOA Using Requirement Specifications and Domain Ontologies

Manoj Bhat, Chunyang Ye, and Hans-Arno Jacobsen

Application and Middleware Systems Research Group
Technische Universität München, Germany
{manoj.mahabaleshwar,yec}@tum.de

Abstract. The composition of web services requires process designers to capture the goals of the service composition in a partial process model. Manually deriving the partial process model from the requirement specifications is not trivial. A clear understanding of the requirements, interaction among services, their inputs and outputs are precursors for developing the partial process models. To reduce the complexity, we propose an approach to guide process designers in deriving the partial process models by reusing the knowledge captured in requirement specifications and domain ontologies. The results of the evaluation shows that our approach is promising in terms of correctness and completeness.

Keywords: Web service composition, domain ontology, requirements engineering, knowledge reuse.

1 Introduction

Services Computing is an interdisciplinary field that covers the science and technology of using computing and information technology (IT) to model, create, operate, and manage services that bridges the gap between business and IT [1]. Increase in the creation and consumption of web services has made the analysis and generation of composition plan challenging [2]. Approaches that tackle the issue of service composition require users to capture the service composition requirements in the form of service templates, service query profiles, or partial process models [8–10]. The requirements include: list of sub-services, inputs, outputs, preconditions and effects (IOPEs) of the sub-services, and the execution order of these sub-services. Henceforth, we refer to the templates that capture these requirements as *partial process models*. The existing approaches assume that the partial process models are readily available to initiate the service composition engine. However, this assumption does not always hold in practice [3].

In this paper, we address the issue of automatically deriving the partial process model for service composition. The goal is to reduce the burden of process designers to a great extent, especially for non-domain experts. Our experiment discussed in Section 3 indicates that the main challenges for process designers include: understanding the composition requirements of complex services, correctly correlating the inputs and outputs of sub-services, and designing the business

X. Franch et al. (Eds.): ICSOC 2014, LNCS 8831, pp. 403–410, 2014.

logic of the process model. To address these issues, we propose to use domain ontologies, user stories in the requirement specification documents (RSDs), and user queries to recommend a set of services along with their inputs, outputs, and execution order to describe the partial process model.

Ontologies are extensively used in different phases of software engineering [4]. In recent years, organizations are putting in the extra effort for manually creating domain ontologies due to their significant advantages as a means of knowledge sharing and reuse. There also exist automatic and semi-automatic approaches for ontology creation. For instance, LexOnto [5] uses the web services in the Programmable Web directory [6] to create classification ontologies. As ontologies are generally available or they can be generated using existing tools, we consider using ontologies to facilitate the automatic generation of partial process models.

On the other hand, the popularity of agile methodologies has made the use of user stories to capture requirements a common practice. The user stories are expressed in a standard format such as "As a *role*, I want *goal* so that *benefit*." To simplify the algorithm, we focus only on the user stories. However, our approach can be generalized to the individual statements in the RSDs.

Since a service composition may involve services from different domains, one of the main challenges of our approach is to link domain ontologies to handle requirements from multiple domains. To address this challenge, we extended the existing approach by Ajmeri et al. [7] that helps requirement analysts visualize how requirements span across multiple domains. The ontologies are linked using the semantic similarity of concepts. The linking of ontologies is used to derive a conceptual model of the requirements to help requirement analysts improve the completeness of requirements. Furthermore, we use natural language processing (NLP) to link the concepts in the ontologies with the terms in the user stories and to classify the concepts as either services or input-output (i/o) of services. Once the atomic services and their inputs and outputs are identified for a queried service, the data dependency constraints determine the execution order.

The main contributions of this paper are two-fold. First we propose an approach to automatically generate the partial process model for service composition. Our approach complements the ideas behind the existing ontology-based and NLP-based service composition approaches. Second we realize our approach as a recommender system that can integrate ontologies and user stories to substantially reduce the time and effort involved in service composition.

2   Related Work

Artificial Intelligence (AI) Planning and Ontology Based Solutions: To address the problem of service composition, different planning techniques have been proposed. These approaches require capturing the requirements as a partial process model which is given as input to the composition engine. The engine generates a plan by comparing the requirements against the services in the repository. For instance, in [8] the goals are captured in a goal language and the planner generates a plan that satisfies these goals. Similarly, in [9] the similarity between the user requests and the services is computed based on the syntactic, semantic and operational details. Furthermore, Grigori et al. [10] propose a method to transform the behavior matching of services and user requests to a graph matching problem. Capturing the requirements in a partial process model is a non-trivial task. We address this issue in our approach by automatically deriving the partial process model from the RSDs and the domain ontologies.

Tag-Based Service Composition: The tag-based approaches for service composition are becoming popular [11]. They are easy to implement and to use. However, they have their own shortcomings, for instance, tags are usually too short to carry enough semantic information and most services have only a few tags. These tags can belong to different types such as content-based, context-based, attribute, and subjective. This results in a large tag-space and low efficiency and effectiveness in semantic matching. Therefore, these approaches are oriented towards mashup. They do not address how to generate traditional workflows which involve sequentially and parallel executing tasks.

Publish/Subscribe-Based Distributed Algorithm: Hu et al. [12] propose a distributed algorithm to enable service composition via a content-based pub/sub infrastructure. Even though the distributed approach seems promising, it considers matching of services at a syntactic level, whereas our solution concerns both syntactic and semantic levels.

Service Composition Using NLP: The service composition system proposed in [13] addresses the shortcomings of the existing NLP-based solutions [14]. The solution proposed in [13] comprises of an integrated natural language parser, a semantic matcher, and an AI planner. The parser extracts the grammatical relations from the requirements and generates the service prototypes comprising of process names and input values. The service prototypes are further used by the semantic matcher to identify services from the repository and the AI planner generates a composed service. In this approach, a clear set of patterns used to identify the process names and their input values from the requirements is not captured. Furthermore, a detailed evaluation of the system with respect to correctness and completeness of the generated composed services is missing.

Although, there exist a large body of knowledge addressing service discovery and composition, understanding the technical and domain specific requirements for process designers to use these approaches still remains a challenge.

3 Case Study of Service Composition

As part of the course curriculum [15], participants are required to complete a project comprising three milestones (M). In M1, each group is required to develop three web services. In M2, participants develop a search engine to look up services from the server. Finally, in M3, each group is required to develop a Travel Agency (TA) service by composing the existing services.

Out of 76 deployed services in M1, 47 services were correctly implemented. However, in M3, 8 groups deployed the TA service and only 1 group correctly implemented the service. The drop in the performance is overwhelming but understandable. One of the main challenges for the participants was to address the problem at a conceptual level. The requirements of M1, to develop atomic services were straightforward and easy to comprehend. The participants success-fully developed a conceptual model which helped them implement the services. On the other hand in M3, the TA service consisted of several sub-services which were from different domains and implemented by different groups. The partici-pants were unsuccessful in creating a conceptual model due to the lack of a clear understanding of the complex relationships among the services.

This example shows that manu-ally creating a correct partial process model is challenging. Our investiga-tion indicates that the main difficul-ties include how to design the business logic of the process correctly and how to correlate their inputs and outputs correctly. If the participants were pre-sented with a process model as shown in Figure 1, understanding the com-position requirements would be easier and the time and the effort involved would be substantially reduced.

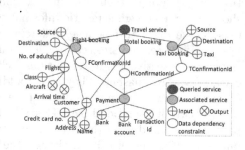

Fig. 1. Partial process model for TA service

4 Approach

The challenges that we address in our approach include: mapping of domain ontologies using semantic similarity mapping approach, identifying if a concept is a service or an i/o of a service, capturing the data dependency of services, and integrating the recommendation with user preferences.

Overview: In this section, we briefly introduce how the partial process model is generated. As shown in Figure 2, the process designer inputs the keywords cor-responding to the service he plans to develop. He also selects the relevant domain ontologies and provides the list of user stories to the system. The system maps the concepts in the domain ontologies to the terms in the user stories and identi-fies the candidate sub-services. The concepts in the domain ontologies associated with the candidate services are identified as i/o concepts of sub-services. Users' past preferences filter the candidate services and tag the i/o concept as either input to a service or output of a service. Tagging of concepts as inputs and out-puts of sub-services establishes the data-dependency constraints to determine the execution order of the sub-services. The process designers' selection iteratively updates the user preference repository to improve the recommendations. Process designers can also suggest the missing concepts to evolve the ontologies, which are validated by a domain expert before updating the ontologies. The partial process model created based on the recommendations is further given as input to the composition engine that retrieves services from the service repositories.

Cross-Domain Ontology Mapping: Ajmeri et al. [7] propose an approach to identify the concepts that link different ontologies using semantic similar-ity mapping. The semantic similarity between concepts is calculated based on

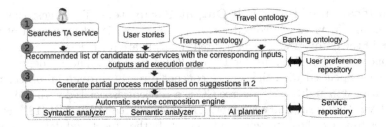

Fig. 2. Service composition using user stories and domain ontologies

syntax, *sense*, and *context* similarity. The *syntactic similarity* matches concepts based on the string equivalence. The *sense similarity* matches concepts based on the similar usage sense determined using a set of synonyms called synset [16]. The *context similarity* matches concepts based on the similarity of their neighborhood. The neighborhood of a concept is determined based on the inheritance relationships from the parent concept to the child concept. The *semantic similarity* between the concepts is computed as a weighted mean of syntactic, sense, and context similarity. The semantically similar concepts identified using the above approach are the concepts which map two different domain ontologies (cf. [7] for a detailed description of the cross-domain ontology mapping algorithm).

Identification of Candidate Services: Once the domain ontologies are linked using the semantic similarity mapping approach, we identify if the concepts in the ontology that are associated with the user query are services. We use the following criteria in [7] to identify if the concept represents a service: the concept or its equivalent concept in the ontologies must be present in the user stories, and the concept or its substring should be part of a verb phrase (VP). However, if it is part of a noun phrase (NP), it should be prefixed by a VP.

For example, in the user story "As a customer, I want *flight booking* functionality, to book flight from source to destination city" the substring *booking* of the concept *flight booking* is part of a VP and hence the concept *flight booking* is suggested as a candidate service. To parse a sentence and to create a constituent tree of objects, we use the open-source Link Grammar library [17].

service(c_1) = US_i.contains(c_1) and (c_1.parseType = "VP" or (c_1.parseType = "NP" and c_1.parent.parseType = "VP")) ? true : false;
where US_i is the ith user story; c_1.parseType is the tag associated with the concept c_1 w.r.t. parse tree of US_i; c_1.parent is the parent token in the parse tree.

Constituent parse tree: (S (PP As (NP a customer)), (S (NP I) (VP want (NP (NP flight) (*VP booking* (NP functionality, (PP to (NP book flight) from source city to destination city.)))))))

Also, if the concept is part of a NP, it should be prefixed by a VP. In the user story "As a customer, I want to *make payment* for flight, taxi, and hotel booking using credit card", *payment* is in NP but is prefixed by verb *make*.

Identification of Input and Output Parameters: To suggest the i/o of the identified services, we consider the concepts associated with each of these services in the ontologies. The associated concepts are referred to as complementary concepts (CC). We consider 1st and 2nd degree CC. The 1st degree CC is a concept associated with the service concept directly through an object property relationship and the 2nd degree CC is a concept associated with the service concept via an intermediary concept. The open-source OWL API [18] provides interfaces to parse the ontologies and to identify the object and data properties.

User Preference Integration: Based on the users' past preferences of services and their i/o, the identified services are filtered and the complementary concepts are tagged as either inputs or outputs. When the user selects services from the recommended list, the confidence of these services is incremented. However, if a service is considered irrelevant for a specific query, the confidence score of that service is decremented. For a specific query, the recommended services are sorted based on the confidence score. Similarly, as the user tags the concepts as either inputs or outputs of a service, the corresponding confidence-input or confidence-output is incremented. If the user deletes the complementary concept, the corresponding confidence-input and confidence-output is decremented. For the subsequent queries, the complementary concept is tagged as input or output by comparing the score of confidence-input and confidence-output.

Data-flow Analysis: The tagging of complementary concepts as inputs and outputs of a service establishes the *data dependency constraint* which helps to compose the services to meet the requirements of the queried service. For instance in a *Travel Agency* service, the output of *Flight, Hotel*, and *Taxi Booking* service are the inputs to the *Payment* service, indicating that *Flight, Hotel*, and *Taxi Booking* service should be executed before the *Payment* service.

5   Evaluation

To evaluate the system developed based on the approach discussed in Section 4, we have considered two practical use-case scenarios which are commonly used as the benchmark examples for service composition[1]. We also conducted an empirical study to evaluate the quality of the recommended partial process model.

Empirical Study: We introduced our system in the course assignment which had the same requirements as the assignment in Section 3. The participants were assigned groups and each group was required to submit three milestones. M3, involved developing the TA service by composing other services. The participants were given a brief introduction on how to use our recommender system.

27 groups deployed their services for M3 and 33% of the groups correctly implemented the service. Services implemented by 44% of the groups failed to pass the test cases due to syntactical errors such as *incorrect variable initialization* and *incorrect namespaces*. However, these services were complete with respect to the requirements; in the sense that, the TA services included invocation of all the

---

[1] Due to space limitations, the case studies are available online via
https://sites.google.com/site/wsccs2013

necessary services, assignment of input-output variables and also maintained a correct execution order. The performance of the groups in this assignment (33% correctly implemented and 44% partially completed) is significantly higher than the groups in the assignment discussed in Section 3 (12%).

On completion of the project, 27 groups provided their feedback regarding the recommender system. A five-point Likert scale [19] is used to capture the responses. In the five-point scale, 1 indicates strongly disagree, 2 indicates disagree, 3 indicates neutral, 4 represents agree and 5 indicates strongly agree. We refer to this scale in the following observations *(O)*:

Understanding Service Composition Requirements: *O1*: 37% of the groups strongly agree and 25% of the groups agree that the recommended process model helps in understanding the requirements of service composition.

Quality: *O2*: 40.7% of the groups strongly agree and 14.8% of the groups agree that the recommended services fulfill the service composition requirements. *O3*: 51.8% of the groups agree and 14.8% of the groups strongly agree that the data dependency constraints help to define the execution order of services.

O4: The average rating for the satisfaction of recommended inputs and outputs for each of the suggested service is 3.89. 46.8% of the groups strongly agree that the recommended inputs and outputs for all the suggested services are correct and complete with respect to the requirements. Moreover, 92% of the groups rate between 3 to 5 on the scale and only 8% of the groups, rate 1 and 2 on the scale (strongly disagree and disagree) in O4.

O5: 59% of the groups indicate that the recommended process model is the same as the manually created service composition.

Time: *O6*: The groups that used the recommender system for developing the TA service spent on average 9.68 hours less than those groups that did not use our recommender system.

Difficulty: *O7*: The feedback also indicates that the challenges in service composition are: "understanding the BPEL syntax (48%)", "handling i/o parameters in BPEL (30%)", and "invoking the external services (18%)", apart from "constructing the control-flow of the process (26%)" and "understanding the requirements (11%)". These results show that although our approach has addressed the issues related to conceptual modeling of services, some technological issues need further effort (e.g., high percentage of failure of services due to syntactical errors and difficulties in adapting to service specification languages).

6 Conclusions

Our approach, realized as a recommender system derives the partial process model using domain ontologies and user stories. The observations based on the evaluation indicate that our approach not only helps in understanding the requirements of service composition but also reduces the time and effort involved in the development of service composition. Our evaluation is based only on the case study and the empirical study. In our future work, we plan to extend the recommender system by integrating a composition engine so as to retrieve desired service compositions in a specific service specification language. Also, in our approach, we have only considered data dependency constraint to identify the execution order of the composed services. Inferring similar constraints and non-functional requirements (e.g., QoS) on the services would further improve the recommendations for service composition.

References

1. Yan, Y., Bode, J., McIver, W.: Between service science and service-oriented software systems. In: Congress on Services Part II. SERVICES-2 (2008)
2. Xiao, H., Zou, Y., Ng, J., Nigul, L.: An approach for context-aware service discovery and recommendation. In: ICWS (2010)
3. Srivastava, B., Koehler, J.: Web service composition - current solutions and open problems. In: ICAPS Workshop on Planning for Web Services (2003)
4. Happel, H.J., Seedorf, S.: Applications of ontologies in software engineering. In: Proc. of Workshop on SWESE on the ISWC (2006)
5. Arabshian, K., Danielsen, P., Afroz, S.: Lexont: A semi-automatic ontology creation tool for programmable web. In: AAAI Spring Symposium Series (2012)
6. The Programmable Web, http://www.programmableweb.com
7. Ajmeri, N., Vidhani, K., Bhat, M., Ghaisas, S.: An ontology-based method and tool for cross-domain requirements visualization. In: Fourth Intl. Workshop on MARK (2011)
8. Traverso, P., Pistore, M.: Automated composition of semantic web services into executable processes. In: McIlraith, S.A., Plexousakis, D., van Harmelen, F. (eds.) ISWC 2004. LNCS, vol. 3298, pp. 380–394. Springer, Heidelberg (2004)
9. Cardoso, J., Sheth, A.: Semantic e-workflow composition. Intell. Inf. Syst. (2003)
10. Grigori, D., Corrales, J.C., Bouzeghoub, M., Gater, A.: Ranking BPEL processes for service discovery. IEEE Trans. on Services Comput. (2010)
11. Liu, X., Zhao, Q., Huang, G., Mei, H., Teng, T.: Composing data-driven service mashups with tag-based semantic annotations. In: ICWS (2011)
12. Hu, S., Muthusamy, V., Li, G., Jacobsen, H.-A.: Distributed automatic service composition in large-scale systems. In: Second Intl. Conf. on Distributed Event-Based Syst. (2008)
13. Pop, F.C., Cremene, M., Vaida, M., Riveill, M.: Natural language service composition with request disambiguation. In: Service-Oriented Comput. (2010)
14. Lim, J., Lee, K.H.: Constructing composite web services from natural language requests. In: Web Semantics: Science, Services and Agents on the WWW (2010)
15. Introduction to Service Comput., https://sites.google.com/site/sc2012winter
16. Miller, G.A.: WordNet: A lexical database for English. Commun. of the ACM (1995)
17. Sleator, D.D., Temperley, D.: Parsing English with a link grammar. arXiv preprint cmp-lg/9508004 (1995)
18. Horridge, M., Bechhofer, S.: The OWL API: A Java API for OWL ontologies. Semantic Web (2011)
19. Allen, I.E., Seaman, C.A.: Likert scales and data analyses. Quality Progress (2007)

Estimating Functional Reusability of Services

Felix Mohr

Department of Computer Science, University of Paderborn, Germany
felix.mohr@uni-paderborn.de

Abstract. Services are self-contained software components that can be used platform independent and that aim at maximizing software reuse. A basic concern in service oriented architectures is to measure the reusability of services. One of the most important qualities is the *functional reusability*, which indicates how relevant the task is that a service solves. Current metrics for functional reusability of software, however, either require source code analysis or have very little explanatory power. This paper gives a formally described vision statement for the estimation of functional reusability of services and sketches an exemplary reusability metric that is based on the service descriptions.

1 Introduction

During the last decade, the focus in software development has moved towards the service paradigm. Services are self contained software components that can be used platform independent and that aim at maximizing software reuse.

A basic concern in service oriented architectures is to measure the *functional reusability* of the services in general or for specific tasks. Such a metric would support the analysis of relations between services, allow to estimate the potential impact of new services, and indicate the suitability of automatization techniques like composition; Fig. 1 shows this information gain. Usually, we have no knowledge about how services in a network are related; they are merely members of a homogeneous set (Fig. 1a). Analyzing their specifications helps us recognize relations between them and identify reuse potential (Fig. 1b).

Surprisingly, there is no metric of which we could say that it is even close to be satisfactorial in regards of measuring reusability. The main problem is that most reusability metrics are based on code analysis [7], e.g. the Halstead metric and others. However, the idea of services is precisely that the implementation needs not to be available. Reusability metrics for black box components exist [4,9,10] but are notoriously inexpressive; that is, they do effectively not say anything about functional reusability even though that was the design goal.

This paper gives a vision statement for the service reusability question and hints to possible solutions for the problem. Intuitively, the reusability of a service s is based on the number of problems for which there is a solution that contains s. Instead of simply using this number directly as a metric for reuse, it should be somehow weighted, since the complexity and likelihood of occurrence of problems strongly varies. Unfortunately, it seems to be very hard, or even impossible,

X. Franch et al. (Eds.): ICSOC 2014, LNCS 8831, pp. 411–418, 2014.

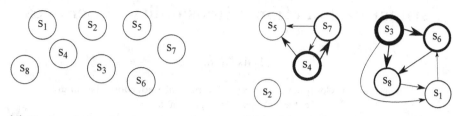

(a) No knowledge about services relations   **(b)** Insights in how service are related

Fig. 1. A metric for reusability helps us learn more about how services are related

to effectively compute such a metric in practice. As a consequence, I argue that the reusability must be *estimated* by another metric that is reasonably related to reusability. I give a sketch of an exemplary metric that measures the *contribution* of services in a service set on the basis of their description. Note that I use the terms service and component synonymously in this paper, because the distinguishing feature (way of execution) is irrelevant for us.

Summarizing, this paper contributes to the question of how reusability of services can be measured. I present a formal problem description for reusability estimation and give an example for a reusability metric.

The rest of this paper is organized as follows. Section 2 gives a deeper background for the motivation of this paper. Section 3 introduces the formal problem definition, and Section 4 sketches one approach to tackle the defined problem.

2   Background and Motivation

First of all, this paper is not about reuse but about *reusability*; more specifically, a *metric for functional reusability*. Reuse means that there is a software artifact s_1 that actually *is* employing another existing software artifact s_2. Reusability, in contrast, talks about the *potential* that, for a software artifact s, there is a set S of yet nonexistent software artifacts that *would* use s. Hence, reusability is dedicated to what *could be done* and not to what *is* done with a software component. Much has been said about *principles* of software reuse and reusability [2,3,6,8], but that debate is mostly about how to *increase* reusability through sophisticated design. In contrast, I assume a certain service architecture as given and (try to) *estimate* the reusability under these conditions.

While metrics for software *reuse* have been around for decades, most of them are unsuitable for services [7] and do not contribute to the *reusability* question.

In contrast to classical reuse metrics, metrics that estimate the functional reusability of black box components are alarmingly poorly studied. The only two metrics I am aware of are Washisaki [10] and Rotaru [9]. However, none of the two has an acceptable expressiveness power, since Washizaki only considers the *existence* of meta information and Rotaru only counts the *number of parameters* in order to express reusability. A comprehensive and exhaustive survey of these and other works is found in [1].

An important property of development environments that aim at increasing reuse is that software components are described *semantically*. We know that two key activities in component based software development are that components are *(i) stored for later reuse* and *(ii) identified as candidates for a solution of a current task* [2, 3]. The second step (look-up problem) requires a sufficiently abstract description of what a component does in order to avoid or reduce reading natural language documentation or even source code analysis. The latter may work in very small environments but not in large organizations with hundreds of components. Hence, reuse, which is the main goal of services, requires a formal specification that reasonably *abbreviates* their functional behavior.

Although software is currently rarely semantically described, current trends in software development suggest that this may change in near future. This can be mostly observed in a shift in the programming style that is less technical than before and that tends towards *workflows* [5]. Business workflow oriented software is much more suitable for business domain specific descriptions than former, rather technical component models.

Assuming that this trend continues, this paper presents one way to estimate software reusability by analyzing semantic descriptions.

3   Problem Description

This section describes the formal frame of this paper. First, I describe my idea of an ideal reusability metric in terms of composition problems to whose solution a service may contribute. Second, I explain the obstacles that occur with that metric and the necessity for alternatives. Third, I introduce the formal service model that underlies the rest of the paper.

3.1   An Ideal Metric for Functional Reusability

An ideal metric for the functional reusability of a service would be based on the number of *composition problems* to whose solution it contributes. This is because a service is (re)used if and only if there is a program that invokes it. In the service world, we would call such a program a service composition. A service composition, in turn, is only created if there is a problem that it solves. If $\mathcal{P}$ is the set of all imaginable (composition) problems, let $\mathcal{P}_s \subseteq \mathcal{P}$ be the set of composition problems $p \in \mathcal{P}$ for which there is a service composition that solves p and that invokes s.

Instead of just counting the number of problems, consider the probability that $p \in \mathcal{P}_s$ occurs at all, which yields the following ideal reusability metric:

$$r^*(s) = \sum_{p \in \mathcal{P}_s} probabilityOfOccurrence(p)$$

This metric only captures the functional reusability and ignores other factors that may affect the practical *suitability* of solutions. In fact, non-functional aspects may cause that a service s is never part of a *chosen* solution for problem p. However, we shall focus on the purely functional aspect here.

The problem set $\mathcal{P}$ is usually infinite, but we may expect the metric to converge towards a finite number for every service s. Of course, divergence is an issue, because there will be probably infinitely many "potential" problems where a service s could be part of a solution. However, I think that the number of actually occurring problems to whose solution a service s may contribute is quite limited. The probability of occurrence of other problems to whose solution s may contribute, hence, is either zero or converges to zero very fast. Concludingly, we may assume that $r^*(s)$ takes a fix value in $\mathbb{R}_+$ for every service s.

The reusability of a reference service may *normalize* the metric. Using service s^* as the reference service, the normalized reusability of a service s is:

$$||r^*||(s) = \frac{r^*(s)}{r^*(s^*)}$$

This allows us to say that a service is, for example, twice as reusable as the reference service; this makes the metric more intuitive.

3.2   The Need for Estimation

It is not possible to compute the metric r^* in practice. Computing $\mathcal{P}_s$ requires to actually *solve all composition problems* in $\mathcal{P}$ under the condition that s is part of the solution. Even if $\mathcal{P}$ is finite, it is probably very large and cannot efficiently be traversed, not to mention solving a complex composition task in every iteration. Apart from that, the probability of occurrence is usually not known and estimating it can be cumbersome.

Consequently, the task is to find a function that *estimates* the normalized ideal reusability. Formally, for a set S of services, the task is to find an efficiently computable function $r : S \to \mathbb{R}_+$ that comes reasonably close to $||r^*||$.

Due to the lack of benchmark possibilities, I argue that it would not be appropriate for this task to speak of approximation. Approximation usually is associated with an approximation error $\epsilon \in \mathbb{R}_+$ that describes the maximum discrepancy between the approximation and the optimum. For example, we would like to have $(r(s) - r^*(s))^2 < \epsilon$ for all $s \in S$. It is anything but clear how this kind of assertions about $||r^*||$ can be achieved, so, strictly spoken, we cannot claim to approximate reusability.

However, it is absolutely possible to define other metrics that, due to some semantic link to reusability, are *indicators* for reliability. As a consequence, approaches for estimating reusability must qualitatively explain why it is reasonable to *believe* that they are a reliable indicator of reusability.

3.3   The Formal Framework for the Service Environment

To obtain commonsense about the nature of problems in $\mathcal{P}$, we shall not rely on natural language descriptions but on formal descriptions. In this paper, I assume that services are described through inputs, outputs, preconditions, and effects (IOPE), and where problems are characterized by an initial state and a goal state that must be reached from the initial state through the application of services.

Definition 1. *A **service description** is a tuple* (I, O, P, E). *I and O are disjoint sets of input and output variables. P and E describe the precondition and effect of the service in first-order logic formulas without quantifiers or functions. Variables in P must be in I; variables in E must be in $I \cup O$.*

As an example, consider a service *getAvailability* that determines the availability of a book. The service has one input b for the ISBN of a book and one output a for the availability info; we have $I=\{b\}$ and $O=\{a\}$. The precondition is $P = Book(b)$ and requires that the object passed to the input b is known to have the type *Book*. The effect is $E = HasAvInfo(b, a)$ and assures that the object where the output a is stored contains the info whether b is available.

I acknowledge that this formalization may not always be adequate, but it is the by far most established service description paradigm besides finite state machines (FSM), and even FSM service representations can often be efficiently transformed into an IOPE representation. The introduction of a(n even) more sophisticated formalism is beyond the scope.

Definition 2. *A **composition problem** is a tuple* $(S, pre, post)$ *where pre is a precondition that must be transformed into the postcondition post by arranging services from a set S described as in Def. 1. pre and post are first-order logic formulas without quantifiers and functions.*

For simplicity, I leave a knowledge base out of the model. A knowledge base is usually used to express ontological information and logical implications in the model but is not needed to explain the idea of this paper.

4   Estimating Reusability Using Semantic Descriptions

This section gives a brief sketch about one possibility to use semantic service descriptions to estimate their reusability. A service s is most likely to be reused if there are many other services that can do something with the effect of s; then s *contributes* to those services. This section defines the relevance of a service based on its contribution to other services and the relevance of those services in turn. The higher the relevance of a service, the higher the number of problems that can be solved with it; this relevance is a good estimation for reusability.

4.1   The Service Contribution Graph

We can capture the direct relation of two services in a *service contribution graph*. Given a set of services S with descriptions as in Def. 1, a service contribution graph is a graph (V, E) with exactly one node in V for every service in S and with an edge $(s_i, s_j) \in E$ if and only if at least one literal in the effect of s_i and the preconditions s_j can be unified. Intuitively, there is a link between from

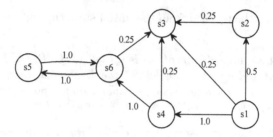

Fig. 2. An exemplary contribution graph for 6 services

s_i and s_j if the effect of s_i has something to do with the precondition of s_j. A service contribution graph is directed and usually cyclic.

The service contribution graph exploits the idea that a service composition contains a service only if it is necessary for a (possibly indirect) successor service or for the desired result of the entire composition. An edge between u and v indicates a chance that there may be compositions that invoke v after u. Thereby, the service contribution graph gives a rough insight into how control flows of service compositions in this environment could look like.

To give consideration to the fact that contributions of services to the preconditions of other services usually vary, the edges in the service contribution graph should carry a weight. A weight function $w : E \rightarrow [0,1]$ indicates for an edge (u, v) to which *degree* service u contributes to v. That is, to which extent the effects of u cover the preconditions of v. An example is depicted in Fig. 2.

A good implementation for the weight function is a modified leveled matching. Usually, a leveled matching algorithm determines to which degree the preconditions of services s_1 and s_2 match and to which degree the effects of s_1 and s_2 match. In this case, however, we want to know to which degree the *effect* of s_1 matches the *precondition* of s_2; the precondition of s_1 and the effect of s_2 are not of interest here. If preconditions and effects are conjunctions, a basic matcher could return the percentage of literals in the precondition of s_2 that are contained in the effects of s_1. For other precondition structures, the matcher would need more sophisticated techniques.

The matcher should take into account the *explanatory power* of the different description elements. For example, a data type information is much less significant for the service description than an ontological concept or even a relation.

4.2   Basic Service Relevance

A basic reusability estimation could measure the *recursive* contribution of a service to the preconditions of other services. For example, if a service s_1 only contributes to a service s_2 that does not contribute to any other service, s_1 is probably less reusable than a service s_3 that contributes to a service s_4 that contributes to five services, each of which contributing to another five services.

Since the contribution graph is usually cyclic, we must be cautious to avoid an infinite recursion for the relevance metric. We can reasonably avoid infinite recursion by assuming that no service is called twice in one composition. A good argument to do this is that we want to measure the relevance of a service by its benefits to *other* services. Otherwise the relevance of a service value would be increased only due to the possibility to invoke itself, which does not make sense. There will be compositions that are excluded by this assumption, but this should not be the usual case. In addition and in order to reduce computational efforts, we reduce a bound $k \in \mathbb{N}$ for the considered recursion depth.

The formal basis for the metric is a *composition tree*. Every node in that tree corresponds to a sequence of services, and the root corresponds to the sequence of length 1 that is just the service s itself. There is an edge from node $(s_1, \ldots, s_n)$ to node $(s_1, \ldots, s_{n+1})$ if (s_n, s_{n+1}) is an edge in the contribution graph and if s_{n+1} is not already in $\{s_1, \ldots, s_n\}$. The relevance of the service s sums up a default value of each node (here 1), weighted with the multiplied path weights from that node to the root.

The basic relevance of a service s for depth k is then:

$$r(s,k) = \begin{cases} 1 + \sum\limits_{s' \in c(s)} w(s,s') \cdot r(s', k-1) & \text{if } k > 0 \\ 1 & \text{else} \end{cases}$$

where $c(s)$ are the child nodes of service s in the composition tree[1] and $w(s,s')$ is the weight of the edge in the contribution graph. Since the maximal recursion depth k will usually be a parameter that is chosen once and then remains unchanged, let the relevance value of a service be denoted as $r_k(s) := r(s,k)$.

4.3   Discussion

The above metric is obviously very rudimentary, but it gives a clue of what a reusability estimating metric may look like. For example, the constant factor of a node could be substituted by an expert's estimation. Also, it would be a good idea to not only consider the outgoing edges of a service, but also its incoming edges in the contribution graph. However, compared to the absence of information as depicted on the left of Fig. 1, this metric already gives very useful insights. We can argue even for this simple measure that it is an estimator for reusability: The more compositions that start with a service are imaginable, the more problems will exist for which that service may be part of a solution.

Note that the alleged redundancy of execution paths that are merely permutations of each other is intended. For example, a service s_0 may contribute to both s_1 and s_2 while in turn s_1 contributes to s_2 and vice versa. Thereby, the relevance of s_0 is increased twice, once by s_1, s_2 and once for s_2, s_1. This may seem unreasonable at first, but it is actually quite what we want. The edge (s_1, s_2) only has a high weight if s_1 contributes for s_2 and vice versa. If one of the paths does not make sense, it will have a low weight anyway and will only marginally affect the relevance value of s_0.

---

[1] More precisely, the last service in the child, since nodes are service sequences.

5   Conclusion

This paper gives a vision statement for metrics of functional reusability of services and sketches service relevance as one possible such metric. It defines an ideal reusability metric and explains why such a metric is usually not computable. The sketched metric tackles this problem by estimating service reusability through service relevance, a recursive metric based on the contribution of services to the preconditions of other services in the network. Its explanatory power is limited by the quality of the service descriptions.

This paper is merely a first step into the direction of analyzing functional reusability, so there is great potential for future work; I just mention some options. First, it would be interesting to estimate the reusability of services in a completely different way; for example, we could use a simplification of the service model that makes the number of composition problems tractable. Second, the presented metric only works with forward edges in the contribution graph, yet we could take into account the provision of required service inputs. Third, the weights in the composition tree could be discounted depending on the depth in order to consider possible noise between the model and the real services that may affect composition. Fourth, the proposed metric could be integrated with a learning approach that collects information about how services are used together.

Acknowledgments. This work was partially supported by the German Research Foundation (DFG) within the Collaborative Research Center "On-The-Fly Computing" (SFB 901).

References

1. Fazal-e Amin, A., Oxley, A.: A review of software component reusability assessment approaches. Research Journal of Information Technology 3(1), 1–11 (2011)
2. Caldiera, G., Basili, V.R.: Identifying and qualifying reusable software components. Computer 24(2), 61–70 (1991)
3. Cheesman, J., Daniels, J.: UML components. Addison-Wesley, Reading (2001)
4. Choi, S.W., Kim, S.D.: A quality model for evaluating reusability of services in soa. In: Proceedings of the 10th IEEE Conference on E-Commerce Technology, pp. 293–298. IEEE (2008)
5. Frakes, W.: Software reuse research: status and future. IEEE Transactions on Software Engineering 31(7), 529–536 (2005)
6. Frakes, W., Terry, C.: Software reuse: metrics and models. ACM Computing Surveys (CSUR) 28(2), 415–435 (1996)
7. Gill, N.S., Grover, P.: Component-based measurement: few useful guidelines. ACM SIGSOFT Software Engineering Notes 28(6), 4 (2003)
8. Krueger, C.W.: Software reuse. ACM Computing Surveys 24(2), 131–183 (1992)
9. Rotaru, O.P., Dobre, M.: Reusability metrics for software components. In: Proceedings of the 3rd ACS/IEEE International Conference on Computer Systems and Applications, p. 24. IEEE (2005)
10. Washizaki, H., Yamamoto, H., Fukazawa, Y.: A metrics suite for measuring reusability of software components. In: Proceedings of 5th Workshop on Enterprise Networking and Computing in Healthcare Industry, pp. 211–223. IEEE (2003)

Negative-Connection-Aware Tag-Based Association Mining and Service Recommendation

Yayu Ni[1], Yushun Fan[1,*], Keman Huang[2], Jing Bi[1], and Wei Tan[3]

[1] Tsinghua National Laboratory for Information Science and Technology,
Department of Automation Tsinghua University, Beijing 100084, China
nyy07@mails.tsinghua.edu.cn, {fanyus,bijing}@tsinghua.edu.cn
[2] School of Computer Science and Technology, Tianjin University, Tianjin 300072, China
victoryhkm@gmail.com
[3] IBM Thomas J. Watson Research Center, Yorktown Heights, NY 10598, USA
wtan@us.ibm.com

Abstract. Service recommendation facilitates developers to select services to create new mashups with large-granularity and added value. Currently, most studies concentrate on mining and recommending common composition patterns in mashups. However, latent negative patterns in mashups, which indicate the inappropriate combinations of services, remain largely ignored. By combining additional negative patterns between services with the already-exploited common mashup patterns, we present a more comprehensive and accurate model for service recommendation. Both positive association rules and negative ones are mined from services' annotated tags to predict future mashups. The extensive experiment conducted on real-world data sets shows a 33% enhancement in terms of F1-Score compared to classic association mining approach.

Keywords: Service Recommendation, Negative Mashup Patterns, Tag Collaboration Rules.

1 Introduction

In Web 2.0 era, a growing number of interactive web services have been published on the Internet. By combing chosen web services, web developers now are able to create novel mashups (i.e., composite services derived from services) to meet specific functional requirements from web users. This programmable paradigm produces an enlarging ecosystem of web services and their mashups [1].

Rapid increasing of available online services makes manual selection of suitable web services a challenging task. Automatic service integration architecture, like SOA [2], and service recommendation algorithms [3-6] are proposed to facilitate service selection and integration in mashup completion. Recently, an increasing number of

---

* Yushun Fan is with Tsinghua National Laboratory for Information Science and Technology, the Automation Department Tsinghua University, Beijing, 100084 China. (Corresponding, E-mail: fanyus@tsinghua.edu.cn).

X. Franch et al. (Eds.): ICSOC 2014, LNCS 8831, pp. 419–428, 2014.

researchers are becoming interested in analyzing and summarizing common service composition patterns from historical mashups. In order to instruct future mashup creation, a plenty of mashup pattern models are proposed to enable automatic service integration [1,7-9]. There are also techniques that focus on finding collaboration rules between services [4,10,11] and complete service composition based on rule reasoning.

Besides these common patterns or rules, there are also relationships indicating improper service combinations. Consider two very popular services, *"Google App Engine"* and *"Yahoo Video Search"*, on ProgrammableWeb.com[1], the largest services/mashups repository on the Internet. Even if both of them have been frequently used in the creation of thousands of mashups, they've never been co-used in the same mashup even once (until Dec. 31th, 2013). In the collaboration network of programmable ecosystem, there exist a large number of never-collaborate connections between services, formally named negative connections in this paper. Straightforwardly, the ever-collaborate connections among services can be named as positive connections. Based on the previous work [12,13], the collaboration network is a rare sparse network. Hence the number of the negative connections are much greater than the positive connections, which brings the data imbalance problem. On the other hand, some current automatic integration techniques just use the positive connections but tend to ignore all these negative connections, which will lose some useful information.

In order to consider the negative connections in a suitable way to improve the recommend performance, this paper proposes a novel method to collect negative connections between services as well as positive ones. The main contribution of this paper is a novel association mining model based on both positive and negative connections for service recommendation. More specific:

- We introduce a training dataset generation strategy to collect both positive and negative connections between services from the collaboration network.
- We propose a rule-based decision tree algorithm, i.e., *RuleTree*, to mine both positive and negative tag collaboration rules from the annotated tags of service connections in the training dataset. A rule scoring strategy, named *RuleScore*, is presented to score the collaboration rules. Combing RuleTree and RuleScore, the novel service recommendation approach is introduced to recommend service for the user.

Experiments on the real-life ProgrammableWeb dataset shows that, compared with the classic association-based approach, our negative-connection-aware approach gains a 33% improvement in terms of F1-Score for service recommendation.

The rest of the paper is organized as follows. Section 2 gives the concepts and problem formulation of tag-based service recommendation. Section 3 presents the details of tag-based association model for service recommendation. Section 4 presents experimental results on mashup ecosystem. Section 5 summarizes the related work and section 6 concludes the paper.

---

[1] http://www.programmableweb.com

2   The Problem Formulation

2.1   Preliminary Definitions

Let $S = \{s_1, s_2, \ldots, s_P\}$ denote all the web services, $M = \{m_1, m_2, \ldots, m_N\}$ denote all the mashups, and $\langle S, M \rangle$ the collaboration network between services and mashups. If a mashup m is composed by several services $s_m^{(1)}, s_m^{(2)}, \ldots, s_m^{(r)}$, then $m = \{s_m^{(1)}, s_m^{(2)}, \ldots, s_m^{(r)}\}$. Let $T = \{t_1, t_2, \ldots, t_N\}$ denote all tags that used to annotate services and $\Gamma = \{a | \forall a \subseteq T\}$ denote all the subsets of T. For an service s, its annotated tags are $T_s = \{t_s^{(1)}, t_s^{(2)}, \ldots, t_s^{(K)}\} \in \Gamma$.

Definition 1: Service Connection.
For two services $s_1, s_2 \in S$, a service connection between them is denoted as $c = \langle s_1, s_2, f(s_1, s_2) \rangle$, where $f(s_1, s_2)$ is a function indicating whether the two services have ever been co-used or not. If s_1 and s_2 have ever been co-used in mashups, then $f(s_1, s_2) = 1$; otherwise $f(s_1, s_2) = -1$. Furthermore, c is called a positive connection if $f(s_1, s_2) = 1$; otherwise c is called a negative connection.

Definition 2: Service's Popularity.
Service's popularity is the function $n(s)$ indicating the number of mashups that contain service s. Hence:

$$n(s) = |\{\forall m \in M | s \in m\}| \tag{1}$$

where $|\cdot|$ means the number of elements in set.

Definition 3: Tag Collaboration Rule.
A tag collaboration rule $r = \langle T_{r1}, T_{r2} \rangle \in \Gamma \times \Gamma$ is a combination of two tag sequences. Given a service connection $c = \langle s_1, s_2, f(s_1, s_2) \rangle$, as well as the annotated tags of services T_{s_1} and T_{s_2}, then c is said to satisfy rule $r = \langle T_{r1}, T_{r2} \rangle$, formally denoted as $c \Vdash r$, if

$$(T_{s_1} \supseteq T_{r1} \text{ and } T_{s_2} \supseteq T_{r2}) \text{ or } (T_{s_1} \supseteq T_{r2} \text{ and } T_{s_2} \supseteq T_{r1}) \tag{2}$$

2.2   Tag-Based Service Recommendation

For most of the popular online repositories, like ProgrammableWeb.com, each web service is annotated with several tags to describe its category, functionalities and properties. Consider two web services published in the repository, denoted as s_1' and s_2'. Each service is annotated by a sequence of tags: s_1' is annotated by tags $T_{s_1'} \in \Gamma$, and $T_{s_2'} \in \Gamma$ for s_2'. The problem of tag-based service recommendation can be defined as follow:

Given two services s_1', s_2' with their annotated tags $T_{s_1'}$ and $T_{s_2'}$, find out whether they will collaborate with each other to construct mashups, based on the potential tag collaboration rules lying in the historical mashups in the collaboration network $\langle S, M \rangle$.

3   Tag-Based Association Model for Service Recommendation

3.1   Service Connection Generation

Due to the sparsity of collaboration network and the incompleteness of historical mashup dataset, there is an extreme imbalance between positive and negative samples: the number of never-collaboration connections is much greater than that of ever-collaboration ones. Thus, this section proposes a strategy utilizing a service popularity criterion to collect a balanced set of both positive and negative connections.

For two services s_1 and s_2 which have been co-used in at least one mashup, a positive connection between them is generated. Thus given all the historical mashups, a set of positive service connections can be defined as follow:

$$C_p = \{\langle s_1, s_2, 1 \rangle | \forall s_1, s_2 \in S, s_1 \neq s_2, f(s_1, s_2) = 1\} \tag{3}$$

For two services which have never collaborate with each other in the same mashup, there exist a negative connection among them. Due to the incompleteness of the dataset, the negative connections cannot be simply considered as the services cannot collaborate to compose a mashup. However, if two services are very popular but never collaborate with each other, it is reasonable to believe that these two services are not capable to construct a mashup in the near future. Hence this paper defines the negative connections between popular services as the credible negative connection. Here the popular service is defined as follow:

Given the popularity threshold k, if the service's popularity is larger than k, i.e. $N(s) \geq k$, then this service is popular.

Then a set of credible negative service connections can be generated as follows:

$$C_n = \left\{ \langle s_1, s_2, -1 \rangle \rangle \middle| \begin{array}{l} \forall s_1, s_2 \in S, n(s_1) \geq k, n(s_1) \geq k, \\ s_1 \neq s_2, f(s_1, s_2) = -1 \end{array} \right\} \tag{4}$$

3.2   Mining Tag Collaboration Rules: RuleTree Algorithm

This section presents a rule-based decision tree algorithm, named *RuleTree*, to mine tag collaboration rules from the training set of positive service connections and credible negative connections. RuleTree algorithm constructs a decision tree which contains collaboration rules as its non-leaf nodes and composability labels, positive or negative, as its leaf nodes. The RuleTree algorithm contains two steps, which is shown as follows.

Step 1: Generate Candidate Rules.
A rule r can only be considered as a candidate rule that can probably be used to construct the tree, if there is at least one service connection in the training set $C = C_p \cup C_n$ satisfies it. Hence the set of candidate rules can be defined as follows:

$$R = \{\forall r \in \Gamma \times \Gamma | \exists c \in C_p \cup C_n, c \Vdash r\} \qquad (5)$$

Step 2: Construct Decision Tree.
The construction step of RuleTree algorithm employs a procedure similar with ID3 [14]: at each iteration of the algorithm, the most significant rule is chosen from candidate rule set, which could distinguish between positive service connections and negative connections to achieve the minimal entropy. Hence the detail of training procedure is given as follows:

```
Algorithm 1. RuleTree: Construct Decision Tree
Require: the connection set C
Require: candidate rule set R
Require: pre-defined maximal depth n of decision tree
RuleTree(C,R,n):
1. if all samples in C are of one class, or R = φ, or n = 0 do
2.    if the majority of connections are positive do
3.         return the single-node tree with label=1
4.    else do
5.         return the single-node tree with label=-1
6. else do
7.    r ←the rule from R that best classifies C according to
      minimal entropy metric
8.    C₊ ← {∀c ∈ C|c ⊩ r},  C₋ ← C − C₊,  R ← R − {r}
9.    return a RuleTree with root node r , left branch
      Rule_Tree(C₊,R,n − 1) and right branch Rule_Tree(C₋,R,n − 1)
```

3.3 Scoring Collaboration Rules: RuleScore Algorithm

RuleScore algorithm scores the tag collaboration rules previously found out by Rule-Tree. RuleScore employs the classic Adaboost algorithm [15] to construct a sequence of shallow rule-based decision trees whose depths are restricted to 1 and assign each of these trees with a coefficient indicating its contribution to composability. At each iteration of main loop, RuleScore constructs a tree over current training dataset of service connections with current weights and then updates the weights of all training samples according to the fact whether they are correctly classified by generated rule stumps. The detail of RuleScore algorithm is given as follows:

```
Algorithm 2. RuleScore: Score Collaboration Rules
Require: the connection set C
Require: candidate rule set R
Require: number of maximal iterations q
RuleScore(C,R,q):
1. Initialize every connection i of C with weight D₁(i) = 1/|C|
2. Initialize every rule r of R do with Score(r) = 0
3. for j = 1,…,q do
```

4.   training a tree $h_j(r)$ ←RuleTree($C, R, 1$) over C with respect to
       the weight distribution D_j where r is the root rule of $h_j(r)$
5. ϵ_j ←the misclassification rate of $h_j(r)$ over C
6. $\alpha_j \leftarrow 0.5\ln\left((1 - \epsilon_j)/\epsilon_j\right)$
7. $Score(r) \leftarrow Score(r) + \alpha_j$
8.   **for** connection i that is correctly classified by h_j **do**
9. $D_{j+1}(i) \leftarrow D_j(i)e^{-\alpha_j}$
10.   **for** connection i that is misclassified by h_j **do**
11. $D_{j+1}(i) \leftarrow D_j(i)e^{\alpha_j}$
12.   **return** $\{\forall r \in R | Score(r) \neq 0\}$ **as** $Scored\_Rules$

3.4   Rule-Based Service Recommendation

Consider two web services s_1 and s_2. Given the annotated tags T_{s_1} and T_{s_2} of them, as well as the scored collaboration rules $Scored\_Rules$ generated by RuleScore, then the set of scored rules that can be satisfied by $\langle s_1, s_2, f(s_1, s_2)\rangle$ is denoted as follows:

$$R(s_1, s_2) = \{\forall r \in Scored\_Rules | \langle s_1, s_2, f(s_1, s_2)\rangle \Vdash r\} \tag{6}$$

Hence the composability score of service s_1 and s_2 can be calculated by summing up the scores of all satisfied rules $R(s_1, s_2)$:

$$F(s_1, s_2) = \sum_{\forall r \in R(s_1, s_2)} score(r) \tag{7}$$

The more positive rules and less negative rules are satisfied by $\langle s_1, s_2, f(s_1, s_2)\rangle$, the greater $F(s_1, s_2)$ is, and two services are more probably composable. Therefore if the estimated value $F(s_1, s_2) > 0$, then services s_1 and s_2 are regarded composable, and if $F(s_1, s_2) < 0$, then s_1 and s_2 are considered as none-composable in mashups.

4   Experiments

An experiment is conducted to evaluate our proposed model compared with some baselines. This paper employs the real-life dataset of web services and mashups obtained from ProgrammableWeb.com. By removing mashups containing less than two services and services that never collaborate with others, we obtain a filtered collection of 1301 services and 3557 mashups (Dec. 31th, 2013).

4.1   Baseline Algorithms

Baseline I: Apriori-based Service Recommendation.
In this approach [11], each mashup is represented as the union of annotated tags of its component services. Apriori [16] mines positive rules of tags from the transactions of mashups. Then composability of any two services s_1 and s_2 is estimated as:

$$F(s_1, s_2) = \sum_{r \in R(s_1, s_2)} \beta * support(r) + (1 - \beta) * confidence(r) \qquad (8)$$

where $R(s_1, s_2)$ denotes the rules satisfied by $\langle s_1, s_2 \rangle$, and β is a weighting coefficient. If $F(s_1, s_2)$ is greater than a predefined threshold, s_1 and s_2 are considered as composable; otherwise not.

Baseline II: RuleTree-based Service Recommendation.
In this approach, service recommendation is made by utilizing decision tree constructed by RuleTree algorithm. The maximal height of constructed tree is restricted to 1000. For every two services with their annotated tags, decision tree returns a binary value, 0 or 1, indicating whether they can collaborate in mashups.

Baseline III: Subsampling for Negative Service Connections.
In this approach, subsampling technique [17] is utilized to handle the dataset imbalance, instead of popularity-based selection strategy in our proposed model. By randomly sampling without replacement, a portion of negative service connections is selected for model training to equal the size of positive connection dataset.

4.2 Performance of Service Recommendation

Table 1 shows the average precision, recall and F1-Score values of proposed service recommendation model in a ten-fold cross validation experiment compared with baseline algorithms for dataset introduced above. Empirically, the threshold of popularity for credible negative connections generation is set 10 in the proposed model, and run 20000 iterations for it to stop. The weighting coefficient of Apriori-based approach is set $\beta = 0.5$, and threshold to determine composability is set 0.4.

Table 1. Performance of Four Recommendation Approaches

Recommendation Approach	Precision	Recall	F1-Score
Apriori-based Recommendation	17.44%	83.58%	0.2885
RuleTree-based Recommendation	70.23%	46.83%	0.5619
Subsampling For Negative Connection Generation	76.12%	62.57%	0.6868
The Proposed Model	*78.85%*	*66.03%*	*0.7187*

It can be observed that our proposed model has the best performance in terms of F1-Score, which can be interpreted as a weighted average of the precision and recall. The classic Apriori algorithm results in an extreme low prediction precision because of its incapability of modeling negative associations and it misclassifies a large portion of negative connections as positive ones. Our proposed model outperforms RuleTree-based approach because of the additional adoption of RuleScore, which enhances the accuracy of RuleTree by utilizing Adaboost meta-algorithm. Our model also outperforms the baseline method that utilizing subsampling for negative connection generation, because popularity-based selection strategy of our model produces a more credible set of negative connections than random sampling.

5   Related Works

In the researches of automatic service composition, service association learning is emerging as a new technique for automatic mashup creation. Most current service association models is on the basis of Apriori algorithm: [4] presents a global Co-utilization service Ranking (gCAR) strategy using association rules inferred by Apriori from historical service usage data, to recommend best services for mashup completion. [7] defines a three-level model of service usage data, from which service association rules is mined to model service usage patterns based on Apriori algorithm. [11] uses Apriori to find association rules of social tags and predict future mashups based on mined rules. [18] utilizes Apriori to mine service association rules from service logs to build a knowledge repository to instruct mashup creation.

Some researches try to extend Apriori algorithm by including negative rules. [19] presents a pruning strategy to reduce the size of candidate negative rules, so that the generation of negative rules can be achieved in an acceptable time. [20] defines a more generalized form of negative rules and generates both positive and negative rules based on the correlation metric. However, these researches merely take the positive samples into consideration, ignoring the latent existence of negative samples.

From a different perspective, we employ both positive service connections and negative ones generated based on service popularity metric from service collaboration network. Hence a more comprehensive service association mining model is formed for automatic service recommendation and gains a better performance.

6   Conclusion

The paper proposes a tag-based association model for service recommendation, combining positive mashup patterns and negative ones. This combination gives a more comprehensive and meaningful illustration of current trend for mashup creation. To the best of our knowledge, we are the first to mine negative tag collaboration rules from service collaboration network, shedding new light on service usage pattern discovery. Our model also produces a more accurate prediction than the well-known Apriori-based service recommendation approaches, making a great accuracy improvement in service collaboration prediction.

In the future work, we plan to develop a distributed version of our model to improve the efficiency of rule mining, which enables it to scale to a massive number of services and service tags in big data applications.

Acknowledgement. This work is partially supported by the National Natural Science Foundation of China (No. 61174169, No. 61033005), the National Key Technology R&D Program (No. 2012BAF15G01) and Doctoral Program Foundation of Institutions of Higher Education of China (No. 20120002110034).

References

1. Han, Y., Chen, S., Feng, Z.: Mining Integration Patterns of Programmable Ecosystem with Social Tags. Journal of Grid Computing, 1–19 (2014)
2. Erl, T.: SOA: principles of service design. Prentice Hall Upper Saddle River (1) (2008)
3. Keman, H., Yushun, F., Wei, T., Xiang, L.: Service Recommendation in an Evolving Eco-system: A Link Prediction Approach. In: International Conference on Web Services, pp. 507–514 (2013)
4. Tapia, B., Torres, R., Astudillo, H., Ortega, P.: Recommending APIs for Mashup Completion Using Association Rules Mined from Real Usage Data. In: International Conference of the Chilean Computer Science Society, pp. 83–89 (2011)
5. Dou, W., Zhang, X., Chen, J.: KASR: A Keyword-Aware Service Recommendation Method on MapReduce for Big Data Application. IEEE Transactions on Parallel and Distributed Systems PP, 1 (2014)
6. Xi, C., Xudong, L., Zicheng, H., Hailong, S.: RegionKNN: A Scalable Hybrid Collaborative Filtering Algorithm for Personalized Web Service Recommendation. In: International Conference on Web Services, pp. 9–16 (2010)
7. Liang, Q.A., Chung, J.Y., Miller, S., Yang, O.: Service Pattern Discovery of Web Service Mining in Web Service Registry-Repository. In: IEEE International Conference on E-Business Engineering, pp. 286–293 (2006)
8. Chien-Hsiang, L., San-Yih, H., I-Ling, Y.: A Service Pattern Model for Flexible Service Composition. In: International Conference on Web Services, pp. 626–627 (2012)
9. Vollino, B., Becker, K.: Usage Profiles: A Process for Discovering Usage Patterns over Web Services and its Application to Service Evolution. International Journal of Web Services Research 10(1), 1–28 (2013)
10. Spagnoletti, P., Bianchini, D., De Antonellis, V., Melchiori, M.: Modeling Collaboration for Mashup Design. In: Lecture Notes in Information Systems and Organization, pp. 461–469 (2013)
11. Goarany, K., Kulczycki, G., Blake, M.B.: Mining social tags to predict mashup patterns. In: Proceedings of the 2nd International Workshop on Search and Mining User-Generated Contents, pp. 71–78 (2010)
12. Keman, H., Yushun, F., Wei, T.: An Empirical Study of Programmable Web: A Network Analysis on a Service-Mashup System. In: International Conference on Web Services, pp. 552–559 (2012)
13. Huang, K., Fan, Y., Tan, W.: Recommendation in an Evolving Service Ecosystem Based on Network Prediction. IEEE Transactions on Automation Science and Engineering PP, 1–15 (2014)
14. Mitchell, T.: Decision tree learning. Mach. Learn. 414 (1997)
15. Friedman, J., Hastie, T., Tibshirani, R.: Special invited paper. additive logistic regression: A statistical view of boosting. Annals of Statistics, 337–374 (2000)
16. Agrawal, R., Srikant, R.: Fast algorithms for mining association rules. In: Proceedings of the 20th International Conference on Very Large Databases, pp. 487–499 (1994)
17. Galar, M., Fernandez, A., Barrenechea, E., Bustince, H., Herrera, F.: A review on ensembles for the class imbalance problem: bagging-, boosting-, and hybrid-based approaches. IEEE Transactions on Systems, Man, and Cybernetics, Part C: Applications and Reviews 42(4), 463–484 (2012)

18. Bayati, S., Nejad, A.F., Kharazmi, S., Bahreininejad, A.: Using association rule mining to improve semantic web services composition performance. In: International Conference on Computer, Control and Communication, pp. 1–5 (2009)
19. Wu, X., Zhang, C., Zhang, S.: Efficient mining of both positive and negative association rules. ACM Transactions on Information System 22(3), 381–405 (2004)
20. Antonie, M.-L., Zaïane, O.R.: Mining positive and negative association rules: An approach for confined rules. In: Boulicaut, J.-F., Esposito, F., Giannotti, F., Pedreschi, D. (eds.) PKDD 2004. LNCS (LNAI), vol. 3202, pp. 27–38. Springer, Heidelberg (2004)

Choreographing Services over Mobile Devices

Tanveer Ahmed and Abhishek Srivastava

Indian Instititue of Technology Indore, India
{phd12120101,asrivastava}@iiti.ac.in

Abstract. Owing to the proliferation of web services, service oriented architecture (SOA) is widely acknowledged as an ideal paradigm for both enterprise applications and compute intensive scientific processes. In todays world, the present scenario of conducting business has found a new inclination towards the Mobile Device. Mobile devices, however, are constrained by battery power, processing capability, availability and network outages. Achieving service composition in such dynamic environment is challenging. In this paper, we propose a technique inspired by Electromagnetism in Physics to enact service choreography over mobile devices. The focus of the work is to minimize the waiting time and to balance load between services of a similar kind, thereby preserving battery power. The technique is validated through a real prototype. We prove the model minimized battery consumption and achieved a reduction in the waiting time.

Keywords: Service Composition, Service Oriented Architecture, Mobile Phones.

1 Introduction

Service oriented architecture owes its popularity to web services and their temporal collaboration, commonly referred to as web service composition. Using web service composition, an organization can achieve a low operation and maintenance cost. As is evident, the Internet today is constantly evolving towards the 'Future Internet' (FI). In the FI, a mobile device is envisioned to become the center of computation in all aspects of daily and professional life, specially for the applications related to *Internet of Everything*[1].

At the moment, service orchestration is a widely accepted standard to accomplish service composition. In the context of the Future Internet, especially the IoS and IoT, service orchestration is expected to run into several hurdles. The biggest problem is: Considering an ultra large scale of the FI, orchestration is not scalable and the coordination between consumers and providers is impossible [4]. In addition, an orchestrator can become a potential communication bottleneck and a single point of failure [3]. In this context, we believe service choreography is *'the'* solution. However, even on a wired network, enacting service choreography successfully for an ultra large scale Future Internet is a challenge. This is further

---

[1] http://www.cisco.com/web/about/ac79/innov/IoE.html

X. Franch et al. (Eds.): ICSOC 2014, LNCS 8831, pp. 429–436, 2014.

exacerbated in a wireless setting, where the network is highly unpredictable, uncertain and error prone. There are several atypical issues, e.g. availability, battery power, application response time and several others that have to be tackled for a mobile device. In addition, composition over Mobile Devices, specially those owned by ordinary people exacerbates the problem even more. In such cases, the Quality of Experience of a person (both the consumer and provider) must never be compromised, since good user experience is a valuable asset in the service industry.

In this paper, we propose a technique customized from physics to enact service choreography over mobile devices, in particular, Cell Phones. We use the fundamental principles of electromagnetism to select a service from a set of similar services. The focus of the technique is to minimize the waiting time a user request experiences and at the same time preserve battery power. The foundation of the work presented here is the proposal of the electric field and the magnetic field. The proposed electric field is a non-user centered parameter capable of bypassing the hotspots to help conserve battery power. Further, in the World of Devices, user centric computation is one of the objectives, therefore magnetic field is designed to incorporate the preferences of a user in service selection. The magnetic field uses the intuition of a human being to select services. Thus, the electric field circumvents congested services and the magnetic field provides a user centric QoS aware composition parameter. We combine the two fields to make the dynamic service selection decision.

2   Proposed Model

In the real world, whenever a charged particle, e.g. an electron, moves in an electromagnetic field, it experiences an electro-magnetic force (EMF). The particle experiences acceleration (purely electric) and a drift in the direction of motion perpendicular to both the electric and the magnetic field. If we assume the two fields to be in the X and Y axes respectively, then the particle will drift in the Z axis. The Electromagnetic force experienced by the particle is known as the Lorentz's force [8].

In this paper, we have taken inspiration from such a phenomenon in the physical world. In our model, the movement of an electron is analogous to the control flow between services. We have assumed that each service hosted on a mobile device offers both electric and magnetic fields, consequently each node offers an electromagnetic force (EMF) to the next incoming service request. The EMF offered by a service is the selection criterion in our model. Next, we present the definitions of Electric and Magnetic Fields, and show how we make the dynamic service selection decision.

2.1   The Electric Field

To formulate the definition of the electric field, we have used the principle of potential gradient. In physics, electric field is defined as the rate of change of potential with respect to displacement [8].

$$E = \frac{dV}{dx} \qquad (1)$$

where, dV is the change in Electric Potential and dx represents the change in displacement, E is the electric field. The electric potential is the amount of work done to transfer a unit positive electric charge from one position to another position.

In the proposed work, the electric potential experienced at a service is defined in terms of the waiting time experienced at a service node. Mathematically,

$$V_x(i) = tw_x(i) \qquad (2)$$

and,

$$V_y(i+1) = tw_y(i+1) \qquad (3)$$

where, $tw_x(i)$ is the waiting time at a service x realizing the ith step (the current service/step in the composition), y is the index of the next service to be selected and $tw_y(i+1)$ is the waiting time. Here, service y realizes the $(i+1)^{th}$ step (the next process-step). From equations (1), (2) and (3), the proposed definition of the electric field offered by a mobile node is:

$$E(y) = \frac{tw_x(i) - tw_y(i+1)}{td(x(i), y(i+1))} \qquad (4)$$

where, $E(y)$ is the Electric Field offered by the service realizing the next process step, $td(x(i), y(i+1))$ is the data transfer time, defined as *"the amount of time required to pass all the parameters and control from a service at a particular step to a service at the subsequent step"*. In mobile devices, the data transfer time also represents latency between two individual devices. It can be seen from the above equation that if a service (realizing the next process step) has less waiting time, then Electric Field value is high. It is understood that the waiting time experienced at a service gives a measure of the congestion experienced at a node. Also, congestion is directly related to battery consumption. Therefore, selecting services offering a high Electric Field value can help preserve battery power. Further, driven by this Field requests will be passed to services that are not overloaded.

2.2   Magnetic Field

From the discussion in the previous sub-section, it is clear that though the Electric Field is runtime dependent, it is not *user-centered*. Today, the consumers are the center of attention in the world of mobile devices. Therefore, '*User-Centricity*' has become one of the most important criteria. In the proposed work, we made an attempt to include this criterion in service composition.

It is a well known fact that human beings have a varied sense of understanding and perception. Human beings exhibit *cognitive bias* preferring certain objects over others. In services computing, if a service is selected via QoS attributes, then human beings will tend to favor certain properties over others. Therefore, selecting a service following such a biased approach should not be the ideal way forward. A feasible strategy would be to select a service based on conscious reasoning as well. In other words, the subjective approach of the human being must be complemented by a reasonable objective approach. The same line of reasoning could be applied to services computing i.e. while selecting a service based on QoS attributes, one must follow a human oriented subjective approach complemented by a reasoning based objective approach. Taking this line of reasoning, we propose Magnetic Field as a preference and QoS based selection function incorporating both the subjective and the objective behavior. An ideal candidate to merge both the two choices is the subjective-objective weighted approach. Therefore, the proposed definition of the Magnetic Field is as follows.

$$M(y) = \beta * wQ + (1 - \beta) * w'Q \tag{5}$$

where, Q is a matrix containing QoS attributes' values. w, w' are the subjective-objective weight matrices respectively. β is bias parameter in the range [0,1]. The QoS attributes chosen for weight calculation and the purpose of experimentation were chosen from attributes commonly found in literature[2]. The method used to calculate weights was taken from [7].

2.3 Coalition of Electric and Magnetic Fields

So far we have presented the definitions of the electric field and the magnetic field. The electric field makes the algorithm congestion aware, thus, aids battery conservation. It is obvious, the combination strategy of the two fields will play an important role in service composition and battery conservation. Basically, the degree of influence each field will have in composition will depend on the method and the parameter of combination. To combine the two fields, there are two broad categories: Linear and Non-Linear. In a mobile environment processing capabilities are limited. Therefore, considering simplicity and computational efficiency, we have chosen a linear combination strategy. It was outlined previously that a node offering electric and magnetic fields offers electromagnetic force (EMF). Therefore, the proposed definition of EMF is:

$$F(y) = \alpha * E(y) + (1 - \alpha) * M(y) \tag{6}$$

where, α is a parameter in the range of [0,1] representing biasness towards either the Electric Field or the Magnetic Field. Using concepts of classical physics, the request (control flow) will move to a service node that has the maximum force value. Therefore, a node is chosen iff it offers the maximum EMF.

$$\forall s \in S_i; s' \in S_i \quad F_{s'} > F_s; s' \neq s \tag{7}$$

where S is a set of all services for a particular process-step, s' is the chosen service, F_s is the EMF offered by a service.

---

[2] https://www.ibm.com/developerworks/library/ws-quality/

Since we are achieving Mobile service composition in a decentralized environment, therefore EMF values must be exchanged between the participants. In the proposed work, the exchange mechanism is based on event based updates. The motivation for event based updates comes from the fact the such an exchange mechanism allows a throttled load on the underlying network. In mobile devices, such a throttled load is beneficial owing to power constraints.

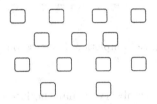

Fig. 1. Experimental Workflow

3   Real World Prototype Implementation

A simple composite application, with a list of redundant services shown in Fig. 1 was chosen for the purpose of experimentation. Though, the Figure represent a simple composition, our motive is to check the feasibility of the model in minimizing the waiting time and balancing load equally. To demonstrate the feasibility of the proposed technique in actual deployment, we have developed a prototype for the mobile device. The procedure for the development and deployment of web services, with a sample service, has been uploaded on github repository[3]. The application container to host the war (Web Archive) files was i-Jetty v3.1. Services were developed using Java and RESTLET[4] framework. Several services were hosted on multiple Android based devices. The battery consumption was monitored via the application GSam Battery (it is freely available at Google play store). The underlying network was the Institute's own WiFi network.

3.1   Behavior of Completion Time

To test the behavior of completion time, Volunteers, hosting services on their devices were asked to stay go around their normal business while service composition was in progress. We tracked the application completion in such a situation. The corresponding result concerning the application completion time is shown in Fig. 2.

It is visible from the Figure that the completion times is less, infact it is almost similar. Therefore, the *Instant-Availability* constraint is not violated. Moreover, we can say with concrete proof that the technique didn't make compromises in the real world.

---

[3] https://github.com/mb-14/RestDroid
[4] http://restlet.org/

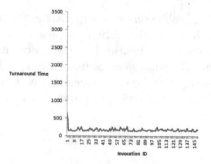

Fig. 2. Completion Time (seconds)

During experimentation we observed that the latency factor kept varying all the time. This observation was due to the fact that mobility played a major role here. Because of the nature of the devices, ignoring such factors during composition is not the best of ways. In the proposed model, we have considered this factor. Therefore, the application completion time is less.

3.2 Behavior of Battery Consumption

In this paper, our motive is to respect 1) *Battery Constraint* 2) *Instant Availability Constraint*. We demonstrated the latter was satisfied by having fast application completion time. For the former constraint, one of the ways is to have a low queue size at a service. A low queue is achievable via load balancing. In this regard, to demonstrate the effect the proposed technique on the battery of a mobile device, we have experimented in two different ways: 1) Service Composition without the electric field i.e no load balancing 2) Service composition with Electric Field. The results concerning the extent of battery consumption for the former case is shown in Fig. 3 (i-jetty Server), and the results concerning the observation for the latter scenario is shown in Fig. 4. Owing to space constraints,

35.6% of battery consumed by:		
i-Jetty		17.0% >
Android System		6.9% >
GSam Battery Monitor		6.4% >
Kernel (Android OS)		3.5% >
AppLock		0.6% >
System (com.androi...		0.6% >

Fig. 3. Power Consumption Without Load Balancing

Fig. 4 shows a snapshot of a few devices only. It can be observed from the two Figures that when there is no load balancing the battery consumption of the device is high, 17%. This is theoretically expected, since all the service requests kept arriving at this service node. A lot of work in literature suffer from this drawback, i.e. repeated selection of a service. Therefore, they violate the battery power constraint, hence degrade the QoE of a user. Looking at the result in Fig. 4, one can clearly see that the battery consumption saw a significant drop. The battery consumption in this case varied from 5.7%-10.7%. This reduction is due to the fact that requests were distributed across devices. Previously we outlined the effect of congestion on battery consumption. Therefore, efficient distribution of requests imply a low queue size, consequently a reduced CPU access, and hence a reduction in power usage. Therefore, in addition to providing a human oriented QoS aware composition parameter, Magnetic Field, the technique performed well in preserving the battery life of person's mobile device.

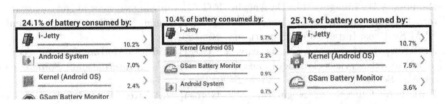

Fig. 4. Power Consumption With Load Balancing

4 Related Work

Service choreography has become one of most important topics of research in the service computing field. However, there only a few techniques purely developed and deployed on real mobile devices. A Technique to enact a service choreography using the chemical paradigm is proposed in [2], [3]. Fernandez et al [3] propose executing a workflow using the chemical paradigm. However, the focus of the proposed middleware is to execute a workflow in wired networks. We have proposed a physics based approach for the mobile platform. Further, the authors in [3] do not focus load balancing, dynamic adaptations. A technique to achieve choreography in peer-peer network is proposed in [2]. The work presented in [5] studies the effect of QoS metrics in message integrity and accuracy of choreographies. A self-* framework for configuring and adapting services at runtime was proposed in [1]. The framework, PAWS, delivered self-optimization and ensured guaranteed service provisioning even in failures. A comprehensive review of service choreographies is available in [6]. However, we did not found any technique with a special focus towards the IoS, let alone a Mobile Device.

5 Conclusion

In this paper, we proposed a technique customized from the behavior of a charged particle in physics to achieve service choreography over mobile devices.

We developed a prototype and conducted experiments with real mobile devices. We showed how the developed prototype achieved a low battery consumption. We achieved a low battery consumption by balancing load between services of a similar kind. Further, we also showed the model produced a reduction in the application turnaround time.

References

1. Ardagna, D., Comuzzi, M., Mussi, E., Pernici, B., Plebani, P.: Paws: A framework for executing adaptive web-service processes. IEEE Software 24(6), 39–46 (2007)
2. Barker, A., Walton, C.D., Robertson, D.: Choreographing web services. IEEE Transactions on Services Computing 2(2), 152–166 (2009)
3. Fernández, H., Priol, T., Tedeschi, C.: Decentralized approach for execution of composite web services using the chemical paradigm. In: 2010 IEEE International Conference on Web Services (ICWS), pp. 139–146. IEEE (2010)
4. Hamida, A.B., Linagora, G., De Angelis, F.G.: Composing services in the future internet: Choreography-based approach. iBPMS: Intelligent BPM Systems: Intelligent BPM Systems: Impact and Opportunity, 163 (2013)
5. Kattepur, A., Georgantas, N., Issarny, V.: Qos composition and analysis in reconfigurable web services choreographies. In: 2013 IEEE 20th International Conference on Web Services (ICWS), pp. 235–242 (2013)
6. Leite, L.A., Oliva, G.A., Nogueira, G.M., Gerosa, M.A., Kon, F., Milojicic, D.S.: A systematic literature review of service choreography adaptation. Service Oriented Computing and Applications 7(3), 199–216 (2013)
7. Ma, J., Fan, Z.P., Huang, L.H.: A subjective and objective integrated approach to determine attribute weights. European Journal of Operational Research 112(2), 397–404 (1999)
8. Rothwell, E.J., Cloud, M.J.: Electromagnetics. CRC Press (2001)

Adaptation of Asynchronously Communicating Software

Carlos Canal[1] and Gwen Salaün[2]

[1] University of Malaga, Spain
canal@lcc.uma.es
[2] University of Grenoble Alpes, Inria, LIG, CNRS, France
gwen.salaun@inria.fr

Abstract. Software adaptation techniques aim at generating new components called adapters, which make a set of services work correctly together by compensating for existing mismatch. Most approaches assume that services interact synchronously using rendez-vous communication. In this paper, we focus on asynchronous communication, where services interact exchanging messages via buffers. We overview a method for automatically generating adapters in such asynchronous environments.

1 Introduction

Software Adaptation [22,9] is a non-intrusive solution for composing black-box software services (*peers* in this paper) whose functionality is as required for the new system, but that present interface mismatch which leads to deadlock or other undesirable behaviour when peers are combined. Adaptation techniques aim at automatically generating new components called *adapters*, and usually rely on an *adaptation contract*, which is an abstract description of how mismatch can be worked out. All interactions pass through the adapter, which acts as an orchestrator and makes the involved peers work correctly together by compensating for mismatch. Many solutions have been proposed since the seminal work by Yellin and Strom [22], see, *e.g.*, [5,7,21,16,13,14]. Most existing approaches assume that peers interact using synchronous communication, that is rendez-vous synchronizations. Nonetheless, asynchronous communication, *i.e.*, communication via buffers, is now omnipresent in areas such as cloud computing or Web development. Asynchronous communication complicates the adapter generation process, because the corresponding systems are not necessarily bounded and may result into infinite systems [6].

In this paper, we rely on the *synchronizability* property [3,18] in order to propose an approach for generating adapters for peers interacting asynchronously via (possibly unbounded) FIFO buffers. A set of peers is synchronizable if and only if the system generates the same sequences of messages under synchronous and unbounded asynchronous communication, considering only the ordering of the send actions and ignoring the ordering of receive actions. Synchronizability can be verified by checking the equivalence of the synchronous version of a given

X. Franch et al. (Eds.): ICSOC 2014, LNCS 8831, pp. 437–444, 2014.
© Springer-Verlag Berlin Heidelberg 2014

system with its 1-bounded asynchronous version (in which each peer is equipped with one input FIFO buffer bounded to size 1). Thus, this property can be analysed using equivalence checking techniques on finite systems.

More precisely, given a set of peers modelled using Labelled Transition Systems and an adaptation contract, we first reuse existing adapter generation techniques for synchronous communication, e.g., [10,16]. Then, we consider a system composed of a set of peers interacting through the generated adapter, and we check whether that system satisfies the synchronizability property. If this is the case, this means that the system will behave exactly the same whatever bound we choose for buffers, therefore this adapter is a solution to our composition problem. If synchronizability is not preserved, a counterexample is returned, which can be used for refining the adaptation contract, until preserving synchronizability. It is worth observing that the main reason for non-synchronizability is due to emissions, which are uncontrollable in an asynchronous environment, hence have to be considered properly in the adaptation contract.

The organization of this paper is as follows. Section 2 defines our models for peers and introduces the basics on synchronous software adaptation. Section 3 presents our results on the generation of adapters assuming that peers interact asynchronously. Finally, Section 4 reviews related work and Section 5 concludes.

2   Synchronous Adaptation

We assume that peers are described using a behavioural interface in the form of a Labelled Transition System. A Labelled Transition System (LTS) is a tuple (S, s^0, Σ, T) where S is a set of states, $s^0 \in S$ is the initial state, $\Sigma = \Sigma^! \cup \Sigma^? \cup \{\tau\}$ is a finite alphabet partitioned into a set $\Sigma^!$ ($\Sigma^?$, resp.) of send (receive, resp.) messages and the internal action τ, and $T \subseteq S \times \Sigma \times S$ is the transition relation.

The alphabet of the LTS is built on the set of operations used by the peer in its interaction with the world. This means that for each operation p provided by the peer, there is an event $p? \in \Sigma^?$ in the alphabet, and for each operation r required from its environment, there is an event $r! \in \Sigma^!$. Events with the same name and opposite directions ($a!$, $a?$) are complementary, and their match stands for inter-peer communication through message-passing. Additionally to peer communication events, we assume that the alphabet also contains a special τ event to denote internal (not communicating) behaviour. Note that as usually done in the literature [15,2,20], our interfaces abstract from operation arguments, types of return values, and exceptions. Nevertheless, they can be easily extended to explicitly represent operation arguments and their associated data types, by using Symbolic Transition Systems (STSs) [16] instead of LTSs.

Example 1. We use as running example an online hardware supplier. This example was originally presented in [11] and both participants (a supplier and a buyer) were implemented using the Microsoft WF/.NET technology. Figure 1 presents the LTSs corresponding to both peers. The supplier first receives a request under the form of two messages that indicate the reference of the requested hardware (**type**), and the max price to pay (**price**). Then, it sends a response indicating if the request can be replied positively or not (reply). Next, the supplier may receive and reply other requests, or receive an order of purchase on the last reference requested (buy). In the latter case, a confirmation is sent (ack). The behaviour of the buyer starts by submitting a request (request). Upon reception of the response (reply), the buyer either submits another request, buys the requested product (purchase and ack), or ends the session (stop).

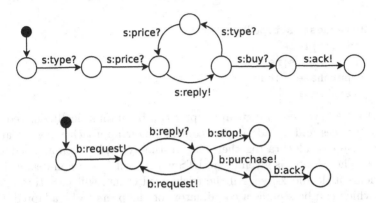

Fig. 1. LTS interfaces of supplier (top) and buyer (bottom) peers

As shown in the example, typical mismatch situations appear when event names do not correspond, the order of events is not respected, or an event in one peer has no counterpart or matches several events in another one. All these cases of behavioural mismatch can be worked out by specifying adaptation rules. Adaptation rules express correspondences between operations of the peers, like bindings between ports or connectors in architectural descriptions. Rules are given as adaptation vectors. An adaptation vector (or vector for short) for a set of peers $\{\mathcal{P}_1, ..., \mathcal{P}_n\}$ with $\mathcal{P}_i = (S_i, s_i^0, \Sigma_i, T_i)$, is a tuple $\langle e_1, ..., e_n \rangle$ with $e_i \in \Sigma_i \cup \{\epsilon\}$, ϵ meaning that a peer does not participate in the interaction.

In order to unambiguously identify them, event names may be prefixed by the name of the peer, e.g., $\mathcal{P}_i : p?$, or $\mathcal{P}_j : r!$, and in that case ϵ can be omitted. For instance, the vector $\langle p_1 : a!, p_2 : \epsilon, p_3 : b?, p_4 : c? \rangle$ represents an adaptation rule indicating that the output event $a!$ from peer p_1 should match both input events $b?$ and $c?$ in p_3, and p_4 respectively, while peer $p2$ does not participate in this interaction. For more details on the syntax and expressiveness of adaptation vectors, we refer to [10].

An adaptation contract for a set of peers is a set of adaptation vectors for those peers. Writing the adaptation contract is the only step of our approach which is not handled automatically. This step is crucial because an inadequate contract would induce the generation of an adapter that will not make the composition of peers to behave correctly (for instance, some expected interactions may be discarded by the adapter, in order to avoid deadlock). However, the adaptation methodology that we propose (Section 3) is iterative, which helps in writing the adaptation contract.

Example 2. Going back to our running example, we observe several differences between both interfaces. For instance, the buyer submits a single message for each request, while the supplier expects two messages; the name of the message for carrying out a purchase is not the same, etc. The vectors below are proposed for composing and adapting the whole system. The correspondence between request! and messages type? and price? can be achieved using two vectors, V_{req} and V_{price}. The mismatch between purchase! and buy? can be solved by vector V_{buy}.

$$V_{req} = \langle b:request!, s:type? \rangle$$
$$V_{price} = \langle b:\varepsilon, s:price? \rangle$$
$$V_{reply} = \langle b:reply?, s:reply! \rangle$$
$$V_{buy} = \langle b:purchase!, s:buy? \rangle$$
$$V_{ack} = \langle b:ack?, s:ack! \rangle$$

In [10,16] we have shown how an adapter can be automatically derived from a set of interfaces and an adaptation contract. Our approach relies on an encoding into process algebra together with on-the-fly exploration and reduction techniques. The adapter is given by an LTS which, put into a non-deadlock-free system yields it deadlock-free. All the exchanged events will pass through the adapter, which can be seen as a coordinator for the peers to be adapted. Code generation is also supported by our approach, thus BPEL adapters can be automatically synthesised from an adapter LTSs. All these steps are automated by the Itaca toolset [8]. Notice that the adaptation algorithms in [10,16] generate *synchronous* adapters, that is, they assume a synchronous communication model for peers. In our present work we show how our previous results can be applied to asynchronous adaptation, where peers communicate asynchronously and are equipped with an input message buffer.

Example 3. Figure 2 presents the adapter LTS generated for our running example. Since the adapter is an additional peer through which all communications transit, all the messages appearing in the adapter LTS are reversed with respect to those in the peers. Note, for instance, how the adapter receives the request coming from the buyer, and splits this request into messages carrying the type and price information. This LTS also shows how the adapter interacts on different names (purchase? and buy!) to make the communication possible.

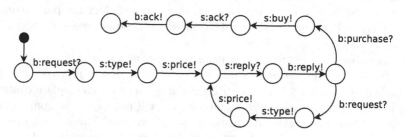

Fig. 2. Adapter LTS for the case study

3   Asynchronous Adaptation

Our asynchronous adaptation techniques rely on the synchronizability property [3,18]. A set of peers is synchronizable if and only if the system generates the same sequences of messages under synchronous and unbounded asynchronous communication, considering only the ordering of the send actions and ignoring the ordering of receive actions. Focusing only on send actions makes sense for verification purposes because: (i) send actions are the actions that transfer messages to the network and are therefore observable, (ii) receive actions correspond to local consumptions by peers from their buffers and can therefore be considered to be local and private information. Synchronizability can be verified by checking the equivalence of the synchronous version of a given system with its 1-bounded asynchronous version (in which each peer is equipped with one input FIFO buffer bounded to size 1). Thus, this property can be verified using equivalence checking techniques on finite systems, although the set of peers interacting asynchronously can result in infinite systems.

The synchronizability results directly apply here, considering the adapter as a peer whose specificity is just that it interacts with all the other peers. It was proved that checking the equivalence between the synchronous composition and the 1-bounded asynchronous composition is a sufficient and necessary condition for branching synchronizability [18]. In the rest of this section, we show how we reuse the synchronizability property for generating adapters that work in asynchronous environments.

Given a set of mismatching peers modelled as LTSs and an adaptation contract (a set of vectors), an adapter LTS can be automatically synthesised as presented in Section 2. Then, we check whether the adapted synchronous composition and the 1-bounded adapted asynchronous composition are equivalent. If this is the case, it means that the system is synchronizable and its observable behaviour will remain the same whatever bound is chosen for buffers. Thus, the adapter generated using existing techniques for synchronous communication can be used as is in an asynchronous context. If the system is not synchronizable, the user refines the adaptation contract using the diagnostic returned by equivalence checking techniques. This counterexample indicates the additional behaviour present in the asynchronous composition and absent in the synchronous one, which invalidates synchronizability. The violation of this property has two main causes: either the adapter does not capture/handle all reachable emissions, or the adapter is too restrictive *wrt.* message orderings, *e.g.*, the adapter requires a sequence of two emissions, which cannot be ensured in the asynchronous composition because both emissions can be executed simultaneously. We apply iteratively this process until the synchronizability property is satisfied.

Our approach is supported by several tools: (i) we reuse the Itaca toolbox [8] for synthesising synchronous adapters, and (ii) we rely on process algebra encodings and reuse equivalence checking techniques available in the CADP verification toolbox [12] for checking synchronizability.

Example 4. As far as our running example is concerned, given the LTSs of the peers and the set of vectors presented in Section 2, we can automatically generate the corresponding adapter (Figure 2). However, if we check whether the composition of this adapter with the peers' LTSs satisfies synchronizability, the verdict is false, and we obtain the following counterexample: b:request!, s:type!, s:price!, s:reply!, b:reply!, and b:stop!, where the very last event appears in the asynchronous system but not in the synchronous one. Note that synchronizability focuses on emissions, hence the counterexample above contains only messages sent by a peer to the adapter (b:request!, s:reply!, b:stop!) or by the adapter to a peer (s:type!, s:price!, b:reply!). This violation is due to the fact that the emission of stop is not captured by any vector, and consequently it is inhibited in the synchronous system, while it is still possible in the asynchronous system because reachable emissions cannot be inhibited under asynchronous communication.

In order to correct this problem, we extend the adaptation contract by adding the following vector: $V_{stop} = \langle b:stop!, s:\varepsilon \rangle$. The corresponding adapter is generated and shown in Figure 3. The system composed of the two peers interacting through this adapter turns out to satisfy the synchronizability property. This means that the adapter can be used under asynchronous communication and the system will behave exactly the same whatever bound is chosen for buffers or if buffers are unbounded.

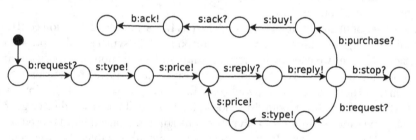

Fig. 3. Adapter LTS generated after addition of V_{stop}

4 Related Work

Existing proposals for software adaptation present interesting approaches tackling this topic from different points of view. However, most of them assume that peers interact synchronously, see, *e.g.*, [10,1,17,16,14,4] for a few recent results. There were a few attempts to generate adapters considering asynchronous communication. Padovani [19] presents a theory based on behavioural contracts to generate orchestrators between two services related by a subtyping (namely, subcontract) relation. This is used to generate an adapter between a client of some service S and a service replacing S. An interesting feature of this approach is its expressiveness as far as behavioural descriptions are concerned, with support for asynchronous orchestrators and infinite behaviour. The author resorts to the theory of regular trees and imposes two requirements (regularity and contractivity) on the orchestrator. However, this work does not support name mismatch nor data-related adaptation. Seguel *et al.* [21] present automatic techniques for constructing a minimal adapter for two business protocols possibly involving parallelism and loops. The approach works by assigning to loops a fixed number of iterations, whereas we do not impose any restriction, and peers may loop infinitely. Gierds and colleagues [13] present an approach for specifying behavioural adapters based on domain-specific transformation rules that reflect the elementary operations that adapters can perform. The authors also present a novel way to synthesise complex adapters that adhere to these rules by consistently separating data and control, and by using existing controller synthesis algorithms. Asynchronous adaptation is supported in this work, but buffers/places must be arbitrarily bounded for ensuring computability of the adapter.

5   Conclusion

Most existing approaches for adapting stateful software focus on systems relying on synchronous communication. In this paper, we tackle the adapter generation question from a different angle by assuming that peers interact asynchronously via FIFO buffers. This complicates the synthesis process because we may have to face infinite systems when generating the adapter behaviour. Our approach uses jointly adapter generation techniques for synchronous communication and the synchronizability property for solving this issue. This enables us to propose an iterative approach for synthesising adapters in asynchronous environments. We have applied it in this paper on a real-world example for illustration purposes.

Acknowledgements. This work was partially funded by the European Commission FP7 project SeaClouds (FP7-ICT-2013-10) and by the Spanish Government under Project TIN2012-35669.

References

1. van der Aalst, W.M.P., Mooij, A.J., Stahl, C., Wolf, K.: Service Interaction: Patterns, Formalization, and Analysis. In: Bernardo, M., Padovani, L., Zavattaro, G. (eds.) SFM 2009. LNCS, vol. 5569, pp. 42–88. Springer, Heidelberg (2009)
2. de Alfaro, L., Henzinger, T.A.: Interface Automata. In: Proc. of ESEC/FSE 2001, pp. 109–120. ACM Press (2001)
3. Basu, S., Bultan, T., Ouederni, M.: Deciding Choreography Realizability. In: Proc. of POPL 2012, pp. 191–202. ACM (2012)
4. Bennaceur, A., Chilton, C., Isberner, M., Jonsson, B.: Automated Mediator Synthesis: Combining Behavioural and Ontological Reasoning. In: Hierons, R.M., Merayo, M.G., Bravetti, M. (eds.) SEFM 2013. LNCS, vol. 8137, pp. 274–288. Springer, Heidelberg (2013)
5. Bracciali, A., Brogi, A., Canal, C.: A Formal Approach to Component Adaptation. Journal of Systems and Software 74(1), 45–54 (2005)

6. Brand, D., Zafiropulo, P.: On Communicating Finite-State Machines. Journal of the ACM 30(2), 323–342 (1983)
7. Brogi, A., Popescu, R.: Automated Generation of BPEL Adapters. In: Dan, A., Lamersdorf, W. (eds.) ICSOC 2006. LNCS, vol. 4294, pp. 27–39. Springer, Heidelberg (2006)
8. Cámara, J., Martín, J.A., Salaün, G., Cubo, J., Ouederni, M., Canal, C., Pimentel, E.: ITACA: An Integrated Toolbox for the Automatic Composition and Adaptation of Web Services. In: Proc. of ICSE 2009, pp. 627–630. IEEE (2009)
9. Canal, C., Murillo, J.M., Poizat, P.: Software Adaptation. L'Objet 12(1), 9–31 (2006)
10. Canal, C., Poizat, P., Salaün, G.: Model-Based Adaptation of Behavioural Mismatching Components. IEEE Trans. on Software Engineering 34(4), 546–563 (2008)
11. Cubo, J., Salaün, G., Canal, C., Pimentel, E., Poizat, P.: A Model-Based Approach to the Verification and Adaptation of WF/.NET Components. In: Proc. of FACS 2007. ENTCS, vol. 215, pp. 39–55. Elsevier (2007)
12. Garavel, H., Lang, F., Mateescu, R., Serwe, W.: CADP 2010: A Toolbox for the Construction and Analysis of Distributed Processes. In: Abdulla, P.A., Leino, K.R.M. (eds.) TACAS 2011. LNCS, vol. 6605, pp. 372–387. Springer, Heidelberg (2011)
13. Gierds, C., Mooij, A.J., Wolf, K.: Reducing Adapter Synthesis to Controller Synthesis. IEEE T. Services Computing 5(1), 72–85 (2012)
14. Inverardi, P., Tivoli, M.: Automatic Synthesis of Modular Connectors via Composition of Protocol Mediation Patterns. In: Proc. of ICSE 2013, pp. 3–12. IEEE / ACM (2013)
15. Magee, J., Kramer, J., Giannakopoulou, D.: Behaviour Analysis of Software Architectures, pp. 35–49. Kluwer Academic Publishers (1999)
16. Mateescu, R., Poizat, P., Salaün, G.: Adaptation of Service Protocols Using Process Algebra and On-the-Fly Reduction Techniques. IEEE Trans. on Software Engineering 38(4), 755–777 (2012)
17. Nezhad, H.R.M., Xu, G.Y., Benatallah, B.: Protocol-Aware Matching of Web Service Interfaces for Adapter Development. In: Proc. of WWW 2010, pp. 731–740. ACM (2010)
18. Ouederni, M., Salaün, G., Bultan, T.: Compatibility Checking for Asynchronously Communicating Software. In: Fiadeiro, J.L., Liu, Z., Xue, J. (eds.) FACS 2013. LNCS, vol. 8348, pp. 310–328. Springer, Heidelberg (2014)
19. Padovani, L.: Contract-Based Discovery and Adaptation of Web Services. In: Bernardo, M., Padovani, L., Zavattaro, G. (eds.) SFM 2009. LNCS, vol. 5569, pp. 213–260. Springer, Heidelberg (2009)
20. Plasil, F., Visnovsky, S.: Behavior Protocols for Software Components. IEEE Trans. on Software Engineering 28(11), 1056–1076 (2002)
21. Seguel, R., Eshuis, R., Grefen, P.W.P.J.: Generating Minimal Protocol Adaptors for Loosely Coupled Services. In: Proc. of ICWS 2010, pp. 417–424. IEEE Computer Society (2010)
22. Yellin, D.M., Strom, R.E.: Protocol Specifications and Components Adaptors. ACM Trans. on Programming Languages and Systems 19(2), 292–333 (1997)

Handling Irreconcilable Mismatches
in Web Services Mediation*

Xiaoqiang Qiao[1], Quan Z. Sheng[2], and Wei Chen[1]

[1] Institute of Software, Chinese Academy of Sciences
Beijing, 100190, China
{qxq,wchen}@otcaix.iscas.ac.cn
[2] School of Computer Science, the University of Adelaide
Adelaide, SA 5005, Australia
michael.sheng@adelaide.edu.au

Abstract. Service mediation provides an effective way to integrate a service requester and a service provider, by reconciling the mismatches between the two. The techniques to assess the mediation degrees of services, to analyze irreconcilable mismatches, and to provide resolutions for irreconcilable behavioral mismatches are therefore essential. To address these challenges, we introduce in this paper two quantifiable metrics, called *service mediatability* and *modification complexity*, to evaluate the feasibility and complexity of mediating a requester and a service. We also propose a pattern-based approach for analyzing service behaviors that cannot be automatically mediated. We further offer resolutions for each irreconcilable mismatch pattern, which help developers to adjust and improve the service behaviors to fulfill the interaction requirements.

1 Introduction

In order to interact seamlessly, a service requester and a Web service should be compatible both in *signature* and in *behavior* [3]. Service mediation is a feasible technique to deal with incompatible services by introducing extra components such as *service mediators* (or adaptors) [11]. Most existing approaches for Web service mediation only focus on how to synthesize service mediators semi-automatically or automatically in the case when services could be mediated. If there are irreconcilable mismatches, the services are simply considered as "not mediatable" and no further solution can be taken for mediation.

However, in practice, interactions among many services may not be fully mediated due to irreconcilable mismatches. Therefore, it is of great significance for analyzing and resolving irreconcilable mismatches between Web services. On the one hand, the irreconcilable information could be readily applied to measure i) the mediation degree of a given service and ii) the difficulty degree in amending the service request for a service mediation. Since there are usually multiple

---

* This work has been partially supported by the National High Technology Research and Development Program of China (863) under Grant No. 2012AA011204, the National Natural Science Foundation of China under Grant No. 61100065.

X. Franch et al. (Eds.): ICSOC 2014, LNCS 8831, pp. 445–452, 2014.

candidate services available for a specific request, such a measurement could be extremely useful for selecting the most suitable service with low cost. On the other hand, the irreconcilable information could also be used as a guide to modify the service request in order to mediate some selected Web services.

This paper focuses on services that could not be automatically mediated and advances the fundamental understanding on Web services mediation by proposing an approach for analyzing and assessing the irreconcilable behaviors of Web services. The main contributions of our work include: i) the concept of *mediatability* enabling a quantifiable measurement of mediation degrees between services, ii) a pattern-based method for analyzing service behaviors that cannot be mediated, iii) the corresponding solution for each irreconcilable pattern, and iv) a research prototype based on the proposed approach.

2   Mediation Degree Assessment for Service Interactions

Our proposed procedure for assessing the mediation degrees of services is illustrated in Fig. 1. First, the mediation model is constructed after defining the service and message mapping. Next, the mediation model is checked for verifying the existence of the mediator and calculating the mediatability of the services. Finally, if a service is mediatable, the corresponding mediator protocol will be automatically synthesized. Otherwise, a pattern-based analysis of the irreconcilable mismatches between the requester and the service will be conducted.

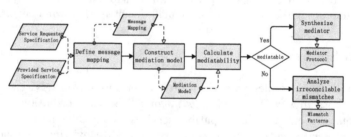

Fig. 1. The procedure of the proposed approach

2.1   Defining Service and Message Mapping

Definition 1. (Service). *A service is defined as a triple:* $S = (\mathcal{M}_{in}, \mathcal{M}_{out}, \mathcal{P})$:

- $\mathcal{M}_{in}$ *is the finite set of messages that are received by service S, and $\mathcal{M}_{out}$ is the finite set of messages that are sent by the service;*
- $\mathcal{P}$ *is the interaction protocol of service S* $\square$.

We adopt the process concept in Communicating Sequential Processes (CSP) [4] to model a service protocol. The language of CSP used in this paper is given in [8]. Message mapping indicates the message correlations between two services.

Definition 2. (Message Mapping). *Let interactive services be* $\mathcal{S}^A=(\mathcal{M}_{in}^A, \mathcal{M}_{out}^A, \mathcal{P}^A)$ *and* $\mathcal{S}^B=(\mathcal{M}_{in}^B, \mathcal{M}_{out}^B, \mathcal{P}^B)$, *the message mapping between them comprises two sets:* $Map_{<A,B>}$ *and* $Map_{<B,A>}$.

- $Map_{<A,B>}=\{synth_i(m_r, \mathcal{M}_D)|m_r \in \mathcal{M}_{in}^B, \mathcal{M}_D \subseteq \mathcal{M}_{out}^A, 1 \leq i \leq n\}$ *is a set of mapping rules from* $\mathcal{M}_{out}^A$ *to* $\mathcal{M}_{in}^B$. m_r *is a receiving message of service* $\mathcal{S}^B$ *and* $\mathcal{M}_D$ *is the set of sending messages of service* $\mathcal{S}^A$. $synth_i$ *is the mapping function to construct* m_r *from* $\mathcal{M}_D$;
- *Similarly,* $Map_{<B,A>}$ *is a set of mapping rules from* $\mathcal{M}_{out}^B$ *to* $\mathcal{M}_{in}^A$ □.

Based on the provided message mapping, we can apply behavior checking methods to determine whether irreconcilable mismatches exist. The mediation model specifies how two services exchange messages through a mediator, which could be automatically constructed based on message mapping.

Definition 3. (Mediation Model). *Let interactive service protocols be* $\mathcal{P}^A$ *and* $\mathcal{P}^B$, *the mediation model between them is:* $[Pipes||(\mathcal{P}_M^A||\mathcal{P}_M^B)]$, *where:*

- $Pipes = (||_{i \leq n}Pipe\_m_i)$, *here n is the number of the target messages defined in the message mapping. For each* $synth_i(m_r, \mathcal{M}_D)$, *there exists a corresponding message pipe* $Pipe\_m_i$ *and its behavior is described as:* $Pipe\_m_i = (||_{j \leq l}left?m_{dj}) \rightarrow synth_i \rightarrow right!m_r \rightarrow SKIP$ *where* $m_{dj} \in \mathcal{M}_D$, *l is the number of source messages that* m_r *depends on. A message pipe receives data with its left channel and writes the result message to the right channel.*
- $\mathcal{P}_M^A$ *and* $\mathcal{P}_M^B$ *are processes that in charge of reading messages from or writing messages into the corresponding pipes, which could be constructed from* $\mathcal{P}^A$ *and* $\mathcal{P}^B$ *respectively by replacing corresponding events based on the rules:*
  - $\forall !m \in \alpha\mathcal{P}^A (or \; \alpha\mathcal{P}^B)$, *if m is a source message in the message mapping,* $!m \Rightarrow (||_{i \leq n}Pipe\_m_i.left!m)$. *Here n is the number of target messages that depend on m. Otherwise,* $!m \Rightarrow WriteNull$. *WriteNull is used to indicate that there is no specified reception for the sending message.*
  - $\forall ?m \in \alpha\mathcal{P}^A (or \; \alpha\mathcal{P}^B)$, *if m is a target message in the message mapping,* $?m \Rightarrow Pipe\_m.right?m$. *Otherwise,* $?m \Rightarrow ReadNull$. *Likewise, we use ReadNull event to represent the required message could not be sent by the partner service.* □

We use the deadlock process concept in CSP to check the existence of mediator and locate the irreconcilable mismatches. To automatically perform the checking process, we further improve the algorithm in [9] to quantify the mediation degree of a service.

2.2 Calculating Mediatability

In order to check the mediation model for verifying the mediator existence and calculating the mediatability, we use algebraic laws of non-deterministic choice (⊓) to obtain *interaction paths*, which represent possible interactive processes between two services in a certain interaction with the aid of the mediator. Due to space constraints, the details of the algebraic laws are described in [8].

Definition 4. (Interaction Path). *Suppose the standard forms of non-deterministic choice of* $\mathcal{P}_M^A$ *and* $\mathcal{P}_M^B$ *are* $(p_1^A \sqcap p_2^A \sqcap \ldots \sqcap p_n^A)$ *and* $(p_1^B \sqcap p_2^B \sqcap \ldots \sqcap p_l^B)$ *respectively, the behavior of* $\mathcal{P}_M^A \| \mathcal{P}_M^B$ *is:* $(p_1^A \| p_1^B) \sqcap (p_1^A \| p_2^B) \sqcap \ldots \sqcap (p_1^A \| p_l^B) \sqcap (p_2^A \| p_1^B) \sqcap \ldots \sqcap (p_n^A \| p_l^B)$. *Each non-deterministic branch sub-protocol of* $\mathcal{P}_M^A \| P_M^B$, $(p_1^A \| p_1^B)$, $(p_1^A \| p_2^B)$,..., $(p_n^A \| p_l^B)$, *is a interaction path between* $\mathcal{P}_M^A$ *and* $\mathcal{P}_M^B$. $\square$

Algorithm 1 shows the procedure to check and record the deadlock events of each interaction path between the requester and the provided service. Function *move* is invoked alternately to traverse all events of the input sub-protocols (line 2). The return value of function *move* has four types. *NoMove* indicates no event is checked during this invocation, while *Moved* means some events have been checked in the invocation. *SKIP* indicates the checking is finished and *ReadNull* means a *ReadNull* is encountered.

Algorithm 1. Deadlock Event Checking

Input: a sub-protocol of $\mathcal{P}_M^{Requester}$: p_1, a sub-protocol of $\mathcal{P}_M^{Service}$: p_2
Output: the deadlock event set: *events*
1. **while** (*true*) **do**
2.   result$_1$:= *move* (p_1), result$_2$:= *move* (p_2);
3.   **if** (result$_1$ = *ReadNull* ∨ result$_2$ = *ReadNull*)
4.   **if** (result$_1$ = *ReadNull*) *record* (*events*, p_1); **end if**
5.   **if** (result$_2$ = *ReadNull*) *record* (*events*, p_2); **end if**
6.   **else if** (result$_1$ = *NoMove* ∧ result$_2$ = *NoMove*)
7.   *record* (*events*, p_2);
8.   **else if** (result$_1$ = *NoMove* ∧ result$_2$ = *SKIP*)
9.   *record* (*events*, p_1);
10.   **else if** (result$_2$ = *NoMove* ∧ result$_1$ = *SKIP*)
11   *record* (*events*, p_2);
12.   **else if** (result$_1$ = *SKIP* ∧ result$_2$ = *SKIP*)
13.   **return** *events*;
14.   **end if**
15. **end while**

If either result$_1$ or result$_2$ is *ReadNull* (line 3), or both of them cannot move forward (return *NoMove*, line 6), the corresponding events can cause a deadlock and should be recorded (i.e., the function *record*). In order to check the remaining parts of p_1 and p_2, we assume the deadlock is resolved and continue the algorithm (line 2). It is noted that the checking is performed from the perspective of the requester. In the scenario when both p_1 (i.e., the requester) and p_2 (i.e., the service) return *NoMove* (line 6), the corresponding event in p_2 firstly will be resolved (line 7). If either result is *SKIP* and the other result is *NoMove* (line 8 and line 10), all of the remaining events in the corresponding protocol will be recorded. If both result$_1$ and result$_2$ are *SKIP* (line 12), the checking procedure is finished. Algorithm 2 shows the details on function *move*.

Based on the recording of the deadlock events, we can calculate the mediatability between the requester and the service. The mediatability of one interaction path is computed as follows:

$$MD_{path} = 1 - \left(\frac{N_{deadlocks}}{N_{total}}\right) \tag{1}$$

where $N_{deadlocks}$ is the number of the recorded deadlock events and N_{total} is the number of all receiving events in the interaction path. If N_{total} is 0, $\left(\frac{N_{deadlocks}}{N_{total}}\right)$ should be 0. Clearly, the value of the mediatability of one interaction path lies in the range of 0 and 1.

Algorithm 2. Move

Input: a protocol to be checked: p
Output: the checking result: $result$

1. **if** $(isSequential(p))$
2.   **for each** $subSequentialProtocol\ p_i$ **do**
3. $result := move(p_i)$;
4.   **if** (result=$SKIP$)
5.   hasMoved := $true$;
6.   **else if** (result=$ReadNull$)
7.   **return** $ReadNull$;
8.   **else if** (hasMoved=$true \lor$ result=$Moved$)
9.   **return** $Moved$;
10.   **else return** $NoMove$;
11.   **end if**
12.   **end for**
13. **return** $SKIP$;

14. **else if** $(isParallel(p))$
15.   **for each** $subParallelProtocol\ p_i$ **do**
16. $result_i := move(p_i)$;
17.   **end for**
18.   **if** (all $result_i = SKIP$)
19.   **return** $SKIP$;
20.   **else if** ($\exists\ result_i = ReadNull$)
21.   **return** $ReadNull$;
22.   **else if** ($\exists\ result_i = Moved$)
23.   **return** $Moved$;
24.   **end if**
25.   **return** $NoMove$;

26. **else if** $(isExternalChoice(p))$
27.   **for each** $subChoiceProtocol\ p_i$ **do**
28.   **if** $(isChosen(p_i))$
29.   **return** $move(p_i)$;
30.   **end if**
31.   **return** $NoMove$;
32. **end for**

33. **else**
34.   **for each** $event\ a_i$ **do**
35.   **if** $(isWriting(a_i))$
36. $writePipe(a_i)$;
37.   hasMoved := $true$;
38.   **else if** $(isReading(a_i))$
39.   **if** $(canRead(a_i))$
40.   hasMoved := $true$;
41.   **else if** (hasMoved)
42.   **return** $Moved$;
43.   **else return** $NoMove$;
44.   **end if**
45.   **else if** $(a_i = ReadNull)$
46.   **return** $ReadNull$;
47.   **end if**
48.   **end for**
49.   **return** $SKIP$;
50. **end if**

The mediatability between the requester and the service is calculated using:

$$MD_{service} = (\sum_{i=1}^{n} MD_{path}^{i})/n \qquad (2)$$

Here MD_{path}^{i} is the mediatability of $path_i$ in the mediation model and n is the number of the interaction paths. Larger values of the mediatability indicate fewer deadlock events and higher mediation degrees.

2.3 Analyzing Irreconcilable Mismatches

We present here a pattern-based method to further analyze the irreconcilable behaviors. A *mismatch pattern* refers to those mismatches that can be reused to identify the irreconcilable behaviors between services.

The mismatch patterns identified in this paper and their corresponding resolving method are presented in Table 1. The interactions between the requester and the service with these mismatches could not be achieved through automated mediation method, but only through manual efforts to modify the protocol and construct the mediator. It is noted that the cost on modifying the requester protocol may be very different. For example, patterns 2 and 4 need the requester to improve and offer more interactive messages or branches, the cost involved will be higher than that of patterns 1 and 5. Since mediatability only measures the quantity of the deadlock events that need to be modified, and cannot reflect the cost and difficulty of the modification, we introduce another metric, named *modification complexity*. The modification complexity of each atomic operation, valued between 0 and 1, is listed in Table 2.

Table 1. Irreconcilable mismatch patterns

ID	Name	Description	Illustration	Checking Method	Resolving Method
1	Missing Requester Message	The service can not send a message that the requester expects to receive.	service requester: $!M_1$, $?M_2$, $?M_3$ ⟺ provided service: $?M_1$, $!M_3$	The deadlock events that are recorded when $result_1$ is Read-Null.	The requester deletes the corresponding event.
2	Missing Service Message	The requester can not send a message that the service expects to receive.	service requester: $!M_1$, $?M_3$ ⟺ provided service: $?M_1$, $?M_2$, $!M_3$	The deadlock events that are recorded when $result_2$ is Read-Null.	The requester adds the corresponding event to provide the required message.
3	Irreconcilable Ordering Mismatch	The message ordering mismatch that leads to a circular dependency.	service requester: $?M_1$, $!M_2$ ⟺ provided service: $?M_2$, $!M_1$	The deadlock events that are recorded when $result_1$ and $result_2$ are NoMove.	The requester switches the ordering of the messages.
4	Missing Choice Branch in Requester	The entire choice branch in the service protocol has no counterpart.	service requester: $?M_1$, $!M_3$ ⟺ provided service: $!M_1$, $!M_2$, $?M_3$, $?M_4$	The deadlock events belong to a choice branch of the service and the start event of the branch is WriteNull.	The requester provides the required choice branch.
5	Missing Choice Branch in Service	The entire choice branch in the requester protocol has no counterpart.	service requester: $!M_1$, $!M_2$, $?M_3$, $?M_4$ ⟺ provided service: $?M_2$, $!M_4$	The deadlock events belong to a choice branch of the requester and the start event of the branch is WriteNull.	The requester deletes the required choice branch.
6	Missing Loop in Requester	A loop structure in the service protocol interacts with a non-loop structure in the requester protocol.	service requester: $?M_1$, $?M_2$, $!M_3$ ⟺ provided service: $!M_1$, $!M_2$, $?M_3$	When p_2 ends with the loop flag while p_1 ends with SKIP, the receiving events in the loop structure would be recorded.	The requester changes the non-loop structure into the loop structure.
7	Missing Loop in Service	A loop structure in the requester protocol interacts with a non-loop structure in the service protocol.	service requester: $!M_1$, $!M_2$, $?M_3$ ⟺ provided service: $?M_1$, $?M_2$, $!M_3$	When p_1 ends with the loop flag while p_2 ends with SKIP, the receiving events in the loop structure would be recorded.	The requester changes the loop structure into the non-loop structure.

Table 2. Modification Complexities of Atomic Operations

Operation	Patterns	Complexity
Add an event	Pattern 2 and 4	0.8
Delete an event	Pattern 1 and 5	0.4
Change the ordering of an event	Pattern 3	0.6
Change the execution times of an event	Pattern 6 and 7	0.6

Furthermore, the complexity of the control structure makes it difficult to modify the protocol, which should be also considered in calculating the overall modification complexity of the requester protocol. The formulas of calculating complexities for structural operators are shown in Table 3. The recursive structure involves a decision event and are executed multiple times. For the choice structures, the influence of the modification on other branches should be considered. In parallel structure, the execution of different branches should be synchronized. Therefore, these structures introduce extra difficulties to the protocol modification, and the corresponding weights are assigned to them.

Table 3. Complexity Formulas for Control Structures

Operator	Formula	Weight
$\rightarrow$	$MC_{a \rightarrow \mathcal{P}} = MC_a + MC_{\mathcal{P}}$	
$\square$	$MC_{\mathcal{P}_1 \square \mathcal{P}_2 \ldots \square \mathcal{P}_n} = W_\square * (MC_{\mathcal{P}_1} + MC_{\mathcal{P}_2} + \ldots + MC_{\mathcal{P}_n})$	$W_\square = 1 + (\text{n-1})/\text{n}$
$\sqcap$	$MC_{\mathcal{P}_1 \sqcap \mathcal{P}_2 \ldots \sqcap \mathcal{P}_n} = W_\sqcap * (MC_{\mathcal{P}_1} + MC_{\mathcal{P}_2} + \ldots + MC_{\mathcal{P}_n})$	$W_\sqcap = 1 + (\text{n-1})/\text{n}$
;	$MC_{\mathcal{P}_1 ; \mathcal{P}_2 \ldots ; \mathcal{P}_n} = MC_{\mathcal{P}_1} + MC_{\mathcal{P}_2} + \ldots + MC_{\mathcal{P}_n}$	
$\|$	$MC_{\mathcal{P}_1 \| \mathcal{P}_2 \ldots \| \mathcal{P}_n} = W_\| * (MC_{\mathcal{P}_1} + MC_{\mathcal{P}_2} + \ldots + MC_{\mathcal{P}_n})$	$W_\| = 1.2$
$\mu \mathcal{X} \cdot \mathcal{F}(\mathcal{P}; \mathcal{X})$	$MC_{\mu \mathcal{X} \cdot \mathcal{F}(\mathcal{P}; \mathcal{X})} = W_\mathcal{X} * MC_\mathcal{P}$	$W_\mathcal{X} = 1.5$

3 Prototype Implementation and the Related Work

We have implemented a prototype system to validate the approach proposed in this paper. It provides editors to graphically specify the service protocol and edit the message mapping rules. It also provides facilities for the mediator existence checking. The interface of the prototype system is developed based on the Eclipse Plug-in technique and wrapped into an Eclipse Rich Client Platform (RCP) application. Due to space constraints, we will not give the details. Interested readers are referred to [8].

The works [1,6] analyze the possible types of mismatches between services and propose mediation patterns for developing mediators. [2,10,11] focus on automatic synthesis of mediator protocols. [5] adds semantic dependency relationship in the service description and presents a general process to derive concrete mediators from mediator specifications. However, none of these works analyzes the irreconcilable behaviors that lead to failure of mediated service interaction.

Nezhad et al. [7] provide some evidences that help to construct missing messages, and a very recent work by Zhou et al. [12] computes the number of irreconcilable interaction paths using a mechanism called *walk computation*. In this paper, we go a step further by focusing on quantitative assessment of mediation degree and modification complexity, pattern-based irreconcilable behavior analysis, and mismatch resolution. Our proposed approach takes irreconcilable services into consideration when selecting Web services, thus increasing the range of candidate services. The resolutions for the irreconcilable patterns also reduce the complexity of manual adjustment for mediated service interactions.

4   Conclusion

In this paper, we advance the existing works on service mediation by proposing an approach to analyze and measure the irreconcilable behaviors for service mediation, including a quantifiable metric for measuring mediation degrees, a pattern-based method for mismatch analysis, a set of resolutions for irreconcilable patterns, and a further metric for measuring complexity and cost of modification in service mediation. Our proposed approach, particularly the two metrics, can also help developers in Web services selection. Our future work will extend the approach to support more complicated processes and investigate techniques developed by semantic Web initiatives to automate the service mediation process.

References

1. Benatallah, B., Casati, F., Grigori, D., Nezhad, H.R.M., Toumani, F.: Developing Adapters for Web Services Integration. In: Pastor, Ó., Falcão e Cunha, J. (eds.) CAiSE 2005. LNCS, vol. 3520, pp. 415–429. Springer, Heidelberg (2005)
2. Canal, C., Poizat, P., Salaün, G.: Model-Based Adaptation of Behavioral Mismatching Components. IEEE Trans. Softw. Eng. 34(4), 546–563 (2008)
3. Dumas, M., Benatallah, B., Nezhad, H.R.M.: Web Service Protocols: Compatibility and Adaptation. IEEE Data Engineering Bulletin 31(1), 40–44 (2008)
4. Hoare, C.: Communicating Sequential Processes. Prentice-Hall (1985)
5. Kuang, L., Deng, S., Wu, J., Li, Y.: Towards Adaptation of Service Interface Semantics. In: Proc. of the 2009 IEEE Intl. Conf. on Web Services, ICWS 2009 (2009)
6. Li, X., Fan, Y., Madnick, S., Sheng, Q.Z.: A Pattern-based Approach to Protocol Mediation for Web Services Composition. Info. and Soft. Tech. 52(3), 304–323 (2010)
7. Nezhad, H., et al.: Semi-Automated adaptation of service interactions. In: Proc. of the 16th Intl. Conf. on World Wide Web, WWW 2007(2007)
8. Qiao, X., Sheng, Q.Z., Chen, W.: Handling irreconcilable mismatches in web services mediation. Tech. Rep. TCSE-TR-20140501,
   http://otc.iscas.ac.cn/cms/UploadFile/20140731050648880/
9. Qiao, X., Wei, J.: Implementing Service Collaboration Based on Decentralized Mediation. In: Proc. of the 11th Intl. Conf. on Quality Software, QSIC 2011 (2011)
10. Tan, W., Fan, Y., Zhou, M., Zhou, M.: A Petri Net-Based Method for Compatibility Analysis and Composition of Web Services in Business Process Execution Language. IEEE Trans. Autom. Sci. Eng. 6(1), 94–106 (2009)
11. Yellin, D.M., Strom, R.E.: Protocol Specifications and Component Adaptors. ACM Transactions on Programming Languages And Systems 19(2), 292–333 (1997)
12. Zhou, Z., et al.: Assessment of Service Protocol Adaptability Based on Novel Walk Computation. IEEE Trans. on Systems, Man and Cybernetics, Part A: Systems and Humans 42(5), 1109–1140 (2012)

Evaluating Cloud Users' Credibility of Providing Subjective Assessment or Objective Assessment for Cloud Services

Lie Qu[1], Yan Wang[1], Mehmet Orgun[1], Duncan S. Wong[2],
and Athman Bouguettaya[3]

[1] Macquarie University, Sydney, Australia
{lie.qu,yan.wang,mehmet.orgun}@mq.edu.au
[2] City University of Hong Kong, Hong Kong, China
duncan@cityu.edu.hk
[3] RMIT University, Melbourne, Australia
athman.bouguettaya@rmit.edu.au

Abstract. This paper proposes a novel model for evaluating cloud users' credibility of providing subjective assessment or objective assessment for cloud services. In contrast to prior studies, cloud users in our model are divided into two classes, i.e., ordinary cloud consumers providing subjective assessments and professional testing parties providing objective assessments. By analyzing and comparing subjective assessments and objective assessments of cloud services, our proposed model can not only effectively evaluate the trustworthiness of cloud consumers and reputations of testing parties on how truthfully they assess cloud services, but also resist user collusion to some extent. The experimental results demonstrate that our model significantly outperforms existing work in both the evaluation of users' credibility and the resistance of user collusion.

1 Introduction

Due to the diversity and complexity of cloud services, the selection of the most suitable cloud services has become a major concern for potential cloud consumers. In general, there are three types of approaches which can be adopted to conduct cloud service evaluation prior to cloud service selection. The first type is based on cloud users' subjective assessment extracted from their subjective ratings [5]. The second type is based on objective assessment via cloud performance monitoring and benchmark testing [10] provided by professional organizations, such as CloudSleuth[1]. The third type is based on the comparison and aggregation of both subjective assessment and objective assessment [7,8].

Whichever type of approaches are adopted, the credibility of cloud users providing assessments has a strong influence on the effectiveness of cloud service selection. In cloud environments, cloud users can be generally classified into two classes according to the different purposes of consuming cloud services. The first class comprises ordinary cloud consumers whose purpose is to consume a

---

[1] www.cloudsleuth.net

X. Franch et al. (Eds.): ICSOC 2014, LNCS 8831, pp. 453–461, 2014.

cloud service having high quality performance and spend as little money as possible. They usually offer subjective assessment of cloud services through user feedback. The second class comprises professional cloud performance monitoring and testing parties whose purpose is to offer objective assessment of cloud services to potential cloud consumers for helping them select the most suitable cloud services. To the best of our knowledge, there are no prior approaches in the literature, which can effectively evaluate the credibility of both types of cloud users in cloud service evaluation.

In this paper, we propose a novel model for evaluating cloud users' credibility of providing subjective assessment or objective assessment, where subjective assessment is from ordinary cloud consumers (called Ordinary Consumers, OC for short), and objective assessment is from professional cloud performance monitoring and testing parties (called Testing Parties, TP for short). The credibility of OCs and TPs providing subjective assessment or objective assessment is respectively represented by *trustworthiness* of OCs and *reputations* of TPs. For an OC, an authority center computes the *relative trustworthiness* of the other OCs who consume the same cloud services as the OC. Relative trustworthiness represents other OCs' trustworthiness from the OC's prospect. The relative trustworthiness can also be affected by the difference of variation trend between the other OC's subjective assessments and TPs' objective assessments over time. Then, the authority center selects the OCs who are considered trustworthy enough by the OC as his/her virtual neighbors according to all the relative trustworthiness values. The neighborhood relationships of all the OCs form a social network. The global trustworthiness of an OC on how truthful he/she provides subjective assessment is computed based on the number of OCs who select him/her as their virtual neighbor.

In the meantime, the reputation of a TP on providing truthful objective assessment is modeled in a different way based on the difference among the TP's objective assessments, the majority of objective assessments from other TPs and the majority of subjective assessments from OCs. That implies that the trustworthiness of OCs and the reputations of TPs can be influenced by each other. For this reason, our model can resist collusion among cloud users providing untruthful assessments to some extent. Through our model, a successful collusion attack would become very difficult in practice since a large number of cloud users would have to be involved in such collusion. In contrast to the existing user credibility evaluation model which is based on subjective ratings only, our experimental results show that our model can significantly improve the accuracy of evaluating user credibility, and enhance the resistance capability of user collusion in cloud environments.

2   The Proposed Model

In this section, we first introduce the framework of our proposed model for evaluating cloud users' credibility, and then present the details of our model.

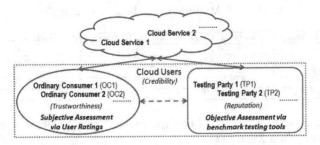

Fig. 1. The Framework of Our Model

2.1 The Framework

Fig. 1 illustrates the framework of our model consisting of two sub models, each of which targets one class of cloud users, i.e., OCs or TPs, respectively. In our framework, subjective assessments for cloud services are extracted from ratings submitted by ordinary consumers, and objective assessments are offered by testing parties using their own benchmark testing tools. After that, subjective assessments and objective assessments will be aggregated in the further cloud service selection process, e.g., the process specified in [7]. In our framework, there is an authority center which is in charge of managing assessments of cloud services and evaluating the trustworthiness and reputation of every OC and TP. Without loss of generality, we focus on the situation, where both subjective assessments and objective assessments evaluate one performance aspect of cloud services. For example, the *response time* of a cloud service can be quantitatively tested by TPs. Meanwhile, an OC consuming the same cloud service can also give his/her subjective ratings for the service response time by sensing how long the cloud responds to his/her requests. The situation of considering multiple performance aspects can be modeled based on multi-criteria decision-making, which will be the object in our future work. In addition, we assume that all assessments are given in similar circumstances.

2.2 The Sub Model for Computing Trustworthiness of OCs

The basic idea of evaluating trustworthiness of OCs in this sub model is that, an OC is considered trustworthy to provide truthful subjective assessments if there are many other OCs or TPs whose subjective assessments or objective assessments are similar to his/hers. To this end, we improve Zhang *et al.*'s work [9], in which, an incentive mechanism is proposed based on modeling the credibility of both buyers and sellers for eliciting truthful ratings of sellers from buyers. Firstly, a series of multiple ratings commonly employed by most rating systems for cloud services are employed instead of binary ratings (i.e., "0" and "1") in Zhang *et al.*'s work to express OCs' subjective assessments. Secondly, in our model, the trustworthiness of an OC can also be influenced by the reputations of TPs. If the variation trend of an OC's subjective assessments over time is more similar to those of objective assessments from TPs having high reputations, the OC's subjective assessments are considered more trustworthy. Finally, in our model, we apply the PageRank algorithm [6] to compute *global trustworthiness* of OCs

Table 1. A Multiple Fuzzy Rating System [7]

Linguistic Ratings	Fuzzy Ratings	Crisp Ratings	Normalized Ratings (r_i)
Very low (VL)	$(0, 0, 0, 3)$	0.75	0
Low (L)	$(0, 3, 3, 5)$	2.75	0.235
Medium (M)	$(2, 5, 5, 8)$	5	0.5
High (H)	$(5, 7, 7, 10)$	7.25	0.765
Very High (VH)	$(7, 10, 10, 10)$	9.25	1

instead of Zhang *et al.*'s method. The experimental results demonstrate that our method is fairer than Zhang *et al.*'s.

Distance Measurement between Multiple Ratings: In this sub model, we apply the rating system defined in Table 1, which is frequently used in prior literature, such as [1,7], to express OCs' subjective assessments. In order to compare two ratings, we adopt the approach proposed by Li and Wang [2], which maps the *rating space* into a *trust space*, to measure the distance between two ratings. As shown in Table 1, fuzzy ratings are first converted into crisp ratings through the signed distance defuzzification method [1]. Then, the crisp ratings are normalized into the interval $[0, 1]$ according to their values. Due to space limitations, we omit the detailed procedure of mapping the rating space into the trust space. In short, a trust space for a service is defined as a triple $T = \{(t, d, u)|t \geqslant 0, d \geqslant 0, u \geqslant 0, t+d+u = 1\}$. Through Bayesian Inference and the calculation of *certainty* and *expected probability* based on a number of sample ratings, normalized ratings can be put into three intervals, i.e., for a normalized rating $r_i \in [0, 1]$, we have

$$r_i \text{ is } \begin{cases} distrust, & \text{if } 0 \leqslant r_i \leqslant d; \\ uncertainty, & \text{if } d < r_i < d + u; \\ trust, & \text{if } d + u \leqslant r_i \leqslant 1. \end{cases}$$

A rating in the *distrust* range means the consumer who gave this rating deems that the service provider did not provide the service with committed quality, and we have a contrary conclusion when a rating is in the *trust* range. A rating in the *uncertainty* range means the consumer is not sure whether the service is provided with committed quality. Here, we call such a range a **trust level**.

The Trustworthiness of OCs: The computation of the trustworthiness of an ordinary consumer OC_A consists of two steps: in Step 1, the authority center computes all the other OCs' *relative trustworthiness* based on OC_A's own experience, and selects a fixed number of top OCs according to the descending order of all their relative trustworthiness values, where these top OCs are considered as OC_A's virtual neighbors. Here, relative trustworthiness represents other OCs' trustworthiness from OC_A's prospect. In Step 2, all these neighborhood relationships form a virtual social network, based on which, the *global trustworthiness* of all OCs are computed.

The details of these two steps are provided below:

Step 1. Computing Relative Trustworthiness of OCs: Suppose there are two ordinary consumers denoted as OC and OC', both of whom consume a group of cloud services, denoted as $\{s_1, s_2, \cdots, s_i, \cdots, s_l\}$. The relative trustworthiness of OC' based on OC is denoted as $RTr(OC \sim OC')$, where $OC \neq OC'$, and computed as follows:

$$RTr(OC \sim OC') = \overline{R_{TP}(OC')} \times$$
$$[\omega \times S_{pri}(OC \sim OC') + (1 - \omega) \times S_{pub}(OC' \sim ALL)]. \tag{1}$$

The details in Eq. (1) are introduced below:

1. $S_{pri}(OC \sim OC')$ (private similarity between OC and OC'): All ratings for a service s_i rated by OC and OC' are ordered into two rating sequences, denoted as $\overrightarrow{r_{OC,s_i}}$ and $\overrightarrow{r_{OC',s_i}}$ respectively, according to the time when the ratings are provided. The rating sequences are then partitioned in mutually exclusive time windows. The length of each time window may be fixed or determined by the frequency of the submitted ratings for s_i. Moreover, it should be considerably small so that the performance of s_i can hardly change in a time window. After that, a pair of ratings $(r_{OC,s_i}, r_{OC',s_i})$, each of which is from its own rating sequence, is said *correspondent* only if they are given in the same time window. If there are more than one correspondent rating pairs in a time window, the most recent r_{OC,s_i} and r_{OC',s_i} are put together as the correspondent rating pair for this time window.

Let N_{s_i} denote the total number of correspondent rating pairs for s_i in all the time windows, then the total number of such pairs for all cloud services is computed as $N_{all} = \sum_{i=1}^{l} N_{s_i}$. If the two ratings of a correspondent rating pair are in the same trust level, such a pair is said *positive*, otherwise *negative*. Thus, if there are N_p positive pairs, then the number of negative pairs is $N_{all} - N_p$. a positive correspondent rating pair means the ratings submitted by OC and OC' respectively in this time window are similar; A negative pair means quite different. In Eq. (1), $S_{pri}(OC \sim OC')$ is called the *private similarity* of OC' which presents the similarity between the ratings provided by OC and OC', and computed as follows:

$$S_{pri}(OC \sim OC') = \frac{N_p}{N_{all}}. \tag{2}$$

2. $S_{pub}(OC' \sim ALL)$ (public similarity between OC' and all other OCs): If there are insufficient correspondent rating pairs between OC and OC', OC''s *public similarity*, denoted as $S_{pub}(OC' \sim ALL)$ in Eq. (1), should be calculated. The public similarity of OC' depends on the similarity between his/her ratings and the majority of ratings submitted by the other OCs. In each time window, the most recent r_{OC',s_i} and the average of the other ratings submitted by the other OCs for s_i are put together as a correspondent rating pair, denoted as $(\overline{r_{s_i}}, r_{OC',s_i})$. Suppose the total number of such correspondent rating pairs for all cloud services is N'_{all}, where there are N'_p positive pairs. The public similarity of OC' is computed as follows:

$$S_{pub}(OC' \sim ALL) = \frac{N'_p}{N'_{all}}. \tag{3}$$

3. ω (weight for private similarity): ω is the weight for how much the private similarity and the public similarity of OC' can be trusted if there are insufficient correspondent rating pairs between OC and OC'. Such a weight can be calculated based on the Chernoff Bound [4] as follows:

$$N_{min} = -\frac{1}{2\varepsilon^2}ln\frac{1-\gamma}{2}, \quad \omega = \begin{cases} \dfrac{N_{all}}{N_{min}}, & \text{if } N_{all} < N_{min}; \\ 1, & \text{otherwise,} \end{cases} \quad (4)$$

where ε is a small value (e.g., 0.1) representing a fixed maximal error bound which OC can accept, and $\gamma \in (0,1)$ is OC's confidence level about his/her own subjective assessments.

4. $\overline{R_{TP}(OC')}$ (average reputation of similar TPs with OC'): $\overline{R_{TP}(OC')}$ represents the weighted average of reputations of TPs, the variation trends of whose objective assessments over time are similar to that of OC''s subjective assessments. Suppose there are m TPs, denoted as $\{TP_1, TP_2, \cdots, TP_j, \cdots, TP_m\}$, providing objective assessments for the l cloud services mentioned above. Following the time window partition method introduced above, we build *correspondent* assessment pairs between OC''s subjective assessments and TP_j's objective assessments for each cloud service, denoted as $(r_{OC',s_i}, oa_{TP_j,s_i})$, where oa denotes the value of objective assessments. All r_{OC',s_i} and oa_{TP_j,s_i} are then put together to build two assessment sequences ordered by the time of every time window, denoted as $\overrightarrow{r_{OC',s_i}}$ and $\overrightarrow{oa_{TP_j,s_i}}$ respectively. After that, each assessment sequence is converted into a ranking sequence according to the assessment values. Suppose the converted ranking sequences for $\overrightarrow{r_{OC',s_i}}$ and $\overrightarrow{oa_{TP_j,s_i}}$ are $\overrightarrow{x_{OC',s_i}}$ and $\overrightarrow{y_{TP_j,s_i}}$ respectively. Then, the similarity, denoted as $\rho(OC' \sim TP_j, s_i)$, between these two ranking sequences are computed via Spearman's rank correlation coefficient [3] which is a common method to compute ranking similarity. Hence, the average similarity of assessment variation trends between OC' and TP_j for all cloud services can be computed as follows:

$$\rho(OC' \sim TP_j) = \frac{1}{l}\sum_{i=1}^{l} \rho(OC' \sim TP_j, s_i). \quad (5)$$

All the TPs with $\rho(OC' \sim TP_j) > 0$ are then selected as the TPs whose objective assessments are similar to OC''s subjective assessments. Suppose there are p such TPs for OC', then the weighted average reputation of these TPs in Eq. (1) is computed as follows:

$$\overline{R_{TP}(OC')} = \frac{1}{p}(\sum_{q=1}^{p} \rho(OC' \sim TP_q) \times R_{TP_q}), \quad (6)$$

where R_{TP_q} represents TP_q's reputation on how truthfully its objective assessments are offered. The details of such reputations will be introduced later.

Step 2. Computing Global Trustworthiness of OCs: Through Eq. (1), the authority center selects a fixed number of virtual neighbors for an OC according to the descending order of all other OCs' relative trustworthiness values, and maintains a virtual social network according to all these neighborhood relationships. Then, we apply the PageRank algorithm [6] in our model. Given a directed graph of neighborhood relationship G, and an OC is a vertex in G, then the *global trustworthiness* of the OC denoted as $Tr(OC)$ is computed as follows:

$$Tr(OC) = \frac{1-d}{N} + d\sum_{OC_i \in G(OC)}^{G(OC)} Tr(OC_i), \quad (7)$$

where $G(OC)$ is the set of all vertices who select the OC as their neighbor, N is the total number of vertexes in G and d is a damping factor which is commonly set to 0.85 in the PageRank algorithm. In our model, $Tr(OC)$ is equivalent to the probability that a random OC' selects the OC as his/her neighbor.

2.3   The Sub-model for Computing Reputations of TPs

In the sub model for computing reputations of TPs, every TP offers objective assessments for the same cloud performance aspect assessed by OCs. The reputation of a TP depends on comparing its objective assessments to the majority of subjective assessments from OCs and the majority of objective assessments from other TPs. We assume that there exists a conversion function [7], through which the values of objective assessments can be converted into normalized ratings introduced in Table 1. Suppose that, for a cloud service s_i, there is a sequence of normalized ratings, which is ordered by time and denoted as $\overrightarrow{r_{TP_j,s_i}}$, corresponding to the sequence of objective assessment values provided by a testing party TP_j. Then, $\overrightarrow{r_{TP_j,s_i}}$ is partitioned in the same way of time window partition introduced in Section 2.2. In a time window, for s_i, there is one normalized objective rating r_{TP_j,s_i} from $\overrightarrow{r_{TP_j,s_i}}$, some subjective normalized ratings from OCs and some objective normalized ratings from other TPs. Let $r_{\overline{TP},s_i}$ denote the average of the objective ratings for s_i provided by all TPs except TP_j in a time window, and $r_{\overline{OC},s_i}$ denote the average of the subjective ratings provided by all OCs of s_i in a time window. In each time window, the authority center gives TP_j a reputation payoff to judge its behaviors in the time window. The reputation payoff matrix is illustrated in Table 2, where "1" means that the two corresponding ratings in a rating pair are in the same trust level, "0" means in different trust levels, and ε_a, ε_b, ε_c and ε_d are the reputation payoffs.

In a time window, the reputation payoff that TP_j can obtain depends on four cases as shown in Table 2:

Table 2. Reputation Payoff Matrix

Cases	Payoffs (TP_j)	$(r_{TP_j,s_i}, r_{\overline{TP},s_i})$	$(r_{TP_j,s_i}, r_{\overline{OC},s_i})$
1	ε_a	1	1
2	ε_b	1	0
3	ε_c	0	1
4	ε_d	0	0

Case 1: If r_{TP_j,s_i}, $r_{\overline{TP},s_i}$ and $r_{\overline{OC},s_i}$ are all in the same trust level, which means a high probability of TP_j providing truthful objective assessments of s_i.

Cases 2&3: If $(r_{TP_j,s_i}, r_{\overline{TP},s_i})$ or $(r_{TP_j,s_i}, r_{\overline{OC},s_i})$ is in the same trust level, but $(r_{TP_j,s_i}, r_{\overline{OC},s_i})$ or $(r_{TP_j,s_i}, r_{\overline{TP},s_i})$ is not, the probability of TP_j providing truthful objective assessments should be lower than that in Case 1. Because objective assessments are usually considered more reliable than subjective assessments, the payoff in Case 2 should be higher than that in Case 3.

Case 4: If both $(r_{TP_j,s_i}, r_{\overline{TP},s_i})$ and $(r_{TP_j,s_i}, r_{\overline{OC},s_i})$ are all in the different trust levels, then TP_j is penalized by giving the least reputation payoff. The reputation payoffs can be defined in the inequality: $\varepsilon_a > \varepsilon_b > \varepsilon_c > \varepsilon_d > 0$.

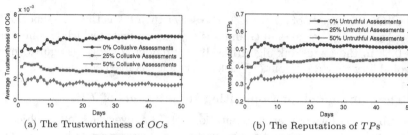

(a) The Trustworthiness of OCs   (b) The Reputations of TPs

Fig. 2. Experimental Results with Collusion

Suppose that the total reputation payoffs that TP_j obtains by assessing s_i in the total t time windows are denoted as ξ_{TP_j,s_i}, then the reputation of TP_j based on s_i and the reputation of TP_j for all cloud services are computed as follows:

$$R_{TP_j,s_i} = \frac{\xi_{TP_j,s_i}}{t\varepsilon_a}, \qquad R_{TP_j} = \frac{1}{l}\sum_{i=1}^{l} R_{TP_j,s_i}. \tag{8}$$

3   Experimental Results

Because no suitable testing environment exists to evaluate our model, we simulate a cloud service environment based on our proposed framework. We collect the data of *response time* from CloudSleuth for 59 real cloud services. To the best of our knowledge, there is no data set of subjective assessments published for those 59 cloud services. Hence, we select 8 similar cloud services from these cloud services, and then simulate subjective assessments from 300 OCs and objective assessments from 36 TPs for the 8 cloud services. We simulate the assessment behavior of all the participants in the cloud environment for a period of 50 simulated days. The trustworthiness of every OC and the reputation of every TP are computed and recorded at the end of each day. In our model, a collusion attack refer to that some users colluding to provide similar untruthful (too high or too low) assessments for a cloud service in order to manipulate the cloud service's reputation, and collusive assessments refers to such similar untruthful assessments. We require that each OC or TP has his/her/its own percentage of providing randomly untruthful or collusive assessments.

In our experiments, all the OCs or TPs are divided into three groups. The OCs or TPs in each group provide different percentages of randomly untruthful or collusive assessments. We have conducted experiments in many different settings. The experimental results demonstrate that our model can effectively detect the OCs or TPs who/which provide randomly untruthful or collusive assessments. Due to space limitations, we only present the experimental results in Fig. 2 when some OCs provide collusive subjective assessments and some TPs provide randomly untruthful objective assessments. Fig. 2 demonstrates that the more collusive assessments/randomly untruthful assessments the OCs/TPs provide, the lower the trustworthiness of the OCs/the reputations of the TPs.

Next, we test the *tolerance* of our model, i.e, the maximum percentages of randomly untruthful or collusive assessments that our model can withstand to stay effective. We compare our model with Zhang *et al.*'s work [9] and the version of our model without TPs, i.e., only OCs' subjective assessments are used to compute their trustworthiness. The experimental results of *tolerance* in Table 3 shows that our model with/without TPs can achieve approximately 83%/43% improvement compared to Zhang *et al.*'s model in the case of providing randomly untruthful assessments, and 38%/14% in the case of providing collusive assessments.

Table 3. Randomly Untruthful or Collusive Assessment Tolerance of Different Models

Models Subjective Assessments	Zhang *et al.*'s model [9]	Our model without TPs	Our model with TPs
Untruthful Assessments	30%	43%	55%
Collusive Assessments	21%	24%	29%

4   Conclusion

We propose a novel model for evaluating cloud users' credibility of providing subjective assessment or objective assessment for cloud services. Our model considers two different classes of cloud users (i.e., ordinary users and testing parties). The trustworthiness of OCs and the reputation of TPs are computed respectively to reflect how truthfully they provide subjective or objective assessments. Moreover, our model have the ability to resist user collusion to some extent. The experimental results demonstrate that our proposed model considering both subjective assessment and objective assessment significantly outperform the exist work considering users' subjective assessment only.

References

1. Chou, S.Y., Chang, Y.H., Shen, C.Y.: A fuzzy simple additive weighting system under group decision-making for facility location selection with objective/subjective attributes. EJOR 189(1), 132–145 (2008)
2. Li, L., Wang, Y.: Subjective trust inference in composite services. In: AAAI Conference on Artificial Intelligence (2010)
3. Marden, J.I.: Analyzing and Modeling Ranking Data. Chapman & Hall (1995)
4. Mui, L., Mohtashemi, M., Halberstadt, A.: A computational model of trust and reputation for e-businesses. In: HICSS, p. 188 (2002)
5. Noor, T.H., Sheng, Q.Z.: Trust as a service: A framework for trust management in cloud environments. In: Bouguettaya, A., Hauswirth, M., Liu, L. (eds.) WISE 2011. LNCS, vol. 6997, pp. 314–321. Springer, Heidelberg (2011)
6. Page, L., Brin, S., Motwani, R., Winograd, T.: The pagerank citation ranking: Bringing order to the web. Technical Report 1999-66 (November 1999)
7. Qu, L., Wang, Y., Orgun, M.A.: Cloud service selection based on the aggregation of user feedback and quantitative performance assessment. In: IEEE International Conference on Services Computing (SCC), pp. 152–159 (2013)
8. Qu, L., Wang, Y., Orgun, M.A., Liu, L., Bouguettaya, A.: Cloud service selection based on contextual subjective assessment and objective assessment. In: AAMAS 2014, pp. 1483–1484 (2014)
9. Zhang, J., Cohen, R., Larson, K.: A trust-based incentive mechanism for E-marketplaces. In: Falcone, R., Barber, S.K., Sabater-Mir, J., Singh, M.P. (eds.) Trust 2008. LNCS (LNAI), vol. 5396, pp. 135–161. Springer, Heidelberg (2008)
10. Zheng, Z., Wu, X., Zhang, Y., Lyu, M.R., Wang, J.: QoS ranking prediction for cloud services. IEEE Trans. Parallel Distrib. Syst. 24(6), 1213–1222 (2013)

Composition of Cloud Collaborations under Consideration of Non-functional Attributes

Olga Wenge, Dieter Schuller, Ulrich Lampe,
Melanie Siebenhaar, and Ralf Steinmetz

TU Darmstadt, KOM, Rundeturmstr. 10, 64283 Darmstadt, Germany
{firstName.lastName}@KOM.tu-darmstadt.de

Abstract. Cloud markets promise virtually unlimited resource supplies. Some providers set up distributed data centers at different geographical locations and jurisdictions and may not always be able to offer effectual physical capacity to serve large customers in one location. A solution is cloud collaborations, where multiple providers unite to conjointly offer capacities. Both Quality of Service and security properties of such collaborations will be determined by the "weakest link in the chain", therefore resulting in a trade-off between monetary aggregates, cumulative capacity and non-functional attributes of a collaboration. Based on our previous research, we examine in our paper efficient composition of cloud collaborations from the broker's perspective, considering Quality of Service and security requirements of cloud providers and users. We propose a Mixed Integer Programming-based heuristic approach CCCP-HEU.COM with deterministic and stochastic variants and provide its quantitative evaluation in comparison with our prior optimal approach.

Keywords: cloud computing, collaboration, QoS, security, cloud broker.

1 Introduction

Cloud markets promise unlimited resource supplies, standardized commodities and proper services in a scalable, pay-as-you-go fashion [1]. Some providers set up distributed data centers at different geographical locations and jurisdictions and may not always be able to offer effectual physical capacity to serve large customers in one location. A solution is cloud collaborations within cloud markets, i. e., the cooperation of multiple providers to aggregate their resources and conjointly satisfy users demands. Supposably, such cloud collaborations have both Quality of Service (QoS) and security impacts. As a user may potentially be served by any provider within a collaboration, the aggregated non-functional service attributes (e. g., availability, security protection level, data center location) will be determined by the "weakest link in the chain", i. e., by the provider with the lowest guarantees. Consideration of country- and industry-specific data protection laws and regulations is another concern by building cloud collaborations, as providers can act in different jurisdictions (the European Union, Canada, Singapore, or the United States), where data privacy laws differ [4].

X. Franch et al. (Eds.): ICSOC 2014, LNCS 8831, pp. 462–469, 2014.

Based on our previous research [5], we examine the Cloud Collaboration Composition Problem (CCCP) with a focus on a broker, who aims to maximize his/her profit through the composition of cloud collaborations from a set of providers and assignment of users to these collaborations. In that assignment, QoS and security requirements, i. e., non-functional attributes, are to be considered and fulfilled. This work extends the previously introduced exact optimization solution approach with a heuristic approach that improves the computational time in the context of cloud markets.

The remainder of this paper is structured as follows: In Section 2, we briefly describe the problem and the formal optimization model, we discussed in our position paper [5]. Section 3 introduces a heuristic approach CCCP-HEU.COM with deterministic and stochastic variants, which is quantitatively evaluated and compared with the previous results. Section 4 concludes the paper.

2   Cloud Collaboration Composition Problem

In our work, we take the perspective of a broker, who acts within a cloud market and unites cloud providers to build cloud collaborations and provides assignment of cloud users to these collaborations. So, the cloud market consists of a set of providers $P = \{1, 2, \ldots, P^\#\}$ and a set of users $U = \{1, 2, \ldots, U^\#\}$. We define resource demand of each user $u \in U$ as $RD_u \in \mathbb{R}^+$ units, for which he/she is willing to pay a total of $M_u^+ \in \mathbb{R}^+$ monetary units. Resource supply of each cloud provider $p \in P$ is defined as $RS_p \in \mathbb{R}^+$ units at a total cost of $M_p^- \in \mathbb{R}^+$.

We define QoS and security constraints as *non-functional* constraints and distinguish two sets of quantitative $A = \{1, 2, \ldots, A^\#\}$ and qualitative $\hat{A} = \{1, 2, \ldots, \hat{A}^\#\}$ non-functional attributes. Quantitative attributes represent numerical properties, e. g., availability. Qualitative attributes depict nominal properties, e. g., applied security policies. The providers make certain guarantees with respect to the non-functional attributes. For each quantitative attribute $a \in A$, the value guaranteed by provider $p \in P$ is denoted as $AG_{p,a} \in \mathbb{R}$. For each qualitative attribute $\hat{a} \in \hat{A}$, the corresponding information is given by $\hat{AG}_{p,\hat{a}} \in \{0, 1\}$. The users specify certain requirements concerning their non-functional attributes. With respect to each quantitative attribute $a \in A$, the value required by user $u \in U$ is denoted as $AR_{u,a} \in \mathbb{R}$. Likewise, $\hat{AR}_{u,\hat{a}} \in \{0, 1\}$ denotes the requirement for each qualitative attribute $\hat{a} \in \hat{A}$, i. e., indicates whether this attribute is mandatory or not.

Based on these notations, the CCCP can be represented as an optimization model, as shown in Model 1. We define $x_{u,c}$ and $y_{p,c}$ as the *main* decision variables in the model (cf. Equation 11). They are binary and indicate whether user u or provider p are assigned to collaboration c or not. We introduce $y'_{p,c}$ as auxiliary decision variables, which are binary as well and indicate the non-assignment of a provider p to a collaboration c. Furthermore, $z_{a,c}$ and $\hat{z}_{\hat{a},c}$ are defined as real and binary, respectively, and represent the cumulative value of the non-functional property a or $\hat{a}$, respectively, for collaboration c (cf. Equation 12).

Model 1. Cloud Collaboration Composition Problem

$$\text{Max. } Pr(x, y, y', z, \hat{z}) = \sum_{u \in U, c \in C} x_{u,c} \times M_u^+ \tag{1}$$

$$- \sum_{p \in P, c \in C} y_{p,c} \times M_p^-$$

such that

$$\sum_{c \in C} x_{u,c} \leq 1 \quad \forall u \in U \tag{2}$$

$$\sum_{c \in C} y_{p,c} \leq 1 \quad \forall p \in P \tag{3}$$

$$y_{p,c} + y'_{p,c} = 1 \quad \forall p \in P, \forall c \in C \tag{4}$$

$$\sum_{u \in U} x_{u,c} \times RD_u \leq \sum_{p \in P} y_{p,c} \times RS_p \quad \forall c \in C \tag{5}$$

$$z_{a,c} \leq y_{p,c} \times AG_{p,a} + y'_{p,c} \times \max_{p \in P}(AG_{p,a}) \tag{6}$$

$$\forall p \in P, \forall c \in C, \forall a \in A$$

$$\hat{z}_{\hat{a},c} \leq y_{p,c} \times \hat{AG}_{p,\hat{a}} + y'_{p,c} \tag{7}$$

$$\forall p \in P, \forall c \in C, \forall \hat{a} \in \hat{A}$$

$$z_{a,c} \geq x_{u,c} \times AR_{u,a} \quad \forall u \in U, \forall c \in C, \forall a \in A \tag{8}$$

$$\hat{z}_{\hat{a},c} \geq x_{u,c} \times \hat{AR}_{u,\hat{a}} \quad \forall u \in U, \forall c \in C, \forall \hat{a} \in \hat{A} \tag{9}$$

$$C = \{1, 2, \ldots, \min(P^\#, U^\#)\} \tag{10}$$

$$x_{u,c} \in \{0, 1\} \quad \forall u \in U, \forall c \in C \tag{11}$$

$$y_{p,c} \in \{0, 1\} \quad \forall p \in P, \forall c \in C$$

$$y'_{p,c} \in \{0, 1\} \quad \forall p \in P, \forall c \in C \tag{12}$$

$$z_{a,c} \in \mathbb{R} \quad \forall a \in A, \forall c \in C$$

$$\hat{z}_{\hat{a},c} \in \{0, 1\} \quad \forall \hat{a} \in \hat{A}, \forall c \in C$$

The monetary objective function for a broker consists in profit maximization, i. e., maximization of the difference between the revenue from the served cloud users and the spending on the used cloud providers (cf. Equation 1).

Equations 2 and 3 make sure that each user and provider are assigned only to one collaboration simultaneously. Equation 4 determines the inverse variable $y'_{p,c}$ for each decision variable $y_{p,c}$ (cf. Equations 6 and 7). These equations determine the cumulative non-functional values for quantitative and qualitative attributes and are formulated such that quantitative properties are given by the "worst" value among all providers in a certain collaboration. Equation 5 prevents the resource demand from exceeding the resource supply. Equations 8 and 9 make sure that users can only be assigned to collaborations with sufficient non-functional guarantees. Equation 10 defines a set of potential cloud collaborations, its cardinality is given by the number of users or providers, whichever is lower.

3 Heuristic Optimization Approach CCCP-HEU.KOM

In our previous research [5], we implemented the described model and evaluated the optimal approach CCCP-EXA.KOM in order to obtain an exact (i. e., profit maximal) solution. We used a Mixed Integer Program (MIP) and a branch-and-bound optimization algorithms [2]. The evaluation results indicated that the computation time of the proposed CCCP exact solution grows in dependence on the number of market participants and in the worst case it is exponential, thus indicating the need for development of heuristic approaches. In the following, we propose a heuristic optimization approach CCCP-HEU.KOM with the improved computation time. Our CCCP-HEU.KOM approach is based on the Divide-and-Conquer principle, i. e., we recursively breaking down the CCCP problem into sub-problems and combine the solutions of sub-problems to provide a solution to the original problem [3]. It consists of four components (sub-problems):

1. ASSIGN: Assignment of cloud users to cloud providers
2. COLLAB: Building of cloud collaborations
3. RCHECK: Checking of resource constraints
4. COMPOSE: Composition of cloud collaborations

ASSIGN: Assignment of users to providers. In this step, the assignment of users to providers will be performed with respect to the fulfillment of NFAs - non-functional requirements of users and non-functional guarantees of providers, as shown in Algorithm 2. The algorithm starts with two empty lists: $assign.P_p$ - a list of all assigned users $u \in U$ of a provider p, and $\hat{P}$ - a list of all providers who can satisfy at least one user. Non-functional guarantees (quantitative AG and qualitative $\hat{AG}$) of each provider will be compared with non-functional requirements (quantitative AR and qualitative $\hat{AR}$) of each user; if a provider p can fulfill the requirements of a user u (or has even better guarantees), then this user u will be added to provider's p list $assign.P_p$ (lines 5-8). Providers who cannot fulfill requirements of any user will be deleted (line 9). Users who cannot be served by any provider will be not added to the lists; thus, the number of users and providers will be reduced. At the end, a set $\hat{P}$ of NFAs-valid assignments (provider - users) is built with respect to the defined NFAs. Resource demand/supply constraints are not considered in this step.

COLLAB: Building of collaborations. In this step, we build cloud collaborations $\hat{C}$, i.e., we bring together providers, who can serve the same users. Thereby, Equations 6 and 7 are to be considered, i.e., the aggregated NFAs of collaborative providers will be defined by the worst ones. The set of valid collaborations is the intersecting set of $\hat{P}$. Applying of the intersection can be examined in two ways: deterministic and stochastic. By the deterministic approach (Algorithm 3), the complete set $\hat{P}$ will be searched through: all permutations of users $\hat{u} \in \hat{U}$ from the $assign.P_{\hat{p}}$ lists will be compared (lines 7-12). Thus, we have $\hat{P}^{\#} * 2^{\hat{U}^{\#}}$ possibilities (single provider sets and empty sets are exclusive), that leads in the worst case to asymptotical exponential runtime for $\hat{U}$, namely $O(\hat{P} * 2^{\hat{U}^{\#}})$. By the stochastic approach, we generate a random subset from the set $\hat{P}$ (Algorithm 4), where not all permutations are considered. The replacement of the Input ($\hat{P}$) of Algorithm 3 by the subset generation improves the algorithm and leads to asymptotical polynomial runtime.

RCHECK: Checking of resource constraints. In this step, we check resource constraints (as defined in Model 1). As shown in Algorithm 5, firstly, the quotients $Q_{\hat{u}} = M_{\hat{u}}^{+}/RD_{\hat{u}}$ (willingness to pay for a resource unit) will be calculated for all users from the provider-users assignments list $\hat{P}$. These quotients are then will be sorted in the descending order with respect to our objective function, namely, profit maximization (lines 5-9). So, the users with the best willingness to pay will be considered first.

COMPOSE: Composition of cloud collaborations. In this step, the best composition of cloud collaborations will be selected. As only one collaboration is allowed for providers and users simultaneously, the duplicates of them must be eliminated. So, the cloud collaborations with the same collaborative partners will be examined and the best constellation with respect to the maximum profit for a broker will be selected. The selected collaborations build then the complete solution of CCCP - $CCCPsol$. As shown in Algorithm 6, each collaboration $c \in C$ produces a certain profit PR_c. To provide an optimal solution, mostly profitable collaborations must be selected to fulfill the objective function. We apply here again the greedy principle and go through all collaborations. In lines (3-7) the collaborations that include the same collaborative partners will be compared - and the collaboration with the best profit $CCCPbest$ will be added to the complete solution $CCCPsol$. So, the composition of cloud collaborations occurs in a polynomial time.

3.1   Evaluation

To assess the required computation time of CCCP-HEU.KOM for different problem sizes and compare it with the exact optimization approach CCCP-EXA.KOM we provided before in [5], we prototypically implemented our heuristc approach in Java and used the same set up for our evaluation (JavaILP and IBM ILOG

Algorithm 2. Assignment

1: Input: set of providers $P = \{1, 2, \ldots, P^{\#}\}$; set of users $U = \{1, 2, \ldots, U^{\#}\}$
2: Output: set NFAs-valid provider-users assignments $\hat{P}$
3: $\hat{P} = \varnothing$; $assign.P_p = \varnothing$
4: **for** all $p \in P$ **do**
5:     **for** all $u \in U$ **do**
6:         **if** $AG_p \geq AR_u$ and $\hat{AG}_p \geq \hat{AR}_u$ **then**   ▷ check the NFAs fulfillment
7:             $assign.P_p = assign.P_p + u$ ▷ assign user u to provider p
8:             **if** $assign.P_p = \varnothing$ **then** delete p
9:                 $\hat{P} = \hat{P} + P_n(assign.P_p)$
10:            **end if**
11:        **end if**
12:    **end for**
13: **end for**

Algorithm 3. Building of collaborations (Full set)

1: Input: set $\hat{P}$ ▷ set of NFAs-valid provider-users assignments
2: Output: set of collaborations $\hat{C}$
3: $\hat{C} = \varnothing$
4: **for** all $\hat{p} \in \hat{P}$ **do**
5:     intersect $assign.P_{\hat{p}}$ with $assign.P_{\hat{p}+1}$ ▷ check shared users in assignment lists
6:     **if** intersect $\neq \varnothing$ **then**
7:         $userxs_{\hat{p},\hat{p}+1} = intersect(assign.P_{\hat{p}}/assign.P_{\hat{p}+1})$
8:         $\hat{C} = \hat{C} + \hat{c}_{\hat{p},\hat{p}+1}(users_{\hat{p},\hat{p}+1})$ ▷ build collaboration
9:         ...   ▷ go through all permutations of users u
10:        $AG_{\hat{c}} = min(AG_{\hat{p}})$ and $\hat{AG}_{\hat{c}} = min(\hat{AG}_{\hat{p}})$ ▷ aggregated NFAs are
11:   ▷ determined by the worst ones
12:    **end if**
13: **end for**

Algorithmus 4. Building of collaborations (Random sub-set)

1: Input: set $\hat{P}$ ▷ set of NFAs-valid provider-users assignments
2: Output: subsets of $\hat{P}$
3: size=$\hat{P}.length$; $\hat{P}.subset = \varnothing$;
4: **for** $size < counter$ **do**
5:     **for** all $\hat{p}$ **do**
6:         subset = generate random subset from $\{1...size\}$
7:         $\hat{P}.subset = \hat{P}.subset + subset$
8:     **end for**
9:     counter=counter+1
10: **end for**

CPLEX framework). We regard *computation time* as the *dependent* variable of our evaluation. As *independent* variables, we include again the number of considered users and providers, i. e., $U^{\#}$ and $P^{\#}$. Each specific combination of $U^{\#}$ and $P^{\#}$ results in a *test case*. For each test case, we created 100 specific CCCP instances with the according dimensions and used the same parameters. The results

---

Algorithmus 5. Checking of resources constraints

1: Input: $\hat{C}$
2: Output: set of built collaborations C with valid resources demand/supply
3: $\hat{RD}_{\hat{c}} = 0$ ▷ resource demand for collaboration $\hat{c}$
4: **for all** $\hat{c}_{\hat{p},\hat{p}+1} \in \hat{C}$ **do**
5: **for all** $\hat{u} \in (users_{\hat{p},\hat{p}+1})$ **do**   ▷ all users in the collaboration $\hat{c}_{\hat{p},\hat{p}+1}$
6:   calculate $Q_{\hat{u}} = M_{\hat{u}}^{+}/RD_{\hat{u}}$ ▷ quotients Q - willingness
7:               ▷ to pay for a resource unit
8: **end for**
9: sort $\hat{u}$ descending according to $Q_{\hat{u}}$ ▷ sorted list $\hat{U}_{\hat{c}}$
10: **for all** $\hat{u} \in \hat{U}_{\hat{c}}$ **do**
11:   **if** $RS_{\hat{c}_{\hat{p},\hat{p}+1}} = RS_{\hat{p}} + RS_{\hat{p}+1} > RD_{\hat{u}}$ **then**
12:    $\hat{RD}_{\hat{c}} = \hat{RD}_{\hat{c}} + \hat{RD}_{\hat{u}}$
13:    **if** $RS_{\hat{c}} = RD_{\hat{u}}$ **then** stop   ▷ maximum supply reached
14:    **end if**
15:   **end if**
16: **end for**
17: **end for**

Algorithmus 6. Composition of cloud collaborations

1: Input: set of collaborations C
2: Output: solution of CCCP - $CCCPsol$
3: $CCCPsol = \varnothing;$ ▷ complete solution
4: **for all** $c \in C$ **do**
5: **if** $c_n \cap c_{n+1} \neq \varnothing$ **then**   ▷ intersect set of c_n and c_{n+1} not empty
6:   $CCCPbest =$ insert c with $maxPR(c_n, c_{n+1})$ ▷ insert the collaboration
7:                ▷ with the best profit
8: **else**
9:   $CCCPbest = c_n$
10:   $CCCPsol = CCCPsol + CCCPbest$
11: **end if**
12: **end for**

---

of our evaluation, i. e., the observed ratio of solved instances and the ratio of the mean computation times in comparison to the CCCP-EXA.KOM approach, are summarized in Table 1. As can be clearly seen, the mean computation times are drasticaly improved, and even the test case (12,18) by CCCP-HEUfull.COM (a heuristic with the full set COLLAB component) takes only 3.46% of the previosly computation time used by the exact approach. This variant shows rather optimal ratio of solving instances in all test cases. CCCP-HEUsub.COM (a heuristic with the sub-set COLLAB component) has better computation times, but the ratio of the solved instances (from 100 problem instances) goes already down with the test case (8,8). It explains also drastical improvement in CCCP-HEUsub.COM computation times for test cases (8,12)-(12,18), as not all solution will be examined - only in the randomly generated sub-sets.

Table 1. Evaluation results of CCCP-HEUfull.KOM and CCCP-HEUsub.KOM

Test case $P^{\#}$, $U^{\#}$	Ratio of solved instances HEUfull / HEUsub	Ratio of mean computation times HEUfull / HEUsub
4, 4	100% / 89,79%	0.94% / 0.50%
4, 6	98.23% / 81.78%	1.57% / 0.99%
6, 6	96.56% / 78.19%	1.87% / 1.13%
6, 9	92.47% / 67.77%	2.45% / 1.22%
8, 8	92.33% / 66.81%	2.62% / 1.45%
8, 12	87.34% / 63.93%	2.85% / 0.60%
10, 10	87.26% / 54.87%	3.30% / 0.45%
10, 15	85.20% / 54.84%	3.37% / 0.56%
12, 12	88.30% / 45.16%	3.40% / 0.40%
12, 18	82.52% / 49.96%	3.46% / 0.23%

4 Conclusions

While cloud markets promise virtually unlimited resources, the physical infrastructure of cloud providers is actually limited and they may not be able to serve the demands of large customers. A possible solution is cloud collaborations, where multiple providers join forces to conjointly serve customers. In this work, we introduced the corresponding *Cloud Collaboration Composition Problem* with our new heuristic optimization approach CCCP-HEU.KOM, as a complement to our prior exact optimisation approach. Our evaluation results indicated drastic improvement in the computation times, but showed also that the proposed heuristic optimization approach CCCP-HEU.KOM is still rather limited and needs further improvements, as a broker acts under rigid time constraints. In our future work, we aim at the development of heuristic approches with meta-heuristics and dynamic changes. In addition, we plan to extend the proposed model with more complex non-functional constraints.

References

1. Buyya, R., Yeo, C.S., Venugopal, S., Broberg, J., Brandic, I.: Cloud Computing and Emerging IT Platforms: Vision, Hype, and Reality for Delivering Computing as the 5th Utility. Future Generation Computer Systems 25(6), 599–616 (2009)
2. Hillier, F., Lieberman, G.: Introduction to Operations Research. McGraw-Hill (2005)
3. Jonson, D.S.: A Brief History of Np-completeness. In: Documenta Mathematica (2012)
4. Wenge, O., Lampe, U., Müller, A., Schaarschmidt, R.: Data Privacy in Cloud Computing–An Empirical Study in the Financial Industry. In: 20th Americas Conference on Information Systems (AMCIS) (2014)
5. Wenge, O., Lampe, U., Steinmetz, R.: QoS- and Security-Aware Composition of Cloud Collaborations. In: 4th International Conference on Cloud Computing and Services Science (CLOSER), pp. 578–583 (2014)

Bottleneck Detection and Solution Recommendation for Cloud-Based Multi-Tier Application

Jinhui Yao[1] and Gueyoung Jung[2]

[1] Palo Alto Research Center (PARC), USA
jinhui.yao@xerox.com
[2] AT&T Research Labs, USA
gjung@research.att.com

Abstract. Cloud computing has gained extremely rapid adoption in the recent years. In the complex computing environment of the cloud, automatically detecting application bottleneck points of multi-tier applications is practically a challenging problem. This is because multiple potential bottlenecks can co-exist in the system and affect each other while a management system reallocates resources. In this paper, we tackle this problem by developing a comprehensive capability profiling of such multi-tier applications. Based on the capability profiling, we develop techniques to identify the potential resource bottlenecks and recommend the additional required resources.

Keywords: Cloud, Bottleneck Detection, Multi-tier Application.

1 Introduction

Cloud computing has gained extremely rapid adoption in the recent years. Enterprises have started to deploy their complex multi-tier web applications into these clouds for cost-efficiency. Here, the cloud-based multi-tier application consists of multiple software components (i.e., tiers) that are connected over inter- and/or intra-communication networks in data centers. Detecting application bottleneck points of multi-tier applications is practically a challenging problem, and yet it is a fundamental issue for system management. Hence, it is desirable to have a mechanism to monitor the application performance changes (e.g., application throughput changes) and then, to correlate system resource usages of all components into the application performance saturation for system diagnosis.

However, automatically pinpointing and correlating bottlenecked resources are not trivial. One of important factors we should focus on is that multiple potential bottlenecks can co-exist typically by oscillating back and forward between distributed resources in the multi-tier applications[6, 9], and they affect each other while a management system performs resource reallocations to resolve the immediate bottlenecks observed individually. Therefore, certain potential and critical bottlenecks may not be timely noticed until other bottlenecks are completely resolved. In this paper, we tackle this problem by developing a comprehensive capability profiling of such multi-tier

X. Franch et al. (Eds.): ICSOC 2014, LNCS 8831, pp. 470–477, 2014.

applications in the cloud. Based on the capability profiling, we develop techniques to identify the potential resource bottlenecks and recommend the required resources to provide adequate performance without the bottleneck oscillation between current and potential bottleneck resources.

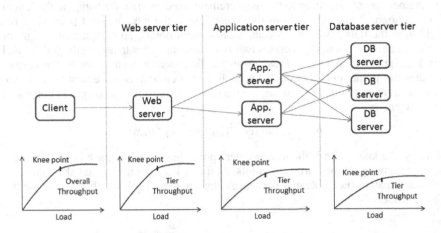

Fig. 1. A 3-tier web transaction application and throughput curves of tiers

2   Bottleneck Detection Using Knee Point Detection

The upper part of Figure 1 illustrates a 3-tier web transaction application that consists of the front-end web server, the middle application servers, and the back-end database servers. Servers in the middle and the back-end tiers handles web transactions in parallel. The lower part of Figure 1 illustrates bottleneck patterns of these tiers. The bottleneck pattern of the application throughput can be described as a knee point of throughput curve, while the workload to the application increases.

As shown in these bottleneck patterns, despite of the initial rapid increase in the application throughput, after the knee point, the throughput cannot increase further because some of system resources of tiers are bottlenecked. Similar bottleneck patterns are shown in all tiers, but at different observation points. This is because a bottleneck in one of the tiers will eventually trigger bottleneck patterns in the other tiers. With these observations, it is important to first capture such knee points, which represent the starting point of bottleneck pattern, of all involved tiers and resource usages of each tier. Then, we can identify the bottleneck causes, in the context of system resources, by analyzing the temporal relations among the bottleneck patterns of all tiers and resource.

2.1   Individual Knee Point Detection

The application throughput can be defined as the number of user requests that successfully get through all tiers. The throughput of the application will keep increasing as the load increases until a certain point, after that point, throughput cannot increase further more because the system bottleneck occurs. Figure 2 illustrates the bottleneck pattern of the throughput. In the figure, we have plotted normalized throughput of the application against normalized load to the application. To capture the knee point, our system first generates a linear line that connects the first measurement point to the last measurement point and then, computes its length (i.e., z in the figure). Second, at each measurement point according to the measurement window size, we compute the length of the orthogonal line drawn from the linear line to the measurement point (i.e., the height h_k in the figure, where k is each measurement point). To compute the height of each measurement point, it generates two lines and computes their lengths (i.e., x_k and y_k in the figure). First line is drawn from the first measurement point to the current measurement point, and the second line is from the current measurement point to the last measurement point. Then, using cosine rule and sine rule, the height is computed as following,

$$ h_k = \; x_k \; sin \; (cos^{-1}((x_k^2 + z^2 - y_k^2)/2x_kz)) $$

Finally, the knee point is the measurement point that has the highest height from the linear line among all measurement points. And this knee point indicates the capability of this application (i.e., potential bottleneck starting point of the application or the tier being considered).

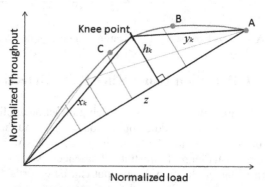

Fig. 2. Bottleneck pattern

2.2   Performance Profiling for Identifying the System bottlenecks

In our approach, we capture the change rate of resource usage (i.e., slope) of each resource type and the change rate of workload throughput until the capability is reached (i.e., knee point), while load increases. The resource usage change rate before the knee point can approximately indicate the degree of contribution of each resource type to the throughput change and the performance capability. These change rates are directly used to build our performance model of the multi-tier application, which is used to infer which resources are the current and potential bottlenecks.

Figure 3 shows the change rates of resource usages and three representative resource types, while load increases over the time. In this illustration, the change rate of CPU is higher than memory usage and disk I/O. It can indicate that CPU contributes more to the workload throughput than memory and disk I/O, and CPU can be bottlenecked first on its knee point. Note that the knee points of three resource types occur at different measurement points.

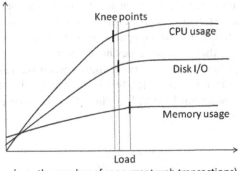

Load
(e.g., the number of concurrent web transactions)

Fig. 3. The change rates before knee points

As shown in Figure 3, throughput increases until the performance capability is reached at knee point. The performance capability is determined by some resource types that consume the most of their available capacities (i.e., bottlenecked).Following this intuition, one straightforward method to find the bottlenecked resource is to sort the knee points to find out which one occurs first. However, a more challenging question will be to find the capability gap (i.e., resource shortage), between the currently bottlenecked resources and the required performance. The capability gap will indicate the additional resource needed for such potential bottleneck resources. And then, it will indicate when the bottleneck is transferred to the other potential bottleneck resources after the management system resolves the current bottleneck by allocating the additional amount of resources. Our system tackles this challenge by defining a quantitative performance model for each individual resource type to identify its correlation to the performance capability of application. Specifically, for each resource type j, a quantitative performance model can be defined as,

$$T_j = f(U_j| (C_j = c, \exists j \in R) \wedge (C_{r'} = \infty, \forall r' \in R, r' \neq j)) \tag{1}$$

, where T_j is the application throughput to be achieved with the normalized resource usage rate, U_j, over given resource capacity (i.e., $C_j = c$) of a resource type j. R is a set of all resource types for the application, and r' is a resource type in R, where r' is different resource type from j. We consider r' has unlimited capacities so that we can compute the correlation of only j to T_j.

While the throughput of the system is determined by the usage of different resources, the resource usage itself is driven by the amount of the load that the system is undertaking. The correlation between the load and the resource usage can be defined as a linear function (note that the correlation between the load and the resource usage can be defined as a non-linear function, however, we have focused on the resource usage before the knee point in our performance modeling, and observed the linear function):

$$U_j = \alpha_j L + \gamma_j \tag{2}$$

, where L is the amount of load, α_j is the change rate of resource usage (e.g., a slope in a linear function), and γ_j is an initial resource consumption in the system. We can obtain α_j and γ_j by calibrating the function to fit into actual curve observed. In this fitting, we use the change rate of resource usage before knee point.

According to Equation 1, the throughput T_j equals to a function of the resource usage U_j, given that all other resource types have unlimited capacities (i.e., $C_{r'} = \infty$). Therefore, this implies that T_j reaches its maximum when the resource being considered is completely utilized (e.g., $U_j = 1$, when it is normalized). Thus, from Equation 1, we can derive the maximum load L_j^{max}, which this resource can undertake at its knee point, as follows:

$$L_j^{max} = \frac{1-\gamma_j}{\alpha_j} \tag{3}$$

We can compute the maximum loads of all different types of the resources with the same way, to produce a set of maximum loads as $\{L_1^{max}, L_2^{max}, L_3^{max} \dots, L_n^{max}\}$, where n is the number of resource types in the system. Once we have obtained the set of all maximum loads, finding the bottleneck resource, intuitively enough, is to find the resource that has the lowest maximum load, since the resource having the lowest maximum load has the earliest knee point $r^{Bottleneck} = \text{argmin}_j L_j^{max}$.

3   Estimating Resource Shortages for Potential Bottlenecks

Using the performance model (Equations 1-3), we can identify the bottleneck in the current configuration of the multi-tier application. However, other resource types may potentially become the next immediate bottleneck after an additional amount of the bottlenecked resource is allocated. Since multiple potential bottlenecks may co-exist in the system configuration as a form of bottleneck oscillation [6, 9], it is necessary to evaluate the total shortage of all resource types of interest in order to consistently achieve the target throughput. These resource shortages indicate the gap between the amount of resource needed and the amount that is currently utilized.

Based on Equation 1 and 2 in the previous section, we can follow the same intuition to define the correlation between the load L and the throughput T of each component, before reaching the knee point of the throughput curve, as a linear function.

$$T = \beta \, L \tag{4}$$

, where L is the amount of load and β is the change rate of throughput. Similarly, we can obtain β by calibrating the function to fit into an actual curve. As mentioned earlier, the correlation between the load and the application throughput can be defined as a non-linear function. However, we have focused on the throughput before the knee point in our performance modeling, and observed the linear function is a good approximation while calibrating the function. By substituting Equation 4 into Equation 2 in the context of L, we have

$$U_j = \frac{\alpha_j}{\beta} T + \gamma_j \tag{5}$$

In Equation 6, if we define the target throughput as T^*, and the required performance capability value as U_j^* of a resource type j (i.e., the usage rate U_j required to achieve T^*), we can replace T and U_j with T^* and U_j^*, respectively, in the equation. Here, (α_j / β) indicates the normalized increase rate of the resource usage to increase a unit of throughput. Thus, the equation indicates how much resource capability is required to meet T^*. Note that if U_j^* is more than 1, it indicates that more resource capability is required to meet T^* than currently available in the configuration, and in this case the normalized resource shortage is thus $U_j^\Delta = U_j^* - 1$. With this equation, the required capability of component x, defined as $U^{x,*}$, for the workload and its throughput goal is a set of such required performance capability values:

$$U^{x,*} = \{U_1^*, \; U_2^*, \; U_3^*, ..., \; U_n^*\} \tag{6}$$

, where n is the number of resource types in the component being considered. Then, the capability shortage for all corresponding resource types in Equation 6 is represented as $U^{x,\Delta} = \{U_1^\Delta, \; U_2^\Delta, \; U_3^\Delta, ..., U_n^\Delta\}$. Similarly, the same method can be applied to all other components in the multi-tier application.

4   Preliminary Evaluation

To evaluate our approach, we have used an online auction web transaction workload, called RUBiS (http://rubis.ow2.org) that is deployed as a 3-tier web application including Apache web server, Tomcat servlet server, and back-end MySQL database server. The workload provided by RUBiS package consists of 26 different transaction types such as "Home," "Search Category". Some of transactions need database read or write transactions, while some of them only need HTML documents. We have created a database intensive workload by increasing the rate of database read/write to making the MySQL server tier being bottlenecked.

Figure 4 shows 3 throughput curves of Apache web server, Tomcat server, and MySQL database server. The figure points out 3 knee points (the red circles in the figure) that have been computed by the technique described in Section 2.1. The earliest knee point has been observed in the database tier as shown in the figure, and it correctly indicates the database tier is bottlenecked for the database intensive workload. As mentioned above, we intentionally set up the workload to make the database server bottlenecked. Note that throughputs of 3 servers are different since, by workload setup, some user requests are controlled not to go through all tiers. As shown in Figure 5, obviously, CPU is the bottlenecked resource type in the current configuration. This can be identified by computing the earliest knee point, similar with the way of identifying bottlenecked tier above. Note that the knee points of disk I/O and network I/O are located at the last measurement points. This is because there are no obvious knee points of these resource types, so the last measurement point is used.

Alternatively, we can identify the bottlenecked resource type by computing the maximum load that each resource type can handle as described in Section 2.2. The result is the set $\{925.5, 2762.5, 15840.4, 79204.4\}$, which represents $\{L_{CPU}^{max}, L_{Mem}^{max}, L_{NW}^{max}, L_{disk}^{max}\}$ as the maximum load of CPU, memory, network, and disk, respectively. It also shows that CPU is the bottlenecked resource type because L_{CPU}^{max} has the lowest maximum load. When we see the maximum throughput of the database tier in Figure 4, it shows the similar amount of load at the knee point. Therefore, it indicates that our performance model is accurate enough to compute the resource shortage. Note that we have also measured their source usages in Web and App tiers, and observed significant under-utilizations of all resources so that they have very high maximum loads.

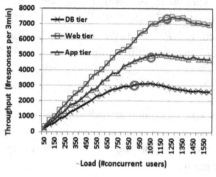

Fig. 4. Knee points of 3-tier application   **Fig. 5.** Resource usages in the DB tier

5   Related Work

Cloud has gathered pace, as most enterprises are moving toward the agile hosting of multi-tier applications in public clouds, many researchers have focused on three different research directions: 1) updating application architecture to move from legacy systems to clouds [3], 2) evaluating different clouds' functional and non-functional attributes for allowing cloud users to correctly make a decision on which cloud to host applications [2, 4, 7, 8], and 3) efficiently orchestrating virtual appliances in a cloud, which may also include negotiations with cloud users. While some highly related previous work has principally focused on estimating rudimentary cloud capabilities using benchmarks [8] and automated performance testing [9],our approach focuses on the precise characterization of application capabilities in a cloud infrastructure.

Analytical models like [1, 5]have been proposed for bottleneck detection and performance prediction of multi-tier systems. They predict system performance based on burst workloads and then, determines how much resource to be allocated for each tier of the application for the target system response time. And there are numerous efforts that have addressed the challenges of managing cloud application performance. For example, [10, 11, 12] are based on very detailed understanding of the system resource utilization characteristics. Performance management solutions like AzureWatch (http://www.paraleap.com/azurewatch) continuously monitor the utilization of the various resource types and send a notification once they are saturated.

6   Conclusion and Future Work

In this paper, we presented an approach to identify the bottleneck resource and to provide the view of potentially co-existing bottlenecks in the cloud-based multi-tier applications. We developed a comprehensive modeling to profile the resource capabilities of the target system. Based on this profiling, we correlated the performance degradations to the resource bottlenecks. The preliminary evaluation results show that our approach is feasible to be used for bottleneck detection and resource shortage estimation for cloud recommender system.

References

1. Urgaonkar, B., Shenoy, P., Chandra, A., Goyal, P.: Dynamic provisioning of multi-tier internet applications. In: Int. Conf. on Autonomic Computing, pp. 217–228 (2005)

2. Jayasinghe, D., Malkowski, S., Wang, Q., et al.: Variations in performance and scalability when migrating n-tier applications to different clouds. In: Int. Conf. on Cloud Computing, pp. 73–80 (2011)

3. Chauhan, M.A., Babar, A.M.: Migrating service-oriented system to cloud computing: An experience report. In: Int. Conf. on Cloud Computing, pp. 404–411 (2011)

4. Cunha, M., Mendonca, N., Sampaio, A.: A declarative environment for automatic performance evaluation in IaaS clouds. In: Int. Conf. on Cloud Computing, pp. 285–292 (2013)

5. Casale, N.M., Cherkasova, G.L., Smirni, E.: Burstiness in multi-tier applications: symptoms, causes, and new models. In: Int. Conf. on Middleware, pp. 265–286 (2008)

6. Wang, Q., Kanemasa, Y., et al.: Detecting Transient Bottlenecks in n-Tier Applications through Fine-Grained Analysis. In: Int. Conf. on Distributed Computing Systems, pp. 31–40 (2013)

7. Calheiros, R., Ranjan, R., Beloglazov, A., DeRose, A.C., Buyya, R.: CloudSim: A toolkit for modeling and simulation of cloud computing environments and evaluation of resource provisioning algorithms. Software: Practice and Experience 41, 23–50 (2011)

8. Yao, J., Chen, S., Wang, C., Levy, D., Zic, J.: Accountability as a service for the cloud. In: IEEE Int. Conf. on Services Computing (SCC), pp. 81–88 (2010)

9. Malkowski, S., Hedwig, M., Pu, C.: Experimental evaluation of n-tier systems: Observation and analysis of multi-bottlenecks. In: Int. Sym. on Workload Characterization, pp. 118–127 (2009)

10. Abdelzaher, T.F., Lu, C.: Modeling and performance control of internet servers. In: Int. Conf. on Decision and Control, pp. 2234–2239 (2000)

11. Diao, Y., Gandhi, N., Hellerstein, J.L., Parekh, S., Tilbury, D.M.: Using MIMO feedback control to enforce policies for interrelated metrics with application to the Apache web server. In: Network Operation and Management Symposium, pp. 219–234 (2002)

12. Diao, Y., Hu, X., Tantawi, A.N., Wu, H.: An adaptive feedback controller for sip server memory overload protection. In: Int. Conf. on Autonomic Computing, pp. 23–32 (2009)

Towards Auto-remediation in Services Delivery: Context-Based Classification of Noisy and Unstructured Tickets

Gargi B. Dasgupta, Tapan K. Nayak, Arjun R. Akula,
Shivali Agarwal, and Shripad J. Nadgowda

IBM Research, Bangalore, India
{gaargidasgupta,tapnayak,arakula,shivaaga,nadgowdas}@in.ibm.com

Abstract. Service interactions account for major source of revenue and employment in many modern economies, and yet the service operations management process remains extremely complex. Ticket is the fundamental management entity in this process and resolution of tickets remains largely human intensive. A large portion of these human executed resolution tasks are repetitive in nature and can be automated. Ticket description analytics can be used to automatically identify the true category of the problem. This when combined with automated remediation actions considerably reduces the human effort. We look at monitoring data in a big provider's domain and abstract out the repeatable tasks from the noisy and unstructured human-readable text in tickets. We present a novel approach for automatic problem determination from this noisy and unstructured text. The approach uses two distinct levels of analysis, (a) correlating different data sources to obtain a richer text followed by (b) context based classification of the correlated data. We report on accuracy and efficiency of our approach using real customer data.

1 Introduction

A *Service System (SS)* is an organization composed of (a) the resources that support, and (b) the processes that drive service interactions in order to meet customer expectations. Due to the labor intensive processes and their complex inter-dependencies, these environments are often at the risk of missing performance targets.

To mitigate this risk and conforming with the underlying philosophy of "what gets measured, gets done", every SS defines a set of measurement tools that provide insights into the performance of its operational processes. One such set of tools include the event management and ticketing tools. Event management is a key function for monitoring and coordinating across several infrastructure components. Ticketing systems record problems that are logged and resolved in the environment. When integrated with the event management setup, ticketing systems enable proactive and quick reaction to situations. Together they help in delivering continuous up-time of business services and applications.

Figure 1 shows an integrated event management and ticketing system, that traces the life-cycle of a problem ticket in the customer's domain. Lightweight agents or probes

X. Franch et al. (Eds.): ICSOC 2014, LNCS 8831, pp. 478–485, 2014.

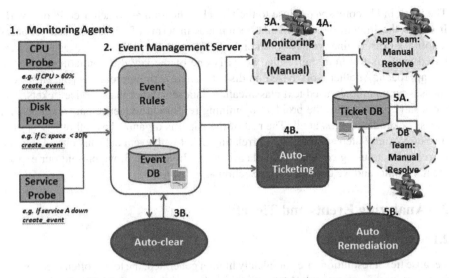

Fig. 1. Integrated event management and ticketing system

(shown on the left of Figure 1) are configured to monitor the health of the infrastructure including servers, storage and network. The collected data is fed into the event management server (i.e. component 2) whose main functions include: (a) continuous collection of real time data from probes on endpoints. (b) For each of the data streams, configure individual event rules to indicate when an event should be triggered. Some examples of an event rule are: *CPU usage is above a utilization threshold, available disk space is below a space threshold, service not running* etc. All the generated events are stored in event management database which can process up to a million events per day. All events could be routed to a manual monitoring team (3A). That team monitors the consoles for alerts, clears the ones that are informational, and raise tickets (4A) in the Ticket DB for the critical ones. Manual handling of large volume of events results in an human-intensive component. In contrast, automated handling (3B) of events, enables auto-clearing of certain classes of bulk alerts. Some event management systems also allow remediation actions to be automatically triggered on event occurrence. If the action is successful the event is auto-cleared and no ticket is created. If not, a ticket is raised automatically (4B). The path:1-2-3A-4A comprises the manual workflow for event-to-ticket handling whereas path:1-2-3B-4B comprises auto-ticket handling. At present majority of the systems continue to operate in manual workflow mode. The main reason for this is that the auto-ticketing causes large volume of tickets. In the absence of reliable auto-clear systems, all tickets have to be manually closed by the monitoring team, thereby adding more manual work in the system.

Thus in a service delivery environment (SDE), the auto-classification of the ticket symptom, and auto-remediation through a corrective action is critical. There has been many relevant works [6], [7], [4], [1], [3], [5] in the area of ticket analytics on structured and unstructured data. What makes SDE data particularly challenging is that it is extremely noisy, unstructured and often incomplete. In this paper we present a novel approach for automatic problem determination from the noisy and unstructured text.

The work in [1] comes very close to the text classification approach used in our work. It shows the limitation of SVM-like techniques in terms of scalability and proposes a notion of discriminative keyword approach. However, it falls short of using context based analysis to refine the results which is one of the key differentiating factors in our approach. Another work based on discriminative term approach is [2]. This work focuses on commonly used text classification data sets rather than service tickets. The work in [7] approaches the problem by mining resolution sequence data and does not access ticket description at all. The rest of the paper is organized as follows. Section 2 introduces our 2-step approach for correlating ticket with event data and classifying the correlated data using context based classification. In Section 3, we present our experimental results and we conclude with Section 4.

2   Analyzing Events and Tickets

2.1   Correlation Model

Because ticket resolutions are completely human generated, the text is often incomplete, noisy and highly contextual. Hence off-the shelf tools that are domain independent fail miserably while trying to understand context. However since every ticket originates from an event, and event data contains regularized text expressions, correlating the event data with ticket data can improve the classification.

If an event is auto-ticketed, then the automatic methods are reliable enough to ensure that the ticket identifier mapping exists in event and in the ticket data. In this case correlation is a simple join operation on ticket numbers. However when tickets are manually generated, this correlation is lost. Operators creating the tickets often do not update event data with the ticket numbers. As discussed in section 1 in reality majority of tickets continue to be generated manually. Hence in the absence of ticket numbers, for joining events and tickets we need smart correlation methods to decipher the event which created the ticket. We propose a correlation method based on multiple parameters and domain information available from the event and ticket information systems.

1. *Timestamp:* A ticket occurrence is *always* preceded by an event. Hence we use a timestamp threshold to narrow down the possible event choices for a ticket. Next, the following specific identifiers help further narrowing-down the correct original event.
2. *Server Name:* Matching server names in the event and ticket problem description indicate higher probability of correlation.
3. *Problem Description:* Similar descriptions in ticket and event fields have a higher probability of correlation. For example, if a ticket and event both describe database connectivity issues, then they are likely to be correlated. Text descriptions are matched w.r.t. syntax and context similarity using methods described in the following section.
4. *Group:* Additional information like application groups can help in event and ticket correlation. However this information may not be present in all data sources.

When the above heuristic is able to successfully identify the original event, the resulting text is enriched. The event text can be used for generic problem determination while the ticket text gives context specific details. This combination is used for classification as described in the following section. In cases where the heuristic fails to identify the correct relevant event and the confidence is low, we proceed with ticket text only.

2.2 Classification Model

In this section we present our approach to classify the noisy and unstructured event and/or ticket text to pre-defined output categories. For the rest of this section, we use the term tickets to refer to both noisy event and ticket text descriptions. Firstly, we define a logical structure for the unstructured and noisy tickets. Next we categorize and classify the tickets based on the contextual information in logical structure.

Logical Structure for Unstructured and Noisy Tickets: Semantics is required to understand the contextual information in tickets. Identification of semantic information in the unstructured and noisy service delivery tickets is difficult. Furthermore, these tickets are syntactically ill-formed sentences. Hence we define a logical structure for these tickets as shown in Figure 2. The logical structure contains two sub-structures: category dependent and category independent. Category dependent structure stores the information corresponding to the specific output category. Category independent structure stores the information present in ticket which is independent of the output categories. Below we describe components of each of these two sub-structures.

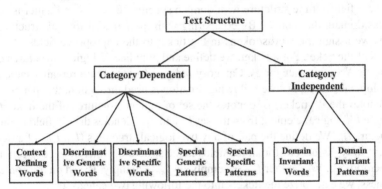

Fig. 2. Logical structure of Text

(a) *Discriminative specific words*: help in discriminating a output category from other categories.
(b) *Discriminative generic words*: help in discrimination of categories but less specific in comparison to discriminative specific words.
(c) *Context defining words*: constitute the contextual keywords. They by themselves do not help in discrimination but are useful to capture the contextual information of a category.
(d) *Special specific patterns*: regular expressions which help in discriminating a output category from other categories.
(e) *Special generic patterns*: regular expressions for discrimination but less specific in comparison to special specific patterns.

(f) *Domain invariant words*: help in identifying the contextual information. Context defining words help in identification of contextual information related to a particular category, whereas domain invariant words help in identification of contextual information in general.

(g) *Domain invariant patterns*: regular expressions which help in identifying the contextual information.

Table 1. Sample words and patterns for discriminating Disk C Full category

Category Dependent					Category Independent	
Context defining words	Discriminative generic words	Discriminative specific words	Special generic patterns	Special specific patterns	Domain invariant words	Domain invariant patterns
physical, percent, threshold, free	storage, space, volume, full	disk, drive	<none>	*c: drive*	too, not, need	*db2*, *.com*

For example, consider the *Disk C Full* output category. For discriminating this category from other output categories, words such as *disk, drive* and patterns such as *c: drive* will help most when compared to words such as *percent, threshold*, etc (Table 1). Words such as *not, too, db2* help in identification of contextual information.

For each of the pre-defined output categories, we instantiate a logical structure and populate the fields of the structure with domain specific keywords and patterns (which we call as domain dictionary). By comparing with the fields of logical structure of a category, we assign the words/tokens in the ticket to the appropriate fields of logical structures of the ticket. For a ticket, we define and populate N logical structures corresponding to N output categories. Category independent structure remains same in all these N logical structures. The following notation is used throughout this paper: Let t_i denotes the ith ticket, L_i denotes the set of logical structures of the ticket t_i, l_{ik} denotes the kth logical element from the set L_i and f_{jik} denotes the jth field in the logical structure l_{ik}. We define the pair of any two logical structures (l_{ij}, l_{ik}) of a ticket t_i as **contextually disjoint** if, for all the fields in the structure, either of the corresponding fields is empty. i.e. $\forall m$, either f_{mik} = empty *or* f_{mij} = empty. Based on the contextual disjointness, we categorize the tickets into the following two categories:

(a) *Simple Tickets*: if all the highly ranked logical structures of a ticket are contextually disjoint.

(b) *Complex Tickets*: if any two highly ranked logical structures of a ticket are not contextually disjoint.

Classification of simple tickets: We use a linear weight based approach to score the logical structures of ticket. The output category corresponding to highest scored logical structure is assigned to the ticket. Weights are assigned to various fields of logical structure based on their discriminative capability. For example, keywords belonging to discriminative specific words gets higher weight compared to discriminative general words.

Classification of complex tickets: As the logical structures of complex tickets are not contextually disjoint, linear weight based approaches may fail to discriminate between the logical structures. Hence we need deeper level of context based analysis to classify complex tickets. We use supervised learning approach to learn the contextual information from complex tickets. The keywords belonging to various fields of logical structure of output categories are used as features. Feature weights are assigned based on the discriminative capability of keywords.

To learn the global contextual information about all the output categories together, a large amount of training data is required. To circumvent this, we build a separate model for each category. A model for category i will have the knowledge about whether a ticket belong to category i or not (local contextual information). We used the Support Vector Machine (SVM) method with a Radial Basis Function (RBF) Kernel to build the classification engine. Complex tickets pass through all the individual models of output categories. Since each individual model knows about tickets belonging to it, globally all the tickets will be correctly classified.

Using rule/weight based approach for classifying simple tickets increases recall but can lower the precision. To maintain higher precision, one can further validate the output of rule based approach using context based analysis to filter out any misclassifications.

3 Evaluation

This section outlines the experimental analysis of the proposed approach. The methodologies have been implemented as part of a Ticket Analysis Tool from IBM called BlueFin and deployed to analyze events and tickets for several key customer accounts. We evaluate the performance of **BlueFin** in comparison with another popular ticket analysis tool **SmartDispatch** [1], a SVM-based text-classification tool, based on large datasets from some well-known real customer accounts.

For unbiased evaluation, we randomly select tickets from 7 different accounts and first manually label them into categories. For the analysis here, we consider 17 different categories of tickets for classification as shown in Table 2. Finally we choose 5000 tickets labeled with one of these 17 categories as the ground-truth data. To measure the accuracy, we computed the Precision, Recall and F1-score for each of these category. Note that in a multi-class or multinomial classification, precision of ith category is the fraction of tickets classified correctly in i (true positives) out of all tickets classified as i (sum of true and false positives). Recall of category i is the fraction of tickets classified correctly as i (true positives) out of all tickets labeled as i in the ground-truth data (sum of true positives and false negatives). F1-score is the harmonic mean of precision and recall. Alternatively, these can be computed from the confusion matrix, by summing over appropriate rows/columns. Note that F1-score is a well-known measure of classification accuracy. The accuracy measures are computed for both BlueFin and SmartDispatch and the results are shown in Table 2. In addition, we also compute the overall accuracy measures for all the categories and present in Figure 3. Observe that the precision measure for each individual categories and the overall precision are extremely good for BlueFin. Moreover, it also maintains high recall values and thus the F1-score and results significantly better performance in comparison to the existing approach in SmartDispatch for all categories.

The major improvement in precision is attributed to the context based analysis in BlueFin while the higher recall is due to the enriched text set using event-ticket correlation model. To understand this in detail we look at the confusion matrix of BluFin

Table 2. Comparison of Precision, Recall and F1-Score for a labeled dataset

Category	BlueFin			SmartDispatch		
	Precision	Recall	F1-Score	Precision	Recall	F1-Score
Database Space	0.65	0.70	0.67	0.14	0.59	0.22
Non-actionable	0.98	0.98	0.98	0.98	0.67	0.79
Job Failed	0.99	0.21	0.35	1.00	0.04	0.07
Server Down	0.97	0.92	0.94	0.83	0.26	0.39
Agent Offline	0.98	0.98	0.98	0.05	1.00	0.10
CPU Utilization High	0.97	1.00	0.98	0.84	0.96	0.89
Paging/Swap space	0.88	0.98	0.92	0.45	0.98	0.61
Zombie Processes	1.00	0.60	0.75	1.00	0.40	0.57
Network Down	0.98	0.45	0.61	0.31	0.73	0.43
Password Expired	1.00	0.83	0.90	0.99	0.79	0.87
Linux Space Full	0.94	0.98	0.95	0.16	0.07	0.10
Backup Failure	0.85	1.00	0.91	0.59	0.99	0.73
Database Inactive	0.94	0.44	0.59	NA	0.00	NA
Process Missing	0.99	0.38	0.55	NA	0.00	NA
Disk C Full	0.82	1.00	0.90	NA	0.00	NA
Win Non C Drive Full	0.89	0.84	0.86	NA	0.00	NA
Service Alert	1.00	0.59	0.74	NA	0.00	NA

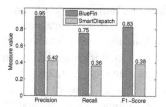

Fig. 3. Comparison of classification accuracy

(Figure 4) and SmartDispatch (Figure 5). Deeper color shades in cells represent higher volumes of tickets. The diagonal elements represent the correct classifications and the non-diagonals are the mis-classified tickets. SmartDispatch has a higher number of overall mis-classifications. For example, consider the tickets that are originally "Windows non C drive full ", but are mis-classified as "backup failed". There are 83 such mis-classifications in case SmartDispatch while BlueFin has only 11. SmartDispatch on the other hand, mis-classifies the ticket due to absence of contextual information. The performance of BlueFin far exceeds smartDispatch in all categories. The reason smartDispatch underperforms, it only uses discriminative keywords and completely ignores contextual keywords, special patterns, which provides important discriminations in case of noisy data.

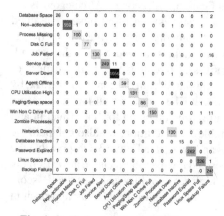

Fig. 4. Confusion matrix for Blufin

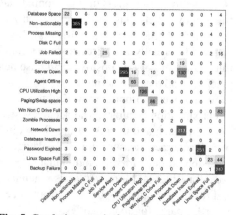

Fig. 5. Confusion matrix for SmartDispatch

4   Conclusion

In this paper, we proposed a novel approach for automatic problem determination from noisy and unstructured service delivery tickets. Central to our theme is the use of two distinct levels of analysis, namely, correlation of event and ticket data followed by context based classification of the correlated data to achieve higher precision and improved recall. Furthermore, we evaluated our approach on real customer data and the results confirm the superiority of the proposed approach. In the future, we plan to improve the precision of our approach by using bi-grams, tri-grams etc. as features and the recall by increasing the size of domain dictionaries.

References

1. Agarwal, S., Sindhgatta, R., Sengupta, B.: Smartdispatch: Enabling efficient ticket dispatch in an it service environment. In: Proceedings of the 18th ACM SIGKDD International Conference on Knowledge Discovery and Data Mining, KDD 2012, pp. 1393–1401. ACM, New York (2012), http://doi.acm.org/10.1145/2339530.2339744
2. Junejo, K., Karim, A.: A robust discriminative term weighting based linear discriminant method for text classification. In: Proceedings of the Eighth IEEE International Conference on Data Mining, ICDM 2008, pp. 323–332. IEEE (2008)
3. Kadar, C., Wiesmann, D., Iria, J., Husemann, D., Lucic, M.: Automatic classification of change requests for improved it service quality. In: Proceedings of the 2011 Annual SRII Global Conference, SRII 2011, pp. 430–439. IEEE Computer Society, Washington, DC (2011), http://dx.doi.org/10.1109/SRII.2011.95
4. Parvin, H., Bose, A., Van Oyen, M.P.: Priority-based routing with strict deadlines and server flexibility under uncertainty. In: Winter Simulation Conference, WSC 2009, pp. 3181–3188 (2009), http://dl.acm.org/citation.cfm?id=1995456.1995888
5. Potharaju, R., Jain, N., Nita-Rotaru, C.: Juggling the jigsaw: Towards automated problem inference from network trouble tickets. In: Presented as part of the 10th USENIX Symposium on Networked Systems Design and Implementation (NSDI 2013), pp. 127–141. USENIX, Lombard (2013), https://www.usenix.org/conference/nsdi13/technical-sessions/presentation/potharaju
6. Shao, Q., Chen, Y., Tao, S., Yan, E.A.X., Anerousis, N.: Easyticket: a ticket routing recommendation engine for enterprise problem resolution. Proc. VLDB Endow. 1, 1436–1439 (2008), http://dx.doi.org/10.1145/1454159.1454193
7. Shao, Q., Chen, Y., Tao, S., Yan, X., Anerousis, N.: Efficient ticket routing by resolution sequence mining. In: Proceedings of the 14th ACM SIGKDD International Conference on Knowledge Discovery and Data Mining, KDD 2008, pp. 605–613. ACM, New York (2008), http://doi.acm.org/10.1145/1401890.1401964

ITIL Metamodel

Nelson Gama[1,2,3,*], Marco Vicente[2], and Miguel Mira da Silva[1,2]

[1]Instituto Superior Tecnico, Lisboa, Portugal
[2]INOV, Lisboa, Portugal
{nelsongama,marco.vicente,mms}@ist.utl.pt
[3]CINAV-PT Navy Research Center, Escola Naval, Portugal
nelson.gama@defesa.pt

Abstract. IT Infrastructure Library (ITIL) has become the *de facto* standard for IT Service Management (ITSM). Despite the advantages in the adoption of ITIL's best practices, some problems have been identified: different interpretations due to the complexity of concepts with poor specification and formalization; different approaches to the same problems; difficulties exchanging process models in different process model languages. Besides all published work, is still missing a metamodel expressing the core concepts, their relationship, and constraints. In this paper, we propose an ITIL metamodel to reduce conceptual and terminological ambiguity, addressing the identified problems, namely: (1) describing the core concepts of ITIL to be used by other approaches; (2) allowing the integration, exchange, sharing and reutilization of models; and (3) the use of different modelling languages following the defined principles.

Keywords: ITIL, metamodel, modelling.

1 Introduction

Abstract. IT Infrastructure Library (ITIL) has becoming the de facto standard, currently the most widely accepted framework in the world, for implementing IT Service Management (ITSM) [1-3].

Despite the advantages in the adoption of ITIL's best practices, many organizations follow ITIL's best practices without a reference model and some problems have been identified: (1) the complexity of ITIL concepts with poor specification and formalization, which leads to misunderstandings about these concepts; (2) different tools and methodologies that are not harmonized or grounded in a shared reference model leading to different approaches to the same problems; (3) the exchange of process models in different process model languages still remains a challenge [4].

Besides all published work and books about ITIL, a metamodel expressing the core concepts, the relation between them, their constraints and limitations is still missing, especially with academic support.

Once a model is an instance of a metamodel, an ITIL metamodel will be a model to shape ITIL. A metamodel of ITIL as an explicit model of constructs and rules,

---

* Corresponding Author.

X. Franch et al. (Eds.): ICSOC 2014, LNCS 8831, pp. 486–493, 2014.

defining logical structures and generating semantics is warranted to specify models within this defined domain of interest.

In this paper, we propose an ITIL metamodel addressing the identified problems, namely: (1) describing the core concepts of ITIL so as to be used by other approaches; (2) allowing the integration, exchange, and reutilization of models developed based on the proposed metamodel; and (3) the use of different modelling languages following the defined principles supported by the metamodel.

2 Related Work

There are a few academic or professional publications concerning the conceptual modelling or metamodels of IT services. They are mostly process-oriented describing how to generalize service processes into universal patterns or conceptual models [5].

To define an ITIL metamodel, firstly we analysed the ontological constructs of ITIL's model definition from ITIL books, identifying modelling limitations. In general, the concepts and processes, as well as necessary databases and interfaces, are defined at a high abstraction level [5]. Only a linguistic description of concepts is provided [1], while its processes are usually depicted as sequences of activities.

We evaluated several ITIL graphical representations searching for the best approach to represent and relate concepts. We found disparate ad-hoc diagrams, different approaches and notations from distinct organizations. These were mainly in-house sketches, diagrams and flowcharts expressing the ITIL views of its authors. ITIL representations are often depicted using BPMN [6] but some have also come across proprietary commercial solutions. In common, all ITIL representations come from one author's interpretation of concepts and relationships from a linguistic description in ITIL books. We acknowledge the added value of these models and tools and we are not claiming they are incorrect, but instead we pointing out their lack of completeness and the absence of a common referential – a metamodel providing a uniform basis in terms of concepts and their relationships.

Afterwards we evaluated some architectural frameworks (MDA core standards [7], and MOF specification [8]) to develop a model and metamodels. Despite valuable, these approaches are software development oriented. A rigid perception of "layered metamodel architecture" may be confused and limitative when considering metamodels to a widespread use [5].

There are many publications and research strands on process metamodel and we also made an overview of published work in this area [4, 5, 9, 10]. However, research work or professional publications regarding the definition of an ITIL metamodel is quite limited. Most of them focused on the previous ITIL version (v2) and are mostly process-oriented, stressing few processes. On the other hand, we did not find a holistic description on how to generalize service lifecycle and neither defining universal patterns nor conceptual models for ITIL's concepts.

Despite all valuable work regarding the definition of an ITIL metamodel we did not identify a proposal focused on the current version of ITIL neither covering the principal ITIL concepts that allows defining a metamodel. An ITIL metamodel as a description of a language's abstract syntax in order to define a set of constructs that allows the creation of grammatically valid models [11].

3   Research Problem

ITIL processes, concepts, and relationships are specified in natural language. Without a formal and commonly accepted semantics, modelling graphical representation is complex [10]. In addition to the aforementioned problems in ITIL adoption, we identified some weaknesses in ITIL representation: (1) unclear concepts definition leading to different interpretations; (2) models developed from a language description and not from a universal referential; (3) lack in formal notation and representation leading to loosely depicted graphical diagrams; (4) focus on logical description of processes; (5) different approaches and methodologies to the same problems, making exchange and knowledge sharing difficult; (6) lack of holistic visibility and traceability from the theory; and (7) different approaches to implementations and tools development.

A metamodel of ITIL, as an explicit model of constructs and rules, is still needed to specify models within this defined domain of interest. The most important contribution of an ITIL metamodel would be the convergence of approaches and applications of leading vendors and motion towards the ITIL compliant solutions [5].

Metamodels are also closely related to ontologies. Both are often used to describe relations between concepts [12], allowing us to understand the logical structures and generating semantics for best practice frameworks [13]. We acknowledge the difference between ontologies and metamodels, once their characteristics and goals are different. However, without an ontology, different knowledge representations of the same domain can be incompatible even when using the same metamodel for their implementation [14]. While an ontology is descriptive and belongs to the domain of the problem, a metamodel is prescriptive and belongs to the domain of the solution [15]. Ontologies provide the semantics, while metamodels provide a visual interpretation of the syntax of specific languages that approximate as closely as possible to the ideal representation of the domain [16]. As a semantic model, the relation to the reality and the interrelation of concepts are true if they obey to a mathematical structure for all axioms and derivation rules of the structure [17]. To the best of our knowledge, there is no universally accepted ITIL metamodel as a reference that allows the modelling development and a language basis for graphical representation.

4   Proposal

Following some previous published work [4, 5, 13, 18, 19] we considered two separate orthogonal dimensions of metamodelling: one dimension concerned with language definition and the other with representation. A language can be defined as a set of valid combinations of symbols and rules that constitute the language's syntax [11].

Firstly, we identified the core concepts from the ITIL glossary [20], by reducing the concepts to the fundamental ones, with representation needs, that should be part of the metamodel. To that aim we followed an ontology engineering process [19] and analysed ITIL domain, clarifying abstract concepts from ITIL' books specifications developing the proposed metamodel. Secondly, we defined linguistically all concepts for an ontological common understanding adding a mathematic representation to concepts and relationships. This clarification provided design rules and a modelling process, decreasing the concept's abstraction but allowing the fundamental distinction of the concepts relation and interoperability. In a next step, we defined the notation, clarifying the ontological metamodel and, thus, the metamodel. The metamodel's quality was validated through the guidelines of modelling defined by Schütte [17].

4.1   Concepts Identification and Characterization

As stated before, we used an ontology-engineering methodology [19] to identify concepts and relationships from ITIL's five books and through the collaboration of ITIL practitioners. We started by defining the domain, the terms, their properties, and purposes. Having identified terms, we created the concepts and determined their relationships, providing the ontological vocabulary and symbols used to define a domain's problems and solutions [21, 22].

Since the subjectivity of modelling cannot be eliminated (only managed), a demand for rules that have to be carried out in the modelling process should be found. Therefore, before developing the metamodel we defined a basis for the development of a language (metamodelling language capability), identifying the core concepts by description and, especially, by definition in order to outline the abstract syntax of a modelling language as follows in Table 1. The language definition (Table 1) clarifies concepts and provides an ontological clarification through the definition of linguistic concepts. This proposed metamodel allows a hierarchy of metamodel levels where each level is "an instance" of the level above. We may have concepts' extensions that allow multilevel instantiations establishing its own kind of metalevel definitions.

Table 1. ITIL metamodel core concepts - modelling language

Concept	Description	Definition
Service Portfolio	The service portfolio S represents the current complete set of services. S is a key element and it is used to manage the entire lifecycle of each service $s_i \in S$. It includes three categories: (i) Service Pipeline P with $P \subseteq S$ (proposed or in development); (ii) Service Catalog C with $C \subseteq S$ (live or available for deployment); and (iii) Retired Services R with $R \subseteq S$.	$S = \{s_1, s_2, \ldots, s_n\}$ $S = P \cup C \cup R$ $\exists\, s_i \in S : s_i \in P \vee s_i \in C \vee s_i \in R$
Service	A Service s_i definition covers from an ITIL book to an IT service. Both cases can share the same metamodel despite having different levels. A Service s_i is a vector performed by a Role ρ as defined as a Contract c_i and in function of a Process Π	$s_i \in C$ $s_i = (\rho, f(\Pi), c_i)$
Process	A Process π_i from the set of Processes Π is a structured set of Activities Δ designed to conduct a Service s_i under a defined Role ρ and triggered by an Event ε^i and delivering an Event ε^o.	$\pi_i \in \Pi$ $\pi_i = (f(\Delta), \varepsilon^i, \varepsilon^o, \rho)$
Activity	A set of actions a_{ij} designed to achieve a particular result in a Process π_i. An Activity Δ can have one or "n" actions a_{ij}.	$\Delta = \sum_{i=1}^{n} a_{ij}$ $1 \leq \Delta \leq n$

Table 1. (*Continued*)

Action	*An atom activity α_{ij} with defined procedure from a set A_{ij} of possible actions. Actions can be performed by a Stakeholder or automatically by an Application Service as$_i$*	$A_i = \{\alpha_{i1}, \alpha_{i2},...\alpha_{in}\}$ $\alpha_{il} = f(as_i)$
Role	A role ρ from a set of roles R is defined as a specific behavior of a stakeholder σ (a business actor) participating in a defining a set of responsibilities in a Process π or in a Service s$_i$	$\rho_i = f(\sigma_i)$ $\forall\, x \in R\; \exists\; \sigma \in \Sigma$: $\rho(x) \in R$
Stakeholder	A stakeholder σ represents a person in a set of Stakeholders Σ with a defined Role ρ at a given moment t.	$\sigma_t = (\sigma_{1t}, \sigma_{2t},..., \sigma_{nt}) \in \Sigma_t$ $\forall x$: $\sigma(x) \rightarrow \rho(x)$
Contract	A compromise c$_i$ between two or more parties.	$c_i = \{OLA, SLA, Agreement, UC\}$
Event	A set ξ of events e$_i$ triggering a Process π$_i$ as input of a Process or e$_o$ produced as output, referring any change of state or anything that happens (internally or externally).	$\xi = \{e_{i1}, e_{i2},...e_{in}\} \cup \{e_{o1}, e_{o2},...e_{on}\}$ $\forall e_{i,o}$: $e_{i,o} \in \xi$
Application Service	An externally visible unit of software functionality as$_i$, provided by one or more components, exposed through well-defined interfaces, and meaningful to the environment [23]	$as_i = f(af_i)$ $as_i \in AS_i$
Application Function	A software component af$_i$ that provides Functions through an Application Service as$_i$ required by an Action α$_i$. Each Application may be part of more than one IT Service. An Application runs on one or more Infrastructure Service $f(\sigma_{ij})$	$af_i = f(\sigma_{ij})$ $af_i \in AF_i$
Infrastructure Service	Externally visible unit of Infrastructure functionality σ$_{ij}$, from the overall organization's technologic infrastructure I$_{ij}$ provided by one or more Infrastructure Function, exposed as service to the Application Function.	$I_{ij} = \sum_{i,j}^{n} \sigma_{ij},$ $\sigma ij \in Iij$

4.2 Metamodel Representation

We mapped the ITIL concepts in the language's metamodel. The proposed ITIL metamodel formalizes expressiveness through the definition of concepts and corresponding visual representation as the following graphical representation (Fig. 1). The proposed ITIL metamodel is based on the structure illustrated in Fig. 1, which relies on concepts presented in Table 1.

5   Demonstration and Evaluation

To demonstrate the widespread use of the proposed ITIL metamodel, we modelled several models of ITIL [24, 25] (not included due to paper size restrictions) and used the ITIL metamodel to model ITIL with ArchiMate [26] in the datacentre organization of the Portuguese Defence Ministry.

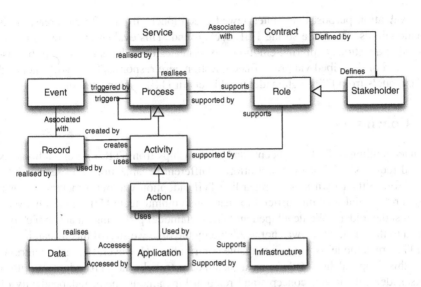

Fig. 1. Proposed ITIL Metamodel

We used the ArchiMate's [26] notation to graphically represent the metamodel for no other reason than making it easy to use, but we may represent the metamodel in any other notation. This generalization makes it possible to model in different languages, and the integration and reuse of models.

We have modelled an overview of all ITIL's five books [24, 25] to understand which services (and from which books) ITIL can provide to its external environment. We have also modelled each ITIL book, showing which are the applications ITIL uses to support its processes, and also the infrastructure components that support those applications. It provides a top view, having ITIL core processes as a black box system providing services to the environment while using all the ITIL processes. We modelled each one of ITIL's processes showing a deeper fine-grained representation, which allow us to look inside the ITIL's processes and see all of its individual activities. These models are consistent, since the processes' inputs and outputs, business, application and infrastructure services are the same, although at different granularity levels. We also mapped the activity sequence of ITIL's Incident Management process from two different notations (ArchiMate [26] and BPMN [6]), which matched almost completely. We realized that it would be harder to integrate two approaches if they did not speak the same language. Therefore, a common frame of reference provided by the ITIL metamodel is warranted. Even in the absence of a formal graphical language we are able to model ITIL using the proposed metamodel.

For the purpose of our research, a high-level checking of utility, correctness, consistency and completeness of ITIL metamodel has been performed. Schu☐tte [17] defines guidelines to metamodel's quality evaluation, which are very similar to the set of design criteria for ontologies [15]: clarity, coherence, extendibility, minimal encoding bias, and minimal ontological commitment.

To evaluation purposes, we interviewed practitioners from different areas, skills and nationalities, all with a strong ITIL background. This evaluation allow us to ask open-ended questions exploring emotions, experiences or feelings that cannot be easily observed or described via pre-defined questionnaire responses [27]. We concluded that the models from ITIL metamodel would benefit ITIL implementation.

6   Conclusion

The understanding of ITIL's concepts and relationships from ITIL referential books is hard and requires a lot of time and effort. Different organizations and service providers develop their own models regarding ITIL adoption without a metamodel or a common referential, making difficult to share and communicate ITIL models between different stakeholders. We developed an ITIL metamodel providing an academic contribution to this area, which was not available by the time we started this research.

An ITIL metamodel is per se a valuable contribution. However, the main contribution of this proposal lies in defining a metamodel to help the ITIL adopters with a universal identification of concepts and relationships among them, independently of approach, language or tool used. We identified the core concepts of ITIL's service lifecycle and the relationship among them, proposing an ITIL metamodel. Our approach keeps the semantics of the core concepts intact and thus allows for the reuse of models and reasoning over the customized metamodel.

Our proposed metamodel might represent a basis to model and to implement ITIL. Moreover, it provides the sharing and the reutilization of the models from one approach to another, even with different modelling languages, to improve the representation of ITIL concepts, and to help promote ITIL discussion and validation within the ITIL community itself.

References

1. Hochstein, A., Zarnekow, R., Brenner, W.: ITIL as Common Practice Reference Model for IT Service Management: Formal Assessment and Implications for Practice. In: International Conference on e-Technology, e-Commerce and e-Service (EEE 2005), pp. 704–710. IEEE Computer Society (2005)
2. Correia, A., Abreu, F.B.E.: Integrating IT Service Management within the Enterprise Architecture. In: 4th International Conference on Software Engineering Advances (ICSEA), pp. 553–558. IEEE, Porto (2009)
3. Gama, N., Sousa, P., Mira da Silva, M.: Integrating Enterprise Architecture and IT Service Management. In: 21st International Conference on Information Systems Development (ISD 2012), Springer, Prato (2012)
4. Shen, B., Huang, X., Zhou, K., Tang, W.: Engineering Adaptive IT Service Support Processes Using Meta-modeling Technologies. In: Münch, J., Yang, Y., Schäfer, W. (eds.) ICSP 2010. LNCS, vol. 6195, pp. 200–210. Springer, Heidelberg (2010)
5. Strahonja, V.: Definition Metamodel of ITIL. Information Systems Development Challenges in Practice, Theory, and Education 2, 1081–1092 (2009)
6. Object Management Group: Business Process Model and Notation (BPMN). V 2.0 (2011)
7. OMG: MDA Guide Version 1.0. The Object Management Group (OMG) (2003)

8. OMG: MetaObject Facility (MOF) 2.0 Core Specification Version 2.4.1. OMG Adopted Specification. The Object Management Group (OMG) (2003)

9. Jantti, M., Eerola, A.: A Conceptual Model of IT Service Problem Management. In: International Conference on Service Systems and Service Management (ISSSM 2006), Troyes, France, vol. 1, pp. 798–803 (2006)

10. Valiente, M.-C., Garcia-Barriocanal, E., Sicilia, M.-A.: Applying an Ontology Approach to IT Service Management for Business-IT Integration. Knowledge-Based Systems 28, 76–87 (2012)

11. Guizzardi, G.: On Ontology, ontologies, Conceptualizations, Modeling Languages. In: Vasilecas, O., Ede, J., Caplinskas, A. (eds.) Frontiers in Artificial Intelligence and Applications, Databases and Information Systems IV, pp. 18–39. IOS Press (2007)

12. Söderström, E., Andersson, B., Johannesson, P., Perjons, E., Wangler, B.: Towards a Framework for Comparing Process Modelling Languages. In: Pidduck, A.B., Mylopoulos, J., Woo, C.C., Ozsu, M.T. (eds.) CAiSE 2002. LNCS, vol. 2348, pp. 600–611. Springer, Heidelberg (2002)

13. Neto, A.N.F., Neto, J.S.: Metamodels of Information Technology Best Practices Frameworks. Journal of Information Systems and Technology Management (JISTEM) 8, 619–640 (2011)

14. Calero, C., Ruiz, F., Piattini, M.: Ontologies for Software Engineering and Software Technology. Springer (2006)

15. Gruber, T.R.: Toward principles for the design of ontologies used for knowledge sharing. International Journal of Human-Computer Studies 43, 907–928 (1995)

16. Baioco, G., Costa, A., Calvi, C., Garcia, A.: IT Service Management and Governance Modeling an ITSM Configuration Process: A Foundational Ontology Approach. In: International Symposium on Integrated Network Management-Workshops (IM 2009) IFIP/IEEE, New York, pp. 24–33 (2009)

17. Schuette, R., Rotthowe, T.: The Guidelines of Modeling - An Approach to Enhance the Quality in Information Models. In: Ling, T.-W., Ram, S., Li Lee, M. (eds.) ER 1998. LNCS, vol. 1507, pp. 240–254. Springer, Heidelberg (1998)

18. Atkinson, C., Kühne, T.: Model-Driven Development: A Metamodeling Foundation. IEEE Software 20, 36–41 (2003)

19. Ostrowski, L., Helfert, M., Xie, S.: A Conceptual Framework to Construct an Artefact for Meta-Abstract Design. In: Sprague, R. (ed.) 45th Hawaii International Conference on System Sciences (HICSS), pp. 4074–4081. IEEE, Maui (2012)

20. OGC: ITIL Glossary of Terms, Definitions and Acronyms (2007)

21. Hevner, A.R., March, S.T., Park, J., Ram, S.: Design Science in Information Systems Research. MIS Quarterly 28, 75–105 (2004)

22. Vaishnavi, V.K., William Kuechler, J.: Design Science Research Methods and Patterns: Innovating Information and Communication Technology. Auerbach Publications, Boston (2007)

23. Lankhorst, M.: Enterprise Architecture at Work. Springer (2009)

24. Vicente, M., Gama, N., Mira da Silva, M.: Using ArchiMate to Represent ITIL Metamodel. In: 15th IEEE Conference on Business Informatics (CBI), IEEE (2013)

25. Vicente, M., Gama, N., da Silva, M.M.: Using archiMate and TOGAF to understand the enterprise architecture and ITIL relationship. In: Franch, X., Soffer, P. (eds.) CAiSE Workshops 2013. LNBIP, vol. 148, pp. 134–145. Springer, Heidelberg (2013)

26. The Open Group: ArchiMate 2.0 Specification. Van Haren Publishing (2012)

27. Oates, B.J.: Researching Information Systems and Computing. Sage Publications (2006)

Formal Modeling and Analysis
of Home Care Plans

Kahina Gani, Marinette Bouet, Michel Schneider, and Farouk Toumani

LIMOS, CNRS, Blaise Pascal University, France
{gani,michel.schneider,ftoumani}@isima.fr,
marinette.bouet@univ-bpclermont.fr

Abstract. A home care plan defines all the services provided for a given patient at his/her own home and permits the coordination of the involved health care professionals. In this paper, we present a DSL (Domain specific language) based approach tailored to express home care plans using high level and user-oriented abstractions. Then we describe how home care plans, formalized as timed automata, can be automatically generated from these abstractions. We finally show how verification and monitoring of the resulting care plan can be handled using existing techniques and tools.

Keywords: Timed Automata, Domain Specific Language, Business Process Management, Home Care Plan, UPPAAL.

1 Introduction

A general trend that can be observed these recent years is to enable as much as possible patients to stay at their own homes instead of having long-term stays at hospitals or health establishments. This trend is motivated by obvious social and economic reasons. Several types of care may be provided at a patient's home including health services, specialized care such as parenteral nutrition or activities related to daily living such as bathing, dressing, toilet, etc. All the medical and social activities delivered for a given patient according to certain frequencies are scheduled in a so-called *care plan*. Hence, the notion of a care plan is a key concept in home care area. As part of the project Plas'O'Soins[1], we are interested by the problems underlying the design and management of home care plans.

The design of a care plan is however a difficult task. Indeed, process modeling in the medical field is not trivial because it requires complex coordination and interdisciplinary cooperation due to involvement of actors from various health care institutions [7]. Furthermore, care plans are essentially unstructured processes in the sense that each patient must have his/her own specific care plan. Therefore, it is simply not possible to design a unique process capturing in advance the care plans of all the patients. Another important feature of care plans lies in their associated complex temporal constraints. Indeed, the design of a

---

[1] http://plasosoins.univ-jfc.fr/

X. Franch et al. (Eds.): ICSOC 2014, LNCS 8831, pp. 494–501, 2014.
© Springer-Verlag Berlin Heidelberg 2014

care plan requires the specification of the frequencies of the delivered home care activities. Such specifications are expressed by healthcare professionals in natural language, using usually a compact form: Every day morning, each Monday morning, etc. The home care activities are generally repetitive but may have irregularities or exceptions. Given the crucial role played by temporal constraints in home care plans, it appears clearly that such specifications could take benefit from existing theory and tools in the area of timed systems [3]. In this paper, we use *timed automata* [1], one of the most used modeling formalism to deal with timing constraints, as a basis to develop a formal framework to analyze care plans.

Solving the above problem and supporting design, analysis and verification, execution and monitoring of home care plan require tackling a number of challenges. The first challenge consists in the design and modeling of care plans. Due to the aforementioned features of care plans, it is not feasible to ask home care professionals to describe directly a care plan using a formal language such as, for example, timed automata. To cope with this difficulty, we first propose a DSL (Domain Specific Language) and a user centered specification language tailored to express home care plans using high level abstractions. We then define an automatic transformation of user specifications into timed automata. The resulting automaton is used to support automatic verification and monitoring of home care plans.

The paper is organized as follows. Section 2 describes the DSL based approach in which we mainly identify elementary temporal expressions. The general modeling process is presented at section 3 together with the construction of the proposed automata, i.e., pattern automata, activity automata and care plan automata. Section 4 presents some verification and monitoring issues. We discuss the result of this work at section 5.

2   A DSL-Based Approach for Specifying Home Care Plans

The design of a care plan is a complex collaborative process, managed by a primary medical coordinator and carried out by an interdisciplinary team. In order to understand such a design process and also to understand how a medical coordinator approaches the problem, we conducted in the context of the *Plas'O'Soins* project a thorough on-sites analysis of current practices in the field of home care.

This study showed the central role played by care plans as primary components of effective care coordination at patient's home. It appears therefore appropriate to provide tools to assist as much as possible the medical coordinator in the design of individual care plans as well as automated support for verification of the plan and monitoring of their executions. This is why in the Plas'O'Soins project, we propose a DSL based approach, tailored to express home care plans using high level abstractions.

A domain specific language (DSL) is a language designed to express a solution to a problem within a specific domain [10]. The proposed DSL provides high level abstractions that can be used by a medical coordinator to design a care plan for a given patient. The main building block in a care plan is the notion of activity. Our DSL includes several predefined activities identified by our analysis of the application domain. Each activity of the care plan is associated with a set of elementary temporal specifications. These specifications provide the information about the time when the activity should be performed, expressed as a quadruplet (Days, Time ranges, Period, Duration). In [6], we proposed a language that enables to express regular or irregular repetitions of an activity within some period in a condensed form, similar to that used by doctors. Figure 1

Predicted acts								
Act Id	Act	Temporalities			Duration	Main actor	Nbr of	Int Id
		Days	Time ranges	Period		type	actors	
A1	Toilet	Monday Wednesday Friday	Morning, evening	01/01/13-03/31/13		Nurse auxiliary	1	I1
		Sunday	Morning	01/01/13-03/31/13	30	Nurse auxiliary	1	
A2	Dress	Every day except(04/20)	Morning, evening	01/01/13-03/31/13		Nurse auxiliary	1	I1, I2
		04/20/13	Morning	01/01/13-03/31/13	10	Nurse auxiliary	1	

Fig. 1. Specification of activities Toilet and Dress

shows a simple example of a specification using this language. Each row of the table corresponds to an elementary temporal specification. In the quadruplet (Days, Time ranges, Period, Duration), Days and Time ranges fields can take different forms (patterns) to reflect the various possibilities encountered in the medical world [6]. Combination of elementary specifications permits to express superposition of different repetitions. Exceptions are introduced via the keyword except. Roughly speaking, the notion of a legal schedule of a care plan activity is defined as a sequence of allowed instances of this activity which satisfies the set of temporal specifications. An appropriate external representation of the care plan is crucial to facilitate the work of the coordinator. Figure 1 shows the current GUI (Graphical User Interface) developed to support a coordinator in designing a care plan using the proposed DSL.

3   General Modeling Process with Timed Automata

As said previously, we used formalism of timed automata (see for details [1]) to model home care plans. We consider in our work timed automata with ϵ-transitions (i.e., silent transitions) and *invariants* (i.e., guards on the states). The activities of care plans are not instantaneous but have a duration. This is why we need to capture the notion of duration of an activity in our timed automaton. This is achieved by considering three kinds of states: the *start states*, the *waiting states* and the *execution states*. More formally, a timed automaton used to model home care plans is defined as follows: $A = (S, s_0, \Sigma, X, Inv, T, F, W, E, St)$ where: S is a finite set of locations or states of the automaton with s_0 the initial state, $F \subseteq S$ is the set of final states, $W \subseteq S$ is the set of waiting states, $E \subseteq S$ is the set of execution states, and $St \subseteq S$ is the set of start states. Σ is a finite set of transition labels including $\{\epsilon\}$. X is a finite set of clocks. Inv: $S \to \phi(X)$ associates an invariant to each state of the automaton and $T \subseteq S \times \Sigma \times \phi(X) \times 2^X \times S$ is a set of transitions.

As an example, Figure 2 shows the timed automaton corresponding to an activity A having a duration d. At the beginning the automaton is at the state $s_0 \in St$ then it starts the execution of the activity A when it enters the state $s_1 \in E$. The automaton stays at this state for the whole duration d of the activity A then it moves to the state $s_2 \in W$. The automaton uses the clocks $\{x_d, x_t\}$, invariants and transitions guards to control the execution of the activityA.

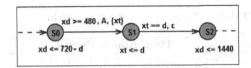

Fig. 2. Example of a timed automaton for a task A

We recall that our main objective is to build a care plan automaton for a given patient. To achieve this objective, we propose a three-steps approach which consists in: (i) mapping each elementary temporal specification into a pattern automaton, (ii) combination of pattern automaton to build an Activity automaton, and (iii) construction of global care plan automaton by composition of activity automata. These different steps are described below.

3.1   From Elementary Temporal Specifications to Pattern Automata

An elementary temporal specification is based on a temporal pattern chosen among several ones. We focus in this section on the case of the relative days pattern (the other patterns are described in [8]). Relative days pattern is used to express a regular repetition of the activity of the care plan. An example of relative days pattern can be found in the line 1 of the Figure 1. For each row of temporality defined for an activity a of the care plan, the corresponding timed automaton pattern $A_{RD} = (S, s_0, \Sigma, X, Inv, T, F, W, E, St)$ is defined as follows:

- S is a finite set of states, with s_0 the initial state. The total number of states is: NbStates = 3+(NbTimeRanges - 1) * 2 * NbDays+ NbDays where NbTimeRanges is the number of times ranges and NbDays is the number of specified Days;
- F is the set of final states. We always have one final state;
- $\Sigma = \{$Activity name$\} \cup \{\epsilon\}$ is the set of transition labels;
- $X = \{x_d, x_t, x_p, x_w\}$ is the set of clocks, where x_d is used to control the execution of the activity within a day, x_t is used to control the activity duration, x_w is used to control the execution of the activity in a day of the week and x_p is used to control the execution of the activity in a day of the period. W.l.o.g., we assume that the time unit is the minute;
- $Inv = \{\forall s \in S, Inv(s) = (x_d \leq EndTimerange - d)$ and $s \in St, Inv(s) = (x_d \leq 24)$ and $s \in W, Inv(s) = (x_t \leq d)$ and $s \in E\}$;
- $T \subseteq S \times \Sigma \cup \{\epsilon\} \times \phi(X) \times 2^X \times S$ is the set of transitions. Each transition corresponds to a day of the week. The number of transitions is: NbTransitions = 3+(7 − NbDays)+NbDays*2+NbTimeRanges-1 * 2 * NbDays

3.2   Activity Automata

This section gives the principles to construct an activity automaton by combining its associated patterns automata. This construction is illustrated on the example of the activity Toilet given at Table 1. Given a set of elementary temporal specifications of a given activity (expressed as rows of a table T), the corresponding activity automaton is built in the following steps:

Table 1. Elementary temporal specifications

Activity	Days	Time ranges	Period	Duration
Toilet	Monday Thursday	Morning	01/01/14-12/31/14	30
	Sunday	Evening	01/01/14-12/31/14	

Table 2. A modified table after step 1

Activity	Days	Time ranges	Period	Duration
Toilet	Monday Thursday	Morning	01/01/14-12/31/14	30
	Sunday	Evening	01/01/14-12/31/14	
	Everyday except(Monday Thursday Sunday)	None	01/01/14-12/31/14	

- Step 1: Add the following elementary temporal specification to T: Everyday except(specified Days) this specification is used to scan all days of the period.
- Step 2: Build pattern automaton for each elementary temporal specification except the last one (i.e., the one added in the previous step).
- Step 3: Build for each pattern automaton A, the corresponding special timed automaton $\hat{A}$. Informally, $\hat{A}$ recognizes timed words that encompass a timed word of A in sequences where the considered activity can also be executed anytime between two occurrences of this activity on the word of A.
- Step 4: Build for the added elementary temporal specification the corresponding special timed automaton $\tilde{C}$. $\tilde{C}$ recognizes timed words which enable the execution of the considered activity at anytime within the exception Days.
- Step 5: Build the intersection of special timed automata constructed at steps 3 and 4. The intersection is achieved following the classical construction defined in [2]. Figure 3 depicts the intersection automaton which encompasses all the possible schedules of the activity Toilet specified in Table 1.

3.3   Care Plan Automata

A care plan can be also described by means of a timed automaton which is obtained by composition of activity automata. For this purpose, we define a specific composition operator which mixes the asynchronous product (or shuffle) on some states and a specific synchronous product on other states (waiting states) in addition to blocking actions (in the execution states). Blocking is used to prevent the interleaving of activities in a care plan while synchronization is

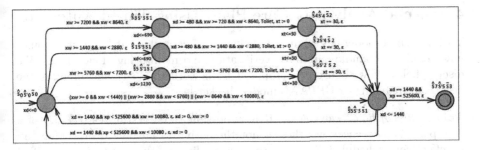

Fig. 3. Activity timed automaton (intersection of pattern automata)

needed when the activity automata are at waiting states in order to synchronize the reset of the day and week clocks (respectively, the variables x_d and x_w). In particular we propose to synchronize on ϵ -transitions (with reset) [5] when their origin states are waiting ones. We will see in what follows a more formal definition.

Definition 1. *(Composition of timed automata)* Let $A_1 = (S_1,\ s_0^1,\ \Sigma_1,$ $X_1,\ Inv_1,\ T_1,\ W_1,\ E_1,\ St_1)$ *and* $A_2 = (S_2, s_0^2, \Sigma_2, X_2, Inv_2, T_2, W_2, E_2, St_2)$ *be two timed automata. The composition of* A_1 *and* A_2, *denoted* $A_1 \times A_2$, *is the timed automata* $(S_1 \times S_2, s_0^1 \times s_0^2, \Sigma_1 \cup \Sigma_2, Xs_1 \cup X_2, Inv, T)$, *where* $Inv (S_1, S_2)$ $= Inv (S_1) \wedge Inv (S_2)$ *and the transitions* T *is the union of the following sets:*

1. $\{((s_1, s_2), \epsilon, \phi, \lambda, (s_1', s_2'))$: $(s_1, \epsilon, \phi_1, \lambda_1, s_1') \in T_1$ *and* $(s_2, a, \phi_2,\ \lambda_2, s_2') \in T_2$, s_1 *and* s_2 *are both* $\in W$ $\}$.
2. $\{((s_1, s_2), a, \phi, \lambda, (s_1', s_2'))$: $((s_1, a, \phi_1, \lambda_1, s_1') \in T_1$, $s_2 = s_2')$ *or* $((s_2, a,\ \phi_2, \lambda_2, s_2')\ ) \in T_2$, $s_1 = s_1')$, s_1 *and* s_2 *are both* $\in St$ $\}$.
3. $\{((s_1, s_2), a, \phi, \lambda, (s_1', s_2'))$: $((s_1, a, \phi_1, \lambda_1, s_1') \in T_1$, $s_2 = s_2'$, $s_2 \in W/St$, $s_1 \in E)$ *or* $((s_2, a, \phi_2, \lambda_2, s_2') \in T_2, s_1 = s_1', s_1 \in W/St, s_2 \in E)\}$.
4. $\{((s_1, s_2), a, \phi, \lambda, (s_1', s_2'))$: $((s_1, a, \phi_1, \lambda_1, s_1') \in T_1$, $s_2 = s_2'$, $s_2 \in W$, $s_1 \in St)$ *or* $((s_2, a, \phi_2, \lambda_2, s_2') \in T_2, s_1 = s_1', s_1 \in W, s_2 \in St)\}$.

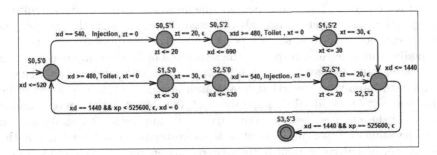

Fig. 4. Care plan timed automaton

Figure 4 shows the result of composition of the Toilet and Injection automata. The resulting automaton encompasses all the possible schedules of the activities Toilet and Injection.

4   Formal Analysis of Care Plans Using Timed Automata

With a formal model describing the behavior of care plans at hand, it becomes now possible to handle automatic verification and monitoring of care plans. We discuss below how to use the proposed framework to verify and monitor the home care plans using UPPAAL model checker [4].

Realizability of home care plans. It is important to check the realizability of a care plan, i.e., to check whether or not the activities included in the plan can be effectively scheduled and performed according to the constraints specified in the plan. In other words, a care plan is realizable when each activity can be performed without interruption in the imposed time range in any specified period. Checking realizability of a care plan can be reduced to the emptiness problem of the corresponding timed automaton.

Monitoring of home care plans. Note that most of the activities of a care plan are manual. In current state of affairs, the activities that have been performed are often recorded manually on paper. Our goal is to enable electronic recording of executed activities in order to keep track of the execution traces of care plans. Such information can then be used to monitor care plans. For example, compliance of executions traces w.r.t. a care plan may be checked by reducing this problem to the membership problem in the timed automata framework. Also, the monitoring system may be used to detect executions that deviate from the specification. More generally, a monitoring system can be enhanced with rules that enable to trigger alerts when particular deviations are detected.

Grouping activities into interventions. Grouping together activities that can be performed by a same type of actor (nurse, ...etc) and which occur in the same time range is called Intervention. The concept of intervention is really important in the sense that, it allows to reduce the waiting time between each activity in order to avoid multiple movings at the patient's home. The analysis of activities to specify interventions is a complex task since it requires to ensure compatibility of time ranges by taking into account the duration of each activity (multiple configurations are possible). It is also necessary to ensure that the grouped activities can be made by a same type of actor. The composition operator can be modified in order to incorporate the interventions in the computed car plan automaton (the obtained automaton is called interventions automaton). This is achieved by modifying the activity automaton in order to take into account the Intervention state. In addition, a specific clock variable, denoted Tmax, is added to control the *idle time* between the activities within the same intervention. In fact, the value of Tmax can be used as a parameter that can be defined by the coordinator and given as input to the composition operator to compute an interventions automaton. It is necessary to add an additional rule in the definition of the composition operator to take into account the new state intervention state. The rule is defined as follows: $\{((s_1, s_2), a, \phi, \lambda, (s_1', s_2')) : ((s_1, a, \phi_1, \lambda_1, s_1') \in T_1, s_2 = s_2', s_2 \in W/E, s_1 \in Int)$ or $((s_2, a, \phi_2, \lambda_2, s_2') \in T_2, s_1 = s_1', s_1 \in W/St, s_2 \in Int \}$.

5 Discussion

We described in this paper, an approach to generate formal specifications of home care plans, expressed as timed automata, from a set of high level and user-oriented abstractions. We briefly discussed then how verification and monitoring of the resulting care plan can be handled using existing techniques and tools. The paper focuses on specific pattern (i.e., the relative days pattern). An extension of this work to the other patterns is described in [8].

Our specification language can easily be extended in order to increase its expressivity and usability. Extensions are performed by introducing other patterns for defining elementary temporal expressions. For example, patterns such as n times per day or per week, would be useful in a medical context.

In this study we considered only the activities of a single care plan relative to one patient. We intend to combine care plan automata to allow the planification of the interventions of several patients. It is necessary to take into account movements between patient homes and availability of human resources. Some works [9,11] have already highlighted the interest of automata for the activities planification. But in these works automata are directly designed by experts. In our approach, automata would result from high-level specifications produced by the administrator users.

References

1. Alur, R.: Timed automata. In: Halbwachs, N., Peled, D.A. (eds.) CAV 1999. LNCS, vol. 1633, pp. 8–22. Springer, Heidelberg (1999)
2. Alur, R., Dill, D.: A theory of timed automata. TCS (1994)
3. Alur, R., Henzinger, T.: Logics and models of real time: A survey. In: de Bakker, J.W., Huizing, C., de Roever, W.-P., Rozenberg, G. (eds.) REX 1991. LNCS, vol. 600, pp. 74–106. Springer, Heidelberg (1992)
4. Behrmann, G., David, A., Larsen, K.G.: A tutorial on UPPAAL. In: Bernardo, M., Corradini, F. (eds.) SFM-RT 2004. LNCS, vol. 3185, pp. 200–236. Springer, Heidelberg (2004)
5. Bérard, B., Petit, A., Diekert, V., Gastin, P.: Characterization of the expressive power of silent transitions in timed automata. Fundam. Inf. (1998)
6. Bouet, M., Gani, K., Schneider, M., Toumani, F.: A general model for specifying near periodic recurrent activities - application to home care activities. In: e-Health Networking, Applications Services (Healthcom) (2013)
7. Dadam, P., Reichertand, M., Kuhn, K.: Clinical workflows - the killer application for process-oriented information systems? Business (2000)
8. Gani, K., Bouet, M., Schneider, M., Toumani, F.: Modeling home care plan. Rapport de recherche RR-14-02, Limos, Clermont Ferrand, France (2014)
9. Abdeddaïm, Y., Maler, O.: Job-shop scheduling using timed automata. In: Berry, G., Comon, H., Finkel, A. (eds.) CAV 2001. LNCS, vol. 2102, pp. 478–492. Springer, Heidelberg (2001)
10. Menezes, A.L., Cirilo, C.E., de Moraes, J.L.C., de Souza, W.L., do Prado, A.F.: Using archetypes and domain specific languages on development of ubiquitous applications to pervasive healthcare. IEEE Computer Society (2010)
11. Paneka, S., Engella, S., Strsberg, O.: Scheduling and planning with timed automata. ISPSE, Elsevier (2006)

Effort Analysis Using Collective Stochastic Model

Vugranam C. Sreedhar

IBM TJ Watson Research Center,
Yorktown Heights, NY, 10598, USA
vugranam@us.ibm.com

Abstract. In this paper we consider the problem of work order (WO) arrivals and time spent on work orders in service delivery to derive the asymptotic behavior of a strategic outsourcing contract. We model both the work order arrivals and time spent on the work orders, also known as effort, as a collective stochastic process. We use the resulting model to derive the probability that a contract will exceed the allocated budget for resolving work orders, and also to calculate the staffing requirement for resolving work orders.

Keywords: Collective Stochastic Model, Poisson Process, Renewal Process, Workload, Effort, Service Delivery.

1 Introduction

Strategic outsourcing (SO) happens when one company outsources part of its business to another company. A service provider and a service consumer negotiate a contract that outlines different kinds of work that needs to be done in terms of managing the consumer's business. A strategic outsourcing company, such as IBM, manages Information Technology (IT) infrastructure and applications for many different companies. A breach of contract happens when services are not delivered as negotiated in the contract. Very often, even when services are delivered that are in par with what is negotiated in the service level agreements (SLAs), a service consumer can quickly become unhappy when things go wrong. There are many reasons why a contract can become troubled or risky, incurring loss to a service provider. A service provider strives very hard to provide services that will increase profitability, customer loyalty and customer value. An SO contract often include SLAs that when violated, the service consumer can impose penalty on the service provider.

A large service provider, such as IBM, have service delivery centers to manage several customers. The management of IT of a customer is broken down into different kinds of work orders (WOs). A work order can be as simple as a request to change someone's password to as complex as migrating 100 physical servers (along with the applications) to a cloud environment. Very often complex WOs are broken down into smaller WOs that are easy to track and manage. Different WOs take different amount of time to resolve. A key question is then to ask is:

X. Franch et al. (Eds.): ICSOC 2014, LNCS 8831, pp. 502–509, 2014.

How much time (or effort) is needed, and hence how many full time employees (FTEs) are needed to resolve work orders, say in a month or a year?

In this article we develop a collective stochastic model (CSM) to determine the total time or *effort*, and hence the number of FTEs, needed to resolve work orders over certain time period such as a month or a year. The main contribution of this paper is to apply the well established theory of collective stochastic process model, and in particular ruin theory developed in actuarial science, to model services delivery system [7]. Modeling services delivery system is a non-trivial exercise, and developing mathematical models will allow future researchers to optimize and gain deeper insights into the complex behavior of services delivery system. To the best of our knowledge, ours is the first comprehensive attempt to leverage concepts from actuarial science and ruin theory to model portions of services delivery system, and in particular, to model effort, contract loss probability, and staffing requirements.

2   Collective Poisson Model

Work orders arrive one at a time and each work order is independent of each other. Let $\{N(t), t \geq 0\}$ denote the number of work orders that was processed before time t. We assume that $N(0) = 0$, and $N(t) \geq 0, \forall t \geq 0$. In other words, there are no work orders before $t = 0$, and there cannot be negative number of work orders. Therefore, $N(t)$ is non-decreasing in t. For $s < t$, we also have $N(t) - N(s)$ equals the number of work orders in the time interval $(s, t]$. We can now define the nth work order arrival as $T_n = \inf\{t \geq 0 : N(t) = n\}$ and the inter-arrival time of work order as $A_n = T_n - T_{n-1}$. The model described above captures the basic set of assumptions needed to describe a work order arrivals. It is important to keep in mind that $N(n)$, T_n, and A_n are all random variables and for $n \geq 0$, they form a stochastic process.

A (homogeneous) Poisson process is a very simple stochastic process that has two important properties: independence property and stationary property. The independence property states that for $\forall i, j, k, 0 \leq t_i \leq t_j \leq t_k, N(t_j) - N(t_i)$ is independent of $N(t_k) - N(t_j)$. In other words, the number of events in each disjoint interval are independent of each other. The stationary property states that $\forall s, t, 0 \leq s < t, h > 0$, $N(t) - N(s)$ and $N(t+h) - N(s+t)$ have the same distribution.

A homogeneous Poisson is too restrictive when we include the time it takes to resolve a work order. We next assume that the time it takes to resolve a work order, that is, the *effort*, itself is a random variable. We use Collective Poisson Process to model the aforementioned situation. A stochastic process $\{X(t), t \geq 0\}$ is called a collective Poisson process if it can be represented as follows:

$$S(t) = C_1 + C_2 + \ldots C_{N(t)} = \sum_{i=1}^{N(t)} C_i, t \geq 0 \tag{1}$$

where $\{N(t), t \geq 0\}$ is a Poisson process and $C_1, C_2, \ldots C_{N(t)}$ are iid random variables and are independent of $\{N(t), t \geq 0\}$. Here C_i represents the effort or time spent on a work order. The total effort during the period $(0, t]$ is then given by $S(t)$.

3   Renewal Process Model

In this section we extend the Poisson process by assuming the inter-arrival times for work order arrival using *Renewal Process* [8]. Let $\{A_n, n > 0\}$ be a sequence of random variable representing the inter-arrival times of work orders, and let $T_{n+1} = T_n + A_n$ be the arrival times of work orders. We define a renewal process for $\{N(t), t \geq 0\}$ so that

$$N(t) = \max\{i \geq 0 : T_i \leq t\} \tag{2}$$
$$= \min\{i \geq 0 : T_{i+1} > t\} \tag{3}$$

To ensure that the work orders do not all collapse at $A_i = 0$, we also assume that $P(A_i = 0) < 1$. Once again we assume both the independence and stationary properties for work order arrivals. It can easily be shown that $N(t)$ as defined by Equation 2 cannot be infinite for some finite time t [8]. In renewal process the inter-arrival times A_n is distributed with a common distribution function F_A, and $F_A(0) = 0$ and $T_n = 0$. The points $\{T_n\}$ are called the renewal times. Notice that the function F_A is a Poisson distribution function for Poisson process. Let us assume that the distribution function F_A has mean μ, one can then show the following result:

$$\lim_{t \to \infty} \frac{N(t)}{t} = \begin{cases} \mu^{-1}, & \text{if } \mu < \infty \\ 0, & \text{if } \mu = \infty \end{cases} \tag{4}$$

Recall that with collective Poisson process it was simple to derive a model for aggregated work order (see Equation 1). On the other hand it is almost impossible to determine the distribution F_A for renewal process $\{N(t), t \geq 0\}$. So we use the *central limit theorem* to get an approximate work order distribution. Let $0 < Var[A_i] < \infty$ and $\mu = E[A_i]$, then $\forall x \in \Re$

$$\lim_{t \to \infty} P\left(\frac{N(t) - t\mu^{-1}}{\sqrt{ct}}\right) = \Phi(x) \tag{5}$$

where $c = \mu^{-3}Var[A_i]$, and $\Phi(x)$ is the standard normal distribution function. The above results allows us to look for $E[N(t)]$ for which we can use *renewal function*. We then define the renewal function as the average number of renewals in the interval $(0, t]$ as $M(t) = E[N(t)] + 1$.

Let $F^{(k)}$ denote the k-fold convolution of F_A, which is the underlying distributions of the renewal process $\{N(t)\}$. Since $\{N(t) \geq k\} = \{A_k \leq t\}$ for

$k = 1, 2, \ldots$ we can derive the following result relating the mean value and the distribution.

$$M(t) = 1 + \sum_{k=1}^{\infty} P(N(t) \geq k)$$

$$= 1 + \sum_{k=1}^{\infty} P(A_k \leq t)$$

$$= \sum_{k=0}^{\infty} F_A^{(k)}(t) \qquad (6)$$

The mean or the expected number of renewals $M(t)$ is a non-decreasing and continuous on $\Re$ and it uniquely determines the distribution F_A. The renewal function for Poisson process is $\lambda t + 1$. We can now extend the collective Poisson process model (Equation 1) to collective renewal process model by assuming $N(t)$ is a renewal process. In actuarial science, the collective renewal process is often called as the Sparre Anderson Model [9].

4 Effort Size Distribution

In this section we will address the random nature of work order effort size. Recall that when a system administrator (SA) works on a work order, he or she will spend some amount time to resolve the issue related to the work order. The amount of time spent on a work order, called the *effort*, is itself a random variable. The effort size depends on various factors including the complexity of the work order, SA experience, etc. To simplify the presentation we will assume *effort* to include all of these marginal costs, and use the term *effort size* to be the representative random variable.

We will focus on two kinds of distributions for effort size. First one is the Light-Tailed Distribution (LTD) and the second one is the Heavy-Tailed Distribution (HTD). The tail of a distribution $F(x)$ is defined as $\bar{F}(x) = 1 - F(x)$, which is nothing more than the upper part of the distribution. It is the tail of the distributions that dictates that governs both the magnitude and the frequency of extreme events. The light-tail distribution has more "mild" form of extreme events, whereas the heavy-tail distribution has more "heavier" form of extreme events.

A distribution $F(x)$ is called a light-tailed distribution if there exits constants $\lambda > 0$, $a > 0$ so that $\bar{F}(x) \leq ae^{-\lambda x}$. Light-tailed distribution have "nice" properties that do not put service delivery in greater risk of contract loss when claim size exceeds the budgeted. Exponential distribution with $\lambda > 0$, Gamma distribution with $\alpha > 0, \beta > 0$, and Weibull distribution with $\beta > 0, \tau \geq 1$ are some examples of light-tailed distribution [8].

A distribution $F(x)$ is called a heavy-tailed distribution if there exits constants $\lambda > 0$, $a > 0$ so that $\bar{F}(x) > ae^{-\lambda x}$. We can also express heavy-tailed (and hence light-tailed) distributions using properties of moment generating functions.

A distribution function $F(x)$ is a heavy-tailed distribution if its moment generating function $M_x(t) = E[e^{tx}]$ is infinite $\forall t > 0$. Pareto distribution with $\alpha > 0, \lambda > 0$ and Weibull distribution with $\beta > 0, 0 < \tau 1$ are examples of heavy-tailed distribution. Even though claim size of work orders cannot be infinite, it is possible for claim sizes to exceed the budget size, which can eventually lead to troubled contracts.

5   Contract Loss Probabilities

In the previous two sections we developed models for WO arrivals and WO effort. In this section we will combine the two models to calculate *the probability that a contract will exceed the allocated budget for resolving work orders.*[1] The Contract Loss Probability (CLP) gives a good indication of the health of a contract. This quantity can be used for staffing decision, resource allocation, staff training, and work order dispatch optimization.

In a typical SO contract during engagement phase, the customer environment is "discovered" and "analyzed" for sizing the cost of the contract. Various factors, such as the number of servers, types of servers, number of historical tickets that were generated and resolved, management process, etc., are used to determine the cost of the contract. A typical cost model include unit price such as cost per server per month. The way these unit prices are computed is more of an art than science. Productivity factors, market competition, economy of scale and other external factors are also incorporated into the pricing or cost model. Once a contract is signed, service provider allocate quarterly or monthly budget for different services of the contract and when operational cost exceeds the allocated budget, the contract is considered to be "troubled" and management systems are put in place to track the services.

Let us assume that each client account has a periodic (say, quarterly) budget $q(t) = rt$, which is the budget rate, and so $q(t)$ is deterministic. We can then define the following *contract loss process*: $Z(t) = a + rt - S(t), t \geq 0$, where a is some initial base budget allocated for resolving work orders. We can see that if $Z(t) < 0$ for some $t \geq 0$, then we have a contract loss for that time period, that is, effort spent exceeds the allocated budget for resolving work orders. Assuming collective Poisson process, a minimum requirement in determining the contract budget rate r is then given by $r > \lambda E[S]$, where λ is the Poisson WO arrival rate. The above condition is called the net profit condition. A safer condition would be to include a safety factor ρ, so that $c > (1 + \rho)\lambda E[S]$.

We can define the contract loss time as $\tau_0 = inf\{t \geq 0 : S(t) > 0\}$, and the contract loss probability as $\phi(z) = P(\tau_0 < \infty | S(0) = z) = P_z(\tau_0 < \infty)$. If we assume that $X(t)$ is a collective Poisson process, we can then calculate the contract loss probability $\phi(z)$ as a closed form solution by focusing on the tail

---

[1] It is important to keep in mind that a contract will allocate budget for different activities, and resolving work order is one of the major activities of a contract. In this article we will just focus on budget for resolving work orders.

end of the claim size distribution. Let $\psi(t) = 1 - \phi(t)$ denote the tail of the contract loss probability, then

$$\psi(t) = \frac{\theta}{1+\theta} \sum_n^{\infty} \frac{1}{(1+\theta)^n} F^{*(n)}(t), t \geq 0 \qquad (7)$$

where $F^{*(n)}$ is the n-fold convolution of the distribution function $F(x)$, and $\theta = (\frac{r}{\lambda\mu} - 1)$, $\mu = E(C_i)$, r is the budget rate, and λ is the Poisson arrival rate of the work orders. Now when the effort sizes are (light-tailed) exponentially distributed $P(C_i > c) = e^{-c/\mu}$, we can derive the following contract loss probability:

$$\psi(t) = \frac{1}{1+\theta} exp\left(-\frac{\theta}{(1+\theta)\mu}t\right), t \geq 0 \qquad (8)$$

Notice that we made two assumptions when deriving the above contract loss probability: (1) work order arrivals follows a Poisson process, and (2) effort or time spent on work orders follows (light-tailed) exponential distribution.

6 Pricing and Staffing Requirements

A key problem in service delivery is determining the staffing requirement for handling work orders. We make a simplifying assumption that a staff or a system administrator can work one work order at a time, with no multi-tasking or context switching. Let $\Pi(S) \in \Re$ denote the budget, and hence staffing requirement, to handle work order effort S. We can then identify the following properties for calculating the staffing budget for an account:

1. $\Pi(S) \geq E[S]$. In this case we have nonnegative effort loading.
2. If S_1 and S_2 are independent, then $\Pi(S_1 + S_2) = \Pi(S_1) + \Pi(S_2)$
3. $\Pi(aS) = a\Pi(S)$, and $\Pi(S + a) = \Pi(S) + a$.
4. Let M be the finite maximum effort, then $\Pi(S) \leq M$.

There are several methods for calculating the staffing budget. The Expected Value principle can be stated as follows [6]: $\Pi(S) = (1 + a)E[S]$, where a is a safety loading factor. The expected value budget is very simple, but it does not take into account the variability in the effort. We can extend this model to include variability as follows: $\Pi(S) = E[S] + aVar[S]$

One issue with the above Variance principle is that different delivery center may have custom staffing budget, depending on local labor policy, pay scale, monetary values, etc. To handle such changes to loading factor, we can use the following modified Variance principle: $\Pi = E[S] + a\frac{Var[S]}{E[S]}$

7 Discussion and Related Work

Our focus in this paper is not to develop a new compound stochastic process model, but to apply concepts from ruin theory in actuarial science for modeling IT service delivery system, and in particular to model "effort" needed to manage a customer IT environment, and to understand under what condition a contract can become troubled. To the best of our knowledge, ours is the first work that models IT service delivery leveraging ruin theory from actuarial science. A lot more work is needed to fully model IT services delivery system. Please refer to the technical report that explains in details on modeling effort, contract loss probability, and staffing requirements, beyond what is explained in the current article [10].

IT service delivery is a complex process with many intricate processes, management systems, people's behavior, and tool sets. Diao et al. proposed a modeling framework for analyzing interactions among key factors that contribute to the decision making of staffing skill level requirements [3,4]. The authors develop a simulation approach based on constructed and real data taking into consideration factors such as scheduling constraints, service level constraints, and available skill sets. The area of optimal staffing with skill based routing is a mature area. Analytical methods are typically complex and do not capture full generality of real IT service delivery systems. The main focus of our paper is not to model the full generality of IT service delivery system. We focus on developing a compound stochastic process model to model effort needed to handle service requests. We focus on understanding the underlying stochastic model for when a contract can become "troubled".

Staffing problem based on queuing theory is old problem and several solutions have been proposed to model in the past. The staffing problem can be simply stated as the number of staff members or agents required to handle work orders, such as calls in a call center, as a function of time. Skill based routing problem is an extension of staffing problem where skills set are incorporated to determine which staff skill is needed as a function of time [5]. Staffing problem are typically modeled a queuing problem rather than as a compound stochastic process. Coban models staffing problem in a service center as a multi-server queuing problem with preemptive-resume priority service discipline and uses Markov chain to model [2].

Buco et al describe a method where in they instrument a management system to capture time and effort when SAs work on work orders [1]. They collect this information from multiple SAs working on different kinds of WOs. The collected data is a sample of the universe of IT service environment. One can use the sampled data to estimate the staffing requirement of a contract.

8 Conclusion

IT services delivery system is a complex system. There has been very little work done to model such a system, mostly due to lack of mathematical maturity in this field. Fortunately, actuarial science and ruin theory provides a foundational mathematics that can be applied to modeling IT services delivery system. We have made several simplifying assumptions such as WOs are independent of each others, all WOs are the same, etc. We are currently refining the mathematics to relax some of these simplifying assumptions. The resulting analytical model will become even more complex, and so can use a combination of estimators and Monte Carlo simulation for understanding the asymptotic behavior of a contract.

References

1. Buco, M., Rosu, D., Meliksetian, D., Wu, F., Anerousis, N.: Effort instrumentation and management in service delivery environments. In: International Conference on Network and Service Management, pp. 257–260 (2012)
2. Coban, E.: Deterministic and Stochastic Models for Practical Scheduling Problems. Ph.D. thesis, Carnegie Mellon University (2012)
3. Diao, Y., Heching, A., Northcutt, D., Stark, G.: Modeling a complex global service delivery system. In: Winter Simulation Conference, pp. 690–702 (2011)
4. Diao, Y., Lam, L., Shwartz, L., Northcutt, D.: Sla impact modeling for service engagement. In: International Conference on Network and Service Management, pp. 185–188 (2013)
5. Gans, N., Koole, G., Mandelbaum, A.: Telephone call centers: tutorial, review and research prospects. Manufacturing and Service Operations Management 5(2), 79–141 (2013)
6. Geiss, C.: Non-life insurance mathematics (2010), http://users.jyu.fi/~geiss/insu-w09/insurance.pdf
7. Rolski, T., Schmidli, H., Schmidt, V., Teugels., J.: Stochastic Processes for Insurance and Finance. Wiley (1999)
8. Ross, S.: A First Course in Probability. Pearson Prentice Hall (2006)
9. Sparre, A.: On the collective theory of risk in case of contagion between claims. Transactions of the XVth International Congress of Actuaries 2(6) (1957)
10. Sreedhar, V.: Effort analysis using collective stochastic model. Tech. rep., IBM Technical Report (2014)

A Novel Equitable Trustworthy Mechanism for Service Recommendation in the Evolving Service Ecosystem

Keman Huang[1], Yi Liu[2], Surya Nepal[3], Yushun Fan[2], Shiping Chen[3], and Wei Tan[4]

[1] School of Computer Science and Technology, Tianjin University, Tianjin 300072, China
victoryhkm@gmail.com
[2] Department of Automation, Tsinghua University, Beijing 100084, China
{yi-liu10,fanyus}@mails.tsinghua.edu.cn
[3] CSIRO, Digital Productivity and Services Flagship, Australia
surya.nepal@csiro.au
[4] IBM Thomas J. Watson Research Center, Yorktown Heights, NY 10598, USA
wtan@us.ibm.com

Abstract. Trustworthy service recommendation has become indispensable for the success of the service ecosystem. However, traditional trustworthy methods somehow overlook the service equality which result into a "rich-get-richer" effect and become a barrier for the novice services to startup and grow. This paper addresses this problem through a novel equitable trustworthy mechanism, which distinguished the difference between the novice and mature services over the trustworthy service recommendation. The results based on the real-world service ecosystem, i.e. ProgrammableWeb, show that our method achieves a better performance in equality guarantee and white-washing prevention. Thus it can promote the service ecosystem's healthy growth in a fair manner.

Keywords: Evolving Service Ecosystem, Equality Trustworthy Recommendation, Equality Guarantee, White-washing Prevention.

1 Introduction and Related Work

With the wide adoption of Service Oriented Architecture (SOA), more and more services are available over the Internet. Many trustworthy recommendation approaches [1-7] have been proposed to help the developers to select the desirable services against many other alternatives. Though these approaches have been successful in addressing this information overload problem to certain extent, most of them somehow overlook the equality and fairness in the evolving service ecosystem. Firstly, the assignment of initial trust value to new services, which is known as the trust bootstrapping issue [8], did not get much attention while it will affect the robustness of the trust model. Additionally, as only the services with high trust value are recommended while the new services may not be able to win a consumer's trust to build the reputation, these traditional trustworthy mechanisms become barrier for the use of new services and result into a "rich-get-richer" effect in the system [5]. Thus how to provide global equality for both existing services and newcomers becomes important for the healthy growth of service ecosystem.

X. Franch et al. (Eds.): ICSOC 2014, LNCS 8831, pp. 510–517, 2014.
© Springer-Verlag Berlin Heidelberg 2014

Equality, also known as fairness, has been studied in many disciplines [9]. For the service ecosystem, we define equality as both existing services and newcomers have a fair chance of being selected and building trust. Some try to offer fairness from the bootstrapping aspect [8,10-12]. However, it is non-trivial to assign an equitable bootstrapping trust value for the new services. Actually, the problem of the unfairness in the traditional trustworthy methods arises from the situation that the new services have to compete with the ones which have built trust over time as soon as they enter the ecosystem. Thus the basic idea here is to split all the services in the same domain into the novice service queue and the mature service queue so that the new services only compete with new ones until they grow matured. Difference mechanisms for the novice and mature services over the four-step trustworthy service recommendation (trust bootstrapping, service organization, recommendation generation and trust updating) need to be designed to distinguish the difference between them. Hence the major contributions of this paper can be summarized as follows:

- The formal definition of equality guarantee in the evolving service ecosystem is presented.
- A four-phase equitable trustworthy recommendation model is proposed to guarantee the global fairness.
- The empirical experiments shows that the proposed approach can achieve a better performance in equality and promote the healthy growth of the ecosystem.

The remainder of this paper is organized as follows. Section 2 describes the formal definition of equality guarantee. Section 3 presents the proposed four-phase equitable trustworthy recommendation model. Section 4 reports the experimental result. Section 5 concludes the paper.

2   Equality Guarantee

Equality measures are based on the proportions of shared resources in the system. In the service ecosystem, services with the similar functionality will compete with each other to gain the opportunity of being selected by consumers. As a consequence, in this paper, the resource in service ecosystem can be defined as *the opportunity of being selected in the composition*.

Equality Metric:
Gini Index has been widely used for fairness measure [13]. Here we reuse Gini Index as service equality metric in a service ecosystem. Suppose S is the set of services in the service ecosystem. According to the number of resources allocated to each service, they can be divided into x subset. Let $S_{r=i}$ present the services with i resource, then our Gini index is defined as:

$$Gini = 1 - \sum\nolimits_{i=1}^{x} (\frac{|S_{r=i}|}{|S|})^2 \tag{1}$$

Here the function $|*|$ refers to the number of item in any given set. Additionally, in a similar manner to how Shannon defines information, the entropy-based fairness [14] in the service ecosystem can be defined as:

$$EnFair = -\sum_{i=1}^{x} \frac{|S_{r=i}|}{|S|} \log(\frac{|S_{r=i}|}{|S|}) \tag{2}$$

As the traditional trustworthy recommendation approaches may harm usage diversity and become the entry barrier for the new services, here we also considered the recommendation diversity which is defined as follows:

$$ReDi = \frac{|RS|}{|S|} \tag{3}$$

Here RS refers to all the unique services which are recommended to the consumers.

White-washing Prevention:
White-washing phenomenon means that services may re-enroll into the ecosystem as new services to white wash their historical records. Suppose $ARB(s_i)$ refers to the allocated resource number of service s_i if it keeps the same behavior as before, $ARA(s_i)$ refers to the one after it white-washes its historical information. Thus we can define the white-washing prevention effect for this service as follows:

$$WWP(s_i) = \frac{ARB(s_i)}{ARA(s_i)} \tag{4}$$

Then the white-washing prevention effect for the service ecosystem can be considered as the average of the white-washing prevention effect for each service:

$$WWP = \frac{1}{|S|} \sum_{s_i \in S} \frac{ARB(s_i)}{ARA(s_i)} \tag{5}$$

If $WWP > 1$, the system can prevent the white-washing phenomenon. A larger WWP indicates a better performance in white-washing prevention.

3 Equitable Trustworthy Recommendation Mechanism

In the evolving service ecosystem, new services are published into the ecosystem over time and the initial trust value is assigned to each service. Then the services with similar functionality are organized into the same service domain. In order to fulfill the composition requirements raised by the consumers, the requirements will be decomposed into different domains and mapped to the related service domain. The candidates will be selected from the domain and presented to the consumers. Finally, each service will build its trust based on its usage and feedback. Hence the trustworthy service recommendation consists of the following four important steps: trust bootstrapping, service organization, recommendation generation and trust updating. Notes that the requirement decomposed and domain mapping are not included as they are dealt in the same way for both novice and mature services. Hence our equitable trustworthy recommendation mechanism (ETRM) works in four steps as follows:

Trust Bootstrapping (TB):
The goal for the trust bootstrapping phase is to assign an initial trust value T_{ini} to the new services. This paper considers the following strategies:

Default-based Bootstrapping (DB):
The default-based bootstrapping strategy assigns a default trust value to the new service [12]. The default value can vary between 0 and 1. If a low initial value is given, this strategy turns out to be the punishing approach [11].

Adaptive Bootstrapping (AB):
The adaptive bootstrapping approach calculates the initial trust value based on the rate of maliciousness in the system [8]. Instead of using the maliciousness rate, we straightforwardly assign the new services with the average trust value in the system.

Service Organization (SO):
The services in each domain are organized into the novice and mature service queues. Some novices are expected to build enough reputation and grow into matured. Hence, we need to consider the migration rule to move a novice services into mature:

Migration Principle. Given the trust threshold T_{mature} and the protection time-window A_{mature}, for the novice service ns, if $T(ns) \geq T_{mature} \parallel A(ns) \geq A_{mature}$, then migrate ns into the mature queue.

Here $T(ns)$ refers to the service's trust, $A(ns)$ refers to the service's age in the ecosystem which means the time since it is enrolled into the system.

If the trust threshold is set lower than the initial trust value $T_{mature} < T_{ini}$ or the protection-time-window is set as $A_{mature} = 0$, then the organization strategy become the same as the traditional trustworthy approaches. Hence, the traditional service organization strategy can be considered as a special case in our proposed model.

Recommendation Generation (RG):
For each requirement of a consumer for a particular functionality in a service domain, the goal for a recommendation system is to generate k service candidates from the service domain and then presented to the consumer. This task includes two steps:

Candidate Picking (CP):
In this step, q services with top q trust value in the mature services queue and the other $k-q$ services with top $k-q$ trust value in the novice services queue are selected to

generate the recommendation list. Obviously, the proportion of the mature services in the recommendation candidates is adjustable to reflect an ecosystem's principal and business model. For example, if the system is conservative, q can be very big (even q = k, *where being equivalent to no* novice services queue). If the system welcomes and encourages new services, a smaller q would be selected, e.g., $q = k/2$.

Recommendation Presentation (RP):
Based on whether the q mature service candidates and the k-q novice service candidates are merged together, two different presentation strategies (*ps*) to present the recommendation list to the consumers can be offered:

- *Single List Presentation Strategy (SLP):* The mature service candidates and the novice service candidates are merged into a single list. Thus it is "One Domain One Recommend List".
- *Double List Presentation Strategy (DLP):* The mature service candidates and the novice service candidates are recommended to the consumer separately using two lists for consumers to select. Thus it is "One Domain Double Recommend List".

Trust Updating (TU):
The service's trust is constructed based on its usage. Also as it has temporal sensitivity and the older perceptions gradually fade, it will evaporate over time. Hence, the trust updating contains two operations:

Feedback Update (FU):
If a service is selected, it will receive a feedback rating from its consumers. Many approaches have been proposed to calculate this feedback trust based on the user ratings. Here we use a simple approach from our previous work. Suppose that in time interval t, the feedback trust for a service s_i from its jth composition $c_{t,j}$ is $CT_{t,j}(s_i)$, then its trust after $c_{t,j}$ occurs is:

$$T_{t,j}(s_i) = (1-w)T_{t,j-1}(s_i) + w \times CT_{t,j}(s_i) \qquad (6)$$

where $w = [0,1]$ refers to the weight of the feedback trust which varies from 0 to 1.

Evaporation Update (EU):
The empirical study shows that the service's trust is temporal sensitivity and will evaporation over time [5]. Similar to our previous work [4], the evaporation factor can be obtained via the following equation:

$$T_t(s_i) = T_{t-1}(s_i) \times e^{-\lambda} \qquad (7)$$

where $T_t(s_i)$ refers to the service's trust at the end of time interval t and λ is the parameter to control the evaporation speed. Obviously, we can use different λ for mature and novice services so that the trust values will evaporate in a different speed.

Hence we note λ_m as the evaporation speed control parameter for mature services and λ_n for novice services.

4   Experiments Based on ProgrammableWeb

To examine the performance of the proposed approach and make the simulation experiment fitting with the actual data, the same to our previous work [4], we obtain the data set from ProgrammableWeb, by far one of the largest online service ecosystem, which contains 7077 services and 6726 compositions over 86 time intervals. Each service contains the information such as name, domain and publication date. Each composition contains the information such as name, creation date, the invoking services' domain list and its visited number as well as the user rating which are used to calculate the composition's feedback trust for the invoking services.

As discussed before, by setting the protection-time-window as 0, the proposed ETRM will reduce to the traditional trustworthy model. The recommendation candidates will all be mature and the presentation strategy will only be *SLP*. Also, only one evaporation speed control parameter will be considered. Thus, we can get the traditional trustworthy models by setting $A_{mature} = 0$, $q = k$, $ps = SLP$, $\lambda_m = \lambda_n$. Hence based on the different bootstrapping strategies, we consider the following baselines:

- Tradition Trustworthy with Default Initial Trust

    The bootstrapping strategy is set as *DB* and the initial value T_{ini} is given. If a high initial value is used, $T_{ini} = 0.7$, we get the *None Approach* [12], named as *nTTDIT*; If a low initial value is used $T_{ini} = 0.3$, we get the *Punishing Approach* [11], named as *pTTDIT*.

- Tradition Trustworthy with Adaptive Initial Trust

    The bootstrapping strategy is set as *AB* and the average trust value in the community is used as the initial trust value. We get the *Adaptive Approach* [8], named as *TTAA* in this paper.

Result and Discussion

Equitable Guarantee
First of all, we consider the three ETMs which have different parameter combinations. Here, for *nETMDIT* and *pETMDIT*, we set the $T_{mature} = T_{ini} + 0.2$ so that the novice services can move to the mature queue after they build their trust. For the *ETMAA* with the adaptive initial strategy, we just use the average trust value over time as the threshold, which is 0.7 in our experiment. Then we set $A_{mature} = 15$ to make sure the length of the mature and novice queue in the system is comparable. The evaporation speed for both mature and novice services are set as 0.005.

White-washing-prevention

In order to simulate the white-washing prevention phenomenon, given a time interval t_w, all the mature services in the ecosystem are republished. Each service's status is set as novice and the initial trust value are assigned to these services. Then, the total selected frequency of these services after white-washing is collected and the WWP can be calculated. Here, we set t_w as the time interval when the number of the published compositions is half of the total number over the whole period. In order to remove the random effect, we run 5 round simulations for each models and the average WWP is used.

Table 1. Equitable Guarantee Performance Comparision

	None		Punishing		Adaptive	
	nTTDIT	*nETMDIT*	*pTTDIT*	*pETMDIT*	*TTAA*	*ETMAA*
Gini	0.8394	0.5785	0.8453	0.5883	0.8429	0.6801
EnFair	0.6724	0.8755	0.6687	0.9057	0.6706	0.8088
ReDi	0.1573	0.5335	0.1573	0.4965	0.1573	0.5184
WWP	1.1407	1.3355	1.1439	1.4069	1.1523	1.2124

From Table. 1, we can conclude that the three ETRMs gain better performance than the traditional trust methods. They achieve a 19.31%~31.08% reduction in Gini index, 20.61%~30.21% increases in entropy-based fairness and 215.64%~ 239.16% diversity improvements. This is because of the separation between novice and mature services that makes the novice services gain an equitable opportunity to be recommended and selected by the consumers for the compositions. Also all the three ETRMs gain a 5.22%~22.99% higher WWP than the traditional methods. It means that the white-washing services in our ETRMs g a lower possibility to be reused.

5   Conclusion

The trustworthy service recommendation has become indispensable for the success of a service ecosystem. However, traditional approaches overlook the service equality for the usage of services, which harms the extension and growth of the service ecosystem. To our best knowledge, this is the first work to: (a) identify the service equality problem in the service ecosystem as well as the evaluation metrics including the equality measurement and the white-washing-prevention effect; (b) propose an equitable trustworthy mechanism which distinguishes the difference between mature and novice services to ensure the equality. The empirical experiments based on ProgrammableWeb show the effectiveness and usefulness of the proposed approach for equality guarantee and white-washing-prevention.

In the future, we will further work on the affection of the parameter combinations to the performance and then construct the mathematical model for the equitable trustworthy model as well as the approach to optimize the evolution of service ecosystems.

Acknowledgement. This work is partially supported by the National Natural Science Foundation of China under grant No. 61373035.

References

1. Wang, X., Liu, L., Su, J.: Rlm: A general model for trust representation and aggregation. IEEE Transactions on Services Computing 5(1), 131–143 (2012)
2. Malik, Z., Akbar, I., Bouguettaya, A.: Web Services Reputation Assessment Using a Hidden Markov Model. In: Baresi, L., Chi, C.-H., Suzuki, J. (eds.) ICSOC-ServiceWave 2009. LNCS, vol. 5900, pp. 576–591. Springer, Heidelberg (2009)
3. Yahyaoui, H.: A trust-based game theoretical model for Web services collaboration. Knowl.-Based Syst. 27, 162–169 (2012)
4. Huang, K., Yao, J., Fan, Y., Tan, W., Nepal, S., Ni, Y., Chen, S.: Mirror, mirror, on the web, which is the most reputable service of them all? In: Basu, S., Pautasso, C., Zhang, L., Fu, X. (eds.) ICSOC 2013. LNCS, vol. 8274, pp. 343–357. Springer, Heidelberg (2013)
5. Huang, K., Fan, Y., Tan, W.: Recommendation in an Evolving Service Ecosystem Based on Network Prediction. IEEE Transactions on Automation Science and Engineering 11(3), 906–920 (2014)
6. Sherchan, W., Nepal, S., Paris, C.: A Survey of Trust in Social Networks. ACM Comput. Surv. 45(4), 41–47 (2013)
7. Malik, Z., Bouguettaya, A.: Rateweb: Reputation assessment for trust establishment among web services. The VLDB Journal—The International Journal on Very Large Data Bases 18(4), 885–911 (2009)
8. Malik, Z., Bouguettaya, A.: Reputation bootstrapping for trust establishment among web services. IEEE Internet Computing 13(1), 40–47 (2009)
9. Seiders, K., Berry, L.L.: Service fairness: What it is and why it matters. The Academy of Management Executive 12(2), 8–20 (1998)
10. Yahyaoui, H., Zhioua, S.: Bootstrapping trust of Web services based on trust patterns and Hidden Markov Models. Knowledge and Information Systems 37(2), 389–416 (2013)
11. Zacharia, G., Moukas, A., Maes, P.: Collaborative reputation mechanisms for electronic marketplaces. Decis. Support Syst. 29(4), 371–388 (2000)
12. Marti, S., Garcia-Molina, H.: Taxonomy of trust: Categorizing P2P reputation systems. Computer Networks 50(4), 472–484 (2006)
13. Yitzhaki, S.: On an extension of the Gini inequality index. International Economic Review, 617–628 (1983)
14. Elliott, R.: A measure of fairness of service for scheduling algorithms in multiuser systems. In: IEEE Canadian Conference on Electrical and Computer Engineering, pp. 1583–1588 (2002)

Semantics-Based Approach for Dynamic Evolution of Trust Negotiation Protocols in Cloud Collaboration

Seung Hwan Ryu[1,*], Abdelkarim Erradi[1], Khaled M. Khan[1], Saleh Alhazbi[1], and Boualem Benatallah[2]

[1] Department of Computer Science & Engineering,
Qatar University, 2713, Doha, Qatar
{deepryu@gmail.com, erradi,k.khan,salhazbi@qu.edu.qa}
[2] School of Computer Science & Engineering,
University of New South Wales, Sydney, NSW, 2051, Australia
boualem@cse.unsw.edu.au

Abstract. Many techniques for addressing trust negotiation issues is little concerned with managing the dynamic evolution of trust negotiation protocols (policies), particularly in cases where there exist ongoing negotiations when a protocol has been changed. We propose an approach that automatically determines how consequences of changing a protocol affect ongoing negotiations. In particular, our approach allows to capture the semantics and intention of protocol changes, memorize and apply them in effectively analyzing the impact of protocol changes on negotiations.

Keywords: Trust Negotiation, Semantics, Content, Evolution, Protocol.

1 Introduction

Collaboration environments have been widely adopted for diverse domains, from scientific domains to end-user communities on the Web. Recently the resources sharing among people in collaborative environments have been managed using cloud computing platforms [1]. In cloud collaboration environments, making access control decisions to resources managed in cloud platforms is a hard task because of the size and dynamics of the users [2,3].

Trust negotiation has been proposed as a viable authorization solution for addressing the issue [7,3]. A *trust negotiation protocol*[1] describes a negotiation process between negotiation parties, in the sense that it specifies which credentials (e.g., digital versions of passports or credit cards) a service provider and users should exchange for the users to access protected resources [6].

Although existing approaches for addressing trust negotiation issues have made significant progress (see [3] for a recent survey), little work has been done on the problem of *dynamic protocol evolution*, which refers to managing the ongoing negotiations when an existing protocol has been changed. In

---

* Most of the work was done when the author was as a postdoc at Qatar University.
[1] In this paper we use "trust negotiation protocol" and "protocol" interchangeably.

X. Franch et al. (Eds.): ICSOC 2014, LNCS 8831, pp. 518–526, 2014.
© Springer-Verlag Berlin Heidelberg 2014

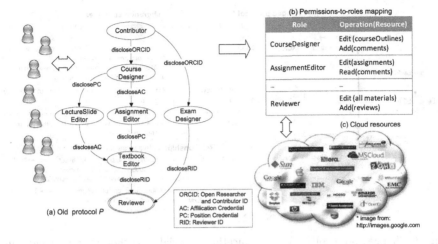

Fig. 1. Protocol P for an education material co-authoring service in cloud collaboration environments. Credentials are disclosed when exchanging messages.

dynamic collaborative environments, trust negotiation protocols can constantly over time because the collaboration contexts change. To tackle the problem, previous works [4,5] proposed techniques that analyze how ongoing negotiations (instances) are impacted by protocol changes to determine the successful migration of negotiations, e.g., migration to a new protocol. For this, the authors focused on *protocol level constraints* on the message (or credential) sequences exchanged between negotiation parties. In the constraints, they have *not* considered the actual message contents exchanged in the message sequences.

What is missing is a technique that takes into account *both* the sequence of messages and their contents as they are *interdependent* and *interrelated*. The consideration of message contents between sequences would be beneficial for improving the rate of successful replacements, which is critical in minimizing discomfort and disruptions to active negotiations. In this paper, we extend the previous works towards more comprehensive management of the dynamic protocol evolution. In particular, we make the following contributions:

- We present *composite change operators* that allow to express the semantics behind applied changes, i.e., a changed message sequence is semantically equivalent with an original one in terms of message contents (Section 3).
- We show how to *enhance* the change impact analyses of previous works by considering the change semantics (Section 4).
- We present the promising results that show we could achieve up to 89% *successful migration improvement*, compared with the prior works (Section 5).

2 Preliminaries

In what follows, we explain the protocol model for representing trust negotiation protocols and then present an example scenario.

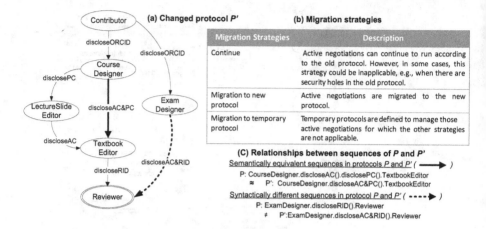

Fig. 2. Changed protocol P' for the education material co-authoring service and some migration strategies applicable to ongoing negotiations

2.1 Trust Negotiation Protocols Modeling

Following previous works [4,6], we model protocols as a finite state machine (FSM). FSM consists of states and transitions. *States* represent the levels of trust that a service provider establishes during its interaction with clients. As in [6], we map permissions (privileges) for accessing certain resources (e.g., service operations) to specific roles (e.g., researchers or administrators), instead of individual users, and then map such roles to states. Thus, once a client reaches at a state, she can access some resources with the role associated with the state. On the other hand, *transitions* are triggered by messages sent by clients to the provider. In our model, states are labeled with an assigned role while transitions with a message, corresponding to the invocation of a service operation.

2.2 An Example: Education Material Co-authoring Collaboration

Consider an education community in cloud collaboration environments. The community users from different countries, such as lecturers, senior lecturers, and professors, could collaboratively work with each other and share their knowledge and experiences in preparing education materials (e.g., lecture slides, assessments, online textbooks, etc). These education materials are (i) stored and managed in the cloud resources, such as Google docs, Dropbox, etc; (ii) shared and reused by the community users for their teaching purposes. The education community provides an education material co-authoring service that consists of several operations, which allow the collaborators to access the education resources in the cloud. The collaborators can invoke different service operations, based on the levels of trust established between the service provider and users.

Figure 1(a) shows a trust negotiation protocol for the co-authoring service. The protocol P states that any user is initially in the Contributor state (role). From there, after providing the ORCID (Open Researcher and Contributor ID),

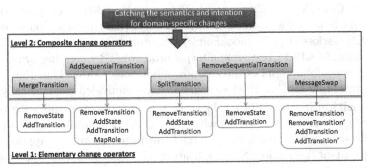

Fig. 3. Layered Protocol Change Operators

lecturers can proceed to state TextbookEditor by sending their position credential (e.g., User.position=Lecturer) and affiliation credential (e.g., User.organization= QU), while senior lecturers proceed to the same state by sending the credentials in the opposite order. In addition, professors can proceed to state ExamDesigner by disclosing their ORCID. Finally, the contributors disclose the reviewer ID (RID) to proceed to state Reviewer and then can access and review all the education materials by invoking the "Edit(all materials)".

3   Layered Change Operators for Evolving Protocols

This section describes two layered protocol change operators, particularly the operators used for catching the semantics and intention of protocol changes.

3.1   Elementary and Composite Change Operators

We distinguish two types of change operators, based on different levels of granularity of changes: elementary and composite change operators (Figure 3). The elementary change operators are used for generic and fine-granular protocol changes, e.g., adding a state or a transition. Such operators have been suggested in the past [4,6]. However, it is "not" possible to represent the semantics and intention behind applied changes using the operators. To fill this gap, we propose the composite change operators that can be applied for making some domain or service-specific changes. For example, if a protocol manager swaps the order in which she receives credentials in a given protocol, she still wants to make sure that both credentials have been received, regardless of their disclosed sequence. The composite change operators are derived by grouping elementary change operators that are executed in sequence.

MergeTransition (State s, State t, Messages $m_1, ..., m_n$): This operator merges n transitions with messages $m_1, ..., m_n$ respectively into a single transition with one message m. It can be applied when (i) a protocol manager wants to modify a message sequence in protocol P, which consists of several messages required to proceed from state s to state t, into another sequence in protocol P', which consists of only one single message; (ii) she regards the sequences as equivalent, from the semantic point of view, due to their contents.

Example 1. Consider the old protocol (Figure 1(a)) and the new protocol (Figure 2(a)). Assume that a protocol manager changes the sequence (CourseDesigner. discloseAC().disclosePC().TextbookEditor) of protocol P to the sequence (CourseD esigner.discloseAC&PC().TextbookEditor) of protocol P' by merging two messages into one message. She applies the composite operator "MergeTransition" to express the intention on that the two sequences are equivalent semantically.

SplitTransition (State s, State t, Message m): This operator splits a transition with message m into n transitions with $m_1, ..., m_n$. It is applied in the opposite case of the situation in which the "MergeTransition" operator is applied.

AddSequentialTransition(State s, State t, Message sm): This operator adds sequentially a transition with message sm between source state s and target state t. It could be used when protocol P' requires an extra message from s to t, which protocol P does not support.

RemoveSequentialTransition (State s, State t, Message sm): This operator removes a sequential transition with message sm between source state s and target state t. It is applied when protocol P needs to receive two messages for clients to access target state t from source state s while protocol protocol P' only requires one of them to grant the access to the same state.

MessageSwap (State s, State t, Message $m1$, Message $m2$) This operator swaps two messages m_1 and m_2 between two states s and t. It is applied in situations where, though the order of exchanged messages is swapped, a protocol manager only makes sure that two credentials has been submitted, regardless of the order.

4 Analysis Considering Both Message Sequences and Their Contents

In contrast to the previous works that only rely on the old and new protocols for syntactically comparing message sequences in the change impact analysis, we exploit the semantic equivalence between sequences in terms of message contents.

4.1 Compatibility Properties as Migration Decision Points

As requirements for determining whether an ongoing negotiation is migrateable, we identify two different degrees of compatibility: sequence and credential compatibility. Sequence compatibility is used for detecting the *syntactic equivalence* between two message sequences, irrespective of their message contents (i.e., disclosed credentials), while the credential compatibility for identifying the *semantic equivalence* between two different sequences, based on the message contents. The compatibility properties are further divided as follows:

- *Forward Sequence Compatibility (FSC)* means that the correct interaction of active negotiations with a given service should be guaranteed after they are migrated to a given new protocol.

  Example 2. In the old and new protocols P, P', if a negotiation in state CourseDesigner of protocol P is migrated to the same state of protocol P', a violation of FSC might occur as it could fail to interact with the changed sequence (path): (CourseDesigner.discloseAC&PC().discloseRID().Reviewer).

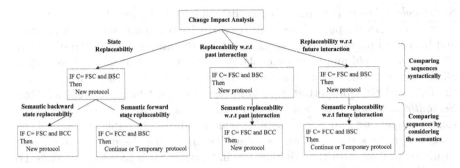

Fig. 4. Replaceability classes and their corresponding migration rules

– *Backward Sequence Compatibility (BSC)* means that, when a negotiation is migrated to the new protocol, the message sequence (followed by the negotiation so far) must be compatible in the context of new protocol.

Example 3. In protocols P, P', assume there is a negotiation in state TextbookEditor of protocol P. If the negotiation has followed the path (Contributor. discloseORCID().discloseAC()...TextbookEditor), a violation of BSC occurs as the sequence is not acceptable by the new protocol P'.

– *Forward Credential Compatibility (FCC)* means that a negotiation can disclose all required credentials when it is migrated to a new protocol, even though it is not guaranteed to correctly interact with a given service.

Example 4. In Example 2, the negotiation is not guaranteed to correctly interact with the changed path, but it satisfies the FCC property as it can send all the required credentials {AC, PC, RID} in the context of protocol P'.

– *Backward Credential Compatibility (BCC)* means that a negotiation has already disclosed all required credentials, even if it followed the message sequence that is incompatible in the context of new protocol.

Example 5. In Example 3, while the negotiation has followed the path incompatible with the new protocol, it satisfies the BCC property as it already sent all the credentials {ORCID, AC, PC} required in protocol P'.

4.2 Analyzing Change Impacts by Different Replaceability Classes

The change impact analysis is based on the notion of replaceability (that is, determining under what circumstances a new protocol can replace an old one to satisfy the above compatibility properties). Each replaceability class can be represented as a migration rule: if [condition] then [conclusion] (Figure 4). Here, the condition part corresponds to the compatibility properties and the conclusion part to the possible migration strategies, with meaning that all negotiations satisfying the properties are handled with the specified strategies.

State-based Replaceability When a new protocol can replace an old protocol, all negotiations can be safely migrated to the new protocol [5]. If protocols are not replaceable, we look at the current states of negotiations as follows.

State replaceability: This analysis class determines the change-transparent states where their forward paths (message sequences from the states to the final state) and backward paths (message sequences from the initial state to the states) are all the same in old and new protocols. As a migration strategy, we can migrate all the negotiations in these states to the *new* protocol as they satisfy both of the FSC and BSC properties, e.g., in Figure 1(a), like state LectureSlideEditor.

Semantic backward state replaceability: Though a certain state is affected by some changes, we can regard it as a semantically replaceable state, if all the changes are the semantic ones, meaning that the changed sequences are semantically equivalent with the original ones in terms of their message contents. For example, in Figure 1(a), this analysis returns the state TextbookEditor.

Semantic forward state replaceability: Unlike the previous semantic analysis, this analysis determines the states that have the same backward paths, but the *different forward paths* (all of the different paths are changed semantically). Note that the negotiations in such states cannot be migrated directly to the new protocol as they may not be guaranteed to interact with the semantically changed path. As possible migration strategies, they can continue to run under the old protocol, if it is acceptable.

Interaction Path-based Replaceability Note that there are some situations where we cannot determine the successful migration of negotiations at the state level, e.g., when migrating negotiations in a certain state might cause the violations of compatibility properties. In this case, to extract the migrateable ones from such a state, we further look at their past and future interactions as follows.

Replaceability with respect to a past interaction: This analysis is performed on the negotiations in the states that have the same forward paths, but *different backward paths* (one of them is changed *syntactically* with the elementary operators). Given a negotiation, the analysis checks whether its past interaction is compatible in the context of new protocol. For example, in protocols P, P', among the negotiations in the state Reviewer, we extract the ones that only followed the *unaffected* backward path (Contributor.discloseORCID().disclosePC().discloseAC().dis closeRID().Reviewer), since they satisfy the FSC and BSC properties.

Semantic replaceability with respect to a past interaction: Even though a certain negotiation followed an affected backward path, this analysis classifies it as a migrateable one, if it took one of the semantically changed backward paths.

Replaceability with respect to a future interaction: After all the previous analyses, there remain negotiations in certain states, which followed compatible backward paths, but are *not* guaranteed to correctly interact with the new protocol. To identify the negotiations that will take the unaffected forward paths, we can infer the possible future interactions of them by applying some data mining techniques to the past interactions of negotiations (see [4] for the details).

Semantic replaceability with respect to a future interaction: Though a certain negotiation is expected to follow some affected forward paths, this analysis further examines whether it will only take one of the semantically changed paths. If so, the negotiation can be migrated to a temporary protocol.

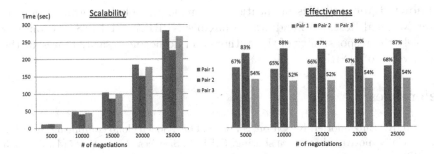

Fig. 5. Evaluation results. X-axis represents the number of simulated negotiations. Y-axis represents the time (sec) taken for the replaceability analysis in Figure 5(a) and the successful migration rate improvement in Figure 5(b).

5   Evaluation

We now present the evaluation results that show how our system can be effectively utilized in the dynamic evolution of protocols.

Evaluation Methodology: We evaluated the performance of change impact (replaceability) analysis in terms of the scalability and effectiveness. For this, we defined three pairs of protocols (each pair consisting of old and new protocols) with different number of states. For example, in pair one, an old protocol had 18 states and 19 transitions and a new protocol 16 states and 17 transitions. We populated the system with a number of artificial negotiations (e.g., 5k, 10k, etc).

Results: Figure 5(a) shows the time taken to perform the replaceability analyses from Section 4.2 for the three pairs of protocols. For example, for 15k negotiations, it took about 100 seconds in performing all the replaceability analyses on the negotiations and determining which ones are migrateable. As we can see from the figure, the time taken to complete the analyses grows linearly with respect to the number of negotiations. In the second evaluation, we measured how much the rate of successful migration could be improved by considering the change semantics as an additional knowledge in the replaceability analysis. Figure 5(b) shows the improvement rate for the protocol pairs. For instance, for 20k negotiations simulated in the pair two, we could obtain the improvement rate 89% ($\frac{(91-48)}{48} = 89$, where the 48% is the successful migration rate from the previous works and the 91% is the rate from this work). In the figure, we can see that we would achieve better migration rate by taking into account the semantics behind protocol changes.

6   Conclusion

This paper proposed an approach for considering both message sequences and their contents in managing the dynamic protocol evolution problem. Particularly, we presented composite change operators for expressing the semantic equivalence between message sequences. We also proposed the change impact analysis that considers the change semantics as an additional knowledge.

Acknowledgments. This publication was made possible by a grant from the Qatar National Research Fund; award number NPRP 7-481-1-088. Its contents are solely the responsibility of the authors and do not necessarily represent the official views of QNRF.

References

1. Chard, K., Bubendorfer, K., Caton, S., Rana, O.F.: Social cloud computing: A vision for socially motivated resource sharing. IEEE T. Services Computing 5(4), 551–563 (2012)
2. Lee, A.J., Winslett, M., Basney, J., Welch, V.: The traust authorization service. ACM Trans. Inf. Syst. Secur. 11(1) (2008)
3. Noor, T.H., Sheng, Q.Z., Zeadally, S., Yu, J.: Trust management of services in cloud environments: Obstacles and solutions. ACM Comput. Surv. 46(1), 12 (2013)
4. Ryu, S.H., Casati, F., Skogsrud, H., Benatallah, B., Saint-Paul, R.: Supporting the dynamic evolution of web service protocols in service-oriented architectures. ACM Transactions on the Web 2(2) (2008)
5. Skogsrud, H., Benatallah, B., Casati, F., Toumani, F.: Managing impacts of security protocol changes in service-oriented applications. In: ICSE (2007)
6. Skogsrud, H., Nezhad, H.R.M., Benatallah, B., Casati, F.: Modeling trust negotiation for web services. IEEE Computer 42(2) (2009)
7. di Vimercati, S.D.C., Foresti, S., Jajodia, S., Paraboschi, S., Psaila, G., Samarati, P.: Integrating trust management and access control in data-intensive web applications. TWEB 6(2), 6 (2012)

Social Context-Aware Trust Prediction in Social Networks

Xiaoming Zheng[1], Yan Wang[1], Mehmet A. Orgun[1], Guanfeng Liu[2],
and Haibin Zhang[1]

[1] Department of Computing,Macquarie University, Sydney, NSW 2109, Australia
{xiaoming.zheng,yan.wang,mehmet.orgun,haibin.zhang}@mq.edu.au
[2] School of Computer Science and Technology, Soochow University, China 215006
gfliu@suda.edu.cn

Abstract. Online social networks have been widely used for a large
number of activities in recent years. Utilizing social network information
to infer or predict trust among people to recommend services from trustworthy providers have drawn growing attention, especially in online environments. Conventional trust inference approaches predict trust between
people along paths connecting them in social networks. However, most
of the state-of-the-art trust prediction approaches do not consider the
contextual information that influences trust and trust evaluation. In this
paper, we first analyze the personal properties and interpersonal properties which impact trust transference between contexts. Then, a new trust
transference method is proposed to predict the trust in a target context
from that in different but relevant contexts. Next, a social context-aware
trust prediction model based on matrix factorization is proposed to predict trust in various situations regardless of whether there is a path from
a source participant to a target participant. To the best of our knowledge,
this is the first context-aware trust prediction model in social networks
in the literature. The experimental analysis illustrates that the proposed
model can mitigate the sparsity situation in social networks and generate more reasonable trust results than the most recent state-of-the-art
context-aware trust inference approach.

Keywords: Social Networks, context, trust prediction, social recommendation.

1 Introduction

In recent years, a growing and large number of users have joined e-commerce,
online employment and social network web sites while online social networks
have proliferated to be the platforms for a variety of rich activities, such as
seeking employees and jobs, and trustworthy recommendations for products and
services. In such activities, *trust* (the commitment to a future action based on a
belief that it will lead to a good outcome, despite the lack of ability to monitor
or control the environment [2]) is one of the most critical factors for the decision
making of users. It is context dependent and it is rare for a person to have

X. Franch et al. (Eds.): ICSOC 2014, LNCS 8831, pp. 527–534, 2014.

full trust on another in every facet. For example, the case of full trust in all aspects is less than 1% at popular product review websites of Epinions.com and Ciao.co.uk [12]. In real life, people's trust to another is limited to certain domains.

Trust prediction is the process of estimating a new pair-wise trust relationship between two participants in a context, who are not directly connected by interactions in the context [14]. Recently, some studies suggest to predict trust taking into account some kind of social contextual information. Liu et al. [7] propose a randomized algorithm for searching a sub-network between a source participant and a target one. In this work, contextual factors, such as social intimacy and role impact factor, are taken into account as constraints for searching, rather than simple trust inference or propagation. Wang et al. [12] propose a probabilistic social trust model to infer trust along a path in a social network exploring all available social context information. However, this method only relies on trust paths and ignores participants off the path who might also have an impact on the predicted trust.

In the literature, most trust prediction models suffer from the following drawbacks: (i) The property of trust values has not been studied sufficiently. For example, the similarity of people's trust can be modeled not only from the trust values but also from their distributions [14]. (ii) The diversity of social contexts is not well dealt with. In real life, the connection between two people can be any of friendship, family member, business partnership, or classmate etc. Even the same relationships—say friendship, their interaction frequency and interaction contexts can be largely different [12]. (iii) The ways to incorporate social information require further study as inappropriate introduction of social information may introduce noise and degrade the trust prediction quality. (iv) Differences of contextual information are not handled properly. For example, how to model the relationship of two contexts? To what extent, the trust in context C_i can be transferred to context C_j?

In order to address the above drawbacks, we first present a social context-aware network model taking into account both personal properties (i.e., features extracted from personal preference, habit, expertise and active context revealed in historical data) and interpersonal properties (i.e., features extracted from two participants including social relationship, social intimacy, similarity etc.) of participants. Then, we propose a new approach to compute the trust transferred from interaction contexts to a target context considering both the properties of participants and the features of contexts in which they have interactions. Finally, we modify matrix factorization methods, by introducing indicator functions of both interaction trust and transferred trust, to predict the trust of a participant in others' minds regarding a certain target context.

The main contributions of our work are summarized as follows: (i) we introduce relevant context information into our model; (ii) we propose a context-aware trust transference method that can mitigate the sparsity problem and enhance the trust prediction accuracy; and (iii) we propose a matrix factorization based method that can predict the trust between two participants in a target context regardless of whether there is a path connecting them.

2   Contextual Social Networks

Context is a multi-faceted concept across different research disciplines with various definitions [10]. In this paper, we define *context* as any information available for characterizing the participants and the situations of interactions between them. If participant p_1 has an interaction with participant p_2, the context about p_1 and p_2 in the social society is referred to as the *social context*, among which the *interaction context* refers to any information about the interaction including time, place, type of services etc. If p_2 recommends a service to p_1, then the information about the service is referred to the *target context*.

2.1   Social Context

Social context describes the context about participants. Before it can be used to predict trust of participants, the properties of each aspect must be extracted modeling the characteristics of participants and the relationship between them. Therefore, social contexts can be divided into two groups according to the characteristics of each impact factor: *personal properties* (e.g., role impact factor, reliability and preference) and *interpersonal properties* (e.g., preference similarity, social intimacy and existing trust).

Role Impact Factor: Role impact factor (denoted as $RIF_{p_1}^{c_i}$) has a significant influence on the trust between participants in a society [7]. It illustrates the impact of a participant's social position and expertise on his/her trustworthiness when making recommendations based on that the recommendation from a person who has expertise in a domain is more credible than others with less knowledge. There are various ways to calculate the role impact factor in different domains. For example, the social position between email users is discoverd by mining the subjects and contents of emails in Enron Corporation[1] [4].

Recommendation Reliability: In a certain context, the reliability of recommendations $(RLB_{p_1}^{c_i})$ measures the rate of a participant's recommendations accepted by recommendees [3]. On the dataset MovieLens[2], the leave-one-out approach is used in [3] to calculate the deviation between the predicted rating and the actual ratings as the reliability of a participant.

Preference: Preference $(PS_{p_1,p_2}^{c_i})$ is an individual's attitude or affinity towards a set of objects in a decision making process [6]. This property may differ greatly between different contexts in real life. The similarity of two participants' preferences can impact the trust between them to some extent [12]. Here, $PS_{p_1,p_2}^{c_i} = PS_{p_2,p_1}^{c_i}$. It can be calculated from the rating values given by users using models such as PCC and VSS [8].

Social Intimacy: Social intimacy $(SI_{p_1,p_2}^{c_i})$ refers to the frequency of connections between participants in a social network. The degree of social intimacy can impact trust as people tend to trust these with more intimate social relationships [1]. Here, $SI_{p_1,p_2}^{c_i}$ is not equivalent to $SI_{p_2,p_1}^{c_i}$. Models like PageRank [11], are able to calculate the social intimacy degree values.

---

[1] http://www.cs.cmu.edu/~enron/
[2] http://movielens.sumn.edu/

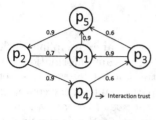

(a) Social network graph

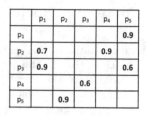

	p_1	p_2	p_3	p_4	p_5
p_1					0.9
p_2	0.7			0.9	
p_3	0.9				0.6
p_4			0.6		
p_5		0.9			

(b) Trust matrix

Fig. 1. The social network in a context

2.2 Social Context Similarity

Interaction context is the information about the situation when the interaction happens between participants p_1 and p_2. For example, suppose that p_2 has recommended mobile phones to p_1 many times in the past. As a result, p_1 trusts p_2 with the value $T^{c_i}_{p_1,p_2} = 0.8$ in the context of mobile phones. Now p_2 recommends p_1 a laptop. As there is no historical recommendation in the context of laptops, and there does exist similarity between the contexts of mobile phones and laptops, we need to calculate the context similarity in order to determine how much p_1 can trust p_2 in the target context of recommending laptops. Let $CS^{c_i,c_j} \in [0,1]$ denote the similarity between two contexts c_i and c_j. Only when c_i and c_j are exactly the same context, $CS^{c_i,c_j} = 1$. And $CS^{c_i,c_j} = 0$ indicates that the information in context c_i is not relevant to c_j at all and cannot impact participants' trust in context c_j. Here, $CS^{c_i,c_j} = CS^{c_j,c_i}$. We adopt the classification of contexts introduced in [12] with a number of existing methods to compute similarity [13,12], such as Linear discriminant analysis and context hierarchy based similarity calculation. In addition, the interaction context c_j is relevant to the interaction context c_i if $CS^{c_i,c_j} > \mu$ (μ is a threshold, e.g., 0.7), denoted as $c_i \sim c_j$. Otherwise, if c_j is irrelevant to c_i, denoted as $c_i \nsim c_j$.

2.3 Contextual Presentation of Trust

In order to apply our prediction model on the trust information in different contexts, we present a contextual trust matrix to represent the contextual information and social properties. Fig. 1(a) shows a social network graph in a context c_i, in which the arrows between nodes mean the existing trust resulting from past interactions. In context c_i, we construct a $N_p \times N_p$ matrix R, where N_p is the number of participants. In this 2-D matrix, if we put the trust value between participants at each context, the structure can be shown as in Fig. 1(b).

The contextual social network graph is shown in Fig. 2(a) with the trust links in all contexts, where the superscript c_i, $i = 1...5$ indicates the context in which the trust exists. Taking all contexts into consideration, the matrix R turns into a $N_p \times N_p \times N_c$ matrix as shown in Fig. 2(b), where, N_c is the number of contexts.

In Fig. 1(b) and Fig. 2(b), only the trust vales are shown in the matrix for illustration purposes. Actually, each element in the matrix is a social property vector containing all the relative properties discussed in detail in this section.

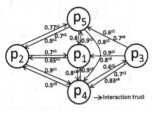

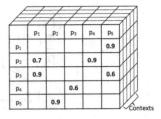

(a) Social network graph

(b) Contextual trust matrix

Fig. 2. Contextual social network

3   Contextual Trust Prediction

The process to predict the trust between participants p_x and p_y in the target context of c_j can be divided into two situations based on available information. They are discussed in the following subsections.

3.1   Trust Transference between Contexts

The trust in relevant interaction contexts can be transferred to the target context. The result is called *transferred trust*. This process is *trust transference*.

As introduced in Section 2, the personal properties and interpersonal properties can impact how much of the trust in interaction contexts can be transferred to that in a target context, which is termed as *trust transference degree*. Thus the transference degree of trust to p_y in p_x's mind from interaction context c_i to target context c_j can be calculated from the following equation:

$$\alpha_{p_x,p_y}^{c_i,c_j} = \omega_1 \cdot PS_{p_x,p_y}^{c_i} + \omega_2 \cdot SI_{p_x,p_y}^{c_i} + \omega_3 \cdot CS^{c_i,c_j} \tag{1}$$

This equation assumes that participant p_x trusts participant p_y with the trust value $T_{p_x,p_y}^{c_i}$ after interactions in context c_i in the past. It calculates the transference degree from the trust in interaction context c_i to the trust in target context c_j, when participant p_y makes recommendations to participant p_x. Here, $\{\omega_i\}, i = 1...5$ are the weights of the properties that impact the trust of p_y in the mind of p_x, and $\sum_i \omega_i = 1$. Therefore, the trust value to p_y in the mind of p_x regarding the context c_i, $T_{p_x,p_y}^{c_i}$, can be transferred to the one in the target context c_j by $\alpha_{p_x,p_y}^{c_i,c_j} \cdot T_{p_x,p_y}^{c_i}$.

However, in the target context c_j, even if participant p_x has no interaction with participant p_y, p_x can trust p_y to some extent primarily due to p_y's social effect and his/her ability to give an appropriate recommendation, which can be depicted by the role impact factor and recommendation reliability. We use the term *"basic trust"* [9] to refer to this kind of trust, which can be formulated as:

$$BT_{p_x,p_y}^{c_j} = \delta_1 \cdot RIF_{p_y}^{c_j} + \delta_2 \cdot RLB_{p_y}^{c_j} \tag{2}$$

where, $\delta_1 + \delta_2 = 1$. Finally, based on the trust in all the interaction contexts C and the basic trust in the target context c_j, the transferred trust representing

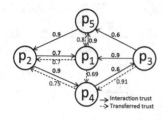

(a) Social network graph

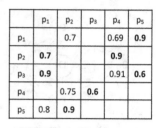

(b) Contextual trust matrix

Fig. 3. Contextual social network with transferred trust

how much participant p_x can trust p_y in the target context c_j can be formulated as follows:

$$\tilde{T}^{c_j}_{p_x,p_y} = \beta_1 \max_{c_i \in C}\{\alpha^{c_i,c_j}_{p_x,p_y} \cdot T^{c_i}_{p_x,p_y}\} + \beta_2 BT^{c_j}_{p_x,p_y} \tag{3}$$

where, $\beta_1 + \beta_2 = 1$; $\max_{c_i \in C}\{\cdot\}$ means the maximum trust value among all the trust values transferred from relevant contexts without basic trust. These coefficients can be calculated using leave-one-out approach [3] in the historical data.

3.2 Trust Prediction Using Matrix Factorization

A more complicated situation is to predict trust between a source participant and a target participant when they have no interaction trust between each other in both the target context and relevant contexts, but they do have interactions with other participants respectively. In such a situation, even if all the trust in all the interaction contexts has been transferred to the target context using the method introduced in Subsection 3.1, the trust we want to predict in the target context is still absent. For instance, we want to predict the trust between p_2 and p_3 in Fig. 3.

As shown in Fig. 3(b), the trust matrix R is a $N_p \times N_p$ matrix representing the trust from trusters (recommendees) to trustees (recommenders). The matrix factorization model maps trust values to a joint latent factor space of dimensionality l so that each trust value r_{ij} in matrix R is the inner product of truster vector $u_i \in \mathbb{R}^l$ (the relationship between truster i and the l latent factors) and trustee vector $v_j \in \mathbb{R}^l$ (the relationship between trustee j and the l latent factors).

$$r_{ij} \approx u_i^T v_j \tag{4}$$

Accordingly, the truster-trustee trust matrix R is modeled as the inner product of a truster-specific matrix $U = \{u_i\}$ and a trustee-specific matrix $V = \{v_j\}$.

$$R \approx U^T V \tag{5}$$

The factorization process is approximated by minimizing the following equation:

$$\min_{U,V} \frac{1}{2} \sum_{i=1}^{n} \sum_{j=1}^{n} (I_{ij} + \eta \tilde{I}_{ij})(r_{ij} - u_i^T v_j)^2 + \frac{\lambda_1}{2}||U||^2 + \frac{\lambda_2}{2}||V||^2, \tag{6}$$

where $||.||_F^2$ represents the Frobenius norm; I_{ij} is an indicator function of inter-action trust. $I_{ij} = 1$ *iff* participant p_i (truster) trusts participant p_j (trustee) in the target context originally, $i \neq j$. Otherwise, $I_{ij} = 0$. In addition, $\tilde{I}_{ij}$ is an-other indicator function of transferred trust. $\tilde{I}_{ij} = 1$ *iff* participant p_i (truster) has trust calculated by Eq. (3) to participant p_j (trustee), $i \neq j$. Otherwise, $\tilde{I}_{ij} = 0$. $\eta \in [0, 1]$ is a coefficient controlling the weight of transferred trust. Once the learning process of the method is achieved by Eq. (6), the trust we want to predict can be calculated by Eq. (4).

4   Experiments

We evaluate the effectiveness of our model in typical scenarios including the basic cases of social networks in real world and compare our model with the state-of-the-art approach social context-aware trust inference (SocialTrust) [12], as well as the prevalent multiplication strategy (MUL) [5]. Due to space limitations, only the comparison of trust inference between contexts is presented here.

In real life, a typical situation needing trust prediction is that a recommender and a recommendee do not have any interactions in the target context c_j. However, they have many interactions in the past in other relevant contexts $C_h = \{c_i\}$, $i = 1, ...n$ and $i \neq j$. Without any loss of generality, the trust val-ues between two participants are generated using a random function in Matlab. We adopt the coefficients from SocialTrust giving the same weight for each co-efficient, where applicable, and set $\omega_1 = \omega_2 = \omega_3 = 0.333$, $\delta_1 = \delta_2 = 0.5$, $\beta_1 = \beta_2 = 0.5$, $CS^{c_1,c_2} = 0.8$, $CS^{c_1,c_3} = 0.1$. The context information we used in this case study can be found in Table 1. In this situation, the trust values to p_2

Table 1. Contextual tust to p_2 in p_1's mind

ID	Context	Context Relation	T_{p_1,p_2}	PS_{p_1,p_2}	SI_{p_1,p_2}	RIF_{p_1}	RIF_{p_2}	RLB_{p_1}	RLB_{p_2}
c_1	Teaching VC	$c_1 \sim c_2$ & $c_1 \nsim c_3$	?	0	0	0	0.8	0	0.9
c_2	Teaching Java	$c_2 \sim c_1$ & $c_2 \nsim c_3$	0.7	1	1	0.5	0.8	0.5	0.9
c_3	Car repair	$c_3 \nsim c_1$ & $c_3 \nsim c_2$	0.8	1	1	0.5	0.8	0.5	0.9

in p_1's mind calculated by Eq. (3) and SocialTrust are 0.57 and 0.74 respectively. MUL does not apply in this case, as it does not deal with trust between contexts.

SocialTrust neglects the concept of basic trust while taking the role impact factor of p_1 in the target context c_1 into account. In real life, this value should be 0 consistently, because when a participant seeks suggestions from others, he/she usually has no experience in the target context. Otherwise, he/she has his/her own trust in the target context already and may not need recommendations. Therefore, our result is the most reasonable one in this scenario. It fits the case in real life that, a VC teacher is usually also good at teaching Java, as teaching Java and teaching VC are similar contexts.

5   Conclusions

As trust prediction is a dynamic and context sensitive process. In this paper, we have first analyzed the properties that can impact trust transference between different but relevant contexts. Based on these impact properties, we have proposed a new trust transference method to transfer trust from interaction contexts to a target context considering personal properties and interpersonal properties. Then, a social context-aware trust prediction model has been proposed to predict trust from a source participant to a target participant. The proposed approach analyzes and incorporates the characteristics of participants' trust values, and predicts the missing trust in the target context using modified matrix factorization. The conducted experiments show that our proposed model transfers trust between contexts in a reasonable way and is able to predict trust between source and target participants.

References

1. Brehm, S.: Intimate relationships. Random House (1985)
2. Golbeck, J., Hendler, J.A.: Inferring binary trust relationships in web-based social networks. ACM Transactions on Internet Technology 6(4), 497–529 (2006)
3. Jia, D., Zhang, F., Liu, S.: A robust collaborative filtering recommendation algorithm based on multidimensional trust model. JSW 8(1), 11–18 (2013)
4. Klimt, B., Yang, Y.: Introducing the Enron Corpus. In: CEAS (2004)
5. Li, L., Wang, Y., Lim, E.-P.: Trust-oriented composite service selection and discovery. In: Baresi, L., Chi, C.-H., Suzuki, J. (eds.) ICSOC-ServiceWave 2009. LNCS, vol. 5900, pp. 50–67. Springer, Heidelberg (2009)
6. Lichtenstein, S., Slovic, P.: The Construction of Preference. Cambridge University Press (2006)
7. Liu, G., Wang, Y., Orgun, M.A.: Social context-aware trust network discovery in complex contextual social networks. In: AAAI, pp. 101–107 (2012)
8. Ma, H., Zhou, D., Liu, C., Lyu, M.R., King, I.: Recommender systems with social regularization. In: Proceedings of the Fourth ACM International Conference on Web Search and Data Mining, WSDM 2011, pp. 287–296. ACM (2011)
9. Marsh, S.P.: Formalising Trust as a Computational Concept. Ph.D. thesis, University of Stirling (April 1994)
10. Sherchan, W., Nepal, S., Paris, C.: A survey of trust in social networks. ACM Comput. Surv. 45(4), 47 (2013)
11. Tang, J., Zhang, J., Yao, L., Li, J., Zhang, L., Su, Z.: Arnetminer: Extraction and mining of academic social networks. In: Proceedings of the 14th ACM SIGKDD International Conference on Knowledge Discovery and Data Mining, KDD 2008, pp. 990–998. ACM, New York (2008)
12. Wang, Y., Li, L., Liu, G.: Social context-aware trust inference for trust enhancement in social network based recommendations on service providers. World Wide Web Journal (WWWJ) (2013) (accepted)
13. Zhang, H., Wang, Y., Zhang, X.: Transaction similarity-based contextual trust evaluation in e-commerce and e-service environments. In: IEEE International Conference on Web Services, pp. 500–507 (2011)
14. Zheng, X., Wang, Y., Orgun, M.A., Zhong, Y., Liu, G.: Trust prediction with propagation and similarity regularization. In: Twenty-Eighth Conference on Artificial Intelligence, Quebec City, Quebec, Canada, July 27-31 (in press, 2014)

Decidability and Complexity of Simulation Preorder for Data-Centric Web Services

Lakhdar Akroun[1], Boualem Benatallah[2],
Lhouari Nourine[1], and Farouk Toumani[1]

[1] LIMOS, CNRS, Blaise Pascal University, Clermont-Ferrand, France
{akroun,nourine,ftoumani}@isima.fr
[2] CSE, UNSW, Sydney, Australia
boualem.benatallah@gmail.com

Abstract. This paper studies the problem of checking the simulation preorder for data-centric services. It focuses more specifically on the underlying decidability and complexity issues in the framework of the Colombo model [1]. We show that the simulation test is EXPTIME-complete for Colombo services without any access to the database (noted $Colombo^{DB=\emptyset}$) and 2EXPTIME-complete when only bounded databases are considered (the obtained model is noted $Colombo^{bound}$). This is a decidability border since we have shown in previous work that the simulation test for unbounded Colombo is undecidable. Moreover, as a side effect of this work, we establish a correspondance between $Colombo^{DB=\emptyset}$, restricted to equality, and Guarded Variable Automata (GVA) [2]. As a consequence, we derive EXPTIME-completeness of simulation for GVA.

Keywords: data-centric services, simulation preorder, variable automata, verification and synthesis.

1 Introduction

Business protocols, and associated representation models (e.g., state machines [3, 4], , Petri-nets), are used for specifying external behavior of services. They open the opportunity for formal analysis, verification and synthesis of services. For example, business protocols have been used as a basis to develop techniques for compatibility and replaceability analysis of web services [5] and also to study the web service composition problem [6]. In the aforementioned research works, the *simulation preorder* [7] plays a fundamental role to solve the considered problems. Indeed, simulation preorder enables to formalize the idea that a given service is able to faithfully reproduce the externally visible behavior of another service.

Recently, the need of incorporating data as a *first-class citizen* in business protocols has been widely recognized and a number of research works has been carried out in this direction, laying the foundations of a *data-centric* approach to web services [1, 8, 9]. Formal models used to describe such specifications, called *data-centric services*, are essentially communicating guarded transitions systems

X. Franch et al. (Eds.): ICSOC 2014, LNCS 8831, pp. 535–542, 2014.

in which transitions are used to model either the exchange of messages between a service and its environment (i.e. a *client*), or service's actions (i.e., read, write) over a global database shared among the existing services. A configuration (or a state) of a data-centric service is made of a control state of the transition system augmented with the current instance of the global database. The incorporation of data turns out to be very challenging since it makes service specifications infinite which leads, in most cases, to undecidability of many analysis and verification problems.

In this paper, we investigate the decidability and the complexity issues of service simulation in the framework of the Colombo model [1]. A Colombo service is specified as a guarded transition system, augmented with a global database as well as a set of variables that are used to send and receive messages. Two sources of infiniteness makes the simulation test difficult in this context: (i) the variables used by a service range over infinite domains and hence the number of potential concrete messages that can be received by a service in a given state may be infinite; (ii) the number of possible initial instances of the global database is infinite which makes the number of configurations of a service infinite.

In a preliminary work [10], we showed that checking simulation in a Colombo model with unbounded accesses to the database, called $Colombo^{unb}$, is undecidable. To complete the picture and provide a decidability border of simulation in the Colombo framework, we study in this paper the simulation problem in the case of Colombo services with bounded databases (i.e. the class of Colombo services restricted to global databases having a number of tuples that cannot exceed a given constant k). Such a class is called $Colombo^{bound}$. We show that the simulation is 2EXPTIME-complete for $Colombo^{bound}$. The proof is achieved in two steps: (i) first we show that checking simulation is EXPTIME-complete for Colombo services without any access to the database (called DB-less services and denoted $Colombo^{DB=\emptyset}$). $Colombo^{DB=\emptyset}$ services are also infinite-state systems, because they still manipulate variables ranging over infinite domains. However, a finite symbolic representation of such services can be obtained by partitioning the original infinite state space into a finite number of equivalence classes. As a side effect of this work, we establish a correspondence between $Colombo^{DB=\emptyset}$, restricted to equality, and Guarded Variable Automata (GVA) [2]. As a consequence, we derive EXPTIME-completeness of simulation for GVA; (ii) then we show that the simulation test for $Colombo^{bound}$ services exponentially reduces to checking simulation in $Colombo^{DB=\emptyset}$. The exponential blow-up is an unavoidable price to pay since we prove that simulation in $Colombo^{bound}$ is 2EXPTIME-complete. For space reasons, the proofs are omitted and are given in the extended version of this paper [11].

Organization of the paper. We start by giving an overview of the Colombo framework in Sect.2, then we present our results on $Colombo^{DB=\emptyset}$ and $Colombo^{bound}$ in Sect.3. Finally, we discuss related work in Sect.4 while we conclude in Sect.5.

2   Overview on the Colombo Model

A *world* database schema, denoted $\mathcal{W}$, is a finite set of relation schemas having the form $R(A_1, \ldots, A_k; B_1, \ldots, B_n)$, where the A_is form a key for R. A world database (or a world instance) is an instance over the schema $\mathcal{W}$. Let $R(A_1, \ldots, A_k; B_1, \ldots, B_n)$ be a relation schema in $\mathcal{W}$, then $f_j^R(A_1, \ldots, A_k)$ is an access function that returns the *j-th* element of the tuple t in R identified by the key $(A_1, \ldots, A_k)$ (i.e. $j \in [1, n]$). Given a set of constants C and variables V, the set of accessible terms over C and V is defined recursively to include all the terms constructed using C, V and the f_j^R functions.

Example 1. Figure 1(c) depicts an example of a world database. For example, the access to the relation Inventory(<u>code</u>, available, warehouse, price) is only possible through the access function $f_j^{Inventory}(code)$ with $j \in [1, 3]$.

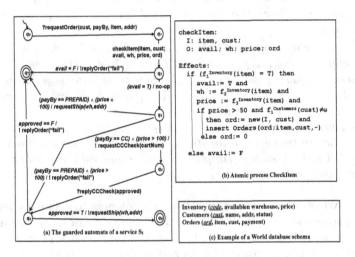

Fig. 1. Example of Colombo service (from [1])

In the Colombo model, service *actions* are achieved using the notion of *atomic processes*. An atomic process is a triplet $p = (I, O, CE)$ where: I and O are respectively input and output signatures (i.e., sets of typed variables) and $CE = \{(\theta, E)\}$, is a set of conditional effects, with:

- Condition θ is a boolean expression over atoms over accessible terms over some family of constants[1] and the input variables $u_1, \ldots, u_n$ in I,
- A set of effects E where each effect $e \in E$ is a pair (es, ev) with:
  - *es*, effect on world database, is a set of modifications on the global database (i.e., expressions of the form insert, delete or modify),

---

[1] The symbol ω is used to denote an *undefined* (or null) value.

- ev, effects on output variables, is a set of assignment statements of the forms: $v_j := t, \forall v_j \in O$ such that either $t = \omega$ or t is an accessible term over some set of constants and over the input variables $u_1, \ldots, u_n$.

A *message type* has the form $m(p_1, \ldots, p_n)$ where m is the message name and $p_1, \ldots, p_n$ are message parameters. Each parameter p_i is defined over a domain $\mathcal{D}$ (w.l.o.g., we assume that all the messages parameters are defined over the same values domain $\mathcal{D}$). The behavior of a Colombo service is given by the notion of *guarded automaton* as defined below.

Definition 1. *A **guarded automaton** (GA) of a service S is a tuple $GA(S) = \langle Q, \delta, q_0, F, LStore(S) \rangle$, where :*

- Q *is a finite set of control states with $q_0 \in Q$ the initial state,*
- $F \subseteq Q$ *is a set of final states,*
- $LStore(S)$ *is a finite set of typed variables,*
- *the transition relation δ contains tuples (q, θ, μ, q') where $q, q' \in Q$, θ is a condition over LStore (no access to world instance), and μ has one of the following forms:*
  - *(incoming message) $\mu = ?m(v_1, \ldots, v_n)$ where m is a message having as signature $m(p_1, \ldots, p_n)$, and $v_i \in LStore(S), \forall i \in [1, n]$, or*
  - *(send message) $\mu = !m(b_1, \ldots, b_n)$ where m is a message having as signature $m(p_1, \ldots, p_n)$, and $\forall i \in [1, n]$, each b_i is either a variable of $LStore(S)$ or a constant, or*
  - *(atomic process invocation) $\mu = p(u_1, \ldots, u_n; v_1, \ldots, v_m, CE)$ with p an atomic process having n inputs, m outputs and CE as conditional effects, and $\forall i \in [1, n]$, each u_i (respectively, v_i) is either a variable of $LStore(S)$ or a constant.*

Semantics. We use the notion of an *extended automaton* to define the semantics of a Colombo service. At every point in time, the behavior of an instance of a Colombo service S is determined by its *instantaneous configuration (or simply, configuration)*. A configuration of a service is given by a triplet $id = (l, \mathcal{I}, \alpha)$ where l is its current control state, $\mathcal{I}$ a world database instance and α is a valuation over the variables of *LStore*.

An execution of a service S starts at an initial configuration $id_0 = (l_0, \mathcal{I}_0, \alpha_0)$, with l_0 the initial control state of $GA(S)$, $\mathcal{I}_0$ an arbitrary database over $\mathcal{W}$ and $\alpha_0(x) = \omega, \forall x \in LStore(S)$. Then, a service makes a move denoted $id_i \xrightarrow{\mu_i} id_j$ according to the mechanics defined by the set of transitions of $GA(S)$. More specifically, given an $id_i = (l_i, \mathcal{I}_i, \alpha_i)$ and a transition $(l_i, \theta, \mu, l_{i+1}) \in \delta$ such that $\alpha_i(\theta) \equiv \text{true}$ then $id_i \xrightarrow{\mu_i} id_j$ where:

- if $\mu = ?m(v_1, \ldots, v_n)$ then only $(v_1, \ldots, v_n)$ receive new values. The others variables and the database do no change.
- if $\mu = !m(b_1, \ldots, b_n)$ then there is no modification on the variables nor the database.
- if $\mu = p(u_1, \ldots, u_n; v_1, \ldots, v_m, CE)$ then

- if there is no $(c, E) \in CE$ where c is verified (or there is more than one) then there is no modification of the variables nor the database.
- let (c, E) be the unique conditional effects in CE s.t c is verified, and let (es, ev) be a non-deterministicall chosen element of E, then :
  * for each statement $insert$ $R(t_1, \ldots, t_k, s_1, \ldots, s_l)$, $delete$ $R(t_1, \ldots, t_k)$, or $modify$ $R(t_1, \ldots, t_k, s_1, \ldots, s_l)$ in es, apply the corresponding modifications. The obtained instance is the database $\mathcal{I}_{i+1}$.
  * for all $v_j := t$ in ev, execute the affectations, all the other variables v of $LStore(S)$ do not change.

The semantics of a Colombo service can be captured by the following notion of an extended infinite state machine.

Definition 2. *(extended state machine) Let $GA(S) = \langle Q, \delta, l_0, F, LStore(S) \rangle$ be a guarded automaton of a service S. The associated infinite state machine, noted $E(S)$, is a tuple $E(S) = (\mathbb{Q}, \mathbb{Q}_0, \mathbb{F}, \Delta)$ where:*

- $\mathbb{Q} = \{(l, \mathcal{I}, \alpha)\}$ *with* $l \in Q$, $\mathcal{I}$ *a database over* $\mathcal{W}$ *and* α *a valuation over the variables of $LStore$. The set $\mathbb{Q}$ contains all the possible configurations of $E(S)$.*
- $\mathbb{Q}_0 = \{(l_0, \mathcal{I}_0, \alpha_0)\}$, *with* $\mathcal{I}_0$ *an arbitrary database over* $\mathcal{W}$ *and* $\alpha_0(x) = \omega$, $\forall x \in LStore(S)$. $\mathbb{Q}_0$ *is the infinite set of initial configurations of $E(S)$.*
- $\mathbb{F} = \{(l_f, \mathcal{I}, \alpha) \mid l_f \in F\}$. *$F$ is the set of final configurations of $E(S)$.*
- Δ *is an (infinite) set of transitions of the form* $\tau = (l_i, \mathcal{I}_i, \alpha_i) \xrightarrow{\mu_i} (l_j, \mathcal{I}_j, \alpha_j)$.

We define now the notion of simulation between two Colombo services.

Definition 3. *(Simulation) Let S and S' be two Colombo services and let $E(S) = (\mathbb{Q}, \mathbb{Q}_0, \mathbb{F}, \Delta)$ and $E(S') = (\mathbb{Q}', \mathbb{Q}'_0, \mathbb{F}', \Delta')$ be respectively their associated extended state machines.*

- *Let $(id, id') \in \mathbb{Q} \times \mathbb{Q}'$. The configuration $id = (l, \mathcal{I}, \alpha)$ is simulated by $id' = (l', \mathcal{I}', \alpha')$, noted $id \preceq id'$, iff:*
  - $\mathcal{I} = \mathcal{I}'$, *and*
  - $\forall id \xrightarrow{\mu} id_j \in \Delta$, *there exists* $id' \xrightarrow{\mu'} id'_l \in \Delta'$ *such that* $\mu = \mu'$ *and* $id_j \preceq id'_l$
- *The extended state machine $E(S)$ is simulated by the extended state machine $E(S')$, noted $E(S) \preceq E(S')$, iff $\forall id_0 \in \mathbb{Q}_0, \exists id'_0 \in \mathbb{Q}'_0$ such that $id_0 \preceq id'_0$*

- *A Colombo service S is simulated by a Colombo service S', noted $S \preceq S'$, iff $E(S) \preceq E(S')$.*

Informally, if $S \preceq S'$, this means that S' is able to faithfully reproduce the external visible behavior of S. The external visible behavior of a service is defined here with respect to the content of the world database as well as the exchanged *concrete* messages (i.e., message name together with the values of the message parameters). The existence of a simulation relation ensures that each execution tree of S is also an execution tree of S' (in fact, a subtree of S'), modulo a relabeling of control states.

3   Main Results

3.1   DB-Less Services ($Colombo^{db=\emptyset}$)

We consider the simulation problem in the class of Colombo services without any access to the database, called DB-less services and denoted $Colombo^{DB=\emptyset}$. Let S be a $Colombo^{db=\emptyset}$ service. The associated state machine is a tuple $E(S) = (\mathbb{Q}, \mathbb{Q}_0, \mathbb{F}, \Delta)$. A configuration of $E(S)$ has the form $id = (l, \emptyset, \alpha)$ while there is only one initial configuration $id_0 = (l_0, \emptyset, \alpha_0)$ with $\alpha_0(x) = \omega$, $\forall x \in LStore(S)$. Moreover, in $Colombo^{db=\emptyset}$ services, atomic processes can only assign constants to variables of $LStore(S)$ or affect value of a variable to another. Note that $E(S)$ is still an infinite state system. This is due to the presence of input messages with parameters taking their values from a possibly infinite domain. Using a symbolization technique, it is possible however to abstract from concrete values and hence turns extended machines associated with $Colombo^{db=\emptyset}$ services into finite state machines. The main idea is to use the notion of *regions* to group together states of E(S). Interestingly, the obtained representation, called $Colombo^{db=\emptyset}$ *region automaton*, is a finite state machine and hence a simulation algorithm can be devised for this case.

Theorem 1. *Given two DB-less Colombo services S and S', checking whether $S \preceq S'$ is* EXPTIME-*complete.*

The detailed proof of this theorem is given in the extended version of this paper [11]. As said before starting from a test of simulation between two DB-less Colombo services S and S', we construct a test of simulation between two corresponding (finite) $Colombo^{db=\emptyset}$ region automaton R^S and $R^{S'}$. The problem is clearly exponential because the numbers of symbolic states in R^S and $R^{S'}$ is exponential in the size of the two services S and S'. The proof of hardness is obtained from a reduction of the problem of the existence of an infinite execution of an alternating Turing machine M working on space polynomially bounded by the size of the input [12] to a simulation test between two DB-less Colombo services.

3.2   Bounded Services ($Colombo^{bound}$)

We consider now the simulation problem in the setting of a Colombo model with a *bounded* global database, denoted $Colombo^{bound}$. A service belonging to $Colombo^{bound}$ is restricted to use during all his executions a global database $\mathcal{W}$ whose size never exceed a given constant k. Given two services S and S', we say that S is *k-bounded simulated* by S' (noted $S \preceq_k S'$) if S' does simulate S if we restrict the attention to executions where the size of the database is at most equal to k.

Theorem 2. *Let S and S' be two Colombo services, then testing $S \preceq_k S'$ is* 2-EXPTIME *complete.*

The proof of decidability of Theorem 2 is achieved by mapping the *k-bound* simulation test $S \preceq_k S'$ into a standard test of simulation between two DB-less Colombo services $\mathcal{M}(S) \preceq \mathcal{M}(S')$. The main idea of the reduction is to encode the bounded databases into a set of variables.

4   Related Works

Data-centric services and artifact-centric business processes attracted a lot of attention from the research community these recent years [8, 9]. Most of these research works focus on the verification problem. In the context of data-centric services, the verification problem is undecidable in the general case. Existing works focus on identification of specific models and restrictions in which the verification problem can be solved. In [13], the author consider the problem of verifying artifact system against specifications expressed in quantified temporal logic. The verification problem is undecidable in the general setting. So, the paper considers a restricted fragment obtained by bounding the number of values stored in a given execution state of the system. The authors use a specific abstraction technique to construct a finite symbolic system which is bisimilar to the original infinite system. By this way, model checking can be carried out over the (finite) symbolic model instead of the original infinite artefact system. The upper bound time complexity of the proposed procedure is doubly exponential. In [14], the authors study the composition problem for data-centric services using an approach based on the simulation relation. Like our approach, they prove the decidability of simulation by bounding the size of database instance, but the model is less expressive than $Colombo^{bound}$.

Independently from the Web service area, the simulation problem between infinite transition systems has been addressed. This problem is undecidable in the general case but there are few classes, e.g., one-counter nets [15], automate with finite memory [2], where the problem is known to be decidable. Close to our work, [16] introduces a new formalism *Variable automaton*, which is an automaton where transitions are labelled with letters from an alphabet or variables. During an execution, the values assigned to variables are fixed and only one special variable can be *refreshed* (reinitialized). In [2], the authors define a variable automaton where variables are *refreshed* at specific states, named FVA (Fresh Variable Automata). They prove the decidability of the simulation for this model. Then, they extend FVA model with equality guards over variables. The obtained model is called GVA (Guarded Variable Automata). The authors show the decidability of the simulation for GVA and provide an upper bound (EXPTIME).

5   Conclusion

We studied decidability and complexity issues related to the simulation problem in the framework of the Colombo model. Our results, ranging from EXPTIME to undecidability show that the marriage between data and web service business protocols gives rise to some challenging issues. The decidability and complexity results, EXPTIME-complete for $Colombo^{DB=\emptyset}$ and 2EXPTIME-complete for $Colombo^{bound}$ are far from being straightforward, due to the fact we are dealing with infinite state systems. This paper proposed also a *symbolic* procedure based on the notion of *region automata* to handle the infiniteness of the framework. Finally, as side effect of our work, we derived a tight complexity of the simulation problem for automata over infinite domain, namely GVA. Our future works will be devoted to the definition of a generic framework that enables to capture the main features of data-centric services and which can be used as basis to study the problems underlying formal analysis, verification and synthesis of data-centric services.

References

[1] Berardi, D., Calvanese, D., Giacomo, G.D., Hull, R., Mecella, M.: Automatic composition of transition-based semantic web services with messaging. In: VLDB, pp. 613–624 (2005)

[2] Belkhir, W., Chevalier, Y., Rusinowitch, M.: Guarded variable automata over infinite alphabets. CoRR abs/1304.6297 (2013)

[3] Bultan, T., Fu, X., Hull, R., Su, J.: Conversation specification: A new approach to design and analysis of e-service composition. In: WWW 2003. ACM (2003)

[4] Benatallah, B., Casati, F., Toumani, F.: Web service conversation modeling: A cornerstone for e-business automation. IEEE Internet Computing 08, 46–54 (2004)

[5] Benatallah, B., Casati, F., Toumani, F.: Representing, analysing and managing web service protocols. DKE 58, 327–357 (2006)

[6] Muscholl, A., Walukiewicz, I.: A lower bound on web services composition. In: Seidl, H. (ed.) FOSSACS 2007. LNCS, vol. 4423, pp. 274–286. Springer, Heidelberg (2007)

[7] Milner, R.: Communication and concurrency. Prentice-Hall, Inc., Upper Saddle River (1989)

[8] Hull, R.: Artifact-centric business process models: Brief survey of research results and challenges. In: Meersman, R., Tari, Z. (eds.) OTM 2008, Part II. LNCS, vol. 5332, pp. 1152–1163. Springer, Heidelberg (2008)

[9] Calvanese, D., De Giacomo, G., Montali, M.: Foundations of data-aware process analysis: A database theory perspective. In: PODS, pp. 1–12 (2013)

[10] Akroun, L., Benatallah, B., Nourine, L., Toumani, F.: On decidability of simulation in data-centeric business protocols. In: La Rosa, M., Soffer, P. (eds.) BPM Workshops 2012. LNBIP, vol. 132, pp. 352–363. Springer, Heidelberg (2013)

[11] Akroun, L., Benatallah, B., Nourine, L., Toumani, F.: Decidability and complexity of simulation preorder for data-centric web services (extended version). Technical report (2014), http://fc.isima.fr/~akroun/fichiers/journal_version_colombo.pdf

[12] Chandra, A.K., Kozen, D., Stockmeyer, L.J.: Alternation. J. ACM 28, 114–133 (1981)

[13] Belardinelli, F., Lomuscio, A., Patrizi, F.: Verification of deployed artifact systems via data abstraction. In: Kappel, G., Maamar, Z., Motahari-Nezhad, H.R. (eds.) ICSOC 2011. LNCS, vol. 7084, pp. 142–156. Springer, Heidelberg (2011)

[14] Patrizi, F., Giacomo, G.D.: Composition of services that share an infinite-state blackboard (extended abstract). In: IIWEB (2009)

[15] Abdulla, P.A., Cerans, K.: Simulation is decidable for one-counter nets. In: Sangiorgi, D., de Simone, R. (eds.) CONCUR 1998. LNCS, vol. 1466, pp. 253–268. Springer, Heidelberg (1998)

[16] Grumberg, O., Kupferman, O., Sheinvald, S.: Variable automata over infinite alphabets. In: Dediu, A.-H., Fernau, H., Martín-Vide, C. (eds.) LATA 2010. LNCS, vol. 6031, pp. 561–572. Springer, Heidelberg (2010)

Market-Optimized Service Specification and Matching*

Svetlana Arifulina[1], Marie Christin Platenius[2], Steffen Becker[2],
Christian Gerth[1], Gregor Engels[1], and Wilhelm Schäfer[2]

[1] Department of Computer Science, University of Paderborn, Germany
[2] Heinz Nixdorf Institute
University of Paderborn, Germany
{s.arifulina,m.platenius}@upb.de

Abstract. Various approaches in service engineering are based on service markets where brokers use service matching in order to perform service discovery. For matching, a broker translates the specifications of providers' services and requesters' requirements into her own specification language, in order to check their compliance using a matcher. The broker's success depends on the configuration of her language and its matcher because they influence important properties like the effort for providers and requesters to create suitable specifications as well as accuracy and runtime of matching. However, neither existing service specification languages, nor existing matching approaches are optimized in such way. Our approach automatically provides brokers with an optimal configuration of a language and its matcher to improve her success in a given market with respect to her strategy. The approach is based on formalized configuration properties and a predefined set of configuration rules.

Keywords: Service-Oriented Computing, Service Engineering, Service Specification, Service Matching, Service Brokers, Service Market.

1 Introduction

Many approaches in service engineering deal with emerging service markets, where service providers provide software services for trade [10,11]. In order to buy and use these services, service requesters have to discover services that satisfy their requirements. For this reason, various approaches introduce *service brokers*, who serve as intermediaries between requesters and providers [1]. Requesters and providers engage such brokers for a successful service discovery because the brokers have expertise in software services for certain markets [4]. For the discovery, a broker *matches* the requesters' requirements specifications to specifications of the provided services. For this, brokers use a special software called *matcher*. The goal of a matcher is based on specifications to determine

---

* This work was supported by the German Research Foundation (DFG) within the Collaborative Research Center "On-The-Fly Computing" (CRC 901).

X. Franch et al. (Eds.): ICSOC 2014, LNCS 8831, pp. 543–550, 2014.

the extent, to which a provider's service complies with the requesters' requirements. Furthermore, providers and requesters often use different *specification languages*. Thus, the broker has to translate their specifications into her own language, which is supported by a certain matcher. This translation is out of the scope of this paper as it can be done automatically based on existing approaches [7].

In the market, different brokers compete with each other for customers [5]. Customers prefer a broker, who delivers most suitable services fast and with the least possible effort for them. Thus, in order to succeed in this competition, brokers can distinguish themselves by providing a fast and accurate service discovery with low effort for their customers. For that, brokers have to develop their own business strategies, which they adjust to the given market. A main part of this strategy is to find the configuration of a language and a matcher, which is optimal wrt. the service discovery and the customer's effort. Depending on the broker's strategy and the market characteristics, different configurations can be optimal because they are subject to multiple trade-offs. For example, a comprehensive specification language enables very accurate matching, but it requires quite a lot of effort for providers and requesters to create such detailed specifications. In contrast, simpler specifications can be matched much faster, but matching accuracy may suffer. Therefore, a broker becomes successful if she has several languages and matchers optimized according to her different strategies in the given market. However, there are too many different variations of languages and matchers to explore them manually as it is a tedious and error-prone task.

In this paper, we present a fully automated approach called LM Optimizer. LM Optimizer supports brokers to find an optimal "language-matcher configuration" (*LM Config*) in a service market. An LM Config refers to a pair of a service specification language and a corresponding matcher, working on instances of this language. Both the language and the matcher are configured in a certain manner. Configuration possibilities are determined by five kinds of configuration rules. Depending on the configuration, matching accuracy, matching runtime, and specification effort can be improved. LM Optimizer takes as an input market characteristics and the broker strategy described in the form of so-called configuration properties (CPs). Based on the given CPs, a configuration procedure applies well-defined configuration rules to configure a holistic service specification language and its matchers (provided as a part of LM Optimizer). As an output, the broker receives an LM Config optimal for the given CPs.

To sum up the contribution, our approach provides brokers with an optimal configuration of a language and a matcher customized for their business strategy and the given market. This allows brokers to obtain the best possible results in the service discovery. Thereby, our approach contributes to the development of successful service markets.

The paper is organized as follows: In the next section, we introduce a running example. Section 3 presents an overview of our approach, while its details are explained in Section 4 and 5. Section 6 briefly presents related work and Section 7 draws conclusions. A longer version of this paper, including an evaluation, has been published in form of a technical report [2].

2 Running Example

As a running example, we use a service market for University Management (UM). In this market, customers request software services that facilitate management tasks at a university. For that, they engage a broker, as shown in Fig. 1. In the market, three services are available: Course Manager, Exam Manager, and Room Manager. The broker matches the given requirements to the specifications of the provided services, in order to find the most suitable one.

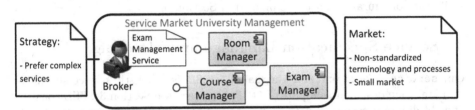

Fig. 1. Example service in the UM market

As shown in Fig. 1, the UM Market has certain characteristics that influence matching. For example, university structure and its management varies significantly from university to university. Therefore, neither terminology nor processes are standardized for services and their specifications in this market. In addition, the market is small because there are currently only few offers. According to the broker's strategy, this specific broker wants to trade only complex services because she expects the most profit from them. As a result, the broker needs an optimal LM Config in order to become as successful as possible.

3 Overview: LM Optimizer

We call our approach for finding an optimal LM Config LM Optimizer. LM Optimizer is fully automated in order to solve the high effort of finding an optimal LM Config manually, as elaborated in Section 5.2. Figure 2 provides an overview of our approach. LM Optimizer takes configuration properties as an input and delivers an optimal LM Config as an output. The configuration properties represent characteristics of the given market and properties of the broker strategy. As an output, we obtain an optimal LM Config consisting of a configured specification language and a set of matchers for it. The matching results delivered by the matcher (based on the service specifications in the configured language) are optimal for the given configuration properties.

LM Optimizer consists of three parts: (1) A holistic service specification language called SSL. (2) A set of matchers called SSL Matchers, which realize

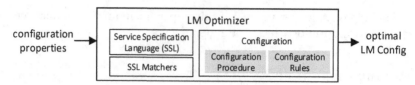

Fig. 2. Overview of the Approach

matching for this language. (3) SSL and SSL matchers are configured by the Configuration, which is responsible for obtaining an optimal LM Config for the given configuration properties. It consists of a set of configuration rules and a configuration procedure. The configuration procedure applies the configuration rules for the given configuration properties, in order to configure the SSL and its matchers optimally. SSL and its matching are described Section 4, while the configuration part is explained in Section 5.

4   Service Specification Language and Matching

Our service specification language, or SSL, is a holistic service specification language designed as a part of LM Optimizer (see Section 3). SSL consists of eight different *service specification aspects* which describe different structural, behavioral, and non-functional properties of a service. Each service specification aspect consists of a set of *language constructs* which describe a certain part of the corresponding service aspect. SSL can be used for comprehensive service specification in many different markets. For each aspect in the SSL, there is one matcher that is able to compare specifications of that aspect. A matcher may implement different matching approaches. Each matcher can run as a matching step in a so-called matching process. The technical report [2] explains in detail the SSL, properties of matching steps, and the matching process.

Matching with the SSL delivers matching results of high accuracy as diverse properties of services are compared. However, the performance of the matching is rather low because comparing all these service properties requires much computation time. Furthermore, writing specifications, which cover all aspects, costs providers and requesters a lot of effort. Thus, we propose a mechanism to configure the SSL and its matchers so that only service properties are considered, which are essential for matching in the given market according to a certain broker strategy. Configuration possibilities for the matchers include ordering, adaption, and weighting of matching steps. Correspondingly, accuracy, runtime, and effort can be balanced in an optimal way for this market and the broker strategy.

5   Configuration

In this section, we describe the configuration performed by LM Optimizer. This includes a set of configuration rules presented in Section 5.1 and a configuration procedure presented in Section 5.2.

5.1 Configuration Rules

LM Optimizer uses configuration rules to find an optimal LM Config. Configuration rules contain the knowledge of how certain configuration properties (CPs) influence service matching with SSL and its matchers. Thus, they determine the configuration of the SSL and its matchers for an optimal LM Config.

CPs formalize the properties of a market or the broker's strategy. One benefit of CPs is that the configuration knowledge condensed in the configuration rules is defined over a formal notation, which can be applied to every market. Thereby, we leverage market knowledge using a systematic, repeatable approach. Furthermore, we allow the broker to control the choice of an optimal LM Config by explicitly setting the relevant CPs. For these CPs, the broker describes her target market and her strategy by assigning concrete values to them.

Configuration rules are grouped in five types: (1) *Selection of specification aspects* – serves to select specification aspects needed in an optimal LM Config. (2) *Selection of language constructs* – helps to select language constructs needed within individual aspects. These two rule types are applied for configuring the SSL. (3) *Configuration of matching process* – are applied to determine an optimal order of matchers based on matcher dependencies and their runtime. (4) *Configuration of matcher properties* – sets certain matcher properties, e.g., a concrete algorithm of a matcher suitable for the current configuration. (5) *Configuration of aggregation of matching results* – puts the focus at certain matching steps, which are weighted higher during the aggregation in the final matching result.

Table 1 shows some example configuration properties and rules. For an extended list of rules as well as a complete overview of all configuration possibilities, refer to our technical report [2].

In order to understand the rationales of the example rules, let us consider the CP Standardization. A CP serves as a basis for the rules and has a range defined as a set of values, which can be assigned to that CP. The CP has the range of true for standardized terminology and processes, terminology_only for a standardized terminology, processes_only for standardized processes, and false for no standard for both. Well-established terminology can replace behavioral specifications of single operations because the semantics of the used names is commonly understandable. If the processes are standardized, matching of the order of operations is not needed as the behavior of equally named services is understood in the same way. Thus, according to Rule 1, Signatures are needed in an optimal LM Config but no Pre- and Postconditions or Protocols.

In Rule 2, the internal behavior of a service should be matched additionally to Signatures. For that, we can use Pre- and Postconditions. Protocols have to be considered as well, in order to match different orders of service operations in the non-standardized processes. Rule 3 is used to select language constructs within the Signatures aspect. Due to the lack of standardization in the market, matching cannot rely on either operation or parameter names. Thus, they should not be considered for matching.

Example rules configuring the matchers are Rule 4 – Rule 6. Rule 4 states to decrease all matching thresholds for a market with a small size by 0.2 resulting in

Table 1. Example configuration rules

Rule no.	Rule type	Rule definition
Rule 1	Selection of specification aspects	Standardization = true → select Signatures
Rule 2	Selection of specification aspects	Standardization = false → select Signatures & Pre-/Postconditions & Protocols
Rule 3	Selection of language constructs	Standardization = false → do not consider Operation and parameter names in Signatures
Rule 4	Configuration of matching process	Market size = small → configure: decrease all thresholds by 0.2
Rule 5	Configuration of matcher properties	Standardization = true → use string similarity matching
Rule 6	Configuration of aggregation of matching results	Privacy important = true → configure privacy weight: multiply with 2

more services returned. Since in a small market, the probability of a perfect match is rather low, we can receive more matching results by decreasing the thresholds. In the matching process, matchers with a higher threshold are moved to the beginning because after their execution fewer services have to be matched. Thus, this decreases the runtime of the matching process. Rule 5 sets the matching algorithm to string similarity matching if the market has standardized terminology and processes. This allows sparing the runtime because names in the standardized market are reliable for matching. Rule 6 configures the aggregation of matching results by increasing the weight of the privacy matching result by the multiplicity of 2 if privacy is important for the broker in this market.

We rely on the knowledge of a broker to assign reasonable range values to her CPs. As future work, we plan to introduce measurable metrics for market properties, which will allow setting the range values at least semi-automatically.

5.2   Configuration Procedure

In this section, we present the part of LM Optimizer responsible for the configuration of the SSL and its matchers. It applies the configuration rules to a set of CPs assigned with concrete values given as input by the broker.

The configuration procedure configures the SSL by building a view on a subset of its specification aspects. Each aspect is also reduced to a subset of its language constructs. Thus, the whole aspects like Signatures or their language constructs, e.g., parameter names, can be omitted. Matching of an SSL configuration is limited to aspects and constructs defined in this configuration. We show three different example configurations in the technical report [2].

There are two phases in the configuration procedure (their order is important as the configuration of matching steps depends on the preceding selection):

1. Language Configuration: In this phase, the necessary service aspects are selected by applying the rule types *Selection of specification aspects* and *Selection of language constructs* described in Section 5.1.

2. Matcher Configuration: In this phase, for each selected language aspect, a corresponding matcher is added as a matching step in the matching process. The matching process is configured by ordering the matching steps. Then, the matching algorithms and the aggregation of results are configured.

LM Optimizer is a fully automated approach as a manual approach cannot cope with the high theoretical complexity of the configuration procedure. SSL consists of 8 aspects, where each one has 1 to 10 language constructs to configure with the mean number of 4.4 language constructs per aspect. The mean number of configurations per service aspect is 148. Including the possibility to arbitraryly combine these configurations, the number of all possible SSL configurations becomes $3.4 \cdot 10^{10}$. Then, we compute the number of possible matching configurations considering that thresholds and weights can be changed in a certain rate within a given interval. The number of configurations is exponential in this case. Currently, LM Optimizer supports 128 different language configurations and 256 different matching configurations enabling the choice between $1.6 \cdot 10^4$ LM Configs. These numbers are based on the extended list of rules from our technical report [2] also containing an evaluation of our approach.

6 Related Work

In the following, we briefly discuss the approaches mostly related to our work. We also explain why they do not solve the problem we stated in this paper.

Two comprehensive service specification approaches established in academia are the Unified Specification of Components (UnSCoM) framework [9] and the Unified Service Description Language (USDL) [3]. These two aim at comprehensive description and matching of a variety of existing service aspects and language constructs for them. In comparison to our approach, the authors of these two approaches do not provide any configuration possibilities either of the languages or of the corresponding matchers. Furthermore, neither the languages nor the matchers are optimized for any market characteristics or broker strategies.

Di Ruscio et al. propose a framework called BYADL to create a customized architectural description language (ADL) by tailoring it, e.g., for domain specifics or operations like analysis or visualization [6]. The authors tailor an ADL by extending it with another language. In comparison, we configure the SSL by view building. In addition, we also configure the operation of matching.

Furthermore, there are some configurable service matchers [12]. However, their configuration possibilities are limited to different signature matching strategies and not selected automatically. Similarly, there are matchers that configure their aggregation strategies (but no other features) automatically [8]. Furthermore, their configuration only influences the matcher but never the specification language, and thereby the considered language constructs, as in our approach.

7 Conclusions

In this paper, we presented a fully automated approach LM Optimizer that supports service brokers to create a language-matcher configuration that is optimal for a given service market as well as a broker's strategy. Using this configuration, a broker can distinguish herself from other brokers competing for customers of their service discovery commissions. Thereby, LM Optimizer supports brokers to be most successful. Three different case studies showed that LM Optimizer returned configurations with a high quality.

In the future, we want to extend our approach by extending the configuration rules and the configuration procedure in order to integrate more rules that are sophisticated. Furthermore, we want to apply our approach to other activities of a service broker in addition to service matching. For example, we expect tools for service certification or quality prediction to be configurable in similar ways.

Another field of future work is to adapt a broker's language matcher configuration already in use. Since service markets are changing rapidly [10], a broker needs to adapt the used matching approaches continuously. For that, the broker can use our approach to configure the most suitable language and the matcher for the current changed marker characteristics or the changed strategy. This allows the broker to remain competitive by being flexible to its changing characteristics.

References

1. Alonso, G., Casati, F., Kuno, H., Machiraju, V.: Web Services: Concepts, Architectures and Applications, 1st edn. Springer (2010)
2. Arifulina, S., Platenius, M.C., Gerth, C., Becker, S., Engels, G., Schäfer, W.: Configuration of Specification Language and Matching for Services in On-The-Fly Computing. Tech. Rep. tr-ri-14-342, Heinz Nixdorf Institute (2014)
3. Barros, A., Oberle, D. (eds.): Handbook of Service Description: USDL and Its Methods. Springer, New York (2012)
4. Benatallah, B., Hacid, M.S., Leger, A., Rey, C., Toumani, F.: On automating web services discovery. The VLDB Journal 14(1), 84–96 (2005)
5. Caillaud, B., Jullien, B.: Chicken & Egg: Competition among Intermediation Service Providers. The RAND Journal of Economics 34(2), 309–328 (2003), http://www.jstor.org/stable/1593720
6. Di Ruscio, D., Malavolta, I., Muccini, H., Pelliccione, P., Pierantonio, A.: Developing next generation adls through mde techniques. In: Proceedings of the ICSE 2010, USA, vol. 1, pp. 85–94 (2010)
7. Kappel, G., Langer, P., Retschitzegger, W., Schwinger, W., Wimmer, M.: Model Transformation By-Example: A Survey of the First Wave. In: Düsterhöft, A., Klettke, M., Schewe, K.-D. (eds.) Conceptual Modelling and Its Theoretical Foundations. LNCS, vol. 7260, pp. 197–215. Springer, Heidelberg (2012)
8. Klusch, M., Kapahnke, P.: The iSeM Matchmaker: A Flexible Approach for Adaptive Hybrid Semantic Service Selection. Web Semantics: Science, Services and Agents on the World Wide Web 15(3) (2012)
9. Overhage, S.: UnSCom: A Standardized Framework for the Specification of Software Components. In: Weske, M., Liggesmeyer, P. (eds.) NODe 2004. LNCS, vol. 3263, pp. 169–184. Springer, Heidelberg (2004)
10. Papazoglou, M.P., Traverso, P., Dustdar, S., Leymann, F.: Service-Oriented Computing: A Research Roadmap. International Journal of Cooperative Information Systems 17(2), 223–255 (2008)
11. Schlauderer, S., Overhage, S.: How perfect are markets for software services? an economic perspective on market deficiencies and desirable market features. In: Tuunainen, V.K., Rossi, M., Nandhakumar, J. (eds.) ECIS (2011)
12. Wei, D., Wang, T., Wang, J., Bernstein, A.: Sawsdl-imatcher: A customizable and effective semantic web service matchmaker. Web Semantics: Science, Services and Agents on the World Wide Web 9(4), 402–417 (2011)

Designing Secure Service Workflows in BPEL

Luca Pino, Khaled Mahbub, and George Spanoudakis

Department of Computer Science, City University London, London, United Kingdom
{Luca.Pino.2,K.Mahbub,G.E.Spanoudakis}@city.ac.uk

Abstract. This paper presents an approach that we have developed to support
the design of secure service based applications in BPEL. The approach is based
on the use of secure service composition patterns, which are proven to preserve
composition level security properties if the services that are composed according to the pattern satisfy other properties individually. The secure service composition patterns are used for two purposes: (a) to analyse whether a given
workflow fragment satisfies a given security property, and (b) to generate compositions of services that could substitute for individual services within the
workflow that cause the violation of the security properties. Our approach has
been implemented in a tool that is based on Eclipse BPEL Designer.

1 Introduction

An important concern in the development of a service-based application (SBA) is the
ability to assure that the application will have certain security properties. Assuring
security is important for any application but acutely so in the case of SBAs. Such
applications, in fact, are based on services which might not be under the control of the
SBA provider and can compromise critical security properties (e.g., the integrity and
confidentiality of data passed to, stored or produced, or the availability).

An increasingly accepted view on how to best assure security is that security properties should be achieved by design rather than be dealt with as an aftermath concern.
Despite being increasingly adopted in the design of normal software applications
security-by-design is not so well supported in the case of SBAs. SBA design is typically iterative focusing on the development of an orchestration model to coordinate
the services that will constitute the SBA [3]. During it, it is necessary to discover
services that can fit with the orchestration model that is being designed or, where this
is not possible, to change the orchestration model in a systematic manner in order to
make it fit with the available services whilst preserving required properties.

Existing approaches are effective in discovering individual services (e.g., [1,2,3])
and service compositions that have functionality and quality properties that are compatible with SBA designs (e.g., [4,5,6]). However, they do not support effectively the
discovery of individual services and service compositions with required security
properties, and the validation of the overall security of a service orchestration process
when the discovered individual services are composed into it. This paper presents an
approach that we have developed to address this problem.

X. Franch et al. (Eds.): ICSOC 2014, LNCS 8831, pp. 551–559, 2014.

Our approach supports the design of secure SBAs. It is based on the use of *Secure Service Composition patterns* (SSC patterns), which are proven to preserve certain composition level security properties if the services that are composed according to the pattern satisfy other properties individually. SSC patterns are used for two purposes: (a) to analyse whether a given workflow fragment satisfies a given security property, and (b) to generate service compositions that could substitute for individual services within a workflow that cause the violation of the security properties required of it. Our approach supports also the replacement of individual services, which violate given security properties, by other individual services or compositions that are discovered based on properties identified by the patterns. The satisfaction of security properties at the service level is determined by digital service security certificates. We implemented our approach in a tool that extends Eclipse *BPEL Designer* [7].

The paper is structured as follows. Section 2 presents scenarios of secure SBA process design. Section 3 introduces the SSC patterns. Section 4 presents the validation and adaptation supported by the SSC patterns. Finally, Section 5 reviews related work and Section 6 summarizes our approach and outlines directions for future work.

2   Scenarios for Secure Workflow Design

To exemplify our approach, assume an SBA, called *StockBroker* allowing stock investors to buy and/or sell stocks in different stock exchanges. Upon receiving a request from an investor, *StockBroker* retrieves the investor's portfolio of stocks, and fetches the trading values of a selected stock and index of the relevant stock market (e.g. NASDAQ, Dow Jones). It then matches these values with the preferences of the investor and contacts different services to carry out the trade and to pay for it.

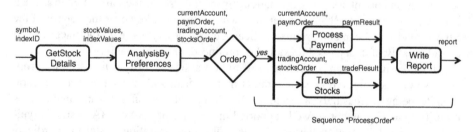

Fig. 1. The *StockBroker* BPEL workflow

Fig. 1 shows the workflow that realises *StockBroker*. This workflow receives a stock symbol and a stock market index ID; invokes a stock information service (cf. activity *GetStockDetails*) to get the details for the given stock in the particular market; matches these details with preferences (cf. activity *AnalysisByPreferences*); and, if a trade order is to be placed, it invokes in parallel the payment service (cf. activity *ProcessPayment*) and the trading service (cf. activity *TradeStocks*)[1]. Finally, a report of all results is produced by the reporting service (cf. activity *WriteReport*).

---

[1] Carrying trading in parallel with payment is possible as clearing of payment transactions can be completed after the trade transaction has taken place.

In designing secure service workflows, we have identified two scenarios. In the first scenario (Scenario 1), an SBA designer wants to verify if an external service operation, used in the workflow through an *invoke* activity, satisfies a required security property. In this scenario, if the service that is currently bound to the activity does not satisfy the property, support is offered to discover alternative services that would satisfy the required property and, if no such individual services can be found, to explore if it is possible to build a composition of other services that satisfies the security property and could, therefore, be used as a substitute for the original service. An example of a composition is shown in Fig. 2. The composition *ParallelStockDetails* shown calls two service operations in parallel, namely *GetStockValues* and *GetStockMarketIndex*.*GetStockValues* returns the trading value for a stock, identified by its symbol, and *GetStockMarketIndex* returns the value of a stock market index.

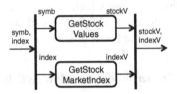

Fig. 2. Service composition *ParallelStockDetails* to be substituted for *GetStockDetails*

The second scenario arises in cases where the SBA designer wishes to verify that a part of a workflow (as opposed to an individual activity of it) satisfies a given security property. Workflow fragments are identified (delimited) by a control flow activity. In the *Stock Broker* workflow, for instance, a designer might wish to verify whether the sub sequence of activities designated as *ProcessOrder* in Fig. 1 preserves the confidentiality of the personal current account information of *Stock Investor*.

3   Secure Service Composition Patterns

SSC patterns are used to specify how security properties of whole abstract workflows (i.e., composition level security properties) can be guaranteed via security properties of the individual services used in the workflow. The causal relation between workflow and activity level properties specified in such patterns is formally proven.

An SSC pattern is composed of: (a) an abstract workflow structure (*Pattern.WF*), called *workflow specification*, that indicates how services are to be composed and the data flows between them; (b) the composition level *security property* that the pattern guarantees (*Pattern.CSP*); and (c) the *security properties* required of the *partner services* that may be bound to the workflow specification (i.e., to the abstract *invoke* activities of the workflow) to guarantee the security property specified in (b) (*Pattern.ASP*). SSC patterns are expressed as rules of the production system Drools [9], to enable their application for workflow security validation and adaptation.

In the following, we present an example of an SSC pattern that we have encoded specifying the effect of composition on the security property of *separability*. Separability is a security property introduced in [20] and has been defined as complete independence between high (confidential) and low level (public) sequences of actions. For this property to hold there should be no interaction between confidential and public sequences of actions (e.g., running these actions as two separate processes without any communication between them). The composition of separability, proven in [20,21], is used for specification of the SSC pattern in Drools as given in Sect. 4.1.

4   Application of SSC Patterns

SSC patterns are used to infer the security properties that the individual services should have for the workflow to have another security property as a whole. This allows to: (a) analyse whether a given workflow (or a fragment of it) satisfies a given security property (security validation); and (b) generate compositions of services that could substitute for individual services, which prevent the satisfaction of the security properties required (security driven workflow adaptation). In the following, we present the approaches that enable these forms of applications.

4.1   Inferring Security Properties of Workflow Activities

SSC patterns are used to infer the security properties, which have to be satisfied by the individual activities (services) of a composition, for the whole composition to satisfy a given security property. In general, there can be zero, one or several alternative combinations of activity level properties, called *security solutions*, that can guarantee the security property required of the composition. The algorithm that applies SSC patterns for this purpose is given in Table 1.

Table 1. Algorithm to infer security properties for activities within a composition

Algorithm: INFERSECPROPERTY(WF, RSP, InSolutions): OutSolutions
Inputs: *WF* – /* workflow specification of a service composition process */
RSP – /* security property requested for WF */
InSolutions – /* list of security solutions used for recursion. Base case: {RSP} */
Output: *OutSolutions* – /* list of security solutions for the activities in WF */
For each pattern *Patt* such that *Patt.CSP* matches RSP **do**
If *Patt.WF* /* i.e. the workflow specification of Patt */ matches *WF* **then**
For each element *E* /* i.e. individual activity or a sub-workflow */ of *WF* **do**
Properties[E] := security properties for *WF.E* identified by *Patt.ASP*
For each security solution *S* in *InSolutions* **do**
S' := replace *RSP* by *Properties* in *S*
SolutionList$_{Patt}$:= ADD(*SolutionList$_{Patt}$, S'*)
For each element *E* in *WF* that is a sub-workflow specification **do**
SolutionList$_{Patt}$:= INFERSECPROPERTY(*E, Properties[E], SolutionList$_{Patt}$*)
OutSolutions := ADDALL(*OutSolutions, SolutionList$_{Patt}$*)
Endif
Return *OutSolutions*

As shown in the table, given an input service workflow WF and a required security property RSP, the algorithm (INFERSECPROPERTIES) tries to apply all the SSC patterns that would be able to guarantee the requested security property RSP. A pattern is applied if the workflow specification of the pattern (*Pattern.WF*) matches with WF.

If a pattern matches the workflow, then the security solutions computed up to that point are updated to replace the requested security property RSP with the security properties for the matched elements in WF (these can be individual activities or sub-workflows). If a matched element E of WF is an atomic activity, the process ends w.r.t it. If E is a sub-workflow, the algorithm is applied recursively for it.

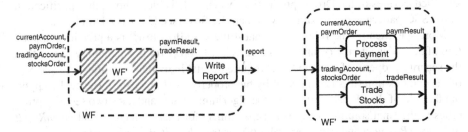

Fig. 3. The workflow patterns of sequence *ProcessOrder*

As an example of applying INFERSECPROPERTIES consider the case where an SBA designer wishes to verify that the subprocess *ProcessOrder (PO)* within the *Stock-Broker* process of Fig. 1 preserves the confidentiality of the Stock Investor current account. This security property can be expressed as *separability*, with *currentAccount* being confidential. *ProcessOrder* can be seen as a sequential workflow consisting of a sub-workflow WF' and the atomic activity *WriteReport* that follows it (see Fig. 3). WF' itself is a parallel workflow involving two atomic activities: *ProcessPayment* and *TradeStocks*.

Table 2. Specification of a pattern in Drools

```
rule "Separability on Parallel Workflow"
  when
    $wf : Parallel( $A1 : act1, $A2 : act2 )
    $csp : Property( propertyName == "Separability", subject == $wf, $cspAttr : attributes )
    $solution : Solution( properties contains $csp )
  then
    Solution newSolution = (new Solution($solution).removeProperty($csp);

    Property asp1 = new Property ($csp, "Separability", $A1);
    asp1.getAttributes().put("public", new Subset($cspAttr.get("public")));
    asp1.getAttributes ().put("confidential", new Subset(new Complement($cspAttr.get("public"))));
    newSolution.getProperties().add(asp1);
    insert(asp1);
    Property asp2 = new Property ($csp, "Separability", $A2);
    asp2.getAttributes().put("public", new Subset($cspAttr.get("public")));
    asp2.getAttributes ().put("confidential", new Subset(new Complement($cspAttr.get("public"))));
    newSolution.getProperties().add(asp2);
    insert(asp2);

    insert(newSolution);
  end
```

Hence, when INFERSECPROPERTIES is applied on to it, in the first iteration an SSC pattern for the sequential flow can be applied on WF, returning two security properties: one for WF' requiring confidentiality for *currentAccount*, *paymResult* and *tradeResult*, and another for *WriteReport*, requiring confidentiality for *paymResult* and *tradeResult*. The second iteration of the algorithm applies another SSC pattern, but for the parallel flow, to WF'. In particular INFERSECPROPERTIES applies SSC patterns specified as rules of the Drools production system [9]. Table 2 shows the specification of the SSC pattern about separability on parallel flow (see [21]) as a Drools rule.

More specifically, the rule defines that if the workflow (wf) is a parallel composition of activities and the composition level security property is separability ($scsp$) then the security property of separability is required of the individual activities $A1$ and $A2$ of the composition (this is expressed by the property *asp1* and *asp2*). Hence, by applying the rule of the SP pattern to WF', the algorithm creates and adds two security properties to the final solution, i.e., *asp1* (separability) for *currentAccount* and *paymResult* of *ProcessPayment* and *asp2* (separability) for *tradeResult* of *TradeStocks*.

4.2   Validation of Security of Individual Services and Workflow Fragments

In order to validate whether a security property is satisfied by a fragment of a workflow, we assume that a fragment consists of a BPEL *scope* or a control flow (i.e., *sequence, flow, if-then-else* or *pick*) activity that can contain multiple service invocations (in the form of *invoke* activities) and further control flow activities.

Given a request to verify whether a workflow fragment (WF) satisfies a required security property (RSP), the algorithm INFERSECPROPERTY is applied to identify the list of alternative security solutions (i.e., combinations of security properties of the individual services in the fragment) that would guarantee RSP. As explained earlier INFERSECPROPERTY tries to apply different SSC patterns in order to identify these alternative solutions. If such solutions exist, each of them is analysed further to check if the security properties required by it are provided by the services in the fragment.

To validate whether an individual service satisfies the security property required of it by a security solution, we express the property as a service discovery query and then use the discovery algorithm described in [8] to match the specification of the individual service with the query and establish if it satisfies the query or not. In applying the service discovery process, we assume the existence of machine-readable security certificates that indicate the security properties that a service S has [8]. If the individual service validation succeeds for all the services of the fragment by even one of the identified security solution, then the fragment is validated. Otherwise, if no security solution can be found, or if none of the found security solution can be satisfied by the services in the fragment, the fragment is reported as not validated.

4.3   Workflow Adaptation

In certain cases, it might be possible to adapt a workflow in order to make it satisfy a required security property. In our approach, this adaptation can take two forms, by: (a) replacing individual services in it by other individual services, or (b) replacing individual services in it by service compositions that are constructed in a way that guarantees the security property required of the service to be replaced. When a workflow fragment is not validated, the SBA designer can compare and select the security solutions for the workflow fragment found by the validation algorithm. This allows to replace the security property over the fragment with security properties over the *invoke* activities within it. Once a specific security solution is selected, the service adaptation mechanism is triggered to adapt the workflow.

4.4   Implementation of the Approach

Our approach has been implemented in a tool called *A-BPEL Designer*. This tool is an extension of *BPEL Designer*, i.e., an Eclipse plugin [7] that offers comprehensive support for the editing and deployment of WS-BPEL processes through Eclipse IDE. In *A-BPEL Designer*, we have extended BPEL by allowing the specification of security properties for *invoke* or *control flow* BPEL. *A-BPEL Designer* offers also support for validating security properties of individual partner services or workflow fragments and adapting BPEL processes to ensure security as described. To offer these functionalities, A-BPEL designer has been integrated with the service discovery engine described in [3] and the service composition tool described in [8].

5   Related Work

Research related to the security of service based applications focuses on making secure an SBA, or verifying its security.

A common approach underpinning research in the former area is to secure SBAs by using additional security services that can enforce the required security properties [12,13,14]. More specifically, an aspect-oriented version of BPEL, called AO4BPEL [12], allows the integration of security specifications in a BPEL process. These specifications are then used to indicate security functionalities that are offered by a special Security Service, and integrate them in the AO4BPEL process.

Sectet [13] is a framework for the implementation of security patterns from design to the implementation of an orchestration. Sectet enables the design of orchestrations as UML message flow diagrams, which are converted into workflows and used to generate stubs for actual orchestrations. In orchestrations, services are wrapped by Policy Enforcement Points, whose purpose is to provide the required security properties.

PWSSec [14] describes a set of complementary stages to be added to the SBAs development phases in order to support security. In particular the WSSecArch is a design phase that takes care of the indications about which security requirements are achieved and where they are in the architecture. The approach makes usage of security architectural patterns to convert the security requirements into architecture specifications, with external security services providing the security functionalities.

Unlike the above approaches, our approach does not use special types of security components or services but supports the discovery of normal services and service compositions that themselves have the security properties required of an SBA.

Attention has been given also to the model based verification of security properties during the design of orchestrations [15,16,17]. These works usually require a UML specification of the system, the security threats associated with it and the description of required properties in order to verify the satisfiability of the latter. Our approach does not require the specification of threats. Furthermore, it does not perform exhaustive verification since its analysis is driven by specific SSC patterns. This is important as it makes security analysis more scalable at the expense of loss of completeness.

Some model based approaches [18,19] support also the transformation of from security requirements into security policies and architectures. This usually happens in an early design phase that must be followed by a subsequent phase where details about the implementation have to be worked out. Our approach offers the possibility to add and address security properties during the workflow design phase, without requiring designer to have a security background.

The METEOR-S project [10] allows annotation of abstract BPEL process to specify semantic-aware QoS properties, including security. The annotations are then used to discover appropriate services for the BPEL process, using an annotated registry. The Sec-MoSC (Security for Model-oriented Service Composition) tool [11] is an extension of the Eclipse BPMN Modeller that allows to design BPMN business processes and to add security properties to them. These two approaches focus only on the validation single service of security properties, while our approach allows the validation of workflow fragments and the substitution of services with service compositions.

6   Conclusion

In this paper we have presented an approach supporting the validation of security properties of BPEL workflows and the security based adaptation of such workflows during their design. A-BPEL Designer implements this approach in the Eclipse platform through the usage of a service discovery engine.

Our approach is based on Secure Service Composition (SSC) patterns, which encode formally proven causal relations between individual service level security properties and composition level security properties. The validation of workflow security is based on identifying (through the SSC patterns) the security properties that the individual partner services need to have for the workflow to have composition level properties. The identified service level properties are used to check if existing partner services satisfy them, discover alternative services for them in case they do not, and discover service compositions satisfying the services if necessary. Our approach supports also the automatic replacement of security non-compliant services.

Our current implementation supports workflows with sequential, parallel and choice control activities (i.e., BPEL *sequence*, *flow*, *if-then-else* and *pick* activities), and the replacement of individual service invocations. Hence, in its current form, its application is restricted to non-transactional and stateless services.

Our on-going work focuses on supporting transactional services. We are also conducting performance and scalability tests, in order to compare our results with competing approaches (especially approaches based on full verification of security).

Acknowledgment . The work presented in this paper has been partially funded by the EU F7 project ASSERT4SOA (grant no.257351).

References

1. Pawar, P., Tokmakoff, A.: Ontology-Based Context-Aware Service Discovery for Pervasive Environments. In: 1st IEEE International Workshop on Services Integration in Pervasive Environments (SIPE 2006), in conjunction with IEEE ICPS 2006 (2006)
2. Mikhaiel, R., Stroulia, E.: Examining usage protocols for service discovery. In: Dan, A., Lamersdorf, W. (eds.) ICSOC 2006. LNCS, vol. 4294, pp. 496–502. Springer, Heidelberg (2006)
3. Spanoudakis, G., Zisman, A.: Discovering Services During Service Based Systems Design Using UML. IEEE Trans. on Software Eng. 36(3), 371–389 (2010)
4. Fujii, K., Suda, T.: Semantics-Based Dynamic Web Service Composition. IEEE Journal on Selected Areas in Communications 23(12), 2361–2372 (2005)
5. Silva, E., Pires, L.F., van Sinderen, M.: On the Support of Dynamic Service Composition at Runtime. In: Dan, A., Gittler, F., Toumani, F. (eds.) ICSOC/ServiceWave 2009. LNCS, vol. 6275, pp. 530–539. Springer, Heidelberg (2010)
6. Pino, L., Spanoudakis, G.: Constructing Secure Service Compositions with Patterns. In: IEEE SERVICES 2012, pp. 184–191. IEEE Press (2012)
7. BPEL Designer Project, http://www.eclipse.org/bpel/
8. ASSERT4SOA Consortium: ASSERTs Aware Service Based Systems Adaptation. ASSERT4SOA Project, Deliverable D2.3 (2012)
9. Drools – Jboss Community, http://drools.jboss.org
10. Aggarwal, R., Verma, K., et al.: Constraint Driven Web Service Composition in METEOR-S. In: IEEE SCC 2004, pp. 23–30. IEEE Press (2004)
11. Souza, A.R.R., et al.: Incorporating Security Requirements into Service Composition: From Modelling to Execution. In: Baresi, L., Chi, C.-H., Suzuki, J. (eds.) ICSOC-ServiceWave 2009. LNCS, vol. 5900, pp. 373–388. Springer, Heidelberg (2009)
12. Charfi, A., Mezini, M.: Using aspects for security engineering of web service compositions. In: IEEE ICWS 2005, pp. 59–66. IEEE Press (2005)
13. Hafner, M., Breu, R., et al.: Sectet: An extensible framework for the realization of secure inter-organizational workflows. Internet Research 16(5), 491–506 (2006)
14. Gutiérrez, C., Fernández-Medina, E., Piattini, M.: Towards a process for web services security. J. of Research and Practice in Information Technology 38(1), 57–68 (2006)
15. Bartoletti, M., Degano, P., et al.: Semantics-based design for secure web services. IEEE Trans. on Software Eng. 34(1), 33–49 (2008)
16. Deubler, M., Grünbauer, J., Jürjens, J., Wimmel, G.: Sound development of secure service-based systems. In: ICSOC 2004, pp. 115–124. ACM, New York (2004)
17. Georg, G., Anastasakis, K., et al.: Verification and trade-off analysis of security properties in UML system models. IEEE Trans. on Software Eng. 36(3), 338–356 (2010)
18. Menzel, M., Warschofsky, R., Meinel, C.: A pattern-driven generation of security policies for service-oriented architectures. In: IEEE ICWS 2010, pp. 243–250. IEEE Press (2010)
19. Séguran, M., Hébert, C., Frankova, G.: Secure workflow development from early requirements analysis. In: IEEE ECOWS 2008, pp. 125–134. IEEE Press (2008)
20. McLean, J.: A general theory of composition for trace sets closed under selective interleaving functions. In: 1994 IEEE Symp. on Sec. and Privacy, pp. 79–93. IEEE CS Press (1994)
21. Mantel, H.: On the composition of secure systems. In: 2002 IEEE Symp. on Sec. and Privacy, pp. 88–101. IEEE CS Press (2002)

Runtime Management of Multi-level SLAs
for Transport and Logistics Services

Clarissa Cassales Marquezan[1], Andreas Metzger[1], Rod Franklin[2], and Klaus Pohl[1]

[1] paluno (The Ruhr Institute for Software Technology)
University of Duisburg-Essen, Essen, Germany
{clarissa.marquezan,andreas.metzger,klaus.pohl}@paluno.uni-due.de
[2] Kühne Logistics University, Hamburg, Germany and
Kühne + Nagel Management AG, Schindellegi, Switzerland
rod.franklin@the-klu.org

Abstract. SLA management of non-computational services, such as transport and logistics services, may differ from SLA management of computational services, such as cloud or web services. As an important difference, SLA management for transport and logistics services has to consider so called frame SLAs. A frame SLA is a general agreement that constitutes a long-term contract between parties. The terms and conditions of the frame SLA become the governing terms and conditions for all specific SLAs established under such a frame SLA. Not considering the relationships between frame SLAs, specific SLAs and QoS monitoring information may lead to partial conclusions and decisions, thereby resulting in avoidable penalties. Based on a real industry case in the transport and logistics domain, this paper elaborates on a multi-level run-time SLA management approach for non-computational services that takes into account those relationships. We describe a cloud-based software component, the BizSLAM App, able to automatically manage multi-level SLAs by extending SLA management solutions from service-oriented computing. We demonstrate the feasibility and usefulness of the SLA management approach in an industrial context.

1 Introduction

Managing Service Level Agreements (SLAs) is an essential task for all kinds of services, be they computational (e.g., cloud services or web services) or non-computational (such as transport and logistics, manufacturing, energy, or agriculture services). The major goals of SLA management are to monitor, check, and ensure that the expected QoS attributes are met during service execution. Expected QoS attributes are expressed in terms of Service Level Objectives (SLOs) that are part of SLAs. In the computational domain, SLA management has been extensively researched. A diversity of languages and tools have been developed [24,2,15,16,19].

SLA management for transport and logistics services is just beginning to be investigated [12]. This especially holds true for automating SLA management, which is fostered by the increasing digitization of SLAs of transport and logistics services together with the need to share SLA information among the participants in a business process. The transport and logistics domain thus significantly would benefit from the techniques

X. Franch et al. (Eds.): ICSOC 2014, LNCS 8831, pp. 560–574, 2014.

and methods developed by the services community for computational services. This paper investigates opportunities for extending techniques developed for computational services to non-computational services in the transport and logistics domain by starting from an understanding of industry requirements and their potential for automation.

Traditionally, managing computational SLAs involves handling two levels of information: (1) QoS monitoring data collected during service execution used, for instance, to check whether the service-level objectives are met; and (2) the actual SLAs that specify expected and agreed to service-level objectives.

SLA management for transport and logistics requires an additional level of information: (3) terms and conditions of so-called *frame* SLAs. A frame SLA is a general agreement that constitutes a long-term agreement (e.g., one year) between parties that have decided to work together. During this period of time, each request for service execution creates a specific SLA (which is equivalent to the SLA at level (2) for computational services). The terms and conditions of the frame SLA become the governing terms and conditions for all specific SLAs established under the frame SLA. In contrast to computational services, the frame SLA is the actual legally binding document between the two partners. The advantage of frame SLAs is that they simplify the execution of services that will be delivered in a repeated manner over an extended time frame. These services can all be executed under the same agreement without having to renegotiate SLAs and SLOs for each service execution.

To automate the SLA management process for transport and logistics services executed under frame agreements requires dedicated solutions capable of handling these three levels of information at run-time in an automated fashion. It is important to consider the multi-level relationships between frame SLA, specific SLA, and actual QoS measurements. Otherwise, SLA management may lead to wrong conclusions and decisions that service levels have or have not been met, resulting in inapplicable and avoidable penalties. Section 2 elaborates on these problems using industry data, thereby motivating the industry needs for such automated solutions.

In our previous work [12], we presented an analyzer component for runtime SLA management of transport and logistics services, providing a computational solution for automatic SLA checking at run-time. In this paper, we integrate this analyzer component into the *BizSLAM* App, which is developed on top of FIspace.eu, a cloud-based business collaboration platform [23]. To this end, we (*i*) define an extensive data model for transport and logistics services and (*ii*) implement dedicated user interfaces for managing SLAs. Section 3 introduces the conceptual foundations and features of app as well as the data model used to express and relate the multiple levels of SLA information. It also describes how our SLA management approach advances the state of the art.

Section 4 discusses feasibility and usefulness of our SLA management approach, applying the BizSLAM App prototype to a specific scenario in SLA management.

2   Problem Statement and Industry Needs

Transport and logistics services can account for between 10% to 20% of a country's Gross Domestic Product, and CO_2 emissions from transport activities amount to 14% of total greenhouse gas emissions. Therefore, an improvement in how efficiently these services are provided can dramatically increase competitiveness and sustainability. Evidence suggests that improved management of transport processes through advanced IT could yield efficiency gains in the range from 10% to 15% [1]. Many opportunities for employing IT to optimize and improve transport and logistics processes can be listed, such as better business collaboration support [23], real-time information handling, better transport and logistics planning tools, predictive process management [17], and enhanced SLA management solutions [9].

In this paper, we focus on enhanced SLA management. More specifically, we look at transport and logistics service level agreements (or SLAs) and their management during the execution of transport and logistics processes. Illustrated by concrete examples from an industry dataset (available from http://www.s-cube-network.eu/c2k), we elaborate on the current situation in industry and the key business requirements for enhanced IT solutions for SLA management in this domain. The industry dataset is based on Cargo 2000 logs covering five months of business operations. Cargo 2000 is a standard established by IATA, the International Air Transport Association, enabling the cross-organizational monitoring of transport processes.

Figure 1 shows the relationship between the actual and planned units of cargo associated with the transportation processes covered by this dataset. The "planned" axis denotes the number of units the logistics service client booked and thus constitutes the number of units that the logistics service provider was expecting to receive from the client. This booked value thus forms part of an SLA between the logistics service client and the logistics service provider. The "actual" axis indicates the effective cargo units received by the logistics service provider at the beginning of the air transport service.

From the perspective of the logistics service provider, all the circles off the diagonal line in Figure 1 would theoretically indicate SLA violations since the actual amount delivered by the customer does not comply with what has been booked. However, the aforementioned information is not sufficient to determine whether an actual SLA

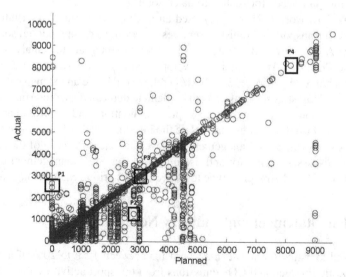

Fig. 1. Planned vs. actual weight of cargo for real-world transport processes (adapted from [8])

violation happened for the transport and logistics service. As discussed in Section 1, the relationships of the three levels of information must be considered, i.e., how the actual measured QoS value, the planned value of the specific SLA, and the frame SLA are related. For instance, assume that the points highlighted by the boxes in Figure 1 are associated with the same frame SLA. Also, assume that this frame SLA establishes that a logistics service client may ship up to 25 containers, each with up to 3000 units of cargo, within the time span of one year. This means that whenever the logistic service client delivers a container with up to 3000 units to be transported, this delivery complies with the frame SLA and the cargo should be transported for the fixed price established under the frame SLA (provided that the number of containers delivered previously does not exceed the established limit of 25). Above this threshold, the fixed price might not apply and may thus require re-negotiating the SLAs.

The boxes P1, P2, P3, and P4 in Figure 1 show the actual amount delivered by the logistics service client (axis Y) versus the planned and reserved amount of cargo to be transported by the logistics service provider (axis X). An analysis of these points without factoring in the frame SLA would indicate that points P3 (3000, 3000) and P4 (8000, 8000) do not constitute SLA violations, while P1 (0, 2900) and P2 (2900, 1200) constitute SLA violations. In this case, penalties should be applied for the service execution of points P1 and P2. Now, taking into account the frame SLA, we actually reach a different conclusion: We find that points P1, P2, and P3 do not constitute violations since the respective amount of cargo in these service executions is under, or equal to, the amount established in the frame SLA (i.e., 3000 units of cargo). In contrast, the service execution represented by point P4 does constitute a violation of the frame SLA.

Currently, industry follows a manual process to check whether the SLOs of the specific agreements (i.e., each individual service execution) conform with the SLOs of the related frame agreement. The numbers provided by a large company from the transport and logistics domain show that in a given month up to 100,000 transports may have to be handled by the logistics service provider [17]. Each of these transports may be associated with a specific agreement, meaning that the number of specific agreements to be checked by a large transport and logistics company could reach up to hundreds of thousands of documents per month. This clearly requires automated support.

The situation faced by industry today, and as presented above, is mainly caused by the following limitations: First, frame SLA information is currently not available in real-time to the down-stream individuals in charge of the actual operations of the logistics service providers. Second, there are currently no standards for representing SLAs in the domain in a structured way. Third, as a consequence from the aforementioned limitations, the SLA management in the transport and logistics domain is manually performed in a "post-morten" fashion (i.e., long after the execution of the service). The remainder of this paper introduces our solution to address these limitations.

3   The BizSLAM App

This section introduces the BizSLAM App, a protoype implementation of a multi-level SLA management component. We first provide the conceptual foundations for multi-level SLAs (Section 3.1) and then introduce the key features of the BizSLAM App

(Section 3.2). One key element of the solution is an extensive data model that includes the major data types found in SLAs for transport and logistics services (Section 3.3). The section concludes with a discussion of related work (Section 3.4).

3.1 Specifics of Transport and Logistics SLAs

Figure 2 depicts the main concepts of transport and logistics SLAs. Each agreement consists of three fundamental aspects. First, the association among the *Logistics Service Provider* and the *Logistics Service Client* as illustrated at the top of Figure 2. Second, *SLOs* that define the expected quality attributes of a transport and logistics service. Third, a set of *Terms and Conditions* including liability and penalty terms that become applicable once a deviation from the SLOs is identified.

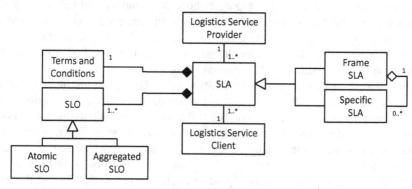

Fig. 2. UML model representing key concepts of Transport and Logistics SLAs

Following from our observations in Section 2, an *SLA* can either be a *Frame SLA* or a *Specific SLA*. Each *Specific SLA* is related to exactly one *Frame SLA*. This also leads to two types of SLOs specified in the domain: An *Atomic SLO* defined in a frame SLA specifies a quality guarantee that has to be met by each of the specific SLAs. In our example from Section 2, the maximum of 3000 cargo units constitutes such an atomic SLO. Each specific SLA established under the related frame SLA may only define a maximum of 3000 cargo units. Another example of an atomic SLO is transit time, defining a maximum time span during which each individual transport must occur. In contrast, an *Aggregated SLO* defined in a frame SLA specifies a quality guarantee in terms of an accumulative value based on the respective SLOs in the specific SLAs. In our example from Section 2, the maximum number of 25 containers per year constitutes such an aggregated SLO. This means that the sum of all containers defined in the specific SLAs may not be more than 25. The two types of SLAs (frame and specific) together with the two types of SLOs (atomic and aggregated) constitute the core for supporting runtime and automated SLA management for transport and logistics services.

3.2 Features of the App

The main purpose of the BizSLAM App is to make SLOs from frame SLAs and specific SLAs available during run-time, thereby fostering conformance and consistency checks.

The BizSLAM App is developed on top of FIspace.eu, a cloud-based business-to-business collaboration platform [23,17]. The app consists of a front-end and back-end. The front-end provides a graphical user interface and is realized as a W3C widget using HTML, CSS and JavaScript. The back-end is implemented in Java and employs the Spring framework to provide REST APIs for connection with the front-end.

The core capabilities of the BizSLAM App are (1) online access to SLA information for all participants while respecting privacy and security requirements (*SLA Operations*), and (2) real-time detection and signaling of SLA violations (*SLA Analytics*).

As part of *SLA Operations*, the BizSLAM App provides support for storing, reading, deleting, updating, and searching for SLA data. The SLA data stored in the BizSLAM App is a subset of the legal contract agreed to by the transport and logistics partners. This subset contains the data (specifically SLOs) to drive the daily activities of transport and logistics service execution. It is out of the scope of the BizSLAM App to engage in the actual contracting negotiation and agreement. Instead, the focus lies on making the agreed SLOs available to participants during runtime. The relevant SLA data is stored in the form of Linked-USDL documents. To this end, the BizSLAM App employs an open source, reusable software component[1]. Details of the data model used for storing SLA data are discussed in Section 3.3.

As part of *SLA Analytics*, the BizSLAM App provides services for an automatic analysis of effective as well as potential SLA violations at runtime. Examples include the detection of repetitive violations of the agreed SLOs together with recommendations for changing the terms of the SLA, checking at a very early stage of the transport and logistics service planning process if the SLOs of a specific SLA comply with the SLOs of the frame SLA established between the parties, as well as proactive notification about opportunities to establish or modify SLAs.

One core element of the BizSLAM App is an analyzer component for automated compliance checks of specific SLAs and frame SLAs. The details of the analyzer component have been presented in our previous work [12]. Basically, the analyzer component translates SLAs into a Constraint Satisfaction Problem (CSP), as agreement terms can be naturally expressed as constraints over a service domain.

3.3 SLA Data Model

Currently, there is no "de facto" standard in the transport and logistics domain that is able to represent different types of SLAs and the diversity of SLOs. Therefore, based on experience gathered from interviews and repeated interactions with transport and logistics partners from industry, we defined an extensive data model for SLAs in that domain. As a result, the data model consolidates all information relevant for SLA management of transport and logistics services. Nowadays, such information is scattered across e-mails, spread sheets, and paper documents.

The data model defines all information constituting a transport and logistics SLA, called *Transport and Logistics SLA Vocabulary*. This model allows for the customization of the SLA and SLO types to meet the specific requirements of different sectors and modes of operations in the industry. Primarily, the data model supports the process of

---

[1] http://catalogue.fi-ware.org/enablers/repository-sap-ri

introducing SLA information during the execution of services. The data model thereby provides a common frame for expressing SLAs. Based on such a common frame, contract terms (and their definitions) can be announced by the logistics service provider and agreed on by the logistics service users, thereby ensuring "semantic" equivalence of the SLOs employed in the various SLAs (e.g., see Section 6 in [21]).

The design of our data model builds upon initial data models proposed by the EU e-Freight project [7]. It is implemented in Linked-USDL, which is a version of USDL (the Unified Service Description Language[2]) that builds upon the Linked Data principles and the Web of Data. To this end, we define our *Transport and Logistics SLA Vocabulary* as an RDF vocabulary, which is depicted in Figures 3–6. Concepts in green and purple indicate the extensions we introduced on top of the e-Freight model. Purple concepts represent transport and logistics concepts defined in existing data models. Blue concepts represent existing vocabularies adopted by Linked-USDL, such as GoodRelations[3] and vCard[4]. Due to space limitations we focus the following description on the most important concepts of the data model.

Part A includes the basic concepts for the *Transport and Logistics SLA Vocabulary*. The central concept is *Contract*, which links to all other concepts in the vocabulary (as explained below). *Contract* holds the information about the established SLA like issue date, issue time, validity period, involved parties and so forth. In order to differentiate between frame and specific SLAs, the *ContractType* concept is used. The links between

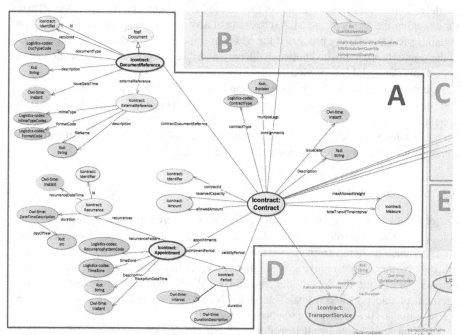

Fig. 3. Data model for Transport and Logistics SLAs represented as RDF graph (Part A)

---

[2] http://linked-usdl.org/
[3] http://www.heppnetz.de/ontologies/goodrelations/v1
[4] http://www.w3.org/Submission/vcard-rdf/

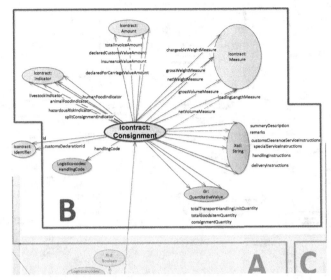

Fig. 4. Data model for Transport and Logistics SLAs represented as RDF graph (Part B)

frame SLA and specific SLAs are realized by means of the *ServicePoint* concept introduced in Part E of the data model.

Part B is designed to enable a very detailed description of the goods that could be transported under the SLA terms. Nonetheless, the attributes and relationships of this section of the SLA are not mandatory and can be used according to the needs of partners establishing the SLA. Examples of concepts that allow for expressing detailed

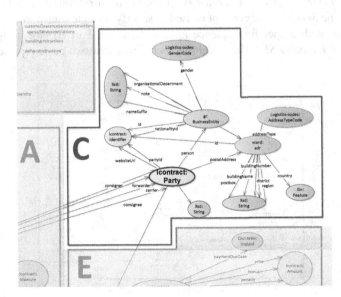

Fig. 5. Data model for Transport and Logistics SLAs represented as RDF graph (Part C)

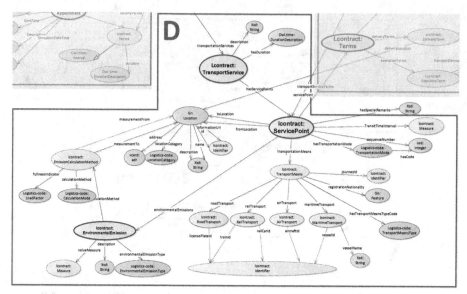

Fig. 6. Data model for Transport and Logistics SLAs represented as RDF graph (Part D)

information of goods include *Measure* (e.g., volume, weight), *Amount* (e.g., amount declared for customs), and *Indicators* (e.g., hazardous).

Part C describes the parties associated with an SLA. The *Party* concept and its associated concept defines the information about the provider and consumer of the agreed contract.

Part D depicts the transportation service agreed among the parties of the SLA. The concepts *Transport Service* and *Service Point* are the most relevant in this part of the vocabulary. The *ServicePoint* concept is used to specify a single transportation service (transport leg) with a specific sequence number (also see Part E). We designed the *Transport and Logistics SLA Vocabulary* in such a way that two basic representations

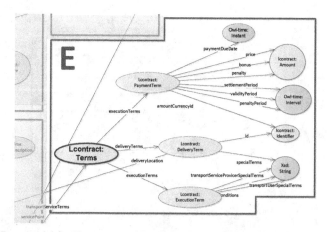

Fig. 7. Data model for Transport and Logistics SLAs represented as RDF graph (Part E)

of transport and logistics SLAs can be chosen depending on the actual situation faced in practice: The first representation uses only one service point to define a transport and logistics SLA. This means that the SLA specifies SLOs for a single transportation leg. The granularity of this leg is irrelevant. For example, the leg could be from Turkey to UK, or from the airport of Amsterdam to the port of Rotterdam. The second representation uses multiple service points, each with individual SLOs. In this case, the vocabulary is able – in a more fine-grained way – to represent SLAs that specify different SLOs for each transportation service. For example, if the SLA specifies that goods from partner P1 should be transported by partner P2 from Turkey to the UK, this may involve two service points with specific SLOs: one for sea transportation from Turkey (i.e., the first leg of transportation service), and a second for road transportation once the goods have arrived in the UK (i.e., the second leg).

Part E associates the terms of the SLA to each *Service Point*. For each of the service points certain terms must be defined. Using the previous data models as a basis, we defined three minimal terms that must be specified for each service point using the contract vocabulary: payment, delivery, and execution. The *ServicePoint* concept can thereby be used to define multi-leg, multi-party, as well as multi-level SLAs.

3.4   Existing Solutions and Related Work

Formalization of contracts and automatic conformance checking of contracts has received considerable interest from a wide variety of research areas since the 1980ies [13]. Work includes approaches for automatic monitoring of formalized contracts [25,13] and for managing multi-party contracts [18]. Recently, contract management has received attention for the management of SLAs associated with web services and service-based applications [22,10,15], as well as cloud services [14,5,20,16]. Approaches that use frameworks such as the ones provided by SLA@SOI [24] and WS-Agreement [19,2] are also available. In summary, all these aforementioned approaches fail to consider frame SLAs and thus the relationships between the three levels of information needed for managing transport and logistics SLAs.

Considering domain-specific approaches for SLA management in transport and logistics many of those efforts rely on Service Oriented Computing principles and techniques, such as the ones presented in [4,27]. They thus also share the aforementioned shortcomings. Complementary efforts have addressed the goal of measuring KPIs among partners in the supply chain. One class of approaches relies on the definition and analysis of contract models for a multi-party collaborative business process, so-called 3PL (3rd Party Logisitcs) or 4PL services [28]. These types of business processes result in a supply chain with collaborative tasks executed by different logistics partners. However, the approach does not provide facilities for runtime SLA management. A different approach developed for transport and logistics services includes a platform based on a service-oriented approach for managing contracts in 4PL businesses [3]. The proposed platform is primarily focused on coordinating business processes among the different partners but not targeted at managing the SLAs among the partners. Finally, different ontology representations of transport and logistics services have been proposed [6,11,26]. They focus on representing services offered by a logistics service provider, match-making for such services and mediation among terms of different information models used by different logistics partners. Yet, they do not focus on representing SLA information once an agreement has been established.

In our previous work [12], we presented a first solution for the run-time management of multi-level transport and logistics services. Specifically, we introduced a computational solution for automatic SLA checking at run-time that employed WS-Agreement to formally represent frame and specific SLAs, and that used CSP solvers to check for inconsistencies. In this paper, we integrate this technical approach into an overall systems perspective and provide evidence for the industrial relevance, applicability and usefulness of such an approach in the transport and logistics domain.

4   Feasibility and Usefulness

This section demonstrates the feasibility of the BizSLAM App (Section 4.1) and discusses the usefulness of applying the App in an industrial context (Section 4.2).

4.1   Feasibility

As described above, the BizSLAM App can be applied to automatically determine inconsistencies in multi-level SLAs during business operations. Figure 3.4 depicts a real-world scenario that shows typical inconsistencies that can be detected. In the given scenario, a logistics service client has established a frame SLA **A** with a logistics service

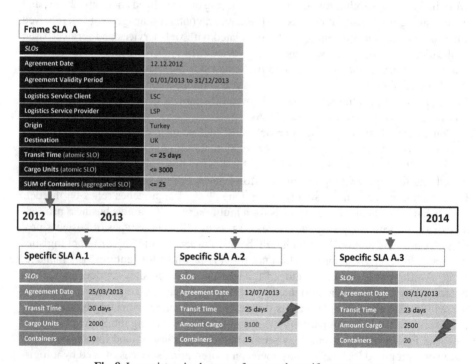

Fig. 8. Inconsistencies between frame and specific agreements

provider. This scenario defines two atomic SLOs as part of the frame SLA: a maximum of 25 days *Transit Time* as well as a maximum of 3000 *Cargo Units*. In addition, the frame SLA defines an aggregated SLO that defines 25 as the *SUM of Containers* to be transported during the validity period of the frame SLA. For each execution of a transport and logistics service under the frame SLA **A**, a specific SLA is created. Figure 3.4 shows three such specific SLAs: **A.1**, **A.2** and **A.3**.

In the scenario depicted in Figure 3.4, two violations occur that are detected by the BizSLAM App as shown in Figure 4.1. The automated conformance check of the BizSLAM App detects these violations immediately, i.e., as soon as they occur, and issues so called pre-violation alerts (the red boxes in Figure 4.1). These alerts inform the logistics service users that if they insist on the chosen SLOs (e.g., in order to ensure timely delivery of goods) this might imply penalties for violating the frame SLA at the end of the validity period of the frame SLA.

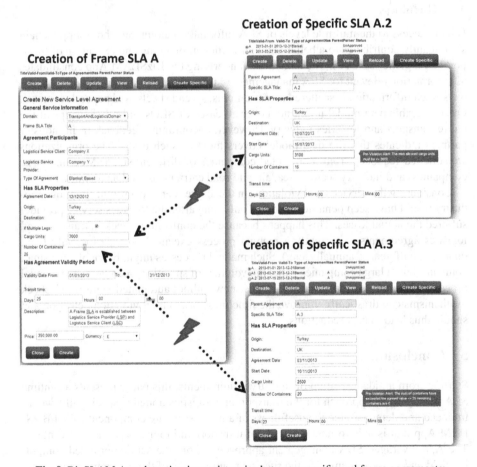

Fig. 9. BizSLAM App detecting inconsistencies between specific and frame agreements

Violation 1: According to the frame SLA, only 3000 cargo units may be transported for each specific SLA. However, the specific SLA **A.2** asks for a cargo volume of 3100 and thus violates the *atomic* SLO *Cargo Units* specified in the frame SLA.

Violation 2: A total of 25 containers may be contracted during the validity period of the frame SLA. When the specific SLA **A.3** asks for 20 containers, 25 containers have already been contracted in the previous specific SLAs **A.1** and **A.2**. Thus, no containers remain to be contracted under the frame SLA, which in turn means that the specific SLA **A.3** leads to a violation of the *aggregated* SLO Containers.

As part of our ongoing research we are preparing an empirical evaluation of our SLA management approach. This includes more sophisticated examples and use cases, as well as controlled experiments that combine real data from the field with simulation to assess performance, scalability, effectiveness and accuracy of the BizSLAM App.

4.2   Usefulness

Having access to the multiple levels of SLA information along the whole supply chain significantly contributes to a better and more efficient planning and execution of transport and logistics services. The data model underlying the BizSLAM App consolidates all information relevant for SLA management of transport and logistics services. Nowadays, such information is scattered across e-mails, spread sheets, and paper documents. Of course, this data model might not cover all cases of SLOs and relationships of the entire transport and logistics industry. However, encouraging feedback from industry partners indicates that the data model covers most of such cases. The organizations we solicited feedback from represented companies of different size (SMEs and large companies) and industry sectors (sea, air, and road carriers, as well as forwarders).

Considering the service level violations in the above scenario, current situation in industry would have seen penalties enforced only long after the logistics service provider suffered the actual losses. This happens because the conformity check in transport and logistics agreements is currently a manual process executed only periodically (e.g., quarterly, half yearly, annually, etc.). Such manual processes might be viable in a small company, but in large companies with high volumes of specific agreements such manual processes become extremely costly. Hence, new online, automated conformity check mechanisms can drastically improve the timeliness of contract violation detection and should thus lead to cost reductions.

5   Conclusion

Starting from an identification of industry requirements, this paper presents a runtime SLA management approach for the transport and logistics domain. Specifically, we introduced and demonstrated the usefulness of a novel software component called BizSLAM App that is able to manage SLAs of transport and logistics services at runtime. The App leveraged SLA management approaches from the service-oriented computing field and adapted them to fit the specific requirements of the transports and logistic domain, especially the need to support both frame SLAs and specific SLAs.

The BizSLAM App was developed on top of FIspace.eu, a cloud-based business collaboration platform that offers novel business-to-business collaboration facilities. This in turn facilitates applying the BizSLAM App capabilities to other non-computational services, as the platform fosters integrating and combining data, services and Apps of various business stakeholders. As part of the FIspace.eu platform, we are currently adapting the BizSLAM App to the agrifood domain, thereby providing facilities to manage contracts from food production to consumption.

Acknowledgements. We cordially thank our industry partners of the FInest and FIspace projects for their valuable contributions to the SLA data model. In addition, we thank Stephan Heyne for supporting us in implementing the Linked-USDL models, as well as Nadeem Bari for his help in implementing the BizSLAM App. We further express our gratitude to Antonio Manuel Gutierrez, Manuel Resinas and Antonio Ruiz-Cortés for earlier collaborations on that subject. Finally, we would like to thank the anonymous reviewers for their constructive comments that benefited this paper.

This work was partially supported by the EU's Seventh Framework Programme (FP7/2007-2013) under grant agreements 285598 (FInest) and 604123 (FIspace).

References

1. Alliance of European Logistics: A technology roadmap for logistics. Technical Report (October 2013)
2. Andrieux, A., Czajkowski, K., Dan, A., Keahey, K., Ludwig, H., Nakata, T., Pruyne, J., Rofrano, J., Tuecke, S., Xu, M.: Web services agreement specification (WS-Agreement). Specification from the Open Grid Forum (OGF) (March 2007)
3. Augenstein, C., Ludwig, A., Franczyk, B.: Integration of service models – preliminary results for consistent logistics service management. In: Service Research and Innovation Institute Global Conference (SRII 2012), San Jose, Calif., USA (2012)
4. Benaissa, M., Boukachour, J., Benabdelhafid, A.: Web service in integrated logistics information system. In: Int'l Symposium on Logistics and Industrial Informatics (LINDI 2007). Wildau, Germany (2007)
5. Cuomo, A., Modica, G.D., Distefano, S., Puliafito, A., Rak, M., Tomarchio, O., Venticinque, S., Villano, U.: An SLA-based broker for cloud infrastructures. Journal of Grid Computing 11(1), 1–25 (2013)
6. Dong, H., Hussain, F., Chang, E.: Transport service ontology and its application in the field of semantic search. In: Int'l Conference on Service Operations and Logistics, and Informatics (IEEE/SOLI 2008), vol. 1, pp. 820–824 (October 2008)
7. e-Freight project: D1.3b: e-Freight framework – information models (March 2010), http://www.efreightproject.eu/
8. Feldman, Z., Fournier, F., Franklin, R., Metzger, A.: Proactive event processing in action: a case study on the proactive management of transport processes (industry article). In: 7th Int'l Conference on Distributed Event-based Systems (DEBS 2013), Arlington, Texas, USA (2013)
9. Franklin, R., Metzger, A., Stollberg, M., Engel, Y., Fjørtoft, K., Fleischhauer, R., Marquezan, C., Ramstad, L.S.: Future Internet technology for the future of transport and logistics. In: ServiceWave Conference 2011, Future Internet PPP Track, Ghent, Belgium (2011)
10. Goel, N., Kumar, N., Shyamasundar, R.K.: SLA monitor: A system for dynamic monitoring of adaptive web services. In: 9th European Conference on Web Services (ECOWS 2011), Lugano, Switzerland (2011)

11. Guihua, N., Fu, M., Xia, H.: A semantic mapping system based on e-commerce logistics ontology. In: World Congress on Software Engineering (WCSE 2009), vol. 2, pp. 133–136 (May 2009)

12. Gutiérrez, A.M., Cassales Marquezan, C., Resinas, M., Metzger, A., Ruiz-Cortés, A., Pohl, K.: Extending WS-Agreement to support automated conformity check on transport and logistics service agreements. In: Basu, S., Pautasso, C., Zhang, L., Fu, X. (eds.) ICSOC 2013. LNCS, vol. 8274, pp. 567–574. Springer, Heidelberg (2013)

13. Hvitved, T., Klaedtke, F., Zalinescu, E.: A trace-based model for multiparty contracts. The Journal of Logic and Algebraic Programming 81(2), 72–98 (2012)

14. Kouki, Y., Ledoux, T.: SLA-driven capacity planning for cloud applications. In: 4th Int'l Conference on Cloud Computing Technology and Science (CloudCom 2012), Taipei, Taiwan, pp. 135–140 (2012)

15. Leitner, P., Ferner, J., Hummer, W., Dustdar, S.: Data-driven and automated prediction of service level agreement violations in service compositions. Distributed and Parallel Databases 31(3), 447–470 (2013)

16. McConnell, A., Parr, G., McClean, S., Morrow, P., Scotney, B.: A SLA-compliant cloud resource allocation framework for n-tier applications. In: 1st Int'l Conference on Cloud Networking (CLOUDNET 2012), Paris, France (2012)

17. Metzger, A., Franklin, R., Engel, Y.: Predictive monitoring of heterogeneous service-oriented business networks: The transport and logistics case. In: Service Research and Innovation Institute Global Conference (SRII 2012), San Jose, Calif., USA (2012)

18. Molina-Jimenez, C., Shrivastava, S., Strano, M.: A model for checking contractual compliance of business interactions. IEEE Trans. on Services Comp. 5(2), 276–289 (2012)

19. Müller, C., Resinas, M., Ruiz-Cortés, A.: Automated analysis of conflicts in WS-Agreement. IEEE Trans. on Services Comp. PP(99), 1 (2013)

20. Munteanu, V., Fortis, T., Negru, V.: An evolutionary approach for SLA-based cloud resource provisioning. In: 27th Int'l Conference on Advanced Information Networking and Applications (AINA 2013), Barcelona, Spain (2013)

21. Papazoglou, M., Pohl, K., Parkin, M., Metzger, M. (eds.): Service Research Challenges and Solutions for the Future Internet: S-Cube – Towards Mechanisms and Methods for Engineering, Managing, and Adapting Service-Based Systems. Springer (2010)

22. Rosario, S., Benveniste, A., Jard, C.: Monitoring probabilistic SLAs in web service orchestrations. In: Int'l Symposium on Integrated Network Management (IM 2009), New York, USA (2009)

23. Verdouw, C., Beulens, A., Wolfert, S.: Towards software mass customization for business collaboration. In: Service Research and Innovation Institute Global Conference (SRII 2014), San Jose, Calif., USA (2014)

24. Wieder, P., Butler, J.M., Theilmann, W., Yahyapour, R. (eds.): Service Level Agreements for Cloud Computing. Springer (2011)

25. Xu, L., Jeusfeld, M.A.: Pro-active monitoring of electronic contracts. In: Eder, J., Missikoff, M. (eds.) CAiSE 2003. LNCS, vol. 2681, pp. 584–600. Springer, Heidelberg (2003)

26. Yahya, B., Mo, J., Bae, H., Lee, H.: Ontology-based process design support tool for vessel clearance system. In: Int'l Conference on Computers and Industrial Engineering (CIE 2010), pp. 1–6 (July 2010)

27. Hua, W.Z., Yousen, H., Yun, D.Z., Wei, Z.: SOA-BPM based information system for promoting agility of third party logistics. In: Int'l Conference on Automation and Logistics (ICAL 2009), Shenyang, China (2009)

28. Zhu, Q., Fung, R.: Design and analysis of optimal incentive contracts between fourth-party and third-party logistics providers. In: Int'l Conference on Automation and Logistics (ICAL 2012), Zhengzhou, China (2012)

Single Source of Truth (SSOT)
for Service Oriented Architecture (SOA)

Candy Pang and Duane Szafron

Department of Computing Science, University of Alberta, Edmonton, Alberta, Canada
{cspang,dszafron}@ualberta.ca

Abstract. Enterprises have embraced Service Oriented Architecture (SOA) for years. With SOA, each business entity should be the Single Source of Truth (SSOT) of its data, and offer data services to other entities. Instead of sharing data through services, many business entities still share data through data replication. Replicating data causes inconsistencies and interoperability challenges. Even when there is a single authoritative source, that resolves inconsistencies, the data copies may end up being out-of-sync and cause errors. This paper describes how to use a SSOT service to eliminate data replication, enforce data autonomy, advocate data self-containment, and enhance data maintenance. Both mutable and immutable SSOT relationships (mappings) are considered. This paper describes the challenges, solutions, interactions and abstractions between the SSOT data service providers and the loosely coupled data consumers. It also assesses the performance and future usage of a SSOT service.

Keywords: Single Source of Truth, Service Composition, Service Oriented Architecture (SOA), Software Design Concept, Software Engineering.

1 Introduction

Before embracing the Service Oriented Architecture (SOA), enterprises or business entities used to share data through data replication. Replicating data across multiple systems gives rise to inconsistencies and interoperability challenges. In some cases, one of the systems is treated as the "authoritative" source or the Single Source of Truth (SSOT). The authoritative source's data is replicated to the clients' databases, resulting in data layer synchronization challenges. Independent client's data transformation or modification can result in data discrepancies that require manual intervention. A better solution is to hide the data layer from the clients in the SOA.

In the SOA, a SSOT should associate with clients through the service layer, instead of the data layer. This would alleviate data replication and the related problems. The authoritative source identified as the SSOT should provide data services for the clients. In this approach, clients maintain mappings to the SSOT data, but do not replicate the SSOT data. Unfortunately, many enterprises have yet to overhaul data layer replication into a SSOT service. Lack of experience in SSOT service implementation may have hindered enterprises from the migration.

X. Franch et al. (Eds.): ICSOC 2014, LNCS 8831, pp. 575–589, 2014.

This paper describes a SSOT service model for two common data sharing scenarios: mutable and immutable data sources. We use two motivating examples to illustrate the variants: (a) the management of Postal Codes (PC) and (b) the management of Electronic Patient Records (EPR). The proposed SSOT service model is useful for any business entity that maintains full ownership of its data, and does not want the clients to duplicate its data, but allows data access by restricted queries. The value of the model will be illustrated by the PC and EPR examples.

Most business applications use addresses. In Canada, Canada Post is the single authoritative agency that manages PCs for mail-delivery addresses. Each address should have exactly one PC, while each PC covers an area with multiple addresses. Most business applications collect address information from their customers, and store customers' addresses with PCs in their local databases. Periodically, business applications also replicate Canada Post's PCs to their local databases for data-validation purpose. For example, an application using billing addresses, which require PCs, may have a Billing_Address table and a Postal_Code table as shown in Fig. 1(a). The Postal_Code table contains all valid PCs periodically replicated from Canada Post. Before adding a new address to the Billing_Address table, the application checks the validity of the provided PC, i.e., whether the PC exists in the Postal_Code table. If so, the application will add the new address to the Billing_Address table. This process can only validate the existence of the PC, but it cannot validate whether the PC is correct for that address. There is a mapping between the PC and the billing address.

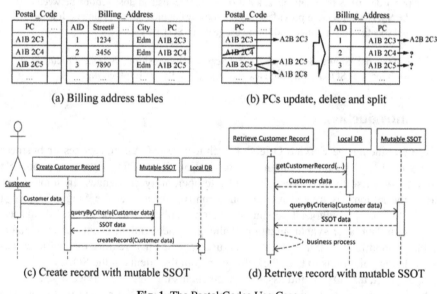

(a) Billing address tables

(b) PCs update, delete and split

(c) Create record with mutable SSOT

(d) Retrieve record with mutable SSOT

Fig. 1. The Postal Codes Use Case

A mapping that changes over time is called a mutable mapping, and a mapping that does not change is immutable. Canada Post changes PCs from time to time. PCs can be inserted, updated, deleted, split or merged. The application needs to synchronize the Postal_Code table with Canada Post, and, if necessary, to correct the PCs in the

Billing_Address table. Since the PC that is mapped to a billing address can change over time, the mapping between PC and billing address is an example of a mutable mapping. Mutable mappings are often subject to synchronization errors. For example, Canada Post only provides PC changes to subscribers monthly. Therefore, the subscribers' Postal_Code tables are out-of-sync with Canada Post most of the time. As shown in Fig. 1(b), when a PC is updated (from A1B 2C3 to A2B 2C3), the corresponding mappings in the Billing_Address table can be updated. However, when a PC is deleted (from A1B 2C4 to none) or split (from A1B 2C5 to A1B 2C5 and AIB 2C8), there is no simple solution to correct the mappings in the Billing_Address table, by using the updated PC list.

As a second example, let us consider a regional Electronic Patient Record (EPR) system that manages patients' health numbers (PHNs), names and contacts. Each patient in the region receives services from multiple healthcare providers, with different specialties. Each healthcare provider obtains patient information directly from the patient during the patient's visit, containing information included in the EPR. Then, each provider independently stores the patient's information in its local database. In this model, a provider-specific patient record may be inconsistent with the regional EPR. In principle, each provider-specific patient record could be mapped to a corresponding EPR in the regional authoritative system. In this case, the mapping between an EPR and a provider-specific record is immutable. The mapping is immutable despite the fact that patient's data may change. For example, when a patient changes his/her name, the patient's EPR will be updated, but the patient's EPR is still mapped to the same provider-specific record. Therefore, the mapping is immutable.

The SOA paradigm can alleviate data synchronization issues. Clients using data that already exists in an authoritative source will not replicate the authoritative data in their local databases. Instead, the authoritative source acts as a SSOT service that provides clients the authoritative data. In the examples above, Canada Post serves as the SSOT service for PCs and a regional health authority provides the SSOT service for EPRs. Clients access PCs and EPRs by invoking SSOT services, without replicating SSOT data in their local databases. Therefore, clients do not need to manage and synchronize data with the SSOT. The SSOT can also shield its autonomy from the clients. We advocate the SSOT service model over data-replication.

This paper is structured as follows. Section 2 and 3 illustrate the challenges and solutions associated with the mutable and the immutable SSOT by the PC and the EPR use cases respectively. Section 4 evaluates the performance of the SSOT service. Section 5 describes the related works. Section 6 recommends future works, and Section 7 concludes the paper by enumerating SSOT's benefits.

2   Mutable SSOT Service

A SSOT service that manages mutable mappings is called a mutable SSOT service. In this case, the mapping between a SSOT record (each individual PC in our example) and a client application record (each billing address in our example) can change over time. Clients need to invoke the mutable SSOT service with query criteria. Therefore, a mutable SSOT service supports at least the query-by-criteria operation.

For example, in the PC use case, Canada Post maintains a mutable PC SSOT service that provides a single web service operation, PC-query. The PC-query operation takes PC query criteria as input. Clients may specify Street Number, Number Suffix, Unit/Suite Apartment, Street Name, Street Type, Street Direction, City, and/or Province as criteria. The PC-query operation returns a set of PCs that match the criteria.

This PC SSOT service can replace data replication. For example, in Fig. 1(a), the PC column in the Billing_Address table and the Postal_Code table are replicated data that can be dropped in favor of invoking the PC-query operation provided by the mutable PC SSOT service. The PC query criteria will come from the remaining columns (e.g. Street#, City) in the Billing_Address table. When the application needs the PC of a billing address, it will use the address data in the Billing_Address table as query criteria to retrieve the PC from the PC SSOT.

The rest of this section will use the PC use case to illustrate how clients can use a mutable SSOT service to replace data replication.

2.1   Client-Record Creation

Fig. 1(c) depicts how an application can use mutable SSOT service for data validation during record creation. In the PC use case, when the application receives a new billing address from a customer, the application queries the PC SSOT using the customer address. If the PC SSOT returns a single valid PC, then the address is valid. The application proceeds to create a new Billing_Address record for the customer.

If the PC SSOT returns more than one PC, then the customer address is not definitive. For example, if the customer address contains only the city field, then the PC SSOT will return all the PCs for the city. In principle, the application should not accept a non-definitive address as a billing address. Therefore, the application would seek additional address details from the customer. Similarly, if the PC SSOT returns no PC for the customer address, the application should alert the customer that the address is invalid and request the user to take remedial action.

In contrast, the data-replication model may allow non-definitive or invalid billing addresses in the application's database. Using a mutable SSOT service not only eliminates data replication, but also enhances data quality.

Different clients may have different processes for the SSOT response. The application in the PC use case expects a single valid PC from the response. Other applications may iterate the response records to select the most desired result. To support different clients' processes, the mutable SSOT query-by-criteria operation may return additional information. For example, the PC-query operation may return other address fields (Street Number, Unit/Suite Apartment, Street Name, etc.) in addition to the PC. Clients can use the additional address fields to filter the response records.

2.2   Client-Record Retrieval

Since the SSOT data is excluded from the clients' local databases, each client needs to combine its local data with the SSOT data to compose the complete data records. The client data retrieval process is depicted in Fig. 1(d).

In the PC use case, the application first retrieves a Billing_Address record from its local database, then uses the local address data as query criteria to invoke the PC-query operation, and retrieve the up-to-date PC from the PC SSOT. If the PC of the billing address has changed since the last retrieval, then the PC SSOT will return a different PC from the last retrieval, but it will be the correct PC.

3   Immutable SSOT Service

A SSOT service that manages an immutable mapping is called an immutable SSOT service. The mapping cannot change over time. Each record in the client application has a permanent static relationship with a SSOT record. To establish this mapping, a client record is associated with a SSOT record using a unique permanent single source of truth identifier (SSOT-ID). A SSOT-ID is conceptually equivalent to the resource identifier in the Resource Description Framework (RDF) [1] and the unique identifier in the Representational State Transfer (REST) [2] architecture. Each record represents a resource in the SSOT. We will use the term resource instead of record since each SSOT resource may contain multiple child-records. For example, an EPR may contain multiple names, addresses and phone numbers as child-records. Each resource has a unique permanent identifier called the SSOT-ID. Clients use the query-by-SSOT-ID operation to retrieve resource details, which include the child-records.

The rest of this section will illustrate the immutable SSOT service through the EPR use case. Assume that a clinic application and a pharmacy application both need patients' health numbers (PHNs), names and contacts, along with their own provider-specific data. Traditionally, in the data-replication model, the clinic application would have a Clinic_Patient table and a Patient_Visit table, and the pharmacy application would have a Pharmacy_Patient table and a Drug_Dispensing table, as shown in Fig. 2(a). The clinic application assigns a county to each patient using the patient's home address, while the pharmacy application does not. In the data-replication model, the PHNs, names and contacts located in the clinic's and pharmacy's databases may have errors or be inconsistent with the authoritative EPR system. When patients move, patients must notify the EPR authority, the clinic and the pharmacy individually.

Actually, PHNs, names and contacts are readily available in the regional EPR system. An immutable EPR SSOT service can eliminate data replication from the clinic and the pharmacy databases. After eliminating the replicated EPR data, Fig. 2(b) shows the new clinic application and pharmacy application tables. In the new Clinic_Patient and Pharmacy_Patient tables, the EPR columns are replaced by the SSOT-ID column. Unlike the PC use case, immutable SSOT clients do not routinely use the query-by-criteria operation to obtain SSOT data. Instead, clients can invoke the query-by-SSOT-ID operation to retrieve SSOT data from the immutable SSOT service.

Each immutable SSOT service should provide at least four operations: (a) query-by-criteria, (b) query-by-SSOT-ID, (c) update subscription, and (d) deletion subscription. The potential risks of using the immutable SSOT service query-by-criteria operation are illustrated in Section 3.1. The rest of the sub-sections describe different usages of the immutable SSOT operations.

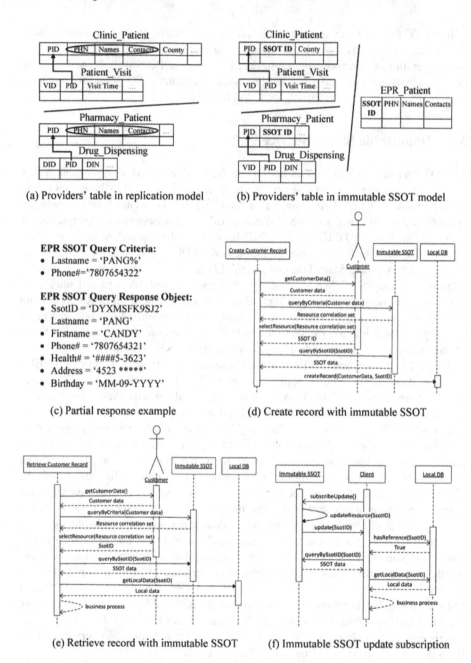

(a) Providers' table in replication model

(b) Providers' table in immutable SSOT model

EPR SSOT Query Criteria:
- Lastname = 'PANG%'
- Phone#='7807654322'

EPR SSOT Query Response Object:
- SsotID = 'DYXMSFK9SJ2'
- Lastname = 'PANG'
- Firstname = 'CANDY'
- Phone# = '7807654321'
- Health# = '####5-3623'
- Address = '4523 *****'
- Birthday = 'MM-09-YYYY'

(c) Partial response example

(d) Create record with immutable SSOT

(e) Retrieve record with immutable SSOT

(f) Immutable SSOT update subscription

Fig. 2. The Electronic Health Record Use Case

3.1   Query-by-Criteria

An immutable SSOT service could provide the same query-by-criteria operation as a mutable SSOT service. Clients could query the SSOT service by criteria and receive a correlated set of results matching the criteria. However, in some situations, the immutable SSOT query-by-criteria operation may sustain a privacy violation risk. In the EPR use case, if the query-by-criteria operation returns all resources matching any given set of criteria, then any client can browse the EPR data, which violate patients' privacy. For example, a client may specify Firstname='JOHN' as the query criteria for the EPR SSOT query-by-criteria operation. In response, the EPR SSOT returns all patients with first name equals 'JOHN'. The large response set may violate many patients' privacy, since many of the set may not be patients of the querying facility.

To avoid browsing, the query-by-criteria operation could specify a maximum number of returned records (i.e. query-limit). If the response set is larger than the query-limit, the service would return an error. At which point the client needs to refine the query criteria and queries again.

A safer query-by-criteria operation may also demand more than one query criterion to avoid brute force hacking. For example, the EPR SSOT query-by-criteria operation could reject single criterion queries to avoid PHN cracking by querying with randomly generated PHN's until a valid resource is returned.

For further privacy protection, the query-by-criteria response set can be filtered to contain partial data. The partial data must include the complete SSOT-ID and sufficient information to identify a SSOT resource. Fig. 2(c) shows a set of query criteria for the EPR SSOT query-by-criteria operation, and one partial response record. The partial record includes the SSOT-ID and only part of the PHN, address and birthday. Using the partial record, a client should be able to determine whether the EPR maps to the targeted patient. Once a partial record is selected, the client can use the SSOT-ID to retrieve the resource details using the query-by-SSOT-ID operation.

3.2   Query-by-SSOT-ID

If the query-by-criteria operation returns only partial data for privacy protection, the immutable SSOT service must provide a query-by-SSOT-ID operation, which takes a SSOT-ID as input. In response to a query-by-SSOT-ID request, the immutable SSOT provides details of the resource corresponding to the provided SSOT-ID, but only the details that the client is authorized to see. This allows the SSOT service to distinguish between client access permissions, providing different information to different facilities, such as pharmacies, clinics and acute-care facilities.

To protect data privacy, the immutable SSOT should include a proper auditing mechanism to detect, identify and stop improper browsing behavior or unlawful use of data. In the EPR use case, if a client continually invokes the EPR SSOT query-by-SSOT-ID operation with randomly generated or guessed SSOT-IDs, the EPR SSOT auditing mechanism should detect and deter the client.

Each SSOT-ID is effectively a foreign key to a remote SSOT resource. Since the SSOT and clients are loosely coupled, the foreign key constraints in the client data cannot be enforced at the SSOT. An alternate foreign key constraint handling mechanism will be discussed in the later sub-sections.

3.3   Client-record Creation

Fig. 2(d) depicts the role of an immutable SSOT service during client record creation. Using the clinic application in the EPR use case as an illustration, when a patient first visits the clinic, the clinic application needs the patient's SSOT-ID. The patient provides personal data to the clinic. The clinic application invokes the EPR SSOT query-by-criteria operation with the patient's data. From the returned set of partial EPRs, the clinic and patient together identify the correct EPR. With the SSOT-ID from the selected partial EPR, the clinic application invokes the query-by-SSOT-ID operation to retrieve the portion of the patient's EPR that is permitted to the clinic. The clinic application then assigns a county to the patient according to the patient's home address in the EPR. With the patient's SSOT-ID and assigned county, the clinic application adds a new record to the Clinic_Patient table for the patient. Similarly, when a patient first visits the pharmacy, the pharmacy application uses the EPR SSOT query-by-criteria operation to retrieve a partial EPR of the patient. The pharmacy application gets the patient's SSOT-ID from the partial EPR. Since the pharmacy data does not depend on data in the EPR, the pharmacy application can add a new record to the Pharmacy_Patient table for the patient with the patient's SSOT-ID.

3.4   Client-record Retrieval

As with the mutable SSOT service, the immutable SSOT clients need to combine the SSOT data with the local data to compose complete data records. The data retrieval process is depicted in Fig. 2(e).

In the EPR use case, when a patient revisits the clinic or the pharmacy, the clinic and pharmacy applications use the EPR SSOT query-by-criteria operation to retrieve the patient's SSOT-ID. With the SSOT-ID, the applications fetch the permission-filtered EPR with query-by-SSOT-ID. Using the SSOT-ID again, the applications retrieve patient's local data from the local databases, i.e. the Clinic_Patient, Patient_Visit, Pharmacy_Patient and Drug_Dispensing tables in Fig. 2(b). Finally, the applications combine the EPR and local data to instantiate a complete patient record.

3.5   Constructing SSOT-IDs

Since the SSOT and the clients are loosely coupled, the clients rely on the SSOT-IDs to be unique and permanent. Therefore, it is important to select a proper data type, length, format and representation for the SSOT-ID. For example, the Canadian Social Insurance Number (SIN) has 9 digits. The first digit of the SIN represents the owner's residential status. Similarly, a SSOT-ID can have embedded representations. The design of the SSOT-ID deserves extraordinary attention to ensure uniqueness and permanency. For example, the SIN is unique, but not permanent. When an owner's residential status changes, a new SIN may be assigned. Therefore, SIN is not a good SSOT-ID candidate. In addition, public data items are not good SSOT-ID candidates.

An SSOT-ID does not need to be a single value. It can also be a composite value, as long as it is unique and permanent. Part of the SSOT-ID can be a fixed-length sequential number, to ensure its uniqueness. Since the SSOT-ID will be shared between systems, it is recommended that the SSOT-ID take a different format from the SSOT database standard, so that the SSOT database standard will not be exposed.

Clients store the SSOT-IDs in their local databases. The SSOT-IDs are guaranteed to be unique and permanent. Therefore, clients may consider using the SSOT-IDs as the primary keys in their local databases. If the SSOT-ID data type and size do not match the local database standard, we recommend that the local database create its own local primary key, and use the SSOT-ID as a foreign key. In the EPR use case, the Clinic_Patient table could have used the EPR SSOT-ID as the primary key. Since the primary key of the Clinic_Patient table will be a foreign key of the Patient_Visit table, the clinic application created its local primary key (PID in the Clinic_Patient table), to preserve data type consistency between tables.

The clients should also consider whether the sequence of the primary keys matter to the local business logic. In the EPR use case, it is likely that a portion of the EPR SSOT-ID is a sequential number. The clinic serves only a relatively small number of patients in the regional EPR system. Therefore, only a small number of the EPR SSOT-IDs will be imported into the clinic's database. If the clinic application uses the EPR SSOT-IDs as its primary key, then the primary key will have a lot of gaps in its sequence. In addition, the order of the primary keys will not represent the order in which patients' records are added to the clinic's database.

3.6   Update Subscription

Data updates for an immutable SSOT may affect clients. In the EPR use case, the clinic application assigns a patient's county based on a patient's home address. When a patient moves, the clinic application may assign a different county for the patient. In this case, data updates in the EPR SSOT affect the clinic application. On the other hand, none of the pharmacy application local data depends on the EPR SSOT data. Therefore, data updates in the EPR SSOT do not affect the pharmacy application.

The SSOT cannot determine how data updates will affect the loosely coupled clients. Clients are responsible for managing their own data. Therefore, the immutable SSOT must provide an update subscription operation. If a client is concerned about data updates in the SSOT, then the client is responsible for subscribing to the SSOT update service through the update subscription operation.

After a SSOT resource is updated, the SSOT will send an update message with the SSOT-ID of the updated resource to the subscribers. When the subscriber receives the update message, the subscriber can check whether the SSOT-ID is referenced locally. If not, the subscriber can ignore the update message. If the SSOT-ID is referenced locally, then the subscriber can fetch the resource details using the query-by-SSOT-ID operation. Based on the latest resource details, the subscriber may update its local data accordingly. The update subscription process is depicted in Fig. 2(f).

In the EPR use case, the clinic application would subscribe to the EPR SSOT update service. When an EPR is updated, the clinic application will receive an update message with the SSOT-ID of the updated EPR. The clinic application determines whether the SSOT-ID is referenced locally. If so, it retrieves the patient details from the EPR SSOT using the query-by-SSOT-ID operation. Then the clinic application can determine whether the patient's latest home address matches the clinic-assigned county in the local database. If not, it updates the local database accordingly. On the other hand, the pharmacy application is not affected by EPR updates. Therefore, the pharmacy application would not subscribe to the EPR SSOT update service. Notice that the pharmacy still relies on the SSOT for the latest EPR patient information. However, it does not subscribe for updates since it does not need to update its own local database, when EPR data changes.

3.7   Deletion Subscription

Just like any other data, the SSOT data can be deleted. Since the SSOT is loosely coupled with its clients, clients cannot put a foreign key constraint on the SSOT to restrain the SSOT from deleting data. Instead, the SSOT provides a deletion service. When a resource is deleted from the SSOT, the SSOT will send a deletion message to the subscriber. Clients need to determine whether they should subscribe to the SSOT deletion service using the deletion subscription operation.

In the EPR use case, deleting a patient from the EPR SSOT may create broken links in the Clinic_Patient and Pharmacy_Patient tables. Therefore, the clinic and pharmacy applications should both subscribe to the EPR SSOT deletion service.

If the SSOT physically deletes the resource, then the deletion message should contain the last version of the resource before the deletion and the reason for deletion. Clients can use this information to determine how to handle the deleted data.

In the EPR use case, a patient may move from the region and be deleted from the EPR SSOT. The clinic and pharmacy applications will receive a deletion message from the EPR SSOT with the last version of the patient's EPR. The applications may store or ignore the EPR in the deletion message. Depending on the reason for deletion, the applications can delete, archive or mark the patient's local record inactive.

Alternatively, the SSOT may logically delete a resource. In this situation, the deletion message will only contain the resource SSOT-ID and the reason for deletion. The client can still fetch the logically deleted resource using the query-by-SSOT-ID operations. The query-by-SSOT-ID operation would return the corresponding resource but flagged as deleted. The query-by-criteria operation could exclude logically deleted resources from the response correlated set, or provide them and flag them as deleted.

In the EPR use case, if patients are only logically deleted from the EPR SSOT, the clinic and pharmacy applications may mark the patient inactive in their local databases. If EPR records are only logically deleted, then clients should always check the deleted flags on the EPR, since logically deleted records may later be undeleted.

3.8   Additional Operations

An SSOT creation subscription operation is not recommended. If clients can subscribe to SSOT data creation, then clients can replicate the whole SSOT database, which violates the purpose of using SSOT. Clients should only link to the SSOT resources related to their operational mandates, but not replicate the SSOT data.

In addition to the four mandatory operations, an immutable SSOT service might provide additional resource create, retrieve, update and delete (CRUD) operations.

In the EPR use case, if a patient has not registered with the regional EPR SSOT, then the clinic and pharmacy applications would not find the patient through the query-by-criteria operation. If the EPR SSOT also provides a patient creation operation, then the authorized clinic or pharmacy personnel can create SSOT EPRs as needed.

If the clinic or pharmacy personnel are not authorized to create SSOT EPRs, then the un-registered patients need to register with the EPR authority later. In the meantime, the applications can create a local temporary file to store the patient's data. An optional column (TEMP FILE#) can be added to the Clinic_Patient and Pharmacy_Patient tables to keep track of the temporary file number. In the absence of the SSOT ID and existence of the TEMP FILE#, the applications will not query the EPR SSOT for patient's information, but retrieve data from the local temporary file. After the patient registers with the EPR SSOT, the applications can insert the EPR SSOT-ID into the Clinic_Patient and Pharmacy_Patient tables, and delete the temporary file. At this point, the application returns to normal processing.

4   Performance and Quality-of-Service (QoS)

Despite the data-synchronization challenges, the data-replication model has a performance advantage over the SSOT service model. In the SSOT service model, client applications make extra service invocations to the SSOT during record creation and retrieval, which may affect user experience. Therefore, we implemented experiments to evaluate how the extra SSOT service invocations might affect user wait times.

The experiments evaluated delay caused by the SSOT service invocations. They were conducted on the institution's network supporting ~40,000 students. The SSOT service was hosted on a workstation in a departmental subnet. In the experiments, client applications accessed the SSOT service through Wi-Fi on the institute's public network during regular office hours. This condition simulated an enterprise network supporting multiple sub-divisions.

The experiment results show that if the SSOT service and the client applications are located within the same enterprise network, then the service invocation costs less than 20 milliseconds per call. This indicates that users should not notice any performance deterioration. If the SSOT service is available across a wide area network, the performance primarily depends on the transmission delay between the public SSOT service and the clients. Clients should benchmark the transmission delay to determine the actual performance effect.

In dynamic web service composition [3], clients select web service providers according to their published quality-of-service (QoS) [4]. Even though, SSOT's clients will likely access the SSOT service statically, the SSOT service should publish the following QoS metrics per operation:

— **Operational hours:** the regular SSOT servicing hours.
— **Maintenance schedule:** the changes and release schedule.
— **Reliability:** the SSOT's ability to perform the operation without errors.
— **Request-processing time:** the maximum and average time required for the SSOT service to complete the operations.

The SSOT may publish additional QoS metrics, such as capacity, performance, robustness, accuracy and more [3]. Clients can design their usage of the SSOT service according to the SSOT's QoS metrics.

If the SSOT service is part of a larger enterprise or jurisdiction, then the SSOT service usually has the same operational hours and maintenance schedules as their clients. Public SSOT services, like Canada Post, are usually available 24x7.

5   Related Work

Most SSOT is implemented on the data layer. Ives et al. [5] suggest synchronizing distributed data on the data layer. Ives et al. propose a "Collaborative Data Sharing System (CDSS) [that] models the exchange of data among sites as update propagation among peers, which is subject to transformation (schema mapping), filtering (based on policies about source authority), and local revision or replacement of data." Since data across multiple sites are continuously "updated, cleaned and annotated", cross-site synchronization has to deal with issues such as data correctness, schema and terminology consistence, and timing. These data layer synchronization hurdles highlight the advantage of our SSOT service model that eliminates data layer synchronization.

Others try to implement SSOT using an Enterprise Service Bus (ESB) [6], in which a SSOT is defined. Clients duplicate the SSOT data locally, and subscribe to ESB for SSOT updates. Whenever the SSOT is updated, clients synchronize with the SSOT by repeating the changes in their local copies. Our SSOT model totally avoids data duplication at the clients' site.

Instead of a data-centric model for SSOT, some research has turned to artifact-centric modeling [7]. An artifact is a set of name-value-pairs related to a business process or task, where data represents business objects. In the artifact-centric model, each artifact instance is shared between all process participants. The participants get information from the artifact and change the state of the artifact to accomplish the process goal. Since the artifacts are shared between process participants, access and transaction control is necessary. Hull [8] suggests using artifact-centric hubs to facilitate communication and synchronization between the participants. Our SSOT service model does not require complicated facilitation or a centralized hub.

Other researchers have proposed the Personal Information Management (PIM) [9] model. In our model, the SSOT does not have any knowledge about its clients' data. However, the PIM model finds, links, groups and manages clients' data references to the source. PIM is a centralized data management model, while SSOT is a distributed data management model.

Finally, Ludwig et al. [10] propose a decentralized approach to manage distributed service configurations. The proposed solution uses RESTful services to exchange configuration data between hosts, and a subscription mechanism to manage changes. This approach endorses a data perspective similar to an SSOT service, where each data source maintains self-contained autonomous data. Data is not synchronized across multiple sites. Sources and clients are statically bound.

6   Future Work

A mutable SSOT service has one standard operation: query-by-criteria. An immutable SSOT service has four standard operations: query-by-criteria, query-by-SSOT-ID, update subscription, and deletion subscription. Based on these standard operations, we defined Web Service Definition Language (WSDL) extensions for the mu-table and immutable SSOT services with corresponding templates. Because of the limited space, we do not include the SSOT WSDL and templates in this paper.

Based on the WSDL extensions and templates, development tools can easily be created to generate SSOT service source code with corresponding client access code. These tools can simplify development for programmers, which encourages the use of SSOT services to replace data-replication. Eclipse is an excellent platform to implement such tools. There are three additional future work topics.

Maintenance and Upgrades: Every active service goes through changes. Besides regular change management, services may experience unexpected emergency incidents. When these incidents occur, the clients should be alerted about their occurrences, side-effects, recovery progress and estimated recovery times. As suggested by Ludrig et al. [10] a subscription service can be used to communicate change, maintenance and emergency notices. Protocols and language extensions can be defined for various types of change, maintenance and emergency activities. Since SSOT introduces a single point of failure, a cloud infrastructure specifically designed for SSOT can improve its availability.

Local Temporary Cache: If the cost of the SSOT service invocation is a concern, clients can cache the SSOT resources temporarily. Once a SSOT resource is obtained, there is a good chance that the client needs the same SSOT resource for related processes. Therefore, temporarily caching the SSOT resource will likely reduce service invocations. The cached SSOT resource can be flushed after a timeout period. The SSOT update or deletion message should also flush the related resource from the cache. The caching functionality would ideally be implemented as middleware that supports the SSOT service architecture.

Schema Synchronization: For existing applications to adopt a SSOT service model, the existing client applications need to map their local data to the SSOT data. Both the SSOT and the clients can make use of existing ontology studies, which define data syntax and semantics for specific industries. For example, HL7 [11] is defined for the health industry; RosettaNet [12] is defined for e-business; EDIFACT [13] is defined for electronic data interchange. Moving toward standard languages will benefit the survival and the long term growth of the industry. The SSOT service model does not define the communication architecture or protocol between the clients (e.g. between the clinic application and the pharmacy application in the EPR use case), but adopting the SSOT service model can simplify communication between the clients. For example, the pharmacy can verify a patient's prescription with the clinic by the patient SSOT-ID and avoid multiple drug dispensing.

7 Conclusion

The SSOT service model described in this paper addresses the data-synchronization problems that arise due to data-layer replication across distributed systems. On the other hand, the SSOT service model introduces a single point of failure in the system. Depending on the Service Level Agreement (SLA), the SSOT may need support from multi-site configurations or cloud-infrastructure with fail-over capability. Although the data-replication model does not have a single point of failure, it suffers from data-synchronization and data-inconsistency issues. Data synchronization usually involves defining a custom peer-to-peer data exchange agreement. The custom agreement tightly couples the data provider and consumer, which makes switching providers very costly. Nonetheless, data synchronization usually happens during the overnight maintenance windows. Data becomes stale between synchronizations. Furthermore, data replication keeps a full copy of the provider's data at the clients' sites. If clients use only a small portion of the provider's data, then the clients are wasting resources. An added benefit of the SSOT service model is that it can control what data each client is authorized to access, while data replication makes all data available to clients.

The SSOT service model allows the provider and clients to be loosely coupled. Clients do not need to pledge infrastructure resources for the foreign data. The SSOT service model also provides up-to-date data. Overall, we believe that the SSOT service model can be used to eliminate data replication, enforce data autonomy, advocate data self-containment, ease data maintenance and enhance data protection. In the long term, these properties will also increase business adaptability.

Within large enterprises or government agencies, managing large amounts of data as a single entity is problematic. Decomposing a large data set into smaller autonomous and independently managed data sets can increase flexibility. As in the EPR case, once the EPR SSOT service is established, a new patient related service can be created without defining and creating its own patient data set. The new service does not need to negotiate with other parties regarding data acquisition or synchronization. The new service can loosely couple with the EPR SSOT and be established quickly. In addition, the SSOT service model allows each individual service to be self-contained and maintain its local database. For example, the clinic application and the pharmacy application in the EPR use case maintain their individual local databases without sharing data with the EPR system. This characteristic is very important in the health industry, where patients' privacy is closely monitored.

The SSOT service model is also applicable to the financial industry. Banking, investment and insurance businesses are often integrated under one corporation. However, legislation may require each of these businesses to be separate entities. The SSOT service model allows the corporation to create a customer SSOT to register each customer once. Banking, investment and insurance services can run as separate entities, while being loosely coupled with the customer SSOT service. With the SSOT service model, new financial services can be introduced more quickly. Similarly, the SSOT service model can benefit any jurisdiction that provides multiple services.

References

1. Lasila, O., Swick, R.R.: World Wide and Web Consortium: Resource Description Framework (RDF) Model and Syntax Specification, W3C Recommendation (1998)
2. Fielding, R.T.: Chapter 5 Representational State Transfer (REST), Architectural Styles and the Design of Network-based Software Architectures, Doctoral dissertation, University of California, Irvine (2000)
3. Dustdar, S., Schreiner, W.: Survey on Web services Composition. International Journal on Web and Grid Services 1, 1–30 (2005)
4. Ran, S.: A Model for Web Services Discovery With QoS. ACM SIGecom Exchanges 4(1), 1–10 (2003)
5. Ives, Z., Khandelwal, N., Kapur, A., Cakir, M.: ORCHESTRA: Rapid, Collaborative Sharing of Dynamic Data. In: The 2nd Biennial Conference on Innovative Data Systems Research (CIDR 2005), Asilomar, CA, USA (2005)
6. Schmidt, M.-T., Hutchison, B., Lambros, P., Phippen, R.: The Enterprise Service Bus: Making servie-oriented architecture real. IBM Systems Journal 44(4), 781–797 (2005)
7. Nigam, A., Caswell, N.: Business artifacts: An approach to operational specification. IBM Systems Journal 47(3), 428–445 (2003)
8. Hull, R.: Artifact-Centric Business Process Models: Brief Survey of Research Results and Challenges. In: OTM 2008, Monterrey, Mexico (2008)
9. Jones, W.: Personal Information Management. Annual Review of Information Science and Technology 41(1), 453–504 (2007)
10. Ludwig, H., Laredo, J., Bhattacharya, K., Pasquale, L., Wassermann, B.: REST-Based Management of Loosely Coupled Services. In: The 18th International Conference on World Wide Web (WWW 2009), Madrid, Spain (2009)
11. HL7 Health Level Seven International, http://www.hl7.org
12. RosettaNet (1999), http://www.rosettanet.org
13. EDIFACT, United Nations Directories for Electronic Data Interchange for Administration, Commerce and Transport, http://www.unece.org/trade/untdid/welcome.htm

Model for Service License in API Ecosystems

Maja Vukovic[1], LiangZhao Zeng[1], and Sriram Rajagopal[2]

[1]IBM T.J. Watson Research Center, Yorktown Heights, NY 10598, USA
{maja,lzeng}@us.ibm.com
[2]IBM India, Chennai, India
srirraja@in.ibm.com

Abstract. Rapid growth and consumption of REST Apis is generating new types of service marketplaces, which are dynamic and complex networks of providers and consumers. Existing models for software licenses and service standards, such as WDSL fall short of providing flexible frameworks for capturing the requirements that this newly created environment demands. Gaps exist in support for multi-pricing agreements across multiple providers and consumers, support for both usage and capacity events and automated generation and composition of licenses. Developers are accustomed to self-serve model, where they create and deploy new applications on the Cloud with a few mouse clicks, employing one or more available APIs. As a result, there is a need to be able to automatically assess existing licenses, compose new ones and understand their dependencies in order to shorten the time-to-value for new services. In this paper, we propose a model-driven approach for defining API service licenses, which provides capabilities to capture business and legal constraints, enable license metric calculation, QoS calculation and service pricing rules. We present API SLA analyzer system, which utilizes proposed license model to uncover SLA violations in real-time.

Keywords: Service License, REST API, Model-driven.

1 Introduction

Simplicity of REST APIs has resulted in rapid development of highly consumable services [1]. As enterprises continue to expose their core capabilities through APIs and enable co-creation of novel business capabilities this opens up a set of challenges in the service-licensing domain. The challenges arise from incomplete models, lack of automation that leads to inefficiencies in end-to-end management of licenses in API ecosystems and ability for consumers to systematically assess license terms.

Firstly, existing API licenses are still designed with intention to be human readable. The legal terminology is not easily understandable by the consumer. As such, it is impossible for machine to parse, understand and assess licenses. Startups and freelancers often customize existing licenses found online. Enterprises rely on legal teams to swift through the agreements, which is labor intense.

Secondly, there is no longer one-to-one relationship between service provider and consumer, requiring license model to capture many pricing models and relationships.

X. Franch et al. (Eds.): ICSOC 2014, LNCS 8831, pp. 590–597, 2014.
© Springer-Verlag Berlin Heidelberg 2014

Thirdly, management of API licenses is a time-consuming, often manual process, which can lead to a lot of human errors. With the shorter development cycle and adoption of DevOps model, manual processing, negotiation and assessment of licenses is no longer an option. Furthermore, as developers build new capability and push them on the Cloud, the licensing model needs to capture both usage-based and capacity-based models.

The main contributions of this work are:

1. A novel, meta-model for representation of service license description (as an XML schema) that facilitates automated license generation and composition. The model provides capabilities to cover comprehensive non-functional properties of service license, including: business constraints, license metric calculation, Quality of Service (QoS) calculation and service price rule.

2. We demonstrate the usability of the proposed license model, as part of the prototype that at real-time uncovers Service Level Agreement (SLA) violations by interfacing and assess the service conditions, in an existing marketplace, and comparing them against real time metrics.

Next section presents the related work. Section 3 describes our proposed model and we discuss how it can be used to automate composition of licenses. Section 4 describes the implementation of SLA analyzer that uses our model. Section 5 concludes and outlines future areas of research.

2   Related Work

Software licenses [2] are centered on the capacity-based model, where the focus is on capacity elements, such as CPU. They are static and data-centric, and computed when the new deployment is complete. They do capture QoS and SLA guarantees.

Web-Service License Agreement (WSLA) framework [3] was designed to capture involved parties, SLA parameters, their metrics and algorithms, and service licensing objectives and the corresponding actions. It does not provide support for automatically creating agreements and it does not capture business and legal terms.

Web Service Agreement Specification (WS-Agreement) [4] provides terms and language to describe services, their properties, and associated guarantees. It is not a generic tool for conflict classification. There is no mechanism for deriving service delivery system based it and claiming a service against the agreement.

Existing efforts addressed compatibility of functional [5,6,7] and non-functional [8, 9, 10] parameters as part of service selection and matching process.

A number of commercial solutions aim to help consumers understand service licenses [11,12,13]. Our prior work presents a classification of common terms and conditions and describes a terms of service management console [14].

3   Service License Model

In this section, we introduce a service license meta-model, shown on Figure 1., which consists of layers: *Information source, Property Function, License Metric* and *License Terms and Conditions Metamodel.* Details about each layer of the metamodel follow.

3.1   Information Source

The information source meta-model provides constructs for defining the service deployment and execution information. The deployment information is related to hardware assets that install software. The execution information describes runtime events that related to execution of software. The runtime event may indicate how many instances are running in a physical server, when the instance is started and terminated, how many CPU cycles, memory, etc. are consumed, etc. Runtime events also report the business usage of the service. For example, when a business transaction is initiated, an event with transaction details is created.

By considering business users, we adopt object-oriented model to construct information metamodel. On the one hand, the deployment information usually is persisted in relational database. Therefore, the proposed metamodel provides constructs to map the deployment information from relational database to object-oriented. In most the case, the deployment information model are static and common to most of the organization and service vendors. Therefore, in practice, most of the organization can adopt pre-defined information model, without creating a new information model from scratch.

On the other hand, the execution information usually is live events that need to be processed before persisted in storage. The information metamodel provides constructs to define the event catalog that can include a collection of event types. It should be noted that the events that related to service usages could be diverse from different service vendors. And usually the service vendors provide definition of these events and event dispatchers that can detect and emit related events in runtime.

3.2   Property Function Metamodel

Property function metamodel provides building blocks to define license terms and conditions. There are two forms of functions, namely *Formula-based Function* and *Table-based Function.* A formula-based function takes a collection of entities defined by information metamodel. Its computation logic is defined by an *Expression* that takes input parameters as operands to construct an expression string by using operators. It should be noted that a formula-based function could be considered as an operand to construct another formula-based function.

3.3   License Metric Metamodel

Above information and property function metamodels provide foundational constructs to define service license metric. There are two major kinds of license metric: capacity-based

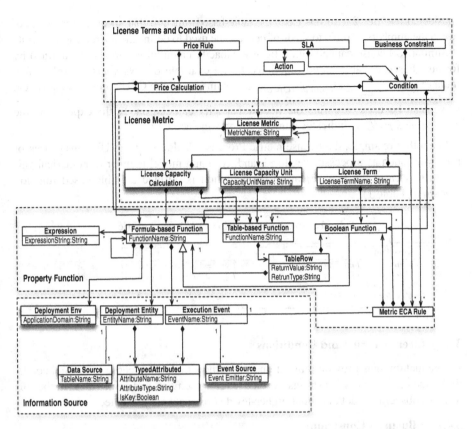

Fig. 1. Simplified UML representation for Service License Metamodel

and usage-based. Capacity-based license metric usually calculates the license requirement by considered the capacity of host that installs or executes the service. The license requirement will not change unless there are hardware upgrades. For example, license metric that measures total number of CPU cores of the physical server that the software deploys to. Unlike capacity-based license metrics, usage-based license metrics are created, calculated and based on live execution event events in realtime fashion. An example of usage-based license metric may measure number of transactions the service executes.

In general, both types of license metrics consist of a *LicenseUnit* and *License Calculations*. The license unit defines denominations that are used to measure the license requirement. In case of capacity-based license metrics, the license unit can be either defined as formula-based function either fixed value or a property function. For example, a license metric bubbled *"NumberOfCore"* that uses total number of CPU cores in the physical server to measure the license entitlement.

In this case the license capacity unit is the fix string *"core"*. In another example, a license metric *"UserTier"* uses number of users as input to map user tiers such as: from one to ten users is considered as *"tier 1"*, and from eleven to hundred users is considered as *"tier 2"*. In this case, the table-based function that specifies mapping between the numbers of users to kinds of tiers can be used to define the license capacity unit.

Similar to license capacity unit, license capacity calculation can also be defined by formula-based or table-based functions. In the example of *"NumberOfCore"*, a formula expression $\sum_{i=0}^{n} CPU_i.numberOfCore$ that sums up all the CPU cores in the physical server can be used to define the license capacity calculation. In the expression, the $CPU_i.numberOfCore$ indicates number of cores in each CPU.

In another example, the license metric Processor Value Unit (PVU) maps processor properties such as processor vendor, brand, type and model number to numerical value. In this case, the license capacity calculation is defined as table-based function (shown in Table 1).

Table 1. Table-based Function PVU license metric

Values	Conditions
120	$Vendor = "IBM", Brand = "Power7", Type = "Multi-core", Model = "AllExisting"$
100	$Vendor = "IBM", Brand = "Power5", Type = "Dual-core", Model = "AllExisting"$
...	...
50	$Vendor = "Intel", Brand = "Xeon", Type = "Multi-core", Model = "5160"$

3.4   License Terms and Conditions

Above metamodels provide foundational constructs to define license terms and conditions, such as business constrains, service level agreement, and price rules. In the following subsections, details about higher-level constructs are presented.

3.4.1   Business Constraint

Business constraints define the conditions that services can be applicable for executions. The condition is defined as a Boolean function that is constructed by using formula-based functions operands. Here are some examples of business constraints.

Data privacy protection constraint:
        Service.Execution.DataPrivacyProtection = "Best Effort";
This business constraint indicates that there is not guarantee on data privacy protection when service is executed.

Data reliable protection constraints:
        Service.Execution.DataReliable.isRetainDataCopy ="True";
        Service.Execution.DataReliable.isReliableForLoss ="False";

Above two constraints indicate that local data copy is retained by the service however, it will not reliable for data lost.

Brand usage constraints:
        Service.Deployment.BrandPermission="Not specified";
        Service.Deployment.LogoUsage="Consumer logo"
Above two constraints indicate that when deploying the service, brand permission is not specified and consumer logo is automatically used.

3.4.2   Service Level Agreement

Service level agreements (SLAs) provide quality guarantee for services. A service level agreement consists of two components: condition and action. Conditions specified the range of value for metrics (related to service quality). An example of condition can be quality guarantee about service availability, such as $Availability > 99\%$. The action of SLA specify the consequence if service quality guarantee is violated, which is usually related to payment or pricing rules.

3.4.3   Pricing Rules

Pricing rules specify the calculation of charges when the customers use services. There are different approaches to charge the service customers, which can include capacity-based or usage-based calculations. The capacity-based pricing rules provide the calculation logic according to hardware capacity that service is deployed to. The usage-based pricing rules provide the calculation logic according to how the service is used, such as number of invocations.

In our implementation, the metamodel is defined as an XML Schema and an editor is provided to facilitate creation of service license definition, which is represented as an XML document.

4   Model in Use

Using the proposed model we have developed the SLA analyzer system, which analyzes the service licenses based on the agreed and actual availability. It also has the capability to analyze licenses based on various other parameters, such as business constraints (e.g. user eligibility and brand permission). User can select one or more APIs and track their violations in a given time window, as shown on Figure 1. Details about the input and output of SLA API are shown in Figure 2.

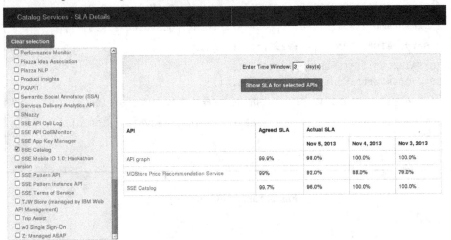

Fig. 2. SLA User Interface Prototype

SLA analyzer service – REST input/output:

Input: `{"apiID":[<list of API ID],"customerId":"<customer ID>","timeWindow":<time Window>}`

Output:

```
{"Results":[{"ServiceID":"<Service ID>","SLA":<Agreed
SLA>,"CustomerID":"<Customer
ID>","QoSAlerts":[{"TimeStamp":"<TimeStamp>","QoSAlert":<true|false>
,"QoSValue":<Actual SLA>}]}]}
```

Sample Input/Output

Input:

`{"apiID":["62","209","19"],"customerId":"10","timeWindow":3}`

Output:

```
{"Results":[
{"ServiceID":"62","SLA":99.9,"CustomerID":"10",
"QoSAlerts":[{"TimeStamp":"2013-11-
05","QoSAlert":true,"QoSValue":98.0},
{"TimeStamp":"2013-11-06","QoSAlert":false,"QoSValue":100.0},
{"TimeStamp":"2013-11-07","QoSAlert":false,"QoSValue":100.0}]},
{"ServiceID":"209","SLA":99.0,"CustomerID":"10",
"QoSAlerts":[{"TimeStamp":"2013-11-
05","QoSAlert":true,"QoSValue":92.0},
{"TimeStamp":"2013-11-06","QoSAlert":true,"QoSValue":88.0},
{"TimeStamp":"2013-11-07","QoSAlert":true,"QoSValue":79.0}]},
{"ServiceID":"19","SLA":99.7,"CustomerID":"10",
"QoSAlerts":[{"TimeStamp":"2013-11-
05","QoSAlert":true,"QoSValue":96.0},
{"TimeStamp":"2013-11-06","QoSAlert":false,"QoSValue":100.0},
{"TimeStamp":"2013-11-07","QoSAlert":false,"QoSValue":100.0}]}
]}
```

Fig. 3. Sample I/O and REST

5   Conclusion and Future Work

Service license definition and management is becoming an increasingly important challenge in the ever-growing service marketplaces. Licenses are still manually created, assessed and composed, which is a very time-consuming effort.

In this paper, we presented a model-driven approach to providing a formal framework for representing service license and capturing both usage and capacity based events. We presented our initial prototype that exposes license management and SLA alert capability via API. As such, we believe that our proposed model can help automate creation, assessment and composition of the service licenses. Moreover, it can help with license reconciliation and conflict detection. Our future work will focus on model evaluation, integration of comprehensive composition methods and optimization of service licenses in multitenant environments.

References

1. Pautasso, C., Zimmermann, O., Leymann, F.: Restful web services vs. big web services: making the right architectural decision. In: 17th International Conference on World Wide Web (2008)
2. Minkyong, K., Han, C., Munson, J., Lei, H.: Management-Based License Discovery for the Cloud. In: International Conference of Service Oriented Computing (2012)
3. Keller, A., Ludwig, H.: The WSLA Framework: Specifying and Monitoring Service Level Agreements for Web Services. Journal of Network System Management (2003)
4. Web Services Agreement Specification. Available at: http://www.ogf.org/documents/GFD.107.pdf
5. Liu, Y., Ngu, A.H., Zeng, L.Z.: QoS computation and policing in dynamic web service selection. World Wide Web (2004)
6. Karmarkar, A., Walmsley, P., Haas, H., Yalcinalp, L.U., Liu, K., Orchard, D., Pasley, J.: Web service contract design and versioning for SOA. Prentice Hall (2009)
7. Verma, K., Akkiraj, R., Goodwin, R.: Semantic Matching of Web Service Policies. In: Second International Workshop on Semantic and Dynamic Web Processes (2005)
8. Reiff-Marganiec, S., Yu, H.Q., Tilly, M.: Service Selection Based on Non-functional Properties. In: International Conference of Service Oriented Computing (2007)
9. Web Services Policy (WS-Policy), http://www.w3.org/Submission/WS-Policy/
10. Gangadharan, G.R., Comerio, M., Truong, H.-L., D'Andrea, V., De Paoli, F., Dustdar, S.: LASS – License Aware Service Selection: Methodology and Framework. In: International Conference of Service Oriented Computing (2008)
11. Digital Trends. Terms and Conditions. Available at: http://www.digitaltrends.com/topic/terms-and-conditions/
12. 500px's Terms Of Service Are Kind Of Awesome. TechCrunc Article. Available at: http://techcrunch.com/2012/04/12/500pxs-terms-ofservice-are-kind-of-awesome/
13. Terms of Service Didn't Read. Available at: http://tosdr.org
14. Vukovic, M., Rajagopal, S., Laredo, J.: API Terms and Conditions as a Service. In: IEEE Service Computing Conference (2014)

Author Index